Political culture and cultural politics in early modern England

Professor David Underdown

Photograph by Philip Underdown

Political culture and cultural politics in early modern England

Essays presented to David Underdown

edited by
Susan D. Amussen
and
Mark A. Kishlansky

Manchester University Press
Manchester and New York
distributed exclusively in the USA and Canada by St Martin's Press

Published by Manchester University Press
Oxford Road, Manchester M13 9NR, UK
and Room 400, 175 Fifth Avenue,
New York, NY 10010, USA

Distributed exclusively in the USA and Canada
by St Martin's Press, Inc.,
175 Fifth Avenue, New York, NY 10010, USA

British Library Cataloguing-in-Publication Data
A catalogue record for this book is available from the British Library

Library of Congress Cataloging-in-Publication Data
Political culture and cultural politics in early modern England:
  essays presented to David Underdown / edited by Susan D. Amussen and
  Mark A. Kishlansky.
    p. cm.
  ISBN 0–7190–4695–5 (hardback)
    1. Political culture—England—History—17th century. 2. Politics
  and culture—England—History—17th century. 3. England—Social
  conditions—17th century. I. Underdown, David. II. Amussen, Susan
  Dwyer. II. Kishlansky, Mark A.
  JN191.P65 1995
  306.2′0941′09032—dc20   95–3505
                                                              CIP

ISBN 0 7190 4695 5 *hardback*

First published in 1995

99 98 97 96 95   10 9 8 7 6 5 4 3 2 1

Typeset in Great Britain
by Northern Phototypesetting Co Ltd
Printed in Great Britain
by Biddles Ltd, Guildford and King's Lynn

Contents

[v]

Contents

Contributors

Susan D. Amussen is Professor of Interdisciplinary Studies at The Union Institute.

Thomas Cogswell is Professor of History at the University of Kentucky.

Richard Cust is Senior Lecturer in Modern History at the University of Birmingham.

Carl B. Estabrook is Assistant Professor of History, Dartmouth College.

Ann Hughes is Professor of History at Keele University.

Maija Jansson is Executive Editor and Lecturer in History at the Yale Center for Parliamentary History.

Lisa Jardine is Professor of English at Queen Mary and Westfall College, University of London.

Mark A. Kishlansky is Professor of History at Harvard University.

Peter Lake is Professor of History at Princeton University.

Molly McClain is Assistant Professor of History at San Diego University.

John Morrill is Reader in History at Selwyn College, University of Cambridge.

Rachel Weil is Assistant Professor of History at Cornell University.

Blair Worden is Fellow and Tutor in Modern History at St. Edmund Hall, University of Oxford.

1

Introduction

Susan D. Amussen and Mark Kishlansky

After years of cleavage, early modern British historians have begun to recon-
nect contrasting approaches to the study of the past. One of the most fruitful efforts has been the integration of social and political history at the
intersection of politics and culture. Whether politics is seen as inscribed
within a matrix of social relations and cultural assumptions or culture is
viewed as an expression of political enfranchisement outside of conventional
institutional arrangements, subjects and approaches which were once carefully cordoned off from each other are now becoming mutually reinforcing.
This can clearly be seen in the work of David Underdown of Yale University
whose recent books, *Revel, Riot and Rebellion* and *Fire From Heaven*, explore
the interconnections between popular culture and political activism at the
local and central levels. Both political culture and cultural politics are fundamental to his work.

The pattern of David Underdown's scholarship – moving as it does from
Royalist conspiracy to the life of seventeenth-century Dorchester – is not
immediately obvious. What is there, after all, that unites mostly well-born
conspirators against Cromwell with the ordinary inhabitants of a country
town? The common themes, though hidden, are there: a central concern with
the English Revolution, its causes and consequences, and an approach which
grants each historical subject their own integrity. Underdown offers as much
respect to the losers as to the winners, whether they be Royalist thugs or the
plebeian Pounceys of Dorchester. He has always been convinced that what
people thought they were doing was important in historical investigation.
Such an approach takes him beyond the myths and masks which so often prevent us from seeing the past clearly.

The consequence of this approach is that Underdown writes with sympathy about people with a wide range of attitudes and positions in society.
While centrally concerned with politics and the workings of the political
process, he has always understood that the process did not exist only for
itself: it served a larger purpose. Thus the whole political culture was rele-

vant: how did people think about politics? How did they define what was important? How did they make their choices? And why?

While Underdown has never been a 'trendy' historian, he has always engaged with questions that connect not just to current scholarly debates, but also to the world around him. History is not just about the past, but about the present. This does not mean that there is any simple correspondence or lessons about the present in the past, but that the ways in which we frame the questions are inevitably shaped by the world we see around us. Since it has now been admitted that MI5 routinely monitored correspondence to and from members of the Communist Party in Britain,[1] it would be curious to know what they made of the chapters on Royalist conspiracy that he sent to his advisor, Christopher Hill! His understanding of the atmosphere of intrigue and fear that he wrote about in *Royalist Conspiracy*[2] was increased by his experience in the United States in the McCarthy era. Similarly, his understanding of the dynamics of groups undertaking serious systemic change in *Pride's Purge* was shaped by curricular debates at Brown University in the 1960s, and that of cultural conflict by the 'culture wars' of the late 1980s.

From his initial work on the Royalist conspirators, Underdown moved to another group of radicals, the revolutionaries of the 1640s, that he studied in his classic work *Pride's Purge*.[3] Here he was influenced both by interest group theories of politics – particularly that which complicated Gardiner's division of the parliamentarians into war and peace parties – and by the methods of prosopography popularized by Sir Lewis Namier. Though Namier's method led him to downplay the significance of ideology in the eighteenth century, Underdown's work led him to emphasize it. Those who became revolutionaries shared a common heritage with those secluded at the purge. It was a commitment to a radical vision of religious transformation which distinguished the groups and it was that commitment which Underdown identified as one of the engines of what he called the 'Puritan' Revolution. *Pride's Purge* was a masterpiece of research as well as of interpretation. Underdown traced the careers of over 450 Members of Parliament through local and central archives, sorting out those identically named from each other and correcting the slips of earlier generations of researchers. His discovery of the parliamentary diary of John Boys added a first-hand account of the crucial months in the winter of 1648 when so many other sources had dried up or been subsequently destroyed.

Work on *Pride's Purge* began one of the most significant transitions in Underdown's work, as he added to his focus on national political issues an examination of local politics, beginning with his native county, Somerset, as a case study. *Somerset in the Civil War and Interregnum*[4] grew out of that work. In it, he has since written, he 'grasped the full implications of the simple, obvious fact that the gentry and commons of that county had followed different paths in the conflict'.[5] That epiphany, and his subsequent travels into the realm of popular politics and political culture, have generated some of his most exciting and innovative work. The countryman's suspicion of the corrupt metropolis which is so much a part of Underwood's small-town background is central here: what happens in the provinces is never secondary.

One of the characteristics, evident in *Pride's Purge* as well as in his later work in *Revel, Riot and Rebellion* and *Fire From Heaven*,[6] that shapes the originality of Underdown's work is his willingness to adopt methodological and conceptual tools from other fields of history and other disciplines when they will help him answer his questions. Thus, the application of Namierite methods to the members of the Long Parliament made it possible to answer some of the important questions about patterns of behaviour. As he moved into popular politics and culture, he read extensively in anthropology to develop the frameworks in which he interpreted the evidence he collected. He reads and thinks about social history as much as political history, but he always bring to social history his knowledge of political history, and vice versa. He has avoided the common tendency of historians to fragment their knowledge.

The theme of *Revel, Riot and Rebellion* was the relationship between forms of popular culture on the one hand, and popular politics on the other. The assumption Underdown made was that politics was, ultimately, an expression of the ways in which people saw the world, a central part of any definition of culture. He also assumed, as he had argued in the Prothero Lecture he delivered in 1980,[7] that the common people of England made their own decisions about who to support in the Civil War; the soldiers were not merely cannon fodder following the lead of local magnates. Perhaps the most controversial aspect of this argument was its association between patterns of settlement and political culture. Underdown argued that nucleated, arable villages in the sheep–corn regions of the west country tended to be more traditional in their popular culture – with maypoles, church ales and so on – less Puritan in their religion and more likely to be Royalist in the Civil War. Pastoral villages with scattered settlement patterns, on the other hand, tended to be more Puritan to eschew traditional festivities and tended to be parliamentarian in their allegiance.[8] The two types of region even had their own characteristic sports: football in the arable areas and stoolball (a bat and ball game) in the pastoral areas.[9] A later article on regional variations in popular culture extends this argument, with an excursion into the early history of Underdown's beloved cricket.[10]

The argument of *Revel, Riot and Rebellion* was a subtle and complicated one, based on the analysis not just of evidence of popular culture from Church Court and quarter sessions records, but a detailed statistical analysis of surviving evidence about the recruitment of soldiers in the Civil War. Underdown noted a number of places where the correspondence did not work – notably the pastoral but Royalist Blackmore Vale in Dorset – but argued that the typology of settlement had a close relationship to political culture.

The argument has been, insofar as it has been addressed, controversial. In a lengthy and thoughtful review of *Revel, Riot and Rebellion* in the *Journal of British Studies*,[11] John Morrill argued that the relationship between settlement patterns and culture was both over-schematic and weak, particularly insofar as it related to patterns of religious belief. Furthermore, Morrill insisted that the surviving evidence of allegiance was too fragmentary to be reliable.

Underdown's response to Morrill defended his argument, and pointed out that he was arguing for a general pattern, not an invariable one. He also suggested that Morrill's alternative – tying Puritanism not to settlement patterns but to clothworking – was less successful at explaining the patterns than was settlement, and more crudely deterministic. The exchange with Morrill reveals another aspect of his work and behaviour. He (and Morrill) were able to disagree respectfully and argue about evidence and ideas. Underdown has had relatively few enemies in a field noted for its contentiousness; his passion for the history has always been central, and obvious to most of his colleagues. So he has encouraged disagreement and debate about important historical issues: his best students were never sycophants.

As part of *Revel, Riot and Rebellion*'s examination of popular culture, Underdown began to explore questions related to both the history of women and the nature of gender. These first arose as he sought to understand why certain offences – like scolding – appeared in some places rather than others.[12] His thinking was stimulated both by his colleague, Joan Scott, and several of his students, undergraduate and graduate (of whom Rachel Weil and Susan Amussen are represented in this collection). He took his interest in gender into the subject of political language in a study of *The Man in the Moon*, a scurrilous Royalist newsbook published in 1649–50.[13] The role of gender as a central political metaphor became one of the organizing themes of the Ford Lectures Underdown delivered in Oxford in January and February 1992. As with so much Underdown has read, he has learned from the work of feminist scholars, and made important contributions to the scholarship on women and gender in the early modern period.[14] At the same time he has used what he has learned from other fields as part of his work on more traditional questions.

In his next work, Underdown moved from the broad regional sweep of *Revel, Riot and Rebellion* to a more focused examination of the development of one place – Dorchester in Dorset. He had discovered the exceptional nature of the Dorchester records – particularly the Mayor's Court Book – while working on *Revel, Riot and Rebellion*, and decided that they would provide the basis for an excellent local study. In *Fire From Heaven*, Underdown was able to examine cultural conflict on the most local level, as he traced the work of the Puritan leadership of the town in the three decades preceding the Civil War. He showed the positive, constructive side of Puritanism, as well as the more familiar punitive side; he also treated those who resisted reformation with sympathy and understanding. It is typical that while some reviewers criticized him for favouring the Puritans,[15] others saw him with 'a soft spot for the unregenerate'.[16] Such divergent perspectives, however, were rooted in the recognition that it was the lives of ordinary people – of whatever political or theological persuasion – that were at the centre of this work.

Fire From Heaven was not just a local study; rather it reflected on issues in local culture through the prism of the national culture. It is informed by the broad range of research and writing that Underdown had undertaken in previous projects. So too was his next project – the Ford Lectures, delivered at Oxford in the winter of 1992.[17] Underdown was the first historian who had spent his career outside of Britain to be invited to give the lectures, and they represented a culmination of much of his work. In them, he sought to connect the two areas in which his work had made such great contributions – the history of elite politics on the one hand, and social history and popular politics on the other.

In his examination of the political cultures of both the elite and the common people, Underdown showed how the two shared common assumptions, even as these ideas were worked out and acted on in different ways, in different contexts. The changes in political culture over the century were, in turn, shaped by the cultural politics of the time, especially the struggles over religion and discipline. At the same time, Underdown argued, there was a greater divergence between elite and popular culture by the end of the seventeenth century. He also showed how certain themes that were common in the early part of the century disappeared from political debate at the end of the century. The Ford Lectures represent the engagement with politics and culture so central to much of his work; these are the interests that are celebrated in this volume.

The essays which follow, written by students, friends and colleagues of David Underdown, reflect the variety and depth of his interests. They range in subject from the political culture of the Long Parliament to the politics of Aesop's *Fables*. They even include a study of the relations between town and cathedral in Underdown's native Wells, a work which places the founding of the school he attended as a boy squarely within the context of the conflict between town and cathedral that is so central to his own mistrust of metropolitan institutions. The essays share with Underdown's work a concern with the integrity of the past, a respect for the people who inhabited it and a fascination with the way historical characters thought and acted. The diversity of both subjects and authors is itself a tribute to Underdown's scholarship and the wide influence of his work.

The most transparent method of studying political culture is in those arenas that contemporaries viewed as political. In early modern England political power was a reflection of wealth, status and privilege rather than the mastering of the techniques of persuasion and manipulation. Only at Westminster, either in the Privy Council or Parliament, were political practices cultivated and developed. Though the 1620s marked a significant advance in the importance of parliamentary politics, it is not until after 1640 that a parliamentary politician actually emerged. John Pym was the first of a series of leaders who mastered the political culture of the institution of Parliament. In 'The unweariableness of Mr Pym: influence and eloquence in the Long Parliament', John Morrill seeks to understand Pym's path to power. Pym was the antithesis of the seventeenth-century magistrate. He had no local base of power, no claim to gentility and little personal wealth. He came into Parliament as a man of affairs, treasurer to the Providence Island Company and a client of the earl of Bedford. Within his circle of hot Protestant laymen, others were seemingly more qualified for political leadership, but it was Pym who gained the garland. Conventionally, Pym's success has been attributed to his mastery of procedure, his 'administrative genius'. But Morrill demonstrates that the two paths to Pym's success were different: the first stemming from his beliefs, the second from his personality. It was his commitment to religious reform that kept him in the forefront of public discussion. Through printed speeches, most of them inexact and some entirely fabricated, Pym became the predominant symbol of parliamentary leadership. This led to vigorous attacks against him, earning him the hostile sobriquet of 'King Pym'. The popular perception that Pym was the leading parliamentarian confirmed the staggering weight of his activity in the House of Commons where he spoke more often, sat on more committees and delivered more messages to the Lords than anyone else. This was the second pillar on which he rested his success, his 'unweariableness', the ability to serve as go-between among groups and individuals within the Commons and as a messenger between the Houses. Pym was a team player rather than an isolated leader on a lonely promontory. Pym was driven not by a desire for an administrative revolution, but by his commitment to a reformed religion that unified the state – traditional erastian Puritanism. Such a portrait fits not only Pym's personal circumstance – unable to lead in wealth, status or standing – but also a political culture in which it was necessary to minimize conflict and to build coalitions.

Pym's commitment to religious reform reflects the centrality of religion in any understanding of the political culture of the seventeenth century. Debates about religion – both in terms of Church polity and doctrine – were heated and pervasive. The controversy between 'Calvinists and anti-Calvinists' or 'Anglicans and Puritans' divided both clergy and laymen and became a lightning rod for power and preferment at the Caroline court. The nature of that dispute has been obscured both by the arcane issues around which it centred – especially the doctrines of assurance, perseverance and double predestination – and the effort of both sides to capture the high moral ground by adopting the rhetoric of tradition and unity. It was the use of this rhetoric, argues Peter Lake in 'The moderate and irenic case for religious war: Joseph Hall's *Via Media* in context', that makes necessary the closest examination of the context in which religious controversialists wrote. In the atmosphere of the early Stuart church, the middle ground was claimed in nuanced argument that actually carried sharp ideological edges. Joseph Hall, who ultimately became a Caroline bishop, was such a master of this strategy that he has been claimed for a partisan by both sides in the debate over Arminianism. One reason for this was Hall's rabid anti-Catholicism. Although he believed the Church of Rome to have been a true church, Hall also believed that it had so fallen from its original purity as to be a veritable sinkhole of corruption. These views, though not original, were more widely shared by the hotter sort of Protestants than the audience to which he preached at court. Thus it was necessary for Hall to camouflage his anti-popery with the rhetoric of irenicism that so appealed to the king. This was, however, just the same rhetoric that led Calvinists to equate Arminianism with Catholicism. The more James I resisted religious war with Spain, the more his court preachers, like Hall, used this coded anti-Catholicism to goad him. In his *Via Media*, Hall again used the rhetoric of moderation, this time to damp down the fiery debate over predestination. His own doctrinal position is difficult to tease out – he thought he had found a middle ground between the extremes – but his pastoral position was clear, the less dispute the better.

As Joseph Hall found, one of the central problems facing anyone in early Stuart England was how to engage in conflict in a political culture that valued consensus. Hall's solution, which used the rhetoric of consensus to exclude other viewpoints, had resonances in other areas. The peaceful resolution of disputes was a central purpose of the local political community which was the arena in which most conflict arose. Richard Cust's essay, 'Honour, rhetoric and political culture', brings us into the world of high politics in early seventeenth-century Leicestershire. There, in the early seventeenth century, the dominance of the Hastings earls of Huntingdon was being challenged by the Greys and their allies among the rising gentry. They competed for office, for influence in the selection of members to Parliament and for prestige at meetings of the county elite. Dispute between the Hastings and Greys came to a head in 1612 when the earl of Huntingdon nominated his relative Walter Hastings Esq. to the commission of the peace. Walter Hastings was a singularly inappropriate nominee. He had a Catholic wife, a meagre fortune and lacked judicial experience, though sixty years of age. Moreover, as kinsman to an earl, Walter Hastings would be given precedence over all other gentry on the bench. But when the Greys challenged the nomination, Huntingdon turned the issue into one of honour rather than power. Adhering to traditional concepts of honour which stressed pedigree and lineage, Huntingdon defended his choice against the Greys whose concept of honour centred on personal merit. Thus their attacks upon Walter Hastings were read by Huntingdon as an attack upon his lineage. From these seemingly irreconcilable positions, the conflict threatened the peace of the entire county. It was composed by the assizes judges, who used a rhetoric of unity that resonated within both codes of honour. For the earl of Huntingdon unity reflected honour through the obligation of obedience; for the Greys, unity reflected honour through piety. Thus confrontation could be avoided by allowing both factions to maintain their differently valued concepts of honour.

By the late seventeenth century, familial disputes quickly became part of national political conflicts rather than local personal ones. The contest for pre-eminence in county society was increasingly bound up with large national issues. In 1678, fifty armed men gathered in Wentwood Forest, Monmouthshire to prevent the felling of trees claimed as private property by the marquis of Worcester and as common waste by the rioters. They drove Worcester's agents from the site and confiscated the valuable timber that was destined for the marquis' ironworks. At first sight, their action appears as another example of the moral economy of the crowd, an attempt by tenants to assert customary rights against efforts by their lord to respond to a market economy. The riot took the form of those enclosure disputes which were so common in the sixteenth and early seventeenth centuries and which had begun to disappear with the conversion of so much land to freehold during and after the English Revolution. But as Molly McClain demonstrates in 'The Wentwood Forest riot: property rights and political culture in Restoration England', it was nothing of the sort. The 'rioters' were nearly all local gentry, their agitation was part of a campaign to prevent the marquis from reaping the windfall of rising timber prices, and this campaign was in turn part of the political conflict in the county that witnessed the division of the Monmouthshire gentry into Whigs and Tories. The group who opposed Worcester included one sitting Member of Parliament and the county sheriff. They had clashed with Worcester at parliamentary by-elections, and though they secured their candidate, a number of the group were removed from the commissions of the peace as a result. But unlike the dispute in Leicestershire in the early seventeenth century, this conflict did not lead to an appeal to unity. Rather, Worcester's opponents took their case to Parliament, declaring that they had been put out of the commission because they were loyal Protestants and suggesting that Worcester was not. Their next gambit, the forest riot, brought their case to the attention of the earl of Shaftsbury and it was briefly caught up in the whirlwind of the Popish Plot. Worcester was forced to defend himself, not in front of local assize judges, but in the House of Lords. His victory came with the Tory reaction after 1681.

The conflict over ecclesiastical doctrine that so dominated the politics of religion in the early seventeenth century was largely conducted by clergymen who attracted a wide audience among the laity. Like its doctrines, the institutions of the Church were equally a matter of concern for laymen. Ecclesiastical and civil jurisdictions overlapped in early modern England, giving rise to disputes about law and authority in local communities. Throughout the late sixteenth century the power of the Church courts eroded under the pressure of the expansion of the role of the justices of the peace. Social legislation like the poor laws and acts against vagrancy had the unintended consequence of making sexual offences more a matter of fiscal than moral concern in the parish. The expansion of the role of secular jurisdiction in towns, especially through charters of incorporation that ceded judicial responsibility to borough magistrates, further eroded the role of the Church in the local community. This left institutions like cathedrals in an anomalous position. As Carl Estabrook shows in 'In the mist of ceremony: cathedral and community in seventeenth-century Wells', the role of these civic institutions was transformed across the seventeenth century. The structure that once defined the very existence of a settlement such as Wells grew less important in the daily life of its citizens. In the early seventeenth century Wells Cathedral exercised an economic stranglehold over the town. The bishop owned the market-place and most of the buildings on the main street, and was the largest employer despite an active cloth industry. Not even the Reformation and the Elizabethan depredations against the Church lands changed this relationship. Yet at the end of the sixteenth century Wells won incorporation after a long struggle against its bishop. Thus began nearly fifty years of jurisdictional conflict in which secular power slowly but steadily encroached upon that of the cathedral. The town took over the function of charity and refused to contribute to the cathedral's almsgiving. The dividing line between the ecclesiastical courts and the borough court blurred. The mayor and aldermen who routinely attended Sunday services at the cathedral in the first decades of the century, withdrew to the parish church by the 1620s. The Civil War was a predictable turning point and the townsmen did not need the formal abolition of bishops to complete the transfer of power. It was a reversal that the Restoration did little to alter. Wells used the occasion of the Caroline charter campaign in the 1680s to assert the economic independence from the cathedral that it had been practising since the 1640s. The charter of 1684 granted rights and privileges to the townsmen that the Elizabethan charter had vested in the bishop. Symbolically, the relationship between ritual and public space was also reversed. In the late sixteenth century the members of the cathedral used the town as the location of their processions, marching from the Close into the square carrying banners symbolic of the power of the bishop. These processions were joined by civic authorities, but organized by the dean. After the Restoration, it was the town which began to use the cathedral for its ritual celebrations, ordering special thanksgiving days or lectures to be held there. Indeed, the cathedral now served the function of public space for the town. After nearly a century of conflict it finally became a symbol of political unity between Church and State.

The inhabitants of cathedral cities were not the only ones who used the upheavals of the Civil War to redress their grievances against institutional powers. The Levellers represented a movement of small property owners against their social and economic superiors. Historians have long noticed the representation of women in Leveller literature, and have argued about its significance. But it is only in recent years that they have become aware of the way gender operated as a category of thinking that informed political debate.

In the early modern period political thought was so imbued with gender that it is difficult to imagine how historians could have overlooked it. With the gendering of the State in patriarchal political theory, gender, family and politics were inextricably connected. To understand the ways in which gender is inflected in politics, historians need to engage in close readings of the texts. Ann Hughes, in 'Gender and politics in Leveller literature', offers her re-evaluation of the Levellers' self-definition through their presentation of women and the family, offers such a reading that demonstrates how this approach can illuminate and clarify our understanding of the past. By examining the rhetoric of the Leveller writings – both the familiar petitions by women, as well as writings about women – she shows how the petitions (even those ostensibly by women) were designed to demonstrate that Levellers were good, solid householders with modest wives. These households were disrupted by the behaviour of the officials who rudely and corruptly arrested their heads. Thus the Levellers' propaganda asserted the credibility of their leaders through their standing as good men. The honesty and commitment of Levellers is contrasted to the corruption of Parliament. The rhetorical strategy employed in these petitions, then, appears less as a claim to female political autonomy, but to respectability by their husbands.

The Civil War and Revolution, like other moments of political crisis, provided an opportunity for outsiders to claim a part in the political process, though their claims were frequently contested, as the Levellers discovered, through attacks on their character and credibility. This process – a struggle over credibility – is extended by Rachel Weil's ' "If I did say so, I lyed": Elizabeth Cellier and the construction of credibility in the Popish Plot crisis', a reading of Elizabeth Cellier's case, especially her pamphlet *Malice Defeated* and the responses to it in the course of the Popish Plot. In the welter of charges and counter-charges that emerged between 1678 and 1680, credibility was central: who would you believe? Since almost all those making accusations had unsavoury reputations, the usual ways of determining credibility were inadequate. Cellier – as a Catholic and a woman – accused the government of using torture to extract confessions from suspected Catholic plotters; at the same time she was accused by Thomas Dangerfield of paying him to concoct evidence of a Presbyterian plot against the Catholics. In *Malice Defeated* Cellier attempts to justify herself by telling the story of her case, including detailed accounts of her hearing before the Privy Council and her trial for treason. Her complicated, and often contradictory, self-presentation reflected the contradictions of her position as an English Catholic married woman before the courts and in politics. Cellier's defence after her acquittal on charges of treason used both her sex and her professional position as a midwife to defend herself. The close reading of Cellier's writings enables Weil to show how the expectations of gender could be manipulated and how Cellier used her professional authority to speak of things that otherwise respectable women could not speak of.

If political debate through the early modern period was gendered, so debates about gender in the period were politicized. The behaviour of individuals in society was never without political implications; and the obsession with proper behaviour reflects its importance in an ordered society. Many of the assumptions and attitudes toward gender, as Susan Amussen argues in '"The part of a Christian man": the cultural politics of manhood in early modern England', are unfamiliar and fundamentally different from those we know today. In spite of the attention given to women and gender, relatively little work has focused on the meanings of manhood. Yet just as we have learned that there were cultural codes surrounding the behaviour of women, so Amussen shows that similar codes operated for men. She argues that we need to see the behaviour of men as socially constructed – a construction that becomes painfully clear in the conflicts between different models of manhood that emerged in the period. These conflicts centred around the role of violence in manliness – a politically charged issue in a time when fighting wars was one of the central activities of government. Amussen also shows that independence, rather than sexuality, was the central marker of manhood. The nature of manhood is a key to understanding many aspects of political and social behaviour in the early modern period.

The difference between early modern and modern conceptions of manhood alerts us to the many ways in which the past was foreign. Just as manhood was viewed differently, so Lisa Jardine argues in 'Companionate marriage versus male friendship: anxiety for the lineal family in Jacobean drama', were intimacy and affection viewed in ways we find strange. Jardine is one of a group of scholars in both history and literature who have struggled with the question of how to read the cultural products of the period. Such readings are rooted in a strong knowledge of both historical and literary trends. Lisa Jardine's analysis of how Jacobean drama reflects on the tensions surrounding the transition to companionate marriage and to freely chosen service in homosocial relationships for men offers an example of the richness of this approach. Both these developments were part of a shift away from an emphasis on lineage and family ties to one on individual ties, rooted in intimacy and emotion. We often see this shift as good and unproblematic. In the seventeenth century, however, such relationships were not only unstable and unpredictable, but also secret and not subject to regulation by outsiders. But the anxieties created by this change were rarely expressed around the bonds of service between masters and men; they were frequently expressed in relation to women who exercised – or tried to exercise – freedom of choice in marriage. Jardine uses an analysis of *The Changeling* to show how some of these cultural anxieties were expressed on stage. Her reading of the historical and literary evidence reminds us that the eventual triumph of affective choice over family control in issues of both marriage and friendship was by no means simple or uncontested.

The cultural politics of *The Changeling* were relatively coded and subtle, but the early modern period had more than enough room for cultural products whose politics were far more explicit. Indeed, the political significance of cultural representations was well known to contemporaries. Genres as different as painting, newsbooks and published pamphlets jostled together with privately circulated verse and broadsides and even books of fables, to describe political events or proffer political points of view. In the seventeenth century the medium was not the message. The separation between elite and popular culture was in production rather than consumption. If only highly skilled artists with aristocratic patrons could propose to paint the walls of the Banqueting House, their intention was to instruct the multitude who passed through its halls. If literacy was confined to a minority of the population, alehouses, inns and market crosses provided gathering places for the illiterate to hear broadsides and newsbooks read. The doggerel libels that circulated in manuscript and were copied in letters from London to the country was itself as likely gathered from the mouths of the 'rude multitude' as from those of city 'wits'. Even elaborately produced folios of Aesop's *Fables* contained politicized morals in easily remembered rhyming couplets.

In a visual age, art was as powerful as literature. Thus it could be harnessed to serve the power of the State. A great set of tapestries commemorating England's deliverance from the Spanish Armada hung first in Whitehall Palace and then in the House of Lords. They were the inspiration for a plan presented to the government of the commonwealth in 1650 by three Dutch artists to represent the great events of the Civil War and Revolution for public display on the walls of the Banqueting House. As Maija Jansson shows in 'Remembering Marston Moor: the culture of politics', even such a seemingly innocuous proposal was fraught with political complications. The artists who proposed to execute it were strongly connected with either the recently executed king or the recently abolished House of Lords. The representations themselves, except where they involved portraits, fed an aesthetic debate between 'adornment' and 'plain' style that was often formulated in the political polarities of Catholic versus Protestant or French versus Dutch. This clash of views was given momentum by the decision to sell King Charles' art collection and the conflict over which epics in it were idolatrous. In this atmosphere the project faltered, making unnecessary this particular form of whitewashing after 1660.

Not all cultural products with explicitly political themes were as respectable as the proposal discussed by Jansson. Indeed, the seditious implications of the most political works made them dangerous, so that while they existed, they often went unpublished. Thomas Cogswell takes as his subject the development of popular political awareness. In 'Underground verse and the transformation of early Stuart political culture' he poses the problem of how the English population could be mobilized for a war that had to be explained in political terms. How had those terms been communicated in the decades before 1642? While constitutional historians have concentrated upon cases in the courts and debates in Parliament, it is doubtful if either made as much impact in the provinces as the reporting of news – both real and specious – and the underground circulation of poetic libels. These were thinly veiled and often scatological accounts of current events and public figures couched in the most extreme language. No one did things by halves in underground ballads: ministers had the blackest characters, the loosest morals, the greediest avarice that could be put into words that might form a couplet. Ministers were helpless against the barbs of the 'pot-poets' and Buckingham and Laud even put a price on the heads of their anonymous libellers. Nor did the government take lightly the impact of underground verse. Court poets were assigned the task of refuting specific libels, though their refined sensibilities and carefully honed skills were just the wrong weapons for the battle. Though dreadful as poetry, the poems helped form a large, politically informed populace and created the pent-up demand for traditional print that was so marked a characteristic of the Civil War period. Once censorship was removed and the Stationers' monopoly broken there was an explosion of publications dominated by 'mercuries', 'curantoes' and savage satires.

Despite the fact that the age was still more visual than literate, the most common form of political representation was the written word. In 'Wit in a Roundhead', Blair Worden underscores the development of the weekly newsbook as a vehicle of political propaganda throughout the English Revolution. Here the uses of the printed word for political purposes were direct and unmediated. Marchamont Nedham was a political propagandist who was variously in the service of Parliament, of Charles I, of the commonwealth and of the Restoration. He believed in the potency of the pamphlet, offering at one point 'to write his majesty back into his throne'. During the first Civil War, Nedham's newsbook *Mercurius Britanicus* was designed both as a counter to the effective Royalist propaganda of Sir John Berkenhead's *Mercurius Aulicus* and as a source of carefully filtered information about the parliamentarian cause. Because he had to convey news, promote his side and refute the enemy in so brief a compass, satire was one of Nedham's chief weapons. His verbal duel with Berkenhead was a brilliant parry and thrust that attempted to diminish the strength of the enemy by ridicule. But his weapon of choice was not always best suited to his audience. Writing to parliamentary and London Puritans at the time that their very survival seemed in doubt, the 'wit' Nedham displayed, whether in ribald jest or breezy jocularity, was unappreciated by the 'sober' sort in the period when he wrote for Parliament and the staunch Royalists in the period in which he wrote for the king. It was this 'wit', Worden argues, that provides a clue to the underlying consistency of a seemingly inconsistent career. His wit was certainly unappreciated by his parliamentary masters. Nedham worked for a publishing syndicate but the 'news' he printed was so vital a part of the parliamentary war effort that he also worked under the watchful eye of parliamentary committees. In 1645 he was thought to have overstepped the bounds of propriety in his criticism of the king and was imprisoned in the Fleet. Even without the formal censorship of the bishops, the political ends to which print culture could be used had clearly circumscribed limits and dire personal consequences.

Nedham was writing in a period that was deeply politicized, a politicization that was relatively new. This can be seen by looking at the changing shape of one publication, Aesop's *Fables*. It was one of the first works printed in English and it remained one of the most popular publications throughout the sixteenth and early seventeenth centuries. As Mark Kishlansky argues in 'Turning frogs into princes: Aesop's *Fables* and the political culture of early modern England', the books of fables were used both to instruct schoolchildren in Latin and to provide entertainment for the newly literate. They were a staple of the publishing houses which reprinted standard editions. But during the 1630s the nature of editions of Aesop's *Fables* began to change. One set of publications became more literary, another more political. Beginning in the 1650s, with John Ogilby, a series of 'editors' produced overtly political publications directed at the well-heeled book purchaser. These editions, many of which were vehicles for copperplate etchings rather than the fables themselves, were staunchly Royalist and monarchist. Authors like Aphra Behn and Sir Roger L'Estrange used their editions of Aesop to inculcate the political values of non-resistance and passive obedience, turning the instructive moral at the end of each fable into a political lesson.

From Pym to Aesop the political culture of early modern England flourished in extraordinary variety. The stimulation that David Underdown provided for a younger generation of scholars proliferates insights and questions through which knowledge grows. Through the care he has taken for his students, the generosity he has given to his friends and the example he has set for his colleagues, Underdown has enriched historical enquiry immeasurably. These essays are affectionately presented to him in gratitude.

Notes

[1] Peter Wright, *Spycatcher: The Candid Autobiography of a Senior Intelligence Officer* (New York, 1987), pp. 45–6.

[2] David Underdown, *Royalist Conspiracy in England, 1649–1660* (New Haven, 1960).

[3] David Underdown, *Pride's Purge: Politics in the Puritan Revolution* (Oxford and New York, 1971).

[4] David Underdown, *Somerset in the Civil War and Interregnum* (Newton Abbot, 1973).

[5] David Underdown, *Revel, Riot and Rebellion: Popular Politics and Culture in England 1603–60* (Oxford, 1985), p. vii.

[6] David Underdown, *Fire From Heaven: Life in an English Town in the Seventeenth Century* (London and New Haven, 1992).

[7] David Underdown, 'The problem of popular allegiance in the English Civil War',

TRHS, 5th series, 31 (1981), pp. 69–84.

[8] This argument was first developed in David Underdown, 'The chalk and the cheese: contrasts among the English clubmen', *Past and Present*, 85 (1979), pp. 25–48.

[9] He further develops the sporting end of things in 'Regional cultures: local variations in popular culture during the early modern period' in Tim Harris (ed.), *Popular Culture in England, 1500–1850* (London, 1995), pp. 28–47.

[10] David Underdown, 'Regional cultures'.

[11] John Morrill, 'The ecology of allegiance in the English Civil War', and David Underdown, 'A reply to John Morrill', *Journal of British Studies*, 26(4) (1987), pp. 451–67 and 469–79.

[12] This theme was more fully developed in David Underdown, 'The taming of the scold: the enforcement of patriarchal authority in early modern England', in Anthony Fletcher and John Stevenson (eds.), *Order and Disorder in Early Modern England* (Cambridge, 1985), pp. 116–36.

[13] David Underdown, 'The language of politics in the English Revolution', in Alvin Voss (ed.), *Place and Displacement in the Renaissance: Essays from the 25th Annual CEMERS Conference* (Binghamton, 1994), pp. 107–31.

[14] It is perhaps noteworthy that in the keynote address at the conference 'Attending to women in early modern England' in November 1990, Lisa Jardine took 'The taming of the scold' as a central focus of her discussion: 'Unpicking the tapestry: the scholars of women's history as Penelope among her suitors', in Adele Seeff and Betty Travitsky (eds.), *Attending to Women in Early Modern England* (Newark, DE, 1994), pp. 123–44.

[15] A. L. Beier, 'Dorset's malignant borough', *Times Higher Educational Supplement*, 2 Dec. 1993, p. 21a.

[16] Richard Ollard, 'Creating Utopia in Dorset', *The Spectator*, 22 Aug. 1992, pp. 26–7.

[17] To be published as *Free Born Englishmen: The Political Nation in the Seventeenth Century* (Oxford, 1996).

Part I

The culture of politics

2

The unweariableness of Mr Pym: influence and eloquence in the Long Parliament[1]

John Morrill

I

In the bleak midwinter of 1643–4, the members of both Houses of Parliament, accompanied by the English members of the Westminster Assembly of Divines,[2] escorted the body of John Pym to what was intended to be its final resting place amongst the tombs of kings in the chapel of King Henry VII in Westminster Abbey. It was the grandest funeral ever given to a commoner in the early modern period, and if the procession did not match the formal splendours of the funeral arrangements for the 3rd Earl of Essex,[3] his resting place within the Abbey was the more striking.[4] In a powerful oration,[5] the Commons' favourite preacher – Stephen Marshall – called him

> a true Christian man, a faithful servant of Jesus Christ, one who had long since beene borne againe of water and the Holy Ghost, engrafted into Christ, adapted to be the childe of God, justified freely by his grace renewed in the spirit of his mind, one who made God his portion, and God's word his guide. In a word he was a true Nathaniel, in whom there was no guile.[6]

Marshall continued with a startling and not unambiguous parallel with another victim of cancer: if Mary Tudor died with Calais engraved on her heart, then

> the publike safety was written in his heart … It was his meate and drinke, his worke, his exercise; his pleasure, his ambition, his all, in what he was, was only to promote the publike good.

But the preacher's main claim for Pym was his sense of call and his extraordinary workaholism – he was daily at his labours from 3 a.m. to almost midnight:

> Such *unweariableness* … this was his constant employment, except only the time of his drawing nigh to God, to be some way or other helpful towards the publike good, burning out his candle to give light to others.[7]

This is perhaps his only uncontested epitaph. It was very much how his contemporaries saw him. Thus when his fellow MP Lawrence Whittaker heard of Pym's death, he wrote in his diary that by ever acting 'his best endeavours for the service of the Parliament, both before the Parliament and since, he hath wasted his estate and his person'.[8] This essay will certainly not seek to disturb that picture of him. His more than 1,000 appearances in the *Commons Journal* (*C.J.*) in the three years of the Long Parliament that preceded his death, his more than 900 recorded speeches, his 33 printed speeches, his domination of the proceedings of the Committee for the Safety of the Kingdom (the executive committee that co-ordinated the parliamentary war effort between the resort to arms and the creation of the Committee of Both Kingdoms to co-ordinate the war of the three kingdoms in 1644–6), all allow him that modest accolade. But was he also – as Jack Hexter claimed more than half a century ago – the master strategist who created the ramshackle but serviceable financial and military structures that allowed Parliament to win the Civil War, the man who combined administrative flair with political artistry in dragging a quailing body of MPs across innumerable constitutional Rubicons?[9] Or do we have to acknowledge, as Sheila Lambert would have us do, that Pym's leadership was a 'myth', that his importance was systematically exaggerated and misrepresented by contemporaries and also by subsequent commentators, so that it has become a convenient fiction built into the historiography of the English Civil War?[10]

It is the simple intention of this essay to explore the parliamentary career of John Pym between 1640 and 1643 more systematically than it has been in the past. It does not attempt a major reassessment of the politics of the period; nor does it add to what has already been established about the links between Pym and other members of both Houses. It seeks to examine and to weigh the significance of his participation in the activities of the Houses, to consider the subjects he spoke on and those he did not speak on and to explain his extraordinary *visibility* in the affairs of the Parliament.

II

Stephen Marshall portrayed John Pym as a man who gave his all to protect the purity of the gospel and the liberties of the people. He led by example. But as so often, behind the hyperbole lay an eloquent silence. Marshall did not address – as Pym himself did in his *Declaration and Vindication* – the charges so often brought against him by his Royalist opponents:

> some charging me to have beene the promoter and patronizer of all the innovations which have been obtruded upon the Ecclesiastical Government of the Church of England; others of more spiteful and exorbitant spirits alleging that I only have been the man who hath begot and fostered all the so lamented distractions which are now rife in this kingdome.[11]

Apart from a caution against too much weight on the Solemn League and Covenant, Pym's last great project,[12] Marshall made no attempt to evaluate Pym's achievement. Marshall credited him with no great religious or constitutional vision and recognized in him no administrative genius or strategic mastery. Rather he applauded Pym's capacity for sheer hard work. Not for Marshall, then, anything along the lines of the encomium of the normally cool and understated Venetian Ambassador: 'the promoter of the present rebellion and director of the whole machine';[13] and certainly not Pym's own rather startling comparison of himself of Cicero:

> In that devilish conspiracy of Catiline against the state and senate of Rome, none among the senators was so obnoxious to anie of the conspirators or liable to traducements as the great orator and patriot of the country, Cicero, because of his counsell and zeale to the commonwealth, their plot for the ruin thereof was discovered and prevented.[14]

Marshall passed over Pym's oratory in silence. S. R. Gardiner was more to the point: 'he worked by influence not by eloquence'.[15] Yet whatever the silences in Marshall's testament, there can be no overlooking contemporary perceptions of Pym as leader of the parliamentary and parliamentarian opposition to Charles I.

From the autumn of 1641 onwards there are repeated references to his having gained the sobriquet 'King Pym'. This may have initially referred to his chairmanship of the committee that exercised executive authority during September and October 1641 while Parliament was in recess and Charles I was in Scotland. Probably the earliest such reference comes from a letter of Edward Nicholas, dated 5 October 1641, followed soon after by Sir Peter Wroth's comment on Pym's signature to committee reports, that 'you know what letter was truly wanting – R' (i.e. J[ohn] R[ex]).[16] By early January 1642, the House of Commons were being told of seditious talk in the streets of London to the effect 'that Mr Pym was King Pym and that that rogue would set all the kingdom together by the ears'.[17] By March 1642 the term was being uttered in Parliament itself.[18] It was a pre-echo of his burial in December 1643 in the vault of kings.

Further evidence of his prominence in public perception comes from the number of libels against him. Most startling was the strange story of the vituperative message sent to Pym in the House of Commons on 25 October wrapped in a plague rag. The message ran 'O trayterous Pym, that betrayeth the king and country and subverteth the fundamental Lawes of the Kingdom, take this as thy reward.'[19] He was the subject of several more published libels throughout 1642 and 1643, hence *The Declaration and Vindication* of himself in April 1643. On 24 January 1643, for example, Simonds D'Ewes records in his journal that 'this day in the forenoon was [a] libell read in the House which was intercepted at Nottingham'. The libel was an entertaining lampoon of the parliamentary leadership, and accused them of obstructing the well-grounded peace for which Londoners had recently petitioned:

> Give eare beloved Londoners
> Fie Fie you shame us all
> Your rising up for peace will make
> The close committee fall.

The next nine verses discuss the leading parliamentarian peers, followed by Speaker Lenthall, the Five Members collectively and then eighteen named Members of the Commons. Pym comes second in that list, after Denzil Holles:

> But I, quoth Pym, your hackney am
> And all your drudgery doe
> Have made good speeches for my selfe
> and priviledges for you
> I sit and can looke downe on men
> Whilst others bleed and fight
> I eate their Lordshipps meate by day
> And give it their wives by night.[20]

Stripped of its coarseness, this image of Pym as go-between and drudge is well worth pondering.

Cumulatively, this is powerful evidence of Pym's dominance in the Long Parliament. Even if we take him to be the spokesman of a bicameral cabal, he appears to have been the most visible and active of the various spokesmen for the several cabals in the Parliament.

III

It seems that contemporaries were fuzzily aware of his leadership, but not necessarily of his greatness or his masterliness. Unweariableness is not the ultimate accolade, or the greatest hyperbole, in the preacher's manual of oratory.

Before embarking on our own analysis of Pym's role in the Long Parliament, we need to remind ourselves of some important constants in Pym's life. There are two admirable accounts of his personal and political development – an account of his life by S. R. Gardiner in the *Dictionary of National Biography* and an analytical essay about his career in the Parliaments of the 1620s by Conrad Russell.[21] Both make clear his untypical background. The early death of his father and remarriage of his mother led him being brought up away from his estates and wider kin. He was married for only a few years and then a widower for almost a quarter of a century; he owned property but preferred not to control it;[22] he owned his own manor houses but preferred to live in the homes of others. All this produced in him a curious rootlessness. He never settled anywhere, he was never a member of a county community, he was never a JP, deputy lieutenant or subsidy commissioner. Rather than administer his own estates, he preferred to serve as a receiver for the royal estates in the south-west, as treasurer of the speculative Providence Island Company, and as a political adviser to the earl of Bedford and to his friends. This – together with the fact that he served in Parliament after Parliament as a carpetbagger for a pocket borough – made him more completely a man of business, ready to vote high taxes for good causes, than almost any of his contemporaries. In the Parliaments of the 1620s this certainly put him out on a limb.

What we know of Pym's life is his life in Parliament. We know little more of where he was or what he was doing in the intervals between the Parliaments of 1614 and 1640 than we knew when Gardiner wrote about him 100 years ago. Pym left no personal papers and few of his letters have survived, even in the papers of others. He has been unlucky in his biographers.[23] He is known to have written only one, insubstantial, account of his beliefs, the six-page defence of himself against the calumnies of his enemies published in early 1643.[24] More than almost any other public figure of the period, we can come to an understanding of him only through his actions and speeches in Parliament – imperfectly recorded as they are. Outside Parliament there are only glimpses of a career as Crown official and colonial administrator.[25] All we can say with confidence is that he can be regularly glimpsed in the relaxed presence of some of the greatest of the malcontent and Puritan peers, and that he had a townhouse in London which was regularly sealed on royal orders at the end of parliamentary sessions.

S. R. Gardiner's distilled account of Pym's career in the 1620s stresses his fierce anti-popery (this conviction that 'papists ... were to not [to be] coerced because of their religion but because it was right "to restrain not only the fruit but even the seeds of sedition, though buried under the pretences of religion"'), his even greater role in the parliamentary pursuit of corrupt ministers (he was manager of three of the impeachment articles against Buckingham) and of clerics (he carried the charges against Montagu to the Lords in 1625, and those against Manwaring to the Lords in 1628) and the key role he was eventually, if not initially, to play in the passage of the Petition of Right.[26] Conrad Russell's account, both in his monograph of the Parliaments of the 1620s[27] and in his detailed essay on Pym in that decade, has an overlapping emphasis: 'there were two obsessive themes which ran through the majority of Pym's speeches in the 1620s ... the purity of the true religion and the sanctity of the King's revenues'.[28] Pym hounded papists from office and sniffed out those whose religious practice had whiffs of popery about it; he called for a crusade against popery abroad and was willing to finance campaigns against it.[29] Like Gardiner, Russell notes that in his first recorded speech Pym called for a new oath of association (based on the 1584 precedent), to combat the threat of militant Catholicism abroad and its fifth column at home. But Russell sees a second insistent theme – the ruthless pursuit of those who deprived the king of his lawful revenue (Mompesson as much as Buckingham) and the willingness to use parliamentary means to enhance that revenue so that Protestantism could be defended and promoted: he proposed an act of resumption,[30] and 'with two exceptions,[31] every speech he made on subsidies was in favour of giving the largest possible number of subsidies in the shortest possible time'.[32]

Already in the 1620s, his belief that a well-counselled king needed a large income to prosper the international Protestant cause put him at odds with many fellow critics of the current ministers and policies, and far away from the 'mere' country gentry massed silently but doggedly on the back benches. There are many pre-echoes of the early 1640s. He looked for accountable but active government; and we see little in him of the fastidious antiquarianism, narrow legalism or localist reflex against centralization of so many of his fellows. And – as Gardiner put it – 'Pym was at bottom a puritan, Wentworth an anti-puritan'. It was a distinction which in the end separated him not only from the future Strafford but from Coke, Phelipps, Digges, Noy, Seymour and a host of others.

IV

Conrad Russell and others have done sterling work in piecing together the contacts between the group around Bedford, Saye and Brooke, their friends, their commoner allies and the Scottish Covenanters during the military campaign of 1639 and the run-up to the elections to the Short Parliament of 1640.[33] The links, however, remain elusive and inconclusive. They certainly cannot be construed as evidence of a willingness on the part of any important group of English politicians deliberately to wreck the Parliament of April–May 1640.

All existing accounts of Pym's part in the Short Parliament – as with every aspect of that Parliament – have been rendered redundant by the discovery and publication of the parliamentary diary of Sir Thomas Aston.[34] For the first time we have a source for the Parliament that allows a sense of its dynamics to emerge. Russell's recent account is an excellent one.[35] Most MPs were willing to barter with Charles: a settlement of English grievances in exchange for hard cash to support a renewed war with the Scots. There was a wide range of opinion about how hard that bargain needed to be; but a majority were willing to sacrifice Scottish interests to secure English ones. Russell is cautious in characterizing the position of Pym and the circle he represented. Pym is shown to be here, there and everywhere in the Parliament, from his two-hour speech on 17 April ('perhaps the most successful of his life'), through his persistent if only partially successful attempts to keep the House to the agenda he there enunciated, to the rumours of his intention to plead for reconciliation with Scotland which seems to have triggered the dissolution on 5 May.[36] It is of the greatest significance that Russell – rightly, I think – believes the record to show that 'if Pym had raised this issue on the floor of the House, he would have lost'.[37]

There is no doubt that Pym was highly visible in the Parliament. Aston records him as speaking on seventy occasions in just over three weeks, more than twice as often as any other MP: only ten members are recorded as speaking more than twenty times, and six of those were the Speaker, and official spokesmen for the government and for the Queen.[38] And yet the great majority of his 'speeches' were in fact only interventions on matters of detail.

Surveying his contribution to the Short Parliament as a whole, what stands out is his outspokenness on religious issues, his prominence as an errand boy between the Commons and the Lords and his abandonment of his natural habitat of the 1620s – impeachment.

Three things are striking about the prominence he gave to religious issues. The first is its striking continuity with the stances he had taken up in the 1620s; the second is its discontinuity with the reticence he famously displayed in the Long Parliament; and third is that much of what he said was as hostile to Scottish ecclesiology as it was to Laudian ecclesiology. Probably his most effective speech (in terms of tangible results) was his 29 April intervention which led to a rapid succession of votes condemning the setting up of images, crosses and crucifixes, protesting about the exclusion from holy communion of those who refused to kneel, and the expression of concern at the introduction of new visitation articles on episcopal authority alone and the deprivation of ministers for non-reading of the Book of Sports.[39] But just as striking was his passionate attack on the principle that Convocation could pass canons or in any way bind the consciences of the laity. This was very much in the tradition of his arguments for the rights of Parliament to judge matters of faith in the 1620s at the time of the York House Conference. It would have made the Scots squirm. Where did that leave the Scottish General Assembly?[40]

His perceived prominence owes most to the fame of his two-hour speech, delivered on 17 April. And yet there are puzzles about this speech. It was not published until the middle of 1641 *The First Speech of Master Pym the Last Parliament*, and it was then reprinted in various versions in 1641, 1642 and again in 1643. Except on the occasion of its initial printing, the implication each time was that it had been delivered to the Long Parliament.[41] And despite Pym's repeated attempts to being the House back to the agenda laid out there, it is not clear that he had much success. Russell's account of the speech highlights Pym's emphasis on the need for annual Parliaments, the iniquity of the 'military charges' in 1639 and the all too real presence of papists around the court. None of these were prioritized in the debates that followed, or in the negotiations with Charles, which focused on Ship Money. Pym represented a minority view in April 1640, and it is far from clear that the failure of the Parliament was any less a defeat for the group he represented than it was a defeat for everyone else. And while most MPs were clearly willing to sacrifice

Scottish liberties in order to secure English liberties, Pym was surely trying to safeguard English liberties without sacrificing Scottish liberties, which is not the same as saying that he gave the protection of the Scots priority over the regaining of English liberties.

V

When we move on to consider Pym's role in the early years of the Long Parliament (1640–3) the account by S. R. Gardiner has been characteristically influential. Gardiner had read the diaries of D'Ewes, Yonge and Whittacre, and he had the *Commons Journals* and the Thomason Tracts open by his side as he wrote.[42] His account recognizes Pym's leading role at all the key moments in the years 1640–3, and the driving force of religion in his life:

> above all existing law, above all popular rights, he placed religion. For him, however, religion did not stand in opposition to the world and the things of the world ... if Pym had been a mere Parliamentarian, wishing to substitute the sovereignty of the many for the sovereignty of the one, his work would have been easy. His difficulties arose from his recognition that more than the form of government was at stake and from his belief that religion ... must be upheld if the nation were to live, even against the will of the nation itself.[43]

There is some anachronism in this judgement, but also much shrewd sense. It needs to be conjoined with the other point that Gardiner saw more clearly than many since him. His encomium on Pym's death also includes the point that in his very first (recorded) speech in the Parliament of 1621, Pym called for a new oath of association to secure the nation against popery and 'that those who should refuse the same should not hold any office in the commonwealth'. This proposal, Gardiner noted, which grew out of the Association of 1584, was the germ of the Protestation of 1641, the Vow and Covenant of 1643, if not of the Solemn League and Covenant itself. Going back to Gardiner often – though not, of course, always – restores a clarity of vision about an aspect of the Civil War. Subsequent historians have not necessarily improved on his intuitions and observation.

VI

For too long the most resonant voice in discussions of Pym's achievement has not been Samuel Gardiner's but Jack Hexter's. His *The Reign of King Pym* is entertainingly written, telling with wit and bravura an essentially dull story of a gifted administrative improviser and skilled political operator. But it is a desperately under-researched and over-written book. It is a chipping from his Ph.D. thesis[44] which sought to establish the dynamics of partisan politics in the later 1640s and which was condensed into his classic article 'The problem of the Presbyterian independents'.[45] The thesis is only marginally concerned with the pre-history of the groups he was concerned with, and the research reflected this. Hexter used the journals of both Houses, and made limited use of the parliamentary diaries of D'Ewes, Whittaker and Yonge. But that is about it. As we will see later, it seriously misrepresents the nature of Pym's contribution to the events of 1643. Lacking back-reference to his actions and words in the months and years preceding the outbreak of the Civil War, taking no account of his published speeches from the last year of his life, and making claims that go beyond what is warranted by the evidence adduced, *The Reign of King Pym* is an extraordinarily cavalier book in all the wrong senses.

In a work concerned exclusively with the months between November 1642 and August 1643, when Pym's steep decline into death from stomach cancer made him a marginalized figure, Hexter makes three major claims. The central one is that in the first years of the Civil War, Pym put himself at the head of a 'middle group' that held the ring between those MPs who would have made peace with the king on almost any terms and those who were deter-mined to impose terms on a king utterly defeated in war. Like the Sinn Fein leadership of the 1980s, seeking to drive the Brits out of Ulster with a ballot paper in one hand and an Armalite rifle in the other, Pym is said to have been obsessed with simultaneously keeping open the lines of communication with the king while escalating the war effort in order to be able to negotiate from a position of strength. He thus co-operated with the war and peace parties by turns and his genius was 'to get what he wanted without doing irrepera-ble damage to the *esprit de corps* of Parliament as a whole'.[46] In a sense the rest of the book is a context for the establishment of this argument.

This argument needs testing far more fully than is possible here, for it is far too unicameral for modern tastes and there are innumerable problems about the stability and cohesion of the alleged middle group.[47] Hexter's other core arguments are independent of it yet they, too, do not stand up to close examination. The first is that Pym was an administrative genius:

> Between November 6, 1642, when the King on a flimsy pretext slighted the first overtures of Parliament after Edgehill, and the middle of the following April, when the treaty between Charles and Parliament was broken off, Pym had either pushed through or thrown open to discussion almost every important adminis-trative, fiscal and military ordinance enacted by Parliament during the Civil War.[48] During the few months of life remaining to him after the treaty collapsed, all his proposed measures were adopted.[49] He left Parliament with an adminis-trative organization in the counties, with an ally ready to march in arms to its assistance, and with three armies of its own to take the field against the King.[50]

The metaphors in defence of this argument lie as thick on the ground as leaves in autumn: 'like an industrious hen, Pym, when he was not busy hatch-ing one batch of schemes, set about laying another';[51] 'Pym's seemingly jerry-built structure survived all the shocks of the civil war';[52] he recognized the need for a weapon of defence 'against a king who when his hands were free had a dangerous itch to lay about on all sides. The forger of that weapon was John Pym and the weapon he forged was the civil-war House of Commons.'[53]

As we will see, this single-handed triumph evaporates in the heat of an inspection lamp; but it is less perniciously wrong than the third part of Hexter's argument, concerning the supreme pragmatism needed to lead a middle group and to build the war machine ('the blueprint of the design mean[t] little, the functioning of the machine mean[t] much').[54]

> If we seek ... for the basis of Pym's policy, we are likely to reverse the custom-ary procedure and miss the one real tree in a futile quest for an imaginary forest. We follow Pym's painstaking labors, his deft craftsmanship in making Parliament a relatively mobile and efficient instrument capable of waging war ... Every effort to define the new goal that Pym was working toward fails. He was not a dog-matic republican like Martin nor a staunch Presbyterian like Harley, and his pre-vious parliamentary career does not incline one to believe that he yearned for a policy of religious toleration ... Not a political theoriest like Ireton, and not a religious theorist like Vane, he had nothing in him of the architect of brave new worlds. He was a political tactician, a political engineer.[55]

It is that influential[56] judgement that this essay seeks to contest.

VII

John Pym's career between the summoning of the Short Parliament and the outbreak of the Civil War has been dealt with as an important aspect of three recent works,[57] and they all have strikingly different emphases. None of them offers us a systematic account of Pym's actions or of his mind, although they all place him centre-stage in their narratives. Anthony Fletcher's is clearly the best account. He takes up Hexter's claim for Pym's tactical brilliance, but combines it with a trait Hexter failed to note:

> one cannot fail to note the contrast between the shrewdness and practicality of Pym's tactics and the emotional basis of his policies. The policies themselves sug-gest the abnegation of reason. The parliamentary leaders were in no position to distinguish between truth and rumour and had no desire to do so.[58]

Thus for Fletcher the near-hysterical tone of the preamble of the Grand Remonstrance[59] 'takes us directly into the inner recesses of Pym's mind',[60] while his speech of 23 June 1641 is seen as the most important of the whole first session, and as 'a theatrical account of the dangers facing the nation shot through with his preoccupation with popery'.[61] Fletcher's Pym is an intuitive politician, at once wily and neurotic, a man who had little understanding of the timidity and paralysing uncertainty of the 'country' members who made up the bulk of the House.[62] He did not so much manipulate a widespread fear of popery as 'impos[e] his own fears of popery [so that] he had many really believe that papists were kindling a civil war'.[63] He was a hater of bishops,[64] he was suspicious of – but willing to use – the Scots,[65] a man of certainty to whom the uncertain turned in an uncertain world.[66]

Russell came to his study of the fall of the British monarchies between 1637 and 1642 from his major study of the Parliaments of the 1620s, with its pendant essay on Pym's career in those Parliaments.[67] Some of the themes of that essay, notably Pym's commitment to sound finances, purged of prerogative pretension, and to sound religion, purged of popish pretension, come through Russell's recent work on the Short and Long Parliaments;[68] and there is a new emphasis on Pym's constitutional radicalism – his apparent allusions to the *Vindiciae contra tyrannos* in his speech introducing the Ten Propositions in June 1641, for example;[69] or his conclusion from studying a draft declaration in Pym's hand from April 1642, that 'this may have been the moment at which the last vestiges of his allegiance to Charles disappeared'.[70] But it must be said that there are some very fuzzy edges to Russell's portrait of Pym in these years. Pym appears sometimes as a free agent, leading by example and intuition, but at other times he is the constrained leader and mouthpiece of a party that was dominated by peers and heavily dependent on serving the ends of their Scottish allies. The Pym of *The Fall of the British Monarchies* is strangely two-dimensional in comparison with the Pym of Russell's *Parliaments and English Politics 1621–1629*, let alone Fletcher's *Outbreak of the English Civil War*.[71]

At least Russell has no doubt of Pym's central role in dividing and ruling the House of Commons. He is treated as the single most important figure in the lower House in the period up to the outbreak of war. This brushes aside the arguments advanced by Sheila Lambert, that Pym's leadership was a 'myth'.[72] Her main argument is that in the early months of the Long Parliament 'it was the role of the peers not the Commons that was crucial'; that there never was unanimity in the Commons against the misgovernment of the past and that there was no Commons consensus for Pym to lead.[73] For Lambert, the fact that Pym was never a teller, that he was 'not in the first rank of committee men in the first session', that his financial proposals were much opposed, so that he cannot be hailed as being 'in charge of finance', and that 'he showed little understanding of bill procedure', all militate against his being accorded the pre-eminent role.[74] Some of Lambert's arguments are clearly overstated – such as the attempt to portray the Long Parliament as 'summoned by the King in the usual manner' and its opening weeks as 'entirely in accordance with the precedents of the early Stuart Parliaments'.[75] This may be constitutionally true but it is politically false. Similarly she seems to me to overstate the claim that a comparison of the behaviour of the Houses following the deaths of Pym and Essex shows the unimportance of the former and the dominance of the latter.[76] But Lambert has presented a case which needs to be answered and not brushed aside. Above all, she has shown that it is wrong to see Pym as a parliamentary jack of all trades who could and did

turn his hand to whatever the occasion required. I hope to show that, insofar as he dominated the politics of the early 1640s, it was by concentrating
on a few tasks at a time. Furthermore, Lambert is surely right to suggest that
he was never in a position to deliver the kind of settlement which could have
prevented war. His financial reforms were no more acceptable in the context
of 1640–2 than they had been in the 1620s. It is striking to go back to Conrad
Russell's classic essay on 'Parliament and the king's finances' and to find that
his discussion of Pym's role in the financial reforms of 1641 suggests it to have
been so limited and so negative.[77] The reform programme consisted of a job
lot of proposals drawn up by the Bedford/Warwick/Pembroke[78] connection
from which Saye was distanced and towards which he was possibly hostile,
and key elements of it were drawn up by Pye, Rudyerd, Gerrard and Vernon
rather than by Pym. Russell indeed notes that all of Pym's own inititiatives
'aroused a good deal of opposition' and that 'some of Bedford's other proposals were much better designed to gain parliamentary support'. If it had
not been for Russell's acceptance of Hexter's argument that the financial programme of 1643, based on this collective programme of 1641, was 'put into
effect by Pym', a claim that we will see does not stand up, then Russell could
have concluded that Pym's part in the 1641 debates was counter-productive.[79]
After all, as Derek Hirst has pointed out, as early as the spring of 1641 Sir
John Hotham (with his great king-defying exploits still to come) 'saw Pym as
a new Strafford, and likened his schemes for reforming the subsidies to a
Turkish despotism'.[80]

VIII

John Pym was certainly the most *visible* figure in the House of Commons in
the first three years of the Long Parliament. His name appears more than
1,000 times in the *Journal* of the House in that period – more times than there
were parliamentary days. This seems to be about twice as many times as the
next most active members, who were almost certainly Denzil Holles, William
Strode and Walter Erle.

After a busy early few weeks – he appears forty times in the *Commons
Journal* during the first eight weeks of the Parliament – he was less dominant
in the period that followed, probably hard at work in committee preparing
the impeachments of Strafford and other evil counsellors. It was with the
resumption of the Houses after the summer recess that his name came to
dominate the *Journal* – appearing at least thirty times every month in all but
two of the months until the onset of his final illness in early October 1643.

His name also appears more than 100 times in the *Lords Journal* – on most
occasions when he is delivering a message from the House of Commons.
There were times when he seemed to have cornered the market in running
important errands between the Houses.[81]

His name also dominates the diaries of those who – often four or five at a time – kept a record of the debates in the House of Commons. It has long been established that only about eighty (of 509) Members of the Commons were recorded as speaking in the House. Again Pym stands out. A count based on seven modern editions which collate most of the diaries for much of the time, supplemented by my own analysis of unpublished diaries for the spring and summer of 1641, suggests that Pym is recorded as having spoken on almost 900 separate occasions, again probably twice as many times as anyone else.[82] The editors of the three volumes of *The Private Journals of the Long Parliament* for the period January to September 1642 conclude that throughout the period an analysis 'based upon the frequency of daily partic-ipation as recorded in the journals of D'Ewes and Moore' puts Pym at the head of the list of 'principal participants' in the activity of the House of Com-mons.[83]

Finally, the *Short Title Catalogue 1641–1700* includes thirty-three published speeches reportedly made by Pym in the years 1640–3,[84] whereas no other MP published more than six speeches in the same period.[85]

There can thus be no mistaking Pym's prominence in the Long Parliament, especially in his role as a link-man for a (perhaps) highly organised group in the two Houses. But visibility is not itself proof of leadership.

IX

And so Sheila Lambert's words come back to haunt us. Pym *was* never a teller, he was 'not in the first rank of committee men in the first session', many of his initiatives encountered strong opposition or ran into the sand. He was not a jack of all trades. Her case could indeed be strengthened. In the period down to the spring of 1642 the king assented to thirty-eight completed public bills and thirteen completed private bills presented to him by the Houses.[86] Many more bills made considerable progress in the House of Com-mons. As far as I can determine, Pym never introduced a bill, and only very rarely did he speak during a debate on a bill at any stage of its progress, except for the Bill of Attainder that finally destroyed the earl of Strafford, and he initially opposed the introduction even of that bill. He was not one of those who publicly identified himself with the view that England's ills needed legislative redress.[87]

If Pym was a dominant force in the House of Commons in the early years of the Long Parliament, it was by becoming ever more a specialist in one or two tasks at a time. Let us take two sample periods. In January and Febru-ary 1641, Pym is recorded as having spoken on forty occasions. He remained silent on many of the principal concerns of the House in these months: the structural reform of the Church; the resolution of franchise disputes and con-tested elections; the Triennial Bill; the Treaty with Scotland; contentious Star Chamber judgements; and above all – dominating these weeks even more than the impending trial of Strafford – the relief of the burdens imposed on the north of England by the English and Scottish armies there.[88] Particularly striking was his determination to keep religious affairs off the agenda, deferring debates on contentious issues[89] and declining to enter into the spiritual wickedness of Laud in an inflammatory address concerned with his usurpation and abuse of jurisdiction and secular authority.[90]

Instead Pym set out regularly to instruct the Houses on procedural matters such as whether MPs could consult the patent rolls in the Rolls Chapel,[91] on the tradition that all committees of the House sent to see the king should contain a Privy Councillor,[92] on the procedure to be followed during divisions and at free conferences,[93] and on the precedents for joint sessions of the two Houses.[94] This reminds us of his seniority in the House of Commons: he was one of the very few veterans to have sat through all the Parliaments of the 1620s and who was active in the Long Parliament. Conrad Russell suggests that, of the twenty most prominent House of Commons men in the 1620s, only Pym and Francis Seymour were present in the Long Parliament.[95] This would obviously give Pym's often specious accounts of custom and tradition an unnatural authority.[96]

But he was more prominent still in pushing forward the cases against Laud and Strafford, sometimes in tandem.[97] He acted pre-eminently as a manager, ensuring that new charges – from the Scots against both of them, for example, or from Sir Henry Wallop against Strafford – were integrated into the proceedings, that the House addressed itself to the relationship between general and particular charges, and that the Lords was kept fully informed of proceedings.[98] In late February he made major set-piece speeches summarizing the charges against Strafford ('the actions of the Minister of the Great Turke or some other Mahumetan Prince, then of a Christian Monarcke and a Gratious King')[99] and Laud ('Mr Pymme spake fully in aggravation of the Archbishopps crimes')[100] linking their treasons one to another.[101]

Perhaps his role is best exemplified in D'Ewes' record that

> it was ordered upon Mr Pymms motion, that all those members in this House that sate in anie chaire in anie of the committees of this Howse who had anie thing prooved before them that might conduce to the making or drawing upp of the charge against the archbishop of Canterburie; that they would meet this afternoone in the chequer chamber.

Twelve months later, in the early months of 1642, his obsession was with Ireland. In the eight weeks after the Attempt on the Five Members, Pym is recorded as having spoken on seventy occasions. These were the weeks during which a number of issues dominated the business of the House: the Militia Ordinance was gestating; the Lords Spiritual were expelled from the House of Lords and twelve of their number were impeached; thirty-six bills were making their way through the House of Commons; extensive treaty negotiations were conducted with the Scots; and the English response to the Irish Rebellion was developed. Forty per cent of all Pym's speeches in these weeks (twenty-seven recorded speeches altogether) were on Irish affairs and he also acted as the key liaison man between the Houses on Irish affairs. He did not speak at all on the militia or the bishops, and only on a handful of occasions on the Scots.[102] He touched on every aspect of Irish affairs: he reported on the seizure of Dunkirk ammunition ships caught heading for Irish ports;[103] he kept the Houses informed about the movement of English troops through Chester to Ireland;[104] he reported the progress of fund-raising for the allied army;[105] he complained about the 'dangerous consequence' of a new catechism in Latin and Irish;[106] and he reminded MPs about the atrocities still allegedly being per-petrated by the rebels.[107] Significantly, his next most visible contributions to the work of the Houses in this period also showed a preoccupation with secu-rity. He made five speeches seeking means to secure the Tower of London in the hands of those in whom the Houses could have confidence, another five concerning the impeachment of the latest evil counsellor to be demonized, George Lord Digby, and (in late January 1642) four speeches reporting on and attempting to exploit the petitions on the state of the kingdom presented by the citizens of London, and by the freeholders of Middlesex, Essex and Hertfordshire. His speech when he delivered these petitions from the lower to the upper House[108] was one of his great set-piece addresses.[109]

An equally detailed review of other periods would produce the same out-come. Pym was neither ubiquitous nor omnicompetent. Looking back over the first session,[110] we find the same obsessions as in the 1620s: in his opening speech to the Long Parliament he called for those who had misled the king into popish and arbitrary policies to be punished, and within days he was car-rying up to the Lords the impeachment articles against Strafford and Laud, and he was pushing through articles against a number of other bishops and churchmen; and he launched the first of several schemes (most of which fell on deaf ears) for an English national covenant, and while he played a lead-ing part in the interim financial arrangements to see England and Scotland through the immediate crisis, his fitful attempts to turn the Commons to long-term financial solutions all nosedived. He was prominent in the impeachment of Strafford before the Lords; in launching the investigation of the Army Plots, and in promoting the Ten Articles. Although he served on the com-mittees that resulted in the Triennial Bill, the Bishops' Exclusion Bill and the Grand Remonstrance, he was barely visible in the debates in the House on these measures. He was not active in the programme of remedial legislation that dominated the Houses in the summer months. His appointment as chair of the Recess Committee sealed his leadership role in developing an innova-tive parliamentary executive and it was in the *exercise* of executive and administrative functions (rather than in the design and enacting of them) that we find him most frequently from the end of the recess until his death. Ini-tially this meant the management of the Irish expedition and the coalition with the Scots to drive the Irish Confederates out of Ulster; but this led nat-urally on to the co-ordination of the defence forces raised against the king from July 1642 onwards and to the development of a three-kingdom defence strategy that was to culminate in the Solemn League and Covenant in the last months of his life.

He thus played little part in the parliamentary activity that led to the remedial legislation of 1641, such as the Acts that dismantled the conciliar courts; he took little part in the major debates on the future settlement of religion and on the Militia Ordinance, and only a subordinate role in the making of the Nineteen Propositions.[111] He was no legislator, and, as Sheila Lambert pointed out, he was not the most prominent committeeman early on, and his real dominance was to come with his key role in all the important executive bodies created by the Houses from the end of the first session onwards – the Recess Committee in the summer of 1641, the Committee for Irish Affairs from June 1642 and the Committee of Safety from July 1642.

Rather he was a man who saw Parliament as the instrument for bringing to justice all those who abused their power and trust as servants of the Crown or servants of the Supreme Governor of the Church. In the years 1641 and 1642, when others promoted bills and acted as tellers as they ground their way through the House of Commons, Pym had very different priorities. In the first session he was overwhelmingly the principal reporter carrying messages between the Commons and the Lords – undertaking eighteen such missions in the first session of the Parliament up to September 1641; twenty in the similar period between the opening of the second session to the outbreak of war and sixteen from that point to his sickening unto death.

His other great initial achievement was to use Parliament as a judicature – the High Court of Parliament calling to account all those miscreants who had abused the king's good name and faith, be they councillors, judges, bishops or popish parsons. But increasingly his achievement was to preside over a radical redefinition of Parliament as a great council of the realm, governing in the king's name. From taking *a* leading part in the impeachment of Strafford, he threw himself into the making of the Scottish Treaty of 1641, the Protestation, the Grand Remonstrance, the Solemn League and Covenant, the creation and resourcing of the English army sent to Ireland in 1642 and of the army under the earl of Essex that took the war to the king from the high summer of 1642 and the creation of a parliamentary executive centred on the Committee of Safety.[112]

X

Was he, then, as Hexter so influentially assured us half a century ago, the craftsman behind the great money ordinances of 1643 – assessment, fifteenths, excise, sequestrations – of the ordinances that set up the associations, the regional structures of war administration, of the ordinance that set up the Westminster Assembly? Amazingly, there is little evidence to suggest that he was. The gloomy D'Ewes, 'recording in his diary the successive outrages per-petrated on the body of his beloved mistress, the common law',[113] does not supply us with any evidence that Pym led any of these outrages. Nor do the diaries of Lawrence Whittaker and Walter Yonge. Nor, for that matter, do the *Journals* of the two Houses. Pym's name appears only rarely in relation to any of these measures. Let us take the evidence of the months November 1642–March 1643 during which most of the ordinances hailed by Hexter as his great and abiding achievement were passed. During those five months Pym makes 102 appearances in the *Journal* of the House of Commons. Just two of them relate to the ordinances referred to in Hexter's account of 'Pym as political artist' – martial law, advance of money, the creation of the associations, weekly assessment, sequestrations. On 25 November he was first named to a joint committee to go to the City to persuade the Common Hall to agree to the levying of assessments for the war effort (a very remote connection with the legislation itself), and on 15 March it was 'ordered that Mr Pym and Mr Lisle do bring in an ordinance of some additions to be made for the Ordinance of Assessments'[114] (note the supplementary nature of this role). The eighteen-page chapter in which Hexter describes Pym's political artistry has eighty-seven footnotes and rather more specific references to the *Journals* of the Houses and to the parliamentary diaries of D'Ewes, Yonge and Whittaker. Just one of the references to the latter actually shows Pym actively and effectively assisting the passage of the great sequence of ordinances which Hexter hails as his great legacy: on 27 March D'Ewes records that 'Mr Pym stood upp and shewed that wee had complaint from all places for the want of money and that therefore we should send upp to the Lords to passe the ordinance for the seizing of the estates of Malignants. It was accomplished.' None of the other footnotes bear out such repeated claims as that 'Pym utilized the momentary indignation ... to add one storey after another to its crazy, ramshackle but otherwise usable financial structure'.[115] Pym had nothing to do with the passage of the martial law ordinance and did not even sit on the select committee to consider it;[116] no evidence is presented that Pym put Sir Gilbert Gerrard up to pushing for the fining of those who had lent on the Propositions. No nudging was necessary – Gerrard was, after all, Treasurer of the Army.[117] The key figure in the debate on the sequestration ordinance – as on many fiscal measures – was Serjeant Wilde.[118] Pym's attempt to promote the Excise in March was a miserable failure; when it returned to the Commons in the summer he played no part in its promotion.[119] It would be otiose to go on.

I am not saying that Hexter's larger purpose – to conjure up a middle group that held the ring between war and peace parties – is an invention.[120] If the middle group existed, there is little doubt that Pym was *an* important member of it. But he cannot be made to be the dominating presence, the mastermind behind all parliamentary good works, and specifically behind parliamentary ordinances. His work in and for the House during the winter months of 1642–3 was dominated by two activities. The first was the management of conferences with the Lords, which he undertook on thirty occasions.[121] These were months during which the Oxford Articles were offered to the king, extensive efforts made to negotiate a ceasefire and 'cessation' (staged disbandment), and Pym was the essential Commons go-between with the Lords on all aspects of these negotiations. He was also frequently sent to the Lords to confer on matters relating to the navy and Ireland and relations with the Scots. His second major activity was as a draftsman of official House of Commons and parliamentary letters and declarations – sometimes alone[122] and more often as one of a team (though he was usually the one who reported back).[123] Beyond this his duties were miscellaneous ones: he was a key figure in linking the Houses to the City of London;[124] he presented to the Commons a list of names of Scottish officers who had volunteered to serve in English armies;[125] he was added to a select committee to look into complaints about vandalism at Lambeth House (i.e. Palace);[126] and he was the first named to a committee instructed to peruse all orders and warrants issued by the House and the Committee for the Safety of the Kingdom in recent months.[127] This was a busy schedule, and it was wholly compatible with his dominating presence at the Committee of Safety which was piecing together management of the war effort. Over the fifteen months of its existence he took his place twice as often as all but one other member of this hub committee, and he also processed far more business than anyone else.[128] Here, surely, lay his real importance. As Simonds D'Ewes wrily tells us, so much business was taken over by the Committee that the House of Commons had little to do 'till they came amongst us and communicated as much as they thought it fit for us to know'[129] and that everything concerning the safety of the kingdom was referred to the Committee 'by a kind of fatalitie and implicite faith'.[130]

His role in the Commons was quintessentially one of co-ordinating the work of the Houses and of this all-important executive committee.[131] Not surprisingly, then, he did not discover at this time a preoccupation with legislation or even with finance. It remains possible that he was the man who behind the scenes persuaded the Houses to pass all these ordinances. Certainly the committees he chaired had the responsibility for enforcing these ordinances. Certainly it seems unlikely that he did not have a strong investment in securing their passage. But he was not the only one. And his agency requires more demonstration than presumption. Hexter's King Pym is an emperor with no clothes.

XI

The other way to get at what drove Pym on is to look more closely at his printed speeches. There is plenty of material but there are also plenty of problems. The printed diaries for 1640–3 and such unprinted diaries as I have studied tell us that in the first thirty-six parliamentary months of the Long Parliament Pym spoke in the Commons on at least 900 occasions. On about

40 per cent of those occasions we have little more than a reference to the fact that he spoke ('Mr Pymme having read the written answeares of Owen Occonelle which were farr shorte of what he had related, wee proceeded'; 'Mr Pym enformed the howse that the Lords were now sett and weere readie to give us a conference'),[132] and on about 50 per cent of occasions what he said was condensed down by the diarist to less than 100 words. Only on about 10 per cent of occasions do we have a substantial account of what he said.

The Lords and Commons *Journals* record the fact that Pym spoke at conferences of the Houses or reported to the Houses on more than 200 occasions in these thirty-six months; but it records his words on only ten occasions, five of them between late October 1641 and late January 1642. Seven of those speeches are very fully recorded and may well represent the most reliable texts we have of his views.

No fewer than thirty-three of his speeches from this period were printed, which was far more than those for any other MP. Fifteen of these were said to have been spoken in the House of Commons, ten in joint conferences with the House of Lords, three in committee and five in conferences with the aldermen and/or Common Hall of London. Many of these are very extensive speeches; their distribution by date of publication is shown in Table 2.1.

Table 2.1: Printed speeches attributed to Pym, Nov. 1640–Oct. 1643[133]

Supposed date of delivery	Supposed place of delivery				
	HoC	HoL	City	Committee	Total
11/40–02/41	2	1			
03/41–06/41	1	2			
07/41–10/41	2	1		1	
11/41–02/42	5	3		2	
03/42–06/42	1				
07/42–10/42	2	1			
11/42–02/43		1	3		
03/43–06/43	2	1	1		
07/43–10/43			1		
TOTAL	15	10	5	3	33

Alan Cromartie has already established that six of the speeches published before 1 August 1642 were fabrications; at least they do not correspond with any occasion when Pym is known to have spoken, and there is nothing in the *Journals* of the Houses or in the private journals of MPs that indicates an appropriate occasion on or near the alleged date of delivery when Pym could have given the speech as published.[134] To Cromartie's list of fabrications I would add a further nine.[135] The pattern of fabrications is shown in Table 2.2.

Table 2.2: Speeches attributed to Pym, Nov. 1640–Oct. 1643 which were probably fabrications[136]

Supposed date of delivery	Supposed place of delivery				Total
	HoC	HoL	City	Committee	
11/40–02/41	0 [2]	0 [1]			0 [3] = 3
03/41–06/41	0 [1]	0 [1]			0 [2] = 2
07/41–10/41	1 [1]	0 [1]		0 [1]	1 [3] = 4
11/41–02/42	4 [1]	1 [2]		2	7 [3] =10
03/42–06/42	1	0 [1]			1 [1] = 2
07/42–10/42	2	1			3 [0] = 3
11/42–02/43		1	0 [3]		1 [3] = 4
03/43–06/43	1 [1]	1	0 [1]		2 [2] = 4
07/43–10/43			0 [1]		0 [1] = 1
TOTAL	9 [6]	4 [6]	0 [5]	2 [1]	15 [18] =33

Note: Figures in brackets represent speeches probably or certainly based on speeches actually made at the time and place claimed.

It will be noted from Table 2.2 that while eight of the nine speeches attributed to the first session were based on speeches actually given, eleven of the fourteen attributed to the period November 1641–October 1642 were fabrications. After that the only publications were five speeches to the City of London and three reputed speeches in Parliament – at least one and probably two of which were fabricated. So, in reality, no more than eleven of his *parliamentary* speeches appear to have been published.

Several of the fabrications were republications of speeches previously published with a new, and false, provenance.[137] At least one is a speech that appears to have been tampered with and republished as though newly minted.[138] Others appear to have been fabricated in order to provide an answer to Royalist propaganda, such as *The report of Mr Pym concerning the King's Majesty* which was appended to a copy of *The Queenes majestys propositions to the States of Holland*.[139] This group are consistent in content but much cruder in tone than Pym's own speeches. One or two of them are simple pastiches of aphorisms from earlier published speeches, drawing not only on Pym's earlier speeches, but on the inflamed rhetoric of others – even Harbottle Grimston's vicious characterization of Laud as the stye of pestilential filth was trotted out.[140]

It remains puzzling that publishers could get away with putting out statements in his name without incurring censure. Yet the themes of all the fabrications were characteristic both of his real publications and evocative of the terrors of any Protestant subconscious. It is also striking how much more daring the fabricators became, building on previous tolerance of their presumption.

Perhaps a nod and a wink were given; perhaps not. Just occasionally, a fabrication is so timely, so sophisticated and on so politically sensitive an issue, that there has to be a presumption that it represented a kite-flying exercise by Pym himself and by the group he represented. The most important of such putative fabrication by Pym is *A most learned and religious speech spoken by Mr Pym at a conference of both Houses ... Sept 23 (1642) declaring ... the necessity and benefitt of the Union of His Majesties three kingdoms in matters of religion and church government*,[141] a speech incongruously printed in a pamphlet together with an item on the coining of farthings and Rupert's sweep from Chester to Worcester. It will be discussed below.

We cannot, of course, be sure of the relationship of the text as printed and the speech as delivered. Conrad Russell has shown that Pym's set-piece speeches were given from notes.[142] Furthermore, close comparisons between the detailed manuscript notes taken by Aston and others on Pym's speech to the Short Parliament show a close correlation,[143] as does a comparison of speeches minuted in the *Lords Journal* and subsequently published.

There is, then, a corpus of extended writing, consisting of eighteen texts that are almost certainly accurate versions of what he said, and more importantly authorized versions of what he wanted it thought he had said, and another five texts which probably fall into the same category. Many of the obsessions which come through in this corpus are the same as in the summaries of his speeches contained in the private journals.

Three obsessions stand out. The first was the relentless pursuit of evil counsellors and the necessity of mechanisms to prevent the king from surrounding himself with polluting advice. As evil counsellors fell by the wayside, others took their place. In the wake of Wentworth and Laud came Digby.[144]

> These ill counsels have proceeded from a spirit and inclination to Popery and they have dependency on popery. The religion of the papists is a religion incompatible with other religions, destructive of all others and destructive of all states and persons that oppose it. Unless these ill counsels be changed it is impossible that any assistance, aid or advice that the Parliament can take to reform wilbe effective for the public.[145]

A year later he was still banging on the same drum in the same key:

> My Lords, your Lordships may observe that the distractions of this Kingdome have beene fomented by the Jesuiticall and Prelaticall Faction, discontented courtiers and selfe-lovers, and how that this Jesuiticall and Prelaticall faction have not onely threatened ruine to the kingdome of Ireland but all other reformed Churches as is evidenced by their late practices.[146]

These speeches are quintessential Pym and could have been given (and with variations of language were given) at any point between November 1640 and

November 1643.

The second obsession, already revealed in the above, was with the integration of secular and religious grievances. Time and again he disaggregates them for analysis only to indicate both that they cross-infect one another and (a theme wholly consistent with his speeches in the late 1620s) how the ultimate source and engine of England's troubles was popery. The language was always the same. In his opening speech to the Short Parliament grievances were put under three heads: 'the first are those grievances which are against the liberties and privileges of Parliament; the second are innovations in matters of religion; the third grievances against the propriety of our goods'.[147] A version of his speech to the Lords when he was sent to deliver the Ten Propositions in June 1641 speaks of three heads: in matters of religion, in the king's private estate, and in the good of the whole kingdom.[148] The fullest of all these addresses was on 25 January 1642 when he introduced a series of county petitions in response to the attempt on the five Members. He spoke of the four dangers ('enemies abroad'; 'papists'; 'tumults and insurrections of the meaner sort of people by reason of ill vent of cloth'; and 'rebels in Ireland'); he talked about the six 'distempers' or 'obstructions' (headed by 'the obstruction of Reformation in matters of religion – no grievances are sharper that those that press upon the tender consciences of men'); and it ends with the 'evil influences which have caused the distractions' ('evil counsellors'; 'discouragement of good counsel'; 'bishops and popish Lords' etc.).[149] The same kind of analysis could be found at any point down to his death. And always the taproot of the evils is found in religion: most graphically in a possibly fabricated speech from June 1642, he argued that their purpose was (in this order) to maintain true religion, to serve the king in preservation of his royal person and dignity, and to procure the common good.

> This may well be called one end, though in respect of the severall relations it comprehends those three branches, they have the same roote, they have the same essence and being. It is impossible that any man should truely affect the king or the common good that is negligent of religion.[150]

His third obsession, then, was with the purity of the true religion. And yet it is exceedingly hard to pin down his own beliefs. Perhaps, like Cromwell, he knew what he would not have but not what he would have. We have already seen that he loathed popery in all its manifestations – both its pure form (adherence to the Bishop of Rome and his false claims) and in its adulterated form – as a theological, liturgical and ecclesiastical contaminant of the Church of England. We have seen how Stephen Marshall hailed him ('engrafted into Christ ... justified freely by his grace, sanctified throughout in spirit, soule and body')[151] – Marshall is convinced that he is one of the elect, with an assurance of saving grace. That makes him a Puritan by any definition. In his *Declaration and Vindication*, Pym asserted straightforwardly that

I am, and ever was, and so will dye a faithful son of the Protestant Religion without having the least relation in my belief to those grosse errours of Anabaptisme,
Brownisme, and the like, everie man hath any acquaintance with my conversation can beare me righteous witnesse. These being but aspersions cast upon me
by some of the discontented clergie and their fautors [*sic*] and abettors because
... I sought a Reformation of some grosse abuses crept into [the Church of England's] government by the cunning and peevishness of the Bishops and their sub-
stitutes. For was it not hightime to seek to regulate their power who instead of
looking to the cure of men's souls when ...

And off he went again into a tirade against the particular wickednesses of the
persecution of preachers and of Prynne in the 1630s.[152]

By my calculation, twenty-nine MPs published or condoned the publication
of their speeches from the debates on episcopacy in the first session of the
Long Parliament. Pym was not one of them. Although he was crucially
involved in the impeachment of Laud and Cosin, and thirteen bishops over
the canons of 1640, and of other churchmen, only one speech dealing directly
with these prosecutions was published – a version of a speech he made at a
conference concerning the impeachment of Laud in February 1641.[153] The evidence of the private diaries suggests that Pym made little contribution to the
major set-piece debates on root-and-branch reform in February,[154] or
May/June 1641.[155] He was much more visible during the heated September
debates which led to the order for the reordering of churches, but typically
his principal role was not in the development of the orders for the removal
of monuments of idolatry and superstition from the churches, but in the management of the conference with the Lords and the decision of the Commons
to stand up to an outraged Upper House which was determined to stand up
for the Elizabethan settlement.[156] More generally, an analysis of his first 100
recorded speeches shows that about twelve focused upon the threat of popery
in general or from particular persons, another ten arose from his management
of Laud's trial, four concerned the prosecution of other delinquent clergy, and
four others were essentially procedural: reporting from a committee on Members taking communion; discussing procedure for a vote on the illegality of
the canons of 1640; moving that a debate on the oaths taken by bishops' chan-
cellors be bought to an end; and (on the same day – just a week before the
heated and divisive debate on the root-and-branch bill itself) seeking a delay
in the debates on the corruptions in the Church.[157]

This does not take us any farther. Similarly, in his 200 recorded speeches
from the winter months of October 1641 to February 1642, he was regularly
to be found denouncing Catholic priests in London and Catholic conspiracies
in Lancashire; he was seeking to impose the oaths of supremacy and allegiance on royal servants; and he was pursuing procedural devices for getting
bishops out of the Lords; but on godly reformation and its lineaments he was
silent. And the same is true of the seventy or so appearances he makes in

Yonge's diary between September 1642 and March 1643. If he had strong views on the religious clauses of the Nineteen Propositions or Oxford Articles, he did not share them with the Houses, let alone the public. Almost his only overtly religious proposal from this period was his call on 3 January 1643 for 'a nationall association betweene us and Scotlande as the popish partie beyonde sea doe unite themselves against the protestants to overthrow our religion'.[158] Certainly that ties in with his last great venture, the securing of the agreement with the Scots in the late summer and autumn of 1643. This was prefigured, with astonishing foresight, in a fabricated speech published in September 1642 calling for

> one Directory or forme of prayer should be observed throughout the three kingdomes ... one catechisme taught ... [and that] the assembly of Divines for reformation of religion and church lyturgy should convene ... and that the 3 kingdomes being under one [Church] government might agree in discipline and unity of spirit.[159]

This seems to get us closer to the heart of his religion. And his enthusiastic endorsement of the Covenant from his sickbed in September 1643, very fully noted by Yonge,[160] bears out his commitment to the military and religious union of 1643. But even then we must be careful. He had not previously shown any interest in a readjustment of the constitutional relations between the three kingdoms. He was one of those happiest to see whatever happened in Ireland as cognizable by the English Parliament or the English courts,[161] displaying no interest in the Scots demands for a federal union in 1641, and a tendency to see the Scots as a separate country with which one might form a political alliance, but not a political union.[162]

In the end we may well get closest to him in a speech not, I think, hitherto noted,[163] which, if it reflected his views, is the most explicit he ever became:

> Religion is the first thing desired to be settled. There hath been many orders made by this present parliament, whereby many corruptions in the ministry and dispensation of the word and sacraments are in some good measure purged, many scandalous vicious teachers in their lives and conversations removed and many powerful and learned men restored ... But yet is there not a thorough reformation ... For want of a thorough reformation men give themselves to all manner of vice and uncleanness, practicing not professing rightly but loosely and profanely any religion, multitudes have forsaken the protestant and joined the Romish religion, many have forsaken our church and become separatists, Brownists and Anabaptists. The whole state seems as if it were composed of naught else but divers factions, sects and schisms, and all through want of a full reformation of religion.

This reeks of the man who ten days earlier really did tell the Lords of 'the agony, the terror, and the perplexity' which was 'universal' in the kingdom. Here we see a man who believes in a state church, whose language is paranoid but not apocalyptic, whose obsession is the purity of the reformed religion, a religion of the Word and the Sword. This is the sober erastian Puritanism of an earlier generation,[164] except for the exceptional venom of the anti-Catholicism. But then this was a man who was five years old and probably living near the coast of Devon as the Armada sailed, and who was almost certainly studying at the Middle Temple at the moment when the Gunpowder Plot was foiled.

XII

It has been the intention of this survey to nuance rather than to transform our understanding of John Pym; to reduce him from an exposed and lonely position as leader of the parliamentarian movement from 1640–3 to a more credible position as an extraordinarily determined and devoted team member.

Let us go back to the influential judgement by Hexter with which we began.

> If we seek ... for the basis of Pym's policy, we are likely to reverse the customary procedure and miss the one real tree in a futile quest for an imaginary forest. We follow Pym's painstaking labors, his deft craftsmanship in making Parliament a relatively mobile and efficient instrument capable of waging war ... Every effort to define the new goal that Pym was working toward fails. He was not a dogmatic republican like Martin nor a staunch Presbyterian like Harley, and his previous parliamentary career does not incline one to believe that he yearned for a policy of religious toleration ... Not a political theorist like Ireton, and not a religious theorist like Vane, he had nothing in him of the architect of brave new worlds. He was a political tactician, a political engineer.[165]

I would suggest that this both underestimates and overestimates him. He was more of a visionary, more of a human dynamo than this allows for, and less of a master politician and much less of an effective leader. By 1640, he was a veteran MP and minor administrator who could be trusted to get up in the House and speak to briefs. He was increasingly used by others to specialize in two very demanding jobs – improving communication between the Houses and running parliamentary committees that had to develop administrative capability as they went along. He was, after all, the former treasurer of a colonial venture who had had to learn to improvise there. For twenty years he had been the friend and confidant but also the hired assistant to a powerful group of social and political leaders with whom he continued to work in the early 1640s. He had been a key member of the think-tank that periodically gathered at Sir Richard Knightley's house at Fawsley in Northamptonshire to ponder the options of those dismayed by Charles' government of England. He was most useful to them in those capacities. He is not a major figure in the debates on religion or, it now transpires, finance. Whenever he spoke on finance, he got his fingers burnt; perhaps he decided to shut up or perhaps he was shut up by others. He lacked, we must remember, the experience of being a country gentleman. His gaunt, austere, State–Church Puritanism, lacking the chiliasm and libertarianism of so many of his colleagues, may also have struck a false note. On the perils of popery, he could be trusted. Otherwise his religious passion drove him, but it did not drive the House or the movement he was part of. Even the impeccable Gardiner stands in need of some modification. 'He worked by influence not by eloquence.'[166] As parliamentary draftsman, as well as manager of awkward conferences, he worked through both.

More than anything else he was the man most convinced by, most expert in identifying and articulating, the great popish design against Protestant and therefore (and thereby) civil liberty. He likened himself to Cicero, the tireless exposer of the Catiline conspiracy with its holistic threat to Roman virtue.

He was a useful front-man. He did not always lead, but his name was used to fly kites and to publicize positions taken up by colleagues and friends. Thus his prominence in the public eye rather exceeded his prominence in the Parliament. He was the busiest MP; but he was not ubiquitous and he was not omnicompetent. Of all the judgements on him, perhaps the highly stylized appreciation by Stephen Marshall is the most appropriate: 'In a word he was a true Nathaniel. in whom there was no guile.' Nathaniel, we remind ourselves, was the fisherman from Cana whom Jesus called to discipleship as he sat below a fig tree trying to puzzle out the Scriptures. For John Pym, the path from the fig trees of Fawsley to the vault of kings was a very different kind of discipleship; but it as a call to serve his God none the less.

Notes

[1] I owe many debts of gratitude in the preparation of this essay. Andrew Barclay spent 100 hours assisting me to identify those printed speeches that Pym could not have made in the Parliament, in producing a list and index of his appearances in private parliamentary diaries, and in sharing with me his impressions of what his work showed; Peter Salt kindly put at my disposal several references I had missed in the unpublished parts of the *Diary* of Sir Simonds D'Ewes – and added to that some quite remarkably perceptive comments on a late draft of the essay; John Adamson and Frances Kelly gave me a list of page numbers in the *Commons Journals* (C.J.) on which Pym's name appears; Derek Hirst, David Smith and Wallace MacCaffrey assisted me with particular enquiries. I would have never have got drawn into the complexities of the Long Parliament if I had not been inspired by the example of David Underdown, in this as in everything he has written about, a scholar who teaches us how to write accurately and empathetically. His *Pride's Purge* remains *the* masterpiece of political analysis on the Long Parliament. Andrew Barclay, Alan Cromartie, Anthony Fletcher and David Smith all read a draft of the article and provided me with sage counsel which much improved it.

[2] The Scottish members were absent because the Scots believed funeral orations in the presence of the corpse could all too readily be seen as part of the popish error of

praying for the soul departed, as though God's eternal decree of salvation and damnation had not already been realized.

[3] S. R. Gardiner, *History of the Great Civil War 1642–1649* (4 vols., 1893), vol. III, pp. 147–50; V. F. Snow, *Essex the Rebel: The Life of Robert Devereux, the Third Earl of Essex* (Nebraska, 1970), pp. 488–94.

[4] Pym was buried (*pace* Snow, *Essex*, p. 466 which implies otherwise without citations) in the chapel of Henry VII (S. Reed Brett, *John Pym 1583–1643: The Statesman of the English Revolution* (London, 1940), pp. 26–7 and sources there given); Essex was buried in the chapel of John the Baptist off the North Choir, alongside many prominent Elizabethan peers (Snow, *Essex*, p. 466 and sources there given).

[5] S. Marshall, *The Churches Lamentation for the Good Man his Loss ... A Sermon Preached at the Funerall of that Excellent Man John Pym Esq.* (1643).

6 S. Marshall, *Churches Lamentation*, p. 34.

[7] *Ibid.*, pp. 34–6.

[8] British Library (B.L.), Addit. MS 31, 116, fo. 99 (entry for 11 December 1643).

[9] J. H. Hexter, *The Reign of King Pym* (Cambridge, MA, 1941). For a critique, see below, pp. 34–6.

[10] S. Lambert, 'The opening of the Long Parliament', HJ, 27(2) (1984), p. 285.

[11] *A Declaration and Vindication of John Pym esquire concerning the divers aspersions which have been cast upon him by sundry base and scandalous pamphlets* (March 1643), pp. 3–4 (there is a sound edition of this tract in an appendix to C. E. Wade, *John Pym* (1912), pp. 334–8).

[12] Marshall said that he 'verily feared lest our relying too much upon the assistance of our brethren from Scotland by their armies may more prejudice their and our successe then the strength of our enemies can do', presumably a caution against 'carnale confidence' rather than an attack on the Scots as such (Marshall, *Churches Lamentation*, p. 13).

[13] *Cal. St Pap. Ven. 1643–7*, p. 53.

[14] *Declaration and Vindication*, p. 7; Wade, *Pym*, p. 337.

[15] S. R. Gardiner, *History of the Great Civil War*, vol. I, p. 258.

[16] For the Nicholas letter, see J. S. A. Adamson, 'Parliamentary management, men-of-business and the House of Lords, 1640-49' in C. Jones (ed.), *A Pillar of the Constitution: The House of Lords in British Politics 1640–1784* (Manchester, 1989), citing Surrey R.O. (Guildford), MS 52/2/19/16. For Wroth's comment, see *Cal. St Pap. Dom. 1641–3*, p. 132. Other letters of Nicholas point to the significance of Pym's role as a lynchpin of a bicameral party at this time, see W. Bray (ed.), *The Diary and Correspondence of John Evelyn*, (4 vols., 1906), vol. IV, pp. 93, 105.

[17] W. H. Coates, A. S. Young and V. F. Snow, *The Private Journals of the Long Parliament, 3 January 1642 to 5 March 1642* (New Haven, 1982), pp. 54–5 (and cf p. 57).

[18] *C.J.* vol. II, p. 478.

[19] *A Coppie of the Bill against the xiii Bishops presented to the Lords by the Commons, October 25 1641 ... whereunto is added the substance of a letter presented to Mr Pym.* The episode is discussed in A. Fletcher, *The Outbreak of the English Civil War* (1981), pp. 128–9.

[20] B. L. Harl.MS 164, fos. 400–1. Note also the passing reference in the doggerel verse on another MP: 'And I, quote Strode, can ly as fast as Mr Pym can trott.' Much of it repeats familiar *canards* (with the inevitable reference to Essex the cuckold) but the reference in the verse on Saye to 'the work ... I plotted ... above these seventeen

years' is noteworthy. The libel as a whole deserves to be better known and studied. This is one of the many important references in this essay drawn to my attention by Peter Salt.

[21] S. R. Gardiner, in his life of Pym in the *Dictionary of National Biography* (*D.N.B.*), vol. 47, pp. 75–83, and (more particularly) C. Russell, 'The parliamentary career of John Pym, 1621–1629' in P. Clark et al. (eds.), *The English Commonwealth 1547–1640: Essays in Politics and Society presented to Joel Hurstfield* (Leicester, 1979), pp. 147–66, which needs to be supplemented by the essay on 'The wardship of John Pym' in C. Russell, *Unrevolutionary England* (1990), pp. 145–63.

[22] As early as 1614 he put all his land in trust and handed over the administration to a distant relation (his step-sister's husband). It remained in trust until at least 1635 (Reed Brett, *Pym*, pp. xxiv–xxv).

[23] Really only J. Forster, *John Pym* (1837); Wade, *Pym*; and Reed Brett, *Pym*. The first two offer useful documentary appendices, but none has more than a loose and anachronistic sense of the period.

[24] *Declaration and Vindication.*

[25] The most recent and best such study is K. Kopperman, *Providence Island 1630–1641: The Other Puritan Colony* (Cambridge, 1993), see esp. pp. 4–6, 300–1, 321–6.

[26] *D.N.B.*, vol. 47, pp. 75–7.

[27] C. Russell, *Parliaments and English Politics 1621–1629* (Oxford, 1979).

[28] Russell, 'Parliamentary career', p. 151.

[29] There is a grim list of his targets in Russell 'Parliamentary career', p. 152 and cf., pp. 158–9.

[30] And this at the very time of Charles' profoundly unpopular attempt to get the Scottish nobility to co-operate in a Resumption scheme.

[31] Twice he spoke out to urge delay until grievances were addressed – namely, to secure Buckingham's impeachment and the Petition of Right.

[32] Russell, 'Parliamentary career', pp. 153–4.

[33] See especially C. Russell, *The Fall of the British Monarchies* (Oxford, 1991), pp. 61–97; P. Donald, *An Uncounselled King? Charles I and the Scottish Troubles, 1637–1641* (Cambridge, 1990), pp. 217–20, 244–50.

[34] J. Maltby (Ed.), *The Short Parliament (1640), Diary of Sir Thomas Aston* (Camden Society, 1988), 4th ser., vol. 35.

[35] no copy.

[36] Russell, *Fall*, pp. 100–23. There is a (for our purposes) less focused discussion in K. Sharp, *The Personal Rule of Charles I* (New Haven and London, 1992), pp. 860–85.

[37] Russell, *Fall*, p. 123.

[38] Maltby, *Aston*, p. 163–70 (appendix B). It is worth noting that the other collection of sources for this Parliament , E. S. Cope and W. H. Coates (ens.), *Proceedings of the Short Parliament of 1640* (Camden Society, 1977, 4th ser., vol. 19) contains very few speeches not also recorded in Acuteness Diary, whereas Aston multiplies the number of known speeches by a factor of at least three. It is possible that he recorded virtually *all* speeches given in this Parliament. What a pity he was defeated in the parliamentary selection in the autumn.

[39] Russell, *Fall*, pp. 114–15; Maltby, *Aston*, pp. 90–1.

[40] Russell, *Fall*, pp. 108–10; Cope and Coates, *Short Parliament*, pp. 168–9; Malt by, *Aston*, p. 31. For Pym's willingness to arrogate to the House of Commons (and to

himself within the House of Commons) the authority to judge matters of true doctrine and practice, see Russell, *Parliaments and English Politics*, esp. pp. 231–2, 410–1. For an outspoken attack on his position, see the letter of Bishops Buckeridge, Howson and Laud to Buckingham, dated 2 August 1625, in W. Scott and J. Bliss (eds.), *The Works of ... William Laud* (7 vols., 1846–60), vol. 6, pp. 244–6. Pym's speeches on religious issues throughout the Parliament are closely linked to the second section of his speech on 17 April, in which 'he defined the title of true religion as a form of property' (Russell, *Fall*, p. 106) – more Scottish squirming?

[41] For the publishing history, see Cope and Coates, *Short Parliament*, pp. 299–302. The resulting confusion was sufficient to cause John Rushworth to publish one of the later versions as Pym's November speech (never actually published) to the Long Parliament. It is not self-evident that its impact was as great at the time as it has been in twentieth-century historiography.

[42] For a hostile account of how Gardiner composed his history, which I find as reassuring as the author found unacceptable, see R. Usher, *A Critical Study of the Historical Method of Samuel Rawson Gardiner, with an excursus on the historical conception of the Puritan Revolution from Clarendon to Gardiner* (St Louis, 1915).

[43] S. R. Gardiner, *Great Civil War*, vol. I, pp. 255–6.

[44] J. Hexter, 'The rise of the Independent Party', Ph.D. thesis, Yale University, 1936.

[45] J. H. Hexter, 'The problem of the Presbyterian Independents', *American Hist. Rev.* (1938), and reprinted in his collected essays, *Reappraisals in History* (1961, 1979), pp. 219–40. The scholar who has done most to refine and deepen Hexter's arguments is of course David Underdown, especially in *Pride's Purge* (Oxford, 1971).

[46] Hexter, *King Pym*, p. 31.

[47] This is where a much greater understanding of prior linkages of friendship and obligation was and is needed. Was Pym a free agent or the agent of others, as he clearly was at other times? Furthermore, like almost all existing narratives of the Long Parliament (the major exception is David Underdown's *Pride's Purge*), the course of politics is explained by reference to the behaviour of organised groups. Too little attention is given to the substantial number of country gentry whose behaviour is determined more by the self-interest of their localities than anything else.

[48] Identified as martial law, assessment of London, association of counties, weekly assessment, sequestration of delinquents' estates.

[49] Identified as fifth and twentieth part, vow and covenant, assembly of divines, impressment, alliance with Scotland, excise, solemn league and covenant.

[50] Hexter, *King Pym*, p. 16.

[51] *Ibid.*, p. 25.

[52] *Ibid.*, p. 26.

[53] *Ibid.*, p. 205.

[54] *Ibid.*, p. 206.

[55] *Ibid.*, pp. 199–200.

[56] See, for example, its full and unquestioned adoption by Derek Hirst, *Authority and Conflict, England 1603–1658* (1986), by far the best-informed and intelligent of the standard textbooks of the period, at pp. 236–8.

[57] Fletcher, *Outbreak*; Russell, *Fall*; Lambert, 'Long Parliament'. Fletcher's account concentrates on the second session of the Long Parliament, Russell's on the first session. For other studies in which Pym makes regular appearances but in ways that add little to the above three accounts, see R. Ashton, *The English Civil War, 1603–1649*

(1978); C. Hibbard, *Charles I and the Popish Plot* (Chapel Hill, 1983); B. Manning, *The English People and the English Revolution* (1976).

[58] Fletcher, *Outbreak*, p. 409.

[59] Most conveniently printed in S. R. Gardiner, *Constitutional Documents of the Puritan Revolution* (3rd edn., 1906), pp. 202–4. The emphasis is on 'the multiplicity, sharpness and malignity of those evils under which we have now many years suffered' and which were fomented and cherished by ... those malignant parties whose proceedings evidently appear to be mainly for the advantage and increase of popery'. This is vintage Pym!

[60] Fletcher, *Outbreak*, p. 82.

[61] *Ibid.*, p. 43.

[62] *Ibid.*, p. 36.

[63] *Ibid.*, p. 410.

[64] *Ibid.*, pp. 168–9 and *passim*.

[65] *Ibid.*, p. 18 and *passim*.

[66] *Ibid.*, p. 72 and *passim*.

[67] Russell, *Parliaments, passim*; Russell, 'Parliamentary career'.

[68] In 'Parliamentary career', p. 51–2, he speaks of 'religion and the sanctity of the king's revenue' as twin obsessions. For these themes in his *Fall* see pp. 20, 32, 115, 194, 242–57, 350–4 and *passim*.

[69] Russell, *Fall*, p. 353 and n.101. I have to say that the quotation he gives from Pym's speech of 26 June 1641 (*L.J.* vol. IV, p. 285), which appears to state that Pym thinks it impossible to work for the good of the commonwealth without serving the king, seems to me incompatible with Huguenot thought. I am grateful to Alan Cromartie for a discussion of this point.

[70] Russell, *Fall*, p. 489.

[71] See Anthony Fletcher's discussion in his review of Russell's recent books, 'Power, myths and realities', in *HJ*, 36(1) (1993), pp. 211–16.

[72] Lambert, 'Opening of the Long Parliament', p. 285.

[73] *Ibid.*, pp. 285–6, 265–8.

[74] *Ibid.*, pp. 267–72.

[75] *Ibid.*, p. 265. This seems to overlook the unprecedented circumstances in which Charles was constrained by the Scots to call that Parliament and the widespread recognition that he had no actual choice but to keep it in being until it had made a treaty with the Scots, which would only follow their remedying the perceived misgovernment of recent years. It was unprecedented for the king to have no *de facto* ability to determine when and for how long a Parliament met.

[76] Pym died at the height of a war going the wrong way, Essex with the war won; the Commons could afford neither to take a day off (although the House of Lords did do so (*L.J.* vol. VI, p. 340) nor to find large sums to settle on his heirs.

[77] In C. Russell (ed.), *The Origins of the English Civil War* (1973), pp. 91–116.

[78] The presence of Pembroke at this early stage – as he moved from high office at court and a seat on the Council to opposition – is rather surprising and is not fully explained.

[79] Russell, *Origins*, pp. 111–13.

[80] Hirst, *Authority and Conflict*, p. 199. This being a textbook, Hirst does not give his source; one of them is almost certainly the diary of Sir Thomas Peyton, where Hotham is quoted as saying that Pym's proposal for the rating of land followed the

pattern of William the Conqueror and that 'the Turks sett their Timarriots on such proportions of land' (W. Notestein, *The Journal of Sir Simonds D'Ewes from the Beginning of the Long Parliament to the opening of the Trial of Strafford* (New Haven, 1923), p. 111 and n. 16.

[81] For example, in the period between 1 November 1641 and 1 March 1642 he was sent to the conferences with the Lords on more than twenty occasions: *C.J.*, vol. II, pp. 832, 833, 836, 845, 849, 856, 879, 886, 916, 917, 924, 925, 946, 947, 948, 956, 958, 959, 969, 972, 974, 978, 983.

[82] Notestein, *D'Ewes*;* M. Jannson, *Two Diaries of the Long Parliament* (Gloucester and New York, 1984); W. H. Coates, *The Journal of Sir Simonds D'Ewes from the first recess of the Long Parliament to the withdrawal of King Charles from London* (New Haven, 1942)*; W. H. Coates, A. S. Young and V. F. Snow, *The Private Journals of the Long Parliament 3 January 1642 to 5 March 1642* (New Haven, 1982) (henceforth, *Private Journals* vol. I); V. F. Snow and A. S. Young, *The Private Journals of the Long Parliament, 7 March 1642 to 1 June 1642* (New Haven, 1982) (henceforth, *Private Journals* vol. II); V. F. Snow and A. S. Young, *The Private Journals of the Long Parliament, 2 June 1642 to 17 September 1642* (New Haven, 1982) (henceforth, *Private Journals* vol. III); C. Thompson, *The Diary of Walter Yonge* (Wivenhoe, 1987).* I am deeply grateful to Dr Andrew Barclay who prepared for me a list and index of all references to Pym in the books asterisked above. I prepared my own list and index for the other volumes; and I have filled the gap between the first and second by reading D'Ewes' diary for the months of March to September 1641 and have also read Whittaker's diary for 1643 (B.L., Addit. MSS 31, 116), and Geoffrey Palmer's diary for 1640–1 (Cambridge University Library, MS Kk. 6.38).

[83] *Private Journals* vol. I, p. xxii; vol. II, p. xvii; vol. III, p. xviii.

[84] See *Short Title Catalogue 1641–1700*, items C2754A, E2729A, H1289, H1465, M400–1, M2939 and P4260–4305, allowing for the duplications involved.

[85] The only qualification to this statement is Sir Edward Dering, imprisoned in the Tower and expelled from the House in February 1642 for publishing a collection of his speeches in a single volume. *See Private Journals*, vol. I, pp. 253–65, 348–54.

[86] *Statutes of the Realm*, vol. V, pp. vi–vii, 178.

[87] The reader of Russell, *Parliaments and English Politics*, will reach the same conclusion with respect to his career in the 1620s.

[88] This list was created by analysis of the index of Notestein, *D'Ewes*, p. 549–98.

[89] Notestein, *D'Ewes*, pp. 308–9.

[90] *Ibid.*, pp. 413 and 413n.

[91] *Ibid.*, p. 239.

[92] *Ibid.*, p. 361n.

[93] *Ibid.*, pp. 363n, 364n.

Ibid., p. 207n.

[95] Russell, *Fall*, pp. 100–1. Seymour was to move towards a constitutional Royalist position in the course of 1641 and was not an assertive presence in the Long Parliament.

[96] As in his account of how Parliament had used to appoint its own clerks, Notestein, *D'Ewes*, p. 264n; or when D'Ewes rebuked him for his claim that the Houses had anciently held joint sessions, *ibid.*, p. 207.

[97] For example, Notestein, *D'Ewes*, pp. 212, 216.

[98] *Ibid.*, pp. 215–16, 244, 256–7, 297–8.

[99] Ibid., p. 305. This had been his line from the beginning; cf. his comment in the first week of the Parliament in introducing Lord Mountnorris' petition that 'when we consider divers points of this petition a man would thinke wee lived rather in Turkie then in Christendome' (ibid., p. 12).

[100] *Ibid.*, pp. 413 and 413n. The versions offered by D'Ewes and Moore differ significantly from the version in Rushworth, *Historical Collections*, vol. IV, pp. 199–202. See below, pp. 37–9.

[101] 'comparing ... how they both endeavoured to subvert religion and the fundamentall lawes of the realm [and] that both were ambitious, proud and insolent', Notestein, *D'Ewes*, pp. 394–5.

[102] The exception to this is that on 24 February he was asked to deliver a message to the Lords about a whole series of matters: the impeachment of the bishops, on guarding the coast of Ireland, on additions to the Scottish propositions and on the bill against pluralities. (*L.J.*, vol. IV, p. 609, and cf., *Private Journals*, vol. 1, p. 449–50).

[103] *Private Journals*, vol. I, p. 50.

[104] *Ibid.*, pp. 99, 301.

[105] *Ibid.*, pp. 239, 243, 296, 300.

[106] *Ibid.*, p. 343.

[107] *Ibid.*, p. 300.

[108] *L.J.*, vol.. IV, pp. 537–43.

[109] See below, p. 40.

[110] What follows is based on an analysis of the *Commons Journals*, Notestein, *D'Ewes* (for the first half of the session) and on an analysis of D'Ewes' manuscript diary (B.L., Harl. MS, 162–3) for the second half of the session.

[111] Again this is most simply demonstrated by reference to the indexes of the various volumes emanating from the Yale Centre for Parliamentary History listed in note 82, checked, of course, against the content. Thus while there is no reference to the Nineteen Propositions in the entry for Pym in the index to *Private Journals*, vols. II and III, it is made clear in the text that although he did not negotiate the propositions themselves through the Commons, he was (what else?) the reporter on 31 May 1642 of the last-minute addition of five propositions to the original fourteen (*Private Journals*, vol. II, pp. 395, 396).

[112] All these positive contributions have been documented in the detailed narratives of the period by Gardiner, Russell and Fletcher referred to above; and are immediately apparent from any browsing the indexes of the various volumes emanating from the Yale Centre for Parliamentary History listed in note 00.

[113] Hexter, *King Pym*, p. 31.

[114] *C.J.*, vol. II, p. 861; *C.J.*, vol. III, p. 2.

[115] Hexter, *King Pym*, p. 16, and the sources there cited.

[116] *Ibid.*, p. 16 n. 10, and the sources there cited.

[117] *Ibid.*, p. 21, nn. 31, 34, and the sources there cited.

[118] *Ibid.*, pp. 22–3, nn. 38–47, and the sources there cited.

[119] *Ibid.*, p. 25, nn. 60–2; although, ironically, he is wrong to say that Pym was not on the committee – *all* members of the Committee for the Advance of Money (of which he was one) were *ex officio* on the Excise Bill Committee.

[120] I have not systematically checked the footnotes beyond page 30.

[121] *C.J.*, vol. II, pp. 832, 833, 836, 845, 849, 856, 861, 879, 886, 897, 905, 916, 917, 924, 925, 946, 947, 948, 956, 958, 959, 969, 972, 976, 978, 983, 991, 999, 1000, 1001;

C.J. vol. III, pp. 2, 3, 4, 7, 10, 19, 20, 24.

[122] C.J. , vol. II, p. 866 (letter of thanks to man who had carried messages to Scotland); p. 873 (to draw up a commission for Mr Strickland); p. 885 (to Hotham about the defence of Hull); p. 892 (for the raising of dragoons in Cambs); p. 893 (to draft an encouraging letter to Sir John Gell); p. 909 (declaration against illegal activities of some sheriffs); p. 940 (to report to Colonel Ruthen on his promised payments out of customs); p. 950 (reply to petitioning seamen); p. 968 (to draw up orders for the deputy lieutenants of Cambridgeshire).

[123] C.J., vol. II, . 838 (letter of thanks to Lord General); p. 839 (Declaration to the Scots); p. 873 (to draw up a defence of Parliament's proceedings); p. 882 (to draft an address to be sent to Holland); p. 901 (rely to Scots complaints about non-payment of their troops in Ulster); p. 902, 915, 928 (to draft declaration about Royalist mistreatment of prisoners); p. 911 (against the earl of Newcastle's illegal assessments); p. 975 (to prepare a declaration for the navy); p. 986 (to vindicate the Houses from aspersions contained in a royal proclamation); C.J., vol. III, p. 26 (to write to Lord General about Surrey assessments).

[124] For example, C.J., vol. II, pp. 861, 927.

[125] Ibid., p. 939.

[126] Ibid., p. 974.

[127] Ibid., p. 994.

[128] L. Glow, 'The Committee of Safety', E.H.R., vol. 80 (1965), pp. 289–313. See Glow's statistical appendix at p. 313. Pym attended on 226 occasions and signed 596 committee orders and warrants. His colourless associate Anthony Nicholls attended on 196 occasions and signed 527 documents; the earl of Pembroke attended 153 times and signed 325 signed times. After that the most frequent attenders were present on 153, 112, 104 and 98 occasions and signed on 325, 304, 289, 278 and 235 occasions.

[129] B. L., Harl.MS 164, fo. 9 (entry for 7 October 1642).

[130] B. L., Harl.MS 164, fo. 10 (entry for 8 October 1642).

[131] Glow, 'The Committee of Safety', pp. 289–313.

[132] Coates, D'Ewes, pp. 75, 111.

[133] Based on the listings in the revised Short Title Catalogue 1641–1700 (STC). The speeches attributed to Pym are listed as C2754A, H1289, H1465, H2422, M400–401, M2939, P4260–4305 and T1118A. This list contains many duplicates.

[134] A. D. T. Cromartie, 'The printing of parliamentary speeches, November 1640–July 1642', H.J., 33(1) (1990), pp. 23–44, esp. at pp. 42–4.

[135] I am deeply grateful to Dr Andrew Barclay who made a careful comparison of the printed speeches against the Journals of the two Houses and modern editions of the private diaries of debates. The Revised Short Title Catalogue 1641–1700 entries for those speeches that he and I propose as fabrications, bearing no relation to matters in those sources, are C2754, H1465, P4270, P4271, P4274, P4283, P4289, P4291 and P4303.

[136] Figures in square brackets are published speeches which appear to be based on speeches actually delivered at the time and place stated.

[137] For example the speech published (STC 1641–1700, M2939, Thomason Tract E172/29) under the title A Motion Presented to the Committee of Parliament ... Also a Speech made by Pym (1641) – and established as a fabrication by Cromartie, 'Printing', p. 41 – was reprinted (STC 1641–1700, C2754, Thomason Tract E155/9) as part of His Majesties Resolution concerning the Magazine in the Tower of London. Like-

wise *A speech spoken in the House of Commons by Mr John Pym* (14 July 1642) and reprinted again as P4272. Similarly, a fabricated speech (see Cromartie, 'Printing', p. 41) published in January 1642 (*STC 1641–1700*, 4287, Thomason Tract E200/4) as *Master Pym, his speech in Parliament ... the fifth day of January ... for his discharge upon the accusation of High Treason* reappeared in September 1642 (*STC 1641–1700*, P4303, Thomason Tract E116/29) as *Mr Pym his Vindication in Parliament*.

[138] For example, *STC 1641–1700*, P4283 (*A speech delivered by Mr Pym at a conference*), purporting to have been delivered on 24 June 1642 looks like a recast version of *STC 1641–1700*, P4299 (*The substance of Mr Pym's speech ... November 9 1641*), itself close to the text in L.J., *vol. IV, pp. 430–2*.

[139] *STC 1641–1700*, H1465 (*Thomason Tract E153/10*).

[140] *STC 1641–1700*, P4290: Mr Pym his speech in Parliament the XXV of January MDCXLI [=1642], p. 2. This claims to be a speech about the twelve impeached bishops and is not to be confused with P4277: *A Speech delivered at a conference January XXV MDCXLI*.

[141] *STC 1641–1700*, P4271 (Thomason Tract E200/65).

[142] Russell, *Fall*, p. 107 and n. 116. Peter Salt pointed out to me that the survival of holograph notes on speeches that were given do not indicate that the speeches were delivered from the notes. For example, Sir Edward Dering informs us that he wrote down notes on his speech introducing the root-and-branch bill and of another speech only *after* he had delivered them (*STC 1641–1700*, D1104: *A Collection of speeches ... in matters of religion*, pp. 63, 78). On another occasion, Dering specifically says he *memorized* a speech, and although he subsequently could not recall it in detail he was willing to own it when a version was printed without his prior knowledge or consent (*ibid.*, pp. 48–9).

[143] *Ibid.*, p. 106 and n. 112.

[144] *STC 1641–1700*, T4304 (Thomason Tract E199/49): *A worthy speech made by Master Pym to the Lords on Fryday the thirty one of December [1641] concerning an information against the Lord Digby.*

[145] *STC 1641–170*, P4299; *The substance of Mr Pym's speech to the Lords in Parliament Novemb. 9 1641.*

[146] *STC 1641–1700*, P4271 (Thomason Tract E200/65): *A most learned and religious speech spoken by Mr Pym at a conference of both Houses the 23 of this instant moneth* [Sept. 1642], p. 1.

[147] *STC 1641–1700*, P4284 (Thomason Tract E198/35): *A speech delivered in Parliament by a worthy member thereof.* Significantly, this was published in July 1641 and does not reveal its origins as a speech of April 1640. For the various versions of this speech and the relationship of the text as published to the text as delivered, see Cope and Coates, *Short Parliament*, pp. 299–302. Cf., the fabricated speech of 1641 which divides grievances into those against the privileges of Parliament, those prejudicial to the religion established and, those that did interrupt the justice of the realm (STC 1641–1700, P4263: *A declaration of the grievances of the kingdom, delivered in Parliament by John Pym, Esq.*).

[148] *STC 1641–1700*, P4268 (Thomason Tract E160/20): *The Heads of a Conference ... June 24 1641.* See also *L.J.*, vol. IV, pp. 285–7.

[149] *STC 1641–1700*, P4277 (and also P4264, P4290): *A Speech delivered at a conference ... January XXV MDCXLI* and cf. *L.J.*, vol. IV, pp. 540–3.

[150] *STC 1641–1700*, E2729A: *Severall Propositions presented from the House of Com-*

mons to the House of Lords by Master Pymm ... under eight several heads ... June 7
1642, p. 2.

[151] See above, p. 19.

[152] Wade, *Pym*, pp. 335–7.

[153] *STC 1641–1700*, P4295 (Thomason Tract E196/33; Rushworth, *Historical Collections*, vol. IV, pp. 195–202): *The Speech and Declaration of John Pymm Esquire ... upon the delivery of the articles of the Commons against William Laud* (1641). Cf. *L.J.*, vol. IV, p. 172. The theme of the speech was 'wickedness in high places' and he treats in turn 'crimes ... various in their Nature ... if you examine them theologically ... they will be found to be against the rule of Faith, against the power of godliness, against the meanes of salvation ... morally to stand against the light of nature, right reason and the principles of human society ... by legall rules ... to be a traytour against His Majesty's Crown, an incendiary against the peace of the state'. This is English Calvinism, uniformed by Covenanting thought from north of the Border, and it draws attention to the absence in Pym of that millenarian edge which is to be found in most Puritan sermons against the Laudians being preached at that time. I am grateful to Alan Cromartie for discussion of this point.

[154] Notestein, *D'Ewes*, p. 336, n. 17, simply records a contribution in passing, which the Scots observer Robert Baillie called short and unprepared.

[155] B. L., Harl. MS 162, fos. 237–319. On 27 May, for example, D'Ewes simply says that amongst those in favour of the bill to abolish bishops were Holles, Pym and Cage, 'who showed that our Bishops had well neare ruyned all religion amongst us and were not willing to yield to any the least reformacon', but he saw the important contribution as Holles'. D'Ewes records that on 10 June 1641 Pym was one of those at a meeting of MPs which had decided to press on with the Bill, but again he is not recorded as having spoken (B.L., Harl. MS 163, fo. 306).

[156] B.L., Harl. MS 164, fos. 89ff.

[157] Notestein, *D'Ewes*, pp. 46 (19 November 1640), 149, (14 December 1640), 308, 309, (1 February 1641).

[158] B.L., Add.MS. 18777, fo. 112^r (as transcribed by Christopher Thompson).

[159] *STC 1641–1700*, P4271: *A most learned and religious speech*, pp. 2–3.

[160] B.L., Add.MS 18778, fox. 29^r–30^v, 43^r (as transcribed by Christopher Thompson).

[161] C. Russell, 'The British background to the Irish Rebellion of 1641', reprinted in his *Unrevolutionary England* (1991), at pp. 263–80 (see esp. p. 272–5). See also the forthcoming study of the Irish Rebellion by Michael Percevell Maxwell.

[162] It is worth adding that, as Karen Kopperman has recently pointed out, Pym was very opposed to the colonies developing constitutionally away from England. They were for Pym, she argues, constitutionally part of England and subject to all its laws, including ecclesiastical laws (Kopperman, *Providence Island*, p. 22).

[163] *STC 1641–1700*, P4292: *Mr Pym His Speech on Tuesday 8th of February* [1642]. It purports to be a speech on the Bill to Exclude the Bishops from the Lords. There is no evidence that it is a version of a speech actually made (checked against the *Journals* of both Houses and the *Private Journals*).

[164] When David Smith read a draft of this paper, he recalled to me the following passage from Russell, *Parliaments and English Politics*, p. 420: 'when Pym, in 1629, tried to include King James in a list of "Fathers of the Church", it seems unlikely that he was indulging in an uncharacteristic piece of courtliness: he was expressing a sincere trust in James's religious dependability'. This seems very just.

[165] Hexter, *King Pym*, pp. 199–200.
[166] S. R. Gardiner, *History of the Great Civil War*, vol. I, p. 258.

3

The moderate and irenic case for religious war: Joseph Hall's *Via Media* in context

Peter Lake

The relationship of ideology to politics has been at the forefront of recent debate on early seventeenth-century English religion and politics. One of the earliest stock criticisms levelled against revisionist scholars was that they had expelled ideology from their account of the period. Certainly, revisionists have tended to replace a vision of the political culture of early modern England centred on ideologically motivated conflict, with one centred on agreement and consensus. On this view, while political conflict could and did occur, its roots lay either in the personal and factional rivalries of the court or in clashes between the interests of the State and those of the ruling class. The resulting disputes were conducted not on the basis of mutually exclusive or antagonistic bodies of political theory or ideology but through the manipulation of shared notions, keywords and concerns. It is thus not fair to say (as is often said) that revisionism ignored ideology. Rather, it radically redescribed the ideological context, the culture, of early seventeenth-century English politics in terms of shared bodies of thought and assumption and a central drive (both ideologically and institutionally constituted) toward agreement and consensus.[1]

Until recently there remained, however, one area where revisionist scholars would allow for the possibility of self-consciously ideological conflict in early seventeenth-century England, and that was religion – hence the prominence of religious disputes in the explanations of the Civil War proffered by both Dr Morrill and Professor Russell.[2] Latterly, however, even this contention has become a subject of intra-revisionist dispute, with some scholars (notably Dr Sharpe, Dr Bernard and Mr White) adopting precisely the same approach to religion as that used by Conrad Russell or Glenn Burgess in their expulsion of ideological conflict from the secular politics of the period. Thus Dr Burgess and Professor Russell have sought to replace what they take to be Johann Sommerville's excessively bipolar vision of a political scene split between contractualists and absolutists, with an account of distinct and yet not incompatible discourses or patterns of argument rubbing along together, always in contact, sometimes in tension but almost never in overt conflict with one another.[3] Now in religion Dr Sharpe and Mr White have sought to supplant what they take to be Dr Tyacke's overly schematic characterization of the theological scene as split into Calvinist and Arminian camps, with a broader and more capacious vision of 'Anglicanism'. On their view, 'Anglicans' were happy to countenance a broad range of opinions on, say, predestination, as they sought to maintain the distinctively moderate and consensual traditions of the English Church, traditions which, for White, Sharpe and George Bernard, had little to do with formal doctrinal dispute and definition and far more to do with the maintenance of order, decorum and Christian consensus within the generous confines of what Dr Bernard has termed England's 'monarchical church'. Common to both approaches is a selective and somewhat over-literal reading of the most self-consciously moderate and consensual aspects of contemporary rhetoric and argument.[4]

One almost perfectly formed example of this mode of analysis can be found in recent treatments of Joseph Hall. Hall, a court preacher, Dean of Worcester, and latterly Bishop of Exeter and then of Norwich, was a self-proclaimed 'moderate'. His career combined a moderate Puritan opening at Emmanuel College, Cambridge and attendance as a delegate at the synod of Dort, with a long career as a bishop and a series of spirited defences of the English Church against separatist and Presbyterian attack. Admired by Nehemiah Wallington but also enlisted by Laud to defend episcopacy against Puritan attack in 1639, Hall personified many of the ideological ambivalences and ambiguities that have stood at the centre of recent debate about the early Stuart Church.[5] His career, in short, almost invites scholarly debate. For, on the one hand, he provides precisely the sort of career trajectory that Professor Collinson has used to exemplify the incorporation of 'Puritan' and evangelical Calvinist strands of thought into that 'religion of Protestants' that, on Collinson's account, dominated the Jacobean Church. On the other hand, Peter White has used Hall and, in particular, his suggestively titled tract of the early 1620s, the *Via Media*, to underwrite a vision of the *via media* of the early Stuart Church very different from that propounded by Collinson. Central to the debate between White, Sharpe, Bernard and Davies, on the one hand, and Collinson, Russell and Tyacke, on the other, has been the alleged 'Calvinism' of men like Hall. For White and Julian Davies the *Via Media* offers proof positive that Hall was not a predestinarian Calvinist at all, but rather a moderate, irenic proponent of a distinctively English middle way.[6] For these scholars (and for Drs Sharpe and Bernard) the use by men like Hall of the language of unity, moderation and order shows that Dr Tyacke and Professor Russell's vision of a Church ideologically divided between Calvinists and Arminians is untenable. Instead, they claim, rightly understood, Hall and his ilk show us that the real line of ideological tension in the early Stuart Church remained that between a moderate Anglican mainstream and a radical, Puritan, predestinarian opposition.

The moderate and irenic case for religious war

In the present chapter I want to address the issues of Hall's 'Calvinism' and of his use of the rhetoric of consensus and moderation through an analysis both of his *Via Media* and of a series of sermons that Hall preached at court in the early and mid-1620s. These sermons, I shall argue, provide the context, both rhetorical and political, in which the *Via Media* should be read. Both the sermons and the tract formed part of a coherent political and polemical strategy to which the rhetoric of moderation, unity and consensus was central, but which in itself was anything but uncontroversial. Both the *Via Media* and the sermons, I contend, have to be read together and as a whole. Quoting sections out of context can make Hall sound like a war-mongering anti-popish bigot, on the one hand, and a moderate, irenic disciple of John Overall, on the other. Only by looking at both those images and by examining the way in which Hall deployed and combined them can we hope to understand what he was up to in the early 1620s.

The essay is intended, therefore, to show that historians should not take even the most enthusiastic invocations of and genuflections before certain fixed points of contemporary debate as a priori evidence of substantive ideological agreement. The claims that, for instance, moderation and unity were good, that extremes and division were bad, that the English Church and commonwealth were moderate, peace-loving and united and could best be kept so by the exclusion and control of certain peccant and fanatic elements bent, for their own private ends, on the disruption of the unity of the State were almost *de rigueur* for any preacher seeking to occupy the high moral ground at the early Stuart court. Again, as Dr Milton has shown, in the wider context of the polemical contest with Rome, claims to moderation, charity and irenicism were increasingly seen as trumps in the struggle to cast the other side as the innovative, schismatic and disruptive party.[7] There was, in short, a discourse of moderation and consensus at or near the centre of religious debate at the early Stuart court. The ability to control that discourse and to type one's opponents as extreme, innovating subversives was a very valuable polemical commodity. But it needs to be remembered that the resulting image of a normative 'middle ground', precisely because it was so valuable, was very far from being unproblematic or uncontested. In fact, the seemingly consensual aims and expectations central to religious disputes conducted in these terms, the precise nature of the extremes between which the golden mean of moderation was to be located, and hence the content of that moderate mainstream itself, were all notions subject to very different readings or interpretations. I want to argue, in short, that the manipulation, for partisan purposes, of even the most calmingly consensual strains of early Stuart discourse often represented a (thinly?) masked form of ideological conflict, the full resonances of which historians can only properly recover by a careful contextual reading of the sources in question.

Part I *The culture of politics*

Peace, unity and catholicity

Let us start with Hall's deployment of the rhetoric of catholicity and Christian unity. Throughout his sermons of the early 1620s Hall stressed the need for unity and moderation in the Church of England and in Christendom as a whole. There was only one holy Catholic Church united around 'one lord, one faith, one baptism'. The difference between 'Catholics' and 'heretics' was to be discerned by applying the tests of the Scriptures, creeds and the primitive councils. Unity, in fact, was of the essence of the Church's being – 'whether ye consider it as the aggregation of the outward, visible, particular churches of Christian professors, or as the inward, secret, universal company of the elect, it is still one'.[8]

Christians should unite around a central core of fundamental doctrines founded on these authorities. The number of such doctrines was small and should not be expanded. Here Hall had recourse to a distinction that played a central role in his sermons from these years – that between Christian articles and theological conclusions:

> Christian articles are the principles of religion necessary to a believer; theological conclusions are school points, fit for the discourse of a divine. Those articles are few and essential; these conclusions are many, and unimporting (upon necessity) to salvation either way. That church then which holds those Christian articles both in terms and necessary consequences, as every visible church of Christ doth, however it vary in these theological conclusions, is columba una.[9]

If Christian unity were to be maintained, Hall explained, it was crucial to keep the number of essential doctrines, the fundamentals of Christian faith and unity, to a minimum. For 'there be some scholastical and immaterial truths, the infinite subdivisions whereof have rather troubled than informed Christendom'. These 'for the purchase of peace, might be kept in, and returned into such safe generalities, as minds not unreasonable might rest in'. Such restraint was the only way in which the Church could avoid needless division and debate over peripheral and inherently doubtful issues, and Hall denounced those who 'like the children of the faithful Abraham, divide the dove; multiplying articles of faith according to their own fancies; and casting out of the bosom of the church those Christians that differ from their either false or unnecessary conclusions'.[10]

On the basis of a core of essential beliefs, stripped down according to these criteria, Hall was prepared to strike an eminently irenic note in some of his dealings even with the papists. 'O for the unity of the spirit in the bond of peace', he cried in one court sermon and introduced another anti-popish diatribe with the (perhaps unlikely) disclaimer 'God knows how little pleasure I take in displaying the enormities of our fellow-Christians.' Indeed, at one point, Hall even denied that it was really the Church of Rome that he was attacking, but rather a ruling faction within it.[11]

[58]

But while members of this faction were ripe for denunciation in this life, and almost certainly doomed to damnation in the next, the Church of Rome herself, because of her retention of the central truths of Christianity, remained a true Church within which it was possible to achieve salvation. Here Hall distinguished between the rulers of the Church, who had created, and now sustained, popery, and 'the ignorant and seduced enemies of God's Church', simple believers 'that follow Absolom with an upright heart'.[12]

Reformed solidarity

But if Hall was prepared to use his notion of a small core of commonly held essential doctrines in order to make irenic noises toward the Church of Rome, he was even more enthusiastic in relation to the foreign reformed churches. He continually contrasted the purity and simplicity of the English Church's profession with the false bombast and vainglorious show of the papists. In England, he boasted in 1622, 'we have nothing but ... the sincerity of scriptures, simplicity of sacraments, decency of rare ceremonies, Christ crucified'. It was on this basis that Hall founded the unity of the reformed churches. 'Surely,' he told the convocation of 1624, 'whosoever willingly subscribes to the Word of God, signed in the everlasting monuments of Scripture, to the ancient Creeds, to the four General Councils, to the common consent of the Fathers for 600 years after Christ, which we of the Reformed Church religiously profess to do; if he may err in small points, yet he cannot be an heretic'.[13]

Hall, of course, could hardly maintain a pretence of unanimity or complete consensus amongst the reformed churches, but on the basis of this distinction he was able to characterize the differences between them as essentially trivial: 'There are certain scholastical opinions of a middle rank, mere theological corollaries, or perhaps some outward ceremonies, wherein we dissent: principles of Christian religion there are not. And, withal, these controversies are but such, as that, when the heat, whether of zeal or anger, shall abate, and either part shall well understand each other, they will easily admit of reconciliation.'[14]

These essentially low-grade disagreements had produced a situation in which tact and judgement were necessary if the unity of the reformed cause were to survive intact. 'We are by God's grace reformed', Hall told convocation in 1624, 'let us take heed lest we be deformed again by mutual dissensions.' Care was necessary in case the existing middle-rank disagreements 'boil forth into more fearful divisions'. Hall deprecated the resulting impulse toward side-taking, name-calling and factionalism. 'Let us all sweetly incline our hearts to peace and unity' he told convocation in 1624, and forswear a factious following of mere men. In another sermon of 1624 he returned to the same theme. 'Since we are one, why are we sundered? One says "I am Luther's for consubstantiation"; another, "I am Calvin's for discipline";

another, "I am Arminius's for predestination"; another, "I am Barrow's or Brown's for separation." What phrensy possesses the brains of Christians, thus to squander themselves into factions?' 'Let us breath nothing, let us affect nothing but Jesus Christ.'[15]

Anglican exceptionalism

Nothing could seem more irenic than that, and yet, as a loyal son of the Church of England, Hall could not get too close to the reformed churches; there were some areas of clear disagreement where the English position had to be defended and praised. Chief of these, of course, was episcopacy. On the continent, Hall argued, the process of reformation had often gone far from smoothly. Admittedly, Hall laid the blame for that initially at the papists' door. For if, at the outset of the process of reform, the papists 'had but reached forth unto us an helping hand ... all had run squarely on ... but they stiffly refused; and, by their forwardness and pertinacity, caused this, so weighty a task, to be cast upon some few; and those both weak, unable and altogether unfit for such a charge. It could not therefore be otherwise, but that the opinions of some single men, not conferred together in such a business, must needs somewhat differ.'[16] This was scarcely an unambiguous endorsement of the course of the continental reformation(s) and Hall was forced to admit that mistakes had been made.

Of these, the most significant had been the failure to retain episcopacy, an omission that allowed Hall to view the foreign reformed churches with a withering and utterly self-satisfied condescension:

O, how oft, and with what deep sighs, hath this most flourishing and happy Church of England wished that she might, with some of her own blood, have purchased unto her dearest sisters abroad the retention of this most ancient and every way best form of government; which might happily also have taken place, if they had met with such a monarchical reformation, as, through the blessing of God, was designed unto us ... The God of heaven raise them up queens for their nurses, and kings for their nursing-fathers, that they may once enjoy with us this happy blessing of the sequence and subordination of degrees.[17]

That passage, with its strident tone of 'Anglican' self-satisfaction and superiority, might seem to be in direct conflict with Hall's equal predilection for a rhetoric of reformed solidarity. For Hall certainly was concerned to laud the achievements and distinctive character of the English Church and he did so, in classically Anglican fashion, by locating the English Church at a moderate mid-point between popish and reformed extremes. Thus in 1628, preaching at Whitehall during Lent, he sought to locate the English position on fasting between a popish formalism and a Puritan subversion. Again, in 1628, addressing the issues of Christian liberty and the way in which purely human laws could bind the conscience, Hall described his position as a studiedly moderate middle way between both popish and Protestant/Puritan extremes. 'I find,' he explained, 'a double extreme of opinion.' The first, popish, position ascribed altogether too much authority to human laws, holding them equal to the positive laws of God, binding the conscience as effectively and directly as genuinely divine injunctions. The second, Puritan, opinion, denied that human laws bound the conscience at all, but controlled only the 'outward' not the 'inward man'. 'We must learn to walk a mid-way betwixt both' Hall concluded. 'The good laws of our superiors, whether civil or ecclesiastical, do, in a sort, reach to the very conscience; though not primarily and immediately ... yet mediately and secondarily as they stand in reference to the law of God with our obedience to his instituted authority; and therefore they tie us, in some sort, besides the case, whether of scandal or contempt.' Here Hall had lined himself up behind the classic conformist defence of the rites and ceremonies of the Church of England, a defence conducted not in terms of any religious value or significance inherent in the ceremonies themselves but simply in terms of the power of the magistrate, ordained of God, over things in themselves indifferent. Here was the perfect basis to resist both 'the Antichristian usurpation' of the papists, on the one hand, and the 'unnecessary differences' generated by baseless Puritan scruples, on the other.[18]

However, this was not Hall's only or even his most usual mode of defending the Church of England. While the issue of Church government and episcopacy served to distance the Church of England from the reformed world, most of the terms in which Hall chose to praise the English or British Church were compatible with his wider notions of reformed solidarity. Here the issue of doctrine was vital. For Hall the English Church was distinguished by her profession of the 'bare, simple, plain, honest, homely truth'. In a court sermon preached at Theobalds in 1623 Hall told his audience 'that no court under heaven hath so rich a stock of truth as this of Great Britain'. It was this common profession of right doctrine that united the Church of England with the Church of the apostles, the fathers, the patriarchs and the martyrs; 'we succeed in their faith, we glory in their succession, we triumph in this glory'. The result was that if the holy dove of God's Church had 'any nest under heaven' 'she is here'. 'Let me never have part in her or in heaven', Hall concluded,' if any church in the world have more part in the universal.' In making this claim Hall laid particular stress on the learning of the English clergy. 'The wonder of the world is the clergy of Britain', Hall told a no-doubt appreciative audience in the convocation of 1624. 'So many learned divines, so many eloquent preachers, shall in vain be sought elsewhere this day, in whatever region under the cope of heaven.'[19]

Here, then, was a Church united in doctrine and polity with the Church of the apostles and fathers, a Church blessed with a godly prince and a learned preaching ministry, a Church and nation, moreover, providentially nurtured and protected by God. To make that point Hall often had recourse to lists of 'the ancient favours of our God' to the English Church and people so typical of Jacobean preaching. To take one example from a court sermon of 1625/6, he started in Elizabeth's reign progressing from 'the memorable frustrations of foreign invasions' through 'the miraculous discoveries of treasons' to 'the successful maintenance of oppressed neighbourhood' and the bloodless accession of James himself. Such deliverances left Hall in no doubt that England was a nation peculiarly blessed of God.[20]

The moderate case for extreme anti-popery

It was no accident that most of the providential deliverances that Hall cited to underwrite his vision of the Church of England involved the frustration of popish and Spanish aggression. For, notwithstanding his irenic rhetoric about the status of Rome as a true Church, about the possibility of salvation for poor, ignorant Catholics, about the need to seek Christian unity, even with Rome, on the basis of a small core of fundamental common beliefs, Hall remained rabidly anti-Catholic. As Anthony Milton's work might lead us to expect, there was a sense in which the elaborate moderation of Hall's irenicism was not calculated to argue in practice for closer links with Rome or for moderation in the treatment of Catholics, but rather to render the continuing errors of the Roman Church altogether inexcusable. In short, Hall's moderation operated very often to license a strikingly immoderate assault on popish error and superstition.[21]

For Hall it was axiomatic that it was the papists, 'our great lords of the seven hills', who 'divide the dove' of God's church', by multiplying articles of faith 'according to their own fancies and casting out of the bosom of the Church those Christians that differ from their own either false or unnecessary conclusions'. On this basis Hall (with many another Jacobean polemicist, including James himself) was able to turn aside popish accusations of Protestant innovation and schism. For Hall, the papists were utterly without excuse for their errors and usurpations. They had deliberately 'turned their backs upon that bright-shining truth, whose clear beams have, these hundred years, glared upon their faces; but also spend their clamorous mouths in barking against this glorious light. What marts of invectives, what bulls of censure, what thunderbolts of anathemas, do we still receive from these spiteful enemies of peace! What doth this argue but the litter of the beast? Rev. xiii?'[22]

Having thus parried the accusation of schism and claimed the moral high ground of moderation and irenicism, Hall lost no time in using this favourable moral terrain to pour upon the papists a stream of very immoderate invective. Hall, in fact, provides us with a very interesting link between the sophisticated, learned world of anti-Catholic polemic, analysed so brilliantly by Anthony Milton, on the one hand, and the somewhat cruder world of slapstick stereotyping and satire, familiar from other more popular and Puritan sources, on the other. Thus Hall had great fun at the expense of the papists' 'pastry deity', 'their God which they know the baker made'. With its 'bread-worship', 'cross-worship' and 'image worship', its belief 'that a man can make the God that made him, and eat the God that he hath made', popery was mere idolatry, a bestial religion. Here 'you would find reason enough why that man of sin, the author of these superstititions, should be called the beast'. In short, for Hall, popery was 'will worship', a false religion of outward show and mere appearance and he derided the papists' 'pretence of antiquity', their 'painted, gilded hobby horse of an outwardly pompous magnificence of the church', 'the baubles of childish superstition'.[23]

The papists' errors were not, however, limited to mere externals. In a sermon with the title the 'True peace maker', preached before James in 1624, Hall accused them of simple heresy on the subject of justification. There was, he explained, 'no possible peace to be made betwixt God and man, but by the perfect justice of him that was both God and man. I would there were a peace in the church about this justice; it is pity and shame there is not. But there must be heresies.' And on this subject Hall was clear that the heretics were the papists. Admittedly, he conceded they did not lapse directly into pelagianism but their errors were patent and of the utmost seriousness none the less:

> It is the main care of our lives and deaths, what shall give us peace and acceptation before the dreadful tribunal of God: what, but righteousness? what righteousness, or whose? Ours or Christ's? ... The Tridentine faction is for the former, we are for the latter. God is as direct on our side as his word can make him; every where blazoning the defects of our own righteousness, the imperfections of our best graces, the deadly nature of our least sins, the radical sinfulness of our habitual concupiscence, the pollution of our best works; every where extolling the perfect obedience of our Redeemer, the gracious application of that obedience, the sweet comfort of that application, the assurance and unfailableness of that comfort, and, lastly, our happy rest in that assurance.[24]

But if Protestantism brought peace between God and man and assurance of salvation to the true believer, popery was incapable of producing such solace. 'Peace is a sweet word,' commented Hall, 'everybody would be glad of it, especially peace at the last', and such peace and papists' 'politick religion' appeared to offer through their 'due satisfactions, undue superogations, patronages of saints, bargains of indulgences, woolward pilgrimages'. Yet 'at the last, after whips and hair-cloths' they leave the 'dying soul to a fear of hell, doubt of heaven'. The only assurance on offer here was an 'assurance of purgatory flames'.[25]

By thus seeking to interpose themselves and their doctrines of merit, satisfaction and penance between God and the sinner the papists not only rendered impossible any true peace between God and fallen humanity, they also usurped or attempted to usurp the royal prerogative of Christ as the only lord of our salvation. Here then were the roots of that antichristian usurpation whereby the papists sought to equate their own laws, ordinances and doc-trines with the laws and ordinances of God.[26]

However, the errors of popery were not restricted to the religious or spir-itual sphere. Hall repeated, often and with all due vehemence, the conven-tional litany of popish oppressions and aggressions in the temporal, political world. After a *tour d'horizon* of popish cruelty which took in the Armada, the Marian burnings, the horrors of the Inquisition and the treatment of Eng-lish captives during the late war, Hall concluded 'false zeal takes pleasure in surfeits of blood, and can enjoy others' torment'. Having dwelt here on popish cruelty, elsewhere he emphasized popish subversion, in another list of popish instigations to treasons, conspiracies, invasions, libels 'and, to make up all, those late bulls, that bellow out prohibitions of justly-sworn alle-giance: those bold absolutions from sacred oaths'. Nothing, Hall concluded, could better demonstrate the antichristian nature of popery. 'In all these, we too well feel that we have to do with the beast; with St John's beast, no whit short of St Paul's.'[27]

For Hall, as for many other anti-papal writers of the period, popery was a contagion, a principal of error and iniquity mere contact with which could prove fatal.[28] Given the seriousness of the threat, Hall felt compelled to call on the authorities to act. In his convocation sermon of 1624 he called on the clergy in the most lurid terms to trample under foot the popish antichrist: 'Rouse up yourselves, O ye holy fathers, if there be any ardour of piety in your breasts, and destroy this Tyberine monster (popery I mean) with the breath of your mouths: and whatever grace and authority ye have with our gracious king, with the peers, and commons of this realm, improve it all with your best prayers and counsels, to the utter extermination of idolatry, to the happy victory and advancement of the sincere truth of God.' As for the sec-ular authorities, Hall exhorted them to enforce the existing recusancy laws with the utmost rigour. For if England would do her part to protect herself against popery, then God would surely do his and step into the breach on her behalf.[29]

Practical applications: the moderate, irenic case for religious war

These, of course, were conventional enough nostrums, applicable, for the intently anti-Catholic, at almost any time and in any situation. But Hall was preaching in the distinctly delicate political circumstances of the early 1620s and his sermons were directed towards a very particular set of policy goals. Following the return of Prince Charles and the Duke of Buckingham from Madrid, the question of open war against Spain over the Palatinate had been forced to the top of the political agenda. The resulting debate within the court and the country centred not merely on whether there should be a war but also on what sort of war it should be. Many felt that a war for the Palatinate must be, in effect, a war with Spain and that a war with Spain would of necessity and, indeed, ought to be, a war for religion, fought in alliance, for the most part, with Protestant powers against the Catholic Habsburgs. On this view, while the Palatinate provided a *casus belli* and its recovery represented a major war aim, the war itself was a wider struggle to defend the godly abroad from Habsburg aggression and popish tyranny. The model for such a conflict was provided by an idealized version of the Elizabethan war with Spain, fought largely at sea but in alliance with the Dutch and the Huguenots. James, of course, took a more limited view. He abhorred war altogether but in particular he was determined to avoid a confessional war. For him this was a specifically German problem, concerning the Palatinate, which he hoped to solve by putting pressure through Spain on the Austrian Habsburgs. If he could not do that through mere negotiation and war became necessary James wanted the resulting conflict confined to Germany. If the war did take on a wider significance it should be seen, not as a religious struggle, but as a war against Habsburg hegemony for which James insisted on Catholic as well as Protestant allies. In short, James did not really want war at all and would not sign off on a religious war at any price. As Tom Cogswell has shown, the tensions this situation unleashed at court, in Parliament and in the wider political nation do much to explain the later political crises of the 1620s. They certainly did much to complicate the lives of court preachers like Hall.[30]

The split between a still pacific *rex pacificus* and his more belligerent son and favourite produced an intensely difficult political terrain which preachers like Hall, preaching at court and often before James himself, had to traverse at their peril. Unsurprisingly, then, we have seen Hall hit many typically Jacobean themes in the sermons analysed above from the early 1620s. The rhetoric of irenicism, of peace and unity, to be achieved by sifting essentials from inessentials, the praise of the English Church as truly catholic, the gestures at wider Christian unity directed both at Rome and the reformed churches: all were authentically Jacobean themes echoed by Hall. However, it is important to remember that the more stridently anti-papal themes in Hall's repertoire also had a respectable Jacobean pedigree. James had cut his theological teeth and made his polemical reputation in argument with the papists, and throughout his reign he had shown no hesitation in deploying established strains of anti-papal argument and denunciation of the sort used so freely by Hall. It is also true, of course, that in the early 1620s he was not keen to emphasize that side of his position and we should see Hall's sermons as an attempt, within the parameters laid down by James' own rhetoric and concerns, to rearrange central elements in the religious discourse of the Jacobean court into a defence of the propriety, indeed, of the necessity, of a religious war against Spain. That this was a task of some delicacy is made clear by a letter written in October 1623 by John Chamberlain. 'Dr Hall made a neat sermon of late at Theobald's,' Chamberlain reported, 'but Dr Whiting went further and dealt more plainly at Hampton Court, for which he was convented before the council and in danger to be committed, but he hath passed it over with being suspended from preaching.' Hall was clearly walking a very fine line indeed.[31]

In a number of remarkable passages – some mere asides, others more purposive argumentative forays – Hall applied the general nostrums and assumptions of the sermons to the particular issue of war. In 'The best bargain', a sermon preached at court in 1623, Hall lauded peace to the rooftops and played up his own role as a peacemaker and reconciler of religious differences. Indeed, so valuable was peace that, Hall suggested, 'if anything in the world may seem a due price of truth, it is peace'. But this was not the best bargain of the sermon's title. 'We may not offer to sell truth for peace' Hall concluded, and ended his discourse with a lament for recent gentry conversions to Rome and an attack on those who seemed prepared to 'truck for the truth of God, as if it were some Cheapside or some Smithfield commodity'. 'Dear Christians, our forefathers transmitted to us the entire inheritance of the glorious Gospel of Jesus Christ, repurchased by the blood of their martyrdom: O, let not our ill husbandry impair it.' There could scarcely be a more direct dig at those crypto-Catholic or politique members of the Spanish faction who had been prepared to make religious concessions in their pursuit of a Spanish match and with it, for Hall, an ignoble and irreligious peace.[32]

By the next year Hall was prepared to be even bolder. In a remarkable sermon titled 'The true peace maker' preached before James at Theobalds on 19 September 1624 Hall concluded his analysis (quoted above) of the faults in the popish doctrine of justification with a peroration that denied the possibility of any true peace with popery at all. Popery was a principle of iniquity, of false order, opposed to all justice and peace. 'What possibility of justice in the long usurped tyranny of the successor to Romulus? Could we hope to see justice once shine from those seven hills, we would make account of peace; but O the miserable injustice of that imperious see! Injustice of claim, injustice of practice.' After another litany of popish abuse and cruelty Hall concluded with a rhetorical question. 'What then? Is it to hope for peace, notwithstanding the continuance of all these? So the work of injustice shall be peace; and an unjust and unsound peace must it needs be that arises from injustice. Is it to hope they will abandon these things for peace? O that the Church of God might once be so happy! That there were but any life in that possibility. In the mean time let God and his holy angels witness betwixt us, that on their part the peace faileth; we are guiltless.'[33]

By 1625, with the outbreak of war, it was safe to be yet more explicit. Now Hall could locate Catholic subversion openly in Habsburg plotting and present the Prince's return unscathed from Madrid as but the latest in the long line of providential deliverances from popish plotting that stretched well back into Elizabeth's reign. Hall was now prepared to declare the war with Spain God's war. 'It is no other than … God's war: God made it, God owns it, God blesses it', he thundered. Given God's support, no matter how great the odds justice would prevail, as the fate, in 1588, of the Armada, 'the pride of Spain, the terror of England', proved. Then, Hall claimed, 'we fought upon our knees, both prince and people. Straight, God fought for us from heaven ... and is the hand of our God shortened? Is he other than what he was? We may be, as we are, weakened and effeminated by a long, luxurious peace: our God is yesterday, and today, and the same forever. If we be not wanting to him in our prayers, he cannot be wanting to our protection.'[34]

True religion, its establishment and defence, thus became the surest bastion for monarchical power and political stability. 'Let the great Caesars of the world then know,' Hall informed the court in 1625, 'that the more subject they are to Christ, the more sure they are of the loyalty of their subjects to them.' 'As ye love your peace, ye great ones, make much of it [true religion]; plant it where it is not, enlarge it where it is; maintain it at home, encourage it abroad.' Of course, as Hall had been implying throughout these sermons, the maintenance of this sort of peace often entailed recourse to anti-papal war. For 'if distressed religion shall come, with her face blubbered and her garments rent, wringing her hands and tearing her hair, and shall prostrate herself at the feet of earthly greatness for lawful succour, with ... come and help ... woe be to the power that fails it! and blessed, thrice blessed from heaven be that hand that shall raise her on her feet, and wipe off her tears, and stretch out itself mightily for her safeguard!'[35] Here, then, was a great opportunity and a great risk confronting England. A nation in a convenant relation to God, if England preserved true religion in order and unity at home and came to the aid of the godly abroad, her cause would be God's and all would be well. But if she failed in her duty there was already the example of the foreign churches, prostrate before antichristian tyranny, to remind her of the consequences of the loss of divine favour.

Puritanism and popery

Here, then, was a very particular spin being put on what remained a recognizably Jacobean agenda of peace, moderation and unity, organized around a nebulous, yet limited, number of core doctrines and the dominating figure of the Christian prince. Hall had taken those themes and, by combining them with a no less authentically Jacobean strain of anti-papal rhetoric, produced a version of peace which involved playing down whatever differences of ceremony or doctrine might divide English Protestants either from one another or from the foreign reformed churches, and insisting on the necessity of war against Antichrist and Spain.

This, of course, was not the only gloss being put on James' rhetoric or on the current situation of Protestant England. Richard Montague, for instance, had taken those same Jacobean themes and organized them into a very different pattern. For Montague the irenic gesture toward Rome had to be taken altogether more seriously. In particular, for Montague, it involved the repudiation of a number of doctrines as Calvinist and even Puritan, many of them

doctrines – ranging from the identity of the Pope as Antichrist, to perseverance and assurance – that Hall himself held dear.[36]

Moreover, Montague's distinctive take on the meaning and consequences
of Jacobean irenicism led him to an account of the relative threats to the
Church represented by popery and Puritanism very different to that produced
by Hall in his sermons before the court. Of course, the equivalence of the two
threats had become a standard feature of Jacobean conformist writing and
yet it was a rare divine indeed who did not dwell with more relish and ideological comfort on one or the other of the two threats. Thus, for all that the
New Gagg was ostensibly a work of anti-Catholic polemic, Montague spent
a good deal of time therein denouncing Puritan and Calvinist errors to which
the Church of England did not, contrary to popular belief and papist accusation, subscribe. Only thus, he claimed, could the English Church sensibly
define and discuss her real points of difference with the Roman Church.[37]

There could scarcely be a clearer contrast with Hall's court sermons of the
early 1620s. There, as we have seen, popery bulked very large indeed, but
Puritanism scarcely figured. For Hall popery was a heresy, on a par with
familism, antinominaism and socinianism. This rendered it very different
from Puritanism, which Hall continued to define well into the 1630s as a
series of mistaken opinions about the ceremonies and government of the
Church. For Hall, unlike Montague (and Peter White), there was no such
thing as Puritan doctrine. Thus, only on a couple of occasions did Hall invoke
the traditional equivalence of the popish and Puritan threats, observing, in the
course of a rabidly anti-popish sermon on 'The beauty and unity of the
church', that the God of the Church could abide neither conventicles nor divisive appropriations of the appellation 'catholic'. In another paean of praise
to unity, Hall denounced the danger to the Church represented by 'that anar-
chical fashion of independent congregations, which I see, and lament to see,
affected by too many, not without woeful success'.[38]

Hall could, therefore, sound a warning note of anti-Puritanism but, given
the stress in his sermons on internal unity and the avoidance and composition of domestic disagreements, it is remarkable how little explicit reference
he made to the traditional areas of Puritan/conformist dispute. As we have
seen, Hall himself espoused the traditional conformist defence of the rites and
ceremonies of the Church as matters inherently indifferent. There was no
trace in his court sermons, unlike those of Lancelot Andrewes, of an avant-
garde conformist defence of the role of ceremony or worship in the life of the
Church. The whole thrust of his position had been to play down the
significance of disputes over mere externals and to emphasize the role of certain areas of doctrinal agreement in preserving English Protestant and, indeed,
wider reformed unity. Hall had appended to his eulogy to the learning of the
English clergy in 1624 a list of recently departed divines which nicely makes
the point. He provided there a spectrum of opinion running from moderate
Puritans like Greenham, Rainolds, Whitaker, Fulke (an ex-Presbyterian),

Perkins and Willett, through Elizabethan conformists like Whitgift and Bab-
bington, to Jacobean Calvinist conformists like Abbot and Mason and finally
to the likes of Richard Hooker and John Overall. It was a list calculated,
through the mere ideological resonance of the names, to play down the
significance of the Puritan/conformist divide in English Protestant thought.[39]

Such a de-emphasis on domestic Puritan disputes fitted very well with the
wider polemical and political purposes of the sermons. A proponent of war
over the Palatinate and of the patriot coalition being put together under such
stress by Charles, Buckingham and their allies in 1623–4, Hall had to argue
against a very different vision of the situation of the Church of England. In
Montague's and, increasingly, James' view the real threat to English stability
lay in Puritanism. Peace, defined conventionally as the absence of war and, in
particular, of war with Spain, was seen as an absolute good and the sort of
moderate and irenic rhetoric that Hall himself used (echoing James) was
taken to involve closer ties with Rome, negotiations with Spain and more distant relations with the foreign reformed churches. Moreover, the opponents
of this view and proponents of war, who had publicly criticized the Spanish
match and were now pushing for war, were increasingly characterized as popular Puritan firebrands, dangerous radicals who pandered to the people and
subverted the power of the prince. No wonder, therefore, that Puritanism
played so relatively small a role in Hall's court sermons and so large a part
in Montague's writings.[40]

Arminianism and the Via Media

Reference to Montague, of course, raises the whole issue of Arminianism.
Although this did not bulk large in Hall's court sermons there were a number
of asides that made his anti-Arminian inclinations clear. Thus, his worried
meditation on the effects of continued division on the once flourishing state
of the English Church, cited above, might have ended with a warning about
the growth of independent congregations, but it was immediately preceded by
a passage excoriating 'our late excutifidians'. Again, the passage cited above,
in which he dissociated the Church of England from the schism of both Puritans and papists, was preceded by what may well have been a reference to
recent English predestinarian disputes: 'O, how is every good heart divided in
sunder with the grief for the late divisions of our Reuben! We do not mourn,
we bleed inwardly, for this distraction.' Another sermon of September 1624
attacked the contemporary addiction to doctrinal innovation and novelty in
a way that might have lent itself to an anti-Arminian gloss.[41]

But these were mere asides, some of them ambiguous ones at that and, on
this basis, one might be tempted to conclude that, for Hall, predestination
was a peripheral issue, of no great concern to the English Church; a topic best
left to the schools rather than handled in the pulpit, even at court. But fortunately we do not have to rely on the sermons alone when reconstructing

Hall's response to the activities of Richard Montague. Hall himself laid out his opinions in his *Via Media*, a tract probably written some time in 1625/6 and prepared and licensed for the press but not published in the summer of 1626.[42] Nor should we be surprised that Hall felt called upon to intervene in the predestinarian disputes of the period. Apart from his considerable ideological stake in the issue, as one of the original English delegates to Dort, the Montague controversy represented a serious obstacle to the political programme contained in Hall's court sermons. Arminianism raised the whole issue of what constituted doctrinal orthodoxy and called into question the doctrinal ties that bound the English Church to the foreign reformed churches – an issue that Hall had left studiously vague. Arminianism, at least in the works of Richard Montague, also raised the question of the English Church's relationship to Rome. Moreover, the political fall-out from these purely doctrinal questions threatened to disrupt the unity of the patriot coalition. After all, the godly elements lined up by Charles and Buckingham to support the war were also precisely the people most likely to be alarmed by Montague's doctrinal claims and polemical posing. Certainly the debates in both the ecclesiastical establishment and the political nation touched off by Montague did not represent that closing of the ranks in the face of the popish and Spanish threats envisioned in Hall's sermons. Hall proceeded to pour oil on troubled waters – hence his *Via Media*.[43]

The rhetorical frame

In this text Hall deployed all the moderate, irenic tropes and devices of the court sermons in an attempt to render Montague's opinions anodyne and thus defuse the theologico-political crisis that his views were threatening to create. Hall's, he told his readers, was a 'heart sincerely devoted to truth and peace' and it was only this impulse that had led him to undertake 'this too necessary, if thankless task'. The task, moreover, was an urgent one. 'That crafty devil that envies our peace takes this perilous season to distract us, that so we might fall as a prey to a common enemy.' But all was not yet lost. 'A few pailsful may yet seasonably extinguish this weak flame, which time will make headstrong and irremediable.'[44]

The way to 'truth and peace', Hall was sure, was not through further scholastic debate. 'It is not disputation, it is not counter writing, that can quench it. These courses are but the bellows, to diffuse and raise these flashes to more height and rage ... There is no possible redress but in a severe edict of restraint to charm all tongues and pens upon the sharpest punishment from passing those moderate bounds which the church of England, guided by the scriptures, hath expressly set; or what both sides are fully accorded on.' The *Via Media* represented Hall's attempt to outline the nature of those limits, and arbitrate between the two sides – which he defined as 'the followers of the tenet of the synod of Dort', on the one hand, and those 'following in the steps of acute Arminius or of our learned and judicious Bishop Overall', on the other. He did so by applying to the disputes his own perspective on the position of the Church of England. He thus arrogated the golden mantle of moderation to himself, to the Church of England and to Bishop Overall, who was now transformed from a party to the dispute into one of its arbitrators. Discussing the decree of election, Hall exclaimed 'but what need I to reconcile these opinions, which have no reason to concern us? The church of England, according to the explication of R[ev.] B[ishop] Overall, goes a midway betwixt both.' Again, treating of the extent of the atonement, Hall broke off his discussion with a repudiation of 'the nice scruples and explications of foreign divines' for 'we have no such cause of strife, if we admit that which our learned bishop commends for the voice of the church of England! who, having laid down the two extreme opinions of the opposite parts, brings in the church of England as sweetly moderating betwixt both'. The 'moderation' of the English Church in these matters, Hall concluded, was 'worthy to be written in letters of gold'.[45]

Here Hall's rhetoric of Anglican exceptionalism, familiar from his court sermons, met his rhetoric of moderation and the golden mean as he searched for the middle ground that could unite all parties and avert further conflict in England, as the scholastic disputes at Dort had so signally failed to do in the Low Countries. It was a procedure that he legitimated by recourse to another central theme in his court sermons – the distinction between 'matters or faith and scholastical disquisitions'. Of matters disputable Hall remarked 'well may the schools pick hence matter enough for their theological problems; but what should either the pulpit or the press do with these busy and bootless brabbles?' Even in the schools Hall urged restraint. 'The infinite subdivisions of those points which we advance to the honour of being the objects of our belief, confound our thoughts and mar our peace.'[46]

Indeed, Hall argued, there were many truths that, for all their certainty, were not fit for the pulpit and, at times, he could speak as though the entire subject of predestination fell under this rubric; at one point, noting approvingly the Dutch remonstrants' assent 'to the judgement of all divines, both ancient and modern, that "these questions of predestination, being perplexed, thorny and troublesome through their obscureness, may, without all detriment of salvation, be either unknown or discussed"'.[47] This, or course, was an odd sentiment for a treatise designed for the press which treated in detail convoluted disputes about predestination. That apparent anomaly should alert us to the need to look very carefully at how, within the *Via Media*, Hall applied his general nostrums about moderation and his dichotomy between matters of faith and matters for scholastic disquisition to particular doctrines, arguments and issues.

The doctrinal core

The *Via Media* took the form of five articles on 'God's predestination', 'Christ's death', 'man's corruption, his free will, his conversion to God', and 'perseverance'. These Hall took to represent the 'chief specialities' around which all right thinking Christians could unite. What was the doctrinal content of Hall's five articles? In the first he asserted a general will of God that all men should be saved: 'There is no son of Adam to whom God hath not promised that, if he shall believe in Christ, repent, and persevere, he shall be saved ... All men, within the pale of the church especially, have from the mercy of God such common helps towards this belief and salvation, as that the neglect thereof makes any of them justly guilty of their own condemnation.' 'Besides the general will of God, he hath eternally willed and decreed to give a special and effectual grace to those that are predestinate according to the good pleasure of his will; whereby they do actually believe, obey, and persevere, that they may be saved.' This decree was not based upon any 'prevision of faith, or any other grace or act of man ... but the mere and gracious good will and pleasure of God'. The resulting decree of election was 'absolute, and unchangeable and from everlasting'. The second article followed naturally from the first, asserting that Christ died for the sins of the whole world and that the 'universal promise and convenant of the gospel, offering remission and salvation to all men through the whole world' was based upon 'this infinite merit of Christ's death'. This offer of supernatural grace was sufficient to 'justly convince the impatient and unbelieving of a wilful neglect, if not a contemptuous rejection'. But again, besides 'this general promise of the gospel, God hath decreed to give a special, more abundant, and effectual grace unto his elect; whereby they may be enabled certainly and infallibly to apply unto themselves the benefit of Christ's death; and do accordingly believe, and persevere, and attain salvation'.

As one might expect from this opening, Hall went on to attribute 'every good motion' of man's fallen will to 'the grace of God preventing, accompanying, following it'. 'In the regeneration,' he wrote, 'God infuseth a new life.' There were certain 'foregoing acts' necessary to salvation. Of these, the outward – 'to go to the church, to sit reverently, to hearken to the word spoken' – were subject to 'freedom of will either way'. The inward, however – 'the knowledge of God's will, the feeling of our sin, the fear of hell, the thought of deliverance' – these were 'by the power of the word and Spirit of God, wrought in the heart of a man not yet justified'. These inward motions could be and often were 'through the fault of the rebellious will, choked and quenched in the hearts of men'. Indeed, this often happened even in the elect who 'oftimes justly deserve, for their neglect and resistance, to be forsaken of God'. But in the case of the elect God did not allow this to happen: 'but such is his special grace and mercy to them, that he notwithstanding follows them effectually with powerful helps, till he hath wrought out his good work in them'. Conversion was, therefore, God's work in his elect: 'when the hearts of his elect are thus excited and prepared by the foregoing acts of grace, God doth by his secret and wonderful work regenerate and renew them'. But he did so in a way that rendered the act of conversion theirs as well: 'While from our new changed will God fetches the act of our believing and coming to him: He gives that power which the will exercises: so as it is at once both ours and God's; ours, in that we do work; God's, in that he works it in us.' Human nature, of course, remained corrupt: we retained not merely 'a possibility but a proneness to resistance' which 'by the gracious and effectual motion of God's spirit' was usually 'so overruled, that it breaks not forth into a present act'. God, however, did not always thus protect his elect 'but sometimes suffers them, through their own fault, to give way to their own sinful desires'. Yet, as Hall observed in his fifth article, 'those who are soundly rooted in a true and lively faith lose not all their right to the inheritance of heaven, neither can either totally or finally fall from grace and truth everlastingly: but, by the special and effectual favour and operation of God, are kept up, and enabled to persevere in a true and lively faith; so that at last they are brought to eternal life'.[48]

In effect this was a fairly uncompromising restatement of the modified hypothetical universalist position adopted after some internal debate by the English delegation at Dort. If these were the central points, fit not only for the schools but for the pulpit, then predestinarian themes would still have a large role to play in English preaching. In the second half of his treatise Hall proceeded to argue, through the admittedly selective quotation of certain passages from the remonstrants and a strategic deployment of some of the opinions and all of the cultural capital attached to the name of John Overall, that the resulting position did indeed represent the middle ground upon which all sound, moderate and reasonable divines could meet and, sinking their differences, agree to differ on whatever other extraneous points remained unresolved, points that, of course, Hall tried hard to categorize as fit only for the schools, not matters of faith at all.

The doctrinal periphery

Identifying three major areas of debate about predestination – '1 the motive or ground, 2ndly. the object, 3rdly. the order of it' – he dealt with each in essentially the same way. Claiming that all agreed that 'there is no other impulsive cause of God's decree of election or reprobation than the free will and pleasure of the Almighty', he identified the area of controversy as whether 'God's decree looks at faith and infidelity as conditions in those who are to be chosen and refused'. At this point Hall turned from the doctrine of predestination to the even more fundamental doctrine of justification by faith. The Calvinists (defendants in Hall's terminology) 'do but desire that faith may be granted to be the mere gift of God: the opponents [remonstrants] profess to grant it'. There was thus nothing left to argue about if 'it is agreed by them that God foresees nothing in us, but the faith of his own giving'.[49]

To drive the point home Hall outlined the three available positions on this subject:

> To hold that faith is so the gift of God, as that it is given to all them who, God foresaw, would dispose themselves by the good use of their free will to receive it, and who should improve the powers of nature to their utmost, is no better than Pelagian ... To hold that faith is so the gift of God, as that it is therefore only not given to all, because all will not receive it, for that God calleth all and gives unto all men sufficient helps to believe if they will, and goes no farther; and therefore that according to the prevision of our free co-working with this sufficient grace his decree determines of us, is but somewhat better than Pelagian. To hold that faith is so the gift of God, as that he doth not only give common and sufficient helps to men whereby they are made able to believe if they will, but so works in them by his grace that they do by the power thereof actually believe and conceive true faith in their soul – this is fair and orthodox.

And yet 'even to this do the Belgic opponents profess to come up in their late dogmatical writings'.

Hall's language in this passage – his opposition between the 'fair and orthodox', 'the pelagian' and the 'somewhat better than pelagian' – shows definitively that for him there were serious doctrinal issues at stake here. It is reminiscent of his treatment of the papists as heretics on the basis of their less than pelagian, but none the less heterodox, attitudes to justification and, in effect, he was pronouncing precisely the same anathema on any genuinely Arminian version of the doctrine of election from foreseen faith, as it was summed up in the first two positions outlined in the passage above. In short, Hall was saying that as long as faith was viewed as a completely gratuitous divine gift, not dependent in any way on the exercise of the human will, then the principle of predestination from foreseen faith ceased to be controversial:

> Neither is this election, according to the plea of the opponents, made ever the more uncertain by this pre-requisition of our faith: since they profess to teach it supposed in our election, not as a condition whose performance God expects, as uncertain; but as a gift, which God, according to his eternal prescience, foresees in man, present and certain ... so as the election of God is not suspended upon the mutability of man's will; but upon the infallible certainty of the foreknowledge of God, to whose eyes our faith and perseverance is not more doubtful than future, and whose prescience hath no less infallibility than his decree. If therefore God may have the sole glory of this work in the gift of that faith which he foresees, and our election hazards no certainty, as they profess to hold, what is there that should need to draw blood in this first quarrel.[50]

In the same way Hall proceeded to invoke the doctrine of justification by faith as a perspective point from which to relegate other questions – such as the object of the decree ('man creable, fallible, saveable', 'man created, but as in his pure naturals' or 'man fallen' or some variant thereon) or the precise order of the decrees – to relative insignificance. 'If this supposed faith may be yielded the mere gift of God, as formerly, I cannot discern any so dangerous inconvenience in this branch of the opinion as should warrant the breach of the common peace.'[51] As Professor Muller has observed, in early reformed orthodoxy the 'doctrine of predestination' simply served to affirm 'the invincibility of divine grace in the ordo salutis'. Hall was here having recourse to the still more basic doctrine of justification by faith to enforce a retreat from 'the defection from the reformed sola gratia' that Muller detects in the theology of Arminius and the remonstrants and which many contemporaries detected in the thought of Richard Montague.[52]

Hall was thus using concessions wrung from the remonstrants on the issue of justification to police and gloss their other opinions on predestination in ways favourable to his own position. At times he almost admitted as much, as, for instance, in the way he described the remonstrants only 'professing' to accept the basic principle that faith was 'the mere gift of God'. 'How fitly it holds suit with their other tenets, let it be their care to approve unto the church of God.' 'Let it be their part to make good their protested sincerity in that assertion; which for peace sake I gladly report from them at the best.' Indeed, Hall was painfully aware that he was open to the accusation that he had 'not fully stated the questions on both sides' nor 'drawn my accorded propositions out of the heart of those tenets which both parts will yield to be their own'. The reason for this was simple, Hall explained: 'my drift is only to pick out of both what may sound towards concord'.[53]

The polemical and political context

In other words, Hall was admitting that his larger argumentative, indeed polemical, purposes were shaping his reading of the works of the remonstrants. The same was true of his use of Overall as a source of authority, a guarantor of his own moderate judgement and impartiality. This, of course, was no accident. For Overall was a man with track record in these matters and, accordingly, his name brought with it a certain ideological or polemical resonance. Back in the 1590s he had crossed swords with the Cambridge Heads over some aspects of predestinarian doctrine; he was regarded by Archbishop Abbot, a proponent of notions of Calvinist orthodoxy still more stringent that Hall's, as a dangerous Arminian influence in the Church and by the remonstrants as a sympathetic spirit. Writing retrospectively about this tract Hall explained that he had come to the view that 'mistaking was more guilty of this dissension than misbelieving' and that in particular Montague, in writing his books, had 'meant to express, not Arminius, but B[ishop] Overall, a more moderate and safe author'.[54] What Hall was doing in the *Via Media* was squeezing Montague between a highly selective and partial reading of the writings of the remonstrants, on the one hand, and his own rendition of the Church of England's position, derived in part and attributed *tout court* to Overall, on the other.

But Hall was not merely invoking Overall's authority for effect. Overall's influence on his position was probably real enough and, as Hall himself explained, that position now contained some serious modifications of high Calvinist orthodoxy. 'The sound of a general and conditionate will [to save all men through Christ's sacrifice for the sins of the world] perhaps seems harsh to some ears; whereto yet they should do well to inure themselves, since it is the approved distinction of worthy, orthodox, and unquestionable divines' – a point he drove home with references to those two pillars of reformed orthodoxy Zanchius and Polanus. This point was crucial to Hall because it allowed him to defend his position from Arminian or remonstrant claims that the necessary concomitant of his relatively uncompromising doctrine of absolute election was a doctrine of reprobation that rendered God the author of sin and called into question the justice of the divine will. It was, of course, one of the major benefits of emphasizing the universality of Christ's sacrifice and the general conditional will of God that all might be saved if they believed that it provided an account of reprobation relatively immune to such criticisms. It was a position that underwrote Hall's crucial claim that positive reprobation 'which is a preordination to punishment, is never without respect and prevision of sin: for, although by his absolute power God might cast any creature into everlasting torment, without any just exception to be taken on our parts; yet, according to that sweet providence of his, which disposeth all things in a fair order of proceeding, he cannot be said to inflict or adjudge punishment to any soul, but for sin.' According to Hall 'the defendants' (the Calvinists) all accepted that and he backed up that assertion with the claim, citing Perkins, that 'even those that are most rigorous' held that 'upon the non-election of some, damnation is "not causally but only consecutively" inferred'.[55]

The result of all this was, therefore, a position almost identical to that of the English delegates at Dort. Hall's was a modified, hypothetical universalist Calvinism well suited to meet some of the most pointed objections of the remonstrants and Arminians. Yet his position retained at its core doctrines of assurance, perseverance and absolute election firm enough to repulse what Hall had called (in his court sermons and elsewhere) the errors of 'our late excutifidians' and hence to preserve, what Professor Muller has termed, the central Protestant tenet of 'the invincibility of divine grace in the ordo salutis'. In the 1590s, of course, Overall had himself been accused of holding that a true justifying faith could be lost and his own refusal, then, to equate the justified with the elect had opened up the possibility of other, rather more 'Arminian' readings of his position than that produced by Hall.[56] The transaction taking place in the *Via Media* between Hall, Overall and the remonstrants was thus very far from simple; Hall was, in fact, using his own particular reading of Overall to underwrite his (self-consciously) partial and tendentious rendition of the remonstrant position as essentially compatible, if not identical, with his own modified Calvinism.

The polemical benefits of this use of the conveniently dead Bishop Overall were very considerable. Where other opponents of Montague – Hall's colleague at Dort, Bishop Carleton and Archbishop Abbott's chaplain, Daniel Featley, among them – were proceeding by direct assault,[57] Hall was proceeding by stealth. In Hall's version of events Montague was not being denounced as an Arminian or a crypto-papist, nor was he being asked to recant or threatened with impeachment. Rather, he was being invited to agree with Hall's version of what he had really meant to say all along – that is, to agree with Bishop Overall of blessed memory and endorse what Hall claimed was the Church of England's distinctive and very moderate position on these matters. Montague's claim to be defending the doctrinal autonomy of the English Church from foreign and Puritan assault was thus being echoed by Hall, but in a way that rendered Montague's substantive opinions virtually identical to the moderate Calvinism of Hall, Ussher and Davenant.

If Montague was being offered a decorous way out of what remained in 1625/6 a distinctly precarious political position so, too, was Charles I being offered advice on how to bring these stirs to a close. The *Via Media* was dedicated to the king who was invited, both in the dedicatory epistle and the text, to intervene in the disputes and confine public statements on the issues in question within the parameters outlined by Hall himself.[58] Had he done so, something like a return to the Jacobean status quo ante would surely have resulted. A modified form of Calvinist predominance would have been confirmed in the Church. Men like Montague would not necessarily have been driven out or impeached. They could have pursued careers, and the king could have preferred them as he saw fit, without provoking any necessary political or parliamentary outcry, so long as all the parties involved accepted Hall's version of acceptable speech on the controverted issues. In this way, peace could have returned to the Church and a major obstacle to co-operation between king and Parliament in the prosecution of the war would have been removed.

Thus, the *Via Media* represents a continuation of both the polemical and political tactics of Hall's court sermons. It belongs in the same rhetorical universe where irenic, moderate tropes and attitudes were enlisted to put the case for rather specific and indeed controversial programmes and positions. The point here is not to argue that Hall was a radical in moderate garb, a reformed *engagé* posing as a reasonable Anglican. After all, Hall's response to Montague *was* a good deal less confrontational and polarized in its language and argumentative procedures than those of Featley or Carleton. Indeed, where the most overtly polemical of contemporary theological treatises operated by assimilating their chosen victim/opponent to the nearest heterodox or heretical stereotype – in Montague's case Arminianism,

Pelagianism and popery[59] – Hall inverted that procedure. He manipulated selected quotations from the remonstrants and highlighted certain passages from Calvinists to create a sense of consensus. Then, by invoking his version of Overall as representing what Montague had really meant to say all along, Hall sought to enlist Montague behind his own version of the middle ground.

The aims of Hall's book were, therefore, *both* irenic and polemical; they constituted a no doubt sincere attempt to find the position upon which the greatest number of people could agree *and* an attempt to close down many of the more objectionably Arminian readings that Montague's works invited. Hence what is being argued here is that the language of moderation, indeed the sincere profession of irenic and moderate attitudes and aims (with which we can surely credit Hall) always took place in specific political and polemical circumstances, and that we will never properly understand their contemporary resonance and meaning without paying full attention to those contexts. In Hall's case the *Via Media* served the same basic purpose as his court sermons – that is, the creation of a common front for an anti-Catholic, anti-Spanish war, united behind a vision of reformed unity as broad as was compatible with what Hall took to be the central saving truths of the Christian religion. And that was a category that excluded both Arminian and popish errors over the issue of justification by faith and, by extension, of predestination, too.

Politically it may be possible to see Hall acting as an agent, spokesman or ally for a group of courtiers centred on the Herberts. He dedicated a crucial and surely controversial court sermon of 1623, 'The best bargain', to Pembroke. Hall also enjoyed links with other Calvinist Privy Councillors like the earls of Norwich and Carlisle.[60] The political strategy implicit in the sermons and the *Via Media* fits well with what we know of Pembroke's line in these years: support for the war and the Protestant cause; a moderate but distinctly anti-Arminian defence of reformed orthodoxy; and a developed sense of the need for compromise between king and Parliament. As Barbara Donagan has pointed out recently, Pembroke's response to the York House Conference was very different from that of Saye or Warwick. They pushed for the meeting and again pushed hard against Montague's doctrinal views. For them York House was clearly a make or break test of the regime's doctrinal credentials. Pembroke seems to have wanted to avoid confrontation on the issue. Hall's strategy in the *Via Media* was entirely congruent with this approach – a regulation of debate on terms favourable to the Calvinists, but giving Montague and his lay and clerical sympathizers a decorous way out. With the doctrinal issues resolved both court and Parliament could return to the serious business of money and war.[61]

Ironically, Hall's book was the victim of its own advice to the king; licensed for the press, it never appeared because of a royal proclamation banning further public dispute on the issue of predestination. We know that Hall's book was seen by the king and Montague at a time when the regime was debating how explicitly anti-Arminian that proclamation should be. If Hall's retrospective account is to be believed Montague both saw Hall's 'reconciliatory papers' and 'professed that he would subscribe to them very willingly'. In fact, the final draft of the proclamation was toned down by Charles himself to avoid any explicit mention of either Montague or Arminianism. Things were clearly in the balance in the summer of 1626. Certainly, the proclamation would have had a very different political and theological resonance if Charles had allowed it to be glossed by the pseudo-official publication of Hall's tract, perhaps with Montague's endorsement attached.[62] Here the very 'moderation' of Hall's pamphlet may well have helped to raise the stakes, if even so carefully hedged a statement as his was now not thought fit for print. Perhaps, for Hall, half a loaf was better than none, but what is certain is that the crucial question of where the practical limits of public speech on the issue lay remained open. For the rest of the decade, and beyond, Hall and others continued to push for their version of doctrinal propriety – but that is another story.

Notes

[1] C. S. R. Russell, *Parliaments and English Politics, 1621–29* (Oxford, 1979); M. A. Kishlansky, 'The emergence of adversary politics in the Long Parliament', *Journal of Modern History*, 49 (1977); *idem*, *Parliamentary Selection* (Cambridge, 1986); K. Sharpe, *Politics and Ideas in Early Stuart England* (London, 1989), esp. chs. 1 and 11 and his introduction to K. Sharpe (ed.), *Faction and Parliament* (Oxford, 1978). This vision of the political culture of the period provides, perhaps, the crucial structuring assumptions of Sharpe's massive *The Personal Rule of Charles I* (London, 1992).

[2] C. S. R. Russell, *The Causes of the English Civil War* (Oxford, 1990) and *The Fall of the British Monarchies* (Oxford, 1990); J. S. Morrill, *The Nature of the English Revolution* (London, 1993), part 1 "England's wars of religion' esp. chs. 3 and 4.

[3] J. P. Sommerville, *Politics and Ideology in England, 1603–1640* (London, 1986); Russell, *Causes*, ch. 6 and his 'Divine rights in the early seventeenth century' in J. Morrill, P. Slack and D. Woolf (eds.), *Public Duty and Private Conscience in Seventeenth Century England* (Oxford, 1993); G. Burgess, 'The divine right of kings reconsidered', *English Historical Review*, 425 (1992) and his *The Politics of the Ancient Constitution* (London, 1992).

[4] Nicholas Tyacke, *Anti-Calvinists* (Oxford, 1987); P. White, *Predestination, Policy and Polemic* (Cambridge, 1992); K. Sharpe, *Personal Rule*, chs. 6 and 12; G. Bernard, 'The Church of England, c.1529–c.1642', *History*, 75 (1990); J. Davies, *The Caroline Captivity of the Church* (Oxford, 1992).

[5] For an outline of Hall's career see R. A. McCabe, *Joseph Hall* (Oxford, 1982), ch. 1 and F. Huntley, *Bishop Joseph Hall* (Cambridge, 1979), *passim*. For Wallington's admiration see P. Seaver, *Wallington's World* (Stanford, 1985), p. 187.

[6] P. Collinson, *The Religion of Protestants* (Oxford, 1982), *passim* and, for his particular use of Hall, see especially pp. 19, 43, 78, 82, 84, 90, 92–5, 137. On White's view of the English middle way see his 'The *via media* in the early Stuart Church', in K. C. Fincham (ed.), *The Early Stuart Church* (London, 1993); for Hall, see especially p. 226

Part I The culture of politics

in Fincham, and White's *Predestination*, pp. 234–6, 244, 247. For Davies' view of Hall see his *Caroline Captivity*, pp. 93–5. For the radical Puritan/mainstream Anglican polarity see White, *Predestination, passim*; Bernard, 'Church of England' and Sharpe, *Personal Rule*, esp. ch. 12.

⁷ James I himself did a great deal to set this tone, for which see K. Fincham and P. Lake, 'The ecclesiastical policy of James I', *Journal of British Studies*, 24 (1985). James' ecumenicism is currently the subject of important research by Brown Patterson, for a foretaste of which see his 'King James I's call for an ecumenical council', in G. J. Cuming and D. Baker (eds.), *Studies in Church History*, vol. VII (Cambridge, 1971). On the wider impact of royal writing in setting the tone for debate and counsel see K. Sharpe 'The king's writ: royal authors and royal authority in early modern England', in K. Sharpe and P. Lake (eds.), *Culture and Politics in Early Stuart England* (London, 1994). On the structures and imperatives of anti-papal polemic see the brilliant article by Anthony Milton, 'The Church of England, Rome and the true church: the demise of a Jacobean consensus', in Fincham, *Early Stuart Church*. Also see Dr Milton's book *Catholic and Reformed*, forthcoming from Cambridge University Press.

⁸ *The Works of the Reverend Joseph Hall D.D.*, ed. P. Wynter, 10 vols. (Oxford, 1863), hereafter cited as Hall, *Works*, vol. V, p. 282, from 'The beauty and unity of the church' preached at Whitehall between 1626 and 1628; also see J. Hall, *Noah's dove bringing an olive of peace to the tossed ark of Christ's church*, an English translation of a Latin sermon preached to Convocation in 1624 and published under the title *Columba Noae* in that year. The Latin text and a later translation are in Hall, *Works*, vol. X, pp. 1–44. For the present quotation see p. 38.

⁹ Hall, *Works*, vol. V, p. 282.

¹⁰ *Ibid.*, p. 182, from 'The best bargain' preached at Theobald's on Sunday 21 September 1623 and printed the same year; *ibid.* p. 283, from 'The beauty and unity of the Church'.

¹¹ *Ibid.*, pp. 349, 350, 359 from 'St Paul's combat in two sermons preached at the court to his Majesty, in ordinary attendance', probably between 1626 and 1628.

¹² *Ibid.*, p. 269, from 'The defeat of cruelty … laid forth in a sermon preached at a solemn fast at Whitehall', probably in 1625–6.

¹³ *Ibid.*, p. 155, from 'The deceit of appearance preached before his Majesty at his court of Theobald's', in 1622; *Works*, vol. X, p. 38, from *Noah's Dove*.

¹⁴ *Ibid.*, vol. X, p. 42.

¹⁵ *Ibid.*, pp. 41, 43–4 from *Noah's Dove*; *Works*, vol. V, p. 283, from 'The beauty and unity of the Church', preached at Whitehall probably in 1625/6.

¹⁶ *Works*, vol. X, p. 41, from *Noah's Dove*.

¹⁷ *Ibid.*, p. 31.

¹⁸ *Ibid.*, vol. V, pp. 386, 388 from 'The Christian's crucifixion with Christ, a sermon preached … March 30 1628 in Whitehall' in preparation for a fast; pp. 400–2, from 'Christian liberty laid forth from a sermon preached … at Whitehall in the time of the parliament', of 1628.

¹⁹ *Ibid.*, pp. 179, 180 from 'The best bargain'; *ibid.*, p. 285, from 'The beauty and unity of the Church'; *ibid.*, vol. X, p. 29 from *Noah's Dove*.

²⁰ *Ibid.*, vol. V, p. 257, from 'A public thanksgiving for the wonderful mitigation of the late mortality preached before his Majesty … at his court of Whitehall, January 29 1625/6 and upon the same command published': *ibid.*, p. 372, from 'The blessings, sins and judgements of God's vineyard, one of the sermons preached at Westminster

on the day of the public fast, April 5, 1628 to the Lords of the High Court of Parliament, and, by their appointment, published'.

²¹ Milton, 'Church of England'.

²² Hall, *Works*, vol. V, p. 283, from 'The beauty and unity of the Church'; *ibid.*, pp. 360–1, 348, from 'St Paul's combat'.

²³ Milton, 'Church of England', for the more popular, Puritan mode of anti-popery see P. Lake, 'Anti-popery: the structure of a prejudice', in R. P. Cust and A. Hughes (eds.), *Conflict in Early Stuart England* (London, 1989); Hall, *Works*, vol. V, pp. 265–6, from 'The defeat of cruelty'; *ibid.*, pp. 348–9, from 'St Paul's combat'; *ibid.*, vol. X, p. 34; *ibid.*, vol. V, p. 183, from 'The best bargain'.

²⁴ *Ibid.*, p. 219–20, from 'The true peacemaker'.

²⁵ *Ibid.*, p. 220.

²⁶ *Ibid.*, pp. 253–4, from 'A public thanksgiving'; *ibid.*, p. 386, from 'The Christian's crucifixion'.

²⁷ *Ibid.*, p. 262–3, from 'The defeat of cruelty'; *ibid.*, p. 349, from 'St Paul's combat'.

²⁸ *Ibid.*, p. 204, from 'The enemies of the cross of Christ, a sermon preached at Hampton Court to King James, in ordinary attendance, in September 1624'.

²⁹ *Ibid.*, vol. X, p. 34, from *Noah's Dove*; *ibid.*, vol. V, pp. 264–5, from 'The defeat of cruelty'.

³⁰ S. L. Adams, 'Foreign policy and the parliaments of 1621 and 1624', in K. Sharpe, *Faction and Parliament*; *idem.* 'The Protestant cause: religious alliance with the west European Calvinist communities as a political issue in England, 1585–1630', D.Phil. thesis, 1973, Oxford University; T. Cogswell, *The Blessed Revolution* (Cambridge, 1989).

³¹ Fincham and Lake, 'Ecclesiastical policy'; T. Cogswell, 'England and the Spanish match', in Cust and Hughes, *Conflict*; N. E. McClure (ed.), *The Letters of John Chamberlain*, 2 vols. (Philadelphia, 1939), vol. II, p. 517, I owe this last reference to the kindness of Dr Peter McCulloch.

³² Hall, *Works*, vol. V, pp. 182, 183, 184.

³³ *Ibid.*, pp. 225, 226.

³⁴ *Ibid.*, pp. 264, 267, 272, from 'The defeat of cruelty'; p. 257, from 'A public thanksgiving'.

³⁵ *Ibid.*, pp. 335, 336, from 'Christ and Caesar, a sermon preached at Hampton Court'.

³⁶ Hall's adherence to the conventional identification of the pope as Antichrist has been illustrated in a number of the references to the Church of Rome as the beast and to the antichristian usurpations of the papists, cited above. For his adherence to essentially Calvinist notions of assurance and perseverance see his slighting reference 'to our late executifidians' who taught 'that a true, solid, radicated, saving faith may be totally, finally lost'. 'I hate the motion', Hall proclaimed, 'it is presumption that I tax; not well-grounded assurance: presumption of outward profession and privileges; not assurance of the inward truth of grace', Hall, *Works*, vol. V, p. 237, from 'Wickedness making a fruitful land barren, a sermon preached to his Majesty, at the court of Whitehall, August 8', probably in 1625. Also see Hall's 'A letter concerning falling away from grace', addressed to 'my good Mr B.' concerning the prevalence of 'our new excutifidians' in Suffolk and taking the same line as the sermon; Hall, *Works*, vol. IX, pp. 520–4.

³⁷ For the polemical context of Montague's works see Fincham and Lake, 'Ecclesi-

astical policy'; for Montague's opinions see his *A Gagg for the New Gospel? No. A New Gagg for an Old Goose* (London, 1624) and his *Appello Caesarem* (London, 1625).

[38] Hall, *Works*, vol. V, p. 285; *ibid.*, p. 237, from 'Wickedness making a fruitful land barren'. For Hall's equivalence of popery with heresies like socinianism, familism and antinominanism see *ibid.*, p. 204.

[39] For a comparison see P. Lake, 'Lancelot Andrewes, John Buckeridge and *avant-garde* conformity at the court of James I', in L. L. Peck (ed.), *The Mental World of the Jacobean Court* (Cambridge, 1991). For Hall's list of departed luminaries see Hall, *Works*, vol. X, p. 29.

[40] On this political and polemical context see Fincham and Lake, 'Ecclesiastical policy'; Cogswell, 'England and the Spanish match', P. Lake, 'Constitutional consensus and Puritan opposition in the 1620s; Thomas Scott and the Spanish match', *Historical Journal*, 25 (1982).

[41] Hall, *Works*, vol. V, pp. 237, 284 from 'The beauty and unity of the Church'; *ibid.*, pp. 202–3, from 'The enemies of the cross of Christ'.

[42] E. Arber (ed.), *A Transcript of the Registers of the Stationers Company of London* (London, 1877), vol. IV, p. 128, entered on 13 August 1626 and licensed by Mr Dr Worall, the bishop of London's chaplain.

[43] On the commotion caused in Church and State by the Montague affair see Tyacke, *Anti-Calvinists*, chs. 6 and 7.

[44] The text of the *Via Media* is in vol. IX of Hall's works, pp. 497–519. These two quotes are at pp. 499 and 497.

[45] *Ibid.*, pp. 497–8, 506, 511, 516.

[46] *Ibid.*, pp. 497–8, 517.

[47] *Ibid.*, pp. 505, 498.

[48] Hall's statement of the five articles is at *ibid.*, pp. 490–7; for the hypothetical universalism of the delegation to Dort see P. Lake, 'Calvinism and the English Church, 1570–1635', *Past and Present*, 114 (1987) and Tyacke, *Anti-Calvinists*, ch. 4; for a rather different view see White, *Predestination*, ch. 9.

[49] Hall, *Works*, vol. IX, pp. 500, 501.

[50] *Ibid.*, pp. 502, 505–6.

[51] *Ibid.*, pp. 502–3, 511.

[52] R. Muller, *Christ and Decree* (Durham, NC, 1986), pp. 130, 171.

[53] Hall, *Works*, vol. IX, pp. 502, 501, 511, 518.

[54] For Overall in the 1590s see P. Lake, *Moderate Puritans and the Elizabethan Church* (Cambridge, 1982), pp. 236–42; for Abbot's opinion see Public Record Offices S.P. 105/95, fo. 9v; and for the more favourable evaluation of the remonstrants see Lake 'Calvinism and the English Church', p. 53. For Hall's retrospective view of Montague and the *Via Media* see his 'Observations of some specialities of divine providence in the life of Joseph Hall', in Hall, *Works*, vol. I, pp. xliii–xliv.

[55] Hall, *Works*, vol. IX, pp. 506–7, 508, 490, 509.

[56] On Overall's views in the 1590s see H. C. Porter, *Reformation and Reaction in Tudor Cambridge* (Cambridge, 1958), pp. 397–413.

[57] See, for instance, G. Carleton, *An examination of those things wherein the author of the late appeal holdeth the doctrines of the Pelagians and Arminians to be the doctrine of the church of England* (London, 1626), or D. Featley and Thomas Goad, *Pelagius redivivus or Pelagius raked out of the ashes by Arminius and his scholars* (London,

1626). For the reaction against Montague in court and Parliament see Tyacke, *Anti-Calvinists*, chs. 6 and 7.

[58] Hall, *Works*, vol. IX, p. 489; also see Hall's autobiographical fragment, *ibid.*, vol. I, p. xliv, where Hall claims to have given the tract to Dean Young of Winchester to show it to the king.

[59] For this propensity see Lake, 'Calvinism and the English Church', p. 69.

[60] Of Hall's sermons published at the time *Columba Noae* (London, 1624) was dedicated to Archbishop Abbot, 'The best bargain' (London, 1623) to Pembroke. 'The hypocrite, set forth in a sermon at the court, Febuary 28, 1629–30' was dedicated to the earl of Norwich. See Hall, vol. V, p. 425.

[61] For a plausible reconstruction of Pembroke's purposes in these years see Adams, 'Foreign policy', 'Protestant cause'; B. Donagan, 'The York House conference revisited: laymen, Calvinism and Arminianism', *Historical Research*, 64 (1991).

[62] Davies, *Caroline Captivity*, pp. 111–12.

4

Honour, rhetoric and political culture: the earl of Huntingdon and his enemies[1]

Richard Cust

I

At Leicester assizes on the afternoon of 27 March 1612, after most of the judicial business had been concluded, the judges held a special hearing in their chamber. Before a large audience of county gentry and freeholders, they attempted to resolve a dispute which had been dividing the shire. On one side was Henry Lord Grey, represented on this occasion by his ally Sir Thomas Beaumont; on the other were Henry Hastings, fifth earl of Huntingdon and his client, and nominee for a place on the county bench, John Bale Esq. The hearing was about whether Bale should be removed from the bench for suborning jurors and generally failing to measure up to the high standards required of a magistrate. But the person who stood to lose most by it was Huntingdon himself, whose credit and prestige were challenged through the suggestion that he had acted improperly in recommending Bale's appointment to the Lord Chancellor.[2] In the event Bale and Huntingdon were vindicated; and this enabled the earl to win the current round of an extended power struggle between his family and the Greys.

Disputes of this sort were not uncommon in early modern England, although the Grey/Hastings feud was one of the more prolonged and notorious.[3] They have been much studied by political historians concerned with local administration, the enforcement of Crown policy, the performance of officeholders and the conduct of parliamentary elections.[4] However, relatively little attention has been paid to what these disputes can tell us about contemporary political culture. This is regrettable because, as anthropologists and social historians have repeatedly demonstrated, studying the records of dispute is one of the most fruitful ways of understanding the assumptions and ideals which bind societies together.[5] The Bale case, and the broader struggle between the Greys and the Hastings, are no exception. Over the period of about ten years they generated a considerable amount of documentation, from letters and petitions and memoranda to a lengthy account of the hearing before the judges written by Huntingdon himself, partly, it would seem, as a reminder of how he had outwitted his enemies and partly as confirmation that his honour and authority had indeed been vindicated. Virtually all of this material was produced from a partisan standpoint, to support a particular line of argument or interpretation of events; but herein lies much of its value. For by studying the terms in which participants sought to legitimate their own actions, and make those of their opponents appear reprehensible, it is possible to gain an understanding of what contemporaries considered acceptable or unacceptable behaviour in such a context. As the legal anthropologist Simon Roberts puts it, within this material we can expect to find

> various kinds of normative proposition; statements in which rules, beliefs and values are either explicitly articulated or emerge by implication. Here we can obtain the disputant's view of the normal and the abnormal through their claims as to what people should or should not have done.[6]

In this respect, it is particularly useful to focus on the concepts of honour which participants espoused and the forms of rhetoric which they deployed. Honour has been described by anthropologists as the means by which the worth of individuals or families is measured in the societies to which they feel they belong. It reflects the ways in which contemporaries sift experience and pass judgements about status and worth, and can thus provide a valuable insight into the values and norms which they espouse.[7] Rhetoric can often be similarly revealing, since it contains the themes which make language and argument attractive in terms of a society's beliefs and assumptions. Both are therefore of central importance to understanding the political culture of early Stuart England; however, before concentrating on these aspects it is necessary to discuss the context and course of the Grey/Hastings dispute.

II

Leicestershire in the early part of James' reign was a divided county. The origins of this could be traced back to the death in 1595 of Henry, third earl of Huntingdon, the redoubtable 'Puritan earl'. In spite of long absences from the county serving as President of the Council of the North, Huntingdon had dominated most aspects of local life. Operating through the agency of three of his brothers – Sir George, Sir Edward and Sir Francis Hastings – he had directed the bench and the lieutenancy, controlled county elections, acted as a 'very good lord' to Leicester Corporation and established a vigorous, Protestant preaching ministry. Because of his massive prestige, this dominance was largely accepted by local gentry and relationships at the top of county society remained harmonious for most of Elizabeth's reign.[8] However, when Henry died without an heir, to be succeeded by his brother George, the Hastings' control began to unravel.

The fourth earl inherited a difficult legacy. His family estates were heavily burdened by debt, and having spent most of his life operating as a country gentleman he lacked the contacts at the centre which had enabled his brother to shore up his position. Much of his time was spent staving off creditors and trying to hold on to his lands in Leicestershire. He also got on much less well with Edward and Francis. Their loyalty to the third earl had been based in part on a common commitment to the Puritan cause. They suspected George, with some justification, of being only a lukewarm Calvinist; and in the case of Francis there appears to have been a certain amount of personal antagonism, which in 1598 led him to abandon a scheme to resettle himself in Leicestershire.[9] This was damaging to the family's influence which the two brothers, particularly Francis, had done an enormous amount to advance during the 1580s and 1590s. The fourth earl's close relationship with Walter, the youngest of the brotherhood, was no compensation. As a suspected Catholic he did not hold local office and his political impact was negligible.[10] All this led to a weakening of Huntingdon's local authority, which became apparent in October 1601 when he was humiliated at the parliamentary election for Leicester.

This arose out of a quarrel with George Belgrave Esq., the origins of which are obscure. It appears to have had something to do with disputes in 1596 over the dismantling of the estate of William Stokes of Beaumanor for whom Belgrave was acting as executor. There was also an ongoing quarrel with Sir Edward Hastings and his son Henry which led to violent clashes and a Privy Council investigation, also in 1596.[11] Belgrave was already 'a noted enemy' of the Hastings clan when Huntingdon wrote to Leicester Corporation warning that on no account should they accede to his request to become a burgess. However, he appeared before the aldermen on 20 October wearing the earl's livery and pretending that he had made his peace with him; and on the strength of this he was elected. The earl felt deeply wounded, the more so when after the election Belgrave 'came openly into the street and pulled off [the livery coat] and threwe it into a channell, saying now thou hast served this turne thou shalt never serve more'.[12] For the following eighteen months he pursued Belgrave through the court of Star Chamber and the Privy Council in an effort to exact the retribution that he felt his honour required. Only when Belgrave had been removed from the commission of the peace, imprisoned by the Council and commanded to make public apology for his actions at Leicester assizes, could he accept that 'the shame of me and my poor ruinat house', 'witnessed by the Parliament, Court and Countrie', had been redressed.[13] However, the damage inflicted in the the meantime had been considerable; and this opened the way for others to challenge the Hastings' hegemony.

The main threat came from the re-emergence into county politics of the Grey family. Since the attainder of Thomas Grey, marquis of Dorset, for his part in the attempted coup at Mary's accession, the Greys had been exiled to Essex; however, through careful cultivation of Elizabeth and the Cecils, and loyal service at court culminating with the lieutenancy of the Band of Gentleman Pensioners, Sir Henry Grey was able to recover the core of his ancestral lands.[14] By the late 1590s the family was ready to resume its former role in local politics. Initially, Sir Henry entrusted responsibility for this to his eldest son, Sir John, who took a prominent role on the commission of the peace after his appointment in 1598. However, following defeat in the 1601 shire election, Sir John seems to have decided to seek his fortunes elsewhere, as a soldier and a courtier, and it was his father who eventually came to reside at the family seat at Bradgate Park, taking the title of Lord Grey of Groby soon after the accession of James.[15] The rivalry between the Greys and the Hastings had long been one of the fixed points of Leicestershire politics. During much of the early sixteenth century, the families had competed on more or less equal terms for dominance of the county.[16] The rivalry resurfaced soon after the Greys' return. At the 1601 shire election, Sir John Grey threw himself into a vigorous campaign for the principal seat and seemed assured of victory, having apparently received the backing of Huntingdon; but at the last moment he was opposed and defeated by Henry Hastings of the Abbey, Sir Edward's son and the earl's nephew.[17] With his credit fully extended, this was profoundly humiliating for Grey and not surprisingly he blamed Huntingdon. The episode was later seen as the point at which the traditional animosity re-emerged; and, soon after, Sir John was joining with Belgrave to allege corruption in Huntingdon's appointments to local offices.[18]

The main cause of aggravation between the two families, however, occurred when the fourth earl died in December 1604. He was succeeded by his grandson Henry who was a minor and therefore ineligible to fill the family's traditional offices of lord lieutenant and *custos rotulorum*. Lord Grey immediately wrote to the earl of Salisbury asking that he be nominated to these offices, along with the Hastings' other Crown appointments of receiver of the Duchy of Lancaster and lieutenant of Leicester Forest, as compensation for surrendering his lieutenancy of the Gentleman Pensioners at James' accession. The fifth earl responded with a counter-petition which pleaded that 'to misse these places might make my house less esteemed where I hope to live and faithfullie serve your majestie', and Salisbury came down on his side. Huntingdon was given the Forest and duchy offices immediately, whilst the lord lieutenancy was left in abeyance until his coming of age.[19]

In spite of this advantageous settlement, the period between the fourth earl of Huntingdon's death in 1604 and the fifth earl's coming of age in May 1607 was an interregnum for the Hastings in Leicestershire. The leading role on the bench of justices passed to the Greys and their allies, the Beaumonts. Lord Grey became unofficial spokesman for the county justices in their dealings with the Privy Council and Leicester Corporation; Sir Henry Beaumont of Coleorton became *custos rotulorum* and, at a by-election in 1606, was chosen alongside his brother, Sir Thomas Beaumont of Stoughton, to serve as knight of the shire; and Sir John Grey, now a Gentleman of the Privy Chamber, provided the all-important point of contact with the court.[20] The shift in power was reflected in some significant revisions to the commission of the peace. Sir John Grey's opponent in the 1601 election, Sir Henry Hastings of the Abbey, found himself demoted in the order of precedence from second to sixth place amongst the county knights, which was a considerable snub. Meanwhile Sir Henry Beaumont's twenty-three-year-old son, Sir Thomas of Coleorton, and Matthew Saunders, an ally of the Greys and Beaumonts, were both brought on to the commission.[21]

These trends, however, were quickly reversed when the fifth earl attained his majority. From the start he was determined to vindicate his honour and authority. This was apparent in his treatment of Leicester Corporation which had been seeking a new charter touching on his rights as steward of the Honour of Leicester. In June 1607 he used his new powers as lord lieutenant to humiliate the mayor for supposedly taking inadequate steps to deal with riots connected with the Midland Rising, and this led to the Corporation climbing down and eventually accepting a settlement.[22] Huntingdon then set about imposing himself on the county gentry. He was required to appoint some new deputy lieutenants to deal with the Rising and in doing so over-looked the claims of established and experienced county leaders friendly to the Greys, such as Sir Thomas Beaumont and Sir William Skipwith.[23] Instead, he turned to Sir Thomas Cave, the long-established Hastings retainer, Sir Thomas' cousin, Henry Cave Esq., and another Hastings ally, Sir William Turpin. When Henry Cave died in 1609, he was replaced by the earl's kinsman, Sir Henry Hastings of the Abbey.[24] The earl pursued a similarly partisan course in recommending appointments to the bench, over which, as the new *custos rotulorum* in succession to Sir Henry Beaumont, he had considerable influence. Those appointed after May 1607 were either established allies of his family, like Sir Thomas Compton, or capable men of business unconnected with the Greys, like Sir Thomas Haselrig.[25] The most controversial of the new JPs was his uncle, Walter Hastings Esq., who came on to the bench in May–June 1607 at the unusually advanced age of sixty, having, so he claimed, never previously served in local office. This was remarkable enough, but what particularly affronted some of his fellow justices was the fact that his wife and family were Catholics and that he himself was suspected of some involvement in the Gunpowder Plot eighteen months earlier. To rub salt into the wound, Walter, as the brother of an earl, was ranked at the head of the local gentry on the commission, directly above Sir John Grey.[26] Sir Thomas Beaumont tried to block the appointment by protesting to Huntingdon that 'he knew that could not be by law, his wife being a recusant, and that he knew it to be against the mynd of parlament, and if he lyved to the next session it should be amended'. But this was simply ignored, and the earl caused further outrage in 1609 when he made Walter a deputy lieutenant in succession to Sir Thomas Cave.[27]

In retrospect, Huntingdon's coming of age can be seen as the moment when county politics began to polarize. But the inevitability of this process should not be exaggerated. Conflict and division could often be overcome through family and social ties. Huntingdon's personal accounts reveal some of these at work. He was evidently on good terms with Sir Henry Beaumont and his son, exchanging visits, using Sir Henry as guarantor for several loans and seeking his guidance in negotiations with Leicester Corporation in 1605. He also appears to have enjoyed a reasonably cordial relationship with Sir John Grey. Grey's servant was carrying letters for him in 1607 and he brought a christening cup for Sir John's eldest son in 1608.[28] Links like these could do much to relieve the competitive tension which often existed between leading county gentry. There was also a strong ethos of unity and harmony within gentry society. This was evident in the alacrity with which Huntingdon and Sir John Grey concluded a truce in 1605. Although this was to prove rather fragile – and Huntingdon was later to dismiss Grey's professions of friendship as mere 'pretences' – it reflected the expectation that gentry would do their best to maintain a state of peace with their neighbours.[29] This also emerged from a letter written some years later by Robert Lord Spencer, a Northamptonshire peer, who was closely related to the Greys and had acted as one of the trustees for Huntingdon's marriage settlement in 1604.[30] He recalled an agreement which the earl had made with him that if the quarrel with the Greys revived 'I should interpose and mediat amety and love which God willing I shall alwayes be ready to doe as long as I live'.[31] These considerations helped to preserve a rough and ready peace within the county until 1610.

Throughout these early quarrels, much of the concern of the Hastings focused on their honour. Honour was described on several occasions as being 'at the stake' and its language was used to express the damage done to the family. It has become something of a commonplace that English men, and women, were particularly concerned with honour in the late sixteenth and early seventeenth centuries. The huge volume of defamation cases which came before the courts, the popularity of duelling and the centrality of honour as a theme in much of the drama of the period, are all indicative of this.[32] And yet it is still an open question what it actually meant to contemporaries.

Amongst the gentry, honour in this period was generally presented in terms of the concept of 'mixed nobleness'. It was seen as an amalgam of personal virtue and noble lineage. However, there was considerable debate about which of these attributes should carry more weight. Broadly speaking, Christian humanists and Calvinists tended to stress the primacy of various forms of virtue, particularly those associated with piety, learning and service of the State, whilst heraldic and antiquarian writers emphasized the enduring significance of pedigree.[33] Modern commentators have generally accepted that the stress on virtue carried the day. In the classic account of the role of honour in sixteenth- and early- seventeeth-century politics, Mervyn James mapped out a pattern of change whereby a concept of honour associated with chivalry and lineage came to be overlaid by a concept linked to humanism, Protestantism and obedience to the Crown. The virtues of wilfulness, stead-fastness and assertiveness gave way to wisdom, temperance and godliness, as the ideal role for a gentleman changed from Christian knight to godly mag-istrate.[34] Elsewhere, James described this as part of the shift from 'lineage' to 'civil' society, from a society structured around the affinities of great landed families to one based on association between the heads of patriarchal, nuclear families.[35] Other historians have generally accepted James' account, and there is no doubt that it provides a valuable framework for understanding social and cultural change amongst the elite. However, insofar as it plays down 'the honour due to blood' and the importance of kinship, it can be misleading.

This point can be illustrated by looking at some of the letters and memo-randa of members of the Hastings family in the late Elizabethan and Jacobean period. Both aspects of honour receive attention; but given that the Hastings were amongst the foremost members of the Calvinist nobility – which has been seen by James and Lawrence Stone as pushing against the older con-cepts[36] – their stress on lineage is particularly striking. A good example is pro-vided by Sir Francis Hastings, who has been portrayed as the quintessential godly magistrate.[37] When he decorated his newly acquired manor house at North Cadbury in Somerset in the 1590s, he installed an elaborate cycle of heraldic stained glass which celebrated the illustrious connections of his ancestors. He may have felt that it was important to remind the gentry of his newly adopted county that his family was as ancient and distinguished as any of them.[38] Certainly he recognized the importance of lineage for underpinning status. In a letter to the third earl in 1592 he lamented that 'poore I shall live with little credite any where and with less comforte if the pillar of our house stande not upright in his full strength'; and he went on to deliver a lengthy piece of advice which was intended to ensure that the earl preserved the pat-rimony of family lands in Leicestershire.[39] This was a classic statement of the importance of kinship solidarity. The earl was reminded of his responsibili-ties to a line which stretched before and after him. Whilst 'the staffe of Ashby house'[40] was entrusted to him he was expected not only to secure a solid inheritance for his heir, but also provide for the various 'branches' of the family. Failure would be disastrous for all of them because 'the honour and credite of the whole house dependeth upon your leaving the heyre of the house in strength and ability to live in his place as an earle'.[41] In return, as head of the family, the earl could expect loyalty and service: if 'everie good member of the house will not adde his best strength therein he is much to blame', insisted Francis on another occasion.[42]

Similar themes emerged in a lengthy set of advice which the fifth earl com-posed for his son in about 1614.[43] The sense of belonging to a lineage which stretched back through the ages was vividly conveyed in his image of the household servants of his father's and grandfather's day, whose continuing attendance on him would not only be 'a brave thinge and a great honour', but would also be 'like pictures to thee, puttinge thee in minde of them by one acte or other that they did in their tyme'.[44] This not only illustrated some of the assurance which derived from belonging to a noble dynasty,[45] it also indicated the credit and inspiration the present head of a family could draw from the deeds of his forebears which was one of the central themes of contemporary discussions of lineage.[46] In addition, Huntingdon devoted considerable attention to 'good lordship' and the duties of the head of the lineage. On the basis of recent experience he urged on his son the importance of wealth for sustaining the family's prestige: 'without means thy house will looke as naked as trees that are cropped ... riches illustrate honour and set forth the dignity of thy place'. He also insisted on the need to 'acknowledge' 'those that be thy kinsmen ... for that house hath the greatest assurance of continuance that hath the most branches'. And, unusually at this date, he was concerned with the giving of livery coats – that 'ancient and honourable custom', as he termed it – which helps to explain why Belgrave's contempt for his grandfather's coat still rankled with him years later.[47]

Lineage and pedigree did much to shape the Hastings' approach to local politics. Again, the fifth earl provides the best illustration of this. Those he trusted were for the most part kinsmen and family retainers. In the years after 1604 he relied heavily for advice and support on his uncle Walter, the brother closest to his beloved grandfather, and to a lesser extent on his mother's kinsman, Sir Henry Harrington, and another uncle, Sir Henry Hastings of the Abbey.[48] They provided much of the loyal guidance envisaged by Sir Francis Hastings. Huntingdon also used his patronage very deliberately to promote family retainers. He explained his backing for Bale's appointment to the commission of the peace in terms of his 'love and former service to my house'; and Sir Thomas Cave, one of his first batch of deputy lieutenants, later wrote of his 'place and calling as well in the long service of his majestie and under many your lord's ancestors as under your good lord'.[49] In return for such preferment Huntingdon expected loyalty, and he was particularly affronted when Sir Thomas Cave's son opposed him in the Bale case.[50]

The other side of this coin was a rooted hostility to those who opposed his family's interests. He advised his son never to trust

> those that have bene enemyes to thy sealfe or thy ancestors ... alwayes carrye a vigilant eye over them, for like ill ground when the fatt of thy courtesies are worne out they will turne to their owne nature, and I never founde any faithful unto me that loved not my ancestors.[51]

This was the language of the feud, in which the social universe was divided between friends and enemies and bitterness and hostility were transmitted from one generation to the next.[52] Although he did not name them, there was little doubt that Huntingdon had in mind the Greys. In a lengthy memorandum about Lord Grey compiled prior to the Bale case he traced the 'differences betwixt his house and myne' back to the reign of Mary Tudor, and displayed a constant distrust of the dealings of him and his son. Belgrave's enmity, although of more recent origin, was represented in similar terms. Both Huntingdon and his uncle Walter described him as someone who 'hath allwaies bene a firebrand of dissention, and hated bothe the roote and branches of my house'.[53] Within this conceptual framework, it was also accepted that any slight must be revenged and there could be no yielding until family honour had been satisfied. Hence Huntingdon advised his son that, although 'no quarrell is lawfull by divinitie, yet to mainteyne thy reputation unspotted thou must not remayne with an injury offered thee'.[54]

The language used by the fifth earl, in particular, was replete with images of lineage, kinship and the feud, and all that these implied. Historians such as James and Stone have tended to see these as concepts characteristic of an honour society which was passing away in England in the latter half of the sixteenth century;[55] but this is a useful reminder of their continuing resonance, even for Calvinist members of the nobility. Early Stuart England continued to exhibit many features associated with the age of chivalry.[56] Honour was still seen as something which was transmitted through the blood and shared by members of a particular line; it was also something which had constantly to be claimed and defended within a highly competitive environment. It could therefore serve to legitimize a code of conduct based on pride, wilfulness and self-assertiveness. However, this is only one side of the picture. The concept of 'mixed nobleness' contained a notoriously ambiguous series of associations, some of them illustrated in Huntingdon's readiness to qualify his call for revenge with acknowledgement of the need to limit quarrels in a spirit of Christian charity. Due weight must therefore be given to the connections between honour and virtue.

For the Hastings virtue took a variety of forms, all of them highly conventional. Principal amongst these was piety, 'the axis and cardo that all the rest run upon', as the fifth earl of Huntingdon advised his son.[57] For Sir Francis Hastings, and also the third earl, piety meant first and foremost a Puritan style of divinity, with an emphasis on the obligations of the elect to promote a purer understanding of the gospel and engage in unremitting struggle against the popish Antichrist.[58] The fifth earl's understanding of piety, however, was much closer to that of the 'Calvinist conformist'. He subscribed to Calvinist doctrine and expressed his abhorrence of popery, but at the same time underlined the need for obedience. 'We are commanded to obey the king in all thinges', he told his son; and on this basis he condemned the ceremonial nonconformity of some puritans as 'a sinne'.[59] Piety was also conceived of in more neutral terms. It meant charity and hospitality to the poor: 'the pitifull regard of ... the poor' which Sir Francis praised in his elder brother.[60] It also meant fulfilling the duty to maintain an ordered and godly household, for which the fifth earl made extensive provision in a set of household regulations for Ashby Castle issued in 1609.[61] And it extended into politics with the Christian duty to reconcile quarrels. 'Blessed are the peacemakers', the fifth earl reminded his son, urging him not only to 'forgive and forget' his own injuries, but also devote time to composing the disputes of his fellow gentry.[62]

Virtue was seen by Christian humanist writers as something which could best be nurtured by learning. This was a view which was also subscribed to by Huntingdon. He gave detailed instruction on when his son should commence the education of his children, which authors they should read and at what stage they should embark on the study of grammar and verse. He also included a passage in the best humanist tradition deriding the ignorance of many of his fellow landowners who 'unless they spend ther tymes in sport they thinke they are noe gentlemen'.[63] For Huntingdon the ends of education were twofold. Firstly, it was a means to securing the praise and esteem which went with being acknowledged as 'a man of parts'. This involved being able to hold one's own at the dinner table, deliver well-turned pieces of rhetoric on 'publique occasions' and behave appropriately at the court – where it was all important not to let 'thy speech ... shewe thee to be but a country gentleman'.[64] Secondly, it was a preparation for the service of prince and commonwealth which most humanist commentators saw as the principal calling of a gentleman.

This was a theme Huntingdon expounded at considerable length in his advice. 'By birth thou art a publique person', he reminded his son, and then launched into a discussion of the various types of service which could be considered honourable.[65] Foremost amongst these was personal service of the prince, which Huntingdon, like many contemporaries, regarded as an important part of the *raison d'être* of the aristocracy. He made much of this in the 1604 petition about his local offices, reminding James that his grandfather had had 'the honour and trust to be your majesties lieutenant', referring to 'his loyaltie, dutie and devotion still living in me to serve our majestie', and claiming that 'I should professe it as a greater honoure to succeede in your favoure then to inheritt an earldom after him.'[66] Huntingdon's fellow peers tended to understand service to the prince to mean service at court; but Huntingdon did not. He was fond of citing Sir Walter Mildmay's maxim that one should 'knowe the court, but spend not thy life there'; and presented a vivid description of 'this glitteringe miserie' compounded of vice, expense, frustration and endless insecurity.[67] His advice to his son was to attend for no more than a 'few dayes' each year in order to remain 'in the king's remembrance and good opinion' and keep up the contacts needed when some favour was being sought. Otherwise he should devote himself to the 'honest delights' of 'a country life' and concentrate on his duties as magistrate and local governor.[68]

Here Huntingdon offered a shrewd appreciation of the way in which local offices could enhance status and esteem. In part this was a matter of being seen to act in ways which were considered virtuous: following one's conscience, displaying wisdom and fairness, avoiding favouritism and bribe taking, protecting the poor and defenceless and so on. 'The world will honour thee seeinge thou hatest vice as much as thou lovest virtue.'[69] However, it was also about a harder-edged ability to exercise power and patronage. This involved being seen to command obedience from those below which, according to Huntingdon, was an essential part of 'the verie nerves and sinewes of nobilitie, without which honorable noblenes is but a painted sheath and cannot consist'.[70] It also meant demonstrating countenance and approval from those above:

> For in generall thou shalt find the most parte of the world to esteeme thee as thou hast power to doe them good or hurt and this must grow chiefly from the king's favour towardes thee.[71]

Huntingdon's analysis of the implications of officeholding further reveal the ambiguities inherent in contemporary notions of honour. On the one hand, it was about aspiring to live up to the noble ideals espoused by authors of conduct books and godly lives; but on the other, it was about being seen to exercise power and compete effectively within a highly contested local arena. The absence of either could reduce honour, in Huntingdon's evocative phrase, to 'a painted sheath'.

Honour, then, emerges from these texts as a range of concepts or discourses of considerable subtlety and complexity. There was a discourse which stressed the importance of ancient blood and lineage, which could legitimize codes of conduct based on competitive assertiveness and the feud; alongside this another which emphasized virtue and extolled wisdom, learning, godliness and restraint; and overlapping both a discourse associating honour with service of the prince and commonwealth. Between them these concepts provided much of the substance of the contemporary noble ethos; but there was no set formula to the ways in which they were mixed together and combined. Each was available to be glossed in different ways and appropriated for different purposes, according to context and circumstance. This allowed for a wide range of roles and positions to be constructed and maintained using common themes and languages. How this happened can be illustrated if we turn back to the Grey/Hastings feud as it resumed in 1610.

III

The re-emergence of open hostilities between the families was prompted initially by the quarrel between Sir John Grey and Sir Henry Hastings of the Abbey which had been simmering away since the county election in 1601. What caused it to flare up at this point is uncertain. It may have had something to do with Sir Henry's efforts to obstruct Lord Grey when he tried to investigate a murder allegedly committed by one of Hastings' servants in January 1610; it may also have owed something to the 'ill offices' performed by Belgrave who had been quarrelling with Sir Henry since the early 1590s.[72] Whatever the reason, Grey challenged Hastings to a duel and in May 1610 the two men travelled to Flushing to fight.[73] Bloodshed was apparently avoided, but the quarrel did not end there because a few weeks later Grey received what he took to be a further slight at the hands of the Hastings. This was in the form of a warrant from Sir Henry and Walter requiring him to assist with the collection of arrears on the county's purveyance composition. They were acting in their capacity as deputy lieutenants, but, according to Grey, had not made this sufficiently clear, which could be taken to imply that they were entitled to give him such orders in a more private capacity. Grey refused to co-operate and, picking on the more vulnerable of the two deputy lieutenants, let it be known that 'neither himself, his friends, servants nor doggs should be under the command of Mr Walter Hastings'. There followed a bad-tempered interview with Huntingdon at which he was told that 'it was the manner of the countie so to gyve notice to men as well borne as himself and that they being at difference he cold not looke to be sent to in anie other fashion then the rest'. After this Sir John and the earl were said never to have exchanged a civil word again.[74]

Huntingdon further inflamed the situation in August or September 1610 by recommending Bale's appointment to the bench.[75] Bale was already a controversial figure within local gentry society. His family was a classic example of upward social mobility in the late sixteenth century, rising from relatively humble peasant origins mainly by dint of profits from agriculture, some of which had been acquired through enclosure and depopulation.[76] Since the 1590s he had been acting as man of business for Sir Edward Hastings and his son Sir Henry, and had made enemies through his interference in county elections and the appointment of local officials. He also had something of a reputation for 'labouring' juries, a talent he had allegedly used to thwart Lord Grey's efforts to convict Hastings' servant of murder. And he had offended Sir Thomas Beaumont of Stoughton by failing to deliver crucial evidence in Star Chamber proceedings in 1607–8 against Walter Hastings' son, Sir Henry of Braunston.[77] The earl's willingness to promote Bale was in keeping with his partisan approach to local appointments; but it was predictably interpreted by his enemies as another act of provocation.

They retaliated by challenging Huntingdon's administration of purveyance. The composition for purveyance – whereby the county agreed to make an annual monetary payment in exchange for the royal household giving up its right to buy cheap produce in local markets – was the heaviest regular demand made on the Leicestershire taxpayer in the early part of James' reign. As such it attracted complaints and queries, most of them directed against the lord lieutenant and his deputies who were responsible for administering the service. Sir Thomas Beaumont and Sir George Belgrave exploited this, casting doubt on the legality of the levy at the time of the debates over the Great Contract in 1610 and alleging corruption in the assessment of arrears.[78] The whole issue came to a head in the summer of 1611 when the Privy Council proposed a change in the manner of compounding. This had to be agreed by the county bench, but Huntingdon and his deputies were unable to carry their colleagues with them which produced a stalemate. It looked as if Leicester-shire would default on the payments, which would lead to all sorts of unpleasant retaliatory action, when suddenly Sir John Grey stepped in and, using his court contacts, took responsibility for meeting the obligation.[79] Once he had his foot in the door and was empowered to act on the county's behalf, however, Grey used this to embarrass Huntingdon. Some-time in June or July he broached the subject with the king and extracted from him a sharp rap across the knuckles for those gentry responsible for the service. James ordered Grey to

> tell the gentlemen of Leicestershire that he tooke it in ill parte the breach of com-posicon, and the rather because yt was at such a time that the whole kingdome tooke notice of yt, to the crossinge of his further purposes.[80]

This must have been particularly wounding to the earl, given his sense that honour derived from the approval of the monarch and that his local prestige depended on being countenanced above. Small wonder that he later described Sir John's initiative as a move 'to crosse me'.[81] For their part the Greys could barely conceal their glee. Lord Grey let slip a reference to the king's words in a letter to Huntingdon in August in which he urged politely, but with more than a hint of blackmail, that further negotiations with the justices were needed to sort out the new composition. This the earl agreed to. New pro-posals were put forward, a deputation to the Privy Council was prepared and, for the first time, officials in the royal household began addressing their let-ters to Lord Grey as well as Huntingdon.[82] The earl was clearly on the run, assailed on all sides and facing the prospect of recriminations from local tax-payers, as well as royal disfavour.

At this point the Greys decided to throw everything behind their offensive. Early in September 1611, Sir John came down to the shire to direct opera-tions. His first move was to join with Beaumont and Belgrave in assuring the Privy Council that Leicestershire did want to agree to a new composition. This was to outflank Huntingdon and his allies who were attempting to retrieve their credit by communicating an offer of annual payment directly to the king.[83] He and his father then extended the scope of the attack on Hunt-ingdon's allies by proposing a general settlement of grievances which became known as 'the overture'. This was intended to cover complaints about unfair assessments for plague relief and the repair of Leicester castle, abuses in ale-house licensing and the exercise of improper influence in the appointment of local officials, all of which had been directed either against Sir Henry or Walter Hastings.[84] Finally, the Greys turned on Bale, sponsoring a letter to Lord Chancellor Ellesmere in which they asked that he be dismissed from the bench and hinted at 'the unadvised purpose of some other that would comende a man of his condicons to any degree or place of authorytie'. This was clearly intended as a further assault on the earl, and the partisan nature of the complaint was betrayed by the fact that, in spite of the best efforts of Beaumont and Belgrave, only six justices actually signed the letter.[85] Nevertheless, even with limited local support there was probably sufficient impetus behind the opposition to Bale to prompt a central government enquiry. Everything depended on getting the right backing at court. But here the strategy of the Grey group was suddenly undermined by a cruel stroke of misfortune: at the beginning of October Sir John Grey contracted smallpox and died.[86]

Grey's death removed the lynchpin of the campaign and tipped the balance decisively in favour of Huntingdon. On 8 October Lord Grey wrote to him proposing further action on 'the overture' and a united front against Bale. Huntingdon stalled by promising an answer within a fortnight, and then simply failing to respond. Meanwhile he raised the stakes by making it clear at a justices' dinner held at Leicester that he personally had recommended Bale's appointment and that any challenge to Bale was a challenge to him.[87] This made it difficult for Grey and his allies to sustain the fiction that they were simply acting in the best interests of the county and in effect asked the gentry to choose sides. Then in November and December the earl shifted his attention to the centre and began some vigorous lobbying of his own. He used his personal contact with the Lord Chancellor via his mother-in-law, Alice Stanley, who had married Ellesmere as her second husband. He also mobilized his uncle Walter, who in the past had proved very effective at working the court through his brother-in-law the earl of Worcester, Master of the House and a Privy Councillor.[88] Huntingdon and his allies concentrated on presenting the actions of the Grey group as 'factious' and 'violent', highlighting in particular the past misdeeds of Sir George Belgrave. Mr Justice Warburton, who rode the midland assize circuit, was shown the letter against Bale to demonstrate 'what troblesome sperittes they are'; Ellesmere was reminded of Belgrave's 'inveterate' malice 'to our house'; and Sir Henry Hastings commenced Star Chamber proceedings against Belgrave, Richard Bowes, a further signatory to the letter against Bale, and others, accusing them of trying to murder him whilst out hunting in September 1611.[89] The Grey group was now very obviously outgunned in the battle for influence at the centre. Lord Grey had allowed his court contacts to lapse after settling for a life in the country; and, in the absence of Sir John, they had to fall back on using Belgrave whose reputation was already compromised. Belgrave responded to the charges being levelled against him by petitioning the Lord Chancellor for protection, having suffered 'xxiii yeres persecution' at the hands of Hastings. But this simply gave Huntingdon and his allies the excuse for a long reply, setting out a detailed response to the accusations made against them and elaborating on the charges of factiousness against Grey and Belgrave.[90] By 22 December the Grey group seem to have felt the game was slipping away from them. They wrote a second letter to Ellesmere, the tone of which was altogether more defensive. It reiterated the charges against Bale, but instead of calling directly for his dismissal, asked for arbitration to vindicate their 'honour and credit'. There were three fewer signatories than there had been to the first letter.[91]

After Christmas the main battle shifted back to Leicestershire as both sides sought to prepare the ground for the expected arbitration. The Grey group had hoped for a special commission to investigate the matter, but as a result of Huntingdon's lobbying the task was entrusted to the assize judges, which gave his side an immediate advantage since Warburton at least had long been on friendly terms with him.[92] The earl was also able to broaden the terms of the inquiry to include not only Bale's actions, but those of Belgrave as well. Preparation for the hearing involved intensive lobbying amongst the local gentry over a certificate which the Hastings camp was drawing up in support of Bale. Huntingdon himself conducted a series of interviews with local JPs to put pressure on waverers; and on the other side Beaumont, his son-in-law, Sir Wolstan Dixie and Matthew Saunders Esq. sought to dissuade potential signatories. Sir Basil Brooke was pestered on his deathbed; Sir Thomas Haselrig was dissuaded with the argument that 'Bale and his children had spoken most vilely of him'; and Sir William Smith was said to have been approached by Beaumont at Oakham assizes asking 'whether he might salute him as a friend or an enymie for that he heard that he had sett his hand to a lre for Mr Bale'.[93] The county gentry were becoming polarized, but at the same time Huntingdon was clearly winning. The certificate vindicating Bale was finally sent to the Lord Chancellor on 8 February 1611/12. It contained the signatures of eleven justices, two former sheriffs and several other senior gentry.[94]

The hearing before the assize judges in March began with Beaumont presenting the case against Bale. His basic argument was that the county needed to ensure that those entrusted with places of authority on the bench possessed birth, education and other qualities equal to their calling. Huntingdon responded by insisting that the attack on Bale was an attack on him, inspired by the factious intent of Grey, Beaumont, Belgrave and their allies. These themes dominated the early exchanges. The judges were eventually able to bring the discussion round to what they saw as more substantive charges: whether Bale had suborned jurors and how recently he had been guilty of depopulation and the conversion of glebe lands.[95] But the debate kept slipping back to broader issues of honour and birth. There was an angry exchange when Belgrave and Sir Henry Skipwith objected to having to stand bareheaded whilst Bale, as a justice, kept his hat on.[96] Then another when Belgrave, in a sneer at Bale's humble origins, suggested that he had 'gotten more by unthatching houses than his father had done by thatching, and that he had walked horses barefoot for threepence'; to which Bale, referring to Belgrave's notorious indebtedness, retorted that 'it was no matter what he said, nothing being to be recovered or gotten of him, he being worth nothing'. Both sides were addressing themselves as much to the large audience of local worthies as to the judges. Eventually, after four or five hours, Bale was vindicated to the satisfaction of the judges and, at Huntingdon's insistence, they passed on to Belgrave. At this point Beaumont attempted to rescue something from the hearing by insisting that the county could only be at peace if Bale was removed, and volunteering to stand down himself to end the controversy. Bale, however, was able to sidestep this by arguing that although he had no personal ambition to keep the place, his removal would be an unjustified slur on Huntingdon. So the hearing ended with Bale confirmed in office and the judges meeting one of the grievances highlighted in 'the overture' by ordering that decisions made at quarter sessions could not be altered by justices acting outside.[97]

Even allowing for the fact that we have only Huntingdon's account of the judges' meeting, it is clear that he had won a considerable victory. Over the following two years he went from strength to strength. He tightened his grip on local government, avoiding further challenges over purveyance, initiating reforms of the militia and also heading off an attempt by Lord Grey to get Sir Brian Cave and Henry Berkeley Esq., two of the signatories to the letters against Bale, put on to the commission of the peace.[98] Meanwhile Bale himself remained an active member of the bench and continued to serve the Hastings family until his death in 1621.[99] In 1614 both Lord Grey and Sir Thomas Beaumont died, and with the passing of his two most powerful antagonists Huntingdon was able to secure a dominance over the shire which was not seriously challenged again until the late 1620s.[100]

The tactics used by the two sides in the Bale case reveal a good deal about the nature of local power struggles in this period. They show the way in which efficient administration often took second place to the pursuit of honour, status and prestige; the importance of the commission of the peace as both a source and a measure of local authority; the vital role of court contacts when it came to the point of appealing to the centre for support or arbitration; and the rather neglected role of the assize judges in settling disputes between gentry. But even more interesting is what the dispute reveals about the values and assumptions which shaped contemporary political culture. The ways in which some of these emerged through differing concepts of honour have already been discussed. Here again one can see a range of themes relating to honour very much to the fore in influencing the conduct of participants. Grey's touchiness about precedence and the proper display of deference, Huntingdon's anxiety about being countenanced above and Bale and Belgrave's verbal fencing over their wealth and social origins, were all evidence of the way in which honour was involved with competition for status; whilst the Grey group's call for high standards of education and conduct in magistrates and Huntingdon's concern to be seen to be serving his prince, illustrated the association of honour with various forms of virtue. However, just as revealing in this context is the rhetoric deployed by the leading participants. By paying close attention to the ways in which language and arguments were shaped to make them attractive to a range of contemporary audiences – from the body of local gentry and freeholders to the Lord Chancellor – it is possible to uncover a range of related themes and beliefs.

One of the most prominent of these was the theme of unity and reconcili-ation. This was deployed particularly by Lord Grey and his allies because it fitted well with their efforts to isolate Bale, and could also deflect the charge of factiousness which was repeatedly levelled against them. The theme of unity and reconciliation had a particularly powerful resonance in the early seventeenth century and was much in evidence at all levels of national and local politics.[101] It drew strength from respect for the Christian principles of love and charity which had been encapsulated in arbitration procedures back into the Middle Ages; and also from the organic analogies which suggested that if the body politic was to function effectively its various parts had to be working in harmony.[102] Both concepts were prominent in 'the overture' which Lord Grey and his son drew up as their manifesto in September 1611.[103] It described their aim as 'a generall, unfeined and faithfull reconciliation ... con-ceaving the occasion to be pleasing to God, full of charitie and benefitt in the countrie'; then went on to explain that

> to the end his Majestie and the countrie may receive the frut of soe good a worke and that all further occasion of offence and injustice may bee removed, and that wee as servants to one master may joyntlie run in an even and upright course in ministering of justice and discharge of our duties, we doe heere in expresse our-selves in our sincere affections both in enterteyning and continuing this just league of frendshipe.

With its stress on reconciliation, duty to the king and service to the country, 'the overture' was a classic example of the rhetoric of unity. And it had a powerful appeal, as was implicitly acknowledged in Huntingdon's hesitant response. He was unable to reject 'the overture' outright, in spite of the bla-tantly partisan terms on which it sought reconciliation, and instead stalled for time and later insisted to the judges that he had done his best to accommo-date it.[104]

The Grey group maintained a similar stance throughout their appeals to the Lord Chancellor and the judges. At no point, they insisted, did they intend any opposition to Huntingdon; the removal of Bale was purely and simply for 'the good and peace of the countrie'.[105] The earl, for his part, responded in kind. An important element in his strategy for substantiating the charge of factiousness against the Grey group was to present himself as the ultimate conciliator. In a letter to the Lord Chancellor in February 1611/12, he insisted that 'my indevors heretofore have been bent and shall still be to winne by the fayrest meanes my greatest enemies'; and this was picked up in various mem-oranda and statements to the judges in which he described his willingness to 'forgive' and 'forgett' earlier injuries by the Greys and Belgrave.[106] The theme of unity and reconciliation, then, was used in a variety of ways: to marginal-ize opponents and reinforce or deflect charges of factiousness. But in this con-text it was only serviceable so far. To sustain the aggressive intent behind the challenge to Bale, the Grey group required a less neutral rhetoric; and for this they turned to the ideal of 'the good magistrate'.

This was an ideal which had been discussed and developed through generations of humanist scholars and commentators, back to Sir Thomas Elyot's *The Book Named the Governor* and beyond. It provided the staple for two of the most common forms of public rhetoric which the gentry experienced in their work as local governors: the jury charge and the assize sermon.[107] The Grey group adopted the theme of the good magistrate to legitimize their attack on Bale. At the outset they focused on the damage which an unworthy justice could inflict on the reputation of authority and the honour of those involved in government. When Grey wrote to Huntingdon on 8 October 1611 to try to entice him into supporting Bale's removal, he urged him to consider that 'all well governed states have as much shunned to grace contumelious persons with power and authoritie as ever Ulisses did to avoyde Silla and Caribdis'. His primary concern, he emphasized, was 'to acquitte and deliver magistracy from such a fowle contempt and indignitye as it must undergoe yf such manner of person be countenanced in place of government ... there we shall doe as much honour to ourselves and as gratefull service unto the country as hath ben done by men of our ranke and qualitie in other places in any time'. The Grey group then sought to apply the rhetoric specifically to Bale. A magistrate, Beaumont argued before the judges, 'ought to be a man of good birth, and not base, and of the like qualities and indowments fit for government'. This was taken to imply he should be born a gentleman, should have attended a university or Inn of Court, should be devoid of ambition and self-seeking and free from the specific offences of suborning jurors, causing depopulation and living 'a lewde and incontynent lieffe'.[108]

Huntingdon readily acknowledged the force of this rhetoric, comparing it to the way 'physitians deale with their patients, to guyld the bitterest pylles that they may goe downe the better'.[109] So instead of resisting directly, he sought to appropriate parts of it for his own purpose, and then challenge some of the more controversial assumptions on which it rested. Part of his overall strategy was based on insisting that Bale's fitness for office must be judged in the light of his own integrity, because he had initially recommended Bale and a verdict against him would reflect on his honour. To establish his integrity, Huntingdon deployed the theme of 'the good magistrate', repeatedly instancing his concern 'to be impartiall in justice' and asking rhetorically 'whether, since I had any charge of government ... I have eiver done, supported or countenanced any badd accon'.[110] This elicited suitably approving comments from the judges which made it that much harder for them to condemn Bale. Huntingdon also latched on to some of the contradictions within contemporary discussion of 'true nobility' to challenge the Grey group's definition of 'the good magistrate'. Against their insistence that he should have been educated at university or Inn of Court, he put the argument, succinctly summarized by Justice Warburton, that 'a man in his natural parts of witt, understanding and reason with observacon might be a wise man and govern well, though he had noe shoole learninge'. More radically he sought to deflect the charge of Bale's lack of pedigree by insisting that, although 'I could not speak much for the worthines of Mr Bale's birth, yett I know many of as mean birth raysed to as great place as he was.'[111] On the earl's account this did much to undercut the case which Beaumont brought at the main hearing and ensured that Bale was judged on the issues of depopulation and suborning jurors, where the evidence was highly ambiguous. He also sought to carry the attack to the Grey group by presenting his own interpretation of their actions.

As we have seen, this was built around depicting them as agents of 'faction'. 'Whether their courses were moved with zeale to honour and government or private ends', he suggested to the Lord Chancellor in February 1611/12, 'the sequill will express.'[112] The charge of 'faction' was constantly reiterated in ways which sought to bring out its odious associations in the eyes of contemporaries. The Grey group were described as 'frends ... by way of faction' which hinted at an element of conspiracy; they were accused of being 'troublesome spiritts', acting out of 'a particular spleane and for satisfying of some humour'; they were charged with dishonesty, having dealt 'untrulye' in portraying the actions of Huntingdon's ancestors; and they were said to have been motivated by 'continuall malice' towards the earl and his family.[113] This approach drew much of its force from a rhetoric developed by humanist and Protestant commentators during the sixteenth century, which castigated those who put selfish 'private' ends before the 'public' good and 'faction' before 'unity'.[114]

To judge by the Grey group's response this approach was highly effective. They were forced on to the defensive, both in their lobbying of the centre and their appeals to the judges. The second letter to the Lord Chancellor showed the extent of this. Instead of reiterating the charges against Bale, most of it was devoted to denying that they had acted out of 'private spleene or faccon' or had 'runne with any violent or factious course into the business'. The charge of 'faction' also raised the stakes, making defeat as potentially damaging for the Greys as it would be for Bale and Huntingdon. In the same letter they accepted that 'there must fall eyther upon him [Bale] or us a most justly deserved blott of disreputacion'.[115] This was perhaps the clearest acknowledgement of the force of the rhetoric being deployed by the two sides.

A close focus on the language and argument deployed in this struggle, then, reveals a series of themes which overlapped with the concepts of honour described earlier. There was the same emphasis on high standards of virtue and putting the 'public' good before 'private' interests. These themes expressed ideals and commonplaces which most contemporaries could readily accept. As a result they exercised considerable force when deployed in a political struggle of this sort. In order to win support, participants were generally concerned to show that their conduct could be justified in terms of these themes, and their actions were shaped accordingly. Like the concept of honour, these themes also displayed considerable flexibility and scope for divergent application. Much of the struggle in the Bale case revolved around the two sides trying to gloss common themes in different ways. Huntingdon proved notably adept at this, subjecting the concept of 'the good magistrate', for example, to a series of readings which undercut the case being put by Beaumont. The fact that these were apparently at odds with concerns he expressed elsewhere about promoting education and extolling pedigree and lineage can be taken as a further indication of their adaptability and openness to being appropriated for differing purposes. Social and political stances in this period were rarely constructed around mutually exclusive sets of ideals. They tended to draw on common themes and rhetorics which could be adapted and synthesized to meet various circumstances and polemical purposes.[116] So just as, in this context, the earl of Huntingdon could play down the significance of lineage, in another his Puritan uncle could emerge as its staunchest exponent.

IV

The dispute between the Greys and the Hastings reveals a world of pride, wilfulness and competitive assertiveness; a world in which gentry struggled constantly to advance the honour and status of themselves and their family line and refused to allow a challenge to either to go unanswered. This is a situation which has become familiar from other studies of factional feuds in late Tudor and early Stuart England, and it bears many similarities to that prevailing in the 'honour and shame' societies which modern anthropologists have studied in Mediterranean countries.[117] Although there was less willingness in early Stuart England to resort to the ultimate sanction of violence, there was the same preoccupation with vengeance, retribution and the satisfaction of honour. Given all this, it is worth asking how it was, none-the-less, that county gentry were so often able to work together with at least the appearance of unity.

The criticisms made of the work of Alan Everitt and other 'county community' historians have established that we cannot simply assume that unity and harmony were somehow 'natural', the necessary consequence of particular patterns of social relations.[118] Because of this, attention has turned to investigating the ways in which notions of community and collegiality were constructed out of the symbols and ideals which comprised gentry political culture. Victor Morgan has led the way in showing how the gentry's experiences at university and their acquisition of county maps helped to develop a sense of loyalty to their county.[119] Perhaps the most perceptive discussion, however, has been provided by Diarmiad MacCulloch in his study of Tudor Suffolk. He has shown how the aggressive self-assertiveness which characterized the dealings of local magnates in the early sixteenth century was gradu-

ally overlaid by a concern to promote harmony and establish the shire's reputation for orderliness and agreement. He points to several influences working in this direction: changes in county government which brought the gentry
of the two halves of Suffolk together more often; the spread of reformed religion which encouraged magistrates and ministers to work together to establish a Protestant social order; and the writings of local antiquarians, such as
Robert Reyce, which encouraged gentry to take pride in the corporate entity
of their shire. Reyce's oft-quoted description of his gentry neighbours encapsulated this communal ideal:

> If differences doe arise which are very seldome, such is the great discretion ever
> tempered with love and kindnes among them, that these devisions are soon
> smothered and appeased. So againe what with the enterlacing of houses in mar-
> riage ... such is the religious unitie wherewith in all good actions they doe con-
> curre, that whatever offendeth one displeaseth all, and whatsoever satisfieth one
> contenteth all.[120]

In some respects, of course, Reyce's description can best be seen as a literary
artifice, an image built up out of Protestant and humanist notions of common
fellowship. At the same time, however, by presenting the Suffolk gentry with
an ideal, towards which they might aspire, it helped to structure the social
'reality' which it purported to describe.

Several of the themes and ideas revealed in the Grey/Hastings feud could
function in a similar way. The images of unity which were continually being
set before them – as manifestations of the Christian ideals of love, peace and
charity and of a healthy body politic – apparently encouraged co-operation
and the settlement of disputes. Similar imperatives have been highlighted by
Professor Kishlansky in his study of the arrangements made to avoide election contests, in which individual ambition was curbed for the sake of preserving the peace of the shire.[121] Again, the ideal of 'the good magistrate' and
the standards of conduct that it implied, served to limit the use of office for
'private' or factious ends. And perhaps the most potent image of all in early
Stuart local politics, that of 'the country',[122] performed a similar shaping and
constraining role. Its use in this case not only suggested the notion of 'the
country' as 'commonwealth' – to which the local gentry belonged and owed
a duty of service – it also alluded to the way in which a county could function as 'a court of reputation', requiring certain standards of behaviour if an
individual was to be adjudged worthy of honour and esteem.[123] It was around
images and ideals such as these – often revealed most clearly in the midst of
dispute – that the fragile notion of 'county community' was constructed.

Notes

[1] I wish to thank David Underdown for his interest in my work and support over
the years.

The research for this article has been financed by the British Academy and the Huntington Library, California, and I am grateful to both of them. I also wish to thank Ann Hughes for her valuable comments and Tom Cogswell and Catherine Patterson for sharing with me their knowledge of all things relating to early Stuart Leicestershire.

² Bodleian Library (hereafter Bodl.L.), Carte MS 78, fos.308–11.

³ A. M. Everitt, *The Local Community and the Great Rebellion* (Historical Association Pamphlet, G.70, 1969), pp. 10–18.

⁴ For example, see A. Hassell Smith, *County and Court* (Oxford, 1974); W. MacCaffrey, 'Talbot and Stanhope: an episode in Elizabethan politics', *Bulletin of the Institute of Historical Research* (hereafter *B.I.H.R.*), 33 (1960), pp. 73–85; G. C. F. Forster, 'Faction and county government in early Stuart Yorkshire', *Northern History*, 11 (1975); A. Wall, 'Patterns of politics in England, 1558–1625', *Historical Journal* (hereafter *H.J.*), 31 (1988), pp. 947–63.

⁵ The best introduction to this subject are the essays collected in J. Bossy (ed.), *Disputes and Settlements* (Past and Present Society, Cambridge, 1983).

⁶ S. Roberts, 'The study of dispute: anthropological perspectives', in Bossy, *Disputes*, pp. 19–20.

⁷ J. Pitt-Rivers, 'Honour and social status', in J. G. Peristiany (ed.), *Honour and Shame: the Values of Mediterranean Society* (London, 1965), pp. 21–38; J. K. Campbell, *Honour, Family and Patronage* (Oxford 1964), ch. 10.

⁸ M. C. Cross, 'The third earl of Huntingdon and Elizabethan Leicestershire', *Transactions of the Leicestershire Archaeological Society*, 36 (1960), pp. 6–21; M. C. Cross, 'Noble patronage and the Elizabethan church', *H.J.*, 3 (1960), pp. 1–16; C. F. Patterson, 'Leicester and Lord Huntingdon: urban patronage in early modern England', *Midland History*, 16 (1991), pp. 46–8; P. W. Hasler (ed.), *The House of Commons, 1558–1603*, 3 vols. (1981), vol. I, p. 192.

⁹ M. C. Cross, *The Puritan Earl* (London, 1966), ch. 3; Huntingdon Library, California (hereafter Hunt.L.), Hastings MS, HA Correspondence, 4714; M. C. Cross (ed.), *The Letters of Sir Francis Hastings 1574–1609* (Somerset Rec. Soc., lxix, 1969), pp. xxiv, 70–1. It is perhaps significant that the fourth earl did not subscribe to the Leicestershire address in support of the Milleniary Petition of 1603, in spite of the lead given by Sir Edward Hastings and Arthur Hildersham, the resident minister at Ashby: British Library (hereafter B.L.), Add. MS 8978, fos.109–10.

¹⁰ Cross, *Puritan Earl*, pp. 34–5; Hunt, L., HA Correspondence, 1021, 5281; Bodl.L., Carte MS 78, fo.418.

¹¹ B. L., Lansd. MS 83, fo.65; Bodl.L., Eng. Hist., C.482, fo.42; *Acts of the Privy Council 1595–6*, p. 216.

¹² Public Record Office (hereafter P.R.O.), STAC 5/A54/2; J. Thompson, *A History of Leicester* (Leicester, 1849), pp. 316–17; Bodl.L., Carte MS 78, fo.310.

¹³ P.R.O., STAC 5/A54/2; B.L., microfilm of the MSS at Hatfield House (hereafter Hatfield MSS), 92/9, 105, 150; P.R.O., SP 12/287/56; C 231/1, fo.127.

¹⁴ *Dictionary of National Biography*, under 'Grey, Lord John'; Hasler, *House of Commons*, vol. II, pp. 203–4, 376–7.

¹⁵ Hasler, *House of Commons*, vol. II, pp. 223–4; P.R.O., C 231/1, fos.52, 110; M. Bateson (ed.), *Records of the Borough of Leicester, 1509–1603* (Cambridge, 1905), pp. 339, 348, 385–6, 393, 414; Bodl.L., Carte MS 77, fos.518–19; B.L., Lansdowne MS 89, fo.44; W. J. Tighe, 'The Gentlemen Pensioners in Elizabethan politics and govern-

ment', Ph.D thesis, University of Cambridge (1983), pp. 72–3, 376–7; Hasler, *House of Commons*, vol. II, pp. 222–3.

[16] L. Fox and P. Russell, *Leicester Forest* (Leicester, 1948), pp. 77–82; D. M. Loades, *Two Tudor Conspiracies* (Cambridge, 1965), pp. 25–34. The Suffolk author of the *Vita Mariae Reginae* in Mary's reign referred to the 'perpetual enmity' between the Greys and the Hastings as an established fact: D. MacCulloch (ed.), 'The *Vita Mariae Reginae* of Robert Wingfield of Brantham', *Camden Miscellany XXVIII* (Camden Soc., 4th ser., xxix, 1984), p. 280 (I am grateful to Diarmiad MacCulloch for this reference).

[17] Bodl.L., Carte MS 77, fos.518–19; Hasler, *House of Commons*, vol. I, pp. 192–3; vol. II, p. 224.

[18] Bodl.L., Carte MS 77, fos.518–19; 78, fo.361.

[19] Hatfield MSS, 189/57, 197/14; P.R.O., SO 3/2, 11 Feb. 1604/5; J. C. Sainty, *Lieutenants of Counties, 1558–1642* (Institute of Historical Research, 1970) special supplement, no.8, p. 26.

[20] H. Stocks (ed.), *Records of the Borough of Leicester 1603–1688* (Cambridge, 1923), p. 21; Hatfield MSS, 103/100; Leicestershire Record Office (hereafter L.R.O.), Borough of Leicester, Hall Papers, vol. VII, fo.618; P.R.O., C66/1662; C219/35/pt.1, no.44; J. Nichols, *The History and Antiquities of the County of Leicester*, 4 vols. (1795–1811), vol. I, p. 456; Hatfield MSS, 214/54; L.R.O., Borough of Leicester, Hall Papers, vol. VII, fo.349.

[21] B.L., Add MS 38, 139; P.R.O., C66/1662, 1682. For Saunders' connections and allegiance, see P.R.O., PCC Wills, PROB 11/125/34 Rudd; Hunt.L., HA Correspondence, 4328.

[22] Patterson, 'Leicester and Lord Huntingdon', pp. 49–58.

[23] For Skipwith's alliance with Sir John Grey in opposition to Walter Hastings and his son, see Hatfield MSS, 214/54. Skipwith was also on friendly terms with the fifth earl, but his antagonism towards another branch of the Hastings family may have disqualified him from preferment as far as the earl was concerned: J. Knowles, 'WS MS', *Times Literary Supplement*, 29 April–5 May 1988, p. 472, 485.

[24] Hunt.L., HA Correspondence, 5419, 1283; Bodl.L., Carte MS 78, fo.309; Hunt.L., HA Financial, Box 6, no.7; Bodl.L., Carte MS 77, fos.518–19.

[25] Bodl.L., Carte MS 78, fo.308; Hunt.L., HA Financial, Box 6, No. 3; P.R.O., C66/1748, 1786, 1822, 1898. For the Comptons' friendship with the fifth earl, see Knowles, 'WS MS', pp. 472, 485.

[26] Although there is no surviving commission of the peace for Leicestershire between 1606 and May 1608, it is clear that the appointment of Walter Hastings Esq. took place between 2 May 1607, when Huntingdon was appointed *custos rotulorum*, and 25 June 1607, when he is described as JP in a letter from the Board of Greencloth: Historical Manuscripts Commission (hereafter HMC), *Report on the MSS of Reginald Rawdon Hastings*, 4 vols. (1928–47), vol. I, p. 364; Hunt.L., HA Correspondence, 4120; Bodl.L., Carte MS 78, fo.318. P.R.O., SP 14/33. Walter Hastings' claim that he had never served in local office prior to 1607 was not strictly true since he had acted as a subsidy commissioner in 1605: P.R.O., STAC 8/55/26.

[27] Bodl.L., Carte MS 78, fos.325–6, 308–9.

[28] Hunt.L., HA Financial, Box 6, nos.3,4; Box 7, nos.3,4; Stocks, *Records of Leicester* p. 34; HMC, *Hastings MSS*, vol. I, p. 373.

[29] Bodl.L., Carte MS 77, fos.518–19.

[30] *Ibid.*, Carte MS 78, fo.418.

[31] Hunt.L., HA Correspondence, 12541.

[32] M. Ingram, *Church Courts, Sex and Marriage in England 1570–1640* (Cambridge, 1987); J. A. Sharpe, *Defamation and Sexual Slander in Early Modern England: The Church Courts at York* (Borthwick Papers, no.58, 1980); L. Gowing, 'Gender and the language of insult in early modern London', *History Workshop*, 35 (1993), pp. 1–21.

[33] R. Kelso, *The Doctrine of an English Gentleman in the Sixteenth Century* (University of Illinois Studies in Language and Literature, 14, 1929); J. P. Cooper, 'Ideas on gentility in early modern England', in *idem*, *Land, Men and Beliefs* (London, 1983), pp. 43–77; Q. Skinner, *The Foundations of Modern Political Thought*, 2 vols. (Cambridge, 1978), vol. I, ch.8.

[34] M. E. James, *English Politics and the Concept of Honour 1485–1642*, Past and Present Supplement, 3 (1978).

[35] M. E. James, *Family, Lineage and Civil Society* (Oxford, 1974); *idem*, *Society, Politics and Culture* (Past and Present Society, Cambridge, 1986), pp. 9–15, 270–307.

[36] James, *English Politics*, pp. 65–72; *idem*, *Society, Politics and Culture*, pp. 430–1; L. Stone, *The Crisis of the Aristocracy 1558–1641* (Oxford, 1965), pp. 743–5.

[37] M. C. Cross, 'An example of lay intervention in the Elizabethan church', in G. J. Cuming (ed.), *Studies in Church History*, vol. II (London, 1986), pp. 273–82. James, *English Politics*, p. 16n cites Sir Francis Hastings as the classic example of a Puritan layman who urged that religious conviction should be put before loyalty to the lineage.

[38] A. J. Jewers, 'Heraldry in the manor house of North Cadbury with the heraldry and monuments in the church', *Proceedings of the Somerset Archaeological and Natural History Society*, 36, pt.1 (1890), pp. 137–67; Cross, *Letters of Hastings*, pp. xxi–xxv.

[39] *Ibid.*, pp. 50–2. On the ideals of kinship solidarity see James, *Society, Politics and Culture*, pp. 274–8.

[40] This phrase is to be found in a similar letter to the fourth earl in 1595: Cross, *Letters of Hastings*, p. 57.

[41] *Ibid.*, pp. 50–2. Elsewhere Francis made much of the third earl's unusually generous provision for his younger brothers and sisters: *ibid.*, pp. 59–60; Cross, *Puritan Earl*, pp. 28–32.

[42] Cross, *Letters of Hastings*, p. 57. He expressed similar sentiments in a letter to the fifth earl in 1605: *ibid.*, p. 100.

[43] Hunt.L., HA Personal, Box 15, no.8. Extracts from this are printed in HMC, *Hastings MSS*, vol. IV, pp. 330–5. The advice was addressed to his eldest son Ferdinando who was born in 1608. It can be ascribed to a date around 1614 on the basis of a reference to it in a later letter of advice to his second son, Henry, and an internal reference to it having been composed over five years after the earl had come of age in 1607: HA Correspondence, 5515; HA Personal, Box 15, no.8, fo.1.

[44] Hunt.L., HA Personal, Box 15, no.8, fo.16.

[45] On this see also the earl's reminder to his son that he was 'descended from noble and honourable parents and allied to most of the nobility either by me or thy mother': *ibid.*, fo.5.

[46] M. Keen, *Chivalry* (London, 1984), pp. 159–61.

[47] Hunt.L., HA Personal, Box 15, no.8, fos.5, 18, 19; Bodl.L., Carte MS 77, fos.518–19.

[48] Much evidence for this comes from the earl's personal accounts covering the period 1606–12: Hunt.L., HA Financial, Box 3, nos.3 and 4, Box 7, no.3. See also HA Correspondence, 9343; Bodl.L., Carte MS 78, fo.418; Thompson, *History of Leicester*, pp. 330–2; Bateson, *Records of Leicester*, pp. 33–6.

[49] Bodl.L., Carte MS 78, fo.326; Hunt.L., HA Correspondence, 1290.

[50] Bodl.L., Carte MS 78, fos.325–6.

[51] Hunt.L., HA Personal, Box 15, no.8, fo.14.

[52] On feuding in this period more generally, see J. Bossy, 'Postscript', in Bossy, *Disputes*, pp. 287–8; K. Brown, *Bloodfeud in Scotland 1573–1625* (Edinburgh, 1986), ch.1.

[53] Bodl.L., Carte MS 77, fos.518–19; Carte MS 78, fo.319.

[54] Hunt.L., HA Personal, Box 15, no.8, fo.18. At the same time, however, Huntingdon appears to have drawn the line at fighting duels. He warned his son that 'I never sawe that hee that had the misfortune to kill a man ever prospered himselfe or his house though the lawe of duells calls it fairely ... blood beinge of that nature that it rises unto God for vengeance and will never rest till it be revenged': *ibid.*, fos.18–19.

[55] James, *Family, Lineage and Civil Society*; *idem*, *Society, Politics and Culture*, pp. 270–307; L. Stone, *The Family, Sex and Marriage in England 1500–1800* (London, 1979), pp. 85–159.

[56] For two studies which illustrate this point from different perspectives, see A. Fletcher, 'Honour, reputation and local officeholding in Elizabethan and Stuart England', in A. Fletcher and J. Stevenson (eds.), *Order and Disorder in Early Modern England* (Cambridge, 1985), pp. 92–115; J. S. A. Adamson, 'Chivalry and political culture in Caroline England', in K. Sharpe and P. G. Lake (eds.), *Culture and Politics in Early Stuart England* (Basingstoke, 1994), pp. 161–97.

[57] Hunt.L., HA Personal, Box 15, no.8, fo.1.

[58] Cross, 'An example of lay intervention', pp. 273–82; *idem*, *Puritan Earl*.

[59] Hunt.L., HA Personal, Box 15, no.8, fos.1–2; HA Correspondence, 5537. On what constituted a 'Calvinist conformist', see P. Lake, 'Serving God and the times: the Calvinist conformity of Robert Sanderson', *Journal of British Studies* (hereafter *J.B.S.*), 27 (1988), pp. 81–116.

[60] Cross, *Letters of Hastings*, p. 60.

[61] Hunt.L., HA Personal, Box 14, no.18; Nichols, *History and Antiquities*, vol. III, pp. 594–8.

[62] Hunt.L., HA Personal, Box 15, no.8, fos.18, 14. For the fifth earl's extensive role in mediating local quarrels, see HA Personal, Box 14, no.24; HA Correspondence, 5435; Bodl.L., Eng. Hist. C.476, fos.31–50 (I am grateful to Tom Cogswell for the last reference).

[63] Hunt.L., HA Personal, Box 15, no.8, fo.15.

[64] *Ibid.*, fos.17–18, 8.

[65] *Ibid.*, fo.13. In the same section of the advice he reminded his son of the Ciceronian precept that as 'We are not borne for ourselves but others, it must not make thee loath or unwillinge to undergoe the trouble, though it is rather *Onus* than *honor*.'

[66] B.L., Hatfield MSS, 197/14. He expressed similar sentiments in 1627 when again threatened with losing his lord lieutenancy: P.R.O., SP 16/67/2.

[67] Hunt.L., HA Personal, Box 15, no.8, fos.7–8. He repeated Mildmay's maxim in a letter to his second son, Henry, in 1627, when he again described the court as '*splendida miseria*': HA Correspondence, 5515.

[68] Hunt.L., HA Personal, Box 15, no.8, fo.7.

[69] *Ibid.*, fos.13–14.

[70] *Ibid.*, Box 14, no.18.

[71] *Ibid.*, Box 15, no.8, fo.7. He anticipated such a reaction in his 1604 petition to James when he complained that 'to misse these places might make my house less esteemed where I hope to love and faithfullie serve your majestie': B.L., Hatfield MSS, 197/14.

[72] P.R.O., STAC 8/54/13; Bodl.L., Carte MS 78, fo.373.

[73] HMC, *Report on the MSS of Viscount De L'Isle*, 5 vols. (1925–62), vol. IV, pp. 200, 204–5.

[74] Bodl.L., Carte MS 77, fos.518–19.

[75] It is hard to establish the date of Bale's appointment with any precision because there is a gap in surviving commissions of the peace for Leicestershire between mid-1610 and late 1611: P.R.O., C66/1897, 1898. Later comments by Huntingdon and the Greys suggest that Bale was recommended to the Lord Chancellor in Aug./Sept. 1610 – and that objections were raised at this time by his opponents – but that he did not actually take his seat on the bench until some time in 1611: Bodl.L., Carte MS 78, fos.308, 326; Hunt.L., HA Correspondence, 4331.

[76] W. G. Hoskins, *Essays in Leicestershire History* (Liverpool, 1950), pp. 128, 142, 156–7; Victoria County History, *Leicestershire*, 5 vols. (1907–64), vol. V, p. 79.

[77] Bodl.L., Carte MS 78, fos.309, 319, 361; P.R.O., STAC 8/54/13; Bodl.L., Carte MS 78, fos.310, 325. The Star Chamber case is dealt with more fully in my article, 'Honour and politics in early Stuart England: the case of Beaumont v. Hastings', *Past and Present*, 149 (1995).

[78] R. P. Cust, 'Purveyance and politics in Jacobean Leicestershire', in P. Fleming and A. Gross (eds.), *Regionalism and Revision: English Provincial Society 1250–1650* (forthcoming).

[79] G. E. Aylmer, 'The last years of purveyance 1610–1660', *Economic History Review*, 2nd ser., vol. 10 (1957–8), p. 82; H.M.C., *Report on the MSS of Lord Montagu of Beaulieu* (1900), p. 86; Hunt.L., HA Correspondence, 4122, 4123, 4327.

[80] Hunt.L., HA Correspondence, 4123; Bodl.L., Carte MS 77, fos.518–19; 78, fo.316.

[81] Bodl.L., Carte MS 78, fos.325–6.

[82] Hunt.L., HA Correspondence, 4327; Bodl.L., Carte MS 78, fos.316,321; Hunt.L., HA Correspondence, 4124.

[83] P.R.O., SP 14/66/9, 17.

[84] Bodl.L., Carte MS 78, fo.322; Folger Shakespeare Library, Washington (hereafter F.S.L.), V.a.402, fo.5.

[85] Hunt.L., HA Correspondence, 4328. The six justices were Lord Grey, Sir John Grey, Sir Thomas Beaumont of Stoughton, Sir Wolstan Dixie, William Cave Esq. and Matthew Saunders Esq. The other signatories were Sir George Belgrave, Sir John Harrington of Exton, Sir Alexander Cave, Brian Cave Esq., Richard Bowes Esq., Henry Berkeley Esq., John Skeffington Esq., and Henry Skipwith Esq.

[86] N. E. MacLure (ed.), *The Letters of John Chamberlain*, 2 vols. (Philadelphia, 1939), vol. I, p. 314.

[87] Hunt.L., HA Correspondence, 4329; Bodl.L., Carte MS 78, fo.308.

[88] For Alice Stanley and the Lord Chancellor, see L. B. Knafla, *Law and Politics in Jacobean England* (Cambridge, 1977), p. 33. For Walter Hastings' connections with Worcester, see Cross, *Puritan Earl*, p. 29; P.R.O., STAC 8/55/26.

[89] Hunt.L., HA Correspondence, 5436; Bodl.L., Carte MS 78, fos.318–19; P.R.O.,

STAC 8/178/2.

[90] Hunt.L., HA Correspondence, 4331; Bodl.L., Carte MS 78, fos.318–19.

[91] Hunt.L., HA Correspondence, 4331. The signatures of Sir John Grey, Henry Berkeley Esq. and John Skeffington Esq. were absent from the second letter.

[92] Hunt.L., HA Correspondence, 5436. For evidence of Warburton acting as an intermediary in securing commissions of the peace which included Huntingdon's nominees Sir Thomas Compton and William Villiers Esq. in Feb. 1607/8, see HA Financial Box 6, no.3.

[93] Hunt.L., HA Manorial, Box 53, no.5b; Bodl.L., Carte MS 78, fos.308–9.

[94] Hunt.L., HA Correspondence, 5437. The justices were Huntingdon, Walter Hastings Esq., Sir Henry Hastings of the Abbey, Sir Thomas Compton, Sir Thomas Humphrey, Sir William Smyth, Samuel Fleming D.D., John Chippingdale D.D., Edward Turville Esq., Henry Smyth Esq. and Bartholomew Laxton Esq. The two former sheriffs were Sir William Fawnt and John Plumbe Esq. and the other signatories were Sir George Manners, Robert Brookesby Esq., Edward Hartopp Esq., William Hartopp Esq., Edward Pate Esq., John Stafford Esq. and one other whose name is illegible. Only five members of the county bench failed to sign for one side or the other: Sir Henry Harrington, Sir William Turpin, Sir Basil Brooke, Sir Thomas Haselrig and Sir Thomas Beaumont of Coleorton.

[95] Bodl.L., Carte MS 78, fos.308–11.

[96] For hat honour, see P. Corfield, 'Dress for deference and dissent: hats and the decline of hat honour', *Costume* (1989), pp. 64–79.

[97] Bodl.L., Carte MS 78, fo.312.

[98] Cust, 'Politics and purveyance', Hunt.L., HA Manorial, Box 53, no.6, fos.5–10 (this is the earl of Huntingdon's lieutenancy book 1614–27 which is discussed more fully in an important forthcoming study by Tom Cogswell of Leicestershire government and politics *c.* 1610–42. I am most grateful to him for allowing me to read this in typescript); HA Correspondence, 2513.

[99] For Bale's continuing attendance at quarter sessions, see the Pipe Roll entries for Leicestershire for the years following: P.R.O., E372/456–60. Bale was knighted when James I stayed at Ashby Castle in 1617: J. Nichols, *The Progresses, Processions and Magnificent Festivities of James I*, 4 vols. (London, 1828), vol. III, p. 422. Bale also stood in as Huntingdon's deputy, representing the Duchy of Lancaster, when the mayor of Leicester was sworn in annually: L.R.O., Borough of Leicester Hall Papers, vol. XII, fo.218; vol. XIV, fo.4.

[100] The next serious challenge to Huntingdon came in 1627–8 when Sir Henry Shirley questioned his running of the lieutenancy. This dispute is fully discussed in Cogswell's forthcoming study.

[101] M. Judson, *The Crisis of the Constitution* (New Brunswick, 1949), pp. 1–107; M. Kishlansky, 'The emergence of adversary politics in the Long Parliament', *Journal of Modern History*, 49 (1977), pp. 619–21; C. S. R. Russell, *Parliaments and English Politics 1621–1629* (Oxford, 1979), pp. 53–4.

[102] M. T. Clanchy, 'Law and love in the Middle Ages', in Bossy, *Disputes*, pp. 47–67; A. B. Ferguson, *The Articulate Citizen and the English Renaissance* (Durham, NC, 1965), pp. 202–4.

[103] Bodl.L., Carte MS 78, fo.322. This was copied into a commonplace book which Brian Cave Esq. used for copying documents on notable local and national events: F.S.L., V.a.402, fo.5.

[104] Bodl.L., Carte MS 78, fo.308.

[105] Hunt.L., HA Correspondence, 4328, 4331; Bodl.L., Carte MS 78, fo.308.

[106] Hunt.L., HA Correspondence, 5438; Bodl.L., Carte MS 77, fos.518–19; 78, fos.308–10, 325–6; Hunt.L., HA Personal, Box 15, no.7.

[107] Skinner, *Foundations*, vol. I, ch.8; R. P. Cust and P. G. Lake, 'Sir Richard Grosvenor and the rhetoric of magistracy', *B.I.H.R.*, 54 (1981), pp. 40–53. For a series of jury charges elaborating on this theme, see the drafts of charges drawn up for delivery at the Warwickshire quarter sessions between 1600 and 1609 by Sir John Newdigate, a friend of Sir John Grey and Sir Thomas Beaumont: Warwickshire Record Office, Newdigate of Arbury MSS, B.633, 659, 669, 679, 683–700, 714, 716–23. These are discussed in V. M. Larminie, *The Godly Magistrate. The Private Life and Public Philosophy of Sir John Newdigate 1571–1610* (Dugdale Society Occasional Paper, no.28, 1982) and in my unpublished paper on 'Humanism and magistracy in early Stuart England'. For Leicestershire assize sermons which deal with these themes, see A. Cade, *A Sermon on the Nature of Conscience* (1620); T. Pestell, *Morbus Epidemicus or the Churles Sicknes* (1615).

[108] Hunt.L., HA Correspondence, 4329; Bodl.L., Carte MS 78, fos.308–10.

[109] Bodl.L., Carte MS 78, fo.308.

[110] *Ibid.*, fo.308; Hunt.L., HA Correspondence, 5438. As an example of his impartiality Huntingdon cited his judgement in favour of a poor man who had brought a suit against his kinsman Sir John Harrington. This, he believed, had led Harrington to sign the letter against Bale: Carte MS 78, fo.310.

[111] Bodl.L., Carte MS 78, fo.309.

[112] Hunt.L., HA Correspondence, 5438.

[113] Bodl.L., Carte MS 78, fos.308–10; Hunt.L., HA Correspondence, 5436; Carte MS 78, fo.318; HA Personal, Box 15, no.7.

[114] Skinner, *Foundations*, vol. I, pp. 221–8.

[115] Hunt.L., HA Correspondence, 4331.

[116] For a fuller discussion of this point, see 'Introduction', in Sharpe and Lake, *Culture and Politics*, pp. 1–20.

[117] Peristiany, *Honour and Shame*; Campbell, *Honour, Family and Patronage*; M. Herzfeld, 'Honour and shame: a comparative analysis of moral systems', *Man*, 15(1980), pp. 339–51.

[118] A. L. Hughes, 'Local history and the origins of civil war', in R. P. Cust and A. L. Hughes (eds.), *Conflict in Early Stuart England* (Harlow, 1989), pp. 224–8; C. Holmes, 'The county community in early Stuart historiography', *J.B.S.*, 19 (1980), pp. 54–73.

[119] V. Morgan, 'Cambridge University and "the country", 1560–1640', in L. Stone (ed.), *The University in Society*, 2 vols. (1975), vol. I, pp. 183–245; *idem*, 'The cartographic image of "the country" in early modern England', *Transactions of the Royal Historical Society*, 5th ser., 29 (1979), pp. 129–54.

[120] D. MacCulloch, *Suffolk and the Tudors* (Oxford, 1986), chs.2–3. The quotation given by MacCulloch on p.120 is from R. Reyce, *Suffolk in the XVIIth Century*, ed. Lord Francis Hervey (London, 1902) p. 60.

[121] M. Kishlansky, *Parliamentary Selection* (Cambridge, 1986), pp. 12–31.

[122] On the potency and varied meanings of 'country', see 'Introduction: after revisionism', in Cust and Hughes, *Conflict in Early Stuart England*, pp. 19–21.

[123] On 'courts of reputation', see Pitt-Rivers, 'Honour and social status', p. 27.

5

The Wentwood Forest riot: property rights and political culture in Restoration England[1]

Molly McClain

I

In June 1678 the free tenants of Wentwood Forest rioted against the alleged invasion of their ancient rights by Henry, marquis of Worcester, the lord of the forest. Worcester had enclosed 3,000 acres of woodlands and had begun to fell oak trees for use in his ironworks at Tintern Abbey in Monmouthshire. The free tenants claimed that the right to take timber from the forest belonged to them by ancient custom and usage. The riot took place when a group of fifty armed men entered the forest and carried away 200 cords of felled wood. The leaders of the rising were arrested and bound to appear at the Monmouth quarter sessions, where they were found guilty of riot and fined.

At first glance, the Wentwood Forest riot appears to be just another example of the numerous enclosure disputes which took place over the course of the seventeenth century. However, on closer inspection, we see that it has some rather remarkable features. The leaders of the riot were not small tenants or landless cottagers with few legal rights. Instead, they were men of wealth and property in Monmouthshire. At issue was access not only to common lands, but also to political power in the county.

The conflict in Wentwood Forest had an impact far beyond local politics. By the end of 1678 the property dispute had become bound up with the national crisis known as the Popish Plot. What began as an apparent enclosure dispute ended as part of one of the most heated political battles in late seventeenth-century England.

II

Enclosure riots, particularly those which took place before 1660 or after 1720, have commanded a good deal of attention from social historians. The upheavals of the sixteenth and early seventeenth centuries have been analysed by Peter Clark, Eric Kerridge, Keith Lindley, Buchanan Sharp and David Underdown.[2] Historians of the eighteenth century have also contributed to the study of rural protest, focusing their attention mainly on resistance to parliamentary enclosure.[3]

The enclosure riots of the Restoration period, by way of contrast, have not been explored in any detail. Max Beloff devoted one chapter to the problem of agrarian disorder in his 1938 study of popular disturbances. However, he qualified his remarks by suggesting that 'the problem of enclosures ... plays little direct part in the history of disorder in this period'.[4] More recently, Buchanan Sharp's study of the forest riots in western England and Keith Lindley's analysis of the fenland riots in Lincolnshire have included some discussion of late seventeenth-century uprisings. However, both authors view the riots as continuations of disputes which had their climax in the years before the English Civil War.[5]

One reason for the apparent lack of interest in Restoration enclosure riots is that they took place during a period of relative social stability. Economic indicators show that both population growth and inflation slowed after 1650, reducing the number of popular disturbances. J. D. Chambers wrote that the demographic depression was 'one of the stabilizing influences that gave the period 1650–1750 a new character of stability and social conservatism so different from the previous century of rampant population growth and social dislocation'.[6] As a result, late seventeenth-century uprisings are thought to have been short-lived and not overtly political. According to one group of historians, such 'bread-and-butter' disturbances 'offered no serious challenge to the governing elite'.[7]

My study of the Wentwood Forest riot argues that enclosure riots, in fact, could be highly political events. The late seventeenth century saw the creation of the Whig and Tory parties and the transformation of politics into an ideological battleground. Party divisions at Westminster often spilled over into the localities, turning seemingly innocuous disputes into serious conflicts. Tim Harris, in his work on London crowds, described how ritualized attacks on brothels were altered in the changed context of the Restoration period. He argued that the bawdy house riots of 1668 served as a 'protest against the policies of the Court'.[8] If popular rituals and celebrations could be used for such purposes, then so could the seemingly more conservative enclosure riots. The following analysis shows how a simple property dispute could become politicized in the highly-charged, partisan atmosphere of late seventeenth-century England.

III

The enclosure of common lands has been defined as a process by which an individual appropriated property which formerly had been at the disposal of the entire community. The lands in question could be open fields, pastures, forests or fenlands. The individual could own the property in question, or he could have gained rights to it by general agreement, parliamentary statute or Crown grant. In any case, he frequently had to contend with people who had used the land for generations and who claimed rights of common over the property. In order to extinguish these common rights, the individual 'enclosed' the land with a fence or a hedge. He could then use the land as he saw fit, without being restrained by the inconvenient usages of custom.[9]

Enclosure was undertaken from the sixteenth through the nineteenth centuries mainly for the purpose of agricultural improvement. Contemporaries believed that the cultivation of overstocked and poorly maintained pastures would maximize both profit and output. As one eighteenth-century gentleman pointed out, such improvements would benefit everyone concerned: 'the landowner will increase the value of his lands, the farmer his profits, labour will be at least as plentiful, and provisions much more so'.[10] However, enclosure also brought great personal profit, particularly when it was employed in forests and chases. Many enterprising gentlemen found that they could gain a lucrative income by fencing in a tract of woodland and stripping it of timber. In so doing, they destroyed the customary economy of the forest for their own personal gain.

During the Restoration period, landowners turned to enclosure in an effort to increase their revenues. The Civil War had plunged many families into acute financial crisis and had burdened them with a tremendous load of debt. By enclosing wastelands and forests, landowners hoped to recoup part of their losses. The earl of Westmoreland, for example, sold off considerable tracts of woodlands in Northamptonshire, gaining £4,576 between 1658 and 1662. Similarly, Lord Hatton realized the clear annual value of £1,030 on his timber sales in Rockingham Bailiwick. J. D. Chambers suggested that disafforestation took place on a considerable scale after 1660 as woodlands were 'subjected more and more to the attrition of enclosure by the large proprietors'.[11]

The ability of landowners to enclose commons came about as the result of a change in the ideology of use-rights. Over the course of the seventeenth century, lawyers and political theorists developed an increasingly absolutist definition of property which favoured the individual owner. This new attitude led to a number of laws which tended toward the dissolution of common right. For example, parliamentary statutes of 1663 and 1671 made it a crime to gather wood and to take game from royal forests. The redefinition of custom as a crime provided what E. P. Thompson described as 'a text-book illustration of the employment of law, as instrument and as ideology, in serving the interests of the ruling class'.[12]

Enclosure, however, was often resisted by local men who fought to preserve their rights of common. Opposition most often took the form of a 'riot' in which a group of small tenants and poor cottagers would gather to pull down the hedges or fences which enclosed a property. During the 1620s and

1630s, the Crown policies of disafforestation and drainage caused many such uprisings. In 1631, inhabitants of the Forest of Dean pulled down the hedges which surrounded Mailescott Woods and cast pieces of felled timber into the river Wye. Meanwhile, in the Lincolnshire fens, hundreds of commoners destroyed drainage ditches and farming implements in order to stop entrepreneurs from converting commonable pasture into arable land.[13]

After the Restoration, enclosure continued to inspire resistance. In 1671, commoners violently destroyed hedges made by the duchess of Cleveland in the Forest of Dean. Several decades later, a series of riots broke out in Northamptonshire following the enclosure of former common lands by the second marquis of Powis. Many of the disturbances took place in the forests and fenlands, regions which had experienced major riots in the years before the Civil War. In 1660, inhabitants of the Isle of Axholme raised a riot which was not dissimilar to the one which had taken place there nearly thirty years before.[14]

Although enclosure riots appear to have been disorderly and dangerous, they were, in fact, highly traditional forms of protest. For one thing, the uprisings were not the work of a 'mindless mob', bent on vandalizing private property. Instead, they were organized by law-abiding members of the working population who wished to preserve their rights of common. Most rioters had a strong parochial orientation. According to David Underdown, 'the most universal outlook was a conservative localism: a stubborn reliance on ancient custom, and a tendency to view national issues through the prism of town or village life'.[15]

Riots also served as a form of extra-legal activity. They provided a venue in which the poor and disenfranchised could express their grievances and compel authorities to respond. Oftentimes, participants appeared armed with petitions which set out their ancient and customary rights. Historians stress the fact that rioters did not challenge the government; instead, they protested against the invasion of their common rights by intruders into local society. Peter Clark found that these uprisings 'were distinctive for their customary, deferential character ... popular disturbance was the engine of last resort – after appeals to the Prince, Common Law, Parliament, and local justices had failed'.[16]

IV

On first inspection, the Wentwood Forest riot appears to have been a classic enclosure dispute. It involved members of the local community who were trying to preserve their rights of common against a wealthy interloper. Moreover, it seemed to be a continuation of a dispute which had taken place nearly forty years before.

Wentwood, located in the country of Monmouthshire, was one of the largest forests in the Welsh border region, encompassing nearly 7,000 acres of woodland and pasture. Wentwood was not a royal forest, but was held by the Somerset family, earls of Worcester, under the great Lordship of Chepstow. The Lords of Chepstow maintained a speech court in the forest and allowed tenants to exercise various rights of common. For example, the tenants were permitted to fell trees in order to rebuild their houses, a right known as *housebote*. They could cut brushwood to make fences (*heybote*) and they could use certain pieces of timber for fuel (*firebote*). The tenants also had rights of pasture (*herbage, primage and pannage*) while the Somersets maintained privileges of fishing, fowling, hawking and hunting in Wentwood Chase. In return, the inhabitants of the forest were required to 'preserve the forest to the Lord's use'. A court roll book of 1597 described the Lords of Chepstow as 'owners of the forest and of the said wood' and stated that 'no tenant shall cut any young oak or beech'.[17]

The common lands in Wentwood Forest had been shared among the Lords of Chepstow and their tenants until 1630, when Henry, fifth earl and, later, first marquis of Worcester, enclosed 3,000 acres in Chepstow Park, Coed Llyfos, the Fedw and Cefn-garw. It is thought that the enclosure of these lands was granted by Charles I as a reward for the Somerset family's financial contributions to the Crown. Having acquired a right to fence in the property, the fifth earl began to cut down timber for the use in his ironworks at Tintern Abbey, located several miles east of the forest along the Wye river.[18]

The fifth earl's enclosures created a great deal of ill-feeling among the inhabitants of Wentwood Forest, many of whom depended on the commons to provide them with grazing rights, firewood, construction timbers and other raw materials. In 1635, and again in 1642, rioters threw open the enclosures and carried away a great quantity of wood. They continued to assert their rights after the Civil War, when Oliver Cromwell became possessed of the Lordship of Chepstow. The Lord Protector continued the fifth earl's policy of selling wood to the ironworks, but he allowed the tenants to collect sufficient timber to support their farms.[19]

After the Restoration, Henry, third marquis of Worcester and grandson of the fifth earl, revived his family's right to enclose one-third of Wentwood Forest. Henry had gained the titles of Chief Forester, Ranger and Keeper of the Forest and Chase of Wentwood and Chepstow Park and he used his new authority to promote his financial interests. During the 1670s, he began to enclose land in Chepstow Park and to fell oak trees for use in the ironworks. He stood to gain a great deal of money. Julian Mitchell, in his recent article on the speech court of Wentwood, estimated that Worcester could make at least £2,500 per annum by providing timber to the forges at Tintern.[20]

The inhabitants of Wentwood Forest were angered by Worcester's proceedings and they responded by organizing an enclosure riot. In April 1678, a group of men set out with their teams and horses to carry away some of the wood which had been cut by the marquis' workmen. The tenants who participated in the expedition exceeded fifty in number and included several gentlemen. According to one witness, the men 'came above 50 of them together into the chase armed with guns, and bells', ready to do their worst. However, their reception was not as dramatic as many had anticipated. Most of the marquis' workmen had gone, leaving only one man to guard the wood. The tenants threatened to kill him, and while he looked on they carried away above 200 cords of wood from the Chase.[21]

On the surface, the Wentwood Forest riot had all the characteristics of the classic enclosure dispute. The rioters had acted to preserve their ancient common rights from an outsider who threatened to destroy the customary economy of the forest. In a petition to the House of Commons, the rioters stated that they 'had done nothing but in order to the preserving of their undoubted right from force'. They claimed that it was Worcester who had invaded their rights by enclosing the forest and 'obstructing the tenants to cut for their necessary occasions'.[22]

The rioters based their claim on legal right and precedent. They cited a number of ancient authorities, including a survey of Wentwood Forest dated 1584 and a presentment of the speech court held in 1271, which showed that the tenants had held common rights in Wentwood Forest for time out of mind.[23] Moreover, they were willing to have their rights determined by due course of law. They claimed that they had committed the riot only because they could not get Worcester to come to a fair trial at law. According to one witness, they 'peaceably carried away some small part of the wood cut down which by their ancient custom they have constantly been allowed lawfully to do and which the tenants would not however in any sort have done but that they could not prevail to have no further destruction made until a trial might be had'.[24]

Because the Wentwood Forest rioters couched their complaints in the traditional language of law and customary right, it is easy to assume that the dispute was no different from the ones which took place earlier in the century. However, if we examine the case more closely, we see some singular differences. In the first place, the leaders and many of the participants were not small tenants or landless cottagers, but members of the gentry. Of the seven men arrested, five were described as 'gentlemen'. Nathan Rogers of Llanvaches was an attorney and a former Member of Parliament for Herefordshire. Nathaniel Field was a grandson of a bishop of Llandaff and Thomas Blethin was a scion of a wealthy county family.[25]

What is unique about the Wentwood Forest riot is that it was orchestrated by some of the most powerful men in the county. A rare tract, published in 1708, reveals that William Morgan of Tredegar, a Member of Parliament for Monmouthshire, played a crucial role in organizing the opposition to this enclosure. In the spring of 1678, Morgan gathered together men who held manors in and around the forest to consider 'what was necessary to be done, and what Method and Course to take, for preserving their Rights in the *Common* and *Estovers* of *Wentwood*'. Members of this group included some of the most influential men in the county, among them Thomas Lewis of St Pierre and William Kemeys of Kemeys, the county sheriff.[26]

The group began by appealing to Worcester to stop what they considered to be illegal proceedings. From their point of view, the marquis had no right to cut down or to sell any timber as he was not the owner of the soil. Morgan insisted that Worcester possessed only three or four manors in the forest and had no more privileges than the other tenants. He apparently 'beseeched his Lordship to forbear further destruction and finally go to a trial of the right'.[27] Worcester, however, disregarded this plea and continued to hire workmen to cut trees and enclose common lands in Wentwood Chase.

Next, Morgan and his associates attempted to put a stop to Worcester's proceedings by forbidding 'the said Workmen to cut or fell any more Wood in the Case, or proceed in their Inclosures'. George and Edward Kemeys, William Blethin and Nathan Rogers were charged with enforcing this decision. According to Morgan, the four men 'did forbid his workmen to proceed, whereupon for some few days they did desist'. This proved to be only a temporary expedient, for the woodcutters soon returned to the forest.[28]

At last, the gentlemen of Monmouthshire decided to test their legal rights by organizing a raid on Chepstow Park. They consulted Sir William Williams and Sir Samuel Baldwin, two prominent lawyers, who 'were of the opinion that the Lord Marquis had unjustly invaded the Rights of the Tenants ... and if the Workmen continue to cut and cord the said Wood, that the Tenants should carry away the Wood so cut, their Custom allowing them so to do, in order to try their Rights'.[29]

The gentlemen who organized the riot all had some financial interest in keeping the common lands free from enclosure. They all held manors in or near Wentwood and they maintained common rights in various tracts of woodlands, including Chepstow Park. Although they were not permitted to sell wood, they received tangible benefits which could be translated into cash. One source suggests that the eight leading tenants in Wentwood Forest each held forest rights worth an average of £40 a year.[30]

However, the potential loss of income does not sufficiently explain the gentry's hostility to enclosure. William Morgan, for example, stood to lose only £80 a year, a relatively small sum when compared to his annual income of £4,000. His associates would not have lost much more. Rowland Gwynne, who had inherited an estate of £1,000 per annum, had forest rights worth no more than £30 per annum.[31]

The Wentwood Forest rioters were motivated less by financial interests than by political ones. Almost all of the gentlemen who helped to organize the uprising shared a history of political opposition to the marquis of Worcester. A decade earlier, in 1667, William Morgan, Thomas Lewis and many other gentlemen had opposed Worcester's candidate in a contested by-election and had selected one of his political enemies instead. Worcester retaliated by purging his opponents from the deputy lieutenancy and the commissions of the peace. His actions only intensified the animosity of the local gentry, and the dispute festered for over a decade. As late as 1678, the House of Commons found that 'there have been great animosities carried on' in Monmouthshire 'upon the occasion of an election ... for member of parliament and the laying by one whom the marquis of Worcester recommended'.[32]

Although the Wentwood Forest riot appeared to be a typical property dispute, it was, in reality, a highly political conflict. The gentlemen of Monmouthshire saw Worcester's selfish pursuit of financial gain as yet another way to advance the Somerset family interest at the expense of the neighbouring gentry. The riot was, in effect, a violent response to the marquis' interference in local affairs.

V

The political conflict between Worcester and the Monmouthshire gentry had its origins in a particular historical situation. For many years, the earls of Worcester had been one of the most powerful Catholic families in south Wales. Their estates stretched from the Black Mountains to the port of Chepstow, from the borough of Monmouth to Wentwood Chase. During the early sixteenth century, the earls had served as marcher lords; later, successive heads of the family acted as lord lieutenants of Glamorganshire and Monmouthshire. The Somersets' extensive landholdings and their military office allowed them to dominate the political life of south Wales.

During the decade of the 1640s, the influence of the Somerset family was swept away by the tide of civil war. The surrender of Raglan Castle to parliamentary forces in June 1646 and the subsequent death of the fifth earl and first marquis of Worcester ended the family's intervention into local political affairs. Instead, their power was redistributed among various individuals, many of whom were associated with Oliver Cromwell.[33]

The developments of the Civil War years encouraged a sense of political independence among the Monmouthshire gentry. After the Restoration, local gentlemen no longer depended on great noblemen to provide them with political leadership. In fact, the county did not have a single resident peer. Blome's *Britannia* (1673) lists Edward, Lord Herbert of Chirbury, William Herbert, earl of Pembroke and Henry Somerset, marquis of Worcester, as three principal noblemen, but none of them retained seats in the county. Lord Herbert of Chirbury rarely visited his properties in Monmouthshire, preferring to concentrate his attention on his north Wales estate. The earl of Pembroke, meanwhile, disposed of great tracts of land in Monmouthshire and Glamorganshire, virtually ending his influence in those two counties.[34]

During the 1660s, members of the gentry began to take a renewed interest in the governance of the county. Sir Trevor Williams of Llangibby came to office after twelve years of inactivity, serving as *custos rotulorum* and deputy lieutenant of Monmouthshire. William Morgan of Tredegar and Sir Charles Kemeys represented the county as knights of the shire. Other leaders of county society became involved in local government, serving as deputy lieutenants and justices of the peace.[35]

The gentry, however, were forced to contend with the ambitious marquis of Worcester, heir to the Somerset estate. A relatively young man, Worcester was determined to restore his family's influence over the political proceedings in Monmouthshire. At first, the gentlemen of the county appeared willing to humour him. In the general election of 1660, they selected him to serve as knight of the shire. However, they stopped short when Worcester asked them to send one of his clients to Parliament after he was raised to the peerage in 1667. Instead, they nominated Sir Trevor Williams to the seat which previously had been held by the marquis. Their choice was a particular insult to the Somerset family. Sir Trevor's role in the Civil War, along with his vehement dislike of Catholicism and his Protestant political connections, allied him with the enemies of the House of Somerset. When Worcester realized that his nominee, James Herbert, might be rejected by the electorate, he took the situation into his own hands. In July, he wrote to his wife that he was 'extremely busy in ... seeing to the writ for Monmouthshire, wherein I perceive there is and will be open defiance'.[36]

The by-election of November 1667 was marked by 'great animosities' between the contesting parties. Worcester used his influence as lord lieutenant of Monmouthshire to sway the election, sending troops from the nearby Chepstow garrison to Monmouth on election day. One observer recalled that '6 files of musketeers were sent to Monmouth to awe the town',[37] However, Sir Trevor received sufficient votes to win the seat. Worcester petitioned the election return, but the Committee of Privileges decided that 'the election was clear for Sir Trevor Williams, he voted to be lawfully elected and his return also lawful'.[38]

The political setback which Worcester experienced led him to take revenge against those he considered to be his enemies in the county. Unable to secure a parliamentary seat for his nominee, he retaliated by removing a number of gentlemen from office in Monmouthshire. In 1667, he ousted Sir Trevor Williams, Henry Morgan and Charles Van from the commissions of the peace and the deputy lieutenancy and replaced them with a number of his supporters. A decade later, he was still taking men out of office for political reasons. In 1677 he removed John Arnold and Henry Probert from the Monmouthshire bench 'pour affronts al duke [of York] and misdemeanors in son office, ut represented per marquis of Worcester'.[39]

Worcester's proscriptions created an influential body of political enemies, many of whom were related by marriage. Two of his chief opponents were William Morgan of Tredegar and his brother-in-law, Sir Trevor Williams of Llangibby. Morgan, the knight of the shire for Monmouth, was one of the wealthiest gentlemen in Monmouthshire. He owned a considerable amount of property in south Wales and his manor house at Tredegar, near Newport, was a model of the classical style. Despite the fact that he was a relatively young man, Morgan's reputation extended far beyond the boundaries of south Wales. One newsletter described both Morgan and his friend Sir Edward Mansell of Glamorgan as 'princes in their own country'.[40]

Morgan's brother-in-law, Sir Trevor Williams of Llangibby, was also an MP and a long-time adversary of the Somerset family. During the Civil War, he had led the clubman movement in Monmouthshire. Both King Charles I and Oliver Cromwell had sought his arrest, the latter describing him as 'full of craft and subtlety, very bold and resolute; hath a house at Llangibby well-stored with arms and strong; his neighbors about him very malignant, and much for him'. After the Restoration, Sir Trevor behaved with somewhat more decorum, acting as *custos rotulorum* and colonel of the militia.[41]

William Morgan and Sir Trevor Williams were related to other opponents of the Somersets, some of whom had fought against the family during the Civil War. Roger Williams of Cefn Ila, Sir Trevor's son-in-law, managed Morgan's ironworks at his forge near Machen. During the Civil War he inventoried the contents of Raglan Castle and took out leases of sequestered lands.[42] Roger Oates of Cefn-tilla, the father-in-law of the above-named Williams, lent his house as Roundhead headquarters during the siege of Raglan castle.[43] Charles Van of Llanwern, who had married William Morgan's sister Blanche, was another enemy of the Somerset family. Van had opposed the marquis of Worcester's interference in election proceedings and had been removed from the commission of the peace in 1667. Thomas Lewis of St Pierre, the high sheriff in 1667, also ranks among the political opponents of the marquis. Lewis was responsible for the election return which brought Sir Trevor to Parliament against the wishes of the marquis. He too was related by marriage to many notable Monmouthshire families, including the Williams of Llangibby and the Oates of Cefn-tilla.[44] Other opponents of the marquis of Worcester included Rowland Gwynne of Pencoed, Henry Morgan of Penllwyn Sarph, Henry Probert of the Argoed and Henry Romsey of Sudbrook.[45]

Not surprisingly, many of these gentlemen had interest in Wentwood Forest. Morgan, for example, was lord of four manors located near the forest: Llanvaches, Lanvihangell, Roggiett and Undy. Rowland Gwynne held the castle of Pencoed in Lanmartin. Thomas Lewis of St Pierre held the lordship of Penhow and had houses and tenements in Walton, Southbrook, Portskewet and Undy. Other free tenants included William Blethin, John Gwyn, George Harris, William Herbert of Caldicot, Thomas Herbert, William Jones of Lantrissent, Sir Charles Kemeys, George Kemeys, Henry Pritchard and Nathan Rogers.[46]

The Monmouthshire gentry had no intention of allowing the marquis to dominate the political life of the county and they set about to stop him. In the spring of 1678 William Morgan and Sir Edward Mansell approached Sir

Joseph Williamson with information about the marquis' recent purges of the deputy lieutenancy and commissions of the peace. Meanwhile, John Arnold, a former justice of the peace in Monmouthshire, told several MPs how he had been ousted from his office by Worcester. He blamed his situation not on his political alliances, but on his Protestant sympathies. He claimed that Worcester had replaced him with gentlemen who 'were kind to their Popish neighbors', in other words, Catholic sympathizers.[47]

Arnold deliberately confused the political dispute in Monmouthshire with an alleged Catholic conspiracy, a sleight of hand which ensured that his information would be given a full hearing. The MPs with whom he spoke were duly shocked and 'advised him to draw a formal narrative touching the Growth and Increase of Popery in Monmouthshire'. Arnold was only too willing to oblige. He drew up a narrative with the aid of John Scudamore of Herefordshire and began circulating it among the neighbouring gentry. Sir Trevor Williams saw to it that the pamphlet was mentioned in Parliament and on 12 April 1678 both the narrative and its authors were called to the House of Commons.[48]

In his report to the House of Commons, Arnold suggested that the marquis of Worcester tolerated the existence of a large Catholic community within his native county of Monmouth. He offered an account of 'the number of Papists' in the county and 'the frequency of Mass [held] privately and publicly' and suggested that Worcester supported a Jesuit college on his estate at Cwm in Herefordshire. Some of Arnold's harshest criticism was directed against Worcester's estate steward, Henry Milborne of Llanrhyddol. Arnold described Milborne as an 'undoubted papist' who only held lands worth £100 per annum in one county, but 'is made justice of the peace in four'.[49]

Worcester's background made the accusations against him seem almost believable. Although he had converted to the Protestant faith in 1658, the marquis was related to some of the leading Catholic families in the kingdom. His sisters Lady Elizabeth and Lady Anne had married two of the principal Catholic noblemen in England, the earl of Powis and Henry Howard, the second son of the earl of Arundel. Worcester's uncle was a priest in the Louvain and his aunt was a nun. He was also related to a number of Catholic families in Monmouthshire including the Scudamores of Treworgan, the Milbornes of Wonastow, and the Vaughans of Courtfield.[50]

However, Worcester's close relationship with Protestant elites put the lie to Arnold's attempt to associate him with popery in south Wales. His marriage to Lady Mary Capel had allied him with Arthur, earl of Essex, an influential Privy Councillor, and Sir Henry Capel, a leading figure in the House of Commons. As a result, few MPs believed that the marquis was actively trying to advance the Catholic cause. In fact, some MPs thought Arnold's report was so poor that they 'were overheard to hiss' as he left the House.[51]

While Arnold's narrative was provocative, it failed to attract the continuing interest of the House of Commons. As a result, Sir Trevor and his allies were forced to look for other ways to discredit the marquis. In Wentwood Forest, they found an opportunity to present Worcester in a truly unflattering light. The property dispute served as a means to illustrate the dangers of allowing a single nobleman to dominate local affairs in Monmouthshire.

Worcester understood only too clearly the political nature of the Wentwood riot and he was determined to take his revenge. Instead of coming to terms with the rioters, as many landlords did, he had them rounded up and punished. Nathan Rogers claimed that the marquis called together his estate agents, the county bailiff and several others 'to terrifie and take up the Tenants and their Servants, that had lately cut or carry'd any Wood for their necessary Occasions'. Some of the leading tenants were arrested and bound to appear at the Monmouth quarter sessions where they were found guilty of riot and fined. Rogers later claimed that the trial had been rigged and the jury 'impannell'd of the lord marquis' own tenants'.[52]

Still, Worcester remained dissatisfied with the prosecution of the rioters and, in June 1678, he took his case before the House of Lords. He moved to obtain a warrant against the seven men whom he had identified as leaders of the raid on Chepstow Park, claiming that they had breached his parliamentary privilege by committing a riot. Three of these men were arrested by officers of the sergeant at arms of the House of Lords and escorted to London where they were kept in custody for nearly a month.[53]

The marquis also used his powers as lord lieutenant to protect his property against any further raids. He ordered the deputy-lieutenant of Chepstow Castle to guard the area where the workmen were cutting wood for use in the ironworks. Soldiers from the garrison stood watch night and day. When a local man came into the Chase to fetch some sprigs of wood, he discovered 'the Governor of Chepstow with six soldiers who had two muskets lying on the ground as though they would have hid them, and glaives and halberts in their hands'.[54] Given the large amount of wood which the rioters had taken from the forest, it is not surprising that Worcester tried to protect his property. However, his employment of soldiers from the Chepstow garrison was seen by many as an ill-disguised attempt at intimidation.

Worcester's aggressive prosecution of his enemies reinforced his reputation as an unjust and 'arbitrary Lord'. The tenants, meanwhile, appeared as the injured party. As lord lieutenant, Worcester was empowered to quell local disturbances, but he was not authorized to use the garrison at Chepstow Castle to settle his personal feud with the county gentry.[55]

The exercise of military power against the Wentwood Forest rioters had great political significance. In the context of 1678, the use of the militia by a former Catholic constituted a serious threat. During the previous winter, Charles II had raised an army to fight against the forces of Louis XIV, a move which alarmed many MPs who feared that the troops would be used instead against Parliament. At the same time, Andrew Marvell had published *An Account of the Growth of Popery and Arbitrary Government*, a tract which crystallized the fears of many Englishmen regarding the king's foreign policy. Many people feared that the standing army would be used 'to change the lawful government of England into an absolute tyranny, and to convert the established Protestant religion into downright Popery'.[56]

The use of the military was an issue which Morgan and his countrymen seized upon. In June 1678, Morgan and his brother-in-law Sir Trevor Williams, the two MPs for Monmouthshire, approached the House of Commons with information about Worcester's proceedings in the forest of Wentwood. They claimed that the marquis had commissioned 'several great numbers of armed men with the Governor of Chepstow Castle' to round up the rioters and 'to overawe the tenants'. The fact that Worcester had used soldiers to defend his property rights appeared to them a clear indication that he was trying to subvert the laws and liberties of the kingdom.[57]

The MPs' report brought the Wentwood Forest dispute into the realm of party politics. Morgan and Williams allied themselves with the Whig party, which designed to preserve the nation from the enslaving designs of courtiers and papists. Their most important ally was the earl of Shaftesbury, the leader of the opposition in the House of Lords. Shaftesbury showed an unusual interest in the case of the Wentwood rioters. He had little real sympathy for the rioters, having opposed the claims of commoners on his own estates. But he was eager to make trouble for the marquis of Worcester, whom he considered to be one of the chief supporters of the court. In July 1678, Shaftesbury petitioned the House of Lords for the release of the three Monmouthshire men who had been taken into custody for breaking Worcester's parliamentary privilege. His actions must have annoyed the marquis, who was in no hurry to see the prisoners set free. On 6 July Worcester wrote to his wife, 'My Lord Shaftesbury offered a new petition today for the Welsh men in custody, which could not be read but is lodged with the Clark and was ordered to be read on Monday, but I think my Lord Feversham's business will jostle it out that day.'[58] However, Shaftesbury's petition must have had the desired effect, for the prisoners were released from custody in early July after paying fines of £40 each and expressing sorrow for their actions.[59]

Shaftesbury's assistance allowed the gentlemen of Monmouthshire to proceed in their efforts to oust Worcester from his position of power in the county. In the autumn of 1678, Sir Trevor Williams began to lobby for the disbandment of Chepstow Castle. He claimed that the garrison was a Catholic stronghold which served to defend the marquis' interests in the county. Shaftesbury aided Williams by taking up the issue in the House of Lords. On 5 December, Worcester wrote to his wife that 'there is not a day has passed this week, that I have not been forced to defend the garrison of Chepstow and the County of Monmouth which Lord Shaftesbury will have to be all papists ... We were at it today for an hour and yesterday as long.'[60]

Sir Trevor used the prevailing fear of popery to remove Chepstow Castle from Worcester's control. During the autumn of 1678, William Bedloe had testified before the House of Commons about an alleged uprising which was supposed to have been organized by Charles Price, the marquis of Worcester's chief steward, and Francis Spalding, governor of Chepstow Castle. His information, however spurious, prepared the way for eventual disbandment of the garrison.[61]

Over the next two years, the Monmouthshire gentry used their influence to frustrate Worcester's efforts to nominate Members of Parliament. At the general election in February 1678/9, the marquis presented the county gentry with a strategy which would have effectively removed Sir Trevor from Parliament. He wanted his son, Charles, Lord Herbert, to share the county seat with William Morgan and he wanted to select Heneage Finch to serve as the single member for the borough of Monmouth. The gentry, however, had no intention of acceding to his demands. Morgan wrote that 'the lord marquis would have one of the knights ... his son, and the nomination of the person for the borough, which the gentry of the county think too much at this time'. They offered him the choice of his son for the first knight with Morgan, 'but he resolved to try for it, though we are sure to carry 3 to one at least. All of his dependency is on the sheriff who he is sure of. But we do not fear to make our interest seen.'[62]

Worcester succeeded in placing his son in the county seat, but he failed to control the borough, which went to Sir Trevor. His small success, however, was not longlasting. When elections were called six months later, Sir Trevor managed to regain control of the county. Charles, Lord Herbert, was left to fight with John Arnold for the borough. He was successful at the poll, only to be set aside in favour of Arnold on the latter's appeal to the House of Commons.[63] Anticipating the marquis' reaction, the gentry met to prevent Worcester from controlling both seats at the next election. In May 1680, John Arnold announced, 'I am very confident we are 20 to 1 against the great lord.'[64]

Having thwarted Worcester's efforts to intervene in the political affairs of the county, the gentlemen of Monmouthshire tried to oust him from his military offices. The frenzied atmosphere surrounding the Popish Plot and the Exclusion Crisis made the House of Commons receptive to their demands. In November 1680, Sir Trevor promoted *A Bill for taking away the Court of Presidents, Vice Presidents and Council of the Marches of Wales*, a measure which would have removed the marquis from his position as Lord President of Wales. The bill passed the House of Commons on 18 December and Sir Trevor was ordered to carry it up to the House of Lords.[65]

Williams also pressed for Worcester's removal from the Privy Council, claiming that the marquis, along with several other councillors, had advised the king to oppose the Exclusion Bill. His suggestion was supported by little, if any, proof. The marquis was not one of Charles II's principal advisors, nor did he influence the king's decisions at this crucial juncture. Still, the suggestion that he had offered counsel on the issue of Exclusion put him in great danger. He all too easily could have ended up like Viscount Strafford, who was condemned to death for his part in an alleged conspiracy against the king.[66]

Worcester was sufficiently worried about the proceedings in Parliament to keep tabs on the debates. At the end of December, he sent a member of his household – possibly his son, Charles, Lord Herbert – to record the discussion in the House of Commons. These notes have been preserved in a book entitled, 'A Journal of the House of Commons proceedings from 18 December [1680] to 8 January, 1681'. Its author took care to record the comments of the Monmouthshire MPs, particularly when they reflected badly on the marquis.[67] During the volatile session of 1680–1, several Welsh MPs spoke out against Worcester. On 3 January, while the Commons was considering a bill for regulating elections, John Arnold told the House that 'he serves for a borough that's governed by an arbitrary lord who pricks mayors as the king pricks sheriffs, and gives them an oath to be for him'. He also took the opportunity to describe election irregularities in Monmouthshire.[68]

A discussion of Worcester's proceedings in Wentwood Forest played a considerable part in the debates in Parliament. Sir Rowland Gwynne, a free tenant and MP for Radnorshire, claimed that Worcester had used the garrison at Chepstow to subvert the laws and liberties of the surrounding countryside, adding that 'the soldiers of Chepstow [were] employed to rob the country of their wood'. He suggested that 'if his parts were equal to his power, his oppressions would be as great as the worst of them'.[69] Gwynne was joined by Sir Trevor and Arnold, both of whom agreed that the marquis had misused his military power. The former stated that 'mass was constantly said' at Chepstow. When confronted with this fact, Worcester allegedly replied, 'you have nothing to do with my garrison'. Arnold confirmed this report and moved that the House of Commons 'dismantle Chepstow and [send an] address against him to the King'. The MPs concurred and requested that the king remove Worcester from 'all places of honour, power, and profit, and from the King's presence for ever'.[70]

The Monmouthshire MPs played a very strong hand; if the nation had broken out in civil war in 1681 they might have succeeded in ousting Worcester from the lord lieutenancy. However, the dissolution of Parliament brought an end to the possibility of civil strife. By the end of 1681, the political tide began to turn against the gentlemen of Monmouthshire. The marquis of Worcester was not turned out of office, as his enemies had desired, but was instead granted a dukedom. Shortly thereafter, the newly created duke of Beaufort crushed his enemies by bringing a successful action of *scandalum magnatum* against both Sir Trevor Williams and John Arnold for their libellous words before the House of Commons. The two men were committed to King's Bench prison, unable to pay their exorbitant fines.

By 1683, it was clear that the Wentwood Forest case had lost its momentum. Several of the leading tenants had died, including Sir Edward Morgan,

William Kemeys and William Morgan of Tredegar. Without these men, the tenants of Wentwood Forest 'lost the chief Support of their Liberties, and Pillar of their Cause'. Moreover, any possibility of further legal action was effectively ended by the Lord Chancellor's judgment in favour of the duke. Although the tenants might have continued to try their case at law, they decided that Beaufort was too powerful to beat. They discontinued their action, claiming that they were 'not able to obtain Right or Justice' against a court favourite like the duke of Beaufort.[71]

Over the course of the seventeenth century, the Wentwood Forest case changed from a simple property dispute to a heated political battle. The transformation was caused, in part, by the Exclusion Crisis, which raised the temperature of political disputes throughout the country. It was also caused by the actions of the marquis of Worcester. His use of the military gave the Monmouthshire gentry a political language in which to express their hostility to aristocratic influence.

The animosities created by the Wentwood Forest case did not fade away with time. Thirty years later, Nathan Rogers, one of the last rioters left alive, published a tract which exhorted the tenants of Wentwood to throw off their 'yoke of bondage' and recover their ancient rights. *The Memoirs of Monmouthshire* described the efforts of Morgan and his fellow patriots to 'put a Stop to the said marquis's arbitrary and illegal Power'. It is not clear whether Rogers was able to influence a younger generation, but he certainly made an impression on Worcester's heir. It was said that the second duke of Beaufort purchased almost every copy of the first edition 'and destroyed them to prevent their circulation'.[72] Long after the Exclusion Crisis had ended, the Wentwood Forest riot remained a symbol of the gentry's struggle for political power in Monmouthshire.

Notes

[1] A shorter version of this paper was presented to the North American Conference on British Studies in October 1993.

[2] Peter Clark, 'Popular protest and disturbance in Kent, 1558–1640', *Economic History Review*, 2nd ser., 29 (1976), pp. 365–81; Eric Kerridge, *Agrarian Problems in the Sixteenth Century and After* (London, 1969); *idem*, 'The revolts in Wiltshire against Charles I', *Wiltshire Archaeological and Natural History Magazine*, 57, (206) (1958), pp. 64–75; Keith Lindley, *Fenland Riots and the English Revolution* (London, 1982); Buchanan Sharp, *In Contempt of All Authority: Rural Artisans and Riot in the West of England, 1586–1660* (London, 1980); David Underdown, *Revel, Riot and Rebellion: Popular Politics and Culture in England, 1603–1660* (Oxford, 1985).

[3] J. L. and B. Hammonds' *The Village Labourer 1760–1832: A Study in the Government of England before the Reform Bill* (London, 1912) and E. P. Thompson's *Whigs and Hunters: The Origin of the Black Act* (New York, 1975) are considered to be two classic works in the field.

[4] Max Beloff, *Public Disorder and Popular Disturbances, 1660–1714* (Oxford, 1938).

⁵ Lindley, *Fenland Riots*, p. 233.

⁶ E. A. Wrigley and R. S. Schofield, *The Population History of England, 1541–1871: A Reconstruction* (London, 1981); A. H. John, 'The course of agricultural change, 1660–1760', in W. E. Minchinton (ed.), *Essays in Agrarian History* (Newton Abbot, 1968), vol. I, p. 232; J. D. Chambers, *Population, Economy and Society in Pre-Industrial England* (Oxford, 1972), p. 29.

⁷ H. T. Dickinson, 'Colloquy on chapter 1', in John Cannon (ed.), *The Whig Ascendancy* (London, 1981), p. 25; Keith Wrightson described the late seventeenth century as an age of declining resistance to agrarian innovation and a 'fading consciousness of traditional popular rights'. Keith Wrightson, *English Society, 1580–1680* (New Brunswick, NJ, 1982), p. 180.

⁸ Tim Harris, 'The bawdy house riots of 1668' *Historical Journal*, 29 (3) (1986), pp. 537–56; *idem, London Crowds in the Reign of Charles II: Propaganda and Politics from the Restoration until the Exclusion Crisis* (Cambridge, 1987), pp. 25, 82–91.

⁹ Joan Thirsk, 'Enclosing and engrossing', in *The Agrarian History of England and Wales, Volume IV, 1500–1640* (Cambridge, 1967), p. 201.

¹⁰ Cited in J. V. Beckett, *The Aristocracy in England, 1660–1914* (Oxford, 1989), p. 172.

¹¹ Philip A. J. Pettit, *The Royal Forests of Northamptonshire: A Study in their Economy, 1558–1714* (Gateshead, 1968), p. 116; J. D. Chambers, *Nottinghamshire in the Eighteenth Century: A Study of Life and Labour under the Squirearchy*, 2nd edn. (London, 1960), p. 147; I am indebted to Robert Ritchie for information about asset stripping in royal forests during the late seventeenth century.

¹² C. B. Macpherson, 'Capitalism and the changing concept of property', in E. Kamenka and R. S. Neate (eds.), *Feudalism, Capitalism and Beyond* (London, 1975), pp. 104–25; Thompson, *Whigs and Hunters*, p. 269.

¹³ Sharp, *In Contempt of All Authority*, p. 95; Lindley, *Fenland Riots*, ch. 2.

¹⁴ Beloff, *Public Disorder*, pp. 76–8; Lidley, *Fenland Riots*, p. 233; The persistence of agrarian disorder led to a series of statutes such as the 1663 *Act for the punishment of unlawful cutting or stealing or spoiling of wood* (15 Car. II, cap 2) and the 1670 *Act against the destruction of enclosures* (22 & 23 Car. II, cap 7). Despite these precepts, riots continued to take place, particularly in woodland regions. E. P. Thompson wrote that 'there cannot be a forest or chase in the country which did not have some dramatic episode of conflict over common rights in the eighteenth century'. Thompson, 'Custom, law and common right', in his *Customs in Common: Studies in Traditional Popular Culture* (New York, 1993), p. 104.

¹⁵ Underdown, *Revel, Riot and Rebellion*, p. 107.

¹⁶ Clark, 'Popular Protest', p. 380; our understanding of early modern enclosure riots has been shaped by the work of E. P. Thompson, particularly his essay on 'The moral economy of the English crowd in the eighteenth century', *Past and Present* 50 (1971), pp. 76–136. In this article, Thompson argued that grain rioters acted to defend their traditional rights against encroachment by outsiders to the community. His model of crowd behaviour has influenced many historians of popular culture. Although I do not seek to find fault with this interpretation, I am not convinced that crowds always had such honourable motives. As I argue in this chapter, the Wentwood Forest rioters used a traditional form of protest for very personal and political reasons. For a comprehensive analysis of Thompson's thesis, see J. Stevenson, 'The "moral economy" of the English crowd: myth and reality', in A. Fletcher and J. Stevenson (eds.), *Order and*

Disorder in Early Modern England (Cambridge, 1985), pp. 218–39.

[17] Joseph A. Bradney, *A History of Monmouthshire* (London, 1904–32), vol. IV, pt. 1, p. 146; National Library of Wales, Badminton Manorial Records 1808.

[18] Arthur Clark, *The Story of Monmouthshire* (Monmouth, 1979), vol. II, pp. 10–11.

[19] Public Records Office (hereafter P.R.O.), C22/478/25; C22/481/47.

[20] National Library of Wales, Badminton Manuscripts and Records II, 11051; Julian Mitchell, 'The speech court of Wentwood', *The Monmouthshire Antiquary*, 6 (1990), p. 66.

[21] National Library of Wales, Badminton Manuscripts Bc 2/41, Box 9, Monmouthshire, 1988 deposit.

[22] National Library of Wales, Badminton Manorial Records 1804; *ibid.*, Tredegar Manuscripts and Documents 64/112.

[23] P.R.O., C5/582/96.

[24] National Library of Wales, Badminton Manorial Records 1804.

[25] Bradney, *History of Monmouthshire*, vol. IV, pt. 2, pp. 157, 187; vol. III, pt. 2; p. 155.

[26] Rogers, *Memoirs of Monmouth-shire, 1708*, p. 81. See also, Julian Mitchell, 'Nathan Rogers and the Wentwood case', *The Welsh History Review*, 14 (1) (1988).

[27] They claimed that without a grant from the Crown 'the said Marquis and his Ancestors had right and liberty to feel, cut and take out of the said Chase such wood and timber only as should be necessary to be spent used and employed in upon and about his or their castle, lordship and manor of Chepstow'. P.R.O., C22/481/47; C5/582/97; National Library of Wales, Badminton Manorial Records 1804.

[28] Rogers, *Memoirs of Monmouth-shire*, p. 81; National Library of Wales, Badminton Manorial Records 1804.

[29] Rogers, *Memoirs of Monmouth-shire*, p. 81.

[30] National Library of Wales, Tredegar Manuscripts and Documents 59/28, 64/114.

[31] B. D. Henning, *A History of Parliament: The Commons, 1660–1690* (London, 1983), vol. II, p. 456; vol. III, p. 99.

[32] Bodleian Library (hereafter Bodl. L.), Carte ms 72, fos. 382–3.

[33] Philip Jones, the ex-Comptroller of the Protector's household, took control of the sequestered Somerset estate and became the dominant source of patronage in the county, A. G. Veysey, 'Colonel Philip Jones, 1618–74', *Transactions of the Honourable Society of Cymrodorion, Session 1966*, 2 (1966), pp. 316–40.

[34] Richard Blome, *Britannia* (London, 1673), pp. 406–7; Philip Jenkins, *The Making of a Ruling Class: The Glamorgan Gentry, 1640–1790* (Cambridge, 1983), p. 20.

[35] CSPD 1668–9, p. 451.

[36] Badminton Muniments, FmF 1/2/24.

[37] *Ibid.*, FmE 3/3.

[38] Caroline Robbins (ed.), *The Diary of John Milward, Esq., Member of Parliament for Derbyshire, September, 1666 to May, 1668* (Cambridge, 1938), p. 181.

[39] Historical Manuscripts Commission (hereafter H.M.C.), *Report on the Manuscripts of Allan George Finch* (London, 1913–22), vol. II, p. 43.

[40] *Ibid.*; Morgan was born 1640, making him 38 years old in 1678.

[41] Henning, *The Commons*, vol. III, pp. 727–8; Sir Trevor had been committed to prison in Abergavenny for his part in hindering the Royalist efforts to besiege Hereford in 1645. He was released by King Charles I despite the protests of the marquis of Worcester, who had proposed that Williams be hanged along with other traitors in

the county.

[42] Arthur H. Dodd, ' "Tuning" the Welsh bench, 1680', *National Library of Wales Journal* 6 (1949–50), p. 250.

[43] *Idem, Studies in Stuart Wales* (Cardiff, 1952), p. 196.

[44] Bradney, *History of Monmouthshire* vol. III, pt. 1, p. 77; vol. IV, pt. 2, p. 249; vol. IV, pt. 1, pp. 76–7, 81.

[45] Many of these names come from a list of gentlemen who signed the 1667 election return. Worcester recognized these men as his opponents for he deprived a number of them of their place in the commissions of the peace. As time went on, other gentlemen, particularly those with property rights in Wentwood Forest, became enemies of the marquis. Bradney, *History of Monmouthshire*, vol. IV, pt. 1, p. 81; Jenkins found that political factions in Monmouthshire 'were often tied especially closely by marriage and kinship. In the 1670s, for example, there was a powerful Whig party among the county gentry, under the leadership of Sir Trevor Williams of Llangibby, and incorporating the Morgans of Tredegar, the Proberts of Penallt Argoed and the Vans of Llanwern.' Philip Jenkins, 'Party conflict and political stability in Monmouthshire, 1690–1740', *Historical Journal*, 29 (3) (1986), p. 560.

[46] Bradney, *History of Monmouthshire*, vol. IV, pt. 2, p. 185; P.R.O., C22/481/47; Rogers, *Memoirs of Monmouth-shire*, p. 93; National Library of Wales, Badminton Manorial Records 1809; *ibid.*, Tredegar Manuscripts and Documents 64/114, 59/28.

[47] P.R.O., SP 44/43, fo. 96v; Bodl. L., Carte ms 72, fos. 382–3; Jenkins, in his recent study of the south Wales gentry, suggested that the opposition to the marquis of Worcester was caused by religious divisions in post-Civil War Monmouthshire. Worcester, he wrote, 'was widely seen as a crypto-papist, still friendly with local Catholic gentry, and related to Catholic magnates in other shires'. The gentry feared that his Catholic sympathies, combined with his high military office, would lead to religious persecution and dictatorship. Although religious division played an important part in motivating the local gentry, it does not explain how Worcester came to be associated with the Popish Plot. I believe that Jenkins gives too much weight to the gentry's fear of Catholicism, overestimating their credulity and underestimating their capacity for political mischief. Underlying religious division were a number of long-standing personal and political motives for the gentry's actions against Worcester. Jenkins, *Making of a Ruling Class*, p. 125; *idem*, 'Anti-popery on the Welsh marches in the seventeenth century', *Historical Journal*, 23 (2) (1980), pp. 275–93.

[48] Bodl. L., Carte ms 72, fos. 378v, 382–3; Arnold's report was published two years later as 'An Abstract of Several Examinations Taken upon Oath in the Counties of Monmouth and Hereford And Delivered in to the Honorable House of Commons … Together with the Account given to the House of Commons the 12th of April, 1678. By John Arnold and John Scudamore, Esqs. of the Encouragement given to Popery in the Counties of Monmouth and Hereford' (London, 1680).

[49] Bodl. L., Carte ms, 72, fos. 382–3.

[50] Badminton Muniments FmE 4/5/2; Bodl. L., Carte ms 72, fo. 378v.

[51] *Ibid.*, fos. 382–3.

[52] Rogers, *Memoirs of Monmouth-shire*, p. 84.

[53] National Library of Wales, Badminton Manuscripts, Bc 2/41, Box 9, Monmouthshire, 1988 deposit.

[54] P.R.O., C22/478/25.

[55] Badminton Muniments FmE 3/16.

[56] Cited in Barry Coward, *The Stuart Age* (London, 1980), p. 281.

[57] National Library of Wales, Badminton Manorial Records 1804; H.M.C., *9th Report*, Appendix II (London, 1883–84), p. 116b; Sir Trevor Williams, MP for Monmouthshire, aided his brother-in-law by circulating the report to all Members of the House. Worcester wrote to his wife that 'Sir Trevor, being the same extravagant tales man that he ever was, is now spreading about papers to the members of the House of Commons ... on my punishing those that broke mine [privilege] on taking away the wood in Wentwood.' Badminton Muniments FmF 1/2/51.

[58] Badminton Muniments FmF 1/2/52.

[59] Mitchell, 'Nathan Rogers', p. 41; Shaftesbury also took a part in releasing Nathan Rogers from custody. Rogers had been arrested in August 1678, while the House was prorogued. After a month's imprisonment, he was forced to pay £40 and to give bond of £200 to appear at the next session of Parliament. On 12 November Shaftesbury made a motion 'for releasing Rogers as not duly taken into custody because in time of prorogation and without fees (but not agreed to, though it is possible upon the next motion it may)', Badminton Muniments FmF 1/2/58.

[60] Badminton Muniments FmF 1/2/67.

[61] John Kenyon, *The Popish Plot* (London, 1972), p. 95; in January 1679/80, the king ordered the garrison of Chepstow to be temporarily disbanded and the soldiers paid off (P.R.O., PC 2/68, 343). Bedloe, a Chepstow native, was the nephew of William Kemeys of Kemeys, one of the participants in the Wentwood Forest dispute. There is evidence that Bedloe was persuaded to serve as an informant against Worcester. The marchioness wrote to her husband, 'I am very confident and have some reason to be so, that he [Bedloe] is managed by those who are as malicious as can be to you; I hope in a short time to be able to give you a better account than I now can for what I write.' Bradney, *History of Monmouthshire*, vol. III, pt. 2, p. 175; Badminton Muniments FmE 4/1/5.

[62] P.R.O., SP 29/411, pt. 2, fo. 77.

[63] Henning, *The Commons*, vol. I, pp. 318–19.

[64] CSPD 1679–80, p. 483.

[65] Bodl. L., Carte ms 72, fo. 514.

[66] John Miller, *Charles II* (London, 1991), pp. 334–40; Ronald Hutton, *Charles the Second: King of England, Scotland and Ireland* (Oxford, 1990), pp. 395–6; Kenyon, *Popish Plot*, p. 203.

[67] Badminton Muniments FmE 3/3. The journal is printed in H.M.C., *12th Report*, Appendix IV (London, 1891), pp. 98–115. The notes appear to be in a hand similar to that of Charles, Lord Herbert. The young man apparently had been living with his father in London during the Popish Plot and Exclusion Crisis. On 10 November 1678, Worcester wrote to this wife, 'to acquaint Charles, that I am willing he should come to town, for this morning I spoke with my brother Essex, whom I find, as much of opinion, he should be here, as my brother Harry [Capel], and others of my friends'. Badminton Muniments FmF 1/2/56.

[68] Badminton Muniments FmE 3/3. Arnold moved 'for longer than one day for the notice of an election in boroughs', probably referring to the 1679 election for Monmouthshire which was supposed to have taken place at the county court on 28 August. But the sheriffs claimed that they did not have a writ, 'nor did know any thing of it; upon which all then attending were dismissed and the Court regularly adjourned'. However, at one o'clock that afternoon, the high sheriff came to town and called a

new court. The election proceedings continued despite the fact that many of the gentry had left town. National Library of Wales, Tredegar Manuscripts and Documents 59/15.

[69] Badminton Muniments FmE 3/3.

[70] *Ibid.*

[71] Rogers, *Memoirs of Monmouth-shire*, p. 67.

[72] *Ibid.*, pp. 67, 81; Daniel Williams, a bookseller who purchased a first edition of Rogers' *Memoirs* from the late duke of Sussex's estate in 1845, wrote that 'this first edition is exceedingly scarce ... The duke of Beaufort is stated to have bought up nearly all this impression and destroyed them to prevent their circulation'. His note is included in a copy of the *Memoirs* now belonging to the National Library of Wales.

6

In the mist of ceremony: cathedral and community in seventeenth-century Wells

Carl B. Estabrook

As powerful administrative and cultural institutions, English cathedrals brought life of a qualitatively distinct nature to the communities in which they were situated. Any settlement, no matter how small, was said to be a city if it contained a cathedral. For much of their history leading up to the middle of the seventeenth century, English cathedrals had the legal, political, ideological and material means to exercise control more generally over the lives of the communities in which they were located but of which they were not fully a part.[1] Thus, the complicated relationship between cathedrals and the cities in which they stood had significance beyond the spiritual issues and competing standards of moral conduct that were so important to early modern political culture. During the turbulent seventeenth century, the relationship between cathedral and community was altered in ways that point to larger cultural and political trends in English urban life. A closer look at this fascinating relationship allows us to understand in yet another way the incursion of outside authority in the lives of local communities and the resulting tensions which characterized and propelled the process of dramatic change in seventeenth-century England.

It must be said that the presence of a cathedral was not always in the local interest. All English cathedrals were part of a greater reticular power structure, the episcopacy, headed by the Crown at the political centre and administered hierarchically through a remote archdiocese. The corporation in the cathedral city of Durham held its charter not from the Crown but from the bishop of Durham.[2] As a target of recurring inconoclastic violence and armed political contention during the Civil War and again in the 1680s, a cathedral brought real trouble to the community dwelling in its shadow. In the 1640s, attacks on Wells Cathedral, a symbol of the religious opulence of central authorities, spilled over into the city itself where lay residents suffered £10,000 of damage to their homes and shops, according to contemporary estimates.[3] A cordwainer explained under examination in 1698 that when the Monmouth rebellion broke out nearby he actually fled the Liberty of St

Andrew's Cathedral in Wells, despite having secured an apprenticeship there, and headed for what he believed to be the relative safety of Spitalfields.[4] As one historian has remarked, Wells was used as a liturgical 'laboratory' by the infamous William Laud when he was bishop there in the 1620s.[5] In short, cathedrals were part of the centralized apparatus of conformity in a cultural and political landscape characterized by extreme local variation.

The dean and chapter at Wells, as well as the bishop in his palace there, exerted pressure on the local inhabitants in a number of problematic and unsympathetic ways. Like all diocesan officials, those under the bishop at Wells adjudicated, through probate, the evaluation and inheritance of property. A dean and chapter, governing a cathedral's own material interests, controlled land, housing and tenants.[6] Cathedral associates, with fixed incomes, were adversely affected by Elizabethan inflation, but cathedrals seem to have fared better than bishops in managing their estates until the Restoration,[7] perhaps by virtue of the more intimate scale of cathedral operations and the more immediate accessibility of their most important tenants. Bishops, many deans, and some archdeacons (diocesan representatives in cathedrals) presided in cathedral cities over ecclesiastical courts through which the laity, often local tenants of the cathedral itself, could be scrutinized, pressured and harassed.[8] So the complicated questions arise: did the cathedral in Wells enhance or undermine the local autonomy of the lay community dwelling in its shadow, and under what circumstances did the local laity benefit or suffer from the presence of the cathedral in their community?

There was dramatic change over time. The Civil War, although not the subject of this essay, was a pivotal episode, as we should suspect. Relations between cathedrals and the cities in which they were located were generally good in medieval and Tudor England. Civic leaders were principal donors to their cathedrals, especially for the improvement of the buildings themselves.[9] In 1446 the provisions drawn up for the administration of Bishop Bubwith's almshouse in Wells made co-operation between the cathedral chapter and the civic leadership an explicit requirement in that regard. In late medieval Wells, there was little or no apparent barrier between the cultural life of the cathedral and that of the town, especially on festival Sundays when the cathedral liturgy involved processions outside the church where the residents of Wells could hear the choir singing to them from behind the lifelike statues on the cathedral's west front.[10] The Reformation, a watershed that has already received close attention,[11] did remove chantries and other devotional links between cathedrals and local elites. Nevertheless, reformed cathedral charters reinforced the dominant role of cathedrals in those communities where they were located.

The conditions of the mid-seventeenth century, however, produced a lasting power shift in favour of civic autonomy. In Wells, good relations began to deteriorate near the end of Elizabeth's reign. During the generation leading up to the 1640s, cathedral communities like Wells were highly susceptible to objectionable pressures exerted from beyond the sphere of the local community.[12] During the Civil War, and the Interregnum that followed it, this pattern was disrupted by competition for local control, at first under the conditions of regional warfare and later in the institutional power vacuum created by the suspension of episcopacy during this phase. The very spaces occupied by cathedrals became theatres of contention. One Puritan divine installed as lecturer at Wells Cathedral during the 1650s found himself preaching to carefully staged parades of disruptive citizens who marched vociferously, even gaily, up and down the aisle during his services.[13] Even though bishops and cathedral chapters returned in the early years of the Restoration, the 'dilapidated bulks of the former cathedrals and episcopal palaces loomed over English cities as symbols of the defeat of the old order'.[14]

The disruptions caused by civil war and its aftermath produced material, political and symbolic changes in the relationship between cathedral and community in Wells. After 1660, the newly restored dean and chapter, working with barely a roof over their heads, found it difficult to make effective claims on the rents, tithes and markets, the control of which they had been forced to relinquish in the previous decade. As the waning influence of ecclesiastical courts suggest, the powers of cathedrals as agents of social control were in steady decline during the late seventeenth century.[15] For the citizens of Wells, the cathedral was transformed from an imposing object of deference into a civic asset. Indeed, after the Restoration in 1660, during the so-called urban renaissance that followed, Wells Cathedral operated more and more in the role of a cultural and social resource at the disposal of the local community. At the same time, assertions of civic autonomy adopted ritual forms appropriated from the cathedral itself.

The history of the early modern charters of Wells reflects the punctuated evolution of the relationship between cathedral and community.[16] The charters of the late sixteenth century met with opposition from the high clergy in Wells but this gave way, after a century or so, to the robust application and celebration of charters by a civic community seemingly oblivious to the former claims of the bishops and cathedral clergy. The legal status of Wells with respect to the cathedral and bishop was somewhat ambiguous in the seventeenth century, a period of profound transition in this regard shaped by a complex mixture of antagonism, confusion, appropriation and co-operation. In the medieval period Wells was clearly established as an ecclesiastical borough; that is to say, the bishop, dean and chapter were entitled to exact fees, fines and deference from the inhabitants and merchants in Wells. Thus, the 1574 charter of Queen Elizabeth raised so many questions and objections from Bishop Berkeley of Bath and Wells, that it was effectively blocked by him until 1589 when a new charter more favourable to the bishop and cathedral was produced by the Crown. The bishop, who was lord of the manor of Wells, had good reason to suppose that a corporate charter would undermine his position in the very community where his palace and cathedral were located. In 1588 the commonality of Wells resorted to petitioning Chancery to prevail upon the new bishop, Thomas Godwyn, who was withholding permission for a charter.[17] In the end the bishop exacted a fee of £130 from the citizens and agreed to comply with the series of chartered privileges issued as 31 Elizabeth in the summer of 1589.

Within two years Elizabeth proclaimed a charter to 'erect and found' the Cathedral Church of Wells 'anew and to ornament and endow the same with proper officers, dignities, revenues and possessions ... with which it was formerly endowed'. This reaffirmed the cathedral's forty-nine prebends, lands granted to provide revenues for the cathedral clergy; it required the city of Wells to pay £42 2s in 'pension, portion, yearly rent', and the provost of Wells £20 annually, to the dean and chapter; it required the vicarage of St Cuthbert's parish in Wells to pay the dean and chapter £20 annually, in contrast to the yearly fees of less than £1 so required of other Somerset parishes, including Freshford whose rectory was required to pay only 8d annually; and it granted the dean and chapter governing power over the existing almshouse, its inmates, endowments and revenues, a power which the cathedral in effect continued to share with the civic leadership until the Civil War.[18]

The prominence of the city of Wells and its parishioners as tributaries singled out for disproportionately burdensome financial commitments to the dean and chapter is one of two especially significant aspects of this new cathedral charter. The other is the timing of the charter's appearance. The dean and chapter of Wells Cathedral had asked for new statutes in 1536, but even the circumstances of the Reformation were not enough to promote their request which the Crown at that time ignored.[19] Instead, the granting of the Elizabethan charter to Wells Cathedral followed closely the city's own controversial new shift in status, but it seems to have done little to mollify the tension between cathedral and community which, by the late sixteenth century, the Crown could hardly ignore. Despite whatever good intentions Elizabeth and her advisors may have had, these charters in Wells raised as many contentious issues as they resolved. The boundaries of the city and borough, for example, as carefully laid out by Elizabethan charter, ran directly 'through the orchard of the Bishop of Bath and Wells', rendering the boundary between civic and ecclesiastical space ambiguous at best.

It seems that the Wells charter granted by Elizabeth was surrendered by the city under Charles II not long after the Restoration, but the destruction and theft of records during the intervening period of violence left some details unclear. By 1684 a restoration of privileges was granted to the city by the charter of 35 Charles II. The right to elect mayors and a body of civic leaders for self-governance was made explicit in James II's Letters Patent for Corporations, but because these were awarded to Wells in 1688, as James himself fell from power, their efficacy was questionable.[20] Charles II's charter had designated Richard Hole as the 'first mayor' of Wells, a pointed bit of revision in view of the fact that Wells city recorders had been making references to the mayors of Wells as far back as 1378, the year with which this roll of mayors, uninterrupted until the middle of the seventeenth century, begins.[21] In short, the civic leadership of Wells, the high clergy in their midst and the authors of royal charters, all held views of the local polity that were, in pivotal ways, at odds with one another. There was a medieval charter issued by King John, but its language was so vague on the subject of incorporation that it allowed competing interpretations to develop. Bishop Ralph, in the mid-fourteenth century, simply had the city's charter revoked. At times, however, the cathedral itself appears to have benefited from the *de facto* existence of a mayor in Wells when families with cathedral connections were promoted to that office. Richard Godwyn, for example, had been 'mayor' of Wells in the 1560s, before an Elizabethan charter even existed, and became recorder of the city in 1591 and an MP for Wells in 1593.

In other recurring areas of contention between cathedral and community, the later seventeenth-century Wells city charters provided for new expressions of local autonomy that were less ambiguous. The 1684 charter of 35 Charles II officially granted the city the right to conduct an annual Wells Fair to be held 'Thursday in mid-Lent to last for two days in place of that on Ascension Day' and granted 'two markets, the first on Wednesday in every second week, and on the first Wednesday in every month, the one for wool and the other for horses'.[22] Thus, control over an annual fair and three markets each month finally placed the civic leadership on level footing with the bishop and the cathedral in the city's open commercial space. Indeed, the language of the 1684 charter reflected the Crown's sensitivity toward the volatile nature of relations between the city of Wells and those high clergy whose power base had always been located in that community. The charter pointedly includes the declaration that the rights and privileges so granted to the city were valid 'not being in any thing prejudicial to the Bishop of Bath and Wells and his successors for the time being or his Liberties nor to the Dean and Chapter of the Cathedral Church of Wells or their successors'.[23] The charter also made it very clear that the city was duly incorporated and enjoyed the right to elect its own mayors.

In 1688 the corporation seized an opportunity when William III's call for corporations to elect MPs nearly fell upon the centenary of the city's contested Elizabethan charter. The old charter was ceremoniously produced by the clerk and reviewed by the corporation, who responded to the king on 11 January 1689 that they had held an 'election being made according to the ancient usage and custom of elections for Parliaments within the said city and elected Edward Berkeley and Thomas Wyndham, esquires after due notice of the time and place of such election given to all parties therein concerned'.[24] The corporation included neither cathedral canons nor members of the bishop's family; in fact, it included Mr Hole, the descendant of a city resident known for opposing Bishop Laud during his tenure at Wells, and Mr Broadbeard, who was the most prominent citizen to tangle with the bishop over the shifting locus of control in the market-place.[25] Two days earlier the corporation, clearly inspired by the convergence of politically and symbolically significant moments, made a great show of civic autonomy and localism. 'At this meeting the charter of Queen Elizabeth dated 23 July 31 Elizabeth [1589] of her reign was taken out and delivered to Mr. Mayor with directions to advise upon it and to defend the inhabitants of Wells from appearing at Bruton [Somerset] Sessions which this to be done at the expense of the corporation … also that no burgess shall be put on any jury outside the city.' In September of that year the corporation trotted out the Elizabethan charter once again, this time 'defending the inhabitants of this Citty from appearing at any general Quarter Sessions of the peace' other than those held in Wells, where the mayor and recorder of the city held the right to serve as justices.[26] In these and other meaningful actions, the citizens of Wells in the last decades of the seventeenth century laid claim to their own civic jurisdiction. More significantly, perhaps, they displayed a historical awareness in resuscitating civic privileges that had been trampled upon during the preceding century.

The relationship between cathedral and community, and the shifting balance of power in this relationship, was very much rooted in the control of property and income. In theory, a cathedral had positive redistributive effects on the economy of the host city by virtue of transforming rural rents into urban purchases and payments.[27] But by the sixteenth century the dean and chapter of Worcester Cathedral had acquired nearly 20 per cent of all the houses in that city while in Winchester the High Street was lined with shops belonging to the dean and chapter there. In Wells the dean and chapter owned fifteen buildings in the market square alone. They also owned the city's main inn, The White Hart in Sadler Street, which was within view of the cathedral itself. In short, the cathedral in Wells controlled the entire commercial centre of the community.[28] So to a large extent the flow of payments within a cathedral city was toward the dean and chapter. Perhaps it was only fitting that during the Civil War local residents at St Asaph, Exeter, and Salisbury turned the cathedrals there into wine shops, sugar factories and taverns of their own.[29] In the first half of the seventeenth century the dean and chapter of Wells, who were not bound within the Liberty of the cathedral to honour the protective guild restrictions of the city, drew skilled artisans from outside the community.[30] Of fifty Wells girls and boys whose apprenticeships were arranged by St Cuthbert's overseers between 1662 and 1700, only one secured a position in the Cathedral Liberty.[31] Nevertheless, the condition in which the cathedral was left by the violence and iconoclasm of the Civil War did change matters. In the first year of the Restoration, the dean and chapter paid £1,309 10d to dozens of named artisans and labourers of whom at least some, if not all, were Wells residents at work on the extensive cathedral repairs. William Bartholomew, a tiler and one of the city's poor relief administrators, brought in £33 19s 2d from the work on the cathedral in that year.[32]

Before the Civil War and Interregnum, the bishop, dean and chapter, and their bailiffs were very much in control of the Wells market-place itself as well as physical access to it. Local farmers complained that the bishop drove cattle across their land or allowed them to stray[33] while the bailiff of the dean and chapter routinely confiscated any cattle or other animals that appeared within the cathedral close, a situation which created problems for people in the market-place just outside the cathedral gates. During the Civil War and Interregnum, while diocesan and capitular authority were suspended, the citizens of Wells grew accustomed to moving themselves and their goods freely through the gates of their city. As one elderly deponent explained in 1664, the dean and chapter had always kept gates leading out of town through the Liberty, such as Browne's Gate, closed to community traffic until the 'chains were broken down at the beginning of the late troubles' more than twenty years earlier. After the Restoration, when the cathedral replaced the chains, Wells citizens boldly cut them down again claiming that roads leading to market are 'a common highway'.[34] Some time after 1652, the citizens of Wells began holding their own pig and sheep market and maintaining a pigpen in the High Street.[35] After the Restoration, this enfuriated the bishop whose prerogatives and tolls had been usurped. Armed with a new charter and corporate connections in 1684, Robert Broadbeard, the Wells wine merchant who championed the community's pig and sheep market, successfully stood his ground.[36] In 1660, the newly restored dean and chapter complained on behalf of one of the canons, whose house was among those in the cathedral Liberty, that in the midst of the rubble caused by the war 'there is a great market house built before the door of this canonical house, which hath drawn the market from other parts to the very doors of this house, to the great annoyance of the said house'.[37] By the time of the Restoration, the citizens of Wells had not only claimed control of the city's open spaces for commercial activity, they had transformed cathedral spaces for their own commercial purposes.

The most extensive material relations between cathedral and community were based on tenancy. From the thirteenth century, a major portion of Wells fell within Canon Grange, manorial holdings of the cathedral. By the seventeenth century, the dean and chapter owned over 140 properties in Wells.[38] Prominent Wells families, including those of several mayors and city recorders, were tenants of the dean and chapter.[39] Even the lesser associates at the cathedral wielded this sort of power over the laity in Wells; in the 1620s William Hunte, one of the vicars choral, was the landlord of residential properties in Chamberlain Street.[40] During the Interregnum, Wells residents suffered by virtue of the very fact that they were cathedral tenants. In 1630, Ambrose Martin, a Wells clothier, having paid an initial fine of £4, became a tenant of the dean and chapter in St Andrew's Street, near the Liberty, at an annual rent of 12s.[41] But, when the government surveyors sorted out claims in 1649, Martin could produce no proof of this arrangement, so the ownership of his dwelling was transferred to the city and his rent raised by a factor of five to £3 10*s* per annum.[42] During the war and its aftermath, the city acquired several of the cathedral's properties in Wells, including canonical houses, some of which the city demolished and sold as materials.

It is scarcely surprising, in view of this reversal, that the cathedral's ability to exert power over the local laity was less keenly felt at the Restoration than it had been in the early seventeenth century. In many Wells locations the dean and chapter, after their return, became tenants of the city. In fact, Richard Thomas, the city receiver in 1667, recorded that the dean and chapter were 4*s* behind in their rent payments owed to the city that year.[43] The cathedral's ability to enforce rent collection from its own tenants had been seriously undermined. During the first year of their restoration, the cathedral spent at least £151 5*s* 9*d* more than its own agents could collect.[44] Richard Busby, the communar in 1689, calculated that rents still in arrears to the dean and chapter for the years following the Restoration exceeded £935 and were £227 8*s* 2*d* for the current year alone.[45] As stipulated in the cathedral's Reformation charter, fabric maintenance relied on rents from the cathedral's holdings in the tiny village of Biddisham, Somerset. In 1665 these amounted to £19 13*s* and were grossly inadequate given the cathedral's awesome requirements for recovery.[46] In view of this critical situation, the dean urged the prebendaries to contribute one quarter of their own revenues to repair 'the whole structure of the same [cathedral] which was miserably damaged in the late troubles, almost from the foundations, at great expense, beyond our means, and hardly to be believed'.[47]

Ordinary tenants of the cathedral readily perceived the weakness of the dean and chapter, and the temptation to evade the payment of rents and dues was too great for some to resist. Philip Ball, whose family was known never to deny the dean and chapter their rents before the 1640s, refused in 1665 to pay his annual St Martin's portion of wheat grown on cathedral lands in Easton. Ball swore audaciously in court that for 'neere forty yeares' rent to the cathedral 'was never paid to his knowledge by him or his predecessors and doth deny that taking advantage of the late troubles he did for that reason deny payment thereof'.[48] The posturing of cathedral tenants like Philip Ball should be contrasted with the seeming fearfulness of the lay tenants in the early seventeenth century. At that time some offenders hauled before cathedral courts for failing to attend church pleaded in their own defence that church was where tenants in debt could expect to be apprehended by ecclesiastical authorities, creditors or both.[49]

We should turn here to the disciplinary role of the high clergy in the lives of the laity who lived among them. In 1609 the Bishop of Bath and Wells, James Montague, printed a manual advising clergy, churchwardens and 'swornemen' of the diocese in the preparations for his visitations.[50] Article 5 moved swiftly to the crux of the matter; it stated that it was an offence to 'impugne the government of the Church of England under the King's most excellent Majesty by Archbishops, Bishops, Deanes, Archdeacons and the rest ... affirming that the same is Anti-Christian, or repugnant to the Word of God'. By the authority of ecclesiastical courts, the preface charged the clergy and wardens to enforce these articles governing personal conduct 'with an earnest zeal to maintain truth and suppress vice'. Bishop Montague encouraged agents of the Church to object to anything or anyone they regarded as suspicious or faulty, 'any matter of Ecclesiastical conezance worthy of presentment in your judgement'. In the early seventeenth century, therefore, agents of the diocese and the cathedral exercised arbitrary powers of scrutiny and legal pressure over most aspects of personal, spiritual and, as we have seen, material life. Moreover, it was an offence in itself to deliver 'any railing, reproachful, or disgraceful speeches of the King's Majesties [*sic*] Courts Ecclesiastical or the proceedings thereof'.

Given the bishop's explicit concern over this last matter, we should wonder who, apart from the ungodly, objected to the ecclesiastical courts. There is some evidence showing that parish elites in most villages and towns made enthusiastic use of archdeacon's courts to report the moral offences of their inferiors.[51] By contrast, wardens in cathedral cities could be less than zealous in the official detection of vice and disorder among their lay neighbours. In Winchester, a larger cathedral city than Wells, detailed *detecta* survive for eleven urban parishes during the seventeenth century.[52] The ecclesiastical court presentment records for 1618, probably near the peak of parochial moral vigilance in England, show that Winchester churchwardens made only three presentments concerning moral offences (one for bastardy and two for drunkenness). Recusancy, poor attendance at church and rates evasion were expressed concerns of churchwardens throughout the century. But, unless church fabric or possessions were in need of attention, Winchester churchwardens solicited by the bishop or archdeacon for presentments during the period after the Restoration responded with 'we know nothing presentable' or, more succinctly, 'nil'. And this body of evidence contains only two presentments for moral offences made by Winchester churchwardens over the entire period between 1668 and 1700.[53] It appears that in at least one cathedral city, churchwardens, leading members of the local laity, were reluctant to partake in the disciplinary business of the high clergy at work in their community, before the Restoration as well as after it.

As members of the lay community in Wells sought to express autonomy through the evasion of ecclesiastical courts, they also dissociated themselves from the more objectionable methods of coercion and scrutiny identified with the cathedral. Indeed, the community of Wells strenuously maintained its identity as an autonomous disciplinary body. Civic authorities in Wells took matters of local discipline into their own hands to the extent of detaining clergy, as in the case of the Reverend Thomas Davis who, in May of 1615, was imprisoned there until he could appear at the Wells quarter sessions 'to answer for being drunke and disturbing the watch'.[54] Ordained deputies of bishops frequently attended assizes, and sometimes quarter sessions, in the seventeenth century to ensure that benefit of clergy was granted to such a person as Thomas Davis.[55] In erecting their own ducking stool, iron pillory and stocks as early as 1611, and maintaining them until at least 1706,[56] the citizens of Wells had equipped themselves to deal with the matter of lay discipline without deferring to the authorities at the cathedral and the bishop's palace. This helps to explain why apparitors, special agents and informants employed by a diocese or cathedral, who appear to have been less active in other types of community,[57] were aggressive in and around Wells. A Mr Jackson, the 'perritor' in Wells, was so extortionate in his use of arbitrary power that in 1614 several local villagers testified against him at the Taunton assizes.[58] To be 'detected' by the ecclesiastical court meant a trip under duress to Wells or defiance as a nonconformist or excommunicant,[59] a fact which should prompt us to reconsider how favourably cathedral cities were viewed by people who lived outside of those communities before the decline of consistory courts in the late seventeenth century.

Of course, the ecclesiastical courts in cathedral cities also adjudicated cases initiated by the laity, usually over marital disputes, defamation or competing claims to prominent church pews.[60] In the first half of the seventeenth century, however, Wells citizens were remarkably under-represented among laity who initiated disputes of this sort, suggesting that proximity to the courts of the bishop, dean and archdeacon bred local contempt for them during that period.[61]Indeed, in 1625 the civic leaders at Wells forbade the use of ecclesiastical courts for internal disputes, declaring 'no burgess to sue another in any court but the Mayor's under penalty of the former law'. In related actions, Wells citizens appealed successfully to the civic authorities to avoid suits in the ecclesiastical court. Thomas Midlam, the opponent of John Crees, a former constable in Wells, was forced by the mayor's court to pay Crees the hefty sum of £10 for having tried to sue him in the bishop's Threeweaken court at the cathedral.[62]

After the Restoration, the business of ecclesiastical courts was effectively reduced to cases initiated by the laity on their own behalf concerning defamation or inheritance. Even in this period, Wells residents were significantly under-represented. In three years of bishop's court activity in Wells between 1678 and 1680, out of more than 250 depositions only three were taken from Wells residents, witnesses rather than litigants in all but one testamentary case. Moreover, one witness testified that a Mr Hellyer called a Mr Quirke a 'rogue two or three times and did wonder that the Lord Bishop would keep such rogues about him'.[63] Robert Quirke, identified as a rector of the dean and chapter, cropped up again in 1706 when a Mr Francis Day of Wells repeatedly called him 'an old knave' in front of a group of customers, including the famous Dr Claver Morris, relaxing (of all places) at the Mitre Tavern.[64] By 1705, Mary Fry, a produce vendor in Wells, sued Peter Chinn for his amusing but defamatory remarks made at the Globe Inn concerning

Fry's daughter and her peas. Fry was careful to point out that 'Peter Chinn lives in Walcombe in the outparish of St. Cuthbert's in Wells and within the jurisdiction of the Dean of Wells'.[65] Indeed, this defamation case brought by a Wells resident suggests that, after the seventeenth century, ordinary citizens had begun to view the judicial business of the cathedral as a special resource at the disposal of the city, rather than as an imposition of an external authority. Where local property matters were concerned, this view began developing not long after the Restoration; in 1665 a Wells creditor by the name of William Keeke used the bishop's bailiff to confiscate the cattle of an evasive debtor from the neighbouring village of Dulcote.[66] By 1693 the mayor of Wells, who appointed churchwardens in the parish of St Cuthbert's, used the dean and chapter to enforce rates collection there.[67]

In cathedral cities, which were often the locations of assize and quarter sessions courts, high clergy exercised power in secular courts as well in the first half of the seventeenth century. The dean of Wells Cathedral occasionally heard quarter sessions cases there, as he did in 1607 when those indicted parties who were citizens of Wells refused to recognize the dean's authority in that court.[68] At this stage, royal authority supported the claims of the cathedral. 'Be it known that through the great care and charge of his Majesty's Justices of the Peace of this County, a strong convenient room adjoining to the Cathedral Church of Wells, by consent of the Dean and Chapter there, is provided for the safe keeping of the Indictments, Inrollment of deeds, and the other Records of the Sessions of this County, there to remain for the ever hereafter, whomever shall happen to be the clerk of the Peace.'[69] In 1609, Anthony Hendborowe was harassed through an ecclesiastical court at Wells by a vengeful man whom Hendborowe had identified as the paternal culprit in a bastardy case heard not in the ecclesiastical court but at the Chard assizes. That ecclesiastical courts were perceived by the local laity as being in competition with lay courts, and possibly with the cause of justice itself, was expressed further in Hendborowe's petition to Sir Edward Phelips, a Somerset JP. Hendborowe lamented that the malicious case 'doth vex and molest ... your worship's poor suppliant with the Lord Bishop's court at Wells to the utter overthrow and impoverishing of your poor distressed suppliant unless he may be by this honorable Bench ... freed out of the said Spiritual Court'.[70] Clergy with cathedral connections were among the harshest justices in cases concerning local laity. The JP who ordered in 1630 that the mother of an illegitimate child in St Cuthbert's should be whipped through the streets of Wells was Paul Godwyn, Doctor of Divinity there.[71] In 1634, when Bishop Piers presided over the quarter sessions at Wells, William Bull (probably the same man who had already served as mayor three times) and his friends created such a drunken disturbance over the JPs, whom they 'affronted with very contemptious speeches', that the quarter sessions 'in regard of the example and frequent number of offences of this kinde, thought fitt to commend the consideration thereof unto his Majesty's Attorney General'.[72]

The situation at Wells quarter sessions changed after the Restoration, even before Wells received its undisputed corporate charter in 1684. Certainly by 1675, William Salmon, identified as 'Mayor of the said Cittie or Burough' of Wells, was hearing quarter sessions cases in his city.[73] As the cathedral's role of adjudicator declined and power shifted towards the civic authorities in Wells, the mayor presided over trials concerning religious issues, recusancy in particular, while violent adulterers actually sought refuge in the cathedral court.[74] The reversal must have seemed complete when, in 1682, Charles Baron, identified as Mayor of Wells, presided there over the quarter sessions case of Thomas Lane, the bishop's apparitor in Wells, apprehended for stealing a pound of combed wool from the house of Thomas Salmon, a stocking-maker in St Cuthbert's.[75]

The dean and chapter at Wells had considerable and continuous difficulty disciplining people attached to the cathedral itself. In 1684 two vicars choral 'riotously' assaulted the son of a resident cathedral canon and his attendant at a Wells tavern.[76] In 1691 Thomas Webb, master of the choristers by the end of the seventeenth century, made flagrantly obscene gestures to the presiding canon and son of the former dean in full view of people gathered in the cathedral.[77] By the 1680s, associates of the cathedral appear to have been reduced to squabbling among themselves, but clerical misconduct in the decades before the Civil War surely undermined the credibility of the cathedral and its relations with the local community.

In the generations of disorder before the mid-seventeenth century, Wells Cathedral associates were conspicuously unruly in ways that undermined local respect for the cathedral while promoting resentment and anti-cathedral sentiment within the local community. In 1591 Roger Rugge, one of the vicars choral, had been caught running an alehouse from within the cathedral close.[78] Mary Clark, the wife of one of the vicars choral, while visiting a residence in Wells, said that 'the ministers were whoremasters and drunckards', a remark which came to the dean's attention in 1628 but for which Clark did not do penance until 1635.[79] The wives of vicars choral brawled openly in the cathedral itself, and in one case this led to bloodshed when one wife, using her lifted leg, barred another wife's entrance to her pew of choice.[80] To the dismay of the dean in the early seventeenth century, the vicars choral would stroll about Wells *non togati* (without their robes) spreading gossip about the cathedral canons. John Corne, one of the vicars choral, used 'very irreverent words of the canons ... viz that he cared not a fart for any doctors of this Church'.[81] Associates of Wells Cathedral were notoriously irreligious. It was well known that even the so-called resident canons of provincial cathedrals spent as little time in them as possible. In the 1580s two vicars choral at Wells were known to have gone without communion for four years running and there was little sign that the devotional practices of Wells Cathedral vicars improved over the long haul.[82] A Mr Yarrow, while attending a service in the cathedral quire in 1628, exchanged loud insults with William Clun, one of the vicars choral, whom Yarrow claims called him a 'base scurvy bitinge fellow' who does nothing but 'eate upp poor folks victualls', to which Yarrow replied that the cathedral vicar was 'a base fellow and sheten [*sic*] priest … hackney priest and stone priest'.[83]

Before the Civil War there were several known recusants among the family members of Wells Cathedral associates, a fact that must have been especially annoying to Wells residents at a time when failure to attend cathedral services there left one open to prosecution as a 'popish recusant'.[84] Long before 1626, when Laud took up residence in the bishop's palace in Wells, some local merchants and civic leaders regarded the cathedral as a suspiciously popish influence in the community. Dean Haydon sponsored church ales there in the first decade of the seventeenth century. On one particularly carnivalesque occasion, Haydon openly taunted the Puritan faction in Wells by orchestrating pageants featuring cathedral choristers, dressed as pagan goddesses singing sacred hymns, and miners in unflattering costumes, posing as prominent local Puritans, delivering mock sermons at the market High Cross.[85] In view of the fact that the sixteenth-century cathedral at Wells was known for the reforming zeal of William Turner (the Edwardian dean and author of *The Hunting of the Romish Fox*) and Matthew Sutcliffe (a prebendary and prolific author of anti-Catholic tracts) the popishness of the cathedral in Laud's time was all the more notorious. Despite the fact that the archdeacon of Wells himself had denounced the cathedral's Laudian liturgy as a pernicious 'mist of ceremonies',[86] the presence of the cathedral in Wells saddled the residents of that community with an unpleasant reputation for popishness which survived the Civil War and Interregnum. In 1664, John Hooper of Nether Stowey, twenty miles west of Wells Cathedral, shouted from the door of his cottage that he might as well go to Rome as go to the city of Wells. Hooper complained pointedly that the apparitor from Wells was after him and not the village vicar, a 'raskall' who, in a shaming ritual of the kind once favoured by the cathedral, 'made a poor wench to stand in a white sheet in the church and he himself waring the Whore of Babilon's smock in the pulpit that he taketh himself to be something when he is nothing'.[87]

In the decades leading up to the Civil War, the importance that Wells citizens attached to the sacred space of the cathedral itself diminished. In 1605, the seven aldermen and sixteen common council members were still paying the cathedral sexton to 'provide and kepe decent places for the xxiii to sit when they come to the sermon in [the Cathedral Church of] St. Andrew', and fifteen years later they paid the cathedral to build special seats for the aldermen's wives.[88] But, when a street riot involving weapons broke out in 1615, the city constables were all found at evening prayer in the parish church of St Cuthbert's; none could be found worshipping at the cathedral, much less defending it from possible harm.[89] A clash between civic and cathedral leadership over the control of sacred space in Chester, beginning with the dean's refusal to allow the mayor to process in the cathedral behind his sword of office, resulted in a stunning general boycott of cathedral services by the residents of that city in the 1630s.[90]

Actions of civic and parish leaders clearly illustrate the fact that lay residents of Wells had come to regard St Cuthbert's as the civic space of worship in the early seventeenth century. An alderman, William Bull, disregarded the cathedral in his 1623 will and provided instead for £20 annually toward sermons to be delivered in St Cuthbert's Church 'whereby all may be influenced truly in the right and true fundamental grounding of the Christian religion', leaving us to wonder what regard he had for the preaching of Wells Cathedral canons. He specified that an endowed sermon should be given 'every year yearly forever' before his civic brethren in St Cuthbert's on the Sunday after Trinity in the morning so as not to conflict with the parish's afternoon sermon. The fact that this did conflict with the cathedral sermon was hardly lost on Bishop Lake. He allowed the endowed sermons to take place in St Cuthbert's but required Bull's widow and executrix to reschedule them for afternoons because 'all the parishioners of the parish of St. Cuthbert's in Wells have (every Sabboth day throughout the year yearly in the forenoon) to come up the St. Andrew's (the Cathedral Church) to the sermon there'.[91] At some point between 1640 and the suspension of episcopacy, during the 'sequestration' of St Cuthbert's own vicar, Mr Westley, the civic leaders of Wells petitioned Parliament for the use of two ministers from nearby villages because of 'the sad condition they [Wells residents] were reduced unto for want of the due preaching of God's word amongst them'.[92] The cathedral was within walking distance but, in all its grandness and splendour, it could provide neither the sacred space nor the spiritual guidance that Wells residents sought for themselves; they wished to assemble in their own church and preferred the care of village preachers to that of cathedral canons.

After the Restoration the identification of St Cuthbert's with the collective identity of the lay community in Wells clearly remained. The cathedral had become an attractive option for the residents of Wells, but after their 1684 charter the corporation went so far as to bring preachers of their own choosing into the cathedral on special civic occasions.[93] The corporation's seats in the cathedral cost them £2 15s 6d per annum, and provided a splendid context for visibility, but attendance was no longer compulsory for Wells residents. In fact, in 1672 the dean and chapter produced a rather odd resolution by which it advised its associates that those residents of Wells who wished to attend common prayer at the cathedral should be treated courteously. They added, 'the wives and daughters of both the gentry and the clergy dwelling within the Liberties of the Cathedral may be allowed to occupy the stalls and seats which are usually assigned to persons of their rank; but to others outside this privilege is denied'.[94] As far as the use of sacred space was concerned, the cathedral had come to view itself as the centre of its own intramural community.

The cathedral had always been extraparochial, a fact which created the potential for serious resentment within the community of Wells itself. The Liberty of St Andrew was part of the Canon Grange, or manorial estates, of the dean and chapter and was exempt from the parochial apparatus of poor relief and infrastructural maintenance in Wells. There is no mention of over-seers of the poor among Liberty residents until 1827 when they appear as ten-ants of the grange at 7 St Andrew Street.[95] Not all tourists were drawn to the cathedral purely for inspiration; many came to Wells as beggars while others were, at the very least, a nuisance spreading beyond the confines of the cathe-dral. In the Easter season of 1706, members of the corporation finally com-plained that 'strangers having intruded themselves into the corporation seats in St. Cuthbert's Church and also into the seats of the Masters [aldermen's] wives, the corporation ordered locks to be put on the doors'.[96] The situation was more serious in the seventeenth century up until the last serious plague struck in the 1660s, when the casual almsgiving of the cathedral may have done as much to draw the poor and suffering to Wells as relieve the prob-lems of people residing just outside the Liberty. In the 1640s, special petitions were made to the JPs, in some cases by Liberty residents themselves, to empower constables to make special ratings of the Liberty, exceptions which the exigencies of civil war forced the dean and chapter, on the verge of elim-ination, to allow.[97]

The situation was quite different by the late seventeenth century. Cathe-dral handouts for the poor of Wells amounted to less in 1680 (£8 13s 4d) than they had in 1599 (£12, the sum called for in the chapter acts of the 1590s).[98] The dean and chapter continued to hand out bread to the poor at Michael-mas, seemingly as a gesture in the new spirit of public relations as these events were accompanied by bonfires, bell-ringing and merriment sponsored by the dean and chapter after 1667.[99] The bishops of Wells had always made volun-tary donations to local poor relief and this practice continued after the Restoration, but in qualitatively different ways. Between 1684 and 1691, Bishop Kenn, the famous non-juror, interacted directly with the ordinary res-idents of Wells, the poorest of whom were invited to dine every Sunday night in the massive Great Hall of the bishop's palace.[100] This was within a seven-acre enclosure in which most Wells residents of previous generations never set foot unless they were in trouble and under duress. By 1691 the corpora-tion was asserting the right of approval over applications for settlement within the cathedral's Liberty.[101] Three years later, Mayor Charles Baron actu-ally removed a poor dependent from St Cuthbert's to the Liberty of St Andrew, noting quite pointedly that this action was initiated by the 'citty' while the Liberty and its constable were directed to enforce it.[102]

The administration of almshouses in Wells, a point of co-operative con-vergence for cathedral and community in late medieval and Tudor times, pro-duced revealing divisions during the first half of the seventeenth century. Bishop Bubwith's almshouse in Chamberlain Street was governed jointly, as stipulated in the provisions of 1446, by its own chaplain, the master of the city (mayor) and one representative of the cathedral chapter. In 1609, two years after Bishop Still left £500 to expand the almshouse, it became necessary to draw up an additional agreement among the late bishop's executor, the dean and chapter and the civic leaders to ensure that the inmates for which the new endowment provided were poor 'of the Cittie or Borroughe of Wells' or at least 'have been resident in Wells for the space of not less than seven whole years'.[103] After all, Bubwith's almshouse was next to St Cuthbert's Church, not within the cathedral close, and by 1617 the clerk of the almshouse, viewing it as parochial space, began referring to it as St Cuthbert's almshouse.[104] By his will dated 22 July 1614, Henry Llewellyn, a private citizen of Wells, had left £500 to endow an altogether separate almshouse to be run by the mayor, masters and burgesses without diocesan or capitular control. Land was bought in Wedmore to serve as income property, but it was not until the 1630s that the almshouse in Priest Row was erected with the proceeds from Llewellyn's endowment. In that same period, Mayor Walter Brick negotiated a lease with the dean and two of his chapter consultants, Dr Paul Godwyn and Dr Revett, whereby the city would pay 10s annually to the dean and chapter and £1 10s annually to the old almshouse in exchange for the ground on which housing for more of the city's own alms recipients was built.[105] In short, the community and the cathedral had established control over separate almsgiving institutions within the city. We should wonder why the residents of Wells should have wanted to make this so.

It was not the case that local laity were uncharitable or unco-operative in general. A voluntary collection for the plague victims of Taunton in 1640 raised £36 from the inhabitants of Wells 'except for the dean and chapter and my lord bishop' as the city clerk pointedly observed.[106] In the absence of a cathedral chapter during the Civil War and Interregnum, the almshouses in Wells carried on under the complete control of civic leadership. The hardships of war did present Wells almshouse administrators with occasional revenue problems, such as those expressed by one farming tenant on Llewellyn manor lands who complained that the 'Parliament Armie' exacted 18s 8d from him for provisions, bullets and powder while 'the tropers did with their horses eate upp my grasse at the spring of the year' depriving him of a harvest worth £1.[107] Nevertheless, almsgiving institutions in Wells remained surprisingly solvent despite the war.

Accounts of the various institutions make it clear that members of the lay community supported purely civic almsgiving efforts more readily than those involving the cathedral.[108] In fact, the records of rent collection and arrears for Bishops Still's almshouse in Wells for the middle decades of the seventeenth century show that tenants of almshouse lands were more co-operative during the hardship years coinciding with alms administration free of cathedral influence.[109] In 1630, while the management of that almshouse was still run jointly by cathedral and community, the administrators managed to collect £33 12s 6d, while £75 12s 11d remained uncollected from previous years.

By far the most successful year in the decade before the Civil War was 1637–8 when the administrators brought in £63 16s 1d, an unusually high sum but only a fraction of the £194 13s owed to them. Amounts actually collected, as opposed to simply owed, dwindled as hostilities intensified on the verge of war so that the figure for the year 1641–2 was a meagre £15 13s 4d. At the end of the very next year there was a startling contrast; with the agents of the cathedral newly removed, the civic governors of Still's almshouse collected £40 3s 4d. Significantly, the tenants became steadily more co-operative as the war proceeded and cathedral influence receded. In 1649 the sum actually collected by the lay governors of the almshouse reached £93 5s, £139 3s 4d in 1651–2, and £192 13s 4d in 1652–3. After the dean and chapter resumed their role in the collection of rents during the Restoration, tenants became less co-operative; the governors could collect only £27 10d in 1666–7 and between £31 and £41 per annum for the rest of the decade. Simply put, these remarkable fluctuations in arrears rates reflected, in large part, the anti-cathedral sentiment which the laity found the means to express during a monumental shift in the local balance of power.

The role of high clergy in the political life of Wells also changed considerably during the seventeenth century. The early stages of this period were marked by the direct infiltration of local political institutions and offices by cathedral clergy and diocesan appointees. In 1593, for example, Alexander Towse, a canon at Wells Cathedral, was enrolled among the 'deputy mayors'.[110] A member of the Piers family appeared on the Wells City Convocation Books in the decade before William Piers became Bishop in 1632.[111] Wells was a small place and, in general, the ablest notaries, lawyers and clerks among the local laity were bound to be of use to both the city and cathedral administrators. In the early seventeenth century, members of the ubiquitous Towse family of Wells, tenants of the dean and chapter, were attorneys in the service of the cathedral. The bishop, as lord of the manor of Wells, had the right to appoint a bailiff there who wielded considerable powers over tenants, ecclesiastical court activity and the market-place in the city. In 1590, the dean and chapter stated plainly that the power of this office should not be entrusted to 'any burgiesse or burgiesses of the cyttie, burrowe, or towne of Wells'.[112] This stance was ignored by the bishop on at least one occasion when John Crosse, a gentleman of Wells, was granted the lifetime position of bailiff in 1616.[113] This suggests that the security, power and other rewards of such appointments could attract local laity to loyal service under the high clergy in Wells.

Over the course of the century, however, the cathedral lost direct connections with families whose members dominated the office of mayor. In 1664 Tristram Towse, who had been general receiver of Wells the year before, became the last member of his family to serve as mayor in the seventeenth century. The recurring names in the records of the local oligarchy – Bull, Baron, Meade, Foster, Salmon, Davis, Irish and Cooke – could be found, as they had been all along, among those listed as wardens of St Cuthbert's, the parish identified with the community and corporation as opposed to the cathedral.[114] This was especially so after the granting of the corporate charter in 1684. The Corporation Act of 1661 had effectively forced new civic leaders to be Royalist episcopalians,[115] which makes it difficult to determine how truly sympathetic relations between cathedral and community were in the early years of the Restoration. By the 1680s, however, it was apparent that members of the Wells corporation swore a renunciation of the Solemn League of Covenant as an annual and lasting component of their convocation ritual.[116] At the Restoration, the king created a mixture of political representation in revived cathedral chapters, as on his own councils, to aid the spirit of reconciliation,[117] an aim which the city's higher degree of independence from capitular and diocesan political influence helped to achieve. Moreover, the Restoration, which seems to have produced more rather than less egalitarianism in local government generally,[118] produced a significantly non-clerical political culture in the Wells corporation. That is not to say that the corporation in Wells became less oligarchical; the city government still consisted of a small circle of men rotating through the principal offices. But the civic oligarchy of the later seventeenth century included men whose intellectual and social profiles were more modest than those of earlier city officials whose ties to the cathedral and high clergy had been close. In September 1689, Thomas Arney and Evans Dyre, two newly sworn members of the corporation in Wells, were unable to sign their renunciation of the Solemn League and Covenant. Another illiterate man, Hodges Cooke, became mayor of Wells three years later.[119]

The civic leaders of Wells and the high clergy there had established competing roles in the political culture of the community before the Civil War. This was expressed in part through public ritual. In the early seventeenth century, the high clergy in Wells used the market-place for their own processions in which the civic leaders were subservient. In the summer of 1608, 'the Maior and Corporation went in their gowns to the High Cross to waite on the Bishop at his first comeing to Towne'.[120] When the queen, Anne of Denmark, visited Wells in the summer of 1613, the bishop sent a letter of instructions to the mayor who, in compliance, ordered 'that the streates should be made handsome and the Town be rid of beggars and rogues'.[121] On the latter occasion, however, the civic leadership jostled to position themselves more prominently, and in secular fashion, in the view of their royal guest.

Awaiting Anne in July 1613, the mayor and aldermen, decked out in their scarlet gowns, gathered at Browne's Gate, a barrier point of contention between cathedral and community, and ordered the burgesses to appear there in black gowns or their 'best apparrele'. The mayor ordered the masters of every guild within the city to prepare elaborate shows. These featured biblical and pagan heroes mingled in unorthodox but readily interpreted ways. The tilers and blacksmiths portrayed Vulcan working away at a forge beside

Noah and the ark while Cupid and Venus looked on. A cart of 'old virgins' was drawn by the tanners who were clad like beasts in skins and horns with cow tails dangling from their necks. The tailors were even more daring in their sexual imagery; they presented the seductive daughter of Herodias who, veiled in samples of the company's wares, danced about the severed head of John the Baptist.[122] The streets of Wells were sprinkled with morris dancers, giants and dragons.

This guild procession seems hardly less reformed than the mocking shows orchestrated by Dean Haydon a few years earlier, but there were some meaningful differences. Despite the resulting hostilities between one Puritan clothier, John Hole, and the city's church ale revellers in the earlier episode,[123] the proud identification of the guilds with the city, rather than the cathedral, may explain the spirited contribution of the clothing companies in the queen's entertainment. Moreover, during the queen's visit to Wells, the bishop and other dignitaries were invited by the mayor to a dinner from which the dean and chapter appear to have been excluded. Indeed, the corporation vowed to indict the cathedral at the very next assizes for having refused to open Browne's Gate for civic processions and other purposes of interest to the local laity.[124] In short, the cathedral city of Wells used the ceremonial occasion of the queen's visit to proclaim and celebrate the community's own secular enterprise and identity; a gesture or reference to the cathedral was conspicuously absent from all this.

Eventually, however, the corporation came to appropriate ecclesiastical ritual itself for the expression of civic identity and authority. Civic ceremony in Wells underwent changes beginning in the Interregnum when the community expanded its claims on ritual forms, spaces and times left uncontested by the cathedral. Defiantly disregarding the banning of knells and 'superstitious bellringing' by parishes, as decreed by Bishop Mawe of Bath and Wells in 1629,[125] St Cuthbert's rang seventy knells in 1649, exacting £12 3s 4d in fees.[126] By 1663 the city of Wells retained a full-time bellringer whose successors in office would wear a special civic gown trimmed with a silver bell.[127] In 1674 (which happened to be the centenary of the Wells charter successfully contested by the bishop) St Cuthbert's rang bells on ninety-four non-ecclesiastical occasions, including Oak Apple day, Guy Fawkes day, private requests for memorial knells and the arrival of the assize judges at Wells. The traditional fairs celebrated by the city of Wells had always taken place in Rogationtide (fifth Sunday after Easter) and Trinity (one of the quarter days), thus conforming to times allowed, but not reserved, for the observance of parochial and secular functions after the Reformation.[128] During the Interregnum and the decades that followed, the city strode outside the guidelines of the traditional calendar to celebrate (and profit from) the autumnal fairs of St Calixtus and St Andrew's, no doubt savouring, in the latter case, the usurpation of the cathedral's own patronal feast day.[129]

The mayor ordered that the 1684 charter itself be celebrated. This was done with lavish 'trumpetts ... ringers, morris dancers ... wine and beer' cost-ing £15 5s, on the following Epiphany,[130] a traditional day of popular revel-ling but one which the cathedral observed, with Christmas and Ascension, as a sacred day of purity and white vestments. That spring the mayor himself, rather than a member of the clergy, led a celebratory perambulation at Roga-tion, a day on which the observance of community boundaries was appro-priate but over which ecclesiastical authorities had formerly presided.[131] In the sixteenth and early seventeenth centuries, autumn had been the season during which civic leaders could preside over the riding of bounds.[132] Immediately fol-lowing the charter of 1684, the mayor handed out alms of his own, in cathe-dral fashion, at Michaelmas. The desired effect was somewhat dampened when the mayor's bonfire spread to the private residence of a Mr Merefield. In all the excitement, the mayor neglected to order the reading and posting of a royal declaration at St Cuthbert's, an infraction for which the parish was cited by the bishop's apparitor who levied a seemingly trivial fine of 6d.[133]

Civic celebration in Wells after the Restoration did not so much express former resentment toward the high clergy as it played out the relegation of cathedral and bishop to a lesser status in the city's political culture. When the bishop crossed town for his formal visitation of St Cuthbert's in 1674, the mayor and the corporation did not bother to attend the bishop ceremoni-ously; they left this to the parish sidesmen who entertained his right reverend lordship with 4s of beer at the time of presentments. The parish spent £2 12s 8d on a dinner for the bishop's visitation and £1 15s on a dinner with the dean, but once again the high clergy found themselves mingling with the parish sidesmen on these occasions.[134] In February of 1684, the civic leader-ship, who had been required to make their way to the cathedral in former times, sat comfortably in their parish church where the bishop had been brought to consecrate a silver plate donated to St Cuthbert's by an alderman's mother. Indeed, some of the bishop's own ceremonial jewels were kept at St Cuthbert's by this time.[135] And, in this year of civic celebration, the mayor ordered St Cuthbert's to spare no expense in 'ringing whom [sic] the Char-ter', for which the ringers were paid three times what they had received for ringing in the bishop ten years earlier.[136]

The assertion of civic autonomy by cathedral cities took ·on special significance in view of the so-called English urban renaissance, which got under way during the late seventeenth century. As we have seen, the rela-tionship between cathedral and community had changed dramatically by this time. The emerging relationship placed a cultural resource at the disposal of Wells that was not present in other types of cities and towns. Before this time, cathedral grammar and choristers' schools served very few local boys apart from the sons of canons and other cathedral associates. One resident of Wells in the late sixteenth century argued that the money spent to educate the cathe-dral choristers scarcely helped the community. Despite the survival of the cathedral school in Wells, Barkham's Blue Coat School was founded by a con-

[152]

cerned citizen in 1654 to address the needs of ordinary local boys and girls.[137] Although more work needs to be done on local contributions of English cathedral schools following the Restoration, we do know for Wells that the resolution of a lengthy dispute between the cathedral and its schoolmaster, Charles Thirlby, effected a link between parish life and education at the cathedral.[138] Dismissed by the dean and chapter in the 1660s, Thirlby became vicar of St Cuthbert's where he refused to pay the staggering annual dues to the cathedral. By 1673, the dean and chapter sought reconciliation with Thirlby; thus the former vicar of St Cuthbert's came to preside over the educational resources of the cathedral where he taught until his death in 1680. Thirlby's successors revived the pre-Reformation practice of staging plays in the cathedral for the instruction of the boys and the enjoyment of the public. In 1705, the dean and chapter sponsored a children's production of *Hamlet*.[139]

The cathedral's revived commitment to music and popular liturgy in the late seventeenth century was conspicuous, perhaps even strategic. At Oxford and Cambridge colleges the installation of organs at the Restoration drew crowds and promoted the popularity of 'episcopalian ceremonies'.[140] In 1661, despite operating at a deficit, the dean and chapter dug into their own pockets to supply the cathedral with new liturgy books and a new 'little organ' worth nearly £85.[141] Thirty years later the dean and chapter spent £20 in a single year just to keep the cathedral organ in tune.[142] To be sure, Bishop Laud's expenditure on music had been high,[143] but this was in the interest of ecclesiastical opulence which parishioners at that time resisted to the point of excommunication, even under Laud's successors at Wells.[144] By contrast, the cathedral at the time of the urban renaissance was reaching out to ordinary people, making services and the devotional practices of the cathedral accessible to the community. Dean Bathurst, who presided over the cathedral from 1670 until 1704, transformed the cathedral's midnight service of matins into a more popular morning prayer service held at six o'clock in summer and seven o'clock in winter.[145] At times the canons must have grown weary of the changing atmosphere brought upon them by their concessions to popular practice. In 1673, with an air of resignation, the dean wrote: 'As for the rails before the altar, we conceive that if they be taken any lower, every dog will leap over them.'[146]

The somewhat surprising popularity of cathedrals in the late seventeenth century is almost certainly connected to the prominence of cathedral cities in the urban renaissance.[147] Educational opportunities for girls at Wells and Salisbury ranked most highly among those provided in English provincial communities during the urban renaissance. In 1700 Thomas Naish, preaching in Salisbury Cathedral, reminded the Society of Lovers of Music gathered there that music 'abateth spleen and hatred'.[148] The sacred music revival of the 1690s was directly associated with choir festivals held by cathedrals for the general public, most notably in Worcester, Gloucester and Hereford. The trend of institutionalizing St Cecilia's day concert programmes was established in Wells, Oxford, Salisbury, Winchester and Norwich. Pre-Reformation pilgrimage was replaced by post-Restoration tourism. Celia Fiennes passed through Wells near the end of the seventeenth century and admired breezily, but all in one breath, the stone figures gracing the cathedral's west front, the Town Hall, the 'little stands for selling things ... in all the streets', the assizes in session and the 'large market place and shambles'.[149]

As the public clearly perceived, cathedrals which had dominated their surrounding communities before the Civil War blended into the profiles of those urban communities after the Restoration. As early as 1660, with repairs underway in Wells Cathedral close, a former canonical house was rebuilt as a public assembly and assize hall.[150] While parks sprang up across English cities and towns, the knave of York Minster became recognized, by the 1720s as a promenade for the lord mayor and members of 'fashionable society' in that cathedral city.[151] During the Civil War and Interregnum, the cathedral close at Salisbury was transformed into that city's 'meat market, rubbish dump, and playground.'[152] In the early seventeenth century, the bishop's consistory court at Wells had disciplined parishioners for playing bowls in churchyards and for using the walls of churches for ball games.[153] In the early eighteenth century, however, the townsfolk of Wells frolicked on the lawn of the cathedral itself and struck balls against the west cloister door while the dean and chapter complained to themselves in vain.[154] The cathedral at Wells had become the cathedral of Wells: an extension of public space and identity in which new levels of local autonomy and cultural vigour were openly expressed by the city and its residents.

Notes

[1] K. Edwards, *The English Secular Cathedrals in the Middle Ages* (Manchester, 1967); S. E. Lehmberg, *The Reformation of Cathedrals: Cathedrals in English Society, 1485–1603* (Princeton, 1988), esp. pp. 25–34 concerning inflation and the finances of Tudor secular cathedrals.

[2] M. Weinbaum, *British Borough Charters, 1307–1660* Cambridge, 1943) remains the authoritative work on this subject. I owe the Durham reference to Dr Paul Halliday.

[3] *Exceeding Joyful News from the Earl of Bedford* (1642) cited by J. Guy, 'From the Reformation to 1800', in L. S. Colchester (ed.), *Wells Cathedral: A History* (Shepton Mallet, 1982), p. 159.

[4] Somerset Record Office (hereafter S.R.O.), D/P/W St C/13/3/20 (St Cuthbert's, Wells, Settlement Examinations, 1667–1710).

[5] M. Steig, *Laud's Laboratory: The Diocese of Bath and Wells in the Early Seventeenth Century* (Bucknell, 1982).

[6] F. R. Goodman, *Reverend Landlords and their Tenants* (Cambridege, 1936); F. Heal, 'Archbishop Laud revisited: leases and estate management at Canterbury and Winchester before the Civil War', in R. O'Day and F. Heal (eds.), *Princes and Paupers in the English Church, 1500–1800* (Totowa, NJ, 1981), pp. 129–52; D. A. Heaton, 'A study of the structure of corporate estate management of the lands of the dean and

chapter of Canterbury, 1640–1760', M.A. thesis, University of Kent (1971).

[7] P. M. Hembry, *The Bishops of Bath Wells, 1540–1640: Social and Economic Problems* (London, 1967); C. Hill, *Economic Problems of the Church* (Oxford, 1956); F. Heal, *Of Prelates and Princes: A Study of the Economic and Social Position of the Tudor Episcopate* (Cambridge, 1980).

[8] R. A. Marchant, *The Church under the Law: Justice, Administration and Discipline in the Diocese of York 1560–1640* (Cambridge, 1969); J. M. Potter, 'The ecclesiastical courts in the diocese of Canterbury, 1603–1665', M.Phil. thesis, Royal Holloway College, London (1972).

[9] Lehmberg, *Reformation of Cathedrals*, pp. 21–2, 31.

[10] *Ibid.*, p. 11.

[11] *Ibid., passim.*

[12] See, for example, Winchester Cathedral Library MSS (Chapter Book, 1622–1645, p. 52r). In a heated debate of 1637, the Crown exacted ship money from the city of Winchester but denied the corporation there the right to assess Winchester Cathedral and its associates for the subsidy.

[13] E. H. Bates [Harbin] (ed.), *Quarter Sessions Records for the County of Somerset, vol. III, Commonwealth*, Somerset Record Society 28 (1912), pp. 198–9 concerning S.R.O. Q/SO/5 (Somerset Quarter Sessions Order Books, 1646–56); for more on the disputed nature of Puritan control in Wells see D. Underdown, 'A case concerning bishop's lands: Cornelius Burges and the Corporation of Wells', *English History Review* 78 (winter, 1963), pp. 18–48.

[14] R. Hutton, *The Restoration: A Political and Religious History of England and Wales 1658–1667* (Oxford, 1985), p. 7.

[15] J. Addy, *The Archdeacon and Ecclesiastical Discipline in Yorkshire 1598–1714* (St Anthony Hall, 1963), *passim*; J. A. Sharpe, *Crime in Early Modern England 1550–1750* (Longman, 1984), pp. 87–92.

[16] Somerset Record Society 46 (1931). Note, however, that pp. 15–16 of these transcriptions refer incorrectly to a Wells charter of 25 Charles II, which suggests wrongly that there was a charter of 1674. The correct citation is 35 Charles II (1684).

[17] Wells City Record Office (hereafter W.C.R.O.), Wells City Charters, nos. 28B and 29.

[18] S.R.O. DD/SAS/SE.91 (Serel Collection: Wells Charters). The Archdeaconry of Taunton owed only £3 annually. With annual dues of £25 6s 8d, Chewton was the only parish to approach the annual sum owed the cathedral by St Cuthbert's, Wells.

[19] Lehmberg, *Reformation of Cathedrals*, p. 68.

[20] S.R.O. DD/SAS/SE.91 (Wells City Charters), 314 and 338.

[21] W.C.R.O. (Mr Thomas Serel's Book on Wells, 1874 MSS).

[22] W.C.R.O. (Wells City Charter no. 32, 10 Jan. 1684).

[23] S.R.O. DD/SAS/SE.91 (Wells City Charters), 314; Somerset Record Society 46 (1931).

[24] W.C.R.O. (City of Wells Convocation Book, 1687–1709).

[25] Other members of the corporation who signed this election report were Paynter (mayor), Coward, Salmon, John Davis, Cooke, Baron, Brown, Hipisley, Robert and Nicholas Thomas, Watte, Merrefield, Jeale, Evans, Cupper (Cooper) and Hill.

[26] W.C.R.O (City of Wells Convocation Book, 1687–1709).

[27] Lehmberg, *Reformation of Cathedrals*, pp. 292–3.

[28] D. S. Bailey (ed.), *Wells Manor of Canon Grange* (Gloucester, 1985), *passim*.

[29] Hutton, *Restoration*, p. 143.

[30] Wells Cathedral Library: Dean and Chapter (hereafter Wells C.L.:DC), (Communar's and other Accounts no. 16, 1634–1680). See entry of 28 March 1638 for an example of a Bristol upholsterer's account.

[31] S.R.O. D/P/W St C/13/6/5 (Overseers of the Poor of St Cuthbert's, Wells: Apprenticeship Indentures, 1662–1710). The one case was of the aptly named John Scripture, indentured in 1692. To this we should add the case of the cordwainer's apprentice who fled the Liberty at the time of Monmouth's rebellion.

[32] Wells C.L.:DC (Fabric Account Book no. 24, 1660–3 and 1665–6, 29 September 1660 through 1 January 1660/1).

[33] S.R.O. DD/HI/223 (Letter to John Hippisley, Esq. from Downside, 5 December 1631).

[34] Wells C.L.:DC Series III/156–160 (Plea in King's Court of King's Bench in the case of the Dean and Chapter of Wells v. John Hanham, Michaelmas, 1664). This deposition of Evan Munday concerned the customary practices of the 1620s.

[35] W.C.R.O. (Acts of the Corporation of Wells: Receiver's Book, 1652–1681). See entry of 21 June 1660 for reference to pig-batch maintenance.

[36] S.R.O. D/P/W St C/4/1/1;S.R.O. DD/SAS/SE.5 (Disputes over Wells Market, 1614–1685); S.R.O. DD/SAS/SE.28 (The General Account of Mr Robert Broadbeard, Receiver of the Mayor, Aldermen, and Common Council of the City of Wells, 1684).

[37] *Cal. II* HMC (1914), p. 431.

[38] Bailey, *Wells Manor, passim.*

[39] Pre-war examples include: Crosses (after 1603); Cowards (after 1606); Morgans (after 1619); Babers (1636–49); and Towses (1637–49). See Wells C.L.:DC (Communar's Accounts, 1625–28); (Ledger Book, 1571–1624), fo. 228; (Communar's Accounts, 1636–37); (Steward's Book, 1629–37), p. 126; (Communar's Book, 1602–3); (Chapter Act Books, 1591–1607), fo. 196. See also S.R.O. DD/CC/111733–5 (Parliamentary Survey, June and July, 1649); and S.R.O. DD/CC/112579.

[40] Wells C.L.:DC (Chapter Act Books, 1622–1635, 17 July 1624).

[41] Wells C.L.:DC (Steward's Books, 1625–37), p. 45.

[42] S.R.O. DD/CC/111733–5 (Parliamentary Survey, 1649). p. 24; W.C.R.O. (Acts of the Corporation: Receiver's Book, 1652–81), fo. 22.

[43] W.C.R.O. (Acts of the Corporation: Receiver's Book, 1652–81), fo. 267; W.C.R.O. (Thomas Serel's Book on Wells, 1874).

[44] Wells C.L.:DC (Communar's and other Accounts: no. 16, 1634–1680). See the communar's accounts for 1660–1.

[45] Wells C.L.:DC (Fabric and Communar's Accounts, 1689–1725).

[46] Wells C.L.:DC (Communar's Accounts: Box C, 1603; 1661; 1663–65; 1669–71; 1676–83; 1684–90).

[47] Wells C.L.:DC Series III: Box 3/III/153 (4 July 1664); *Cal. II* HMC (1914), pp. 433–4.

[48] Wells C.L.:DC Series III/155 (Brief in the Case of the Dean and Chapter v. Philip Ball, 1665–66).

[49] See, for example, Canterbury Cathedral Archive DCb J/X.5.10 (Archdeacon's Court, Canterbury: Comperta and Detecta, 1615–24), fos.178 and 202v: Potter, 'Ecclesiastical courts', p. 51.

[50] *Articles to be Ministered and to be Enquired of and Answered in the Trienniall Visitation of the Reverend Father in God James by God's Permission Bishop of Bath and*

Wells (London, 1609); S.R.O. D/D/Vm/S/2340.

⁵¹ Sharpe, *Crime in Early Modern England*, pp. 85–7.

⁵² Hampshire R.O. 21M65 B1/28 (Detecta made at the Visitation of George Abbott, Archbishop of Canterbury in the Diocese of Winchester, 1618); 21M65 B1/37 (Presentments of the Churchwardens within the County of Southampton on the Annual Visitation of George Morley, Bishop of Winchester, 1664); 21M65 B1/41 (Churchwarden's Presentments within the Diocese of Winchester made at the Annual Visitation, *c.*1673); 202M85/3/1311–1342 (Churchwarden's Presentments made at the Visitations of the Archdeacon of Winchester, 1668–1700).

⁵³ Winchester churchwardens presented a bastard in St Thomas (1668) and another one in St Faith and St Cross (1673).

⁵⁴ S.R.O. DD/SAS/SE.28 (Wells Convocation Books, 23 May 1615).

⁵⁵ C. B. Herrup, *The Common Peace: Participation and the Criminal Law in Seventeenth-Century England* (Cambridge, 1987), pp. 48–9.

⁵⁶ S.R.O. DD/SAS/SE.28 (Wells Corporation Records); Q/SR/24 (Somerset Quarter Sessions Rolls). See especially 1616 sessions for petty offenders, including one with an 'incorrigible tongue', pilloried at Wells.

⁵⁷ Sharpe, *Crime in Early Modern England*, p. 85.

⁵⁸ S.R.O. Q/SR/19/68 (Somerset Quarter Sessions Rolls, 1614).

⁵⁹ Excommunication, which carried material as well as spiritual penalties, was in decline in the first half of the seventeenth century. At Canterbury, for example, roughly 17 per cent of those detected by the ecclesiastical courts were excommunicated in the first decade of the century and the rate fell to 10 per cent in the decade before the Civil War. See Potter, 'Ecclesiastical Courts', pp. 75–7. It is unclear, however, whether or not this decline represented increasing leniency on the part of the high clergy or increasing compliance on the part of those presented to their courts.

⁶⁰ In the first half of the seventeenth century, these 'instance' cases were generally on the rise but were far outnumbered by the 'correction' cases initiated by the ecclesiastical authorities. For example, the consistory court of Canterbury heard 452 instance cases in 1623 while it brought 723 correction cases. See Potter, 'Ecclesiastical Courts', p. 40.

⁶¹ Pew disputes were commonly brought before the diocese in Wells, but not by Wells residents. The record of bishop's court depositions provides only one example between 1601 and 1637: S.R.O. D/D/Cd/65 (Bishop's Consistory Court at Wells: Depositions, April, 1630).

⁶² S.R.O. DD/SAS/SE.28 (Wells Convocation Books, 16 Jan. 1625).

⁶³ S.R.O. D/D/Cd/96 (Bishop's Consistory Court at Wells: Depositions, 1678–80), see esp. 11 November 1679.

⁶⁴ S.R.O. D/D/Cd/109/9 (Bishop's Consistory Court at Wells; Depositions, Quirke contra Day, 2 July 1706).

⁶⁵ S.R.O. D/D/Cd/128/11 (Bishop's Consistory Court at Wells: Depositions, Fry contra Chinn, 7 February 1705).

⁶⁶ S.R.O. Q/SR/107/18 (Somerset Quarter Sessions Rolls, 31 July 1665).

⁶⁷ S.R.O. D/D/Cd/126 (Bishop's Consistory Court at Wells: Depositions, Collins contra Ball and Collins contra Holder, 1693).

⁶⁸ S.R.O. Q/SR/2/71 (Somerset Quarter Session Rolls, 29 August 1607).

⁶⁹ Bates [Harbin], *Quarter Sessions Records, vol. I, James I,* Somerset Record Society 23 (1907), p. 247.

[70] S.R.O. Q/SR/6/22 (Somerset Quarter Sessions Rolls: The Humble Petition of Anthony Hendborowe, 1608/9.

[71] Bates [Harbin], *Quarter Sessions Records vol. II, Charles I,* Somerset Record Society 24 (1908), p. 123; see also S.R.O. Q/SR/63/2 (Somerset Quarter Sessions Rolls, Epiphany 1630) and Q/SO/4 (Somerset Quarter Sessions Order Books, 1627–38, 3 April 1630). Godwyn was not the only JP to order harsh corporal discipline in Wells in the first half of the seventeenth century; other JPs ordered two unwed mothers from Somerset villages to be whipped through Wells in 1614/15. Somerset Record Society 23 (1907), pp. 112 and 121.

[72] Somerset Record Society 24 (1908), p. 207; S.R.O. Q/SR/71/2 (Somerset Quarter Sessions Rolls, Epiphany 1633/4) and Q/SO/4 (Somerset Quarter Sessions Order Books, 1627–38, Epiphany 1633/4).

[73] S.R.O. Q/SR/128/28 (Somerset Quarter Sessions Rolls, 24 June 1675).

[74] S.R.O. Q/SR/144/21 (Somerset Quarter Sessions Rolls, 11 October 1680); Q/SR/144./5 and 6 (Somerset Quarter Sessions Rolls, 10 September 1680).

[75] S.R.O. Q/SR/152/10 (Somerset Quarter Sessions Rolls, April 1682).

[76] Wells C.L.:DC (Chapter Act Book 1683–1705, 5 January 1683/4).

[77] *Ibid.,* 14 January 1690/1).

[78] *Cal. II* HMC (1914), p. 321. The vicars choral were cathedral singing men who performed a variety of services but, by the seventeenth century, were by no means required to be priests.

[79] Wells C.L.:DC (Chapter Act Book 1622–35, 23 October 1628 and October 1635).

[80] *Ibid.,* (9 January 1625/6).

[81] Wells C.L.:DC (Chapter Act Book 1591–1607, 26 November 1607).

[82] Lehmberg, *Reformation and Cathedrals,* p. 160.

[83] Wells C.L.:DC (Chapter Act Book 1622–35, 1 October 1628).

[84] See, for example, the cases of Wells gentlemen Beaumont and Evans in Wells C.L.:DC (Chapter Act Book 1622–35, January 1625/6). Mary Clark herself was detected on grounds of non-attendance.

[85] J. Imray, 'Relations between the cathedral and the city of Wells', *The Friends of Wells Cathedral Journal* (Autumn, 1991), p. 13.

[86] D. Underdown, *Somerset in the Civil War and Interregnum* (Newton Abbot, 1973), p. 23.

[87] S.R.O. Q/SR/106/50 (Somerset Quarter Sessions Rolls, 23 May 1664). For examples of Wells residents subjected to cathedral shaming rituals see: *Cal. II* HMC (1914), pp. 328–9.

[88] S.R.O. DD/SAS/SE.28 (Wells Corporation Records, September 1605 and October of 17 James I).

[89] S.R.O. Q/SR/21/82 (Somerset Quarter Sessions Rolls: The Information of Two Constables of the Cyttie of Wells, 1615).

[90] R. V. H. Burne, *Chester Cathedral* (London, 1958), pp. 114–15; Lehmberg, *Reformation of Cathedrals,* p. 275.

[91] S.R.O. DD/SG/17 (Indenture made by Kathleen Ellinor Bull concerning sermons to be preached annually at St Cuthbert's, September 1623).

[92] S.R.O. T/PH/hw/6/c/2227 (Petition of the Mayor, Masters, Burgesses and other inhabitants of the Parish of St Cuthbert's in Wells, to the Right Honourbale the Lords and Cojmmons assembled in Parliament).

[93] S.R.O. DD/SAS/SE.28 (Serel Collection MSS). See esp. the entry concerning 29

September 1684 which records the considerable sum of £1 3*s* 4*d* paid by the corporation to Mr Winchcome for preaching in Wells Cathedral.

[94] D. S. Bailey (ed.), *Wells Cathedral Chapter Act Book, 1666–83*, Historical Manuscripts Commission 20 (1973), p. 44.

[95] Bailey, *Wells Manor*, pp. xx–xxi and 25.

[96] S.R.O. DD/SAS/SE.28 (Corporation Records for the City of Wells, 15 April 1706).

[97] Bates [Harbin], *Quarter Sessions Records vol. III, Commonwealth*, Somerset Record Society 28 (1912), p. 23.

[98] Wells C.L.:DC (Communar's and other Accounts: no. 16, 1634–1680); *Cal. II* HMC (1914), p. 337.

[99] Wells C.L.:DC (Communar's Cash Book, 1667–68).

[100] *Kelly's Directory of Somerset and Bristol* (London, 1889), pp. 387–94.

[101] S.R.O. D/P/W St C/13/3/20 (St Cuthbert's, Wells Settlement Examinations, 1667–1710).

[102] S.R.O. D/P/W St C/13/3/1 (Removal from the In Parish of St Cuthbert's, Wells, 1694–1798).

[103] Wells C.L.: Alms House (hereafter Wells C.L.:AH) s.435A (Indenture between Nathaniel Still, executor of the late Bishop, and James, now Bishop of Bath and Wells, the Dean and Chapter of Wells, and the Mayor, Masters and Burgesses of Wells, 12 December 1614).

[104] Wells C.L.:AH s.442 and s.428.

[105] *Cal. II* HMC (1914), p. 417.

[106] S.R.O. DD/SAS/SE.25 (Wells Corporation Records, 3 September and 25 December 1640).

[107] Wells C.L.:AH s.473 (William Lacham of Wedmore: His Note on Payments for Balls Close, Llewellyn's Almshouse Property, 1643).

[108] Wells C.L.:AH s.457 (Accounts of Bishop Still's Almshouse, 1630–1673); s.466 (Payments of Rents Owing to the Poore People in the Almshouse in Pryston Reow, 1635–1648); s.469 and s.470 (The Rents and Arrearage of Rents Belonging to the Almshouse in Priston, 1639–1644); s.475 (Rentroll of the Hospitall of the Cittie of Wells, 1644–1645); and S.1695 (Report of the Charity Commissioners, Somerset: City of Wells, 1820).

[109] Wells C.L.:AH s.457 (Accounts of Bishop Still's Almshouse, 1630–1673). John Guy speaks of the 'capitular windfall of 1660–63' and earnings of £14,000 by the chapter of Wells Cathedral 'through the leasing and fines of its property'. See Guy, 'From Reformation to 1800', p. 162, in which he cites I. M. Green, *The Re-Establishment of the Church of England, 1660–3* (Oxford, 1978). It seems quite probable, however, that estimates of rent revenues based on capitular records have been inflated in the past. In the Still's Almshouse manor records, for example, the accounting practice was to carry over into the subsequent year the sum of arrears from the previous year as an *asset* and these tended to accrue in a misleading way. Thus *suma oneris*, as accounted in records of this kind, included unrealized earnings.

[110] W.C.R.O. (Thomas Serel's Book on Wells, 1874 MSS); J. Le Neve (ed.), *Fasti Ecclesiae Anglicanae 1541–1857 vol. V* (University of London Institute of Historical Research, 1979), compiled alphabetically by J. M. Horn and B. S. Bailey.

[111] W.C.R.O. (Wells City Convocation Book, 1615–1625).

[112] Wells C.L.:DC (Wells Dean and Chapter Act Book, 23 October 1590); *Cal. II* HMC (1914), p. 320.

[113] Wells C.L.:DC (Chapter Act Book, 13 September 1616); *Cal. II* HMC (1914), p. 371. It is possible that John Crosse was related to Leonard Crosse who succeeded Alexander Towse as 'mayor' in 1607.

[114] S.R.O. DD/SAS/SE.28.

[115] T. Harris, *Politics under the Later Stuarts: Party Conflict in a Divided Society 1660–1715* (Longman, 1993), pp. 39–41; Hutton, *Restoration*, pp. 158–61.

[116] W.C.R.O. (Wells City Convocation Book, 1687–1709).

[117] Hutton, *Restoration*, pp. 172–3.

[118] *Ibid.*, p. 132.

[119] W.C.R.O. (Wells City Convocation Book, 1687–1709).

[120] S.R.O. DD/SAS/SE.28 (Wells Corporation Records, 18 July 1608).

[121] S.R.O. DD/SAS/SE.28 (Wells Corporation Records, 19 July through 16 August 1613).

[122] S.R.O. DD/SAS/SE.28 (Wells Corporation Records, 20 August 1613). For a detailed analysis of the 1613 cordwainers' show as representative of guild street theatre see J. Stokes, 'The Wells cordwainers show: new evidence concerning guild entertainments in Somerset', *Comparative Drama*, 19 (4) (winter, 1985–6), pp. 332–46.

[123] D. Underdown, *Revel, Riot, and Rebellion: Popular Politics and Culture in England 1603–1660* (Oxford, 1985), pp. 55–6.

[124] S.R.O. DD/SAS/SE.28 (Wells Corporation Records, 13 January 1613/14).

[125] S.R.O. D/P.Fiv/23/5(i) (Articles to be Enquired of at the Annual Visitation of Bishop Leonard Mawe, 1629).

[126] S.R.O. D/P/W St C/4/1/1 (St Cuthbert's, Wells, Churchwardens Accounts, 1649–1677).

[127] W.C.R.O. (Acts of the Wells Corporation: Receiver's Book, 1652–1681); W.C.R.O. (Wells Convocation Books, 1687–1709, December 1706).

[128] D. Cressy, *Bonfires and Bells: National Memory and the Protestant Calendar in Elizabethan and Stuart England* (London, 1989), pp. 10–11 and 15–23.

[129] W.C.R.O. (Wells Convocation Books: Receiver's Book, 1652–1681, 14 October and 30 November throughout). The accounts refer specifically to the fairs of St Calixtus and St Andrew; the danger of confusion must be avoided here because 30 November is also the feast of St Cuthbert of Mayne, an Elizabethan Catholic Martyr, not the Saxon St Cuthbert for whom the parish in Wells was named. St Andrew's Day was widely chosen as a fair day by other cities and towns. See Cressy, *Bonfires and Bells*, p. 16.

[130] S.R.O. DD/SAS/SE.28 (The General Account of Mr Broadbeard, Receiver of the Mayor, Aldermen, and Common Council of the City of Wells in the Year 1684).

[131] S.R.O. DD/SAS/SE.28 (Wells Corporation Records, 14 May 1685).

[132] D. M. Palliser, 'Civic mentality and the environment in Tudor York', in J. Barry (ed.) *The Tudor and Stuart Town: A Reader in English Urban History 1530–1688* (Longman, 1990), pp. 212–13; C. Phythian-Adams, 'Ceremony and the citizen', in P. Clarke and P. Slack (eds.) *Crisis and Order in English Towns 1500–1700* (London, 1972), pp. 57–85.

[133] S.R.O. D/P/W C/4/1/2 (St Cuthbert's, Wells, Churchwarden's Accounts, 1677–1727).

[134] S.R.O. D/P/W St C/4/1/1 (St Cuthbert's, Wells, Churchwarden's Accounts, 1649–1677: July and August, 1674).

[135] S.R.O. D/P/W St C/4/1/2 (St Cuthbert's, Wells, Churchwarden's Accounts,

1677–1727: 10 February 1683/4 and the inventory of parish goods taken by William Paris and Richard Collins for the year 1674).

[136] S.R.O. D P/W St C/4/1/1 (St Cuthbert's, Wells, Churchwarden's Accounts, 1649–1677).

[137] *Cal. II* HMC (1914), p. 411; A. Barnes, 'The Church and education in Wells, Somerset, from the eve of the Reformation in Wells, Somerset, from the eve of the Reformation until 1891', D.Phil. thesis, University of Manchester (1990), pp. 199–201; L. S. Colchester, *A History of Wells Cathedral School* (Wells, 1985), pp. 27–31; and Lehmberg, *Reformation of Cathedrals*, pp. 199–200.

[138] *Cal. II* HMC (1914), pp. 437–40; Colchester, *Wells Cathedral School*, p. 32.

[139] *Cal. II* HMC (1914), p. 487.

[140] Hutton, *Restoration*, p. 146.

[141] Wells C.L.:DC (Communar's and other Accounts, no. 16, 1634–1680).

[142] *Cal. II* HMC (1914), p. 470.

[143] Wells C.L.:DC (Chapter Act Book, 1622–1635, 16 August 1626). Laud's budget for cathedral music may have been as high as £44 8s 8d in the summer of 1626.

[144] E. Green, *On Some Excommunications and Public Penances in Somerset* (Bath, 1875), pp. 1–16.

[145] Guy, 'From Reformation to 1800', p. 164.

[146] Wells C.L.:DC Series III: Box 4/III/184. This reference to dogs at cathedral communion services may explain the odd reference to a *flagellatoris canum* listed among cathedral employees in the fabric and communar's accounts of 1689.

[147] See Peter Borsay's *The English Urban Renaissance: Culture and Society in the Provincial Town, 1660–1770* (Oxford, 1989), pp. 29, 111, 123, 129, 132, 139, 147. Even Borsay does not address this observation directly and it is worthy of further study.

[148] T. Naish, *A Sermon Preached at the Cathedral Church of Sarum, November 22, 1700* (London, 1701), pp. 12–13 as cited by Borsay, *English Urban Renaissance*, pp. 269–70.

[149] C. Morris (ed.), *The Journeys of Celia Feinnes* (London, 1949), pp. 241–2.

[150] *Cal. II* HMC (1914), p. 431.

[151] Borsay, *English Urban Renaissance*, p. 163.

[152] S.R.O. D D/Cd/32, 45 and 61 (Bishop's Consistory Court at Wells: Depositions), for examples between 1600 and 1626.

[153] Cal. II *HMC (1914), p. 513.*

7

Gender and politics in Leveller literature[1]

Ann Hughes

I

Historians and literary scholars have agreed that women were a visible and valued element in the Leveller movement, as messengers, money-raisers and petitioners. Individual Leveller women petitioned for the release of themselves and their husbands from prison, but special attention has been given to the collective petitions from Leveller women against the imprisonment of Leveller leaders and the punishment of army mutineers in the spring of 1649, or in support of John Lilburne during his second trial for high treason in summer 1653. For an older generation of radical and liberal historians, such as M. A. Gibb and H. N. Brailsford, the involvement of women was an unproblematic, inevitable part of a precociously progressive movement:[2]

> in their attitude to women the Levellers were ahead of their time. They encouraged women to play their part in politics side by side with their husbands and brothers, because they believed in the equality of all 'made in the image of God'.

The petitioners of 1649, 'with their sea-green ribbons pinned to their breasts may be reckoned in their modest anonymity among the forerunners of Mary Wollstonecraft'. This vision of proto-feminists, working in easy collaboration with their menfolk, now seems anachronistic and too simple. We are more sceptical about visions of English history describing a linear progression towards a more egalitarian, participatory society, whether these 'grand narratives' take a Whig form, or more radically stress the struggles of ordinary people. We are more aware of the contradictions and exclusions accompanying the emergence of 'democracy'.[3]

Feminist scholarship has been a major means by which linear notions of progressive change have been challenged in recent decades. The assumption of equality has been replaced by a darker stress on the contradictory relationships between women and radical movements in the seventeenth or the nineteenth centuries, or indeed on the ambiguities of Mary Wollstonecraft's engagement with eighteenth-century republicanism. More abstractly, Carole Pateman has argued that as early 'liberal' theorists increasingly founded male political rights on abstract notions of natural right or contract, rather than on social rank or family status, so the subordination of women was more and more taken for granted as an unchanging element in a natural world.[4]

Leveller women have been discussed in important and useful ways by both historians and literary scholars influenced by feminism. Here they have been treated as an aspect of *women's* experience rather than, as with Brailsford, as part of a specific political movement. The Leveller women's petitions of spring 1649 now become the climax of a process of female, even feminist, activism unleashed by the political upheavals of the 1640s. Their rhetoric has been carefully analysed as presenting a brave, and much opposed justification for women's political independence and involvement:[5]

> That since we are assured of our creation in the image of God, and of an inter-est in Christ, equal unto men, as also of a proportionable share in the Freedoms of this Commonwealth, we cannot but wonder and grieve that we should appear so despicable in your eyes, as to be thought unworthy to petition or represent our grievances to this honourable house. Have we not an equal interest with the men of this Nation, in those liberties and securities, contained in the Petition of Right, and other the good Laws of the Land?

The opposition faced by Leveller women is seen as demonstrating the radicalism of their claims and the unsettling nature of female intrusion into a 'public sphere' in a society where gender hierarchies were fundamental to conceptions of order. The newsbooks reported that Parliament refused to accept the women's petition on 25 April 1649, recording nothing in the *Journal* of the House, but answered them, through the Serjeant by 'word of mouth':[6]

> Mr Speaker (by the direction of the House) hath commanded me to tell you, that the matter you petition about, is of an higher concernment then you understand, that the House gave an answer to your Husbands, and therefore that you are desired to go home, and look after your owne businesse, and meddle with your housewifery.

Newsbooks attacked the Leveller women as whores, 'oyster-wives', the 'civill-sisterhood of Oranges and Lemmons'.[7] It is here assumed that the Leveller women were challenging strict prohibitions against women's political activism, prohibitions operating both within the movement and in the world outside. Their declarations are thus judged against implicit though variable standards of self-conscious, female assertiveness. On the one hand, Patricia Higgins judges that the women's petitions of 1653 represented a disappointing retreat from a more independent stance in 1649, but on the other Ann Marie McEntee sees the later, 'humbler' petitions as evidence of increasing political sophistication. She argues that the mockery Leveller women faced reveals anxiety about collective female power and an erosion of the 'sex-gender system'. Opposition failed, however, to dissuade the women from political involvement for they 'considered themselves as citizens as well as wives, mothers and widows'.[8]

The identification of a female tradition of petitioning in the 1640s and 1650s is not simply a twentieth-century construction: seventeenth-century commentators, as I shall show, also tended to lump together all kinds of assertive female activity. However, there is some danger of misunderstanding the precise significance of particular interventions by women if we stress only that they were women, and not also recognize that they were Levellers, or supporters of peace, or Quakers. The focus on women's activities and experiences is an essential and enriching part of current historiography. None the less, I will argue that we can enlarge our understanding of both women and the Levellers by using the insights of feminist scholars to analyse Leveller women and Leveller presentations of gender as part of the Leveller movement itself, rather than as an episode in women's activism.

Much of the literature I shall be examining is derived from a third approach to Leveller women, and indeed to the Levellers in general: the biographical approach adopted by Pauline Gregg or Margaret George.[9] Here the stress is on the suffering, supportive wives of the leaders. From the autobiographically structured pamphlets of John Lilburne, in particular, a tragic picture is drawn of the life of his wife Elizabeth: her pregnancies and miscarriages, the births and deaths of her children, the unceasing lobbying, letter writing and petitioning to keep her husband out of prison. In the summer of 1645, heavily pregnant, Elizabeth Lilburne joined her husband in Newgate prison where he was sent for distributing scandalous books; in her absence the agents of the Stationers Company broke into the Lilburne house and stole her childbed linen. This set the pattern for the next twelve years ending on John's death in 1657 during a brief release from yet another prison to visit his wife after yet another confinement.[10] According to John Lilburne's pamphlets, these years were punctuated by virulent public quarrels between husband and wife. The disputes followed a consistent pattern as Elizabeth tried to persuade John to give up the cause he was engaged in, to make his peace with the dominant parliamentarian factions and take proper care of his wife and children. Some of these published conflicts will be discussed below.

Hitherto, most commentators have taken the accounts by John Lilburne at face value, reacting with an understandable sympathy for Elizabeth. Antonia Fraser, for example, comments that Elizabeth's life recalls the definition of a martyr as someone who is married to a saint.[11] Margaret George offers an equally sympathetic picture of Elizabeth, derived from her husband's pamphlets, while noting also the variety of ways in which women and family life figure in the writings of all prominent Levellers:[12] 'they talked openly and artlessly of the assistance of their wives'; 'female efforts were naturally integrated with those of the men'. 'Openly', 'artlessly' – these judgements on

Leveller presentations of themselves, their wives and their domestic life are widely shared. Biographies of John Lilburne as well as accounts of his wife, or of Richard and Mary Overton, all take Leveller autobigraphical writing for granted as a direct reflection of the reality of their authors' lives, as an unvarnished presentation of self. Much current literary and philosophical theory, of course, renders such readings extremely problematic.

Whilst biographers have used Leveller writings as an unmediated source for Levellers' lives, political theorists and historians have closely interrogated the literature in order to discover consistent and coherent abstract 'positions' on political issues – on the franchise, in particular, after C. B. Macpherson's stimulating *The Political Theory of Possessive Individualism* – but also on property, the status of the English legal system, the 'ancient constitution', the nature of grace and salvation. In his response to Macpherson over twenty years ago Keith Thomas regretted the excessive concentration on the franchise issue, and the imposition of an overly coherent or rational framework on Leveller ideas, but little work has been done to develop these insights.[13]

Work on history, politics and literature over the last fifteen years offers fruitful new approaches for an understanding of gender and the Leveller movement. Most importantly for my argument here, the many insights often comprehended under the label 'the linguistic turn', have rendered the relationships between politics, language and identity more complex, more problematic and more interesting. Much recent social theory has blurred 'the boundary between the represented and the real', arguing that language does not reflect some reality beyond itself, rather it is through a variety of languages and discourses that we constitute and understand the world around us. Furthermore, an understanding of individual identity as coherent, fixed and again reflected in language has been challenged by an argument that it is only through language that individual and collective identities are forged. Politics can thus be seen as a cultural and discursive struggle to offer particular identities and visions that encourage people to become involved in political movements and activities; concepts of gender in turn are at the heart of identity.[14] Leveller literature can be explored for the identity and agency offered to its readers; and discussed as a means by which a new political movement was imagined, or called into being, rather than as a straightforward reflection or presentation of pre-existing demands or interests.

More concretely, we have the example of a range of work on nineteenth-century British politics that has examined the political languages, the narrative strategies, the rituals and symbols by which political movements created themselves, understood the world and had an impact on it.[15] Equally, work on eighteenth-century France offers insights and connections that seem relevant to mid-seventeenth-century England. Lynn Hunt and Sara Maza have argued that it was not only through political philosophies and programmes that new visions of the world were created, but also through melodramatic accounts of family conflict – stories of exploitation, deceit and oppression that were seen as having a general relevance. Maza's work shows that sharp distinctions between private and public issues were not drawn; rather, 'private' often simply meant individual or particular, and a glaring example of family scandal might have much public importance.[16] This work, like many of the studies of nineteenth-century British politics, emphasizes the fundamental importance of narrative to human understanding; it is through the telling of stories that we become convinced of what is true, and develop a sense of identity, both individual and collective.[17] What then do the stories the Levellers told about themselves suggest about the movement that was coming into being?

There has hitherto been little attempt at a cultural analysis of radical politics during the English Revolution. Recent 'revisionist' history has been based mainly on literal-minded reading practices, positing a sharp distinction between manuscript and printed sources, and privileging the former.[18] Furthermore, prevailing historiographical scepticism about the importance or even the existence of radical political movements in the 1640s and 1650s has made the Levellers marginal to historical analysis.[19] David Underdown's ambitious work on popular politics in the English Revolution shows the value of attention to cultural practices and to gender relationships in broadening our understanding of the nature of political conflict. *Revel, Riot and Rebellion* necessarily concentrated on the more 'traditional forms' of provincial popular politics rather than on London radicalism.[20] Few connections are drawn in other recent work between popular disturbances and mainstream political divisions of the period; much social and cultural history ends in 1640, or starts in 1660. Only Clive Holmes, in his sophisticated discussion of the links between Lilburne and the troubles in the fens, has challenged these conceptual and chronological divisions.[21]

The impact of this scepticism is seen in a recent, brief but suggestive discussion by a leading literary scholar. Thomas Corns does argue that Leveller publications do not so much reflect as create or define a political movement: they 'work to invent, or to call into being political categories that had not previously existed'. But, for Corns, Leveller discursive strategies are not very convincing, because the movement itself did not amount to much. The Levellers were a mass movement which lacked mass support, and so, 'the characteristic idiom, the assumed collective voice, attempts to disguise the central anxiety'.[22] Of course, the importance of the Levellers cannot be demonstrated simply through their own printed literature. Other kinds of research on radical London politics will be necessary for a full rehabilitation of the interest and importance of the Levellers. This discussion depends, however, on a variety of recent historical scholarship which encourages us to take the Levellers seriously as a radical force in London and parliamentary politics from 1646–9. Drawn mainly from the respectable middling sort of London, given focus by men like John Lilburne and Richard Overton who had a background in both religious radicalism and popular journalism, the Levellers were prominent in the attacks on a 'presbyterian' dominated city and Parliament from the mid-1640s. They acquired some influence, at least, in the army in 1647, and provided a crucial 'ally on the left' for the Revolution of winter 1648–9. Their angry and rapid disillusion with the commonwealth seriously threatened political stability in 1649, but by the end of that year the Levellers were defeated with the crushing of army radicalism and the imprisonment of their leaders.[23] It seems likely that consistently committed Levellers were few in number – support fell away in the crisis of 1649 – but at crucial points in the later 1640s Leveller ideas enthused a much broader following, who constituted a vital element in preventing a settlement with the king. Even in 1653 a London jury would not convict John Lilburne of treason, while the impact of Leveller style on the collective radical memory is seen in the revival of Leveller colours and favours during the Exclusion Crisis.[24]

On the basis of this long historiographical prologue, I want therefore to examine Leveller literature as the avenue through which a self-consciously democratic political movement engaged in a process of self-definition, and in a struggle over meaning – over the meaning, especially, of the cause for which parliamentarians had fought. My concern is not with a search for consistent abstract policies or programmes but with the ways in which Leveller writing offered a more general identity and vision. Within this approach, my focus is on gender – on Leveller portrayals of women, of families and of female activism – but not because these offer necessarily accurate accounts of family life, or of women's opinions. These descriptions, I argue, are by no means 'natural' or 'artless', but strategic and rhetorical evocations of a particular image of the household and its political implications. Gender roles and household relationships, in other words, were a fundamental part of the political identity offered to the readers of Leveller literature. My purpose is partly to re-evaluate the Leveller women's petitioning of spring 1649, but within a broader examination of the uses of gender in Leveller arguments. Rather than taking Leveller literary treatment of women for granted, I want to ask basic questions about how and why Leveller men described and discussed 'their' wives and 'their' families. What do these visions of gender relationships suggest to us about the nature of the political movement being fought for through print? Conversely, what impact does this view of Leveller literature imply for our understanding of the women petitioners?

II

It is well known that the Levellers paid close attention to symbol and ritualized activity, as seen especially in the solemn processions that marked the funeral of the army mutineer, Robert Lockyer, in May 1649.[25] Thousands attended (although newsbooks vary greatly in their estimates):

Officers, souldiers, Citizens, Maids etc every one having a black Ribbon and a small one fastned to it of a sea green colour ... it is said so called not of the sea but of the Republique, for the People in many places of scripture are compared to the great waters, the sea or ocean, which was signified by sea-green. His Horse was led by a footman covered with black.

The procession was apparently ordered by gender and age, 'citizens and women', 'youths and maids', while the coffin was decorated with rosemary dipped in blood.

But it was self-consciously through print, above all, that the Leveller movement was defined and embodied.[26] The Levellers were a group of people who supported certain texts and campaigned for the liberty to communicate them. When John Lilburne presented *England's New Chains* to the House of Commons on 26 February 1649,[27] he told MPs he was,

> desired by a company of honest men, living in and about London, who in truth do rightly appropriate to themselves, the title of the Contrivers, Promoters, Presenters and Approvers of the late Large London petition of the 11 September last ... to present you with their serious apprehensions ... we are those that in the worst of times durst own our Liberties and Freedoms ... Nay, Sir, let me with truth tell you, that to the most of us, our Wives, our Children, our Estates, our Relations, nay our Lives, and all that upon Earth we can call Ours, have not bin so highly valued by us as our Liberties and Freedoms.

This self-naming – against the insulting tag of 'Leveller' – introduces several significant images. The Levellers are a 'company of honest men' (and each element here is important); furthermore they are men with wives, families, estates – but all these they are willing to risk for the sake of their 'liberties and freedoms'.

The Levellers were thus defined especially by their adherence to petitions – to texts that were more than texts, for petitions demanded action, invited support, courted punishment. Furthermore, Leveller pamphlets demanded participation, partly in the process of reading itself:[28]

> Courteous Reader, by reason I am prohibited to have Pen, Ink, and Paper; I am forced now to write a peece, and then a peece, and scarce have time and opportunity seriously to peruse and correct what I write ... I must intreat thee, as thou readest, to amend with thy Pen, what in sence of quotations may be wanting or false; and I shal rest thy true and faithful Country-man, ready to spend my bloud for the fundamentall Lawes and Liberties of England, against any power whatever that would destroy them.

Correcting Lilburne's prose was intended to develop further solidarity in the defence of England's laws and liberties.

Many Leveller publications were composite texts, quoting petitions, official orders, legal and parliamentary precedents within an overall narrative. The same text could thus have many different purposes and appeals. Often there

were copious cross-references to other Leveller publications which again reinforced the definition of the movement as a group of people who were familiar with the same texts, while also combining an image of unity with a sense
of complexity and differentiation. In one of his 1653 pamphlets Lilburne
urged readers, for further information,[29] 'to read the honest papers, already
printed and published by my self and friends or well-wishers, for my vindication and justification'. He listed twenty-three items including 'My three
addresses to the Councel of State' and all his own pamphlets, printed letters
and petitions from that summer:

17. My friends petition of London of the 9 of July 1653 to the Parliament ...

18. The honest women of Londons petition, with their paper to back it unto every
Individual Member of Parliament.

19. The young men and Apprentices of Londons petition.

20. The honest people of Kents petition. ...

23. The honest men of Hartfordshires petition for John Lilburn, which is the
onely thing of all the forementioned that is not printed.

This was printed parallel to the ordering of Robert Lockyer's funeral procession.

Finally, a crucial element in Leveller strategy was to engage literally in a
struggle over meaning, over the meaning of the parliamentary cause, as laid
out in Parliament's own declarations.[30] Parliament's *Book of Declarations*,
published in March 1643 was quoted by Lilburne more than anything else
except the Bible. The declarations and justifications of 1642–3 were endlessly
analyzed, revealing Parliament's perfidy in betraying its early ideals. It was as
if textual analysis in itself could reall Parliament to its original purity.

Where print was so important, the publication of petitions by women, as
individuals or collectively, and the discussion of marital and family relationships must be seen as a strategic move. Both Lilburne and Richard Overton
recounted with pride and approval the activities of their wives on their behalf
during their imprisonments in 1646–7. In 1649, Lilburne remembered how,
through 'a large Petition of my Wives, and accompanied at the delivery of it
with divers of her feminine friends', he got a hearing before a committee of
the House of Commons. At the time Lilburne complained in strongly gendered terms, about the abuse suffered by his wife as she petitioned. She was
attacked, 'at the very Parliament door, when she was peaceably wayting there
with eight Gentlewomen more, for an Answer to her late Petition, and for
Justice from the House, about my illegall sufferings'. The attack, by Richard
Vaughan, a London goldsmith, ensign to the guard at Parliament, was 'a
piece of unmanlike cruelty and barbarism ... which renders him to be one of
the malicious, basest, unworthiest, and cowardliest of men, to use a Gentlewoman in such a manner'.[31] Elizabeth Lilburne's petition on her husband's

behalf was published under her own name, while Mary Overton, in prison herself because, in her husband's words, she 'would not be subject to the arbitrary and diabolicall accustomary proceedings of that house' (of Lords), published a petition for her own release.[32]

Such public interventions by women were presented as uncontroversial, but they were of course carefully limited and controlled. The wives were supporting their husbands and defending their families, and it was made clear that theirs was not an independent voice. As John Lilburne told the House of Commons in February 1647,[33] 'she is my wife, and set at work to doe what she did at the earnest desire of me her (unjust imprisoned) husband, and truly I appeale to every one of your owne consciences, whether you would not have taken it very ill at the hands of any of your wives, if you were in my case, and she should refuse at your earnest desire to doe that for you'. Through his description of his active, but dutiful wife, Lilburne was also constructing himself as a good husband and a true man; ideas about masculinity are a crucial element in Leveller identity and merit further exploration on another occasion. The symbiosis between wives and husbands was demonstrated when Elizabeth Lilburne's and Mary Overton's petitions were republished within pamphlets written by their husbands: in framed narratives the men authorized and appropriated their wives' opinions into a familial whole. Overton, indeed, claimed the authorship of his wife's and brother's petitions, and explained the careful strategy behind women's interventions: 'being reduced to this miserable condition, I prepared a Petition and Appeale (since published in print) in the behalfe of my wife and brother to the House of Commons, which *for the better credence of our miserable condition*, was presented by a competent number of women, but notwithstanding all the agitation and sollicitation that we could use, an admission thereof into the House (so much as to be read) could not ... be obtained'.[34] In *Regall Tyranny* John Lilburne expanded on the points Elizabeth had made in her petition, and adds, 'another thing not mentioned at all', thus reinforcing his superiority in arguing their case.[35] In *The Resolved Man's Resolution*, a pamphlet that also recounted a public argument between the Lilburnes, John Lilburne described the preparations for their appearance before the House of Commons committee:[36] 'I was led presently to take care, to do something for my wife as the weaker vessell ... and for that end, I drew her presently up a few lines, which I read unto her, and gave her instructions ... unto which she readily assented, and set her name to it, which verbatim thus followeth' – and then the pamphlet prints 'The humble addresses of Elizabeth Lilburne, wife to Lieut. Col. John Lilburne, prerogative prisoner in the tower of London'. Hence readers are offered a very carefully nuanced, authorized public appearance by a woman: she is named clearly as a wife, the wife indeed of a prisoner; the man writes for the 'weaker vessell', and gives her instructions; yet her active co-operation and assent is also emphasized. As with Mary Overton's defiance of the Lords, women's participation is important, even encouraged, but the movement is defined by men.

Women were a crucial element in the prison narratives which inevitably loomed large in Leveller publications; exploiting a genre already common in popular literature for broad political ends. Pre-Civil War prison pamphlets focused on individual misdeeds and oppression, whether these are of penitent criminals or sadistic warders; for the Levellers, however, the imprisonment of Lilburne, Overton and the bookseller William Larner revealed the generalized tyranny of an oppressive Parliament. The injustice done them should be challenged for, as the pamphlets always insisted, it could happen to anyone. Larner's experiences were 'published ... to the view of the world, chiefly for the serious Observation of all the Free-men of England, who cannot long enjoy their Freedoms, lives nor Estates, if the Rule of Law be not truly followed, nor Justice duly Administered'.[37]

A melodramatic image of the respectable householder, plucked from the society of family and friends, was central to these prison stories. As Mary Overton put it:[38] 'we, our husbands, brethren, friends and servants, contrary to all law (severally, and in a forced and unjust separation from our husbands) are kept and mewed up in your several starving, stinking, murthering prison houses'. Lilburne complained frequently of close imprisonment, 'without the use of pen, ink or paper, and not suffering his friends, nor wife (that singular comfort and help that the wise God provided for poor frail man) to set foot in this his chamber door for about three weeks together'. Sometimes, indeed, he placed separation from his wife before the lack of a pen.[39]

Political theorists have often stressed the radical individualism of the Levellers. Leveller programmes urged the protection of the individual body from impressment, of the individual conscience from State coercion, of the individual's right to labour and enterprise from interference by monopolistic trading companies.[40] If we turn from programmes of demands to the identities offered to readers, however – the visions of how Levellers were supposed to live, or be – we find that leaders like Overton and Lilburne are hardly ever seen alone. They are not portrayed as individual men, but very overtly as householders, as the heads of mutually supportive, clearly differentiated units of husbands, wives, servants and children. Lilburne's wife, Overton's wife and brother, Larner's wife, parents and servants are all prominent in the prison accounts of 1646–7. Overton lamented 'this our unnaturall and cruell division in three severall prisons, my selfe in one, my wife in another, my brother in the third, and my three children exposed to the mercy of the wide world'. Ellen Larner recounted how her husband had lost two servants in Parliament's military service; how she herself, 'being with childe, seeing the violent apprehension of her husband, fell into a dangerous sinknesse [*sic*]'; how his aged father and mother, lately plundered by Royalists in Gloucestershire, depended on him for support. Finally, in the ultimate demonstration of a harmonious household, two of Larner's servants went to prison rather than give evidence against their master.[41] The Leveller was an honest householder, while the movement brought together networks of honest households, united by friendship. Lilburne wrote in 1652 of 'the affections of thousands of mine honest and indeared Freinds', while the women petitioners of 1649 vowed never 'to rest until we have prevailed that We, our Husbands, Children, Friends, and Servants may not be liable to be thus abused, violated and butchered at men's Wills and Pleasures ... Take the bloud of one more, and take all, Slay one, slay all.'[42] It was on the basis of an idealized image of the household that the Levellers founded the notion of a movement differentiated yet united, as illustrated already at Lockyer's funeral, or in Lilburne's listing of petitions in his support from a variety of places and people, young and mature, male and female.

The visibility of women was essential to this construction of the household, and gender was further implicated in the multiple meanings of 'honest' households, to which we shall return. In turn, accounts of households brought great emotional force to the prevailing Leveller argument of disillusion and betrayal.[43] Parliament had broken its promises, had not fulfilled the declarations which had drawn men to risk all in its service. Through accounts of the sufferings of their wives, the Leveller leaders conjured up a movement of honest, responsible householders who cannot in fact perform their proper roles of protecting and providing for their dependants – because of Parliament's apostasy.

There were several rather different elements in this story, in all of which the Levellers' status as family men was crucial. The first, most obvious, has already been touched on: honest men, on whom many others depended, who had fought for freedom, were now hauled off to prison leaving their wives and children to suffer. Overton's family was 'deprived of all meanes and wayes by industry to procure any livelihood'. Larner, owed £46 6s 6d for his military service, was harassed and then imprisoned; his wife begged for his release on bail, 'to follow his calling, thereby to prevent the apparent ruine of himself, and his whole family'.[44]

But duty to the 'cause' took priority before an individual's responsibility to his family. William Larner, 'out of his good affection to the state, left his Wife, Family and Calling, and voluntarily went in the service of the Parliament against the common Enemy'.[45] Indeed, honest householders had no choice but to fight for freedom because oppression and injustice would destroy their households anyway. This choice that was not a choice is one of the underlying themes of the published confrontations between John and Elizabeth Lilburne. Much of Lilburne's rhetoric of sacrifice of family for the general good comes from the later pamphlets of exile, influenced by specifically republican arguments derived from his reading of Plutarch and Machiavelli. However, it is present in earlier tracts also, as in a 1647 example. John and Elizabeth Lilburne were both in prison and both called for examination by a committee of the House of Commons. In the midst of a long address by John:

my wife seeing Mr Wever so furious upon me as he was, burst out with a loud voice and said, I told thee often enough long since, that thou would serve the Parliament and venture thy life so long for them, till they would hang thee for thy paines.

John Lilburne asked the committee to excuse, 'what in the bitternesse of her heart being a woman she had said unto them', and in his commentary drew on Christian traditions of martyrdom:[46]

And for my wife and children ... shall I for love of them sin against my owne soule, and be silent, when my conscience, from sound grounds tells me God would have me to speake.

His 'native Country' was being enslaved and his wife and children would 'undeniably perish' if he stayed at home and did nothing to defend 'the law and justice of the Kingdome'.

Finally, in a simple, but effective and much repeated motif, suffering wives and widows with their hungry children exemplified the fate of the humble men who had given all they could to service of the Parliament. Soldiers had ventured their lives for 8*d* a day, yet now their 'poore widowes and father-lesse children' were denied 'their small arreares' and risked starvation. Heavy taxes were imposed on poor men, who relied on their own labour to support their families while Parliament's officials lived in 'pomp and gallantry', on salaries of £1,000 p.a. and more. 'Honest, faithfull and experienced men' could have been employed at a tenth of the cost.[47]

Parliament's tyranny was thus revealed in the attacks on the honest house-holds of the Leveller leaders. Leveller pamphlets of 1646–7 offered moving descriptions of the invasion of their homes, and the disruption of their domestic harmony by the agents of the Stationers' Company or the House of Lords. But stories of domestic violation reach a melodramatic peak with the arrests of the Leveller leaders in March 1649, one of the bitterest turning points of the Revolution. Again Leveller narrative strategies echo popular story-telling; their stories follow a familiar pattern in which readers can almost fill in the stages for themselves, embellished with precise and vivid detail to convince of their verisimilitude. The imagery approaches that of rape, as soldiers violently enter their homes, and the men are dragged from their beds in the middle of the night, watched by sick and frightened children, breast-feeding women, and outraged neighbours. What these narratives lack is a comforting resolu-tion or 'closure'; rather they invite an anxious identification, insisting, as so often, that what happened to Lilburne, Overton, Walwyn and Prince could happen to any free-born Englishman.[48]

About four o'clock in the morning, Thomas Prince's house, 'was beset with about 200 Horse and Foot Souldiers with their Arms; one or more of them knocked at my door, my Wife being up with one of my children (who was very sick) ... my wife presently comes running to my chamber and said to me,

Husband, what have you done, here is a Troop of horse and many souldiers at the door for you? I gave my wife this Answer, I fear them not.' The soldiers came in, searched Prince's ovens and beds and then arrested him for high treason. Mrs Prince was as resolute as Mary Overton or Elizabeth Lilburne in 1646–7, and a familiar moral was drawn:[49]

> Forthwith came my Wife unto me, and said unto the souldiers, that she knew her husband had done no harm, and that he cared not for the worst his Enemies could do unto him.

Husband and wife then lamented that the Parliament for whom Prince had risked his life and lent above £1,000 had turned on him, but comforted themselves with their discharge of their consciences against 'tyranny and slavery'.

The other arrests were similar. Richard Overton was lodging with friends when the soldiers ransacked the house, accused Overton of sleeping with 'the Gentlewoman who then sat suckling her childe', insulted most of the other inhabitants, 'and gave it out in the Court and Street, amongst the souldiers and neighbours that it was a Bawdy-house'.[50] Noise, violence, a terrified household and a troubled but loyal neighbourhood were the themes of William Walwyn's account.[51] His maid was left, 'crying and shivering'; his daughter sick, while his wife 'certainly had been much more affrighted, but for her confidence of my innocence'. As usual in Leveller literature the general implications were overtly drawn. Walwyn concluded, 'in like manner, any man or woman in England is liable to be fetcht from the farthest parts of the Land, by parties of horse and foot, in an hostile manner, to the affrighting and ruining of their Families'.[52]

These dramatic narratives of violation and capture form the polemical context for the Leveller women's petitioning of April and May 1649 – a context of invaded homes and ruined families. The petitions present the women as engaged in a controversial and unprecedented activity as a response to this monstrous disruption of their households:[53]

> We are so over-prest, so over-whelmed in afflictions, that we are not able to keep in our compass, to be bounded in the custom of our sex; for indeed we confess it is not our custom to address our selves to this House in the Publick behalf.

Many later discussions have also assumed that the Leveller women's petitioning was a dramatic assertion of female political rights, and some contemporary sources agree. All newsbook accounts agree that many hundreds of women were involved in lobbying Parliament over several days around 22 April, and again two weeks later; such mass action by women was clearly a dramatic and, to many, an alarming development.[54]

None the less we should be cautious before accepting completely that this petitioning campaign was as outrageous as the women themselves insisted. Newsbook accounts, for example, vary in their response. For some, in the weeks that saw the execution of the Welsh ex-parliamentarian Poyer, chosen from his fellow 1648 rebels after a dramatic drawing of lots, the execution and funeral of Lockyer and the army mutinies, the Leveller women were simply not very newsworthy, and treatment was very brief. Other newsbooks report the Leveller petitions as an example, on a larger scale, of women supporting their husbands, coupling their activities with the attempts of Lady Capel, wife of an executed Royalist, to obtain her jointure, or the lobbying by Poyer's wife to prevent her husband's execution. This satirical account is echoed in many more sober newsbooks:[55]

> The Parliament have this week been much troubled with Women; as first this new Prophetesse, secondly by the women Petitioners; thirdly Col Poyers Wife, fourthly my Lady Temple, Nay, and with some Children too, viz. The murder'd Kings Children for means for their livelyhoods; and I would all the oppressed men, Women and Children in England and Ireland were about their ears, for that would make a quick dispatch of them.

Women's petitioning is thus seen as normal in many accounts, irritating or embarrassing perhaps, but a part of political life. Most newsbooks give brief summaries and extracts from the petition; thus even disapproving papers helped to spread the women's message. More extended comment is found especially in the satirical pamphlets, with the greatest hostility coming from Royalist news writers who resorted to sexual slander to discredit their political opponents.[56] 'Hannah Jenks, Ruth Turn-up, Doll Burn it and Sister Wagtayle have petitioned the supream Authority for their man John, and Mr Overton, that they would in their great widsoms spare those worthys for breeders ... Holofernes Fairfax look to thy head, for Judith is a comming, the women are up in armes, and vow they will tickle your members.'

Feminist literary scholars Susan Wiseman and Diane Purkiss have cautioned against assuming too direct a relationship between such sexual slander, or debate about the nature of women, and the activities of 'real' women.[57] As gender hierarchies are symbolically essential to all ordering of power in societies, sexual debate and slander can operate as much on a symbolic level, revealing the broader, unconscious tensions and problems of patriarchal society. The sexual political literature of the 1640s and 1650s may indicate the anxieties of men at their own divisions rather than that women have become more active or more threatening. The unruly female was a potent symbol of disorder, used to mock and discredit political and religious opponents, while reinforcing the absurdity of women's political activities. Of course, in the spring of 1649 many, perhaps hundreds of real women, were intervening in public affairs in a manner that was certainly not just symbolic. However, as Wiseman argues, Henry Marten, often associated with the Leveller women in the newsbooks, was libelled sexually because he was a republican, not because he was a libertine, although his well-known, long-term cohabitation with a woman who was not his wife lent credibility to such slanders.[58] Likewise, Leveller women were opposed as much as Levellers as women. Literary conventions and well-established satirical strategies, as much as genuine alarm at female activism, underlay attacks like the following[59]

> The bony-lasses will try one touch more and if that will not doe they will scale the wall at Westminster, and with boyling water scald the Hornets out of their nests; And when this great assault shall be made, Harry Martin hath promised them they shall not want for a Standard, for he will keep his unshaken till that day, and then hee will mount it amongst them, and display the banner of his mettle right valiantly so long as hee can stand.

Frankly phallic pornographic images ridicule both the Parliament and their radical critics by associating them with unruly and dishonest women, in a manner that recalls the verse libels that attacked pre-Civil War politicians.[60]

Both sympathetic and hostile accounts of the Leveller women in the news-books, carried images from popular literature, and should not be seen as unproblematic direct reporting. Common epithets such as 'Bonny lasses', 'brave lasses', 'Bonny Besses' recalled popular ballads and songs such as a 'country jig' sung by a character in Thomas Deloney's *Thomas of Reading* (1612), or the refrain of the earliest, and one of the most enduring ballads about warrior women, 'Mary Ambree'.[61] It is perhaps significant that Mary Ambree, like the Leveller women, combined a womanly love for her partner with a manly valour necessary in the absence of the male, by avenging her soldier lover after his death in battle.

We should not, then, take for granted that the Leveller women's petitioning of 1649 was unprecedented and outrageous. All petitions are 'humble', and these women are humbly soliciting the parliament's help on behalf of their husbands and families. Rather, we need to examine why the women themselves insisted that it was so controversial and dramatic. On one level it seems clear that the public protests of honest women, mistresses of honest households, were an integral and vital part of Leveller self-presentation as a movement, and a major element in their responses to the violation of Leveller households in March 1649. 'Honest', with its connections with honour, was a term with multiple meanings in early modern England. To the Levellers its use implied sincerity and openness rather than the deceit and deviousness of their opponents; respectability and independence for men; and, very importantly, dedication to the 'public' service. For women, however, 'honest' referred especially to sexual behaviour, meaning chastity or fidelity, while publicly prominent activity by women risked accusations of dishonesty, or unchastity. Indeed, unconventional female behaviour of any kind could be met by sexual slander.[62] What the Levellers seem to have been insisting on was that their households, their women, were so honest that they could intervene publicly without any stains on their character.

Furthermore, the structure of the petitions of 1649 was directed, above all else, at forcing home a sense of the enormity of the violation of Leveller households, and by extension, a realization of Parliament's betrayal of the early Civil War ideals. The calamity was so extreme that of course women, even women, had a duty to act, to take a stance in a 'public' arena. Thus, both petitions counterposed the normal expectations of female behaviour – to be silent, to keep at home – to the extremes of endeavour now required by honest women and householders.[63] 'The grievous weight of the publick Calamity' meant that they were not able, 'longer to sit in silence, for our oppressions are too many and great for us ... if oppression make a wise man mad; how is better to be expected from us that are the weaker vessel? We are so overprest, so over-whelmed in afflictions, that we are not able to keep in our compass, to be bounded in the custom of our sex.' They had sat at home while 'our husbands, our children, brethren and servants' had incessantly waited on the Commons with petitions, to be met only with 'hostile violence'. Now the women were resolved to join the struggle for native freedoms, even if they perished with their menfolk, 'we knowing for our encouragement and example, God hath wrought many deliverances for severall Nations from age to age by the weake hand of women'.

The second petition made similar points through a series of rhetorical questions.[64] How could they be 'so sottish or stupid' as not to realize the threats of arbitrary power? Should they 'keep at home in our houses' when faithful men like the four Leveller leaders were 'fetcht out of their beds, and forced from their Houses by Souldiers, to the affrighting and undoing of themselves, their wives, children and families?' In the circumstances of April 1649, 'Our houses being worse then Prisons to us, and our Lives worse then death', the women were forced to take drastic steps to remedy this great calamity. In 1653, when the Leveller movement no longer really existed, but old contacts were used to campaign against Lilburne's trial, there were significant differences in the rhetoric of the women's petitions. Although it was stressed that[65] 'the thing is so gross that even women perceive the evil of it', the women now spoke of their 'undoubted Right of Petitioning', rather than presenting their interventions as extraordinary.

Leveller definitions of honest households were amplified by the Levellers' own recourse to sexual slander; by frequent use of a vivid language of sexual contrast, particularly the contrast between the honest wife and the whore; and by a connected discourse of the true manliness of political honesty contrasted with the unmanliness of Leveller opponents. Once more, Leveller discursive strategies built on existing cultural resources; their language and arguments drew on the rhetoric of sexual slander used by London women from social milieux similar to those from whom the Levellers sought support.[66] Levellers defended the 'honesty' of their women, forced to enter a public arena to attack the individual or collective wrongs done by the Parliament. Scorning their opponents' accusations that Leveller men were associates of whores, Leveller pamphlets claimed that their enemies themselves promoted whoredom and loose living. In a series of dramatic incidents and polemics, 'honesty' was constructed as a complex of personal standards and political loyalties, and contrasted with the many-sided dishonesty of the parliamentarians who had betrayed the people's cause.

These points can be illustrated only briefly. At the end of a 1647 pamphlet mainly concerned with the sufferings of himself and his wife, John Lilburne discussed the House of Lords' treatment of two apparently unconnected family scandals.[67] One Elizabeth Walker, whose husband had abandoned her, 'for the satisfying of his lust', had spent six years in attendance on the House of Lords, 'for a little relief to keep her and her children alive'. Yet one Mr Staveley, a dedicated servant of the Parliament and high sheriff of Leicestershire, had been imprisoned for refusing to pay alimony to his wife who deserted him to live 'in the highest, professed and open incontinency that a woman can'. The moral was obvious, but as usual Lilburne hammered it home, bringing together chastity, honesty and righteousness to make a political point:

> do not these two forementioned actions visibly declare that they are greater friends to whores and rogues then to honest and chast men and women and whether injustice and oppression be not more delightsome to them then justice, righteousness and truth?

This coupling of individual morality and political conduct is found in later Lilburne pamphlets. Seeking to defend himself from accusations of Royalist intrigue while in exile in the Netherlands, Lilburne counter-attacked by denouncing the sexual associations of both Royalist spies and the republic's 'spy-master' Thomas Scot. Lilburne unmasked Captain Wendy Oxford, who had tried to trap him in Royalist plots, as an agent of Scot's,[68] in order to, 'render him uncapable to receive any more bills of exchange from Mr Thomas Scot, for the paying of him his sallery, to enable him to drinke drunk night and day, to feast, whore it, swear, rant it and domineer, rather like a bedlam than a man; or to send one of his sluts over to give Mr Scot if he wants a tast of her (which kind of flesh is notoriously at Westminster knowne he loves as well as Oxford doth)'.

Church court evidence from before the Civil War indicates that it was women, in particular, whose chastity was an issue in local communities, while men were more likely to be damaged through their association with immodest women, than on account of their own promiscuity. It was a different matter when sexual honesty had political implications.[69] During the Civil War, and in the aftermath of the regicide especially, notions of manhood and male authority were rendered generally problematic; Leveller presentations of the male self participated in broader anxieties and reformulations. Leveller men were clearly concerned to establish their own chastity as well as the honesty of their wives. Partly this was because they had to defend themselves against the sexualized jibes of opponents, but more positively the central Leveller identity of responsible householder necessarily involved a chaste conception of masculinity. Even the long-married William Walwyn whose pamphlets sometimes included cosy political discussions between himself and his wife was forced to deny that he was 'loosely addicted to women'. Clearly this derived from the widespread view of Walwyn as a dangerous religious radical and from the linking of religious heterodoxy with libertinism, but to Walwyn, 'this is such a slander as doggs me at the heels home to my house; seeking to torment me even with my wife and children'.[70]

It was equally necessary for Richard Overton to engage in a struggle over the meaning of his 1649 arrest, which was not universally seen as the shattering of a domestic idyll. In his account of his arrest, Overton offered the testimony of a corporal who had confessed that the soldiers, 'had dealt uncivilly and unworthily with me, and that there was no such matter of taking me in bed with an other woman etc'. He added the deposition of a witness denouncing Lieutenant Colonel Axtell's accusation as false and scandalous; and finally took space in one of the newsbooks to deny the slur printed a week before.[71]

The most striking example of the language of sexual contrast is found in the descriptions of the treatment of Mary Overton in 1647, both in the petition under her own name, and in her husband's more extended narratives. In Richard Overton's magnificently indignant account he presents his wife's chaste modesty as entirely compatible with a determined defiance of the 'usurped jurisdiction' of the House of Lords. Not content with despatching Mary Overton to the gaol at Maiden Lane, the Lords, 'order that she shall be cast into the most infamous Goale of Bride-well, that common Centre and receptacle of bauds, whores, and strumpets, more fit for their wanton retrograde Ladies, then for one, who never yet could be taxed of immodesty, either in countenaunce, gesture, words or action'. Yet, 'to the utmost testimony of her weake power' Mary resisted the illegal order, 'for in plain down-right termes (like a true bred Englishwoman brought up at the feet of Gamaliel) she told the Marshall she would not obey it'. Consequently Mary Overton was dragged through 'the dirt and the mire of the streetes' to Bridewell, 'with the poore Infant still crying and mourning in her Armes', defamed as a strumpet and a whore. Thus she risked losing her reputation for ever, 'that for the future (if ever delivered from her bondage) she should not passe the streets upon her necessary occasions any more without contumely and derision, scoffing, hissing and poynting at her, with such or the like sayings, as, see, see, there goes a strumpet that was dragged through the streetes to Bridewell'. Thus Overton drew on the widespread concern both of urban communities and of popular literature with the sexual reputation of women, to highlight, as so many Leveller pamphlets did, the threats to 'the freedoms of the Commons of England', when honest households were attacked, and the honour of 'modest, chaste and civill women' was literally dragged through the mire. The dangers of the street, a public thoroughfare where only disorderly women ventured, were evoked in vivid prose to highlight the injustice done to a pure woman. Furthermore, the true and complex womanliness of Mary Overton was contrasted with the false, bombastic masculinity of the 'Turky-cock Marshall' who 'with his valiant lookes like a man of mettle assailes her and her Babe, and by violence attempt to pluck the tender babe out of her Armes, but she forcibly defended it, and kept it in despite of his Manhood'. The true men were the 'honest and discreet' porters of the City of London who refused to aid in the abuse.[72]

Finally in this discussion of the stories Levellers told of their family life, we should return to the later Lilburne pamphlets recounting the quarrels between John and Elizabeth, not merely to sympathize with the unfortunate Elizabeth, but to ask what such narratives are intended to suggest. John Lilburne's trial for high treason in September 1649 came only weeks after two of his sons had died of smallpox while Elizabeth herself and a daughter had been gravely ill. From this time, through the many tribulations of his last years – his banishment in early 1652 for a renewed, virulent attack on Sir Arthur Haselrig, his return and second trial in the summer of 1653, the years of imprisonment ending only in death – John Lilburne bitterly described Elizabeth's 'mournfull arguments ... to be quiet', to submit to Cromwell and thus regain his liberty.[73] In general, as I have already suggested, the quarrels demonstrate that commitment to the cause had to come before any personal or family considerations. More specifically, the 1652 pamphlets highlight Cromwell's hypocrisy and deceit in a dynamic narrative: he might be able to convince a weak woman that his promises were genuine, but John Lilburne would not be deflected from defence of his own rights and the broader liberties of English men. Hence male political resolution is defined through its opposite, female personal credulity. 'The general gives my wife good words (which makes her believe him infinitely to be her friend)', but John Lilburne thought immediately of the eighteenth chapter of Machiavelli's *Prince*, and was convinced Cromwell was as 'false as the Devil himself'. 'Honest Besse' urged on John, 'such sneaking terms as my Soul abhorres, and ... no way becomes a man of a gallant ennobled and heroic minde', withholding the books he needed to write defiant pamphlets and petitions, 'through childishnesse, weaknesse or womanlinesse ... filled with womanish passion and anger'. John Lilburne had 'almost made myselfe Blinde', 'readeing, studying and writeing large Epistles to her, to satisfie her with *reason*'.[74] Here there is a much grimmer view of women's capacities than in most of the pamphlets of the 1640s, but it is worth noting that it is Elizabeth Lilburne's lack of commitment to the public good that is attacked when her concern for her husband, home and family is condemned as a weakness, albeit an inevitable one.[75]

Once we move from the central Leveller image of their own honest households, then, the accounts of gender relationships or of the nature of women (especially women who are not Levellers) become more ambiguous and contradictory with the resort to more conventional sexual slander, or assumptions about women's weaknesses. The very definitions of the movement shifted between one of 'honest men', and the more differentiated presentations in processions, or in series of printed petitions, as a movement of men and women, apprentices and masters, Londoners and others; the precision about place seemingly as important as that about age or gender.[76] However, the prevailing language was that of the household. We cannot tell from the pamphlets alone whether an accurate picture is being offered of Leveller family life, whether of the Walwyns' long, comfortable marriage or the more tragic and troubled Lilburne relationship. Rather, Leveller accounts are literary constructions, narratives, arguments used to offer a political identity to readers, and to convey a set of meanings about a movement and a cause – a friendly association of honest households shattered by the betrayal of those for whom they had fought.

The vision of household does, however, echo or presuppose something of the idealized godly household of the Puritan sermons and conduct books, which portrayed an active, affectionate partnership between husband and wife, with the wife a valued, if subordinate associate. The Leveller image does not share the conduct books' assumption that the wife is somehow 'confined' to her home, like a snail, while the 'wider world' was a male preserve. As Susan Amussen and Laura Gowing have stressed, the realities of domestic life, and particularly the participation by women of middling and poorer rank in urban economic life, did not lend themselves to such sharp contrasts.[77] Notions of the 'public' and 'private' are complex and contradictory in Leveller writings, not least when connected to gender. Women's capacities for political actions and their involvement with the public good were on a lesser scale than men's, but there is no clear sense of a public–private political split paralleling gender divisions. The 1649 pamphlets portray Leveller households as a refuge from oppression, yet households are clearly also embedded in a public world; a major thrust of Leveller campaigns between 1646 and 1649 was to stress that the oppression of individual households was a political not a merely personal issue. The story of the calamitous betrayal of the Parliament's cause was told through vivid accounts of the tribulations of honest householders. In these stories an active public role for women, and a defiant public female voice, was a vital, even essential element.

Women's activity was firmly connected with the household, and their interventions were presented as defending and reaffirming family unity. Unity did not mean equality, of course. While a political rhetoric based upon the household validated activity by women (and servants) in certain circumstances, it also offered clear justification for the male head of household's monopoly of formal political rights. The account of Leveller identity offered here thus has important implications for more conventional political analysis. Furthermore, Leveller literature also contains discordant writing on gender, indicating some of the instabilities and tensions surrounding early modern understandings of women. These incoherencies surely reflect some of the contradictions in households where women were seen as clearly subordinate, but also as capable, active partners whose co-operation was essential to the running of the whole enterprise.[78] They are also a product of the discursive problems of establishing a picture of women who were both honest and active in a public world. In the end, for Lilburne at least, women's weaknesses and irrationality made them less dedicated to the public service, especially in a cause that was betrayed and embattled.

I offer no neat conclusions to this chapter. My aims have been twofold: firstly to demonstrate the advantages of examining the Levellers and gender together, rather than as two separate topics, one part of a history of women's protest, the other (a marginal) part of a more conventional political history of the later 1640s. Secondly, in the spirit of David Underdown's own broad work on popular politics and culture, I have tried to open up approaches to the radical, popular political literature of the 1640s and early 1650s. As interesting as their programmes or abstract theories are the political identities Leveller pamphlets offered to their readers. These political identities were constructed to a large extent from stories told about the violations of households and the proper behaviour and relationships of men and women. These stories echoed themes and techniques found in pre-Civil War popular literature, and in the narratives ordinary people presented in courts of law;[79] but the Levellers sought to generalize individual suffering – to place it in an overall context of betrayal, oppression and, they hoped, of resistance.

Notes

[1] I am very grateful to Richard Cust, Mary Fissell, Mark Jenner, Nigel Smith and James Vernon for advice and encouragement with this chapter; and to seminar audiences in Oxford and London for much useful comment and discussion.

[2] H. N. Brailsford, *The Levellers and the English Revolution*, (1961), pp. 316–17; F. M. Leventhal, *The Last Dissenter. H. N. Brailsford and His World*, (Oxford, 1985); pp. 298–9; David Wootton, 'Leveller democracy and the Puritan revolution', in J. H. Burns and M. Goldie (eds.), *The Cambridge History of Political Thought 1450–1700* (Cambridge, 1991), pp. 416–17.

[3] See, for example, James Vernon, *Politics and the People. A Study in English Political Culture c.1815–1867* (Cambridge, 1993), pp. 9–10.

[4] C. Pateman, *The Disorder of Women: Democracy, Feminism and Political theory* (Cambridge, 1989); for some scepticism about Pateman see Rachel Weil, 'And women rule over them: sexual ideology and political propaganda in England 1680–1714', Ph.D. thesis, Princeton University (1991), pp. 64–6, 151; but the point about the unpicking of liberal complacency stands. Dorothy Thompson, 'Women and nineteenth century radical politics: a lost dimension', in J. Mitchell and A. Oakley (eds.), *The Rights and Wrongs of Women* (Harmondsworth, 1976); Anna Clark, 'The rhetoric of chartist domesticity', *Journal of British Studies*, 31 (1992); Barbara Taylor, 'Mary Wollstonecraft and the wild wish of early feminism', *History Workshop Journal*, 33 (spring 1992).

[5] *To the Supreme Authority of England, the Commons Assembled in Parliament/The Humble Petition of divers well-affected WOMEN, of the Cities of London and Westminster, the Borough of Southwark, Hambletts, and Parts Adjacent, Affectors and*

Approvers of the Petition of Sept 11 1648, British Library (hereafter B.L.), Thomason Tracts, 669 f. 14/27; Patricia Higgins, 'The reactions of women, with special reference to women petitioners', in B. Manning (ed.), *Politics, Religion and The English Civil War* (1973); Elaine Hobby, *Virtue of Necessity. English Women's Writing 1646–1688* (1988) pp. 13–17; Ann Marie McEntee, '"The [Un]civill-sisterhood of Oranges and Lemons": female petitioners and demonstrators, 1642–53', *Prose Studies*, 14 (1991), also published as a separate volume: J. Holstun (ed.), *Pamphlet Wars: Prose in the English Revolution* (London, 1992).

⁶ *Perfect Occurrences of Every Daie Journall in Parliament ...* 20–7 April (B.L., E.529/21); the same wording is found in *Mercurius Militaris*, 24 April–1 May (B.L., E.552/2). Higgins, 'Reactions of women', pp. 200–5, is the fullest recent account.

⁷ *Mercurius Pragmaticus*, 23–30 April (B.L., E551/12); *The Man in the Moone Discovering a World of Knavery under the Sunne*, 16–23 April (B.L., E551/10).

⁸ Higgins, 'Reactions of women', pp. 211–12; McEntee, '"The [Un]civill-sisterhood"', pp. 92–3, 101–2, 106–7.

⁹ Pauline Gregg, *Free-born John: A Biography of John Lilburne* (London, 1961); Margaret George, *Women in the First Capitalist Society: Experiences in Seventeenth Century England* (Brighton, 1988), ch. 4: 'Leveller husband/Leveller wife'. George's book is one of the few studies to look at both the 'activist' petitioners and the 'suffering' wives. Although I differ from George's approach, it was her work which first suggested to me the value of looking at how Levellers wrote about women.

¹⁰ John Lilburne, *England's Birthright Justified* (October 1645), facsimile in William Haller, *Tracts on Liberty in the Puritan Revolution*, vol. III (New York, 1965), p. 300; Gregg, *Free-born John*, pp. 122, 345–6.

¹¹ Antonia Fraser, *The Weaker Vessel: Women's Lot in Seventeenth-Century England* (1984), p. 236; cf. Gregg, *Free-born John*, p. 346.

¹² George, *Women in the First Capitalist Society*, pp. 61, 64.

¹³ C. B. Macpherson, *The Political Theory of Possessive Individualism*, (Oxford, 1962); R. B. Seaberg, 'The Norman Conquest and the common law: the Levellers and the argument from continuity', *Historical Journal*, 24 (1981); J. C. Davis, 'The Levellers and Christianity', in Manning, *Politics, Religion and the English Civil War*, pp. 225–50; Keith Thomas, 'The Levellers and the franchise', in G. E. Aylmer (ed.), *The Interregnum: The Quest for Settlement* (1972), esp. pp. 57–8; R. Howell and D. E. Brewster, 'Reconsidering the Levellers: the evidence of the *Moderate*', *Past and Present*, 46 (1970) also attacks the view that the Levellers had a 'coherent and unified programme' (p. 69), but again concentrates on the franchise issue, with a brief look at religious liberty.

¹⁴ Kevin Sharpe and Peter Lake, 'Introduction', in *idem, Culture and Politics in Early Stuart England* (Stanford, 1994), p. 4 is quoted. For other general discussions see Lynn Hunt (ed.), *The New Cultural History* (Berkeley, 1989); Patrick Joyce, 'History and post-modernism', *Past and Present*, 133 (1991).

¹⁵ For example, Gareth Stedman Jones, *Languages of Class: Studies in English Working Class History 1832–1982* (Cambridge, 1984); Patrick Joyce, *Visions of the People: Industrial England and the Question of Class, 1848–1914* (Cambridge, 1991); John Belchem, 'Republicanism, popular constitutionalism and the radical platform in early nineteenth-century England', *Social History*, 6 (1981); James Epstein, 'Radical dining, toasting and symbolic expression in early nineteenth-century Lancashire: rituals of solidarity', *Albion*, 20 (1988); F. R. Donnelly, 'Levelerism [*sic*] in eighteenth and nine-

teenth-century Britain', *Albion*, 20 (1988).

[16] Lynn Hunt, *The Family Romance of the French Revolution* (1992); Sara Maza, 'Domestic melodrama as political ideology: the case of the Comte de Sanois', *American Historical Review*, 94 (1989).

[17] Frederick Jameson, *The Political Unconscious: Narrative as a Socially Symbolic Act* (Ithaca and London, 1981) and the works of Hayden White are the most commonly cited inspirations. For the latter see, for example, 'The value of narrativity in the representation of reality', *Critical Inquiry*, 7 (autumn, 1980), reprinted in *idem, The Content of the Form* (Baltimore, 1987).

[18] For revisionism see Richard Cust and Ann Hughes, 'After revisionism', in Cust and Hughes (eds.), *Conflict in Early Stuart England: Studies in Religion and Politics, 1603–1642* (Longman, 1989). A discussion alert to the rhetorical and discursive constructions of identity through print is J. C. Davis, *Fear, Myth and History. The Ranters and the Historians* (Cambridge, 1986). It focuses, however, on a construction imposed from outside rather than on groups forging their own identity.

[19] The important article by J. S. Morrill and J. D. Walter, 'Order and disorder in the English Revolution', in A. Fletcher and J. Stevenson (eds.), *Order and Disorder* (Cambridge 1985) gives a brief, balanced account of the Levellers and other radical groups, while concentrating on local discontent. Mark Kishlansky, *The Rise of the New Model Army* (Cambridge, 1979) is more trenchant (p. x: 'The decision to exclude the so-called Levellers was a more difficult one ... The source materials leave little impression of radical infiltration or leadership [in the Army], but recent historiography has raised the Levellers to fantastic heights. They are nothing less than the deus ex machina in explanations of the Revolution.').

[20] David Underdown, *Revel, Riot and Rebellion. Popular Politics and Culture in England 1603–1660* (Oxford, 1985; 1987 paperback edition quoted), p. 213; cf. Underdown, 'The taming of the scold: the enforcement of patriarchal authority in early modern England', in Fletcher and Stevenson, *Order and Disorder*. Brian Manning's work stresses the importance of radicalism, but he works within a framework of class conflict, rather than that of the 'new cultural history': Manning, *The English People and the English Revolution* (1976; second edition, 1991); *idem, 1649. The Crisis of the English Revolution* (London, 1992).

[21] B. Sharp, *In Contempt of all Authority: Rural Artisans and Riot in the West of England 1586–1660* (Berkeley, 1980); K. Lindley, *Fenland Riots and the English Revolution,* (London, 1982); Clive Holmes, 'Drainers and fenmen: the problem of popular political consciousness in the seventeenth century', in Fletcher and Stevenson, *Order and Disorder*.

[22] Thomas Corns, *Uncloistered Virtue. English Political Literature, 1640–1660* (Oxford, 1992), pp. 135–42.

[23] Norah Carlin, 'Leveller organisation in London', *Historical Journal*, 27 (1984); Ian Gentles, 'London Levellers in the English Revolution: the Chidleys and their circle', *Journal of Ecclesiastical History*, 29 (1978); *idem, The New Model Army in England, Ireland and Scotland, 1645–1653* (Oxford, 1992), pp. 190–226, and ch. 10; Manning, *1649*; Austin Woolrych, *Soldiers and Statesmen: The General Council of the Army and its Debates, 1647–8* (Oxford, 1987), with more qualifications, represent a range of work that sees the Levellers as a significant force.

[24] Austin Woolrych, *Commonwealth to Protectorate* (Oxford, 1982), pp. 250–61; Gregg, *Free-born John*, pp. 330–2 for 1653; David Allen, 'Political clubs in Restora-

tion London', *Historical Journal*, 19 (1976), especially p. 569 on the 'Green ribbon club'; Richard Ashcraft, *Revolutionary Politics and Locke's Two Treatises of Government* (Princeton, 1986), pp. 143, 164, 247–50.

[25] *The Kingdomes Faithfull and Impartiall Scout*, 27 April–4 May (E529/31); *Continued Heads of Perfect Passages in Parliament ...*, 27 April–4 May (E529/39); *Perfect Occurrences of Every Daie Journall in Parliament ...*, 27 April–4 May (E529/32).

[26] Cf. Wootton, 'Leveller democracy', pp. 414–15. On these issues I have benefited greatly from reading Nigel Smith's chapter on the Levellers from his forthcoming book on literature and the civil war.

[27] *Englands New Chains Discovered* (1649), reprinted in W. Haller and G. Davies (eds.), *The Leveller Tracts 1647–1653* (first published 1944, rept. Gloucester, MA, 1964), p. 168.

[28] John Lilburne, *London's Liberty in Chains Discovered*, (1646), B.L., E.359/17, postscript, p. 72; cf. Lilburne, *The Legall Fundamentall Liberties of the People of England*, published June 1649, reprinted in Haller and Davies, *Leveller Tracts*, p. 449; Joan Webber, *The Eloquent 'I': Style and Self in Seventeenth Century Prose* (Madison, 1968), esp. p. 77, for the active response required to Lilburne's writing.

[29] Lilburne, *The Upright Mans Vindication* (August, 1653), p. 29.

[30] David Wootton, 'From rebellion to Revolution: the crisis of the winter of 1642/3 and the origins of Civil War radicalism', *English Historical Review*, 105 (1990); Andrew Sharp, 'John Lilburne and the Long Parliament's *Book of Declarations*: a radical's exploitation of the words of authorities', *History of Political Thought*, 9 (1988).

[31] *Legall Fundamentall Liberties*, in Haller and Davies, *Leveller Tracts*, p. 411; *London's Liberty*, pp. 32–3.

[32] *To the Chosen and betrusted Knights, Citizens and Burgesses, assembled in the high and supream Court of Parliament, The Humble Petition of Elizabeth Lilburne, wife to Lieut-Col John Lilburne* (September, 1646), B.L. 669 f. 10/68; Richard Overton, *An Appeale from the Degenerate Representative Body of the Commons of England Assembled at Westminster. To the Body Represented, The free people in Generall* (July, 1647), reprinted in D. M. Wolfe (ed.), *Leveller Manifestoes of the Puritan Revolution* (New York, 1944, repr. 1967), pp. 164–5; *To the right Honourable, the Knights, Citizens, and Burgesses, the Parliament of England, assembled at Westminster, the Humble Appeale and Petition of Mary Overton, prisoner in Bridewell* (March 1647), B.L. E381/10. I am not concerned with whether the women 'really' wrote these petitions or simply put their names to their husbands' work. My interest is in the fact that it seemed appropriate for them to be published under women's names.

[33] John Lilburne, *The Resolved Man's Resolution*, (May, 1647), pp. 11–12.

[34] Overton, *An Appeale*, in Wolfe, *Leveller Manifestoes*, p. 166, italics mine; Lilburne, *London's Liberty*, pp. 65–70; *idem*, *Regall Tyrannie Discovered* (January, 1647), B.L., E370/12, pp. 72–7, print Elizabeth's petition. Richard Overton, *The Commoners Complaint* (February, 1647), included as appendices the appeals of his wife, and of his brother. The main pamphlet is reprinted in Haller, *Tracts on Liberty*, vol. III, pp. 373–95. *A true Relation of all the Remarkable Passages and Illegall Proceedings of some Sathannicall or Doeg-like Accusers of their Brethren, Against William Larner* (May, 1646), included, pp. 7–8, a copy of 'The humble Petition of Ellen Larner, wife of William Larner', the radical bookseller imprisoned for distributing scandalous books.

[35] Lilburne, *Regall Tyranny*, pp. 78, 84.

[36] Lilburne, *The Resolved Man's Resolution*, pp. 2–3.

[37] Sandra Clark, *The Elizabethan Pamphleteers. Popular Moralistic Pamphlets, 1580–1640* (London, 1983), pp. 68–82 for pre-Civil War prison literature; *A true Relation of all the Remarkable Passages ... Against William Larner* (1646), title-page; see also Overton, *Commoner's Complaint*, title-page. Cf., Maza, 'Domestic melodrama'.

[38] *The humble Appeale and Petition of Mary Overton*, p. 8.

[39] Lilburne, *Regall Tyrannie Discovered*, p. 47; cf., *Legall Fundamentall Liberties*, in Haller and Davies, *Leveller Tracts*, p. 411; *London's Liberty*, p. 26; *Lieutenant-Colonel John Lilburne, His Apologeticall Narration* (Amsterdam, April, 1652), B.L., E659/30, title-page, p. 10.

[40] From many other examples see Macpherson, *Possessive Individualism*; Leveller programmes are found in the series of 'Agreements of the People' and in successive petitions, notably that of 11 September 1648. Most are reprinted in Wolfe, *Leveller Manifestoes*. A broader view, which has much influenced my account is found in Manning, *The English People*.

[41] Richard Overton, *An Appeale from the Degenerate Representative Body of the Commons of England Assembled in Westminster. To the Body Represented, The free people in Generall* (1647), reprinted in Wolfe, *Leveller Manifestoes*, p. 165; *A true Relation of all the Remarkable Passages ... Against William Larner*, title-page, pp. 7–8.

[42] Lilburne, *As You Were, or the Lord General Cromwell and the Grand Officers of the Armie their Remembrancer* (Amsterdam, 1652), p. 9; *To the Supreme Authority of England, the Commons Assembled in Parliament/The Humble Petition of divers well-affected WOMEN*.

[43] The fragmenting of the friendships of the early 1640s was also an important trope for the story of betrayal. Cromwell, 'my then most intimate and familiar bosome frind' (Lilburne, *Apologeticall Narration*, p. 5) was the most obvious focus, although Lilburne also charted the break-up of parliamentarian alliances through the shifts in his relationship with the baptist William Kiffin: *Legall Fundamentall Liberties*, in Haller and Davies, *Leveller Tracts*, p. 440; *As You Were*, p. 4–5.

[44] Overton, *An Appeale*, in Wolfe, *Leveller Manifestoes*, p. 165; *A true Relation of all the Remarkable Passages and Illegal Proceedings ... against William Larner*, p. 8. There are similarities with Chartist rhetoric: Clark, 'Chartist domesticity'.

[45] *A true Relation of all the Remarkable Passages ... Against William Larner*, p. 9. In 1649, John Lilburne wrote of his wife's 'extraordinary grief' when he refused a place of £1,000 p.a. on his release from a Royalist prison, preferring to fight 'for 8 pence a day till I see the liberties and peace of England settled': *Legall Fundamentall Liberties*, in Haller and Davies, *Leveller Tracts*, p. 407.

[46] John Lilburne, *The Resolved Man's Resolution*, pp. 6, 8, 23; Joan Webber, *The Eloquent 'I'*, amongst many important insights into Lilburne's presentation of himself in print, stresses (p. 68) the influence of Fox's accounts of the Protestant martyrs.

[47] This example is from Lilburne, *London's Liberty*, p. 57, but similar accounts abound in Leveller pamphlets and in *The Moderate*, the Leveller newsbook: see for example the edition of 13–20 March 1649: B.L., E548/2, pp. 362–3.

[48] Cf. Peter Lake on the households (often London households) torn apart by terrifying, intimate crimes as presented in sensational pre-Civil War murder pamphlets: 'Deeds against nature: cheap print, Protestantism and murder in early seventeenth century England', in Sharpe and Lake, *Culture and Politics*. Mark Jenner has pointed out to me the echoes also of biblical stories such as the cruelties of Herod, and atrocity

stories from the Thirty Years War.

[49] *The Picture of the Councel of State, held forth to the Free People of England* (April 1649), reprinted in Haller and Davies, *Leveller Tracts*, p. 234.

[50] *Ibid.*, p. 214–15.

[51] William Walwyn, *The Fountain of Slaunder Discovered* (May 1649), reprinted in Jack McMichael and Barbara Taft (eds.), *Writings of William Walwyn* (Athens, Georgia, 1989), pp. 362–4.

[52] *Ibid.*, p. 364.

[53] *To the Supream authority of this Nation.*

[54] *The Kingdomes Faithfull and Impartiall Account*, 20–27 April, B.L., E529/22 (a sympathetic paper) says 300; *Continued Heads of Perfect Passages in Parliament*, 20–27 April, E529/3, says 'near 500'; *The Moderate*, 17–24 April, E551/20, 'some hundreds'.

[55] *The Man in the Moone Discovering a World of Knavery under the Sunne*, 23–30 April, E552/8. Lady Temple was seeking protection for her indebted husband. Similar couplings of different women's activities are found in *A Perfect Diurnall*, 23–30 April, E529/26; *Perfect Occurrences of Every Daie Journall in Parliament*, 20–27 April, E529/21; *The Moderate Messenger*, 7–14 May, E530/5.

[56] *The Man in the Moone*, 16–23 April; see also *Mercurius Pragmaticus*, 23–30 April, E551/12.

[57] Susan Wiseman, ' "Adam, the father of all flesh", porno-political rhetoric and political theory in and after the English Civil War', *Prose Studies*, 14 (1991), also published as a separate volume, in Holstun, *Pamphlet Wars*, pp. 134–57; cf. Diane Purkiss, 'Material girls: the seventeenth-century woman debate', in C. Brant and D. Purkiss (eds.), *Women, Texts and Histories 1575–1760* (London, 1992).

[58] Wiseman, '"Adam, the father of all flesh"', p. 144; *The Remonstrance or Declaration of Mr Henry Martin and all the whole society of Levellers* (September 1648), B.L., E464/37, claimed Leveller support was drawn from, 'Theeves, petty theeves, whoore-masters, whoore-mongers, drunkards, tiplers, covetous persons ... as also the prayers of all women who have poysoned their husbands, murdered their children, baudy housekeepers, whoores, secret and publick, and all others who desire to live as they list'. I owe this reference to Wiseman's article.

[59] *Mercurius Pragmaticus*, 8–15 May, E555/13.

[60] Alastair Bellany, ' "Raylinge rymes and vaunting verse": libellous politics in early Stuart England, 1603–1628', in Sharpe and Lake, *Culture and Politics*.

[61] *The Penguin Book of Renaissance Verse 1509–1659*, selected and introduced by David Norbrook (1993) pp. 325, 792; Dianne Dugaw, *Warrior Women and Popular Balladry, 1650–1850* (Cambridge, 1989), pp. 1–2, 31–42. For these phrases in the newsbooks see, for example, *Mercurius Militaris*, 8 May 1649, B.L., E554/13, the humourous newsbook edited by the Leveller sympathiser, John Harris.

[62] Laura Gowing, 'Gender and the language of insult in early modern London', *History Workshop*, 35 (spring 1993); *idem*, 'Women, sex and honour: the church courts in London, 1572–1640', Ph.D. dissertation, London (1993).

[63] *To the Supream authority of this Nation ...* pp. 3–4.

[64] *To the Supreme Authority of England.*

[65] *To the Parliament of the Commonwealth of England, The humble Petition of divers afflicted Women, in behalf of M. John Lilburn Prisoner in Newgate* (July 1653), B.L., 669 F.17/26; *Unto every individual Member of Parliament/The humble representation of divers afflicted women petitioners to the parliament on the behalf of Mr John Lilburn*

(July 1653), B.L., 669 F.17/38.

66 Gowing, 'Gender and the language of insult'.

67 Lilburne, *The Resolved Man's Resolution*, pp. 28–9.

68 Lilburne, *As You Were*, p. 2.

69 Gowing, 'Gender and the language of insult', esp. p. 7; cf. Bellany, ' "Raylinge Rymes" '; I have benefited also from reading an unpublished paper by Richard Cust, 'Honour and politics in early Stuart England: the case of Beaumont versus Hastings'.

70 Walwyn, *The Fountain of Slaunder Discovered*, in Taft (ed.), *Collected Works*, p. 358. For a report of the Walwyns' discussions, see William Walwyn, *Walwyn's Just Defence* (1649), repr. in Haller and Davies, *Leveller Tracts*, pp. 372–3.

71 *A Picture of the Council of State*, in Haller and Davies, *Leveller Tracts*, pp. 217, 233. The story about Overton sharing a bed with another man's wife was repeated in *Perfect Occurrences of Every Daie Journall in Parliament*, 23–30 March, B.L., E529/3; it was denied by 'Mr Overton's friends' the following week, 30 March–6 April: B.L., E529/7.

72 The best account is in Overton, *The Commoners Complaint*, repr. in Haller, *Tracts on Liberty*, vol. III, pp. 16–21. Similar narratives are found in Mary Overton, *To the right Honorable, the Knights, Citizens and Burgesses, the Parliament of England*; and Richard Overton, *An Appeale*, repr. in Wolfe, *Leveller Manifestoes*. Cf. Gowing, 'Gender and the language of insult'.

73 John Lilburne, *As You Were, or The Lord General Cromwell and the Grand Officers of the Armie their Remembrancer* (1652), p. 4 provides the quote.

74 John Lilburne, *The Upright Man's Vindication* (August 1653), pp. 5–7; *Lieutenant-Colonel Lilburne Revived* (March 1653), 'Letter to a friend', pp. 1–3 (second pagination).

75 Lilburne announced his conversion to the Quakers in an open letter to his wife, in similar terms, renouncing world and family to serve God, 'even to a final denial of father, kindred, friends, my sweet and deeply beloved (by me) babes or thy own self': *The Resurrection of John Lilburne, Now a Prisoner in Dover Castle* (1656), esp. pp. 4–6.

76 The ambiguities are again revealed in the varying Leveller uses of the creation myth: cf. Lilburne, *Regall Tyranny Discovered*, pp. 6–7, which stressed the original equality of men and women with the more conventional version in Lilburne, *London's Liberty in Chains Discovered*, postscript.

77 For the snail image, see Patricia Crawford, 'Public duty, conscience, and women in early modern England', in J. Morrill, P. Slack, D. Woolf (eds.), *Public Duty and Private Conscience in Seventeenth-Century England. Essays presented to G. E. Aylmer* (Oxford, 1993), p. 59. Susan Amussen, 'Gender, family and the social order, 1560–1725', in Fletcher and Stevenson, *Order and Disorder*, pp. 196–217; *idem*, *An Ordered Society: Gender and Class in Early Modern England* (Oxford, 1988), p. 119; Gowing, 'Gender and the language of insult', pp. 9–12.

78 Cf. Linda Pollock's perceptive account of the complexities of elite women's upbringing, ' "Teach her to live under obedience": the making of women in the upper ranks of early modern England', *Continuity and Change*, 4 (1989), pp. 231–58. Elite women had to be taught subordination, but, like Leveller wives at a lower social level, they had to be capable of running their households in the absence of their husbands.

79 Cf. Gowing, 'Gender and the language of insult', p. 9–10; *idem*, 'Women, sex and honour', pp. 196–207, where the links between stories told in defamation cases, and the themes of popular literature are demonstrated.

8

'If I did say so, I lyed': Elizabeth Cellier and the construction of credibility in the Popish Plot crisis

Rachel Weil

On 8 January 1679 the Catholic midwife Elizabeth Cellier visited Newgate prison to bring charitable aid to Catholic prisoners. She heard 'Terrible Grones and Squeeks which came out of the Dungeon'. Thinking that the cries came from a woman in childbirth, Cellier asked to be allowed to assist her, but was rudely driven away by the turnkey. She stayed around, however, and soon realized that the sounds were those of a man being tortured.[1]

Cellier's story, which she told in her pamphlet, *Malice Defeated*, struck at deeply held beliefs about the English legal system. Torture was supposed to happen in Catholic countries, like Spain, and it was against such practices that English liberties were defined. Cellier's story also cast doubt upon the existence of the notorious 'Popish Plot' (that is, the plot by Catholics to overthrow the government, murder the king and destroy the Protestant religion which had been 'revealed' – or invented – by the informer Titus Oates in 1678). The man being tortured, Cellier suggested, was Miles Prance, the Catholic silversmith who had been arrested in connection with the rumoured 'Popish Plot' and had then turned witness against his fellow Catholics. If Prance's confession had been obtained by torture, it strongly implied that there was no Popish Plot; rather, there was a plot by Presbyterians and their Whig allies to *frame* the Catholics for treason, in order to draw the public's attention away from their own plans to overthrow the government, murder the king and establish a republic.

The fact that Cellier chose to publicize her story is symptomatic of the pervasive uncertainty among the English public as to the trustworthiness of official authorities. It reveals an expansion of the possibilities as to what people might believe, and to whom they might be willing to listen. This paper will not ask whether Cellier was right about the existence of a Presbyterian plot, but what this episode can tell us about the problem of credibility in the Popish Plot crisis. In what context did Cellier's story make sense? What strategies of self-representation did she use to make herself believable? What can the fact that a woman expected to be believed about a matter of political importance tell us about the nature of political culture in the Popish Plot crisis?

The problem of credibility

The Popish Plot crisis might be seen, among other things, as an epistemological one. Stories about plots were central to the propaganda war between Whigs and Tories that emerged in 1679–80, and were widely aired in the press. Whigs used the story of a Popish Plot to garner support for themselves, while Tories countered with a story about a Presbyterian plot.[2] Because, as Peter Lake has argued for an earlier period, anti-popish and anti-Presbyterian rhetorics were dialectically constructed in relationship to one another,[3] competing plot stories became mirror images of each-other, and could be converted into one another. This was especially easy because Whigs and Tories both attributed an infinite capacity for disguise and dissimulation to, respectively, papists and presbyters. It was a Tory commonplace that Presbyterians masqueraded as Jesuits, a Whig commonplace that Catholics masqueraded as dissenters. In this context, it is not at all surprising to find the original story of a Popish Plot being turned by Cellier into a story about the existence of a Presbyterian plot to frame the Catholics. Similarly, as we shall see below, Cellier's story was given a further twist by the informer Thomas Dangerfield, who alleged that there was a Popish Plot to frame the Presbyterians in a plot to frame the papists. Every plot story was weavable into a number of ever more complex frames so that its meaning was subject to continuous reinterpretation.

This suggests that a large part of what would have made a plot story believable hinged not simply on the evidence offered but on the way that the witness and informer was presented. Here, too, uncertainty loomed, because the traditional ways of knowing whom to believe seemed not to apply. Information about the character of witnesses was an important part of legal proceedings in the seventeenth century, determining who could or could not be believed. What made for good character might vary, or be contested. The terms used to denote it might refer to financial status (for example, as in the phrase, 'a person of good credit'), or it might refer more vaguely to moral uprightness or good relations with neighbours.[4] Whatever the case, credibility was an attribute of the person, and this attribute was knowable. The circumstances of the Popish Plot crisis, however, disrupted the relationship between credibility and character. The informers and witnesses who came forward with tales of plots and counter-plots were sometimes criminal, often lower-class, and occasionally female. Moreover, their low status could enhance their credibility. A respectable person was presumably less likely to have first-hand contact with plotters and their dark doings. Criminality might be an asset in a witness. Thus, when he appeared at the Bar of the House of Commons, the informer William Bedloe, who according to historian J. P.

Kenyon was a 'professional criminal, a robber, highwayman and a confidence trickster', said: 'Mr Speaker, I have been a great rogue, but had I not been so I could not have known these things I am now about to tell you.'[5]

At one level, the problems posed by the presence of low-life/criminal informers were not new. The secretaries of state had made use of domestic spies, largely against dissenting conventicles and left-wing plots, since 1660.[6] The secretaries realized, as do today's historians, that the information they obtained by this means was questionable. The informers were of dubious character, and the system of payment created monetary incentives for informers to invent plots. The credibility of informers was thus not a new problem in 1679. However, the Popish Plot crisis posed the problem of credibility more sharply, and in a more public way. The words of informers and stories about them were reported in the press. Moreover, the government lost its monopoly on the practice of spying. The sense that the king was not looking after his own best interest encouraged the development of vigilante spy networks.

An example of such a network can be reconstructed from the testimony of the informer, Thomas Dangerfield. In October 1679, Dangerfield was arrested for trying to frame the Whig politician Roderick Mansel for treason by forging treasonous papers and planting them in Mansel's chamber. Dangerfield confessed to the fraud, but said that a group of Catholics had employed him to do it. He explained that he had been approached by the midwife Elizabeth Cellier, who had been acting as an agent for the Lady Powis, the wife of one of the five Catholic lords imprisoned in the Tower. They had hired him to find (or concoct) evidence of a Presbyterian plot. Lady Powis used her contacts to introduce him to more powerful people, such as the earl of Peterborough. Peterborough promised him help in obtaining a military commission and got him an audience with the king's Catholic brother, the Duke of York, who payed him twenty guineas and promised to make Dangerfield's fortune if he obtained proof of the Presbyterian plot. Dangerfield's train of connections stretched downward as well. They included, for example, Thomas Curtis, a clothworker recently arrived in London from the north, to whom Dangerfield promised £5,000 and an audience with the king, 'besides being taken care of for life', if he could obtain proof of the existence of a Presbyterian army.[7]

The spy network described here was bound together by patron–client links. The hierarchical structure was important to its functioning. The spymaster–patron who hired an informer not only provided him (or her) with material aid but also loaned the information legitimacy through his own respectable reputation. In this sense, vigilante spy networks mirrored and enforced social hierarchy. At the same time, vigilante spymasters were open to having their motives called into question in a way in which (I would speculate) State officials who employed spies were not. In public discussions of spymasters and informers, the flow of moral capital could be reversed: instead of the spymaster conferring respectability on the informer, the informer could taint the reputation of the spymaster. What the social differ-ence between the spymaster and the informer meant about the credibility of each was called into question in a way that might subvert the principles of social hierarchy.

This is what happened when Thomas Dangerfield was confronted by his ex-employers in front of the Privy Council in November 1679. According to Dangerfield's account of the proceedings, the men and women that he accused denied having encouraged him to fabricate evidence of a Presbyterian plot: rather, they insisted that they had heard about this alleged plot from Dangerfield. In defending themselves, they repeatedly pointed to Dangerfield's bad character. Lady Powis said 'she hoped the Oath of an Infamous person should not bring her in danger';[8] Henry Nevil, alias Payne, a pamphleteer who was said to have helped Dangerfield write and distribute anti-Presbyterian propaganda, 'reflects upon me as a Lewd and Infamous person'.[9] Peterbor-ough, 'in a large Discourse appealed to the known Method of his Life and Conversation, his Constant Services to the Crown', and said that he hoped that 'his Lordship's [Peterborough's] actions have been such, as shall exempt him from any shadow of reflection that can happen by such a Creature as I'.[10] Moreover, Peterborough explained his patronage of Dangerfield as a patriotic duty:

> His Lordship told the Board, That he could not but be troubled to have his name mentioned by such a Person as I was; but yet if any whoever should come to morrow to him again and tell him of any dangerous Practices against the King and the Government, whether by the Lord Shaftsbury or any other Lord what-soever, he should hold himself bound in duty to Hearken to any such Person, and to Indeavour to discover any such danger by all the waies he could.[11]

Thus, Peterborough's own status and reputation required that he involve him-self with Dangerfield, but they also guaranteed that the slime would not rub off on him.

Dangerfield, however, called into question the sharp line that his opponents drew between the spymaster and the informer he employed. He made no attempt to refute the aspersions on his character. Rather, he embraced them, and in doing so altered their meaning. In response to Nevil's comment that he was a lewd and infamous person, Dangerfield replied.

> That if I were such as he said, it was the more plain, that I could not proceed in such weighty undertakings as I had managed, without considerable Counsel and Direction; which is agreeable to what I have affirmed.[12]

Dangerfield thus emphasized the fact that people of low character, like him-self, have no motive to plot or deceive unless someone else rewards them for it. Paradoxically, his own bad character could work as proof of his credibil-ity. Moreover, Dangerfield's remarks implied a different understanding of how information about plots was generated. For Peterborough, the information was out in the world, ready to be collected – the use of disreputable persons like Dangerfield to collect it was a necessary inconvenience, but did not taint the spymaster, whose motives were purely patriotic. What Dangerfield calls attention to is the possibility that the informer–spymaster relationship can be conceptualized differently, in a way that puts emphasis on the spymaster's desire for information, for evidence of a plot. The more the informer is revealed to be out for money, the greater the possibility that he is merely giving the spymaster what he wants. Looked at from this perspective, Peterborough could be held responsible for Dangerfield's lies about Presbyterian plots, even if it was Dangerfield who was doing the lying, because Peterborough was providing the incentive.

The problems of credibility that emerged in this encounter before the Privy Council were taken up in the courts and in the press. In the trial of Elizabeth Cellier, where Dangerfield was the most damning witness, Cellier succeeded in having Dangerfield's testimony discredited on grounds that he had a criminal record. As the Lord Chief Justice put it, 'It is a sad thing that People of a vitious profligate Life ... should be suffered to be Witnesses to take away the Life of a worm.'[13] A different line, however, was taken in a picaresque novel, *Don Thomazo: or, the Juvenile Rambles of Thomas Dangerfield* (1680), which purported to tell the story of Dangerfield's education in roguery up until the time that he met his Catholic employers. That a Popish Plot informer could become the subject of a picaresque novel says much about the nature of public discussion during the Popish Plot crisis. The questions that remained central but ambiguous in picaresque novels – can a crook have a sense of honour? is the reformation of the criminal at the end of the story sincere? – were also central to the problem of determining the credibility of Popish Plot witnesses.

The preface to *Don Thomazo* took up these questions. The author reminds us that Dangerfield is now 'under the Protection of his Sovereigns Pardon, to which all true Subjects ought to give an awful respect and obedience'. He then stresses the possibility of reformation: 'the way to amendment is never out of date', as 'St Austin himself had occasion enough to repent the Follies of his Youth'. Finally, the author echoed Dangerfield's reply to Nevil at the Privy Council hearing: 'And it is no small Argument, that his being so proper for the designs for which he was call'd out, was half a proof, that his discoveries were true.'[14]

The Popish Plot crisis thus opened the way for a public discussion of credibility, featuring protagonists of all social classes, in which traditional criteria of status, character and respectability did not hold uncontested sway. What did make for credibility was up for grabs. In pamphlet literature, a variety of strategies can be found. Dangerfield, for example, frames his *Particular Narrative* as a conversion story, in which the hand of God prevents him from carrying out the heinous orders of his Catholic patrons.[15] Elizabeth Cellier begins her narrative, *Malice Defeated*, with a history of her family's loyalty to the Crown.[16] Credibility might be established by appeals to the efficacy of a royal pardon, or the privileges attached to certain professions. We can thus see the Popish Plot crisis as an unusual moment in which people outside of the formal political nation were able to speak on subjects of national importance.

However, the fact that plot stories were the object of political contest meant that no one's claims to credibility went unchallenged. Cellier's story (and Dangerfield's) exemplifies the possibilities for intervening in political affairs that the Popish Plot crisis opened up for ordinary people. It also reveals some of the mechanisms of exclusion, de-authorization and discrediting that it produced. What we see in the Popish Plot crisis is a debate in which the lower classes and women were objects as much as subjects.

So far, we have dealt with issues of credibility as they relate to class and status. But in Cellier's case, gender comes into play as well. As a woman, Cellier was excluded from formal participation in the political system. Moreover, the fact that she she was a midwife raises issues about non-official kinds of 'political power' which hinge on the knowledge of secrets and the ethics of telling them. Gender is also relevant in the responses to Cellier, which focused on both her profession and her sexuality. The next section will examine Cellier's pamphlet, *Malice Defeated*, which she published in the wake of her treason trial, with an eye to how she tried to construct herself as a credible witness, and how issues of gender figured in that construction.

Malice Defeated

It is worth saying at the outset that *Malice Defeated* is a confusing book on many levels. It is written in such a way as to be ambiguous about the claims it is making about the existence of a Presbyterian plot. Cellier tells the story of how she came to learn of the existence of a Presbyterian plot through Thomas Dangerfield, whom she met when he was a prisoner in Newgate. Dangerfield had provided her with information about the torture and abuse of Catholic prisoners, as well as about the efforts of men connected to the Whig leader, the earl of Shaftesbury, to bribe prisoners to give false testimony concerning the mythical Popish Plot. He proved so valuable an informant that Cellier helped him out of prison and gave him a job. In theory, he was to collect overdue debts for her husband. In reality, Cellier employed him as a spy. He frequented coffee-houses and brought her news of the plans of Shaftesbury, the Whigs and the Presbyterians to raise an army to overthrow the government.

What Cellier leaves unclear in this account is whether we are to think that the information that Dangerfield provided about the Presbyterian plot was true. The turning point in Cellier's relationship with Dangerfield came, of course, when he was arrested for planning forged papers in Mansel's chamber and alleged that Cellier had put him up to it. Cellier interprets his betrayal as the result of his having been bribed by the Presbyterians. From that point on, she presents Dangerfield in her pamphlet as a contemptible scoundrel, and she successfully discredited him as a witness at her trial by pointing to his criminal record. But did this mean that Dangerfield had always been a liar? Since Cellier had no proof independent of Dangerfield's information that there was a Presbyterian plot, one would logically think that she could not make any claims for the reality of its existence. Yet, Cellier claims in *Malice Defeated* that the Presbyterian plot was real, that 'Dangerfield once writ Truth'.[17] So there is a gap between what the book can logically be expected to do within its own rules of evidence, and what it seems to be trying to do.

The impact of *Malice Defeated* comes not through the working through of evidential problems but through Cellier's construction of herself. *Malice Defeated* is a strongly self-dramatizing work, in which Cellier's personality seems to leap off the page. We follow her through tribulation and triumph: from her arrest and imprisonment, where she heroically resists the efforts of Dangerfield and others to bribe her to turn witness against the Catholics, to her several appearances before the king's Privy Council which investigates the affair, to her conduct of her own defence at her treason trial. This section will look at a number of aspects of Cellier's self-representation in her narrative: her sense of herself as a martyr; her relationship to the law; her understanding of the relationship between law and truth, and truth and fiction; the significance of her gender; and the significance of her status as a midwife. As will be seen, the terms and tropes through which Cellier presents herself involve a number of agendas, and are not entirely straightforward.

One of the strongest images in *Malice Defeated* is that of Cellier as a martyr for the sake of truth. To Dangerfield, who tries to persuade her to turn witness against the Catholics, she replies, 'I had rather dye ten thousand deaths, than belye myself or others.' To the lords of the Council she announces 'I thank God Death is no terror to me, and she that fears not to die, cannot fear to speak Truth.' Threatened with being locked up for life, she responds 'I am a prisoner for Truth Sake, and that Cause, and the joy I have to suffer for it, makes this Dirty Smoaky hole to me a Pallace ... for I have thrown off all care of Earthly things, and have nothing to do but serve God.'[18]

The claim to be a martyr for the sake of truth proves to be deceptive. Cellier is of course not martyred, since she is triumphantly acquitted at the end of the pamphlet. She also does not consistently tell the truth. At some points, she cheerfully admits to lying. After telling the Privy Council that she has never been out of England, she is confronted with a witness named Richard Adams who deposes that she told him, over a drink at the Devil Tavern, that she had been 'beyond the Sea'. Cellier replies, 'If I did say so, I lyed.' When the president of the Council asks, reasonably enough, 'If you Lyed then, how shall we know you tell Truth now?' she answers, 'My Lord, there is a great deal of difference between what I say at a Tavern, to a Man of his Understanding, and what I say here, where every Word ought to be equal to an Oath.'[19] Similarly, at a hearing before the Privy Council, she confronts her former maid, Margaret Jenkins, who gives testimony against her. Cellier tells the Council that Jenkins should not be believed because she had been dismissed for stealing a spoon. Jenkins objects that at the time Cellier had thought that someone else had stolen the spoon. To which Cellier replies: 'Yes, and I think so still, but being told you accuse me, I must defend myself as well as I can.'[20]

Cellier's ethic might be described as one that sanctions situational lying for the sake of a larger 'Truth'. But her emphasis here on the artificiality of 'truth' as it emerges in a judicial (or in this case quasi-judicial) setting casts a significant shadow over her eventual legal triumph (which is, like her defence against Margaret Jenkins, based on discrediting the chief witness against her on grounds of alleged previous crimes). This raises questions about Cellier's presentation of the legal system, and of the relationship of that presentation to the themes of martyrdom and truth. Exactly what Cellier means to say about the legal system is ambiguous. The early prison scenes of the pamphlet were considered seditious precisely because they presented England as a scene of judicial torture.[21] Yet, the story can be read as a vindication of the ideals of the English legal system against the unscrupulous Whigs who threaten its integrity. Cellier at several points underscores her own commitment to and knowledge of the law. She claims to have enough knowledge 'to make a country justice', and emphasizes the fact that her husband, a Frenchman, cannot handle his legal business without her.[22] To an extent, then, Cellier puts herself firmly within a common law ideological tradition. This contributes to her political agenda by showing that Catholics share the mainstream belief in the superiority of the English legal system and are thus part of the mainstream political community.

And yet, if Cellier is paying a compliment to the legal system by showing herself vindicated through a trial, the compliment turns out to be rather backhanded. The jurors for example, do acquit her of treason … and then ask for a bribe, explaining that they would have been paid if they had convicted her. This introduces an ambiguity as to whether we are to think that the legal system worked, or merely that the jurors erroneously assumed that they would be rewarded. Moreover, Cellier puts such an emphasis on her own skill at defending herself that one is left unsure as to whether the pamphlet is celebrating the justness of the law, or Cellier's capacity to manipulate it. Such doubts, however, might also be seen as necessary to the polemic in which she is engaged. Given the fact that so many Catholics had already been convicted of treason, she could not show the legal system to be unproblematically just. Yet this move works in tension with Cellier's presentation of herself as a martyr for the sake of truth.

The relationship of *Malice Defeated* to the concepts of both truth and martyrdom is further complicated by Cellier's self-conscious use of literary allusions. Cellier writes in a way that tends to place her work on the border between reality and fiction. A stint by Dangerfield in the pillory is assimilated to the illusory knight errantry of Don Quixote: he peeps through the 'wooden engine' like 'Don Quicksot through his Helmet, when he was mounted upon Rosinant, and going to encounter with the Windmil'.[23] Moreover, long passages are written in the form of a dramatic dialogue. The lines between art and life are blurred in a striking way in an extraordinary exchange before the Privy Council. When Cellier asks to be tried soon, a Lord replies: 'Your Tryal will come soon enough, you will be put to death.'

> *Cel*: Blessed be God, then I hope the Play is near an end, for Tragedies whether real or fictitious, seldom end before the Women die.
>
> *A Lord*: What, do you make a Play of it?
>
> *Cel*: If there be no more Truth in the whole Story [i.e. of the Popish Plot] than there is in what relates to me, every Play that is Acted has more Truth in it.[24]

At one level, the literariness of these moments is ironic. Playing on the double-meaning of the word 'plot', Cellier suggests that the Popish Plot which her persecutors imagine to exist is as unreal as a fictional plot. At the same time, however, when Cellier applies fictional tropes to herself (as, in the case above, she does with the image of the doomed tragic heroine), her relationship to the literary image is less ironic. She derives moral capital from the images of her own vulnerability, even as she frames the scenario in which she is made vulnerable as an unreal fiction. This can be seen in her description of the attempts by William Waller, the Whig sheriff, to get her to incriminate her fellow Catholics in return for his assistance. The encounter is described ironically in terms of the conventions of knights rescuing ladies. Here, the convention is in Waller's head, and Cellier delights in refusing the role: 'I am not such a Distressed Damosel to use your Service.'[25] Waller's attempt to put her into a script shows that he is a liar. At the same time, however, the scene does let the notion that Cellier is a damsel in distress in the back door. The encounter with Waller, as she writes it, reads like a narrative of attempted sexual seduction. For example, Waller compliments her, in the manner of Satan to Eve, 'flattering me, telling me what high esteem he had for my Wit and Courage'.[26] The sexual dimension is captured in a *double entendre*, when Cellier decides she 'durst not trust my self with such a Doughty Knight … lest he should make Romances of me' – 'romance' here meaning false story but also carrying sexual connotations.[27] Although she rejects the part of the scenario that would allow Waller to be her rescuer, the scene gains in power from the fact that we are meant to see her as being threatened and vulnerable. Plot lines about female vulnerability – women as martyrs, women as tragic heroines, women as potential victims of seduction – are simultaneously rejected and reinscribed.

Cellier's equivocal relationship to the figure of the doomed tragic heroine might be seen as part of a strategy to exploit the fact of her sex without being constrained by it. Cellier's use of literary conventions centring on female vulnerability thus raises a larger issue of how Cellier understood her position as a woman acting in politics.

The question of whether a woman can play a role in political affairs is not explicitly addressed in *Malice Defeated* itself. In fact, the issue may be most remarkable for its absence. Cellier's attitude stands in contrast with that which the literary critic Catherine Gallagher has ascribed to Royalist women. Basing her argument on the Duchess of Newcastle's remark, 'we are no subjects', Gallagher has argued that women saw themselves as standing completely outside the hierarchical relationship of sovereign and subject.[28] Cellier unapologetically presents herself as a person with political opinions and defines herself as part of a community of loyal subjects on the first page of *Malice Defeated*, in which she explains her choice to convert to Catholicism: the experience of seeing a king murdered by a party calling itself Protestant because he was said to be a Catholic caused her to enquire into the Catholic religion, 'wherein I thank God I found my Innate Loyalty, not only confirm'd, but encourag'd'. Catholic doctrine, she tells us, agrees with her 'Publick Morals' as well as her private ones; she regards herself as being 'in Communion with those who were the humble Instruments of his Majesties happy Preservation'.[29] Her sex does have a bearing on her political identity, however, in the sense that she is married to a French merchant. When William Waller tries to make her take the oaths of supremacy and allegiance, she refuses on grounds that she is a *femme covert* whose husband is a foreign citizen – she thus points out to Waller that to force her to take these oaths is a violation of her husband's privileges. While one might take this to mean that Cellier's sex excludes her from full membership in the political nation, it is important to note that a large part of the point of this scene is to show that Cellier understands the law better than Waller himself.[30]

In general terms, then, Cellier does not seem to worry about the fact that she is a woman with political convictions. She does, however, worry about 'modesty', a quality that she identifies as essential (presumably uniquely essential) for women. Addressing her female readers, she apologizes if her behaviour might be thought to be 'too Masculine', but defends herself with the assertion that 'none can truly say but that I preserv'd the Modesty, though not the Timorousness common to my Sex'.[31] The issue of modesty is at the heart of one of the more peculiar scenes in *Malice Defeated*. Cellier is being questioned before the Privy Council. She has just been confronted by the witness Richard Adams, who, as noted above, catches her out having lied about whether or not she had ever travelled out of England. The fact that she lied is then taken to have implications for her credibility in general. Adams goes on to further impugn her credibility with an apparent *non sequitur*. There is something, he says, that he left out of his testimony against Cellier:

Adams: Your bawdy Story I left out of the Depositions, I was asham'd to speak it.

King: What, can she speak Bawdy too?

Adams: Yes, indeed she did.

L[ord] C[hancellor]: I [aye], she's fit for anything.

Cel: My Lord, I never spoke an immodest word in my Life. Mr. Adams, though you strive to take away my Life, do not take away my Honour; What did I say?

King: What did she say? come tell us the Story.

Adams: She said – She said – that – She said – That if she did not lose her Hands, she could get Mony as long as –

King: As long as what? out with it.

Adams: *made as if he were ashamed, and could not speak such a word.*

Cel: I said, if I did not lose my Hands, I should get Mony as long as Men kissed their Wives.

Adams: By the Oath I have taken, she said their Mistresses too.

Cel: Did I so, pray what else do they keep them for?

L. Chan: That was but witty.

King: 'Twas but natural to her Practice.[32]

The handling of modesty in this scene is complex. For Adams, Cellier's lack of modesty – in the sense of speaking bawdy – is a sign of a bad character, and hence is logically connected to the fact that she lied. However, the scene is set up in such a way as to expose a fallacy in Adams' approach. The joke here is that Adams' equation between modesty and truthfulness leaves him in a bind. He can't tell the truth about what Cellier said because he's too modest to repeat her words. What I think Cellier wants us to see is that there is something wrong with the way Adams thinks. He conforms to a stereotype of the Puritan, ever ready, like Jonson's Zeal-of-the-land Busy in *Bart'lemy Fair*, to detect signs of depravity, and over-squeamish about being in the presence of it. Adams is so afraid of contamination that he cannot distinguish between talking about something and being it. This is true at two levels: that is, he cannot bring himself to repeat Cellier's words, and he cannot see that because Cellier describes a reality it does not mean that she creates it. He does not draw a boundary between the speaker and the thing spoken about.

Cellier sets up for herself an alternative model of the relationship between modesty and truthfulness. What is striking is that she does not retreat to a mythical virgin innocence to make herself honourable. 'Modesty' is not innocence, blindness or silence. At least, not for a midwife, whose job it is to witness and speak authoritatively about matters that would make another person blush. Thus, her speech about men having mistresses can be defined as 'natural to her profession' rather than 'immodest'.

Cellier's status as midwife seems to be central to her construction of herself as a credible witness. It is not surprising that midwifery could form the basis for a woman's self-identification as a political actor, or in particular as a person who has a role to play in bringing justice to pass. It is not an accident that when the jury asks her for a bribe, Cellier, although refusing, does offer her professional services to their wives. In doing so, she draws an equation between midwifery and the carrying out of justice: 'I will with no less fidelity serve them [the wives] in their Deliveries', she writes to the foreman, 'then you have done me with Justice in mine.'[33] Midwives did, in fact, have a role to play in the legal system. Their expertise was called upon when women convicts pleaded their bellies, or when a determination as to whether a woman was pregnant affected the inheritance of an estate. Midwives were also called upon to question women in labour as to the paternity of their children, and to report on the findings in court. Midwifery may thus have been a springboard for women's participation in the legal system and sense of public responsibility.[34] It is significant in this respect that Cellier initially visited prisons in her capacity as a midwife.

We might also speculate that midwifery is especially important in Cellier's case because it helps her to address the problem that faced anyone seeking to tell stories about plots: i.e. how to present information without being tainted by one's own involvement in obtaining that information, and while appearing disinterested. What set midwives apart from other women was not simply their expertise, but the oaths which they took when they were licensed, which obligated them to prevent frauds (such as concealing births, attributing false paternity, faking births, etc.).[35] These gave them a monopoly on the ability to obtain and convey knowledge without having their own moral character compromised by the act of obtaining or conveying it. An ordinary woman who has information about who is the father of another woman's child cannot broadcast it without the risk of being called a scold or gossip. A man who wants to know if a woman is really pregnant cannot examine her himself without an affront to decency. The midwife is the person who can say something about sexual matters without it being immediately asked what it says about her that she knows about that. Cellier's understanding of her privileges as midwife might stand as an allegory for her understanding of the spymaster/informer relationship. As we saw above, Peterborough had tried to set up a clear distinction between the spymaster on the one hand, and the informer and the sordid stories he conveyed on the other. As we also saw, Dangerfield challenged this construction, calling attention to the way in which the spymaster could be said to be implicated in both the informer's disreputable character and in the informer's choice of information to convey or invent. In this context, Cellier's invocation of the special privileges of a midwife to look upon and convey information about potentially shameful things without being herself shamed by it might be taken as an implicit response to Dangerfield's move. Unlike Adams, Cellier stands apart from and untainted by what she witnesses (or brings to light): whether that is the secrets of generation, or the secrets of the Presbyterians.

It is worth nothing, however, that if this passage succeeds in establishing Cellier's 'modesty' in one sense, it does so by skirting on the edge of sedition. Is it an accident that a king notorious for his mistresses and bastards is shown tolerantly chuckling at precisely this subject, bonding with Cellier over their shared knowledge of the ways of the world? What does Cellier mean by presenting this moment? We might conclude that Cellier is politically inept – she is calling attention to, and bonding with the king around, the aspect of his life that his critics are most ready to emphasize, his sexual peccadilloes. On the other hand, one might argue that this is a savvy or at least coherent move. By showing herself bonding with the king around precisely what he has been attacked for, she shows that she, rather than the Whigs, is the truly loyal supporter of monarchy.

Perhaps the question to ask here is not whether Cellier is or is not intending to attack Charles II, but what the political riskiness of this passage might tell us about *Malice Defeated* as a whole. It exemplifies tendencies that we have already seen in the course of this discussion. We have noted a number of other instances in which Cellier makes moves that can be read in negative as well as positive ways. Her depiction of herself as lying about Margaret Jenkins might lead a reader to see her as a defender of a greater a priori truth, or simply as a liar. Her virtuosity with the law might indicate respect for it, or lack thereof. Her casting of her narrative in a self-consciously literary form might help her to capture the emotional force of certain literary tropes, or it might suggest that she is writing fiction. These moves are not, however, arbitrary or merely suicidal, and this discussion has emphasized the way in which they may each fulfil particular ideological agendas. In this sense, the risky character of Cellier's writing may suggest the extent to which the possibilities for political outsiders to construct their identities as credible witnesses or even patriots were open and in flux, and remind us of the complexity of the task confronting such people.

The scene with Charles II also exemplifies Cellier's tendency to make the presentation of herself the centre of the text. It is very much about Cellier, what she can say in front of and about the king, and the peculiar intimacy and privilege that characterizes her relationship with him. The image that Cellier creates of herself in this scene – perhaps it can be described as 'royal jester'? – is one of a number of equally compelling images that she gives her readers of herself: martyr, tragic heroine, clever legal tactician. I suspect that these images stand out more clearly in most readers' minds than the details of the case or the problems associated with proving it. The result is that the persuasiveness of *Malice Defeated* is oddly bound up with Cellier's representation of herself in the text.

This tactic, however, could backfire. The next section will suggest that the conflation of the truth of Cellier's story with both the character of Cellier the author and the representations of Cellier in the text could be turned against Cellier and her book.

Attacks on Cellier

Although Cellier was acquitted of treason, her writing and publishing of *Malice Defeated* led to her conviction for libel. She was fined £1,000 and condemned to stand in the pillory. She also became the object of vituperative attack in the press. Cellier's construction of herself as a disinterested witness was challenged in a variety of ways in the many pamphlets and lampoons written in response to *Malice Defeated*.

Midwifery was at the centre of many of the attacks on Cellier. Her plots, or claims about plots, were frequently depicted as monstrous births or illegitimate children. According to *Modesty Triumphing over Impudence*, Cellier's stories about Presbyterian plots were 'silly abortive Brats, begotten by the Lords and Ladies of the Popish Caballs, and brought into the World by her wicked Paws'.[36] A drawing from the period shows the devil giving birth to plotters through his anus.[37] In one lampoon written 'On Mrs. Cellier in the Pillory', she delivers both plots and Catholics:

> If our belief she studying to persuade
> Some bastard-plots delivered, 'twas her trade
> Her Roman Customers well knew her skill
> And therefore hop'd if they employ'd her still
> They might be freed by their Lucina's power
> From the hard teeming matrix of the Tower [i.e. of London][38]

The most extended treatment of plots and lies as monstrous births (and, conversely, births as lies and plots) comes at the end of *Mr. Prance's Answer to Mrs. Cellier's Libel*. Prance, we may recall, figured importantly in *Malice Defeated* as the man whose screams first alerted Cellier to the practice of torture in Newgate. The pamphlet denies that torture occurred, and rehearses the reasons why the Catholics are lying about it (e.g. in order to cast odium on the Protestant religion and play down the crimes of the Catholics). It ends with a postscript entitled 'The Adventure of the Bloody Bladder; A Tragi-comical Farce, Acted with much applause at Newgate by the said Madam Cellier'. This describes how Cellier, seeking to avoid her just punishment, declares herself pregnant, bribes some midwives and fakes her labour, using a pig's bladder filled with blood to provide verisimilitude. The story is written in a way to echo the prison scenes of *Malice Defeated*. The pillory is ironically described as an 'engine' (i.e. of torture). Cellier, while faking her labour, cries out, 'use not a Woman in my Condition more barbarously then Heathens, more Savagely than Turks and Indians', bellowing so loudly that the keeper of the prison, Captain Richardson, fears 'she would be ready enough to swear he had Rackt and Tortur'd her'.[39] Prance's parody thus discredits both Cellier and the torture story implicitly by setting up dramatic juxtapositions: the illegal engines of torture versus the legal pillory; Cellier's self-proclaimed willingness to die for the truth versus her cowardice when facing her just punishment; real screams of torture versus fake screams of childbirth.

These attacks on midwifery struck at Cellier's claims to disinterestedness and objectivity. The story of the bloody bladder suggests that midwives participate in fraud. Midwifery was also linked in pamphlets both to concealing bastard births and to abortions and procuring. One pamphlet offers a biography of Cellier in which she moves seamlessly from adultery to prostitution to bawding to running a home where courtesans can deliver bastards in secret, to midwifery.[40] Cellier is also shown bragging about the influence that she exerts over the great and powerful because the lives and reputations of their wives and mistresses are in her hands.[41] She is not a disinterested witness to childbirth, but someone who uses her ability to expose or conceal it as a route to power.

Cellier's sexual character was attacked as well. One pamphlet, purportedly written by Dangerfield, reprints lascivious letters between Cellier and someone called her 'Dear Spaniard'. The author spins out the tale of her simultaneous adulterous affairs with an Italian seigneur and his negro slave, which culminates in the birth of a 'Tawny Faced' child, after which she becomes 'very exquisite at the Cracking Trade'; she now brings in business for her husband by 'her modest compliance with Lascivious Requests'. Playing upon clichés about the sexual permissiveness of Catholicism, he tells Cellier directly that 'you would fain be Sainted for your Merits ... and so perhaps you may: as that Strumpet the Egyptian St. Mary; so Famous in your Callandar for exposing her Body to relieve the necessities of the Holy Monks and Hermits of her time'.[42] These accounts of Cellier's alleged sexual adventures are seen as relevant in assessing the truth of *Malice Defeated*. Sexual dishonesty opens the door to perjury.

> In short, Mrs. Elizabeth Cellier is a Woman that has forfeited her Fidelity to her Nuptial Bed, and when a Woman has once lost her Modesty, she is fit for all sorts of Mischief, and there ought to be no farther Credit given to her.[43]

We seem here to be meant to take these stories about Cellier's sex life as real biographical facts, and to judge the truth of her claims in *Malice Defeated* on the basis of her character. The relationship between Cellier's alleged bad sexual character and her untruthfulness, however, is more slippery than it looks. In many cases, it is Cellier's *book*, rather than the alleged true facts of Cellier's life, which is offered as an indication of her lascivious sexuality. Cellier's writing of *Malice Defeated* was itself treated as an act of sexual transgression. First of all, it is seen as a form of cross-dressing. Cellier is frequently associated with Pope Joan, the legendary female pope who passed as a man but was unmasked when she went into labour during a procession. It was suggested that Cellier, had she been there, could have helped Pope Joan hide her sex by providing her with a dildo.[44] In a similar vein, a picture of Cellier standing in the pillory shows her wearing breeches.[45] The

idea that there was something masculine about the writing of *Malice Defeated*
sometimes leads authors to attribute the pamphlet to a priest rather than to
Cellier herself. This does not, however, restore Cellier to proper femininity;
rather, the notion that a priest wrote the book is expressed in sexual language. In *The Scarlet Beast Stripped Naked*, a priest is said to have 'fathered'
the book on Cellier. Or, in an even more complex image, the author is said
to be 'our Wonderful witty thing of a Mid Wife, or a priest got into her Belly,
and so speaking through her, as the Devil through the Heathen Oracles'.[46]
Cellier's book, then, can be seen as an illicit sexual act, or as the product of
one.

Cellier's spying was also transformed into a sexual act. One of the most
frequently repeated stories about Cellier was that she hired Dangerfield
because she lusted after him, that he was employed as her stud. The most
elaborate development in this theme comes in a pamphlet written (purportedly) by Dangerfield himself, *Tho. Dangerfield's Answer* (1680), but it is
repeated elsewhere. In a way, Dangerfield's portrayal of his relationship to
Cellier as that of a male prostitute to a client could be seen as an elaboration
or a sexualization of what he said to Peterborough and the Catholic aristocrats in front of the Privy Council. Once again, he focuses attention on the
desires of the people who hire him. Lust for the evidence he manufactures is
transformed into lust for him.

Dangerfield thus invites readers to see through, or perhaps penetrate, the
flimsy surface of *Malice Defeated* to the sexual narrative that is barely concealed therein. Reading *Malice Defeated* becomes, or is treated as, an act of
voyeurism. Playing on the frequently voiced assumption that *Malice Defeated*
was really written by a priest, Dangerfield treats us to the spectacle of the
priest exposing Cellier's nakedness to the reader through an elaborate ruse of
inadequately covering it up. He reminds us of Cellier's claim in *Malice
Defeated* that she employed Dangerfield to 'collect overdue debts' (as
opposed, of course, to the real reason, i.e. that she wanted his sexual favours).
This is, he tells us, so implausible as to be transparent; the reader of *Malice
Defeated* ought to be able to see through the excuse, precisely *because* the
excuse is so bad. And what the reader sees is a naked woman and a peeping
satyr:

> [The story about overdue debts] Twas an excuse that never will be believed, and
> so therefore it was very Femininely done, to put such an over-ridden stale pre-
> tence upon the Nation. Come, come, Mrs. Elizabeth, your Ramping Dominican
> [i.e. the priest–author], had no mind to hide your nakedness, but only to throw
> a Tiffaney vindication over it; rather by contraction to display, than cover the
> prospect: Where, by my advice, he should be Pictured peeping, like the Satyr in
> Aretine's Postures, with a line and plummet in his hairy fist.[47]

There are several levels of voyeurism here. The priest is a peeping satyr; the
priest is letting *us* peep when we read *Malice Defeated*; at another level, it is

the author of *Tho. Dangerfield's Answer* who is setting up a scene in which we can be voyeurs in a way that we may not have been when we read *Malice Defeated* itself. Reading this, it is hard to pinpoint where the transgressive sexual act is occurring. The premiss of the whole passage is that it is 'out there in the real world', between Cellier and Dangerfield. Yet, the passage works to create for us the experience of a different kind of sexual encounter, between us as readers/voyeurs and Cellier; and it alludes to a third, that between the priest and Cellier. These encounters cannot be said to exist 'out there in the real world'. They are in the text (or in one of two texts: either *Malice Defeated* or *Tho. Dangerfield's Answer*). Thus, we do not need to literally believe the facts in order to perceive Cellier as an emblem of sexual transgression.[48]

What stands out in these attacks is not just the fact that they centre on Cellier's sexuality, but the slippage that they involve between Cellier and her book. They link an attack on her sexual character with an attack on the truthfulness of her book, but the direction in which the link is constructed is not always clear. Her alleged sexual character (immodesty) indicates that the book is untruthful, but the way we know that Cellier is sexually immodest is because the book is untruthful, and/or because we read sexuality in the book. It is hard to tell whether the authors of these attacks are saying that *Malice Defeated* should not be believed because Cellier is a whore, or whether they are saying that Cellier must be a whore because her book is untruthful. The gap between the author, the book and the subject matter is closed: Cellier is collapsed into her book, her political acts are treated as sexual acts, readers are invited to treat *Malice Defeated* as a piece of pornography which exposes its author's nakedness.

A similar slippage between book and author, and between untruthfulness and sexual transgression can be seen in the multiple meanings of the word 'impudent', which was one of the most frequently used terms in attacks on Cellier and *Malice Defeated*. Titles of pamphlets included, for example, *Modesty Triumphing over Impudence* and *A Whip for Impudence*. The meanings of the term are overlapping and complex, involving specifically sexual immodesty but also other kinds of transgression. An impudent book could mean several things: a book written by a sexually debauched person; a book that insults the great; a book that lies; a book written by someone who had no business writing a book (e.g. a woman); a pornographic book; a book which might as well be a public sexual act.

The conflation of meanings evident here, and the slippages that occur between Cellier and her book, creates the illusion that the relationship between character and credibility that was disrupted by the Popish Plot has been restored. That is, there appears to be a connection between Cellier's (bad) character and the (un)truth of her book. The means by which the connection is established, however, is circular. It is easy to see why it would be hard to respond to this kind of attack. Cellier could not vindicate her character by showing that she was truthful, nor could she use her character to establish her truthfulness. It would be interesting to speculate on whether there is something gender-specific about this kind of attack. Were women particularly vulnerable to having their books and their bodies collapsed into one another? Are we seeing in attacks on Cellier the crystallization of a logic which renders all women who write whores by definition? Such questions, alas, cannot be answered in the scope of this chapter. In any case, and for whatever reason, there is no extant printed response by Cellier (or anyone else) to these attacks.

Midwifery and the politics of credibility

This episode marked the end of Cellier's direct involvement in politics in any obvious sense. She did, however, make one more public appearance, this time as a champion of midwifery. In 1687 she proposed to King James II a plan for the establishment of a royal foundling hospital and a 'college of midwives' which would supervise and professionalize their training.[49] She then defended her proposal (against a still unidentified critic) in a pamphlet entitled *To Dr. ——, An Answer to his Queries concerning the College of Midwives* (1688). The pamphlet is interesting because it deals with many of the themes of *Malice Defeated* and with many of the issues around which she and the book were attacked. Surveying the history of midwifery, she tells a story which involves issues of modesty, cross-dressing, false sexual accusations, the perfidy of paid informers, and women's political action. Once upon a time, she tells us, the Athenians made a law that no woman should practice any kind of medicine, on pain of death. Because of this law, 'many Women perished, both in Child bearing, and by private Diseases; their Modesty not permitting them to admit of Men either to Deliver or Cure them'.[50] Finally, a noble maid, Agnodicea, out of pity for the miserable condition of her sex, took it upon herself to dress as a man and learned the arts of healing. She soon became the only physician that women would call to heal them or assist them in childbearing. Her success enraged the physicians. To punish her, they bribed a witness, 'there being Witnesses to be found then (as of late years, that would swear anything for Money)', to say that she had committed adultery with one of the Areopagites' wives. To save herself from the charge of adultery, Agnodicea reveals her true sex, which in turn leads her to be condemned to death for violating the laws against women practising medicine! She is saved, however, by the women of Athens, who assemble *en masse* to tell the chief magistrates 'they would no longer account them for husbands or friends' if they condemned her.[51]

We might see this story, and the pamphlet in general, as a kind of wishful thinking in which Cellier reasserts some of the premises of *Malice Defeated*. Modesty is again a woman's most important quality; and, once again, it is reconcilable with political action and with taking on a role usually monopolized by men. False accusations of sexual impropriety are unsuccessful. Cross-dressing by a woman *promotes* female modesty rather than destroys it. Finally, midwives are given a role as saviours of the nation. The pamphlet begins by reminding us of the Hebrew midwives Shiprah and Puah, who saved the Israelites by refusing to carry out Pharaoh's order to kill the male children. It ends with a fantasy that the exposed children rescued by the new foundling hospital will become soldiers in an army led by the new 'Moses', the Prince of Wales (whose birth Cellier predicts in this pamphlet).

We might, then, think of *To Dr.* —— as an exercise in politics by other means. It is perhaps significant that, as it turned out, Cellier's defence of midwives did have bearing on a political issue: in 1688, the birth of the Prince of Wales and the allegations of fraud surrounding it made the question of who could be relied on to tell the truth about birth an issue of national importance.[52] There is an important similarity between this episode (known as the warming-pan scandal), and the Popish Plot: in both cases, the interests of the nation were seen to hinge on things that could only or best be known by people outside the governing class or formal citizenry. We might broaden our conception of politics in this period to include the politics of knowledge and credibility. That is, we might look at how certain situations, like the warming-pan scandal or the Popish Plot, opened up the public airwaves to people outside the formal political nation, while at the same time making the credibility of those people an object of political struggle.

Notes

Versions of this paper were presented to the European History Faculty Colloquium at Cornell and to the spring 1994 meeting of the Berkshire Conference of Women Historians. I would like to thank the members of those groups, as well as Chris Franquemont, Peter Lake, Jane Marie Law, Mary Beth Norton, Leslie Peirce and Judith Surkis for helpful comments and encouragement.

[1] Elizabeth Cellier, *Malice Defeated* (Elizabeth Cellier, 1680), pp. 2–3.

[2] Tim Harris, *London Crowds in the Reign of Charles II* (Cambridge, 1987), esp. chs. 5 and 6.

[3] P. Lake, 'Anti-popery: the structure of a prejudice', in Richard Cust and Ann Hughes (eds.), *Conflict in Early Stuart England*, (Longman, 1989).

[4] For an interesting discussion, see Susan Dwyer Amussen, *An Ordered Society* (Basil Blackwell, 1988), pp. 152–5.

[5] J. P. Kenyon, *The Popish Plot* (Heinemann, 1972), p. 93.

[6] James Walker, 'The secret service under Charles II and James II', *Transactions of the Royal Historical Society*, 4th series, 15 (1932), pp. 211–35; Peter Fraser, *The Intelligence of the Secretaries of State* (Cambridge, 1956); Richard L. Greaves, *Deliver Us from Evil; The Radical Underground in Britain, 1660–1663* (Oxford, 1986).

[7] This is a broad summary of Dangerfield's account in *Thomas Dangerfield's Particular Narrative* (Henry Hills, 1679). For Cellier's recruitment of Dangerfield, see pp.

1–3, and *passim*; for Powis, pp. 7–8 and *passim*; for Peterborough and the Duke of York, pp. 33–5; for Curtis, pp. 30, 72–3, 55–6.

[8] *Ibid.*, p. 70.

[9] *Ibid.*, p. 70. I believe that this is the Henry Neville Payne (*fl.* 1672–1710) listed in the *Dictionary of National Biography*. He should not be confused with Edward Neville the Jesuit or Henry Neville the republican.

[10] *Ibid.*, pp. 61, 63.

[11] *Ibid.*, p. 64. For Lady Powis' statement that she, like Peterborough, heard about the Presbyterian plot from Dangerfield, see p. 53.

[12] *Ibid.*, p. 70.

[13] *The Trial of Elizabeth Cellier* (Randall Taylor, 1680), p. 16.

[14] *Don Tomazo, or the Juvenile Rambles of Thomas Dangerfield* (William Rumbald, 1680), 'To the Reader' (unpaginated).

[15] *Thomas Dangerfield's Particular Narrative*, pp. 38–9.

[16] Elizabeth Cellier, *Malice Defeated*, p. 1.

[17] *Ibid.*, p. 12.

[18] *Ibid.*, pp. 21, 30, 26.

[19] *Ibid.*, p. 28.

[20] *Ibid.*, p. 26.

[21] For the charges of libel brought against Cellier for publishing *Malice Defeated*, which focus on her presentation of the legal system, see *The Trial and Sentence of Elizabeth Cellier for Writing, Printing and Publishing a Scandalous Libel called Malice Defeated* (Thomas Collins, 1680), pp. 10–13.

[22] *Malice Defeated*, p. 34.

[23] *Ibid.*, p. 13.

[24] *Ibid.*, p. 30.

[25] *Ibid.*, p. 27.

[26] *Ibid.*, p. 23.

[27] *Ibid.*, p. 23.

[28] Catherine Gallagher, 'Embracing the absolute: the politics of the female subject in seventeenth-century England', *Genders*, 1 (spring, 1988), pp. 24–39, esp. p. 28.

[29] *Malice Defeated*, p. 1.

[30] *Ibid.*, p. 17.

[31] *Ibid.*, p. 32.

[32] *Ibid.*, p. 28.

[33] *Ibid.*, p. 42.

[34] This argument has recently been made by Patricia Crawford, 'Public duty, conscience and women in early modern England', in J. Morrill et. al. (eds.), *Public Duty and Private Conscience in Seventeenth-Century England* (Oxford, 1993). See also James Oldham, 'The origins of the special jury', *University of Chicago Law Review* 50 (1983), pp. 137–213.

[35] On the licensing of midwives, and their special responsibilities, see Jean Donnison, *Midwives and Medical Men* (Historical Publications, 1988), ch. 1. A copy of a midwife's licence from 1686 is reprinted on pp. 236–7. See also forthcoming work by Mary Beth Norton on control of information by midwives in colonial America.

[36] *Modesty Triumphing over Impudence* (Jonathan Wilkins, 1680), p. 10.

[37] Virginia and Harold Wayland, *Francis Barlow's Sketches for the Meal Tub Plot Playing Cards* (Pasadena, 1971), p. 7. (sketch 20).

[38] 'On Mrs. Cellier in the Pillory', Bodleian Don. b. 8, p. 611.

[39] *Mr. Prance's Answer to Mrs. Cellier's Libel* (L. Curtis, 1680), p. 17.

[40] *Tho. Dangerfield's Answer to a certain Scandalous Lying Pamphlet Entituled Malice Defeated* (Randall Taylor, 1680), pp. 16–17.

[41] *Modesty Triumphing over Impudence*, pp. 6–7.

[42] *Tho. Dangerfield's Answer*, pp. 17–18, 16–17, 15.

[43] *Ibid.*, p. 3.

[44] *To the Praise of Mrs. Cellier the Popish Midwife: On her incomparable Book* (Walter Davis, 1680). See also *The Scarlet Beast Stripped Naked* (D. Mallet, 1680), last page (i.e. p. 4, but note irregular pagination).

[45] Wayland, *Francis Barlow's Sketches*, p. 37 (sketch 54).

[46] *The Scarlet Beast Stripped Naked*, pp. 2, 4.

[47] *Tho. Dangerfield's Answer*, pp. 9–10.

[48] For another instance in which the act of reading *Malice Defeated* is sexualized, see *The Scarlet Beast Stripped Naked*, p. 2.

[49] 'A Scheme for the Foundation of a Royal Hospital' (1687), printed in White and Cochrane et al. (eds.), *The Harleian Miscellany*, 10 vols. (1808–1813) vol. IV: pp. 142–7.

[50] [Elizabeth Cellier], *To Dr. —— An Answer to his Queries concerning the College of Midwives* (1688), p. 3.

[51] *Ibid.*, p. 4.

[52] See Rachel Weil, 'The politics of legitimacy: women and the warming pan scandal', in Lois G. Schwoerer (ed.), *The Revolution of 1688–1689: Changing Perspectives* (Cambridge, 1992). Interestingly enough, Cellier was sometimes erroneously identified as having been the midwife at the birth of the Prince of Wales.

Part II

The politics of culture

9

'The part of a Christian man': the cultural politics of manhood in early modern England

Susan Dwyer Amussen

Malcolm: Dispute it like a man.
Macduff: I shall do so;
            But I must also feel it as a man.

Macbeth IV, iii, 218–20.

[T]he husband ... ought to be the leader and author of love in cherishing and increasing concord ... he must wink at some things and gently expound all things and to forbear. [*sic*] Howbeit the common sort of men doth judge that such moderation should not become a man, for they say that it is a token of a womanish cowardness, and therefore they think it is a man's part to fume in anger, to fight with fist and staff.

'Homily of the state of matrimony', 1563

I

What did it mean to be a man in early modern England? How was manhood defined and lived? The exchange between Malcolm and Macduff, immediately after Macduff has learned of the murder of his wife and children, suggests that manhood had multiple and sometimes conflicting meanings. These meanings are not always those we would expect: Malcolm wants Macduff, 'like a man', to give himself to revenge, but Macduff insists that 'as a man' he must also give way to grief at the execution of his loved ones. The invocation of manhood as a justification for both reactions alerts us to the complexity of early modern thinking about manhood and masculinity.

A parallel and equally unexpected tension is evident in the 'Homily of the state of matrimony'. In setting up a model of Christian manhood in opposition to 'the common sort of men', the Homily acknowledged competing cultural values.[1] The Homily's argument, that a man should be patient and yielding to his wife, who lacks his 'strength and constancy of mind', defines an alternative to the 'common' values of manhood. The Homily argues that such patience is enjoined by scripture, and that even with it, 'a man may be a man'.[2]

The competing images of manhood in both *Macbeth* and the 'Homily of matrimony' draw our attention to manhood and masculinity as social constructions. As such, they are not fixed or rigid, and their meanings can be deployed for a variety of ideological and social purposes. Although there are apparently archetypal patterns of manhood that appear in most cultures, they vary both in specifics and intensity; they are 'adaptations to social environments'.[3] The social construction of manhood is less visible than that of womanhood, because the attributes of men, as of any dominant group, are naturalized, while those of subordinate groups are made deviant: the 'lenses of gender' in our society make male experience the norm.[4] Yet the energy that went into defining proper masculinity on literary and theoretical levels in late Elizabethan and Jacobean England betrays its artificiality. Few men, apparently, knew how to be men. The negotiation of competing, complementary, contradictory and sometimes novel concepts of manhood was an important source of social tension in early modern England.

The extent of energy necessary to define manhood reflects not only the usual difficulty of enforcing social norms, but conflicting models of manhood that were developed in the period. These competing definitions need to be seen in the context of the 'reformation of manners' that has been described by historians in recent years.[5] Although the 'reformation of manhood' that I will be describing in this essay included norms of sexual behaviour, it is striking how small a role sexuality played in the debate: while 'reformers' may have been more intent than traditionalists on chastity outside of marriage, ideas about men's relationship to women and appropriate sexual behaviour were largely similar in both groups, and unexpected to modern readers.[6] In the scene from Macbeth with which we began, Malcolm – after testing Macduff's loyalty by claiming an unlimited appetite for his future subjects' women and property – admits that 'I am yet/Unknown to woman' (II, 125–6): while the text makes this part of Malcolm's claim to virtue and leadership, it is cut in most modern productions as undercutting his manliness.[7] Yet for early modern audiences, a man's sexual activities were not central to his manhood. The 'Homily of matrimony' locates the conflicts about manhood around the issue of violence, and although that was certainly not the only contested area of manhood, it was a central one. The attack on violence was part of what Norbert Elias has called 'the civilizing process', and is evident not only in the 'Homily', but also in the State's attack on the use of violence by aristocrats in the Tudor period.[8] The importance of violence, however, is in the way men's relationship to it reflected their access to the central characteristic of manhood in early modern England: independence. Not all men were independent, nor were all equally independent; therefore there were different ways of asserting independence, of acting 'as a man'.

Both manhood itself and the power of men were unstable categories of early modern thought. In part this derived from fluid concepts of gender. The role of dress as a marker of gender is suggestive: Shakespeare's cross-dressed heroines need only (apparently) change clothes to change identities, while boys acted the parts of women on the Elizabethan and early Stuart stage.[9] A steady stream of women – often celebrated in ballads – put on male clothing and went to sea; men put on women's clothes and disguises in riots. Outside the theatre, it was impossible to know what the subjectivity of women dressed as men was, so it was assumed to be male and transgressive. The fluidity of gender boundaries was also assumed by prophetic imagery in which men gave birth and women became men.[10]

Dress could be the key to identity because the conception of the body common in early modern England (and Europe generally) did not make a sharp distinction between the bodies of men and women; rather, the common scientific assumption was of the 'one-sex' body.[11] This medical theory held that the sexes were essentially identical, and that the genitals of women were a mirror of those of men: women were deformed men, not a radically different sex. In this model, as with dress, it was possible (though certainly not common) to move from one sex to the other: sex was not fixed, but fluid. Such fluidity made it difficult to sustain a rigid sex/gender system.

The fluidity of gender boundaries exacerbated the general anxiety about patriarchy and patriarchal power that is such a familiar aspect of early modern gender relations.[12] Threats to patriarchal power are central themes in the extended pamphlet debate on women that surfaced at various times between 1560 and 1640, but particularly in the 1610s. In two pamphlets, *Hic Mulier* and *Haec Vir*, dress is a sign of the disordered relations between the sexes which undermines patriarchal authority.[13] *Hic Mulier* complains about women taking on mannish dress, and implicitly, mannish roles. *Haec Vir*, ostensibly written by 'Hic Mulier', retorts that women must do so because men have surrendered their role by dressing – and acting – effeminately. The issue of dress had other repercussions; Robert Greene's *Quip for an Upstart Courtier* (1592) features a debate in which 'Cloth Breeches' and 'Velvet Breeches' stand in for their wearers – and the merits of rival conceptions of gentility and class. It is a confrontation between he who cares about 'hospitality, and ... honour, with relieving the poor' and he, 'richly daubd with Gold, and powdered with pearl', who is ultimately judged to be 'an upstart, come out of Italie, begot of Pride, nursed up by self-love, and brought into this country by his companion Newfangleness, that he is but of late time, a raiser of rents, and an enemy in the commonwealth'.[14] The suggestion that fashion might not be manly – and indeed the court as well – was a powerful one during the reign of James I, as both the corruption of the court, and its moral decay, became increasingly notorious.[15] Such pamphlets, the other traditions relating to cross-dressing, as well as sumptuary legislation, indicate the importance of dress in defining one's place in a gendered hierarchical society.

Inappropriate dress was one sign of the omnipresent threat to patriarchy, standing as it did for women's insubordination in general. In a series of pamphlets and plays, the popular literature of the early seventeenth century debated women's nature and their refusal of obedience. The anti-feminist argument was that women were naturally shrill and combative, shrewish and intemperate. Such pamphlets as Joseph Swetnam's *Arraignment of Lewd, Idle, Forward, and unconstant women* (1615) served to indict women not only for all the vices, but all the problems of the time. Women would not be governed, as they should be, by men. Swetnam argued that 'men for the most part are touched but with one fault, which is drinking too much, but it is said of women that they have two faults: that is, they can neither say well nor yet do well'.[16] Women's nature made the work of manhood that much more difficult. Such pamphlets did not go unchallenged, of course, but the debate highlights the insecurity of patriarchy.

Men and masculinity were threatened both by the very nature of early modern thinking about gender divisions, and by women's insubordination. Men's ability to behave properly as men was not merely an academic question; it had very real political consequences. Men, as heads of household, were responsible for the conduct of their subordinates, and were generally held to represent them. The political role of men as heads of household was sustained throughout the seventeenth century, and was not challenged in any of the political theories of the period. While Hobbes and Locke rejected the organic and familial metaphors for the State, they retained the idea of the male as head of household who stood (implicitly) for the rest of the family. Indeed, the famous title-page of Leviathan presents this image of the State clearly: the State is made up of men, and only men.[17]

The challenges to patriarchy from disorderly women were not the only or even necessarily the central problem relating to manhood. More important were the tensions between normative ideas of manhood and other sets of social relations: appropriate behaviour for men, as well as for women, was context-specific. As a head of household, a man should be prudent but generous, honest, forceful but loving, wise in governing his own house and obedient to those in authority. While martial valour was not needed or desirable in the household, a man might need such skills in military service (practised regularly in the militia) – and less respectably, in the convivial atmosphere of the alehouse.

This range of behaviour properly belonged only to married, property-owning men: these were the men who were independent. Didactic literature distinguished sharply between the roles of husband/father/master on the one hand, and son/servant on the other. The one was the governor, the other the governed. The importance of governing was indicated in part by the length of the sections devoted to it in such works. Those who were governed learned the skills of governing in the process.[18] For the many men who were subordinate in the social system because of either age or status or both, it was impossible to be 'real' men.

Not only was proper behaviour context-specific; being a man – like being a woman – involved negotiating several different codes of behaviour.[19] On the one hand, there was the moral code supported by the Church; it emphasized sexual chastity and living in harmony with one's neighbours, as well as fulfilment of religious obligations. There was a code relating to class, which emphasized the proper behaviour of men who wanted to be leaders in their communities. Finally, and most importantly, there was the idea of manliness itself, which stressed responsibility, independence, self-sufficiency and neighbourliness as sources of honour – though the weight given to each of these varied. This code assumed the possession of property to provide autonomy. Individual men pieced together their identity from these different codes.

Manhood was a cultural construct. It defined a set of behaviours that were expected to demonstrate that English men were above English women, as well as men elsewhere in the world.[20] These ideas existed in a society, however, which placed some men over others. In this context, the reformation of manhood served to further divide men, between those who followed the reformed code, and those who could not do so. Because of the tensions between ideas about manhood and the social structure, we must ask how these ideas moved from the universe of cultural ideas to people's lives.

Most modern observers assume a close relationship between manhood and sexual prowess. We will therefore begin with a consideration of rape. We will then turn to forms of violence between men which were common in early modern England. However, both State policy and the rise of litigation as a mode of settling disputes increasingly distinguished between men on the basis of wealth. By looking at apprentices and clergy, who were dependent in particular ways, the role of independence is highlighted. Finally, reputation – particularly for honesty and sexual behaviour – played a key role in establishing one's position in the community and highlighting one's independence.

II

The 'Homily of matrimony' suggested that violence against women was, for many men, a central component of manliness – though as we shall see later, so too were forms of violence between men. Wife-beating was the most common form of such violence, but it was also represented by rape and attempted rape. The evidence of rape underlines the limits of violence, and suggests that violence was not strongly linked to sexuality in early modern ideas of manhood – though both were certainly important. Rape, like other violent offences short of murder, was rarely reported during the period, and its position is confused by the use of the same word to cover both rape and abduction.[21]

Several aspects of the allegations of rape or coerced sexual activity – and attempts at it – are significant. Rape does not appear to be part of the passage to manhood in the period. To a modern observer, the absence of allegations of gang rapes is remarkable. Most rapes and rape attempts took advantage of the isolation of the woman to act: thus Francis Barber raped Jane Bingley while she was alone in a close milking her mistress' cows, so when she 'cried out for help' there was no one to come.[22] John Cawvert allegedly directed Elizabeth Parker on a short-cut to Leeds, then took advantage of an isolated spot to force her to have sex.[23] Joan Sherre was on the road between Bexwell and Downham Market when a man threatened to rape her, but he left when two other men came along the road.[24]

The experience of Sarah Wood, a London servant, highlights another common theme in rape cases, the use of superior social standing to take advantage of a women. Wood alleged that Mr John Sheffield, a lodger in her master's house, raped her on an evening when her master and mistress were out. Sheffield asked Wood to do her job – to 'light him up to his chamber' – in order to get her away from the men in the kitchen.[25] Masters – or their sons – could also be charged with rape, although convincing a jury would undoubtedly be difficult; Richard Deadman of London raped his servant Joyce Nothall when no one was in the house, taking advantage of his social and physical power to overcome her.[26]

According to popular custom, a woman had to show that she had cried out in order to claim rape. Most accusations of rape either indicate the crying out, or explain that the rapist had stopped the woman's mouth to prevent her from doing so. The cry alerted those around to foul play, and could prevent rape. The use of secluded places, and the choice of times when a house was empty, meant that this defence was ineffective. When the cry was heard, it did help: Joan Knight, a widow of Marshwood, Dorset, made enough noise while Henry Snook was trying to rape her that Elizabeth Pinney came into her house and interrupted the scene.[27]

What is most striking to the modern observer is the way men responded to accusations of rape. The depositions in twenty-eight cases involving rape accusations have survived for the northern circuit assizes between 1647 and 1693. In thirteen of those, there are depositions from both the accuser and the accused. In only one of those does the accused admit to sex but argue that it was consensual; in ten, the accused denied any sexual relationship, and two of those accused claim that they had never seen their accuser before. That men distance themselves not just from the violent assault of rape, but from any sexual activity, is striking: extra-marital sexual activity was not a part of their presentation of themselves to the world.[28]

Those women who bore illegitimate children to their masters or their masters' sons may have frequently been victims of coercive sexual assaults, though there may also have been elements of wishful thinking when the man involved was unmarried.[29] Mary Smyth, a servant of the widower William Ship, a Woodland yeoman, was a member of the Broadmead Baptist congregation in Bristol when she became pregnant. When questioned, she said, 'it was by her master, who she said, at first forced her', but now refused to marry her. Ultimately, members of the congregation convinced him to marry her, but her account suggests that what began as rape became more complex over time.[30]

The accounts of rape which have survived suggest that while rape was not unknown, sexual assault and conquest were not a central part of male identity. Men took advantage of women to whom they had access, but that access often depended on status as well as gender; men could use social and gender power to discredit women who alleged rape.[31] But status did not protect men from rape accusations: in 1557 it was reported that Lord Latimer had attempted to rape the wife of the owner of the house in which he lodged, leading to such an outcry that 'the constables and street rose and fetched him out of his house, and brought him through Cheapside to the Mayor's, and 40 boys at his heels wondering on him'. He was placed in the Fleet prison – a harsh action against a nobleman.[32] The presentment of William Jackson of Little Snoring, who would 'bragg and boast of his lewdness, and that he can command women at his pleasure to satisfy his filthy lust' is a rare linking of sexual conquest to masculine identity.[33] There are few street ballads focused on rape, and even fewer serious accounts of rape in pamphlets or other descriptive sources. While people might enjoy the light-hearted account of coercive sex within courtship, they were not amused by accounts of less ambiguous assaults.[34] Cumulatively, such evidence point to the limited role sexual conquest played in ideas of manhood – and to the shame usually associated with allegations of rape.

The suggestion that sexual violence was not central to male identity is underlined by one set of collective assaults on women. In 1681 Lady Anne Stowe wrote to the Countess of Rutland about life in the capital.

> There is a company of men, they say fifty or more, which are called Whipping Tom, and they deserve that name, for their employment a nights, is to take what women they can light of when it is late, and whip them so cruelly that some has died of it, and others are very ill. One night there was one of them that caught a maid servant, and she being too strong for him called the Constable, and he was taken and proved to be a haberdasher in Holborn; he was just upon marrying one with £600, but she will not now have him, and he is prosecuted with that severity that it will ruin him. I wish all the rest of them may be so served.[35]

For the men involved, manhood was expressed through violence, not sexual prowess. There is no suggestion in Lady Anne's account that the women involved 'deserved' to be whipped: indeed, she shows some glee that the haberdasher will lose his marriage to a wealthy young woman. Such attacks on women were not part of an approved or even tolerated male youth culture.

Men used violence – both inside and outside marriage – to control women. In general, however, that violence was not sexualized. Although men took advantage of women who were isolated, such assaults were not central either to their sexual lives or their identity – just as, apparently, homosexual encounters were not necessarily inconsistent with it.[36] It was not through sexual violence that men acted as men.

Of course, men did not direct all their violence at women; a key component of the 'traditional' model of manhood was a willingness to engage in violence with other men. The traditional model is illustrated by the career of Thomas Pouncey, a Dorchester butcher recently described by David Underdown. Thomas Pouncey was quick with his fists and any other weapons that came to hand, and he beat his wife. Yet he was not entirely disreputable; he was a butcher, a freeman of the town and served as surety on recognizances with some regularity. He was certainly contentious: he threw his meat cleaver at two men he met along the Weymouth Road, and when they had the cleaver, he threw stones instead; when he tried to stab Elizabeth, the wife of William Foote, the beadle reported that Margaret Pouncey, Thomas' wife, had run away and left her children at the church door. But Pouncey's violence was not entirely uncontrolled: when he and Richard Paty quarrelled in an alehouse, they went out and fought, and then returned and continued drinking together.[37]

The violence so central to Thomas Pouncey's sense of himself and his manhood was, of course, often reproved by moralists. On the other hand, he shared with other men a strong sense of the importance of his independence and rights. When he was conscripted for the Ile de Rhé, he complained to the council about the corruption of the constables and deputy lieutenants: instead of conscripting the able and healthy, the constables conscripted many 'boys', and someone accepted bribes from 'able men' to leave the unit: almost half of those conscripted in Dorset had disappeared before they got to Portsmouth.[38]

We cannot simply dismiss Pouncey as a bully. His behaviour reflected a sense of his independence and honesty, not just his propensity to violence. And even his ready use of his fists was, in other contexts, culturally valued. Sir Dudley Digges proudly told the Parliament of 1628 that 'In Muscovy one English mariner with a sword will beat five Muscovites that are likely to eat him.'[39] It was, of course, the freedom of the English that made a difference – the liberty which Pouncey defended when he complained of the abuses of recruiting.

Finally, Thomas Pouncey's offences cluster around times of traditional celebrations – although in Dorchester such festivities were frowned upon: four of the fourteen incidents which brought him before the mayor's court took place during the Christmas season, two around All Saints and Guy Fawkes, one around midsummer, and two around Lammas. His attempted stabbing of his neighbour's wife – and his wife's desertion of him – took place during the week before Lent began – the traditional time for carnival. He was never brought before the court in July, or from mid-August to the 30th of October; only one of his offences occurred during Lent.[40] Thomas Pouncey was not always wild, but his adherence to a traditional conception of manhood was linked to his fidelity to an equally traditional festive – and drinking – calendar.

It is easy to think of the violence of those like Thomas Pouncey as random and uncontrolled, but it was not. Just as Pouncey returned to the alehouse to drink following his fight with Richard Paty, so many brawls appear to have followed a pattern that served to limit violence. Brawls were usually the result of some alleged offence, and in that way were a more immediate way of protecting one's reputation than a defamation suit.[41] John Ward struck at the cleric William Bury when Bury alleged that the coin he had given him was 'too light', and claimed that Bury had substituted a different coin for the one he had originally given him. In the fight that followed, weapons – a bill and a pole – as well as fists were used, but at the end Ward 'set [Bury] on his feet and led him towards one Frowndes house, and said that he was sorry that he was hurt'.[42] While Ward felt it necessary to avenge the slight to his financial honesty, he did not seek to injure Bury seriously.[43] He needed no encouragement to help Bury to a nearby house.

Attempts to limit violence by participants or others were common; even when such limits failed, and someone died, there is often evidence that bystanders had tried to stop a quarrel. On the night in December 1674 when Mr Jonathan Gorges was killed in a London street brawl, the watch had already intervened to break up a fight between his killer, Mr Nathaniel Ludlow, and Mr Robert Blackstone, and friends had stopped another one between Ludlow and Gorges, and tried to stop a second.[44] More than a century earlier, two men who were fighting were first separated, but then 'by and by upon the multiplying of words, Thomas Cobham and Smyth went to it again', resulting in injuries that left Smyth on the verge of death.[45] Such interventions were not limited to the elite; Elizabeth Lovell, a Leeds alehouse keeper, had tried to send Nicholas Holmes home because he was drunk and quarrelsome, and though in the end she could not stop the fight in which Holmes was killed, during the fight one man tried to separate the combatants, and sought help from other bystanders.[46]

Even when justified by insults, there was debate as to whether and when violence was acceptable. Throughout the early modern period the government sought to clamp down on duels, the upper class form of the brawl. James I apparently commissioned Thomas Middleton to write a pamphlet against duels, which appeared as *The Peacemaker* in 1618. Middleton's pamphlet, which moves from international peacemaking to domestic peace to sobriety to duels, stresses the importance of the reformed ideal of manhood: independence, sobriety and self-restraint.[47] Legislation against duels was repeated throughout the seventeenth century, and when there was a death there was a chance of prosecution.[48] Even under Charles II – much less pacific than his grandfather – the campaign against duels continued. The earl of Rochester was reportedly banned from court when he drew his sword in response to a joke made by Mr Thomas Killigrew in the king's presence.[49] By focusing on duels rather than all fights, however, the government reinforced class distinctions, and the cultural distinctions in access to manhood.

Violence was a way of asserting one's place in society, an affirmation of independence. Violence was common in part because it was the easiest way to claim such independence, especially for those whose position in society was not entirely independent. The structure of early modern society made independence impossible for many men; for others it limited it. The tensions around independence and manhood are particularly clear for two groups of men, apprentices and clergy. Apprentices were clearly dependent, and although they reached adulthood while in service, they were unable to marry. The clergy, while apparently independent, depended on elite patrons for preferment, and on the tithes paid by their congregations for their income; their position continued to be defined by status in a society increasingly dominated by relations of class.

Independence and manhood are central issues in the diary of the Lancashire apprentice Roger Lowe. He was apparently in his early twenties when his diary begins in 1663, actively courting a series of women. His social life (especially in drinking) was primarily with other men – though he occasionally accompanied one of them to visit a woman, or was joined by them in his visits. For instance, on 17 September 1663 he 'went with James Naylor to Neawton awooing Ann Barrowe', while the following week Nicholas Corles came to visit, and they went to an alehouse and got drunk. However, he was in service with his master for nine years, and towards the end of that time he strongly resented the subordination represented by continued servitude. His position was unusual, as he lived in a different town from his master and managed his shop without any interference other than the occasional reckoning. This practical independence may have increased his resentment, for in October 1664 he asked Mr Battersbie to speak to his master concerning his 'grievances', saying 'I thought it sad for me to be engaged nine years to stay in Ashton to sell my Master's ware of and get no knowledge' [*sic*].[50] Until he obtained his freedom, Lowe was not 'a man' to himself or the rest of his community; he gained his freedom in November 1665, and while he continued to be employed by others, by March 1668 he felt able to marry.[51]

The tensions caused by apprentices' dependence are also evident in the riots that they regularly led against prostitutes and brothels in London. Since apprentices were forbidden to marry, prostitutes presumably provided a sexual outlet for them. The resentment of their ambiguous position – as apprentices they had not achieved full manhood – was targeted, however, not at the masters who controlled their lives, or at the authorities who barred them from marriage, but at the women who profited from their patronage.[52]

Conflicts around issues of dependence, independence and behaviour are also visible with the clergy. These conflicts are particularly visible because of the regulation of clergy behaviour by the church courts. The quarterly visitations of parishes included a series of questions about the behaviour of the parson, from his conduct of church services to his morals. Thus, church court records include numerous cases against clergy who failed to uphold moral or religious obligations.[53] Complaints about quarrelsome, abusive and litigious clergy were common: Thomas Michelson of Seething, Norfolk called his parishioners fools, dolts and idiots, and stirred up quarrels between neighbours, while Robert Somes of Stalham said uncharitable things about his parishioners in a sermon.[54]George Pilkenton, the vicar of Beddingham, Norfolk, who tried to seduce various women and frequented women of ill fame, also encouraged conflicts among his neighbours with lies, frivolous suits and quarrels.[55]

What is striking is that faults that understandably hindered the exercise of moral leadership were often joined to (to us) less obvious complaints. The agricultural pursuits of some clergy annoyed their parishioners. Jonathan Skynner, the rector of Wolverston, Suffolk, was prosecuted as a scandalous minister in 1640. Not only did he rail at parishioners, seldom preach, excommunicate a twelve-year-old boy and enter vexatious suits against members of his parish, but he also kept cows and pigs in the churchyard. Finally, 'He followed mechanical works and almost all sorts of husbandry.'[56] This final complaint is noteworthy – and not unique. William Naylor of Swanton Novers, Norfolk, his parishioners complained, 'doth not live according to his calling but followeth husbandry as going to cart and following his cattle and keeping them to the offence of the parishioners'. Naylor apparently accepted the standard implicit here; his response was that he kept servants, so that he did not do his own work.[57] In 1669 one parishioner complained that he had seen the rector of Gayton, Norfolk, 'sow barley as an ordinary husbandman'.[58] The agricultural work done by William Jacombe in 1678 was 'servile', 'to the scandal of his function'.[59]

What was it about being an 'ordinary husbandman' that was contrary to being a clergyman – and undermined an important leadership role in the community? And what can this tell us about being a man in early modern England? The income of clergy derived both from tithes – often collected in kind – and for some, the produce of the glebe attached to the living. While some clergy might lease out the glebe, farming it oneself was not an unreasonable choice.[60] Regardless of their wealth, all clergy were accorded the status designation of 'Mr'. Farming oneself – without servants – contradicted the gentle status ascribed to the clergy. Work with their hands therefore undermined their spiritual function.

The clergy were caught, more explicitly than most men, between expectations of independence, self-sufficiency and responsibility, and codes of gentility – between being a man and being a gentleman. This last semi-secular code placed an increasing emphasis in the early modern period on civility, proper behaviour, good manners and refinement; such demands were especially difficult for many of the poorer clergy to meet, and probably represented new expectations.[61] The clergy were a group defined by status in a world increasingly defined by class.

Insults directed at clergy frequently reflect this tension, with claims that the speaker was 'as good a man' or 'as honest a man' commonplace.[62] John Acreman alleged that Robert Hawkins of Beckley, Oxfordshire, 'was a jail keeper's turnkey boy in Holland and had no learning but what he had in a jail in Holland'.[63] Mr Nuttall 'was a proper parson to make a bishop in hell … and a proper parson to lie under a hedge and steal a peck of nuts'.[64] Or the allegation that a vicar 'would speak beyond his book and play the knave and tell a lie as soon as an other man'.[65] While such insults were usually directed against particular clergy, they could be aimed at the clergy in general. John Wassey alleged that 'he did not regard nor value such ministers no more than he did musty dogs', and cursed and swore against ministers and tithe gatherers'; he wanted ministers 'to work for their living as he did'.[66] Edmund Hudson declared that ministers were all 'covetous whoring rogues'.[67]

The position of the clergy was a difficult one: they were supposed to be above their congregations, morally and socially, but they often lacked the resources to meet the social demands placed on them. Even when they did, those resources frequently came from their parishioners. Their uneasy position is marked not only by suits against them and the abuse they received, but also by conflicts over tithes, which underline the importance of independence and prosperity to them and their neighbours. The collection of tithes was the point at which the clergy's lack of independence was most visible. Elizabeth Stone told her rector that 'he was a dumb dog and that he were as good stand by the highway side and take a purse as take his tithes wrongfully'.[68]

The clergy found their ambiguous position difficult, and as a result some directed abuse at their social superiors. The rector of Stradsett, Norfolk, told Mr Francis Piggot that 'I am as good a man as you and an honester man than you and that you have cozened me of £10.'[69] Thomas Ramsie, the vicar of Crostwick, not only complained of the abuses of the rich, but published libels against several, which he read in church.[70] The tension between the poor parson who deserved the respect due a gentleman while his reliance on tithes made him dependent on those he was supposed to lead, created conflicts and difficulties for all those involved.

Attacks on disorderly clergy reflect the expectation that they, like other respectable members of the community, adhere to the reformed ideal of manhood. As recent scholarship has demonstrated, reputation was a central concern of early modern community leaders.[71] Defamation cases focus on many things, but (because of the court's jurisdiction) usually include illicit sexual activity. They alleged the fathering of bastards, the keeping of whores (naming names), pre-nuptial sexual intercourse and the like. But the defamation cases also engaged issues that related to sobriety, honesty and the good government of the household.[72]

The simplest basis for a defamation suit was the insult – the use of abusive words like 'whoremaster', 'whoremasterly knave', 'rogue', 'cuckold', or 'cuckoldly knave' – often imaginatively combined. Insults, by attributing undesirable characteristics or behaviour to their target, sought to deprive him of his standing in the community. In particular, the practical consequences of credible allegations about fathering an illegitimate child led to frequent suits involving accusations that men paid others to take responsibility for – or marry – the women whom they had made pregnant: if believed, a man could become responsible for the financial support of the child.[73] Defamation suits were a way of fighting back, in which men defended their place – and the respect of their neighbours.

Three issues aside from sexual behaviour play an important role in defamation suits. They were honesty, sobriety and the good government of the household. Honesty was a prized virtue, and the word 'honest' referred not only to an absence of lying, but also to chaste behaviour: when Margery Russell alleged that William Gay 'would have had to do bodily with her', she repeatedly said that 'he was a dishonest person'.[74] In a society where reputation was equated with 'credit' – in all its meanings – it was important to be trustworthy.[75] One witness allowed that 'he thinketh it a heinous word to be called a forsworn man'.[76]

Sobriety, like honesty, was a central component of a respectable man's life. In spite of the ubiquity of alcoholic beverages in early modern society, drunkenness was generally condemned: good men drank, but were never drunk. Drunkenness implied being out of control and irresponsible. William Parsley, who acted for the official sealer of stuffs made in Norwich and Norfolk, refused to seal cloths woven by John Castell because he believed Castell was drunk.[77] Drunkenness undermined one's ability to support oneself and one's family.

Allegations about honesty and drunkenness were part of a more general concern about how effectively men ran their households. Good government of oneself and one's family was central to reputation, and to one's ability to play one' proper role in society. Men could and did bring lawsuits regarding allegations that their wives were unfaithful. Richard Wakefield joined his wife in suing Thomas Fawke when Fawke had alleged that Wakefield 'was a cuckold, and he should be his cuckold he should not be an ordinary cuckold, and should have a pair of horns tipped with silver'.[78] William Herring of Norwich sued Elizabeth Brownrick when she alleged that Herring's wife Mary was the concubine of another man.[79] The proper government of the household involved more, of course, than ensuring that one's wife behaved herself, but it was the most easily defined element of good government.

What often gets lost in the discussion of defamation are the real consequences for men if the allegations they complained of were true. Such behaviours undermined the 'credit and reputation' of the accused, and even the punishment for them was damaging. Though historians have often considered the punishments imposed by the church courts – penance, rather than the financial damages available at common law – trivial, early modern villagers did not agree, since the reputation damaged by penance had a monetary value. When John Roleright, alias Fuller, was accused of fathering a child on Joan Cary, he denied any relationship with her, but admitted that two years earlier, he had begotten a child on another of his father's servants, Katherine Taplin, alias Tappin. He asked that he be spared the standard punishment of public penance in return for a contribution of money to charity. He argued 'that it would be a great disrepute to him to do public penance and be also a great hindrance to his preferment in marriage'.[80] Defamation about sexual behaviour mattered because such behaviour was a central element of reputation – itself critical in a face-to-face society.

The ideal of manhood defended against in defamation suits was that of the respectable. Even the use of the courts was itself part of the reformed ideal of manhood. In *Quip for an Upstart Courtier*, Cloth Breeches and Velvet Breeches first plan to fight to decide who is better, but the narrator steps in, asking 'Why, what mean ye, will you decide your controversy by blows, when you may debate it by reason?'[81] By going to law, the site of conflict was moved from the street or alehouse into the courts – and resolution was delayed. Thus defamation cases illuminate how those who wanted to be the leaders of their communities, respected by their neighbours, viewed their reputations. In addition, some of the values expressed may represent new and stricter standards of propriety. Thus the standards implicit in defamation cases, while not confined to the propertied, were particularly expected of them, and depended on the autonomy and independence – and thus the credit – that was more easily available to them.

The use of the law to settle disputes and affirm one's place in society is in sharp distinction to the use of violence described earlier in this essay. The law offered other tools that served to limit violence and uphold reformed ideals of male behaviour. The most frequently used of these was the bond to keep the peace;[82] the penalty was forfeiture of whatever sum – usually £10 or £20 – had been pledged. In 1606 Robert Gardner sought a bond of good behaviour against Edward and John Bagnold of Newcastle under Lyme, whom he suspected of being responsible for his being robbed a year earlier, and who had recently entered Gardner's house with daggers drawn, threatening to kill him.[83] A century later Anne Lombard, a young single woman living in Hawkchurch, Dorset, sought one in response to Edward Mitchell's repeated assaults on her. On several occasions neighbours had intervened, but Lombard evidently felt that the bond represented greater security.[84] A bond was relatively cheap, and it moved a quarrel from being a matter of private to one of public concern. It did not provide certain protection, but it served as a strong deterrent.

III

Manhood, like womanhood, is a social construction. It is particularly easy to see it as a mutable social form when, as in the early modern period, changes in ideas about manhood made it a subject of more overt conflict. There were many forces which sought to move men from the traditional model of manhood to the reformed one. The reformed model was associated with the propertied and the respectable, and it was supported by the institutions of both Church and State. The ideal man in both models was independent, proud and cared for himself; he protected his own honour and that of his family. In the traditional model, this was frequently done through the use of violence; in the reformed model, violence was replaced by self-restraint and the recourse to law. This latter method required property and money as well as patience; those without access to the first two necessarily relied on older methods to assert their manhood and defend their reputations.

Because independence was central to manhood, not all men could be manly. The development of the reformed vision of manliness further restricted access to manliness, and was thus central to the cultural conflicts of the early seventeenth century. Manhood is not a historical constant, and in early modern England it was not based on sexual activity. The question was what constituted independence and how it could or should be asserted and lived. The increasing use of the courts as a means of settling disputes and claiming place by those of property, as well as the attack on duels, increasingly separated the wealthy from their poorer neighbours, who often used violence to assert their place in society, particularly in relation to other men. The reformation of manhood is another piece of the cultural polarization of early modern society.

Notes

The author is grateful to Cynthia Herrup, Jodi Mikalachki, Nancy Grey Osterud and Rachel Weil for comments on earlier drafts of this essay. A very early version was given to Mark Kishlansky's seminar on Early Modern England at Harvard in 1993; the comments and questions at that session helped refine the argument. As always, David Underdown has listened, read, and criticized through the whole process of creating this essay.

[1] 'An homily of the state of matrimony', reprinted in Joan Larsen Klein (ed.), *Daughters, Wives and Widows: Writings by Men about Women and Marriage in England 1500–1640* (Urbana and Chicago, 1992), p. 16.

[2] 'Homily of matrimony', pp. 16, 17.

[3] David D. Gilmore, *Manhood in the Making: Cultural Concepts of Masculinity* (New Haven and London, 1990), p. 224.

[4] Sandra Lipsitz Bem, *The Lenses of Gender: Transforming the Debate on Sexual Inequality* (New Haven and London, 1993).

[227]

[5] The phrase is used by Keith Wrighton as the title of his dissertation 'The Puritan reformation of manners with special reference to the counties of Lancashire and Essex, 1640–1660', Ph.D. dissertation, Cambridge University (1973); the ideas are elaborated in Keith Wrightson and David Levine, *Poverty and Piety in an English Village: Terling, 1525–1700* (New York and London, 1979) and Keith Wrightson, *English Society, 1580–1680* (London, 1982); David Underdown, 'The taming of the scold', in Anthony Fletcher and John Stevenson (eds.), *Order and Disorder in Early Modern England* (Cambridge, 1985), pp. 116–36; David Underdown, *Fire From Heaven: Life in a Seventeenth Century English Town* (London, 1992); for the view of this from the perspective of elite cultural history, see Norbert Elias, *The History of Manners* (New York, 1978).

[6] Alan Bray, *Homosexuality in Renaissance England* (London, 1982).

[7] See, for example, Michael Mullin (ed.), *MACBETH Onstage: An Annotated Facsimile of Glen Byam Shaw's 1955 Promptbook* (Columbia, 1976), p. 193: in this production, a significant argument developed between the actor playing Malcolm and the director precisely centred on how manly Malcolm was: see interview with Trader Faulkner, pp. 251–2. I am grateful to Irene Dash for information on the performance history of the play, and for this reference.

[8] For one study of chivalric ideal and practice, see Georges Duby, *William Marshall: The Flower of Chivalry*, trans. Richard Howard (New York, 1985); Lawrence Stone, *The Crisis of the Aristocracy, 1558–1641* (Oxford, 1965), pp. 234–50; a central text of this attack is Thomas Middleton, *The Peacemaker*, in Gary Taylor et al. (ed.), *The Complete Middleton* (Oxford, forthcoming); see also Susan Amussen, 'Critical introduction to *The Peacemaker*', in *The Complete Middleton Companion* (Oxford, forthcoming).

[9] The intersection of cross-dressed heroines with boy actors created, of course, even more complicated issues: see Lisa Jardine, *Still Harping on Daughters: Women and Drama in the Age of Shakespeare*, 2nd edn. (New York, 1989), ch. 1.

[10] See Rudolf M. Dekker and Lotte C. van de Pol, *The Tradition of Female Transvestism in Early Modern Europe* (Basingstoke, 1989); Dianne Dugaw, *Warrior Women and Popular Balladry, 1650–1850* (Cambridge, 1989); Phyllis Mack, *Visionary Women: Ecstatic Prophecy in Seventeenth Century England* (Berkeley, 1992) for prophetic language; David Underdown, *Revel, Riot and Rebellion: Popular Politics and Culture in England, 1603–1660* (Oxford, 1985), pp. 110–11; Jean Howard, 'Crossdressing, the theatre, and gender struggle in early modern England', *Shakespeare Quarterly*, 34 (4) (1988), pp. 418–40, esp. pp. 420–1 for the treatment of women who dressed as men.

[11] Thomas Laqueur, *Making Sex: Body and Gender from the Greeks to Freud* (Cambridge, MA, 1990), esp. pp. 134–42.

[12] Underdown, 'The taming of the scold'.

[13] For the debate, including texts of the central pamphlets, see Katherine Henderson and Barbara McManus, *Half Humankind: Texts and Contexts in the Debate on Women, 1540–1640* (Urbana and Chicago, 1985).

[14] Robert Greene, *A Quip for an Upstart Courtier* (London, 1592), reprinted in *The Harleian Miscellany*, vol. V (London, 1810), pp. 393–421, esp. pp. 398, 412, 421.

[15] David Underdown, *Free-born Englishmen: The Political Nation of Seventeenth Century England* (forthcoming), ch. 2; *idem*, 'Yellow ruffs and poisoned possets: placing women in early Stuart political debate', in Susan Amussen and Adele Seeff (eds.), *Attending to Early Modern Women* (Newark, forthcoming); by his very nature, the

courtier was, of course, a dependent creature.

[16] Swetnam, 'The arraignment' in Henderson and McManus, *Half Humankind*, p. 205; Swetnam is so pleased with this that he repeats it on p. 207!

[17] The title-page is reproduced as the cover for the Penguin Classics edition of *Leviathan* (London and New York, 1985): the Leviathan is a large male figure whose body is composed of smaller male figures.

[18] Susan Dwyer Amussen, *An Ordered Society: Gender and Class in Early Modern England*, (Oxford and New York, 1988), esp. pp. 36–46; William Whately, *A Bride-Bush: or A Direction for Married Persons Plainely describing the duties common to both, and peculiar to each of them* (London, 1625) devotes sections VIII–XIII (pp. 97–188) to the husband's duties, and section XIV (pp. 189–216) to the wife's duties.

[19] For the competing codes for women see Amussen, *An Ordered Society*, pp. 119–20.

[20] Although there is no room to explore this here, the literature of travel and exploration in the period is full of comparisons, both implicit and explicit, which place English men above others; the political rhetoric of Parliament echoes this as it emphasizes the benefits of English freedom: see Underdown, *Free-born Englishmen* (forthcoming).

[21] John Beattie, *Crime and the Courts in England, 1660–1800* (Princeton, 1986), pp. 124–32; Susan Amussen, ' "Being stirred to much unquietness": violence and domestic violence in early modern England', *Journal of Women's History*, 6 (2) (1994), pp. 70–89; Anna Clark, *Women's Silence, Men's Violence: Sexual Assault in England 1770–1845* (London and New York, 1987); Nazife Bashar, 'Rape in England between 1550 and 1700', in *The Sexual Dynamics of History* (London, 1983); for the law of rape, see Giles Jacob, *A New Law-Dictionary*, 2nd edn. (London, 1732), entries on rape and ravishment; Edward Coke, *Institutes of the Laws of England* (London, 1797), part III, p. 60.

[22] Public Records Office (P.R.O.) ASSI 45 2/1/13, 1647, Examination of Jane Bingley; for the significance of the 'cry', see below.

[23] P.R.O. ASSI 45 1/5/29–30, Examinations of Elizabeth Parker, John Cawvert.

[24] Norfolk Record Office (N.R.O.), C/S3/17, 9 James I, Information of Joan Sherre, 23 August 1611. In almost all of the cases of rape or attempted rape I have found, the perpetrators take advantage of isolation. In one case the allegation includes the assertion that a man's wife helped him to rape their servant – but of course secrecy was possible within the household: Corp. of London R.O., Sessions Papers 1683, Information of Dorothy Taylor of Broadstreet.

[25] Corp. of London R.O., Sessions Papers 1680, Information of Sarah Wood, 19 Nov. 1680.

[26] Corp. of London R.O., Sessions Papers 1675, Information of Joyce Northall, 9 Feb. 1674/5.

[27] Dorset R.O., B7/A4/9, Pta, Lyme Quarter Sessions, 24 Jan. 1731/2, Information of Joan Knight.

[28] The depositions are found in P.R.O. ASSI 45, boxes 2/1–16/3, 1647–1693. I have included all the cases which are listed in the P.R.O. index under rape, although the status of some is ambiguous: Mary, the wife of Thomas Firth of Bolling is convicted of adultery and sentenced to death after accusing John Sharpe of Bolling of having sex with her on several occasions: P.R.O. ASSI 45 5/2/35, ASSI 44/6.

[29] Keith Wrightson, 'The nadir of English illegitimacy in the seventeenth century', in P. Laslett, K. Oosterveen and R. Smith (eds.), *Bastardy and its Comparative History* (Cambridge, MA, 1980), pp. 176–91, finds that between 14 per cent and 23 per cent

of all women bearing bastards in Essex and Lancashire named their master or some-one in a 'magisterial position' as the father: p. 187; for the coercion involved, see Susan Dwyer Amussen, 'Punishment, discipline and power: the social meanings of violence in early modern England', *Journal of British Studies*, 34(1) (1993), pp. 1–34.

[30] Edward Terrill, *Records of a Church of Christ*, pp. 213–14, 215–16, 225, 247: Smyth's experience suggests why reports of rape are rare, insofar as *she* was expelled from the congregation for her sin, only readmitted after nearly two years. Her master had, evidently, not committed any sins.

[31] See for example, N.R.O., DEP/43, Hudson con Noble, fos. 165–7, 222v–27v, 247v–50v, and DEP/44, fos. 13–22; while the role of rape in maintaining patriarchy is not germane here, one weakness of Roy Porter's 'Rape – does it have a historical meaning', in Roy Porter and Sylvana Tomaselli (eds.), *Rape* (Oxford, 1986), pp. 216–36 is that he ignores the dimension of class when he uses elite diaries and jour-nals as evidence for the absence of fear. Young women in service were concerned about the potential for sexual assault, and many clearly had strategies to deal with it. That some such assaults occupied an ambiguous terrain in popular culture – like date rape today – is undoubtedly true, but that does not negate the role of such assaults in maintaining patriarchy; it merely emphasizes that in early modern England, patriarchy was allied to a particular social structure as well, and the experience of women within that structure differed significantly.

[32] HMC, *Twelfth Report*, App. IV (Rutland I), p. 68, letter of Thomas Edwards to earl of Rutland, 16 April 1557.

[33] N.R.O. ANW 1/2, 1580, Little Snoring against William Jackson. Since such slan-derous and immoral boasting would certainly be presentable, the uniqueness of this case in the courts I have examined in Norfolk and Oxfordshire is noteworthy; cf. Laura Gowing, 'Gender and the language of insult in early modern London', *History Workshop Journal*, 35 (1993), pp. 1–21, esp. pp. 7–8.

[34] For street ballads, see Joy Wiltenburg, *Disorderly Women and Female Power in the Street Literature of Early Modern England and Germany* (Charlottesville, 1992), pp. 199–202; Wiltenburg notes that the theme of the battle of the sexes underlies some 'humorous' songs that do indicate the ambiguity of consent in courtship; I am grate-ful to Frances Dolan for information about pamphlets.

[35] HMC, *Fifteenth Report*, App. V (Rutland II), p. 64.

[36] Bray, *Homosexuality*, pp. 69–70; the place of homosexual encounters changed in the early eighteenth century: Randolph Trumbach, 'Sex, gender, and sexual identity in modern culture: male sodomy and female prostitution in enlightenment London', in J. C. Fout (ed.), *Forbidden History: The State, Society, and the Regulation of Sexu-ality in Modern Europe* (Chicago, 1992), pp. 89–106, esp. pp. 90–1.

[37] Underdown, *Fire From Heaven*, pp. 163–4.

[38] *Ibid.*, pp. 180–1.

[39] *Proceedings in Parliament 1628*, ed. R. C. Johnson, M. F. Keeler et al. 6 vols., (New Haven, 1977–83), vol. II, p. 66.

[40] He appeared in the town court on 30 June 1630, 2 Nov, 1631, 8 March, 1 April, 14 August and 11 Dec. 1633; 6 June 1634; 2 Jan., 3–4 Aug and 14 Dec. 1635; 15 Feb., 26 and 31 May and 30 Oct. 1637; the incident reported 8 March 1633 actually occurred the Sunday after Christmas. The absence of offences in Lent is perhaps the most remarkable: as a butcher, Pouncey would have little employment during that season. I am grateful to David Underdown for sharing his notes on Thomas Pouncey with me.

For the calendar, see David Cressy, *Bonfires and Bells: National Memory and the Protestant Calendar in Elizabethan and Stuart England* (Berkeley, 1989), ch. 2.

[41] For more on the pattern of brawl, see Amussen, 'Punishment, discipline and power'.

[42] Oxfordshire Archives (Oxf. Arch.), MS. Oxf. Dioc. papers c. 21, 1572, fo. 240v (Personal answers of William Bury Cler. to articles of John Ward).

[43] The ability to discern which coin one had given the parish priest is also a telling comment on the scarcity of specie in the sixteenth century.

[44] Corp. of London R.O., Sessions Papers 1674, Information re. Death of Jonathan Gorges.

[45] HMC, *Twelfth Report*, App. IV (Rutland I), p. 68 (16 April 1557), Thos. Edwards to Earl of Rutland.

[46] P.R.O., ASSI 45 1/4/23–37, Info re. death of Nicholas Holmes.

[47] For a fuller discussion of these issues, see Amussen, 'Critical introduction to *The Peacemaker*'.

[48] V. G. Kiernan, *The Duel in European History: Honour and the Reign of Aristocracy* (Oxford, 1988); for attempts to limit duels and legal consequences, see pp. 82–3, 94–5, 99–101.

[49] Bodl. L., MS. Don c. 37, no.1040, 23 Feb. 1668/9; the offence was exacerbated by being in the king's presence. Charles II was ambivalent about duels: like his grandfather, he opposed them, but often pardoned those involved: Kiernan, *Duel*, p. 100.

[50] *The Diary of Roger Lowe, of Ashton in Makerfield, Lancashire, 1663–74*, ed. William L. Sachse (London and New York, 1938), *passim*, esp. pp. 33–4, 74–5, 81, 84; in October 1664 he expressed frustration; his service ended a little more than a year later, in November 1665. For sociability in general, see Karl Westhauser, 'Friendship and family in early modern England: the sociability of Adam Eyre and Samuel Pepys', *Journal of Social History*, 27(3) (1994), pp. 517–36.

[51] *Diary of Roger Lowe*, pp. 118–19.

[52] K. J. Lindley, 'Riot prevention and control in early Stuart London', *T.R.H.S.*, 5th ser., 33 (1983), pp. 109–26; Tim Harris, 'The bawdy house riots of 1668', *Historical Journal*, 29(3) (1986), pp. 537–56: Harris suggests that the riots reflected nonconformist resentment of the strict enforcement of religious uniformity as against the lax enforcement of laws against prostitution. This political dimension, of course, would not be present in the earlier period.

[53] Oxf. Arch., MS. Oxf. Dioc. papers c. 29, 1682. Ronald Marchant, *The Church Under the Law: Justice, Administration, and Discipline in the Diocese of York, 1560–1640* (Cambridge, 1989), pp. 214–16; Christopher Hill, *Society and Puritanism in Pre-Revolutionary England*, 2nd edn. (New York, 1967), p. 326.

[54] N.R.O., DEP/24, Christopher Ramsey and Simon Loveleech con Thomas Michelson, Cler., fos. 209–25: there are numerous other complaints about his as well – including his use of the surplice from the parish as a costume in a Christmas masque; N.R.O., DEP/24, Richard Baspole con Robert Somes, Cler., fos. 436–37v.

[55] N.R.O. DEP/22, Offic. domni con George Pilkenton: the case against Pilkenton was also strengthened by the allegation that he preached that Christ was 'craftier than the devil' and the rulers could not know God because of the pomp and pride in which they lived: fos. 228–34v.

[56] Wallace Notestein (ed.), *The Journal of Sir Simonds D'Ewes, From the Beginning of the Long Parliament to the Opening of the trial of the Earl of Strafford* (New Haven,

1923), pp. 200–1; some of these complaints also appear in N.R.O. DEP/45, Book 48b, John Driver and Robert Smith con Jonathan Skinner, Cler, fos. 131–42.

[57] N.R.O., ANW 2/66, 1627, Swanton Novers, presentment by Richard Chapman of Mr William Naylor.

[58] N.R.O., DEP/48, 1669, Gibbs con Brookebanck, Cler., fo. 152.

[59] N.R.O. DEP/50, 1678, Offic. Dmi con William Jacombe, Vicar of Oulton and Guestwick, file 10. For a full discussion of this, see Christopher Hill, *Economic Problems of the Church From Archbishop Whitgift to the Long Parliament* (Oxford, 1956), pp. 216–18.

[60] Clergy with land were, of course, the lucky ones: some received only a small stipend while a wealthy layperson collected the tithes and income from the living: Hill, *Economic Problems*, pp. 134, 200, 272.

[61] Elias, *History of Manners*.

[62] See for example, N.R.O., DEP/36, Samuel Hooker, Cler., con Thomas Chapman, fos. 241v–242v; DEP/33, Samuel Oates Cler. con Peter Hunt, fos. 498v–499v.

[63] Oxf. Arch., MS. Oxf. Dioc. papers c. 28, 1674, Robert Hawkins Cler. con John Acreman, and Anna ux. Robert Hawkins con John Acreman, fos. 66v–7v, 68r–v, 68v–69, 71r–v, 82r–v, 69v–71, and 83r–v, esp. fo. 82; the other insults include the word 'rogue', the assertion that Hawkins frequented 'whores' – 3 or 4 – and got them with child, and that his wife was 'a notorious whore and her children were all bastards and therefore she was a base stinking Queen' (fo. 68).

[64] N.R.O., DEP/37, Mr Nuttall con Edmund Spinke, fos. 30–1, 116–17.

[65] *Ibid.*, DEP/26, Mr Robinson Cler. con Burrell, fos. 275v–276, 277.

[66] *Ibid.*, DEP/48, 1667/8, George Heyho Cler. con John Wasse, fos. 42v–45v, esp. 43, 44v.

[67] *Ibid.*, DEP/48, Offic. Promot per Mr John Hickman con Edmund Hudson, fos. 145–7, esp. 145 r–v.

[68] *Ibid.*, DEP/37, Payne Cler. con Elizabeth Stone, fos. 102v–103.

[69] *Ibid.*, DEP/38, Pigott Gent. con Hodgson Cler., fos. 105–7v.

[70] *Ibid.*, DEP/46, 1663, Thomas LeGros, Ar., con Thomas Ramsie, Cler., fos. 277–84, 339–51: LeGros – who along with Sir William Paston, Bart., was a target of the libels – brought in twenty-five witnesses in the case!

[71] For defamation, see Amussen, *An Ordered Society*, pp. 101–4, 118–19; Martin Ingram, *Church Courts, Sex and Marriage in England 1570–1640* (Cambridge, 1987), esp. pp. 292–302; J. A. Sharpe, *Defamation and Sexual Slander in Early Modern England: The Church Courts at York*, Borthwick Papers no. 58 (York, 1980).

[72] Amussen, *An Ordered Society*, pp. 102/3; Sharpe, *Defamation*, pp. 11, 14/15.

[73] See for example N.R.O., DEP/43 (1638), Bartram con Bell, fos. 76v–77v; Bartram con Gedge, fos. 31v–32, also 78r–v; N.R.O., DEP/10, Book 11, Atkinson con Rookesby, fos. 232r–v; N.R.O., DEP/10, Bk. 11a, Chapman con Harde, fos. 255v, 283.

[74] N.R.O., DEP/10, Bk. 11a, William Gay con Margery Russell, fos. 223v–224.

[75] Amussen, *An Ordered Society*, pp. 152–5.

[76] Oxf. Arch., MS. Oxf. Dioc. papers d. 15, fos. 202v–3; cf. N.R.O., DEP/56 (1713), Robert Colby con Francis Kirby, fo. 319; also N.R.O. ANW /2/66, 1625, Swannington presentment of Nicholas Hunt for calling the questman 'cheating knave'.

[77] N.R.O. DEP/33, John Castell con William Parsley, fos. 385v–386, 386v.

[78] *Ibid.*, DEP/49, file 25, Richard Wakefield et ux. con Thomas Fawke, 1671: whether the silver referred to the status of the alleged lover or the flagrancy of the affair is not

clear.

[79] *Ibid.*, DEP/56, William Herring con Eliz. ux. John Brownrick, fos. 29–31.

[80] Oxf. Arch., MS. Oxf. Dioc. papers c.2, Nov. 1630, fos. 114 (112) and 117 (114) r–v; also 131 (128)v.

[81] Greene, *Quip*, p. 400.

[82] The modern version of this is the restraining order.

[83] *Staffordshire Quarter Sessions Rolls*, vol. V: 1603–6, William Salt Archaeological Society, *Collections for the History of Staffordshire*, 3rd ser., 30 (1940), Easter 1606 sessions, pp. 303–4.

[84] Dorset R.O., Quarter Sessions Rolls, Jan. 1709/10, 29 Dec. 1709, examinations of Anne Lombard, singlewoman, Susanna wife of Abraham Bevil, and Elizabeth, wife of John Swayne, all of Hawkchurch.

10

Companionate marriage versus male friendship: anxiety for the lineal family in Jacobean drama

Lisa Jardine

[A good wife] is a man's best movable, a scion incorporate with the stock, bringing sweet fruit; one that to her husband is more than a friend, less than trouble; an equal with him in the yoke. Calamities and troubles she shares alike, nothing pleaseth her that doth not him. She is relative in all, and he without her but half himself. She is his absent hands, eyes, ears and mouth; his present and absent all.[1]

The companionate marriage, characterized here by Thomas Overbury in 1614, is treated as something of a milestone in household development by early modern social historians.[2] For Keith Wrightson and others it is the reformed Church's contribution to progressive household management: 'In the domestic economy, decision-making, conflict resolution and sexual behaviour, mutuality in marriage, within the context of ultimate male authority, may well have been not only the conjugal ideal, but also the common practice among the English people as a whole.'[3] Historians have tended to see partnership based on free choice, intellectual and educational equality, self-regulation in personal behaviour and shared responsibility as self-evidently desirable as the model for the contracted reproductive household unit. Arranged marriage, strenuous dependency in all household management decision-making and subordination of wife to husband as his 'chattel' (subject to his will in all matters) seem clearly inferior as the organizing principles within the domestic unit.[4] Here, however, I shall argue that the new model raised problems in relation to the contemporary understanding of the structural coherence of 'family' and, in particular, produced anxieties concerning the agency of women within it. And as a further stage in my argument I shall suggest that the perceived possibilities for conflict, or at least inconsistency of goal, between the long-term objectives of the lineal family and the short-term agreements made between consensual marriage partners closely resembled another area of contestation – that between the bonds of kinship and the contracted undertakings between non-kin male 'friends'. In both cases the consenting parties were motivated by the desire to optimize the social and economic possibilities for their own 'domestic' unit. In both cases the result-ing interference with lineal prospects and planning takes place in the private rather than the public domain. And in both cases any value attached to a modern type of 'intimacy' had to be offset against the dangers of secrecy, and of binding relationships invisible to (and impervious to) regulation by the administrative systems of the State.[5]

The problems these issues raise are vividly dramatized in the theatre of the early seventeenth century. They are central and structural to the plots of the plays of an early seventeenth-century dramatist like Thomas Middleton. Here I shall use Middleton's best-known play *The Changeling* (now attributed to Middleton and Rowley) as the basis for an exploration of some of the under-lying features of intimate relationship which created dynastic anxiety. I shall argue that the source of anxiety is less the instrumentality of women them-selves, than the way the new marriage model is in contest with traditional social organization. I shall suggest that the *frisson* caused by the prospect that emotional closeness might prove socially effective charges the relationship erotically – it is intense, secret and powerful. In the same way, the close rela-tionship between men of similar social standing which emerges in the late six-teenth and early seventeenth centuries as the model for household service gains an erotic charge from the way it can exert invisible influence within and beyond a household.[6] In the drama these two forms of socially disturbing inti-macy collide against a backdrop of traditional dynastic and lineal aspiration.

We can already detect a cultural difficulty in the language of the period associated with alliance and duty. The term 'love' modulates during the period we are looking at from a formally acknowledged designation of duty and affection towards the authority figure who governs one's life to a more self-centred, freely-willed directing of emotion generated by a bond of unofficial obligation and indebtedness.[7] The former version of 'love' is vividly captured in Shakespeare's *King Lear*, in Cordelia's description of the nature of her commitment to her father:

> Good my Lord,
> You have begot me, bred me, lov'd me: I
> Return those duties back as are right fit,
> Obey you, love you, and most honour you.
> Why have my sisters husbands, if they say
> They love you all? Haply when I shall wed,
> That lord whose hand must take my plight shall carry
> Half my love with him, half my care and duty:
> Sure I shall never marry like my sisters,
> To love my father all.[8]

Since the obedience and dutiful dependency expected of female kin is des-ignated 'love', regardless of whether it is directed towards father, brother or uncle (in the absence of father), or husband, a moment of representational crisis arises at the point of transfer. As the father 'gives away' his daughter in marriage, her 'love' passes instantaneously from him to her new husband (and this transfer is represented symbolically by the pause of the wedding cortège at the church porch). On the threshold between the woman's belonging to one household and another, the husband specifies the terms of partition of lands and property between himself and his wife (the jointure), as she passes (as currency, but not as agent) from one contractual undertaking to another; she continues passively to 'love', but reactively redirects her emotional attention.[9] Cordelia's two sisters, who do voice their total and permanent love for their father at the beginning of *King Lear* in spite of the fact that they are married and have left the paternal household, turn out, inevitably, to be adulterous wives, as well as feignedly loving daughters.[10]

This structural and formalized version of love has its corresponding type in the male/male relationship between feudal master and his servant – the kind of loyal, no-nonsense relationship Kent describes at the beginning of *King Lear*:

> Royal Lear,
> Whom I have ever honour'd as my King,
> Lov'd as my father, as my master follow'd,
> As my great patron thought on in my prayer.[11]

Even Lear's dismissal and banishment of Kent (for giving him advice he did not wish to hear) does not sever the relationship – it is not within Kent's 'nature' to do other than continue to 'love' and serve, and he merely disguises himself and re-enters his master's service.

David Starkey has represented the shift from this kind of 'loving' relationship between master and servant as an inflection towards intimacy as the basis for trust and service.[12] And whereas 'alliance' and its contractual undertakings rested squarely in the public domain (its negotiations formally recorded and witnessed), 'affection' and individualized emotional attachment establish private and invisible bonds which escape the terms of recognized kinship relationships. In such cases mutual obligation and indebtedness – on which might rest undertakings to further each other's causes, for instance, or to deal financially on each other's behalf – might be entirely undetectable in the public domain. I shall argue that Jacobean theatre dramatizes the way in which developing strategies for male private service within the noble household came into conflict with the equally vital strategies for assuring lineage continuity through marriage alliance, and for consolidating resources in land and monies on the basis of family unions – strategies which necessarily focused on women, and on reproduction as the most valued manifestation of sexuality. In so doing, I shall argue, the theatre preserves the textual trace of anxiety or uncertainty about the consequences of gradual shifts in acceptable social practice which are not clearly articulated in other kinds of 'documentary' historical evidence. In other words, new kinds of liaisons between men, formally unacknowledged in the public sphere, came into competition with the more traditional forms of liaison, or bond-forming, between dynastic houses, with their feudal accoutrements (including lineal retainers). And a play like *The Changeling* allows us to recapture contemporary cultural strategies for responding to such submerged conflict.[13]

The move towards intimacy in male service is vividly captured in Shakespeare's sonnet 29:

> When in disgrace with Fortune and men's eyes,
>   I all alone beweep my outcast state,
> And trouble deaf heaven with my bootless cries,
> And look upon myself, and curse my fate,
> Wishing me like to one more rich in hope,
> Featur'd like him, like him with friends possess'd,
> Desiring this man's art, and that man's scope,
> With what I most enjoy contented least;
> Yet in these thoughts myself almost despising,
> Haply I think on thee, and then my state,
> Like to the lark at break of day arising
> From sullen earth, sings hymns at heaven's gate;
>   For thy sweet love rememb'red such wealth brings
>   That then I scorn to change my state with kings.[14]

Some years ago John Barrell drew attention to this sonnet as exemplifying and deftly manipulating a 'discourse of patronage'.[15] Here, 'love' designates a relationship of dependency of the author to the addressee which is at once passionate and dutiful: a relationship of serving (or, more accurately, service), loyalty, *fides* or good faith, a homosocial bonding on which, by the 1580s, apparently, the smooth and effective running of the households of noblemen depended. Although the tone of this sonnet suggests the kind of intensity of feeling which we associate with courtship of a woman, what is at issue here is an attempt to gain the attention of, and enter a relationship of trust with (in other words, the courtship of) a male patron.

Traces of the intimacy which characterizes the new type of relationship amongst men are to be found in surviving letters exchanged between lord and member of his private household close to his person, in which the terms of passionate commitment are also those of a contemporary love sonnet. Here is an exchange of letters between Anthony Bacon and his employer, the earl of Essex:

My singular good Lord, If God had not sent me the other day so special a defensive of the honour and comfort of your Lordship's presence to fortify my spirits beforehand, they could never have resisted such cruel enemies as have since assailed me without giving me any respite or breathing till this morning.

(Anthony Bacon to the Earl of Essex)

Farewell, worthy Master Bacon, and know that, though I entertain you here with short letters, yet I will send you from sea papers that shall remain as tables of my honest designs and pledges of my love to you from your true and best wishing friend Essex.

(Essex to Anthony Bacon)[16]

The professions of intense feeling in exchanges like these use 'love' to code a kind of mutuality of obligation and indebtedness within which the responsibilities of employer and employed form part of a private undertaking. As in sonnet 29, Anthony Bacon recommends himself as ideally equipped to serve, and Essex responds by valuing that service in personal (intimate) terms. What seems to be at issue here is the kind of access which personable young men can gain to prominent persons in the public sphere via their personal accomplishments including both congeniality as a companion and competence in producing and processing knowledge – expertise at information gathering, and in self-presentation using the discursive skills associated with a humanistic training in letters. The 'secretary' and the 'intelligencer' offer a new kind of service to the nobleman, fit for the world of international diplomacy and embassy.[17] The relationships established are, I think, felt as disturbingly volatile – a far cry from the steady, unchanging and dependable commitment of the feudal retainer.

There is a recognizable emotional affinity between the intensified, private relationship between noble master and gently born intimate servant and the newly mutual and personalized love between partners in a marriage love-match. The similarity is recorded, I suggest, in cultural productions which appear to waver in indecision between a male and a female lover as addressee. It is a comparatively short step, in other words, from the sorts of sentiments exchanged in familiar letters between Essex and Anthony Bacon and the following:

A woman's face, with Nature's own hand painted,
Hast thou, the Master Mistress of my passion;
A woman's gentle heart, but not acquainted
With shifting change, as is false woman's fashion;
An eye more bright than theirs, less false in rolling,
Gilding the object whereupon it gazeth;
A man in hue all hues in his controlling,
Which steals men's eyes and women's souls amazeth.
And for a woman wert thou first created;
Till Nature, as she made thee, fell a-doting,
And by addition me of thee defeated
By adding one thing to my purpose nothing.
      But since she prick'd thee out for women's pleasure,
      Mine be thy love, and thy love's use their treasure.[18]

Since the groundbreaking work of Alan Bray, these kinds of texts have been identified as homoerotic, and used to argue that sodomitical relationships were not clearly censured in the period (though Bray also argues that they were not clearly defined either).[19] Here, however, what I am interested in is the tension sustained between love towards a man and love towards a woman, ambiguously evoked through the term 'love'. The important passage for us is the final two lines:

> But since she prick'd thee out for women's pleasure,
> Mine be thy love, and thy love's use their treasure.

Until the final couplet, the ambivalence of the 'love' has turned on its subject: the 'master–mistress' of the poet's passion, who, in his seductive power towards both men and women is of confused or indeterminate gender. Thus far the sonnet supports my suggestion that the two *were* readily confused, that 'masters' increasingly demanded attentions of an intimate kind, thereby modulating 'favour' towards them from public courtship towards feminized seduction. The clinching couplet, however, turns upon the love actively offered by the sonnet's addressee: directed towards the poet it is 'love'; towards a woman it is 'love's use'. Constructive (intense) mutual commitment between men is here finally contrasted with the merely sexual and reproductive heterosexual activity – love's use.[20] Since this is the 'turn' in the sonnet, it apparently resolves the struggle between the (certainly erotic) interest aroused by the addressee in the author, and the addressee's availability ('prick'd out') for 'women's pleasure'. That resolution takes the form of a preference declared for male bonding ('mine be thy love'), over procreative sex ('thy love's use their treasure').

It would be easy to jump to the conclusion that the import of this (and a significant number of others amongst Shakespeare's sonnets) is that male friendship is socially acknowledged as a superior kind of alliance to courtship of a woman.[21] I am suggesting precisely the opposite – that we should read the tendency of poems of this kind to elide professional male friendship and sodomy in a 'discourse of sodomy' as part of the period's mistrust of concealed, irregular networks of co-operation of all kinds, where these interfered with the recognized, public socially structuring forms.[22]

When the earl of Essex's secretary, the future Lord Chancellor, Francis Bacon, was given the job of 'minding' the Spanish defector Antonio Perez, in 1593, his mother, Lady Anne Bacon, who disapproved of her son's consorting with a Catholic informer, levelled the accusation that this was a sexual, rather than a professional relationship:

> He keepeth that bloody Perez, as a coach-companion and bed-companion, a proud, prophane, costly fellow, whose being about him I verily fear the Lord God doth mislike and doth less bless him in credit and otherwise in his health.[23]

It was a charge readily levelled at any man who apparently neglected bond-forming with women (with a view of marriage) in favour of intelligence-net-working with men. In a recent book on the Elizabethan spy network, Alan Haynes suggests that a similar (and this time formal) charge laid against Francis' brother Anthony was a consequence of Anthony's having given cause for offence in the sphere of *heterosexual* attachments:

> There is substantial evidence that [the source of the accusation against Anthony] was Charlotte Arbaleste, Madame du Plessis, the wife of the chief advisor to Henri of Navarre ... Bacon had ... declined to marry one of the daughters of Madame du Plessis, although it might have provided him with an advantageous cover. His error was to have allowed the notion of marriage to arise.[24]

Where intimacy between men was a feature of the network of relationships on which an activity depended (in this case spying or 'intelligence'), an aggrieved or politically motivated adversary might, apparently, readily mobilize the slur of sodomy (and in this case, more damagingly, the court charge). Although this gets us no further in deciding whether in fact sodomy *was* a customary practice in such households, it does, given the deeply illicit nature of any such relationship, suggest generalized anxiety concerning the difficulty in deciding upon the real nature (and effectiveness) of these kinds of 'privy' loyalties and dependencies.

What happens if we now turn our attention to women, and specifically to marriage in which the woman chooses her partner, rather than complying with an alliance contrived to enhance the prospects of her family or line? Curiously enough, I think the version of 'love' produced by the 'choice' model of marriage tends in the direction of intensifying the problem we are looking at (rather than clarifying or resolving it). Because this model stresses the active participation of the woman in the liaison, it makes her 'love' equivalently more active. No longer a simple reflection of duty, stimulated by context (love's object to be father or husband depending on whose household she inhabits), she now directs her love according to her own will. Hence, ironically, the potential unruliness not only of Cordelia (as I quoted her above), but of Desdemona:

> My noble father,
> I do perceive here a divided duty:
> To you I am bound for life and education,
> My life and education both do learn me
> How to respect you, you are lord of all my duty,
> I am hitherto your daughter: but here's my husband:
> And so much duty as my mother show'd
> To you, preferring you before her father,
> So much I challenge, that I may profess,
> Due to the Moor my lord.[25]

Desdemona's admission that 'she did love the Moor, to live with him', is an admission of her own, wilful choice, which animates the shift of 'duty' from father to husband with a kind of dangerous energy which Cordelia's avowal of duty lacked (however short of the mark it came for her father).

Where the plot involves a conventional courtship, the drama of the period frequently turns on a tension (still residually resonant for us today) between the 'love' of male bonding and the 'love' of heterosexual emotional attraction – can the commitment between the men survive the absorption of one of them with a woman? In Shakespeare's *Much Ado About Nothing* this tension produces a telling moment of confusion in the play. Returning from the wars in the service of Don Pedro, Prince of Aragon, the young nobleman Claudio falls headlong in love – at first sight – with Hero, the daughter of their host Leonato, Governor of Messina. He confesses his love to his master, who offers to gain permission for the match from Leonato, and to woo Hero on Claudio's behalf.

Don Pedro's relationship with Claudio is represented as an *amicitia* or friendship relationship, one in which the authority of the one and the service of the other are sustained by mutual respect, personal indebtedness and obligation, and above all, intimacy and warmth of feeling. Within the play, this produces a curious elision of dynastic and consensual models of marriage: Don Pedro correctly intercedes for Claudio with Leonato, since his rank (and Claudio's dependent relationship with him) will make Leonato's consent to the match more likely. Effectively Don Pedro acts as Claudio's social and financial guarantor. His proposal to woo Hero (disguised as Claudio) to gain her *love*, however, confuses his role in the match.[26] By the time the plan reaches the ears of the troublemaker Don John it has become one for Don Pedro to win Hero's love for himself, and then to make gift of her to Claudio:

> I whipped me behind the arras, and there heard it agreed upon that the Prince should woo Hero for himself, and having obtained her, give her to Count Claudio.[27]

This is a fair version of the plan. Don Pedro has apparently elided old and new forms of alliance-formation: negotiation of a dynastic alliance, and personal courtship aimed at a love-match. A suit to establish lineage is transitive (Don Pedro sues on Claudio's behalf with Leonato). A courtship to gain an individual's 'love' is not – there is a reciprocal service bond of 'love' between Don Pedro and Claudio, and there is Claudio's 'love' for Hero, which he hopes to make reciprocal, but these are independent of one another, and possibly in competition.[28] Hence when Claudio sees Don Pedro successfully gaining Hero's 'love', he reads it as a competitive bid for *her* love, in the face of the challenge offered by the heterosexual relationship to the 'love' between lord and young man in his service. Claudio's close friend Benedict also interprets Don Pedro's wooing as self-interested, counselling Claudio to affect the pose of the forsaken lover 'for the Prince hath got your Hero'.[29] Don John's mischievous insinuations only have the effect of intensifying Claudio's jealousy.

In *Much Ado About Nothing* the confusion caused by the elision of line-match and love-match is short lived. The puzzlement it causes us does, I think, serve to remind us that we have lost the intensity of emotion potentially to be associated with the tension generated between male/male and male/female 'love' bonds. In Middleton and Rowley's *The Changeling*, by contrast, such tension is woven into the play's very fabric. Unpicking the threads allows us access to insights withheld from us by the passage of time in more 'documentary' evidence.

The dramatic power of Middleton and Rowley's *The Changeling* has fascinated generations of critics. The play's obsessive preoccupation with emotional intrigue, female betrayal, murder and corruption, has a vividness which has tempted commentators to link the plot with actual contemporary sensational cases of female interference in dynastic affairs, like the Thomas Overbury/Frances Howard scandal.[30] It is not, however, necessary to propose links of this kind – the play's aura of 'reality' is equally plausibly attributable to skilled writing on the part of the play's two authors. Sub-plot and main plot are unusually closely integrated for a play of the period, with the sub-plot comically highlighting key themes and commenting ironically on some of the play's main preoccupations, and the two parts of the plot are drawn together in the conclusion of the play. Such structural integrity in a jointly authored play tends to bear out the current critical view that Middleton and Rowley took responsibility for writing designated characters, rather than individual scenes (as earlier criticism was inclined at assume).[31]

The Changeling dramatizes tensions created by the competing demands of noble lineage and contracted obligation, duty to family and self-advancement. As elsewhere in Middleton's drama (notably in *Women Beware Women*), the social imperative for hierarchical organization of family and inheritance is endangered by the self-centred plans of a well-born fortune hunter (and Middleton's sympathies appear to be on the adventurer's side). The continued prosperity and social standing of Vermandero's line depends upon his making an advantageous marriage match for his daugher. Alonzo de Piracquo is Vermandero's social superior – an alliance with him will enhance the fortunes of the Vermanderos. By thwarting that choice, and giving rein to her own desires, Beatrice-Joanna intervenes in the public world of courtly position and lineage connections. Her own choice, Alsemero, is a self-made man (though of good birth and background), and in local terms an interloper and adventurer.[32]

The Changeling's plot highlights the potentially damaging effect on Alicante's social order of Alsemero's bid to secure his own fortune in marriage. His inclination becomes Beatrice-Joanna's burning desire. The direct outcome of her arranging for Alonzo de Piracquo to be disposed of is that the union she actually achieves – the forced union with the household servant, De Flores

– is one well beneath her socially, with a 'mere' gentleman (his unsuitability is highlighted dramatically by the fact that he is physically repulsive), thus underlining the socially disruptive consequences of Beatrice-Joanna's meddling with lineage.

The dramatic demonization of the woman who, like Beatrice-Joanna, intervenes on her own behalf in the social process of contracting a lineal marriage is closely linked to the perceived structural importance of traditionally arranged marriage to a family's long-term economic calculations in early modern England. Strategic improvement of the family's fortunes was a significant criterion used in parental choice of a marriage partner, particularly where the only heir was a daughter:

> A suitable marriage, especially among the propertied classes, was one which gave the individual and those closest to him potentially useful new kinsmen, and increased the number of people through whom favours might be sought and advancement achieved. 'Good lordship' and help in recovering lands were among the possible advantages accruing from matches considered by the Paston family, while Alice Wandesford's match with a man of very different religious and political sympathies from her own was made after the civil war in order to free the family's lands from sequestration. The need to use marriage to gain useful allies made for the choice of partners from within one's own region.
>
> Material substance was always a very important consideration.[33]

Whether an advantageous marriage was effected by traditional contracting amongst established families, or by the new-style bargain-making of a more straightforwardly material kind which Houlbrooke describes, the central need for a woman's consent also made it possible to transfer on to her the blame for any failure in the outcome. In *The Changeling* Middleton and Rowley have convincingly designed a plot which shifts the epicentre of blame for the disruption of traditional family alliance from the fortune-seeking man who is ultimately the cause, to the woman whose fortune he seeks.

When, in the final Act of *The Changeling*, Beatrice-Joanna confesses to her father that she has engineered a murder and dishonoured her marriage bed, the metaphor she chooses is one which underlines the fact that family inheritance depends on the guaranteed integrity of shared blood, or blood-relatedness:

> Beatrice: I am that of your blood was taken from you
>   For your better health. Look no more upon't,
>   But cast it to the ground regardlessly;
>   Let the common sewer take it from distinction.[34]

Vermandero's closest blood relation – his only living daughter – represents herself as blood which must be purged from a congested body, a tainted issue of the family's head, to be discarded and wiped from the record (deprived of its 'distinction' or the privilege of its rank). Here Middleton powerfully draws together the positive and negative associations of the hereditary and sexual senses of 'blood'. As a result of Beatrice-Joanna's determined pursuit of her own desires in love, against her father's wishes for posterity of his family, lineage (blood) and the 'hot blood' of the pursuit of carnal gratification have converged and been run together – issue has become corruption, and death is the punishment.

The chastity test to which Alsemero proposes to subject his bride on her wedding night (in Act Four) highlights the importance of pure reproductive descent for the play's male protagonists. Alsemero, the shrewd seaman-adventurer, has been converted by his encounter with Beatrice-Joanna into a love-sick suitor. But the pragmatic Alsemero remains alert to the possibility that the woman who freely returns his love may be fundamentally unreliable as a participant in what is essentially a man's world of contractual undertakings – unlike the courtly Alonzo de Piracquo, whose infatuation clouded his masculine judgement ('Why here is love's tame madness', comments his brother Tomazo[35]). Although Beatrice-Joanna's successful counterfeiting of the symptoms of chastity after the test absolves her temporarily from suspicion, those symptoms themselves remind us of precisely what is at stake in woman's sexual purity: the 'gaping', sneezing and helpless laughter which are Diaphanta's involuntary bodily responses to the potion represent purity as a state of uncontrolled foolishness, entirely available for shaping masculine control. By simulating that state herself, and then by substituting a 'true' virgin for herself in Alsemero's wedding bed, Beatrice-Joanna demonstrates her own ability to manipulate the tokens (and guarantees) of chastity, and thus how vulnerable the marriage bond is to female interference.

Beatrice-Joanna's choice of Alsemero as partner is guided by personal inclination, and the belief that his choice of his closest companions is made with discretion and judgement. She confidently believes that these form a proper basis for a marriage alliance:

> Then I appear in nothing more approved
> Than making choice of him;
> For 'tis a principle: 'He that can choose
> That bosom well, who of his thoughts partakes,
> Proves most discreet in every choice he makes.'
> Methinks I love now with the eyes of judgement,
> And see the way to merit, clearly see it.[36]

Beatrice-Joanna's admiration for Alsmero's judgement relates specifically to his choice of a friend of the utmost discretion in whom to confide – Jasperino. Her assumption that she too can build such intimacy in the form of a friendship-marriage turns out, however, to underestimate the gendered nature of such relationships.

According to Beatrice-Joanna, her own marriage to Alsemero will be a liaison based on emotional and intellectual compatibility. These would be ideal grounds for close personal friendship between men – amity or *amicitia* – the social bond by which men of good birth set considerable store. But such a basis for an alliance between a man and a woman seems regularly in the drama to be suspect (compare the relationship between the Frankfords in Heywood's *A Woman Killed with Kindness*). The liaison which involves the active consent of both parties, and some kind of equal participation, makes female 'love' equivalently more active.

Once marriage is determined on the model of mutual affection and shared preference, it appears to come into direct conflict with the socially acceptable form of close partnership (friendship between adult men of good birth), quite as much as with traditional, parentally sponsored marriage alliance. Like male friendship, its outcome is no longer confined to the continuation of the line, but becomes much more likely to produce networks of relationships and profitable dependencies within and between households. In the case of male friendship, these are the invisible networks of credit and profit around which early modern society built a system of obligation and indebtedness. But where women become involved there is no recognized code of conduct to ensure a socially responsible outcome.

The bargain of mutual obligation which Beatrice-Joanna enters into with De Flores travesties her freely chosen relationship with Alsemero (just as Antonio's 'mad' courtship of Isabella in the sub-plot apes and ironizes the main plot). As soon as Beatrice-Joanna hits on the plan to use De Flores to get rid of Alonzo de Piracquo, the attention she bestows upon him is readily confused with sexual attention: 'Her fingers touched me! She smells all amber';[37] ''Tis half an act of pleasure / To hear her talk thus to me'.[38] De Flores is quite clear, from the instant the compact is made between himself and Beatrice-Joanna, that the request by a desirable woman that he provide her with 'service', will yield carnal intercourse as its reward (he is also clear that such a contract serves the blatant self-interest of the participants):

> *Beatrice*: As thou art forward and thy service dangerous,
>   Thy rèward shall be precious.
> *De Flores*:   That I have thought on;
>   I have assured myself of that beforehand
>   And know it will be precious: the thought ravishes.[39]

Alsemero's intimate servant, Jasperino, is equally convinced that freely chosen intimacy of any kind between a woman and a man is suspect, when he alerts his master to the possibility that Beatrice-Joanna and De Flores are secretly 'allied':

> I heard your bride's voice in the next room to me;
> And, lending more attention, found De Flores
> Louder than she …

Then fell we both to listen, and words passed
Like those that challenge interest in a woman.[40]

A woman's 'interest' – where she invests her affections and duty – is compromised by attention to a man other than her husband-to-be, without the need to prove any suspicious details.

As she embarks on her scheme to do away with the man chosen by her father to be her husband, Beatrice-Joanna is oblivious to the fact that the move she makes actually means that she has freely chosen De Flores, rather than Alsemero, as her alternative sexual match. But it should be stressed that she alone is unaware of the inevitable consequences of her refusing Alsemero's (honourable) proposal that he fight a duel with Alonzo, in favour of De Flores. When Beatrice-Joanna (still operating under the conventional marriage model) protests her elevated birth as an impediment to De Flores's proposal of sexual union, he confidently declares such observations to be irrelevant:

> *Beatrice*: Think but upon the distance that creation
>   Set 'twixt thy blood and mine, and keep thee there.
> *De Flores*: Look but into your conscience: read me there;
>   'Tis a true book, you'll find me there your equal.
>   Push, fly not to your birth, but settle you
>   In what the act has made you: y'are no more now;
>   You must forget your parentage to me:
>   Y'are the deed's creature.[41]

De Flores, like Bosola in Webster's *Duchess of Malfi*, is a household servant of the new model, who offers service for material reward, and whose prospects depend precariously on a balance sheet of obligations and indebtednesses for services rendered.[42] In this world Beatrice-Joanna's appeal to rank has no relevance; the 'true book' is the account book in which service is costed, and where the 'rate' for disposing of a suitor is sexual intimacy with Beatrice-Joanna.

The moment in the play which most vividly conveys the way Beatrice-Joanna's active choice impinges upon the world of men's affairs is the scene in which her adulterous union with De Flores is formally discovered in Act Five. Immediately Alsemero has pronounced his wife 'whore' and she has confessed to having instigated murder, he locks her in his closet: 'Enter my closet: / I'll be your keeper yet'.[43] Twenty lines later, he thrusts De Flores in to join her.

The man of property's 'closet' was the physical place of his greatest privacy.[44] His closet was adjacent to his sleeping quarters, and contained his books, his correspondence and his most private possessions. It was generally locked, and inaccessible to anyone but himself and his most intimate personal servants. The woman of the household might have her own closet or 'cabinet',[45] which might contain her personal effects and toiletries, but she would not have access to her husband's. For a woman to cross the threshold from the general house into the husband's closet is to intrude on the man's most personal and private space. Beatrice-Joanna thus infringes Alsemero's privacy twice in the play, and in both cases the intrusion is sexually fraught.

When Beatrice-Joanna finds Mizaldus' medical treatise, and stumbles upon the concoctions Alsemero has prepared from it for testing her virginity, they are in Alsemero's locked closet, in whose door he has inadvertently left the key. What she discovers is a secret practice, his medical experimenting, the kind of pursuit of knowledge a gentleman might well have been expected to engage in discreetly in private:

> Here's his closet,
> The key left in't, and he abroad i'th' park.
> Sure 'twas forgot; I'll be so bold as look in't. [*Unlocks closet*]
> Bless me! A right physician's closet 'tis,
> Set round with vials – every one her mark too.
> Sure he does practice physic for his own use.
> Which may be safely called your great man's wisdom.[46]

By gaining access to the private space and the secrets which it contains, she is enabled temporarily to dupe Alsemero into believing her chaste when she is already deflowered. Entirely fittingly, then, it is within that same space – the space of intimacy she has already betrayed and violated – that Alsemero confines her when he discovers her guilt. He will be her 'keeper' (jailer), even if he could not guard her virtue. His decision to confine De Flores with her intensifies the sense of violation of his own innermost enclosure, and does, I think (as Garber has argued) load the screams which the audience hears issuing from there with sexual overtones:[47]

> *Beatrice*: [*within*]   O, O!
> *Vermandero*: What horrid sounds are these?
> *Alsemero*: [*unlocking closet*] Come forth, you twins of mischief.
>   *Enter De Flores, bringing in Beatrice [wounded].*[48]

The adulterous couple, confined within Alsemero's most intimate chamber, are heard violating its secrecy. The space of a man's private knowledge is violently entered, and it becomes witness to illicit carnality and unspeakable acts – copulation and murder.

It is against this fundamental violation of male intimacy that we need to set the sub-plot, with its obsessive echoing of enclosure and intrusion. The elderly Alibius confines his young wife and his domestic charges – the madmen and fools of his private asylum – under a single roof. Though notionally a 'secret' enclosure, its confines are breached on a daily basis by 'daily visitants, that come to see [the] brainsick patients'.[49] These are 'Gallants ... of quick enticing eyes, rich in habits, / Of stature and proportion very comely'.[50] This arrangement makes for dangerous proximity within Alibius' household between his officially chaste wife and a large number of men who are not 'kin'. Easily violated by counterfeiting madmen, this renders his wife vulnerable to amorous attentions in his absence ('Alibius' means 'elsewhere'), including those of his personal servant cum keeper, Lollio. Alibius himself is therefore totally gullible, his family virtue entirely open to external penetration. The secret and unsupervised exchanges between the gentleman-intruder Antonio and Alibius' wife, deep in the inner space of his household, raise the immediate possibility that Isabella will be easily unfaithful to this, the first sane man successfully to breach its defences. That these exchanges are observed and spied upon reminds us (as in the main plot) that privacy within the domestic space is a theoretical concept rather than a reality – individual privacy is almost unthinkable in a space filled with minor family members (here supplemented by the 'family' of fools and madmen) and servants going about their business within the household enclosure (as Alice Friedman has vividly shown in her work on Elizabethan domestic architecture).[51]

The integrity of Alibius' marriage in *The Changeling* is only upheld because of a conscious choice by Isabella herself. Isabella is no less wilful, then, than Beatrice-Joanna – faced with the temptation to arbitrary sexual infidelity she merely makes the socially acceptable choice and declines Antonio's advances. This makes her a 'good' wife (a foil for the 'bad' wife Beatrice-Joanna), but without any suggestion that her choice was any more reasonable. She shows no emotional interest in her actual husband, she is easily disobedient when presented with the opportunity to consort with strange men (albeit supposed madmen), and Alibius' intention at the outset to confine Isabella forcibly – to lock her away – underlines the fact that she can be assumed to be fundamentally untrustworthy, simply by being a woman.

In *The Changeling*, the main plot insists on the inevitable downfall of the woman who acts on her own behalf to choose her destination as wife. She is doomed to bring about her own destruction as soon as she woos for herself. Even in the sub-plot, Isabella becomes temporarily threatening when she herself feigns madness, and physically 'touches' Antonio – the man who is trying to force his attentions upon *her*:

> Isabella: [*Touching him*] Let me suck out those billows in thy belly;
>   Hark how they roar and rumble in the straits!
>   Bless thee from the pirates.
> Antonio: [*Pulling free*] Pox upon you! Let me alone.[52]

In spite of this moment of horror (mirroring Alsemero's disgust at discovering his wife's 'active choice' of him over his rival by engineering that rival's death), Antonio's desire revives as soon as Isabella reverts to a socially acceptable passivity before his advances. Any woman, the play suggests, may swerve from desirable acquiescence to disruptive initiative-taking, at any moment and without warning.

De Flores: I see in all bouts, both of sport and wit,
    Always a woman strives for the last hit.[53]

The strongest lines imputing dangerously disruptive motives to the active woman are all put into the mouth of the arch-villain, De Flores. The fact remains, however, that the final message the audience carries strongly away from *The Changeling* is that when a woman freely chooses her sexual partner she moves beyond restraint:

De Flores: I have watched this meeting, and do wonder much
    What shall become of t'other [suitor]; I'm sure both
    Cannot be served unless she transgress. Happily,
    Then, I'll put in for one; for if a woman
    Fly from one point, from him she makes a husband,
    She spreads and mounts then like arithmetic:
    One, ten, a hundred, a thousand, ten thousand –
    Proves in time sutler to an army royal.[54]

The outcome is inevitably spiralling disorder and disaster for those around her. The only remedy, as Isabella insists to her husband, is perpetual male vigilance: 'You were best lock me up.'[55]

When Beatrice-Joanna's father welcomes Alonzo de Piracquo, the man he has selected to marry his only daughter, into his house, he describes his choice in terms of 'love' – a lineage bond between the male representatives of two important families:

[*To Alonzo and his brother*] Y'are both welcome,
    But an especial one belongs to you, sir,
    To whose most noble name our love presents
    The addition of a son, our son Alonzo.[56]

The transforming power of love between men of equal rank intensifies the union by marriage into one of blood: 'our son Alonzo'. When the torrid plot of *The Changeling* has run its course, it is this bond which survives Beatrice-Joanna's treachery and restores social order and harmony. As Vermandero bewails the loss of his family's good name, his son-in-law Alsemero counsels him to wipe the memory of his daughter from the record. By this expedient, 'innocence is quit / By proclamation'.[57] Alsemero offers himself as dutiful son (surviving son-in-law) to fill the gap left by the absent and forgotten daughter:

Alsemero: Sir, you have yet a son's duty living;
    Please you accept it.[58]

His epilogue reaffirms the male line as the bedrock of early modern society, its reassuring indestructible basis:

Alsemero: All we can do to comfort one another,
  To stay a brother's sorrow for a brother,
  To dry a child from the kind father's eyes,
  Is to no purpose; it rather multiplies.
  Your only smiles have power to cause re-live
  The dead again, or in their rooms to give
  Brother a new brother, father a child:
  If these appear, all griefs are reconciled.[59]

The plot of *The Changeling* pivots around a struggle for control of lineage between a network of interested men and a woman set upon her own heart's desire. That plot, I have been suggesting, corresponds to a perceived conflict of interests within contemporary society between the traditionally structuring forms of family alliance and two separately developing versions of 'love' – the bond of mutuality in marriage, and the conduit to service-relationship between men within the household. What, then, does *The Changeling* offer us as a contribution to understanding that conflict?

In *The Changeling* the dynastic alliance which Vermandero has formally negotiated for his daughter is threatened by the 'love' (at first sight) of a less suitable but well-networked and supported man, by the gaining of control over the daughter by a mere household servant, and by that daughter's own amorous desires. Yet of the three, it is the daughter's actions which are made dramatically appalling, and for which the punishments are ritually devastating – a humiliating enforced sexual union with the physically repellant servant she despises, abuse and rejection by the man for love of whom she acted, and violent death. Alsemero's intervention in family matters on his own terms, by contrast, is only temporarily disruptive – he takes his place at the close of the play as successor in the family line.

The personal negotiation and internal flexibility which the reformed Church apparently offered in its marriage model (mutual consent; free choice; partnership) made it readily comparable with intimate male friendship – a type of liaison whose goal was not reproduction (the continuation of the line) but unspecified (and publically untraceable) networks of relationships and profitable dependencies within and between households. In practical terms, the impact of hidden undertakings between men (between, say, the earl of Essex and the numerous gentlemen of his extended household who acted as his intelligence gatherers and secretaries) might have real political consequences – was, indeed, always potentially in conflict with court and ministerial control.[60] Given the constraints on women's behaviour in general, female autonomy in choice of marriage partner was likely to be less really socially and politically disruptive. Yet *The Changeling* shows us this as more psychologically and emotionally disturbing. Beatrice-Joanna's pursuit of her own sexual desires may not, initially, be technically 'illicit', but her action readily arouses the anxiety associated with illicitness. Non-conforming sexual conduct is apparently always culturally disturbing, and symbolically disruptive, then as now.[61] In the final analysis the drama vividly captures collisions between domestic and public interests which might otherwise be lost to us. It does so, however, in a sensationalized form in which, as ever, in the matter of blame we are asked to 'look to the woman'.

Notes

[1] Thomas Overbury, 'Character of a good wife', cit. in A. Macfarlane, *Marriage and Love in England: Modes of Reproduction 1300–1840* (Oxford, 1986), p. 179. Alan Stewart points out to me that this quotation is reminiscent of the standard Ciceronian *amicitia* line on shared adversity. For generalized discussions of the 'good wife' in the period see M. J. M. Ezell, *The Patriarch's Wife: Literary Evidence and the History of the Family* (Chapel Hill, 1987).

[2] See K. Wrightson, *English Society 1580–1680* (London, 1982), pp. 90–104; Macfarlane, *Marriage and Love*; R. A. Houlbrooke, *The English Family 1450–1700* (London, 1984), pp. 96–126; S. D. Amussen, *An Ordered Society: Gender and Class in Early Modern England* (Oxford, 1988). On the ideology of the companionate marriage see V. Wayne, introduction to *The Flower of Friendship: A Renaissance Dialogue Contesting Marriage by Edmund Tilney* (Ithaca, NY, 1992), pp. 13–37.

[3] Wrighton, *English Society*, p. 100.

[4] Apart from humane social historians in general, feminist historians have been naturally hostile to arranged marriage because agnatic kinship structure suggests that such arrangements are made by men and for men. But of course female kin were also extremely active in 'match-making', and the future financial security of a daughter was as important to the strategic choice as was perpetuating of the male line. See Ezell, *Patriarch's Wife*, pp. 20–35.

[5] On the importance of intimacy for the organization of the Tudor and Stuart court see D. Starkey (ed.), *The English Court from the Wars of the Roses to the Civil War* (London, 1987), esp. chs. 3–6.

[6] See L. Hutson, *The Usurer's Daughter* (London, 1994); A. Stewart, *The Bounds of Sodomy* (Princeton, forthcoming).

[7] So although social historians like Wrightson and Macfarlane suggest that it 'seems reasonable to conclude that among the greater part of the common people marriage partners were freely chosen, subject to the advice of friends and a sense of obligation to consult or subsequently inform parents if they were alive and within reach' (Wrighton, *English Society*, p. 78, cit. Macfarlane, *Marriage and Love*, p. 124), Wrightson's full discussion of flexible arrangements for 'consent' of parents (or in the absence of parents, 'friends') to marriages largely formed by the two young people does, I think, suggest that the economic need for some form of lineal endorsement means that 'love' between partners still conforms more closely to the lineage model than appears at first sight.

[8] *King Lear*, Arden edition, I. i. 95–104.

[9] See Macfarlane, *Marriage and Love*, p. 282; J. H. Cooper, in J. Goody, J. Thirsk and E. P. Thompson (eds), *Family and Inheritance: Rural Society in Western Europe 1200–1800* (Cambridge, 1976).

[10] Thus this kind of 'love' follows the agnatic lineage model: 'The daughter is treated

as a marginal member of her father's lineage, and after her marriage, her children will leave it entirely; their allegiance passes to her husband's line' (D. Herlihy, *Medieval Households* (Cambridge, MA, 1985), p. 82).

[11] *King Lear*, Arden edition, I. i. 139–42.

[12] Starkey, *English Court.*

[13] For a related argument about Jacobean drama and social anxiety see S. J. Wiseman, ''Tis Pity She's a Whore: representing the incestuous body', in L. Gent and N. Llewellyn (eds.), *Renaissance Bodies: The Human Figure in English Culture c.1540–1660* (London, 1990), pp. 180–97.

[14] Shakespeare, sonnet 29.

[15] J. Barrell, 'Editing out: the discourse of patronage and Shakespeare's twenty-ninth sonnet', in *Poetry, Language and Politics* (Manchester, 1988), pp. 18–43.

[16] G. Ungerer, *A Spaniard in Elizabethan England: The Correspondence of Antonio Perez's Exile*, 2 vols. (London, 1976).

[17] See L. Jardine and A. T. Grafton, ' "Studied for action": how Gabriel Harvey read his Livy', *Past and Present*, 129 (1990), pp. 3–51; L. Jardine and W. Sherman, 'Pragmatic readers: knowledge transactions and scholarly services in late Elizabethan England', in P. Roberts and A. Fletcher (eds.), *Religion, Culture and Society in Early Modern England: A Festschrift for Patrick Collinson* (Cambridge, 1994), pp. 102–24.

[18] Shakespeare, sonnet 20.

[19] A. Bray, *Homosexuality in Renaissance England* (London, 1982); 'Homosexuality and the signs of male friendship in Elizabethan England', *History Workshop Journal*, 19 (1990), pp. 1–19. In *Sodometries: Renaissance Texts, Modern Sexualities* (Stanford, CA, 1992) Jonathan Goldberg claims that the instability of the term (and understanding of) 'sodomy' in the period gives the critic licence to reinterpret all ambivalent sexuality in Renaissance texts along a sodomitical axis. Whilst at times this produces somewhat 'perverse' reading, it has the virtue of destabilizing the comfortably modern heterosexual bias of most criticism, including some of my own (Goldberg, *Sodometries*, pp. 112–15).

[20] 'Use' here, in other words, has the sense of 'use up' or consumption. Whereas in male friendship there is prolonged reciprocity with the pay-off endlessly deferred.

[21] This is what Goldberg wants to argue in *Sodometries*. Valerie Traub argues along similar lines that in Shakespeare's sonnets the purity of homoerotic attraction is in tension with reproductive sex which is tainted by its inevitable association with the female body. The anxiety she detects is there, I am arguing, but I am tracing it to a different source. See V. Traub, *Desire and Anxiety: Circulations of Sexuality in Shakespearean Drama* (London, 1992), pp. 140–4.

[22] Alan Stewart suggests comparison with a recent article by Lauro Martines, 'The politics of love poetry in Renaissance Italy'.

[23] Ungerer, *A Spaniard*, pp. 219–20.

[24] Alan Haynes, *Invisible Powers: The Elizabethan Secret Services 1570–1603* (Stroud, 1992), p. 105. See also J. M. Archer, *Sovereignty and Intelligence: Spying and Court Culture in the English Renaissance* (Cambridge, 1993).

[25] *Othello*, Arden edition, I. iii. 180–9.

[26] *Much Ado About Nothing*, Arden edition, ed. A. R. Humphreys (London, 1981); 'I will assume thy part in some disguise, / And tell fair Hero I am Claudio, / And in her bosom I'll unclasp *my* heart, / And take her hearing prisoner with the force / And strong encounter of *my* amorous tale' (I.i.301–5, my emphasis).

[27] I.iii.56–60.

[28] Within the conventions of parentally negotiated marriage matches there was a place for proxy wooing. A trusted and personable emissary could seek to endear the proposed partner to the intended spouse where geographical distance or other impediment made personal wooing inappropriate. Holbein's intensely 'humane' portrait of Christina of Denmark is part of such a proxy wooing process – the ambassador 'falls for' the designated princess and the trusted painter records a 'likeness' which captures the personal qualities which recommend her. But where a more personal kind of service relationship pertains, this kind of wooing in one's own person on behalf of another ceases to be appropriate.

[29] II.i.179, Leonato too believes that Don Pedro woos for himself: 'Daughter, remember what I told you: if the Prince do solicit you in that kind [with a marriage proposal], you know your answer' (II.i.61–2).

[30] They also suggest real-life models like the supposedly notorious Dr Crooke for the mercenary madhouse proprietor, Alibius.

[31] According to a manuscript note by Malone in his copy of the 1653 quarto, *The Changeling* was licensed for performance in 1622: 'Licensed to be acted by the Lady Elizabeth's servants at The Phoenix, May 7, 1622, by Sir Henry Herbert Master of the Revels' (Bodleian Mal. 246(9)). The earliest performance recorded is in January 1623/4 at court; the play enjoyed a considerable success up to the closure of the theatres in 1642, and again after 1660. Contemporary accounts suggest that it owed its popularity to the performance of Antonio – the feigning madman, identified as the titular 'changeling' (fool, half-wit) in the list of *dramatis personae* in the 1653 printed text of the play. If so, then seventeenth-century taste valued *The Changeling* for precisely that part of the play which modern critics find least interesting. Recent criticism focuses almost exclusively on the main plot, in which the 'changelings' are those who are turncoats and traitors to rank and lineage – De Flores and Beatrice-Joanna ('Commonly the childe expresseth his sire, and posterity (if not chaungeling) covets to tread the steps of their ancestours' (Lawrence Humphrey, *The Nobles* (1563), cit. Leo Salingar, 'The Changeling and the drama of domestic life', *Dramatic form in Shakespeare and the Jacobeans* (Cambridge, 1986), pp. 222–35)).

[32] In John Reynolds' main source story, the fourth of five 'tragicale histories' in the first book of *The Triumphs of Gods Revenge against The Crying and Execrable Sinne of Wilfull and Premeditated Murther* (entered in the Stationers' Register on 7 June 1621), the distinction between Don Alonso Piracquo, the suitor of good local standing, and Don Pedro de Alsemero, the son of a professional soldier, who has acquired a considerable fortune through trading in the Indies, with a reputation for bravery, but no public presence in Alicante, is equally carefully drawn.

[33] R. A. Houlbrooke, *The English Family 1450–1700* (London, 1984), pp. 73–4.

[34] V.iii. 155–4.

[35] II.i.156.

[36] II.i.8–14.

[37] II.ii.82.

[38] II.ii.86–7.

[39] II.ii.130–3.

[40] IV.ii.95–103.

[41] III.iv.135–42.

[42] The Duchess' future husband Antonio, in the same play, is also such a servant.

The first scene between them plays heavily on this 'balance sheet' version of obliga-tion. When the Duchess finally declares her love to Antonio it is with the words, 'Being now my steward, here upon your lips I sign your Quietus est'. Whereas male service always leaves deferred obligations unfulfilled, when a woman is involved good service inevitably leads to a 'quietus est' – an acquittal of service, and an explicitly (rather than erotically deferred) service/use.

[43] V.iii.86–7.

[44] For the household significance of the closet see Stewart, *The Bounds of Sodomy*. For the importance of such 'privy' Chambers in structuring social relations and facil-itating decision-making in an elite household see Starkey, *The English Court*.

[45] II.ii.6.

[46] IV.i.17–23.

[47] M. Garber (seen in typescript).

[48] V.iii.140–2.

[49] I.ii.53–4.

[50] I.ii.55–7.

[51] A. Friedman, *House and Household in Elizabethan England: Wollaton Hall and the Willoughby Family* (Chicago, 1989).

[52] IV.iii.120–3.

[53] V.i.129–30.

[54] II.ii,57–64.

[55] III.iii.267.

[56] II.i.97–100.

[57] V.iii.187–8.

[58] V.iii.217–18.

[59] V.iii.221–8.

[60] See P. Hammer, ' "The Bright Shininge Sparke": the political career of Robert Devereux, 2nd Earl of Essex, *c.*1585–*c.*1597', Ph.D. thesis, University of Cambridge (1991).

[61] Which raises the question, whether accusations of sodomy against men in intimate service were political mobilizations of an equivalently powerful anxiety against arrangements which were not, in fact, illegal unless they could be shown to be sedi-tious, but where the endlessly deferred expectation of some unspecified 'fulfilment' could readily be eroticized. This is relevant to recent work by Jonathan Goldberg and others, which sees actual sodomitical activity wherever a charge of such was laid against someone (See Goldberg, *Sodometries*).

11

Remembering Marston Moor: the politics of culture

Maija Jansson

God had prevailed. The army triumphed, monarchy was destroyed and a commonwealth born. After seven years of war, in a long and bitter struggle, the Royalists were defeated by the forces of Parliament. Ultimately it was the success at Marston Moor and Naseby, Langport and Preston that paved the way for the execution of the king in 1649. How would these extraordinary events be remembered? Would there be a monumental visual record of the battles, confirming the cause and commemorating victory? Could there have been for contemporaries a vision of Naseby similar to the mammoth canvas painted by Sir John Gilbert 220 years later, or that of Marston Moor by Abraham Cooper that hangs in Chequers today?[1] Three Netherlanders thought so.

Drawing on their European training and familiarity with classical battle scenes and soldiers in continental collections, several painters with Dutch connections proposed to the commonwealth a massive artistic tribute to the victors of the Civil War. It would stand open 'unto the people's view', in the Banqueting House, a memorial to the Roundheads who had defeated King Charles I. The artists, in the order that their names appear in the address to Parliament, at the beginning of the proposal, are Balthazar Gerbier, Peter (or Pieter) Lely and George Geldorp.[2] By looking closely at their proposal and the reasons for its failure we can learn something about the state of English art in the seventeenth century and the artistic values of the governing class between the end of the monarchy and the establishment of the Protectorate.

Although the Rubens ceiling was in place by 1635, the rest of the great hall of the Banqueting House remained bare in 1650.[3] The idea of decorating the walls of the House was not new, however, apparently having been broached a decade before by Sir Anthony Van Dyck. According to Sir George Vertue's notes, later edited and printed by Horace Walpole, around 1640 Van Dyck proposed to King Charles, through Sir Kenelme Digby, that the inside walls of the great hall be decorated with a history and procession of the Order of the Garter.[4] His proposal was accompanied by a small oil chiaroscuro sketch on two pieces of wood, now in the possession of the duke of Rutland. The design is comprised of four parts: first is the picture of the history of the institution of the Garter; second, the procession of the knights in their robes; third, the portrayal of the ceremony of the installation and fourth, the grand feast.[5] According to Vertue, Charles apparently liked the idea but for some reason, perhaps because the price was too high, even 'extravagant', or perhaps because he was sensitive to Digby's tainted relationship with Parliament over the Catholic question, the king refused to support the project.[6] In his observations on Edmund Waller's poem entitled 'To Van Dyck', Elijah Fenton, the poet's editor, says that the demand of fourscore thousand pounds was 'thought unreasonable' (Rubens was paid £3,000 and a gold chain for the ceiling).[7] While the king was negotiating with him for a smaller fee 'the gout and other distempers put an end to that affair and his life [in] 1641'.[8]

In any event, for whatever reason, Van Dyck's plan never came to fruition. What is interesting to the historian, however, regarding the subsequent proposal by Gerbier and his colleagues, is that Van Dyck's sketch remained with the king as part of what came to be called the Royal Collection. At the time of its dispersal after Charles' death, Lely was in possession of the sketch.[9] Lely knew and admired Van Dyck's work and well may have met him personally in the Netherlands. It is certainly conceivable, given the closeness of the community of artists in England, that Van Dyck's chiaroscuro sketch for the great hall was generally known and served as the inspiration for the Gerbier–Lely–Geldorp plan of the commonwealth period.[10]

The proposal by the three artists called for 'the representing in oil, pictures of all the memorable achievements since parliament's first sitting'.[11] Although it is undated, it must have been put forward some time between the fall of the monarchy in 1649 and the dissolution of the Long Parliament in December 1653. Clearly emanating from their continental background, the three artists proposed that England do what 'has been practiced in most parts of the world' and present to the public remembrances of the most 'memorable acts of their general welfare, or those of their deliverance from some eminent danger'.

The precedent for their proposal, they stated, was the set of memorial tapestries commissioned by Charles, Lord Howard of Effingham, the Admiral of the English fleet, to commemorate the English victory over Catholic Spain in 1588. These 'Armada tapestries' were purchased by James I in 1616 to hang in Whitehall and were later installed in the Tower of London. The ten tapestries were designed by Hendrick Cornelisz Vroom for the Brussels weaver, Francis Spierincx, from a series of charts drawn by Robert Adam under the supervision of Lord Howard.[12] They were woven in Flanders with quantities of gold and silver thread. Later, in the early eighteenth century, the battle scenes portrayed on the Armada tapestries were engraved by John Pine and published in a large folio edition.[13] In his brief introduction to the plates Pine ascribes the commission of the tapestries to ancestors determined that the victory over the Armada should not pass into oblivion. Toward that end,

he wrote, they had had the wisdom to employ artists to portray the engagements between the two fleets in 'ten curious pieces of tapestry'.[14] Portraits of
the English captains, taken from life, were displayed in the borders. As a
whole the work was designed 'to remain as a lasting memorial of the triumph
of British valour guided by British counsel', the same rationale used by Lely
and company for including in their design the portraits of parliamentarians
'by whose directions the achievements have been wrought', around the scenes
of battle.

Pine, in undertaking to engrave the scenes of naval engagements and portraits in the tapestries 150 years later was following the inspiration of his
ancestors in preserving their memorial, 'lest time, or accident, or moths may
deface these valuable shadows'.[15] Inexpensive engravings, he proclaimed,
'multiplied and dispersed in various lands', would ensure immortality for the
events presented in the tapestries. Multitudes could then enjoy the pictures
while the originals would be protected from the curious. Perhaps Pine was
acquainted with the story of the boy in 1652 who was caught clipping gold
out of the hangings at Whitehall.[16] Regardless of the particulars Pine was no
fool. The tapestries were destroyed by fire when the Parliament buildings
burned in 1834. But they can be seen today in his engravings and also as the
background to John Singleton Copley's canvas of *The Death of the Earl of
Chatham* (1798) in the Tate Gallery in London.

In 1649, however, the Armada tapestries themselves were quite visible and
probably in excellent repair, being then not much more than fifty years old.
They had hung for some time in the Tower until 1644 when the lords of Parliament had them moved to their meeting place in the White Chamber of the
Old Palace of Westminster.[17] There they stayed until after the king's death
when they fell under the jurisdiction of the various committees and contrac-
tors appointed to dispose of Charles' goods and estate. Cromwell liked them
and apparently wanted to see them hanging in Whitehall. Finally, in April
1650, in order to ensure their survival in the public domain, the Council of
State decreed that 'the hangings containing the story of Eight-Eight [were] to
be reserved for the use of the state'.[18] Clearly they were a revered bit of art
and history.

As the Armada tapestries did for the war with Spain, the Gerbier–Lely–Geldorp plan for the Banqueting House murals was to portray the major battles
and parliamentary victories of the English civil wars, as well as portraits. 'All
the most remarkablest battles and the most considerablest sieges of towns'
that took place in Ireland and Scotland as well as England were to be painted,
'with the portraitures of such generals and commanders as have, during the
parliament's sitting, fought the said battles and gained the said towns'.[19]
Those canvases were to be placed in the great room of the Banqueting House
(with the Rubens ceiling), and in the galleries, and other rooms at Whitehall,
'for the fascination of the present time as also for posterity'. Moreover, there
was an inspirational element in the design, for the scenes of battle were not

only to memorialise but also to infuse with encouragement 'all such as are in authority and command'.

Furthermore, 'as the great hall at Whitehall is very spacious', there was also to be included 'representation of the whole assembly of the parliament by whose directions the said great achievements have been wrought'. The painting of the rump Parliament was to be placed at 'the upper end of the great room, formerly called the Banqueting House'.[20] At the other end were to be placed 'the portraitures of the several members of the Council of State'. Perhaps in deference to the biblical grounding of the Puritan audience they addressed, the artists claimed that these canvases to adorn both ends of the hall would reflect 'a comportment answerable to the saying in the 88th Psalme, verse 11':

Truth shall spring out of the earth and
righteousness shall look down from heaven, etc.

Realistically and practically how was this memorial to be accomplished? Who would pay for oil paintings of battles when the military arrearages from the war were so enormous and not yet settled? Well out of reach of government finance but in regular touch with the art market, the artists themselves conceived of a means of payment that seemed simple enough but most certainly contributed to the reasons for the failure of the project. In the new found freedom of the republic art and patronage were no longer tied to king and court. As in a private contract, the plan proposed that each person to be represented on canvas – Members of Parliament, the Council of State, the Lord General, officers of land and sea forces – pay for his own portrait. That way the State could be 'taken off from the greatest part of the charges'. And by stipulating that each individual be responsible for financing his portrayal the artists anticipated quicker payment that would provide money up-front for brushes and canvas and hence better enable the 'speedy pursuance of the work'. Government could be a long time in paying.

Following the description of the design the proposal mandated that it be completed by 'choice artists, expert both in the representing of personages, battles, and landscapes'. Sir Balthazar Gerbier was the eldest of the three, having been born in Middelburg, Zealand, in 1592.[21] He apparently went to England in 1616 with the Dutch ambassador Noel de Caron and was almost immediately employed as a painter of miniatures and general collector by George Villiers, recently appointed Master of the Horse. He lived with the Villiers family and very quickly became part of their social circle that included Charles, then Prince of Wales. Gerbier accompanied Villiers (created duke of Buckingham in 1617) and Charles to Spain in 1623 where he painted a portrait of Maria, the Infanta, that was sent to James I for inspection.[22] Although Edward Norgate, the illuminer and heraldic draftsman (1581–1660), claimed that 'the best crayons that I ever saw were those made by Sir Balthazar Gerbier after those so celebrated histories done by Raphael',[23] Gerbier's talents as a courtier were more noticed than his abilities as an artist. Buckingham introduced him to artistic circles in Paris where he met, among others, Peter Paul Rubens. After the duke's assassination in 1628, Gerbier went into the king's service and worked for Charles I in several capacities, but primarily as a collector and secret agent. Although he may have painted a miniature of Charles as prince in 1616,[24] it is known for certain that some time around 1629 he oversaw the casting of his design for an equestrian statue of Charles I to stand in the garden at Roehampton. Two years later, in 1631, Charles appointed Gerbier as his agent at Brussels.[25] Back in England in 1638 Gerbier was knighted at Hampton Court,[26] and in the following year, once again in Brussels, he began negotiations with Jacob Jordaens for the paintings to decorate the Queen's house at Greenwich. In 1641 Gerbier returned from the continent, and on the death of Sir John Finet was appointed Master of Ceremonies at the English court.[27] Later, in 1652, he would publicly express his disappointment in not receiving the office of Surveyor General of the king's works when Inigo Jones died. The position went to Sir John Denham, although Gerbier protested to Charles II that the place had been promised to him.[28]

By the 1630s, indeed since he first took his post in Brussels, Gerbier was probably no longer painting. His creative impulses by the 1640s were directed to other schemes and he began a career in pamphlet writing and project design. Finally, overwhelmed by debt, he left England in 1643 and settled in Paris until the English Civil Wars were over and Charles had been tried and executed. He returned to London some time in 1648–9 and established what turned out to be a not very successful academy at his home in Bethnal Green.[29]

By the time Gerbier left England in 1643 he had known Charles personally for twenty-seven years, even as a close friend, and had worked for him a good part of that time. They had met as young men when Balthazar was twenty-four and Charles just sixteen. After the fall of the monarchy when Gerbier returned to London he bought the Van Dyck portrait of Charles on horseback at the sale of the Royal Collection – a warm remembrance of an old friend.[30] Little wonder then that a contemporary would scrawl on the back of the proposal for the Banqueting House murals designed to stand as a memorial to parliamentary victory:

> This proposal came very ill from Sir B. Gerbier who had received such marks of favor from his royal master, K. Charles. G. S.[31]

Having spent most of his life in England, Gerbier was anxious to ingratiate himself with the powers of the new State even at the cost of his loyalty to the monarchy.[32] He sought to provide services in a variety of ways, even offering to reveal the *arcana imperii* of his tour of duty as Crown agent in Brussels. The papers from that tour were, he said, 'no alchemical chimeras nor tenders grounded on mercenary intention'[33] but might be useful in the commonwealth's 'pious designs towards the propagation of Christ and their endeavouring to prove instrumental for the opposing of all anti-Christian forces'. He also put forward an elaborate plan for collecting long overdue debts to England from the cautionary towns.[34] His schemes worked. On 16 January 1651 the Council of State recommended Gerbier to the trustees for the sale of the late king's goods 'to be considered by them ... the Council looking upon him as a person whose endeavours are for the service of this commonwealth'.[35] That was the same year that he published *The None-Such Charles and his Character*, a public condemnation of the character and rule of his old friend.[36]

For Gerbier, however, more than any conviction about victory and remembrance his own personal debt may have been the motive for his role in the proposal for the Banqueting House murals. Ultimately, his relations and schemes with the commonwealth failed and he eventually returned to Holland in 1658 to wait out the interregnum. With the Restoration of 1660 he formally lost his office (and salary) as Master of Ceremonies, although in reality the salary had no doubt gone years before. He contributed to the design for the triumphal arches for Charles II's coronation in 1661, but he seems to have had little steady work under the new king and died impoverished somewhere between 1663 and 1665.

Sir Peter Lely, the second named in the murals proposal, was the youngest. He was born in Westphalia in 1618 of Dutch parents. His father, Johan van der Faces, was a military officer in the army of the States General and came from a house in de Lelye on the western side of the Noordeinde of The Hague. It was from the location of the family house that, by 1637, the young son had acquired the name, Peter Lely, by which he is best known.[37]

Lely began painting under Frans Pietersz Grobber in Haarlem around 1637 and probably went to England in September 1641, the year of Van Dyck's death, perhaps with the wedding entourage of William, Prince of Orange, although that is not certain.[38] Lely's early landscapes, with their resonances of the Dutch-Italianate school whose work he knew in Holland, received little attention in the English art world.[39] He worked for a while in Geldorp's studio then set out on his own and, following in the steps of Van Dyck, turned to portraiture.

It was not until 1647 that he really became established. Perhaps through his ability as a copyist of Van Dyck,[40] Lely received the patronage of Algernon Percy, tenth earl of Northumberland. Northumberland, although bitter about the lack of naval reform in the decade leading up to the calling of the Long Parliament, was always a moderate and supported a negotiated settlement with the king right up through Charles' imprisonment at Newport.[41] In 1645, as a moderate, he had been appointed guardian for the king's children remaining in England – James, duke of York, Princess Elizabeth, and Henry, duke of Gloucester. It was apparently through the Northumberland connection that soon Lely was commissioned to paint the canvas of the *Children of Charles I*, now at Petworth. Charles' favourite artist, William Dobson, whom he may have appointed Sergeant Painter and Groom of the Bedchamber, and who had travelled with the court to Oxford,[42] had died in poverty in 1646. Lely also painted staunch parliamentarians, some time at the end of the decade producing a full-length portrait of Sir Edward Massey that hangs now in the National Gallery of Canada. No other full-length portrait of that size is known to have been done by Lely before the Restoration.[43] That portrait may have been the prototype for the portraits of parliamentarians that Gerbier, Lely and Geldorp envisioned surrounding the murals of battle scene in the Banqueting House. After the successful canvas of the royal children, and again through Northumberland's influence, arrangements were made for Lely to paint the king and his younger son James, duke of York. Richard Lovelace was so taken with a preliminary sketch of the two that in his ode 'To My Worthy Friend Mr. Peter Lilly' he spoke of 'clouded majesty' and wrote that 'None but Lilly ever drew a mind'.[44] Vertue said that Lely had captured in the finished picture a 'sterner countenance' that expressed 'the tempests' which the king had recently endured.[45] The painting remains in the Northumberland Collection at Syon House, a memorial to father and son, once and future kings. Lely at this time also took up commissions from Leicester, Salisbury and Pembroke, the 'noble defectors' who remained near London during the wars.[46]

By 1650 Lely, still in his early thirties, had achieved great acclaim and was considered by many to be England's finest portrait painter of the time. Oliver Cromwell sat for him in 1654 and it was from that commission that the famous story sprang. For Cromwell requested, as Vertue reported, that Lely not flatter him at all, 'but remark all these roughness, pimples, warts, and everything as you see me, otherwise I will never pay a farthing for it'. Reverend Dallaway, who, in the nineteenth century, added commentary to Walpole's edition of Vertue, notes (without reference) that the portrait was painted after Cromwell had become Lord Protector and was commissioned as a present for Sir John Danvers, one of the judges in the trial of the king.[47] Lely's biographer, Oliver Millar, however, discounts both stories and says the portrait was not done *ad vivum* but from Samuel Cooper's miniature, in which case the story 'should probably be associated with Cooper rather than Lely'.[48]

Lely achieved his greatest prominence after the Restoration under the royal patronage of Charles II. He was appointed principal painter to the king in 1661 and knighted in 1679. He died suddenly the following year. One suspects that his interest in the proposal for the Banqueting House murals was essentially artistic. He was not entrenched in government or army. By 1650 he had known Northumberland for only three years and his relationship with Charles was purely as a professional portrait painter. Even during the period of his most prolific studio work in the Restoration Lely apparently managed to steer clear of politics.

The last name on the proposal was that of George Gelders, or Geldorp, of the three the least known both to his own contemporaries and to modern historians. He was born in 1611 in Antwerp (Spanish Netherlands) or Cologne and was a friend of Van Dyck, with whom he first stayed on his arrival in England and whose work he would later make a business of copying.[49] Walpole remarks that Geldorp 'could not draw himself, but painted on sketches made by others'.[50] He eventually purchased a studio and apparently Lely worked for him during his first few years in England. Another one of Geldorp's early apprentices, Isaac Sailmaker, was responsible for the portrayal of the British fleet before Mardyke.[51] Inspired perhaps by the recent discussions of the placement of the Armada tapestries, Cromwell commissioned Sailmaker to produce a view of the English navy before battle. Was Sailmaker's interest prompted by his teacher? It seems unlikely. Geldorp stuck pretty much to portraiture.[52] In the mid-1620s he painted the canvas of the Cecil family that hangs at Hatfield House and he did portraits of a number of Scottish peers – George Gordon, second marquess of Huntley and James Stuart, duke of Richmond, among others – but on the whole his commissions seem to have been few.[53] The reason for that may be apparent in his brief petition to Parliament in 1646. His complaint regarded an order of State that he leave London 'on account of his being a Roman Catholic'. The House of Commons responded that it was 'not their intention in their ordinance against papists to remove merchant strangers' as well.[54] He later was of service to the commonwealth in brokering the sale of 'busts, tapestries, and pictures' from the Royal Collection to the Frenchman M. de Bordeaux.[55] It might be added here, though, that regardless of religious affiliation the London Company of Painter–Stainers protested loudly against foreigners whose success stemmed from court patronage.[56] Under the king, himself a significant collector in Europe, patronage of the arts had flourished and the Caroline court was known for its sophistication. Did the collapse of the court signal the end of an interest in things cultural? Certainly it had an effect on the artistic life of London, the art market, architecture and theatre. Without doubt the absence of court-generated support for cultural activities figured in the rejection of the Banqueting House project, but there were other more immediate reasons for its failure.

What, then, were those reasons? The answer may be as simple as the fact that it was never actually proposed. There is no record in the *Journals* of the House of Commons between the date of the king's execution and Cromwell's dissolution of the Long Parliament to indicate that the proposal was ever read on the floor of the House, ever submitted and withdrawn, or ever rejected. On the other hand, the very fact that it was printed suggests a seriousness of intent on the part of the artists. Unfortunately there are few diary accounts for the period to flesh out the bare notices of business in the *Journal* records and provide a clue about the outcome of the project.

The absence of documents comes as no surprise. As historians know, 'The first thing that goes in a revolution is truth while the first thing that disap-

pears in a rebellion or civil war is papers.'[57] Therefore, in the absence of relevant papers and further evidence, let us assume that the proposal was at least
read and conclude that the lack of record of the reading is the result of a
problem with the sources which are, for this transitional period, less than perfect. If this is so then we must again ask why the proposal did not pass. There
are four considerations that militated against its success, two artistic and two
political: first, the matter of the Puritan aesthetic and the question of the general level of artistic development in England at the time; and, second, the crucial problem of government indebtedness coupled with the issue of national
unity.

Artistic considerations, particularly the matter of a Puritan aesthetic, bring
us face to face with the iconoclasm of the radical element of the Puritan
movement of the sixteenth century. It is well documented. Although it can be
argued that less damage was done to church statuary and decoration under
Oliver Cromwell than during the Protestant Reformation more than a century earlier, none the less iconoclasm was still a very real issue in the middle
of the seventeenth century.[58] There are official and unofficial accounts of the
destruction of religious art that run all through the early Stuart period, from
outcries against imagery to Henry Sherfield's smashing of the stained glass in
the parish church at St Edmunds, to William Dowsing literally defacing the
angel bosses in Norfolk churches.[59] In reference to religious zealots who
trashed the Queen's chapel and heaved a Rubens altarpiece into the Thames,
one historian has said that 'Beauty outraged them as much as holiness.'[60] This
kind of destruction continued in the 1640s authorized by the Commons' committee for demolishing superstitious monuments, chaired by Sir Robert
Harley.[61] On 20 October 1643 the Commons ordered the removal of 'scandalous monuments and pictures' in the chapels at Windsor and Eaton. Later
other chapels were cleansed and, improbable as it seems, the activity was captured on canvas. In 1657 Thomas Johnson, a member of the Company of
Painter–Stainers painted *Iconoclasts in Canterbury Cathedral*. It is an austere,
visual record of a parliamentary committee directing the destruction of
stained glass and carved decoration in that cathedral.[62] These operations, of
course, were acts directed at destroying religious works and images that proliferated under the influence of the Laudian high church. They were more
attacks on the theology that permitted such decorations than on the artworks
themselves, although, in the process, of course, it was the artwork and not
the theology that was destroyed. We know that altars and stained glass,
crucifixes and candlesticks aroused ire, but we are less clear about what decoration was acceptable to Puritans, or that they might even have encouraged
and supported. For some moderate Puritans, like the preacher John Owen,
all church decoration was not an anathema. We are told that as dean of
Christ Church he chose to keep what was 'old and beautiful' and consequently the stained glass there was preserved.[63] Oliver Cromwell himself had
the 'Diana' fountain moved from Somerset House in 1656 to the garden of

his favourite residence, Hampton Court.[64]

More to our point with regard to the Banqueting House is the matter of the Puritan attitude toward secular art. We find here that the same issue that propelled the iconoclastic movement informed secular taste, namely religion. The art and architecture of Counter-Reformation Catholic baroque was decorated, embellished and celebrated the 'material splendour of God's creation'.[65] On the other hand the pragmatism of English and Dutch Protestantism emphasized the simple and the practical rather than the decorative and excessive.[66] One need only compare the work of Rubens, the Flemish painter, with that of the Dutchman, Rembrandt, who was born in Leiden and worked in Amsterdam, to see the differences. In England secular artwork connected with the monarchy was seen to be tainted with high church innuendo and outright papism and was subject to attack. On 27 January 1650 Colonel Berkstead was ordered by the Council of State to 'take care of the pulling down of the gilt image of the late Queen and also of the King ... and the said images are to be broken in pieces'.[67] On the other hand, images and pictures even in churches that were set up as monuments to kings, princes or noblemen, or other dead persons 'not commonly reputed or taken as a saint' were exempted from the ordinance of August 1643 condemning monuments of superstition or idolatry.[68]

In a real sense English art was tied to Holland; not only did those countries share republican notions of government and Calvinism but they also shared painters. The predominantly northern Dutch artists who worked in England in the seventeenth century 'reinforced' what the Church espoused: 'a practical, dignified but decidedly undemonstrative view of greatness and public responsibility'.[69]

The general level of artistic development in England, in part because of the pragmatic nature of English Protestantism, focused on portraiture. Portraits served a purpose in society in 'establishing status, in conferring dignity and conforming worth'.[70] Every country squire who left provision for an almshouse gave his portrait with his monetary gift. Guildsmen and parliamentarians, gentry and military officers, peers and government officials alike sat for their pictures. In a sense portraits were commemorative, and they were certainly safe.[71] Unlike narrative paintings using classical themes and even biblical stories, they conveyed a direct message, and could not be conceived of as superfluous and unnecessary. They represented (and commemorated) the continuity of family, indeed of society as a whole. In fact, this otherwise artistically lean period not only sustained Peter Lely but also produced Samuel Cooper, whom some would argue was 'perhaps the greatest English portrait painter of the age', although a miniaturist.[72] Landscapes were by and large not commissioned in England at this time, even though on the continent pictures of the seasons, such as Rubens' *Summer*, were in vogue as well as rural views and seascapes. Genre paintings were not bought except by those few, the king included, with a sense of European taste.[73] Charles I owned three topographical views of London, precursors to the 'prospect' or 'bird's eye view' of manor house and gardens that gained such popularity in the second half of the century.

In proposing to paint scenes of English military engagements (as opposed to depictions of naval encounters) on the walls of the Banqueting House, Lely and his contemporaries were introducing a new genre that would not take hold in England until later in the century. This lack of interest in battle scenes is attributable to geographical isolation from the arena of European wars and certainly to the extended period of general domestic peace under the Tudors and Stuarts following the conclusion of the Wars of the Roses at Bosworth Field in 1485, and broken only by the battles of Stoke Field in 1487, Flodden in 1513 and Pinkie in 1547.

Just how far behind continental artistic expression was England? When did paintings of battle scenes become popular in Europe? After the creation of the Bayeux tapestry with its depiction of the Battle of Hastings in 1066 there was a long hiatus before drawings and prints of soldiers and military subjects outside of illustrations for chronicles and early histories became popular in the late fifteenth and early sixteenth centuries. More prolific in northern Europe, the focus of our discussion, engravings and woodblocks were a particular 'speciality' of the German and Swiss artists.[74] They took their inspiration from the interest in the infantry that grew out of the Swiss campaigns against Burgundy in the 1470s and Maximilian's exploits in the Netherlands twenty years later. Both Albrecht Altdorfer and Albrecht Dürer, young men at the time of those wars, grew up familiar with them and, lacking first-hand military experience themselves, they learned how to draw scenes of baggage transport and sieges, foot-soldiers and cavalry, as in, for example, Altdorfer's *Baggage Train and Camp Follower* and Dürer's *Standardbearer with Beard*.[75] Mantegna's *The Triumphs of Caesar* (mid-fifteenth century) were known and admired by them both for their composition and content. In 1505 the German artist, Lucas Cranach the Elder, in his woodcut of a *landsknecht halberdier* produced an image of a soldier that would be recognizably the European stereotype for years to come.[76] In Holland, artists caught in 'a flood-tide' of anti-mercenary feeling capitalized on the religious and political outrage toward those soldiers who operated with a freedom from the constraints of the pulpit and society that regulated civilian life.[77] Prints of pillaging, gluttony, drunkenness and debauchery proliferated. At the same time, pictures of warfare inspired by biblical themes, such as the *Massacre of the Innocents* and *The Storming of Jerusalem* declined in popularity; they were eclipsed by these increasingly more secular designs. Interest in the third estate and peasantry, as well as fascination with occupations and costumes, was reflected in the prints and series of the day. Each kind of foot-soldier and cavalry rider was depicted in the dress appropriate to his role, from arquebusier to field surgeon. The image of death itself changed; mortality was disconnected from theology, and the grim reaper became the soldiers' handmaiden and standardbearer. Even glassmakers turned away from religious themes for their windows, and by the sixteenth century we are told by a historian that 'saints were out and soldiers were in'.[78]

On the continent military themes were not limited to prints but also found their way on to canvas. The battle of Pavia in 1525, the great victory of the imperial forces over Francis I, was depicted in at least three contemporary oil paintings to commemorate the event, if not the soldiers who participated.[79] And a hundred years later Melchior Feselen emulated the Pavia pictures in his *Siege of Alesia*, finished in 1633.[80] Albrecht Altdorfer's canvas of the *Battle with the Huns outside Regensburg*, now in the National Museum in Nuremberg, was completed in 1618. Jan Asselyn's *Battle of Lützen* fits here also, it hangs today in Brunswick in the Anton Ullrich Museum. Not surprising, too, was the proliferation of depictions of battle scenes to celebrate the Spanish monarchy. In the salon of the Buen Retiro were visual descriptions of Spanish conquests, such as the capitulation of Breda to Spinola's forces in 1625 and the taking of Bahia shortly thereafter. They furnished subject matter for a whole raft of paintings. Count Duke Olivares oversaw the decorating of the Hall of Realms in the Retiro with painted narratives of twelve Spanish victories, echoing the labours of Hercules.[81]

Later the Thirty Years' War reinspired printmakers and engravers across Europe. Scenes of soldiers and sieges proliferated.[82] Whether these prints could be said to be memorials to common soldiers is open to question, but clearly on the continent warfare had pushed secular art beyond portraiture and, as in Holland, in the case of the customary militia paintings, altered the form considerably. The stiffly set group of half-length portraits of the *Kloveniersdoelen te Amsterdam* done in the sixteenth century is, by 1642, reworked in the Night Watch into full-length figures of guardsmen in action.[83] However, little of this theme and composition had reached England by the mid-century.

It is not surprising that the army theme came to fruition first in Europe and was only later picked up across the Channel. Land battles were simply not part of the experience of the generations of Englishmen that grew to manhood between the battle of Bosworth field and the bishops' wars. And even the latter, although fought on English soil, were contained in a relatively small arena, the skirmishes and fights confined to a limited area in the north. The experience was hardly universal. English mercenaries who fought on the continent knew something about warfare, but for most subjects wars were something that happened elsewhere and were experienced only vicariously from corrantos, newsletters and exotic tales told by returning mercenaries.

The earliest common soldiers remembered by name in England were not those from Crécy and Agincourt made famous by Shakespeare, but those who fought at Flodden in 1513 and were immortalized in stained glass in the parish church of Middleton, Lancashire.[84] By the end of the sixteenth century, with the rise of professional armies and well regulated navies, soldiers and sailors were known for their units and ships. A few prints and engravings began to appear depicting regiments and fleets, often from copies of those produced in northern Europe. By the time of the civil wars in the next century, there were contemporary engravings of the positions of troops at Naseby and Dunbar Hill, but they were set designs, not action pictures.[85] Other than Jan de Wyck's virtual still-life painting, inappropriately titled *The Siege of Oxford*, it does not appear that there were many contemporary English oil paintings of particular battles from either a Royalist or a parliamentary perspective, although there were portraits of a number of participants on both sides.[86]

Sea and naval encounters tell a different story. Surrounded by water, Englishmen's experiences at sea were rich and varied, encompassing exploration and circumnavigation as well as defence. The 1571 victory of the Christian Holy League of Pope Pius V over the heathen Turks at Lepanto was celebrated by Catholics and Protestants alike in most of Europe and England, as well by monarchists as by republicans.[87] Within a year canvases like the south German, H. Letter's *Battle of Lepanto*, now in the National Maritime Museum in Greenwich,[88] were produced in commemoration of Lepanto which may have provided the precedent and example for the plethora of contemporary oil paintings of the Armada seventeen years later. Hendrick Vroom, for example, designer of the Armada tapestries described above, also did a large oil of *The Seventh Day of the Battle of the Armada*, famous for its 'marvellous wealth of details'.[89] The importance of the event also lent itself to annual celebration which, at least on one occasion, in 1590, resulted in a commemorative painting by an unidentified artist, although historians have speculated that it may have been a work of Nicholas Hilliard. That canvas, which currently belongs to the Society of Apothecaries in London, 'provides a loose summary of several aspects of the event, rather than attempting a literal representation of fact'.[90] Two Dutchmen, Jan Theodor de Bry and, again, Vroom, portrayed the English attack on Cadiz in 1596. In both Holland and England there was a perennial interest in navy battles that grew to a groundswell by the end of the seventeenth century and the period of the Dutch wars. 'The commemoration of historical naval events', says the historian M. Russell, 'was one of the mainstays of early marine painting'. Even this genre, however, had not broken completely with portraiture, although in this case the delineation was of an inanimate object. The same historian tells us that a marine artist could not reach the pinnacle of success without 'full proficiency and experience in ship portraiture'.[91] Examine, for example, *The True Portraiture of his Matie's Royall Ship the Sovereigne of the Seas*, 1637.[92]

It was the Dutch who brought marine painting out of the realm of portraiture and scenes painted from memory after the fact into the world of immediate visual record. They were years ahead of the artists who followed cavalry and foot-soldiers into battle. William Van de Velde took to sea in his own galliot to observe and sketch the ships of England and the United Provinces engaged at the battle of Scheveningen in 1653. He was a pioneer capturing for the first time on canvas 'a detailed eyewitness account' of a naval battle.[93] The historian Blair Worden compares the work of the father and son team of Van de Veldes to 'war journalism'. Painting originally in Holland, they both took up residence in England around the end of 1672 where commissions and profits flowed from royal admirals with grand salaries and court connections. Poets, too, may have addressed them. Edmund Waller in his 'Instructions to a Painter' reiterates the inspirational element present in the Banqueting House proposal: 'Let they bold pencil, hope and courage spread'.[94] And Andrew Marvell wrote 'The Last Instructions to a Painter about the Dutch Wars, 1667'. As records of encounters rather than commemorations, their canvases preserve visual records of the Anglo-Dutch wars and in so doing they memorialize the events for generations to come. Their naval scenes complement the famous Lely portraits of the English commanders now hanging in the Queen's house at Greenwich. Samuel Pepys recollects stopping at Lely's studio with Admiral Penn to make an appointment 'when to be drawn among the other commanders of flags [in] the last year's fight'. Pepys also recounts seeing the portraits of the flagmen 'in the late great fight with the Duke of York against the Dutch'.[95]

In 1650, however, still shattered by the recent devastation of war, and with no prior artistic tradition of military themes, England was not ready for images of battle scenes either as memorials or as artworks, although there were other remembrances of the civil wars. The designs for the new coinage celebrated Parliament and the commonwealth.[96] And there were a few commemorative medals struck. Thomas Simon, for example, forged a silver medal in 1650 with a depiction of the two Houses of Parliament and the inscription, 'In the multitude of councillors there is peace'.[97] A 'jeweled enamel' was presented to Fairfax showing himself on a great chestnut horse on one side and the battle of Naseby on the reverse.[98] Mariners who did 'good service' were honoured with a medallion that displayed the arms of the commonwealth on one side with the House of Commons on the other. These were given as rewards to the living, however; they were not meant to commemorate the dead or to immortalize the event.

The political reasons that came into play in the rejection of the Banqueting House proposal centred around the matter of money. At the end of the civil wars the government was heavily in debt. Arrearages to the troops were enormous and widows and orphans cried out for support.[99] Government finance and taxation lacked organization at a local and national level. Everyone was affected. Royalists had lost property through confiscation, and parliamentarians had given generously to support their cause. Few individuals had either credit or cash remaining for extravagances like paintings.

Ironically, at precisely the same moment that the proposal for the murals in the Banqueting House was put forward a glut of pictures flooded the art market. With the death of the king it was decided that the massive personal and royal art collections be dispersed. On 22 February 1649 Parliament ordered that the Council of State should be empowered to dispose of pictures and statues at St James, 'for the present service of the state'.[100] A month later the Commons enlarged its order with a resolution that the personal estates of king, queen, and prince of Wales should be 'inventoried, appraised and sold' with the exception of those goods that the Council saw fit to reserve for the use of the State. The first profits were to pay off the debts of the king, queen, and prince and for 'public uses of this Commonwealth',[101] which included at the outset provision for a loan of £30,000 to the treasurers of the Royal Navy. The amount of goods to be disposed of was enormous and the sale lasted intermittently for three years, from 1649 through 1651. In looking at the length of the detailed inventories one can readily see that a project to commission new murals while literally hundreds of canvases of important artists were on the block would have been difficult for any new government to justify.

Furthermore, and perhaps even more crucial to the question of the murals, is the fact that celebratory artwork is a positive reflection that emanates from unity and strength. After the Powder Treason in 1605 there could have been tapestries or murals. John Goodwin, a London minister, envisioned subsequent fifths of November as 'the anniversary remembrance of that great battle fought between hell and heaven, about the peace and safety of our nation … wherein hell was overthrown and heaven and we rejoiced together'.[102] And the discovery of the Gunpowder conspiracy is still celebrated with bonfires and bells. The situation was different after the wars. England was in disarray in 1649; the Crown was gone and the remaining parliamentarians were unsure of how to lead the country from monarchy to republicanism. The Council of State was barely installed and indecision and confusion reigned regarding its responsibilities. Royalists still roamed the countryside and Scotland was not yet subdued. In short, the immediate atmosphere of apprehension that followed the execution of the king was a far cry from the heady pride that permeated virtually every corner of the island after the defeat of the Spanish Armada.

Although victory in 1649 was in one sense the same as it had been in 1588, the triumph of Protestantism, the civil wars were fought not against foreigners but against brothers. The defeated did not pack up and go home. Royalism was not eradicated by the execution of the king, the country was still torn over the issues of monarchy and Crown. In short, Lely, Gerbier and Geldorp's proposal for a parliamentary memorial by way of murals for the Banqueting House was rejected for issues far broader than a simple visual tribute. The absence of a peculiarly Puritan secular visual aesthetic,[103] and the absence of a precedent in the art world for military memorials, coupled with the indebtedness of the country and a lack of social cohesion all worked against its acceptance. The time was not right for the idea of memorializing events of national importance for the 'people's view'. That would be left to the Revolution in France and Jacques Louis David.[104]

For whatever complex of considerations as to why the idea failed we have only the proposal itself by which to envision the project. There are no sketches or cartoons, and no known detailed descriptions of it in manuscript. But if we let our imaginations take flight we can see in our mind's eye the exquisite proportions of Inigo Jones' Palladian Banqueting House, the Rubens ceiling commissioned by Charles as a memorial to his father, King James, and the great hall decorated with murals inspired by Van Dyck and executed by Peter Lely in a tribute to the victories of the parliamentarians – an artistic unity in political diversity.

Memorials of the English civil wars would appear only in the nineteenth century with the new Houses of Parliament, the parliamentary reform acts and the 'celebration by the whole nation' of the history of Britain. By 1832 the attention of all Englishmen was once again focused on the institution of Parliament and the idea of liberty many believed it embodied. As the movement for reform coalesced historians and journalists found inspiration for change in the example of the struggles of the seventeenth century. Isaac Disraeli published his *Commentaries on the Life of Charles the First*; John Forster wrote the biography of Sir John Eliot, singling him out as 'the most illustrious confessor in the cause of liberty' who died for his belief that 'upon the abandonment or maintenance of the privileges of parliament would turn the future misery or glory of England'.[105] Thomas Babington Macaulay laid tribute at Cromwell's feet, recounting that he 'reformed that system on the same principles on which Mr. Pitt, a hundred and thirty years later, attempted to reform it, and on which it was at length reformed in our own times'.[106] Artists followed suit, producing illustrations of the battles that resulted in parliamentary victories, and their pictures were hung in schools and town halls across England as lessons for generations of schoolboys to come. Great numbers of canvases – like Charles Cattermole's *Cromwell and his Soldiers*;[107] Abraham Cooper's *Oliver Cromwell, Lord Manchester, and General Lambert at Marston Moor*,[108] Ernst Crofts' *Cromwell at the Storming of Basing House*, James Ward's *Marston Moor*[109] and Thomas Woodward's *The Battle of Worcester*[110] – were painted as remembrances of the idea for which men in the seventeenth century were willing to die.[111] These works, as memorials of the civil wars and the men who fought them, provided the visual expression for the writing of those historians that much later would be accused of 'whiggishness'. Their books, however, in combination with the canvases and the larger-than-life statue of Cromwell that still stands in front of the Parliament buildings, served to unify the country. When all was said and done controversy was laid to rest and the reform acts passed. Perhaps the Commonwealth erred in not embracing the Gerbier–Lely–Geldorp proposal.

Notes

[1] Gilbert completed the canvas of the battle of Naseby in 1872. I want to thank Elise Kenney and Peter Hasler for their help with some of the art references in this chap-

ter.

² For 'The humble proposal of Sir Balthazar Gerbier, Kt., Peter Larry [*sic*], and George Gelders [*sic*] concerning the representing in oil, pictures of all the memorial achievements since the parliament's first sitting', see Stowe 184, fo. 283. A shorter version of the proposal is printed from Stowe 211, fo. 3 in C. H. Collins Baker, *Lely and the Stuart Portrait Painters*, 2 vols. (London, 1912).

³ There were paintings that hung on some of the walls in the hall from time to time, but there was no permanent decoration there. See Oliver Millar, *The Age of Charles I, Painting in England 1620–1649* (London, Tate Gallery, Published for the exhibition of 15 November 1972–14 January 1973), p. 37.

⁴ See Horace Walpole, *Anecdotes of Painting in England with Some Account of the Principal Artists ... with additions by the Rev. James Dallaway* (London, 1862), vol. I, pp. 335–6.

⁵ Van Dyck's oil sketches on boards for the great hall were sold in 1650 when the Royal Collection was dispersed and were in Sir Peter Lely's possession at the time of his death. In 1787 they were acquired for the duke of Rutland in whose family they have remained. They are reproduced in *Anthony van Dyck* (National Gallery of Art, Washington DC, for the exhibition, 11 November 1990–24 February 1991), pp. 364–6.

⁶ Walpole, *Anecdotes of Painting*, vol. I, pp. 336 n.1.

⁷ Millar, *The Age of Charles I*, p. 37.

⁸ *The Works of Edmund Waller, Esq.; in Verse and Prose*, published by Mr Fenton (London, 1730), pp. 31, lxv.

⁹ *Catalogue of British Drawings*, ed. Edward Croft-Murray and Paul Hutton, supplemented by a list of foreign artists' drawings connected with Great Britain by Christopher White (London, 1960), pp. 409–16.

¹⁰ There are extant sketches by Lely of the Knights of the Garter that 'have affinities in both size and appearance with Van Dyck's studies'. *Catalogue of British Drawings*, vol. I, pp. 409–10, relating to 'Studies of figures taking part in the ceremonies of the Order of the Garter on St George's Day, April 23rd'.

¹¹ The quotations here and below are from the proposal, Stowe 184, fo. 283, see above, n. 2.

¹² Roy Strong, *Lost Treasures of Britain* (London, 1990), p. 211. For the Armada charts, see *Armada 1588–1988, An International Exhibition to Commemorate the Spanish Armada* (Penguin Books in Association with the National Maritime Museum, 1988), pp. 243–8; M. Russell, *Visions of the Sea; Hendrick C. Vroom and the Origins of Dutch Marine Painting* (Leiden, 1983), pt. II, ch. 2. See also Phyllis Rogers, 'The Armada tapestries in the House of Lords', *Journal of the Royal Society of the Arts*, 125 (Sept. 1988), pp. 731–5.

¹³ John Pine, *The Tapestry Hangings in the House of Lords Representing the Several Engagements between the English and the Spanish* (London, 1739). Pine's engravings are reproduced in *Armada 1588–1988*, pp. 248–51.

¹⁴ Pine, *Tapestry Hangings*, p. 1.

¹⁵ *Ibid.*

¹⁶ See SP 25/27, fo. 519.

¹⁷ *Journals of the House of Lords*, vol. VI, p. 554; Elizabeth Read Foster, *The House of Lords, 1603–1649, Structure, Procedure, and the Nature of its Business* (Chapel Hill, 1983), p. 5.

¹⁸ As early as August 1649 notice was given by the Council 'That the hangings which

are used in the House of Parliament and the several courts of justice be reserved as part of the good [for the use of the commonwealth]'. SP 25/63, fo. 32. See also, SP 25/5 (unfoliated).

[19] Here and through the following three paragraphs the quotations are from the proposal, Stowe 184, fo. 283.

[20] I find no evidence that the name of the Banqueting House changed under the commonwealth or before.

[21] *Catalogue of British Drawings*, vol. I, pp. 328–9.

[22] *Ibid.*, p. 329; Horace Walpole, *Anecdotes of Painting*, vol. I, p. 274. In 1618 he had done a portrait of Villiers that is presently owned by the duke of Northumberland.

[23] Walpole, *Anecdotes of Painting*, Vol. I, p. 275. Edward Norgate was the author of *Miniatura or the Art of Limming*. See Mansfield Kirby Talley, *Portrait Painting in England: Studies in the Technical Literature before 1700* (published privately by the Paul Mellon Centre for Studies in British Art, 1981), pp. 156–70.

[24] There is a pen-and-ink miniature of the prince in the Victoria and Albert Museum inscribed, 'Gerbier fec. 1616'.

[25] *Catalogue of British Drawings*, vol. I, p. 329.

[26] W. A. Shaw, *The Knights of England* (Baltimore, 1971), vol. II, p. 206.

[27] SP 16/482:50. Regarding Gerbier's career see also Eileen Harris, *British Architectural Books and Writers 1556–1785* (Cambridge, 1990), pp. 206–7.

[28] See Gerbier's dedication to Charles II in *Brief Discourse Concerning the Three Chief Principles of Magnificent Building* (London, 1664). Denham had been a councillor of Charles I and attended Henrietta Maria in Paris in 1642 (see *Dictionary of National Biography*).

[29] His lectures for the academy were printed, see Wing, *STC*, vol. I, nos. 538–82, passim.

[30] See *The Inventories and Valuations of the King's Goods 1649–1651*, ed. Oliver Millar, vol. 43, (the Walpole Society, Glasgow, 1972), p. 316; *Catalogue of British Drawings*, vol. I, p. 330. It hangs now in the National Portrait Gallery.

[31] I have not been able to identify G. S. There were six with those initials that sat in the Long Parliament: George Searle, George Skutt, George Snelling, George Starre, Sir George Stonehouse and Giles Strangeways. See D. Brunton and D. H. Pennington, *Members of the Long Parliament* (Archon Books, rep. 1968).

[32] A bill was introduced for his naturalization in 1628 but failed, probably because of his close relationship to the duke of Buckingham. *Proceedings in Parliament 1628*, ed. Keeler, Cole and Bidwell, Index. Sir Francis Nethersole reported to Elizabeth of Bohemia that Gerbier had been 'ill handled' in the House of Commons which showed a 'strange animosity' toward him. *Ibid.*, vol. IV, p. 199.

[33] An uncalendared note in SP 25/63, fo. 247 reveals that some of Gerbier's papers 'were taken to make use of at the trial of the late King'.

[34] 'A Summary Relation of Sir Balthazar Gerbier's Proceedings since this Parliament's Assembly and his final ends thereby'. Dated 4 March 1652, B.L. Add. 32, 093, fos. 305–7.

[35] SP 25/16, fo. 42.

[36] Balthazar Gerbier, *The None-Such Charles and his Character extracted out of divers original transactions, dispatches, and the notes of several public ministers and councillors of state as well at home as abroad* (London, 1651).

[37] Oliver Millar, *Sir Peter Lely 1618–80*, exhibition at 15 Carlton Terrace, National Portrait Gallery, p. 9.

[38] R. B. Beckett, *Lely* (London, 1951), p. 6.

[39] Millar, *Age of Charles I*, p. 106.

[40] *Catalogue of British Drawings*, vol. I, p. 330.

[41] S. R. Gardiner, *History of England from the Accession of James I to the Outbreak of the Civil War 1603–1642*, 10 vols. (London, 1886), vol. 9, pp. 135, 136.

[42] See Malcolm Rogers, *William Dobson 1611–46* (London, National Portrait Gallery, published from the exhibition held from 21 October 1983–8 January 1984), p. 16. There is no record of these appointments in the Calendars of State Papers.

[43] Beckett, *Lely*, p. 11.

[44] *Lucasta*, ed. W. Carew Hazlitt (London, 1864), p. 102: 'To My Worthy Friend Mr. Peter Lilly: on that excellent picture of his Majesty and the Duke of Yorke, Drawne by Him at Hampton-Court'.

[45] Walpole, *Anecdotes of Painting*, vol. II, p. 444.

[46] Millar, *Lely*, p. 11.

[47] Walpole, *Anecdotes of Painting*, vol. II, p. 444; *HMC*, 6th Report pt. 1, 1877, pp. 437b–438a.

[48] Quoted from D. Piper, in Millar, *Lely*, p. 47.

[49] Walpole, *Anecdotes of Painting*, vol. I. p. 339.

[50] *Ibid.*

[51] *Ibid.*, p. 340.

[52] A landscape from his studio was sold on 5 April 1650 from the king's gallery at Oatlands. It was described as 'A landshape of London done by gelderps man', *Inventories and Valuations*, p. 278.

[53] The pictures of the marquess of Huntley and the duke of Richmond were engraved by Robert van Voerst; copies can be found in the Sutherland Collection, Ashmolean Museum, Oxford. See Margery Corbett and Michael Norton, *Engravings in England in the Sixteenth and Seventeenth Centuries*, (Cambridge, 1964), part III, 'The reign of Charles I', pp. 206 and 209.

[54] *C.J.*, vol, 7, p. 591.

[55] *Inventories and Valuations*, p. xxii.

[56] Millar, *Age of Charles I*, p. 89.

[57] David Underdown.

[58] G. E. Aylmer, *Rebellion or Revolution, England 1640–1660* (Oxford, 1987), p. 110.

[59] For the case against Henry Sherfield, Recorder of Salisbury for breaking a painted glass window in the church of St Edmonds in the said city, see Howell, *ST*, vol. III, pp. 519–62; Eric C. Walker, *William Dell, Master Puritan* (Cambridge, 1970), p. 99.

[60] Charles Carlton, *Going to the Wars, the Experience of the British Civil Wars 1638–1651* (London, 1992), p. 277; *Inventories and Valuations*, p. xi.

[61] *Inventories and Valuations*, pp. xi–xii; Aylmer, *Rebellion or Revolution*, p. 110–11; *C.J.*, vol. I, p. 349.

[62] Millar, *Age of Charles I*, p. 109.

[63] R. Glynne Lloyd, *John Owen – Commonwealth Puritan* (Pontypridd, Modern Welsh Publications Ltd., 1972), p. 77.

[64] H. M. Colvin (ed.), *The History of the King's Works* (London, 1982), vol. IV, pp. 147, 269–70.

[65] Andrew Wilton, *The Swagger Portrait, Grand Manner Portraiture in Britain from*

Van Dyck to Augustus John 1630–1930 (London, Tate Gallery, for the exhibition 14 October 1992–10 January 1993), p. 15. Wilton is speaking particularly of portraiture; the same is true for art and architecture.

[66] See J. T. Cliffe, *The Puritan Gentry* (London, 1984), p. 51, where the author remarks that in the routines of daily life 'many Puritan gentry deliberately sought to follow a regime of austerity'.

[67] SP 25/16, fo. 78.

[68] *Acts and Ordinances of the Interregnum*, ed. C. H. Firth and R. S. Rait (London, 1911), vol. I, p. 266.

[69] Wilton, *Swagger Portrait*, p. 15.

[70] *Ibid.*, p. 12.

[71] Richard Wendorf, *The Elements of Life, Biography and Portrait Painting in Stuart and Georgian England*, (Oxford, 1991), p. 10.

[72] Millar, *Age of Charles I*, p. 96.

[73] *Ibid.*

[74] J. R. Hale, *Artists and Warfare in the Renaissance* (London, 1990), p. 1. See, for example, Albrecht Dürer's *Recruiting Scene* (1543), *ibid.*, p. 2; Daniel Hopfer's, *Soldier and a Woman* (*c*.1530) *ibid.*, p. 39; Erhard Schoen's *Siege of Munster* (1535) *ibid.*, p. 19.

[75] Hale, *Artists and Warfare*, pp. 10, 52.

[76] See Herbert Langer, *The Thirty Years War* (Dorset, 1990), pp. 103, 126; and Hale, *Artists and Warfare*, p. 52.

[77] Hale, *Artists and Warfare*, p. 25.

[78] *Ibid.*, p. 52.

[79] *Ibid.*, pp. 188–9.

[80] *Ibid.*, p. 196.

[81] Jonathan Brown and J. H. Elliott, *A Palace for a King, The Buen Retiro and the Court of Philip IV* (New Haven, 1980), pp. 162, 190.

[82] Langer, *The Thirty Years War*, pp. 64–102.

[83] *Interesting Information about the Night Watch* (Rijksmuseum Foundation, Amsterdam, 1987).

[84] Hale, *Artists and Warfare*, p. 263: 'There, in the memorial window to Sir Richard Assheton, the archers who accompanied him at the battle of Flodden in 1513 are named in the inscriptions along their bows'. By 1588 the names of the common soldiers and sailors were lost in the lists of muster masters and press gangs. Tapestries and prints depicted units and fleets, not individual gunners and mates. With the Vietnam memorial in Washington the concept of memorializing the individual has come full circle back to the memorial for the archers at Flodden. See also Smurthwaite, *The Ordnance Survey Complete Guide to the Battlefields of Britain* (London, 1987), p. 126.

[85] See, for example, 'The description of the armies of horse and foot of his Majesty's and Sir Thomas Fairfax his excellency as they were drawn into several bodies at the Battle of Naseby, the fourteenth day of June 1645', engraved from Joshua Sprigg, *Anglica Rediviva*, 1647.

[86] The iconography of William Dobson's portrait of *Charles II When Prince of Wales* (1643? Scottish National Portrait Gallery) suggests that it was painted to commemorate the Battle of Edgehill, which appears as background to the portrait.

[87] A painting commemorating the Battle of Lepanto hung in Philip II's bedroom and another in the Council Chamber of the Doge's Palace in Venice.

[88] The nationality of the painter is in question. The canvas is reproduced in *Armada, 1588–1988*, p. 65.

[89] It was Karel van Mander, contemporary biographer and painter, who described Vroom's canvas of the Armada. The painting is in the Tiroler Landesmuseum Ferdinandeum, Innsbruck, and is reproduced in *Armada, 1588–1988*, p. 252.

[90] The painting is reproduced in *ibid.*, p. 261.

[91] Russell, *Visions of the Sea*, p. 61.

[92] Corbett and Norton, *Engravings in England*, part III, plate 14.

[93] Blair Worden, *Stuart England* (Oxford, 1986), pp. 168–9.

[94] Waller, *Works*, 'Instructions to a painter, for the drawing of the posture, and progress, of his Majesty's forces at sea, under the command of his Highness Royal together with the battel, and victory, obtained over the Dutch, June 3, 1665', pp. 161–17.

[95] *The Shorter Pepys*, ed. Robert Latham (Berkeley, 1985), pp. 643, 607–8.

[96] *Acts and Ordinances*, vol. II, pp. 191–2.

[97] Exhibit of the English Civil War at the Imperial Army Museum (London, 1992). As early as 1625 A. Vanderdort was appointed Chief Medalist for his work in moulding medals and mint stamps. Walpole, *Vertue*, vol. I, pp. 265–8; Thomas Rymer (ed.), *Foedera Conventiones, literae, et cujuscunque generais Acta Publica inter Reges Angliae*, 10 vols. (Joannem Neaulme, 1739–45), vol. 18, p. 100.

[98] Ludlow, *Memoirs*.

[99] Osborn fb 67. Letter from Cromwell to the Justices of Peace of Middlesex (and copies, I assume, to other counties), 12 January 1651, to provide help for widows and orphans of maimed and slain soldiers by acts and ordinances of parliament. Those ordinances for maintenance for 'wives and children of those that are killed' in the service of Parliament began as early as 1642 and continued for a decade. *Acts and Ordinances*, vol. II, pp. 36, 997, 1055, and see index, under Pensions.

[100] *CJ*, vol. 6, p. 148; SP 25/87, 16; 25/62, 7.

[101] *CJ*, vol. 6, pp. 172, 185, 243, 249; SP 25/87, 33, 39, 58, 59; SP 25/62, 130; 25/94, 83. The act, passed in July 1649 is printed in *Acts and Ordinances*, vol. II, pp. 160–8. It is interesting to note that in selling off the art collection the parliamentarians apparently had no interest at all in who bought the religious paintings that they claimed smacked of Catholicism when they were owned by the king. See also *ibid.*, pp. 546–8.

[102] Quoted from David Cressy, *Bonfires and Bells, National Memory and the Protestant Calendar in Elizabethan and Stuart England* (London, 1989), p. 156.

[103] i.e., there was no clearly definable set of regular and positive principles for the creation of secular art.

[104] See Emmet Kennedy, *A Cultural History of the French Revolution*, (New Haven, 1989), ch. 9, 'The fine arts and the revolutionary imagination, music, art, and drama'. The other popular painter of French history, Jean Auguste Dominique Ingres (1780–1867) produced the bulk of his canvases in the nineteenth century.

[105] John Forster, *Sir John Eliot: A Biography 1590–1632*, 2 vols. (London, 1864), pp. xii–xiii.

[106] Lord Macaulay, *The History of England from the Accession of James the Second* (London, 1872), vol. I, p. 140.

[107] Sheffield City Art Galleries.

[108] Chequers.

[109] *The Battle of Marston Moor*, sold at Sotherby's in 1969, originally in the collec-

tion of Edward Spencer-Churchill.

[110] The Worcester Borough Hall.

[111] See the Appendix to Strong, ' *"When did you last see your father?"* Subjects from British history ... exhibited at the Royal Academy 1679–1904'. Strong lists 59 paintings under the subject 'civil wars', as well as 33 under 'Charles I'; 35 under 'Oliver Cromwell'; and 35 under 'Cavaliers', 'Roundheads and Puritans'. The majority of canvases in each category were done in the middle of the nineteenth century and later.

12

Underground verse and the transformation of early Stuart political culture

Thomas Cogswell

I

'What do you think will become of me,' Archbishop Laud asked Strafford in 1637, 'when I am thus used?' From a normally self-possessed archbishop, such anxiety was odd enough, but odder still was the source of his fears. Rather than royal vacillations or aristocratic cabals, what had shaken him was a series of manuscript libels. Equally striking was the rapidity with which his confidence had eroded. Only a few months earlier 'the libels which fly abroad in all places' had merely concerned the prelate. If nothing was done about them, the archbishop understood that he could only be expected 'to be the subject of God knowes how many more'. But the apostle of 'Thorough' had no intention of suffering in silence: 'a little more Quickness in Government', he assured Strafford, 'would cure this Itch of Libelling'. The archbishop's prescription certainly left Prynne, Burton and Bastwicke smarting.[1] Yet these exemplary punishments, far from calming the situation, only inflamed it. Hitherto the archbishop's worries had centred on printed pamphlets, which had a comparatively limited distribution. After the mutilations, however, opposition to him became more ominous, as short manuscript libels began to appear around the City, some in prose, others in verse, and a few set to music. Hence, the prelate had to endure public ridicule such as the 'Arch-Wolf of Cant[erbury]', who held a lease for St Pauls from Satan himself and who led the Devil's army to overthrow the Reformed Church.[2] The new 'liberty everywhere taken to utter slight speeches of authority' understandably transformed the archbishop's concern into alarm. Stung by one of these poems, he had to watch helplessly as the pursuivants searched for an author who, he eventually conceded, 'cannot be found'. Powerless to check the abuse, he could only wax philosophical: 'these were symptoms of some disease in the Government'. His friend in Dublin concurred. While outraged at these 'very unsufferable' attacks, Strafford also acknowledged that in the present circumstances, 'how to help it I know not'. The rapidly deteriorating situation made

Laud's question even more plaintive – 'can you tell me what this will come to?'[3]

To this emotional plea, scholars have generally remained as indifferent as they have been to the political implications of such rude verses.[4] The present essay seeks, at least, to advance the task of correcting this omission by explaining where these libels came from as well as where they were to lead the archbishop. This task, it must be conceded, involves much more than belated justice.

Although contemporary critics were addicted to composing lists of the realm's notorious vices, none of their denunciations of drunkenness, fornication and greed ever mentioned mass murder. This fact only deepens the mystery about how contemporaries were able to begin slaughtering each other in the fall of 1642. Arguably, scholarly attention has wandered of late from this basic question. Some are now busy charting the intricate evolutions of the British problem; others are producing new, and yet more savage judgements on the Personal Monarch, replete with confident assertions that the Civil War is impossible to imagine without Charles I; and a few are lost in wonder at Lord Saye and Sele's ability to be everywhere at once. All of these pursuits are well and good. Yet the fact remains that they can do little to explain the extraordinary display of psychopathology which began at Edgehill. A partial corrective can be found in a minister's exhortation as troops filed to the front: 'it is not onely store of coyne, high spirited horse, good Ammunition, sound skill, fierce resolution, nor a strong Arme,' he reminded them, 'but a strong Cause that makes a compleat soldier'.[5] What exactly was either side's 'strong cause', and how had it formed?

Modern answers have quite rightly highlighted religious and social factors. Religion plainly had a good deal to do with contemporary alignments, while social position and geographical location determined much. Yet having said all that, how did these factors harden in a 'strong cause'? The present essay suggests that these explanations should be broadened to include the emergence of popular political awareness. Simply put, in the decades before Edgehill, a rapidly expanding percentage of the population underwent a crude adult education which left them keen observers of national events and ultimately eager participants in them. In this line of enquiry, the vital question centres on what contemporaries heard and read, which allowed them to translate general predilections into firm ideological positions.

At first glance, this query appears to be a non-starter. The fates of Prynne, Burton and Bastwicke neatly illustrate the real limits to what contemporaries could get into print. And what did, while often surprisingly juicy, was never substantial enough for contemporaries to have cut their political teeth on it. Fortunately, scholars are now becoming aware of the stiff interpretative price which they have long paid for privileging print culture. Printed materials in fact represented only part of the contemporary media. While Whitehall maintained some control over the few presses in the realm, it had almost none over the hundreds of thousands of pens. Once this realization belatedly dawned, scholars have been at once delighted and amazed at the extent of the 'underground' manuscript trade and the audacity of its debates. Political treatises represented a sizable portion of this genre. But arguably the more significant segment, both in terms of sheer distribution and often in visceral impact, were the manuscript poems.

II

In his despair, Laud could have found some comfort; his difficulties with abusive poets were far from unique as the uncompromising response of two of his predecessors illustrated. In 1599 Archbishop Whitgift and Richard Bancroft, then Bishop of London, ordered the public burning of several offensive verses; more dramatically, they also banned the further production of satires and epigrams. Although a few bolder poets evaded their prohibition in later decades, Bancroft and Whitgift at least had the posthumous satisfaction of stunting the growth of an entire literary genre for forty years.[6] Their power to compel the muses to sing a new tune appears impressive until it becomes clear that their success only made Laud's difficulties almost completely intractable.

The extraordinary public execution of these verses culminated an equally extraordinary souring of the literary mood as the 1590s progressed. Profound and unprecedented economic problems cast a pall over late Elizabethan England, which only darkened as Spanish war inclusively dragged on. By 1598, Thomas Bastard could no longer endure the customary laudatory rhetoric about Elizabeth's 'golden age' and 'goolden [*sic*] peace'; instead he offered a more realistic portrait focusing on 'home jarres' among 'so fewe rich and so many poore'. What most exasperated Everard Guilpin was not simply the lofty rhetoric; rather it was 'establishment' poets like Edmund Spencer who created it.[7] This bitter tone assumed more ominous proportions as the prolonged debate over Presbyterianism encouraged contemporaries to develop an impressive ability for raillery in both poetry and prose. Whatever the ecclesiastic results of the extended Marprelate controversy, the literary ones were formidable. Indeed, the irony of the public burning in 1599 was that, a decade earlier, Whitgift and Bancroft, in an effort 'to have answered them [the Martinists] after their own vain writings', had unleashed the likes of Thomas Nashe, the *railleur par excellence*, on their opponents and the reading public.[8]

From this fertile ground arose the late Elizabethan rage for epigrams and libels. This passion attracted the aspiring poets like John Donne, John Davies, John Marston and John Hoskins as well as dozens of lesser lights eager to earn fame as 'a plaine dealing lad, that is not afraid / To speake the truth, but calls a jade a jade'. So popular did this genre prove that well dressed poets had to sport 'some Epigram or Satyre' pinned to his glove.[9] Admittedly some of these works were harmless enough, the mockery com-

paratively gentle and the objects of mirth safely obscure. Yet the more popular efforts, Bastard explained, were 'all rawe with indigested spite / Whose
witt doth droppe inuenymde iniurie' and 'blots of spitefull infamie'. Far more
than with formal poetry, these verses found a broad and receptive audience.
In fact, the defining characteristic of a contemporary malcontent, Joseph Hall
observed, was an obsession with 'nothing but Satyrs and Libels'.[10] About the
aim of these poets, there can be little doubt. Livid with anger, one contemporary objected to these 'insulting Tamberlaynes' who laid the country waste
with their rhymes, while another begged the government to hang 'the devils
Intelligencer' who put 'the States in Vrinalls'. Nothing less was worthy of
those "Shamelesse of shame', who dared to attempt

> to plucke the plume of Englands happiness,
> and Broach the malice of thy base contempt,
> in civil iarres bred by uncivilnesse.

Such an intransigent attitude was not poetic conceit, for the libellers so
incensed the lord treasurer, Lord Buckhurst, that in 1599 he called for the
death penalty to check them.[11]

Such hostile reactions should not obscure the fact that the authors of these
printed works carefully avoided any direct reference to contemporary persons. Given the regulation of the printing trade, such caution had much to
commend it. The author had to secure the approval of a government licen-
sor. If the author sought to hide behind the veil of anonymity, the publisher
could not; all involved in an offensive production could be tracked down
through the printers. John Marston therefore had ample reason for anxiety
about a particularly ill-tempered volume of verse; the true nature of a satire,
he assured his readers, 'is under fayned name to note generall vices'. Nevertheless this logic eluded many who 'will needes wrest each fayned name to a
private unfained person', and particularly to 'some greater personage'. Any
blame for offensive satires therefore belonged to overly imaginative readers
rather than to the author. The ingenuity of Marston's definition ultimately
failed to persuade those in power, and in 1599 his were among those burned.[12]

Yet the government's action was ultimately ineffective. Naturally those
who felt themselves abused rejoiced over the censure, 'for had ye [the satirists]
gone forward with approbation ... you would shortly have proved as mischievous to the Inhabitants of England, as Tyrone hath bene to the Frontiers
of Ireland'.[13] Their delight would have abated, if not evaporated altogether,
with the knowledge that the 1599 decree did not end the practice. Rather it
simply shifted satiric libels into another poetical genre over which the regime
had ever less control.

Raw though some plainly found Bastard's work, the fact of the matter was
that the necessity of securing a licence forced him to pull his punches. Hence
Bastard actually boasted that 'I have taught Epigrams to speake chastlie'.[14] It
followed that if his worries about a licence ever vanished, then so too would

his concern about the modesty of his language disappear. The simplest way to achieve that end was to circulate poems in manuscript. Residents of colleges and the Inns of Court had long been past masters at the production of pasquils and squibs mocking rival scholars and institutions.[15] Likewise, those at court had sometimes expressed their contempt for rivals in verse. The crisis of the 1590s, however, began the transformation of this practice. By writing only in manuscript, thus avoiding any involvement with printers, and by hiding behind the veil of authorial anonymity, contemporary poets could ridicule prominent national figures as easily as they had mocked awkward colleagues. The distribution of these manuscript lampoons underwent a similar revolution. A poet could, of course, simply spread copies among friends in taverns and ordinaries, but if he ever sought a wider audience, he simply had to go a few hundred feet away from the heart of the book trade. Instead of entering the bookshops in St Paul's Yard, he proceeded into the cathedral itself and joined the throng milling about the middle aisle eager for the latest political developments. In the cacophony of hundreds speaking simultaneously, there was poetry; for the passion for the latest news often produced recitations of the most recent verse libels. Admittedly even in the 'Tower of Babel', a few efforts were too sulphurous to be uttered aloud; in that case, the lines could be affixed to a prominent place either in the church or in the churchyard. From there, newsmongers quickly relayed the latest efforts to their friends elsewhere.

With the development of the 'underground' genre came a literary species of the 'pot-companion poet' or, more simply, the 'pot-poet'. Although modern scholars have been largely oblivious of them, contemporaries could spot them easily enough. In a throng of Pauls walkers, Thomas Dekker suggested, look for those 'that spit nothing but ynck, and speake nothing but Poeme'. Thomas Overbury was more straightforward: pot-poets were the ones who looked like 'a dunghill not well laid together'.[16] Their unfortunate appearance was partly a function of their lifestyle. Somewhere between a court literati and a humble balladeer, such a poet found 'a cup of Sack inflames him and sets his muse and nose a fire'. Indeed some insisted that they could not write until 'strong Sir Claret Burdeaux Redcrosse Knight / Dubs him a poet'.[17] In this line of work alcohol was no luxury. Copious amounts of wine and beer helped explain the generally appalling literary quality, and in the composition of lines apt to be slanderous, if not seditious, a tipsy head dimmed the prospect of a flogging and a heavy fine. So too did the potential for financial gain. Given the growing demand for political commentary in verse, poets happily discovered that 'verses are growne merchantable wares'.[18] Topical verse played no small part in Richard Corbett's rapid rise to the deanery of Christ Church and the bishopric of Norwich. While most poets had to accept less impressive rewards, the one who received £2 for a few lines on the duke of Buckingham cannot have been too unhappy with the outcome.[19] All of these factors ensured that by James' accession, a notable event would almost invariably produce a verse commentary, while a serious crisis could be guaranteed a spray of poems.

The discovery of a new world of literary material, vast and largely untouched, is of course a happy event. But even the most intrepid explorer quails on finding evidence of earlier expeditions which had come to grief. Arguably the most evocative of these was one which Mr Dubois launched during the Regency, hardly a period renowned for its prudery. In the end, he became bitterly frustrated with editing rhymes, whose mere mention 'in societies, by no means puritanical, would speedily send the speaker on his travels by the nearest outlet, door or window'. The only possible answer was a privately published volume with a tiny run. The indelicacy of these verses also hampered Mr Fairholt's valiant attempt a few years later to present an edition of poetry relating to the duke of Buckingham. He managed to get his volume into the public domain, but only at the expense of deleting whole passages with the note that 'the lines which follow are too coarse for printing'.[20]

A few examples reveal that problem which bedevilled Dubois and Fairholt was not their excessive delicacy. Francis Bacon's persistent halitosis, one poet maintained, had a simple explanation:

the Muses nine upon a tyme
as gaping he lay winking
Shitt on his tongue, when he was yong,
and made his breath so stinking.[21]

More unsettling still was Sir John Harrington's account of six Puritan women, searching for an alternative to the 'old and popish name of preaching'. After rejecting preaching, teaching, catechizing, exercising and lecturing, they agreed on standing, since 'standing wear more fitt, / Sith preachers seldom in the pulpit sitt'. Only those well acquainted with Harrington's favourite *double entendres* would have readily equated standing with erection and pulpit with vagina. Such humour was too subtle for one pot-poet, who made Harrington's point emerge more directly with the introduction of a stock character, the unfortunately named Dr Prick; thus in the end, the women trooped off to see 'good Mr Prick' stand.[22] As distressing as these examples are, they paled before one poet's extended indictment of Buckingham's family; along with dubbing them a collection of drunkards, adulterers and idiots, the poem depicted Sir Anthony Ashley sodomizing the 'blackarse hole' of the duke's niece. Quite understandably this poem was one of those which Fairholt found himself unable to print fully in 1850.[23] As these examples reveal, this genre flourished somewhere between the crude and the appalling.

Sober modern scholars naturally prefer the more detailed, and more decent discussions found in manuscript tracts. Yet the contemporary distributors did not. At the height of the crisis in 1642, a bitter author complained that a work 'of thirty or forty sheets of papers is not like to sell in this age were the matter never so good'. Meanwhile he had no doubt about what would – 'some reviling tearmes against Monarchy and Hierarchy'.[24] While the raillery could be delivered in either prose or verse, the latter was preferred. It is not hard to see why, with a mass audience whose appreciation of classical prose was as minimal as their attention span. The pursuit of the lowest common denominator resulted in many of these verses being set to music; then they could be 'chanted from Market to Market to a vile tune' so that 'the poor Country wench melts like her butter to hear them'. As one advertisement went, 'buy and read, or sing with me'.[25] Hence when a gentleman wanted to humiliate a local minister, the obvious method was to pen 'a scandalous Libel', which 'a common fiddler' would then perform.[26]

This much is predictable. What is more surprising is the extent to which contemporaries were addicted to versifying almost everything. Condemned men like Raleigh and Strafford spent their last hours fussing over farewell sonnets, while the despondent left suicide notes in couplets.[27] Ponderous tracts often mixed poetry and prose, and even the most technical of them frequently presented their introductions and conclusions in verse. For instance, after the 1621 Parliament degraded 'Sir' Francis Mitchell, he circulated an 'underground' vindication, whose elaborate case rested on a poem with a pointed refrain: 'Spare not, cry out awake Prerogative.' Finally even preachers appreciated the value of verse; one gave his flock couplets summarizing the sermon.[28]

These efforts found an eager audience. In fact the response was so enthusiastic that more formal poets came to resent the competition often bitterly. For John Davies, the only thing more remarkable than Thomas Bastard's dreadful verses themselves was that 'some foule-mouth's Readers ... so slop them up that it would make one spew'. Abraham Holland was equally appalled with the pot-poets' 'heavy Rimes, which ... Would make one quite abiure all Poetrie'. Yet the amateurish rhymes of the pot-poets notwithstanding, the age's greatest poets like Michael Drayton and Ben Jonson could scarcely find an audience. The enormous popularity of pot-poets drove Holland to exclaim that 'The doting world is come unto this passe, / England is all turn'd Yorkshire', that byword for provincial ignorance.[29] Others denounced these verses on moral rather than literary grounds. 'What libelles against Princes,' Dekker asked,

> against Peeres, against the State, or against the Magistrates, were ever (pricking Thornes) thrust into the sides of this Empire, to make it bleed, of which a Pen was not guilty?[30]

A mass of Dekker's contemporaries agreed, and it was precisely the poem's scandalous nature which riveted their attention.

Such denunciations of the manuscript political verse, far from curtailing its circulation, only served to expand it. To be sure, some carefully kept their commonplace books free from the poetic contagion. Yet the reverse was also an accepted practice, as hundreds of surviving poetic miscellanies testify. Still others adopted the sensible compromise of copying out whatever reached them in either form. In his commonplace book, John Rous made quite clear that 'I hate these following railing rimes'; nevertheless he carefully recorded them 'for president of the times'.[31] Furthermore, for topical verse, these rhymes had a remarkably long half-life. Denunciations of Buckingham remained hot items well into the 1630s, and although the cycle of poems addressed to Saint Elizabeth in heaven date from the 1610s, they were still in demand in 1640s.[32] The rage for vintage verses even altered the rules of hospitality, for guests often received access to a host's commonplace books as well as to his cellar and kitchen; thus a visitor to Sir Roger Mostyn's house busily transcribed his host's collections, which in turn had been 'drawen out of the bookes of that truely Noble gentleman, Richard Grosvenor'.[33] Not surprisingly, the latest verses were a common commodity in the brisk epistolary traffic between London and the provinces. Although the Revd Gerrard warned Strafford that some newsletter writers did not 'take Notice of Verses', he hastened to assure the earl that he did.[34] So too did Dr Mede and John Chamberlain, thus allowing their friends whether in Suffolk or Holland to remain poetically *au courant*. Admittedly such thoughtfulness had its dangers. Transmission of one poem made Dr Mede so anxious that he carefully wrote it out on a separate sheet of paper from his newsletter; his correspondent should keep it secret, for if trouble followed, he warned, 'Ile deny it.'[35] If a metropolitan correspondent occasionally forgot, his rural friends were not above reminding him. Hence, a preacher in Essex asked a neighbour, then visiting in Westminster, for the latest production – not for the love of scandal, the minister carefully added, but simply that 'I might see the varietie of wittes'.[36]

Here it is worth stressing the advantage of brevity. While transcribing a pamphlet was a serious chore best left to scriviners, copying out a page or two of verse was child's play. Dissemination was even easier with 'underground' ballads, as prosecutions for singing them reveal.[37] Consequently, the coarseness of these poems should not obscure the fact that there were very few, if any, forms of communication more ubiquitous than these 'underground' squibs.

The genre's importance far exceeded its broad distribution. Few indeed were the poems which analysed issues in a cool, dispassionate manner. Rather, most were by their nature wildly partisan. Robert Cecil, earl of Salisbury, was not merely an overly enthusiastic royal minister; he was 'Oppression's praiser, Taxation's raiser', 'the country's scourger, the cities' cheater', 'the king's misuser, the Parliament's abuser', 'a camel', 'a dolphin', and 'a heart-gripping harpy'.[38] Similar opprobrium rained down on George Villiers, duke of Buckingham, a minister variously renowned for his 'treacherie, neglect and cowardice', 'most gracelesse duke', master of the 'al goe-naughts', 'darling Absolon', 'Lucifer', 'thy kingdom's curse', 'the Romists' friend, the gospells' foe, / the Church and the kingdomes overthrowne'.[39] Even monarchs and their families were not entirely out of reach of bolder 'pot-poets'; one dubbed James I as 'a Price of mickleworth' and 'a redshank' and the young Charles as 'the Duckling of York'.[40]

The flourishing state of the 'underground' media, while an undeniable boon for the general public, was a more dubious mark of appreciation for those who found themselves libelled. Understandably the aggrieved were eager to meet their tormentors; Buckingham himself once offered a £1,000 reward for the privilege. Unfortunately, apprehending anonymous poets was much more difficult than tracking down errant printers. To relieve the frustration of those who had been 'epigrammed', contemporaries developed a few counter measures. Since many of the 'pot-poets' were associated with the theatre, opening night was the best place to exact vengeance. Having paid for a choice seat on stage, the aggrieved party could stalk out in the middle of the play's climax, drawing as many of his friends with him as he could manage. Or he might stay and 'turne plain Ape ... mewe at passionate speeches, blare at Merrie, finde fault with the musicke, [and] whew at the childrens Action'. Baring that, the abused might find some satisfaction amid friends in taverns by calling for a close-stool and then withdrawing 'to wipe his taile' with the offending verses.[41]

Unfortunately any palliative effect of these actions diminished in inverse proportion to the prominence of the libelled. Buckingham did stalk out of the Globe at least once, and it is easy to imagine him on a close-stool. Yet it is equally hard to believe that these actions could have satisfied him after notable public attacks. Thus he and his colleagues in high office generally sought to prosecute the guilty. Regrettably these efforts more often than not merely underscored the tactical advantages of a manuscript libel. First of all, mere possession of a manuscript libel proved nothing; law students found with a nasty ballad neatly slipped out of harm's way by innocently insisting that they had just found it. And while there were arrests and punishments – Alexander Gill and his scrivener suffered for celebrating Felton's execution – most cases only exposed the limits of retribution.[42] Since the government's guiding principle was the cessation of any discussion of affairs of State, punishment often only subverted this goal. One suspect sent to prison found to his great delight that between the inmates and their keepers, the Fleet was a splendid source of 'good intelligence of state occurrences' as well as 'wise discourse'. A public prosecution, moreover, ran the risk of further disseminating the offensive verses. Hence when some fiddlers were hauled before Star Chamber for 'singeing publiqlye verye foule and scandalous songs', the prosecution only referred to the vital evidence, the song itself, by its first and last lines. Much to the audience's disgust, only the judges got to see the complete text.[43]

Under the circumstances, the best response, as Bancroft had discovered with the Martinists, was not to investigate but to counter-attack. While the likely fruitlessness of the former would only underscore one's vulnerability, the latter had an undeniable cathartic effect. Scores of poets were eager to assist the aggrieved in giving as good as they got. Admittedly some took full advantage of the regime's favourable attitude towards their work to hurry into print. Yet most were content to have their works pass from admirers at court to the Pauls' walkers. This practice after all was an accepted convention among most courtier poets, whose poems generally appeared in print decades after their composition, if at all. James' regime could look for help from the likes of John Harrington, Robert Ayton, Robert Stradling, Edmund Bolton and above all Richard Corbett.[44] And in the crisis over the Spanish match, their number received their most distinguished addition – James himself. Decades of labouring in complex metres and rhymes had produced dozens of technically proficient and lyrically awkward poems. Yet in his frustration in the early 1620s the king discovered his voice in the sturdy rhyming couplet, the favourite weapon of the 'pot-poets'. Then he excoriated his critics while exhorting his readers to 'hold you the publique way / Wonder at kings and them obey'.[45] Charles I admittedly was less handy with punchy rhymes; he could barely manage a couplet in honour of a teenage paramour, Lady Diana Cecil.[46] But between the likes of John Suckling, Thomas Carew, William Davenant and John Denham, he too had no lack of poetic champions in this often savage guerrilla war in manuscript.[47]

From this poetic phalanx came a stream of verse, which matched the vigour, if not the volume, of the government's critics. For those hired pens, no position was indefensible. A parliamentary impeachment could not stop William Lewis from waging a spirited defence of Lord Chancellor Bacon. Likewise the bloody carnage of English troops at the Ile de Ré, which scandalized most contemporaries, prompted a lone poet to caution against despair and against allowing the French to 'kill more with their songs / Then twise their swords'. In a similar vein, when mourning over the death of Gustavus Adolphus reached embarrassing heights in 1632, Thomas Carew reminded all that

> though the German Drum
> Bellow for freedome and revenge, the noyse
> Concernes not us, nor should divert our ioyes.[48]

Their defense of untenable positions, impressive though it was, paled before their ability to carry the polemical battle into the enemy camp. Sir Edward Coke discovered this in 1626, when Charles pricked the parliamentary hero as Sheriff of Buckinghamshire. His martyrdom engulfed him in a wave of popularity. It also brought out a long, abusive poem recounting his many embarrassments from his having 'feathered his nest' while on the bench to his daughter's unhappy marriage to Buckingham's lunatic brother; she, the poet suggested, 'will wish (then she had beene well trickt) / her husband had been like her father Prickt'. Another unexpected poetic offensive began with the 1628 opening, when Bishop Corbett satirized the brave new world in which Pym, Prynne and Jordan, 'must define / What Lords are hetr'rodox and what divine'. A passionate rebuttal of this sally simply brought on a powerful apologia of Buckingham. 'I'll give you better counsel', the duke allegedly told the Parliament-men,

> as a friend –
> Cobblers their latchet ought not to transcend
> Meddle with Common matters, Common wrongs –
> To the House of Commons, Common things belong.

The same capacity for pre-emptive strikes can be found in William Davenant's assault in 1630 on the lingering popularity of the Parliament-men who 'would from the Bosome of the State / Chase Truth, or there distract her with debate'. Instead he advocated what was to be the central theme of the Personal Rule: 'When Thrones are rich, the People richer grow'.[49] All these sallies never overwhelmed their opponents, but at least they made sure that the government did not concede its case by default.

Examples of similar poems, for and against, can be produced *ad nauseam*. All of them would simply confirm the obvious; in spite of the regime's remarkable success at sanitizing print culture of all but the most officious political commentary, everything was not tranquil and consensual in early Stuart England. Once we expand our enquiries to include all forms of information, it quickly becomes apparent that the safety of the 'underground' manuscripts allowed contemporaries to conduct a steady, often violent political debate. The audience for these clashes furthermore cut across class distinctions and geographic location so effectively that the 'underground' market arguably was as close to a mass media as early Stuart England ever achieved.

III

Given the development of the 'underground' media, Laud had ample warrant for alarm when he found himself in 1637 being cast as the latest popular bogeyman. Unfortunately, subsequent events, far from diverting the attention of popular poets, only focused it on him more tightly.

In the economic doldrums after the Scottish rebellion, a contemporary remarked that there were only two growth industries. One fashioned nooses to punish Scottish rebels, and the other political verse. In the sitzkrieg along the Tweed the latter figured prominently, with poetic raids into either camp spreading copies of the latest rhymes. While the Scots warned their opponents to remember that 'when wee'r slaine, this rod comes on your breech', the English replied that 'Thou Rebell Scot, wee feare thee not'. Such exchanges, needless to say, found an attentive audience.[50] The regime's public relations problem became a positive disaster with the opening of the Long Parliament. Popular attention could not help being riveted on Westminster. An even more frightening development was Parliament's insistence on the abolition of Star Chamber and High Commission and its failure to establish an alternative method of policing print. Admittedly, in later years an occasional author managed to irritate a majority of the Commons enough to bring punishment upon himself. Yet these occasions were so rare that the pilloried author easily excited popular sympathy. One of the unlucky few wondered aloud about why his verses should have earned such displeasure when the realm was awash with 'the Inumberable [sic] multitude of Pamphlets' and 'Libels'.[51]

The extent of the altered political situation could not escape the archbishop. 'Libels', he noted, 'are continually set up in all places in the city'. After a mob of rioting apprentices, all brandishing the latest slanders, drove him out of Lambeth Palace, Laud could not even find peace in the Tower where he was imprisoned early in 1641. A promising 'Poet', he reportedly noted, 'is accounted of no estimation, whose fansie cannot elevate it selfe so high as to breake my (once stony) heart'. Their success could be heard throughout the city where 'libels and ballads against me were ... sung up and down the streets'. Yet 'how to help it', Laud confessed, 'I know not'.[52]

The crux of the problem was that the realm was undergoing a media revolution. Merchants, once fixated on commercial information 'from Aleppo, Constantinople, the Straits, or Indies', were then only interested in news 'from Yorke, Ireland and the Parliament'. Attorneys likewise were concerned only with 'buying up all the pamphlets and dispersing themselves into corners and reade them'.[53] Even the Church offered no sanctuary from current events; there, a poet lamented, 'All our divinity is news'. This new obsession, furthermore, was not confined to the elite; it also invaded common 'Bake-houses, Barber-shops and Ale-house' and infected women as well as men. Gone too was the customary caution of the lower orders who traditionally discussed public affairs 'under the rose'; instead, 'tongues wrangle and jangle' so vigorously that 'you shall not finde three men agree in one opinion'.[54]

In this radical transformation, the crucial development was that 'cum priviligio's out of date'. The impact of the regime's loss of control over printing was dramatic, for at last much of the political poetry and prose, which had hitherto circulated only in manuscript, reached print. The underground market itself continued largely as an outlet for some of the cruder efforts. Even the new liberty could not entirely relieve publishers' anxieties about poems like that celebrating the London alderman who when 'a Thousand Men / discharged their musketts, he discharged too' and so 'beshit his hose in everye seame'.[55] Nevertheless the bulk of the 'underground' media finally emerged into public view, bringing with it its celebrated backlist. Thus the old favourite about six Northamptonshire Puritans at last reached print as did other vintage verses like Leycester's Ghost and elegies, by then a decade old, on Gustavus Adolphus.[56] Yet it did not require a particularly astute poet to appreciate that more topical verses would truly ensure that 'the Presse is his mint'.[57]

As in earlier crises, those who reigned supreme were 'Owen Dogerell', 'Master Red-Nose', and a host of other pot-poets, all members of

> that shamelesse crew
> Of namelesse Authors, Authors of all lies,
> Of Slanderous Pasquils rayling falicies.[58]

While graver heads bemoaned their existence, the pot-poets themselves were delighted with the work. The outbreak of the Scottish crisis found one nearly bankrupt since 'his Poetry would not bring in enough to feede a Cat'. Afterwards his rhymes brought in three shillings a pamphlet and enough beer for a fortnight.[59] While the material rewards rarely made more serious poets envious, the mass audience was another matter. Acclaimed courtly authors again watched in disgust as the political crisis ensured that 'he who can best rayle, scoffe, and invent, / The greatest lyes, shall give the most content'. Compounding the aggravation was the hitherto novel enthusiasm of religious extremists, eager to prove that 'the Brethren can poetize'. For the literati, therefore, the only consolation was the thought that 'this wicked age must have a biting poet'.[60]

Equally revolutionary was the explosion in the printing trade. Tantalized by the possible profits, Henry Walker, an ironmonger, used his stock of andirons to bankroll what soon became a major publishing concern. By 1642 he boasted a backlist of 300 titles with a total print run of half a million pamphlets, which would 'goe neere (if it were laid sheet by sheet) to cover the whole Kingdome'. Such a vast enterprise necessitated a similar explosion in the retail end of the trade. Immediately after 1640, booksellers reportedly increased tenfold, but an even more striking illustration of the media revolution was the appearance of some five hundred 'mercuries', street-hawkers wandering through the town crying, 'Come buy a new booke, a new booke, newly come forth?'[61] Little wonder then that the massive size of the new industry became a pressing argument against the reimposition of printing controls; after all it employed 'many a poore man in London these dead times of trading'.[62]

The new environment terrified Laud – and with good reason. When a country gentleman rebuked a Londoner for criticizing the government, the citizen urged him to visit the metropolis where 'you shall see divers writings, yea, and Bookes printed, lying on many Booksellers Stals to be sold, that give them as bad language as I have done'. In response the gentleman denounced 'such Satyricall spirits', for such 'tart or bitter speeches … will occasion the readers, or hearers of them, either to hate their persons or jeere at them, or both'. Such an analysis was all too correct, as the archbishop quickly learned. Pamphleteers first encouraged schoolboys to greet the prelate with the cry, 'Give little Laud to the Divell'.[63] Then they urged the apprentices to sack Lambeth Palace, an outrage which they readily endorsed. Meanwhile actors mocked the prelate with a play celebrating his imprisonment.[64] In his greatest trial when apparently everyone, including James I's old court jester, turned on him, he found consolation in the fact 'it is not I alone that have endured … ridiculous pamphlets and ballads'.[65] His fellow bishops in general and Wren of Norwich in particular shared in the public opprobrium.[66] Loyal adherents of the Laudian regime also suffered, ranging from men like Dr Roane of the church courts to Dr Fuller, dean of Ely.[67] Even the symbols of the Church, from medieval crosses to organs, could not escape condemnation.[68] Nor was the pot-poet's contempt strictly ecclesiastical. A volley of 'lamentable Ballads' from 'the ragged Regiment of Poets' drove Secretary Windebacke and Lord Keeper Finch out of the country.[69] Their fate became the envy of many monopolists, who could not escape repeated poetic sallies.[70] As uncomfortable as their experiences were, all of these officials and clerics found some satisfaction in the knowledge that enemies merely wanted to humiliate them. The earl of Strafford, unfortunately for him, was not so lucky. Thus one pot-poet suggested that the archbishop's fate was bound up with that of the Lord Deputy; shortly before his death, the earl allegedly advised Laud that 'in conclusion there must be / A rope for you, an axe for me'.[71]

The systematic debasement of the regime's leading figures could well have been interpreted as the complete collapse of the royal government. Indeed, Whitehall was soon so deserted that the curious 'may pisse in the Porters Lodge, and never feare the losse of your Hat' and even sit on the Chaire of State 'and no body blacks your Eye'. Laud himself gave every indication that he felt himself alone in the face of 'so much hatred, and so many base libels, as have filled the streets against me, and such bitter revilings of me in print'. Yet in fact he and the rest of his colleagues had vocal and sometimes quite effective support. As in earlier crises, some poets were eager to defend beleaguered royal officials, who in turn were keen to encourage their efforts. 'Little Bookes or Ballads' thus quickly became 'a prime peece of policy of state'.[72] Consequently, while the archbishop may have felt himself the target of the media's almost unrelieved scorn, he was in fact caught in the crossfire between two increasingly well-defined sides.

The rapidly developing crisis found the government without a poetic champion. Early on, Scottish spies reported from the royal camp that 'old Iohnson the Poet being dead, great moane is made for one of that quality'. Although no one of his stature ever emerged, a mass of lesser poets none the less vied for the post. Furthermore, a handful like Thomas Herbert, Martin Parker and John Taylor even dispensed with the customary veil of anonymity, thus ensuring that they attracted some of the parliamentary fire. 'What', one poet asked these three, 'wilt thou again lament the losse of those dayes, wherein thou has attended the whole fry of famous whores?' Their contemptible work, another argued, only had value to those who need something either 'to stop vinegar bottles' or to accompany them in visits to 'Sir Ajax his Office'.[73] Such abuse left the nascent Royalists unfazed. Their most telling critic was simply 'some Poet to the short hair'd crew, / Who long since bid to honesty adue'. And while their opponents mocked their unworthiness as 'sons of Ben', they wheeled out the Elizabethan scourge of Puritans; thus forty years after his death, the ghost of Thomas Nashe returned to preside over the construction of the rudiments of the Royalist position. After all, his ghost proclaimed,

> It is as lawfull, for honnest [*sic*] men by either speaking or writing to make the malicious Facts and Acts of Knaves knowne, as it is for Knaves to slaunder and abuse honest men.[74]

As Nashe would have reminded the Royalists the most vulnerable point of their opponent's case was religion. However odd the Laudian church might appear, Laud's opponents could be made to look odder still. Consequently, no one invested too much in a detailed defence of Laud. Martin Parker simply argued against the common assumption that Laud was an agent of Rome, reminding his readers of 'what sad report / Papists may give of the High commission Court'. Even the prelate's most stalwart apologist, Thomas Herbert, announced that 'I shun his actions'.[75] A much easier means to defend Laud, Herbert and Parker recognized, was to go over to the offensive and to emphasize the lunacy of the brave new world of the Roundheads.

The construction of a schismatic 'other' allowed the merits of Laud and his fellow clerics to emerge in contrast. Against those who equated episcopacy with popery, one author set Foxe's *Book of Martyrs*. To jettison the bishops would be to break faith with 'Cranmer, Ridley, Reverend Latimer, / Good Bishop Hooker, zealous Bishop Farrar' and to shun those Elizabethan

> shining Starres,
> Who govern'd decently the Church, held warres
> With Antichrist, and knockt his triple Crowne
> to Hell.

Puritan critics purposed to abandon much more than tradition. In one tract, an extended recitation of the many colleges and hospitals which bishops had founded stunned a rabid anti-Laudian into silence.[76] The abolition of episcopacy would also seal off a traditional avenue of social mobility. Since episcopacy also represented a State Church with thousands of posts, dutiful fathers anxious about 'bringing up their Children', understandably balked at the prospect of no bishop, no parson and no college fellow. Given that the clerical reformation would soon become a social one, parents could scarcely send their sons into law, since 'Lawyers are so little regarded now adayes', one father advised another, 'that I feare before they can procure other men's Suites at Law, they'le want Suites to their owne Backs.' In addition, since the Puritans were intent on looting episcopal wealth 'for the filling of their [Puritan] Stomacks', then Church rates 'had more need to be increased then diminished'. Nor were sorely pressed parishioners likely to find any relief, for , as one poet reminded his readers, 'the politick Saints ... contemne the humble play / of trap, or footeball'.[77]

[291]

If this catalogue of fears failed to give contemporaries pause, then the description of Puritan horrors certainly would. Services would of course be incessant, since Puritans, one poet argued, would insist on nothing less than prayers 'nine times a day'. These would be conducted, not by a learned clergy, but rather by 'predicant Mechanicks' who favoured

> an odde kind of gesture in their Poopits [*sic*], vaporing and throwing heads, hands, and shoulders this way, and that way, puffing and blowing, grinning and gerning, shewing their teeth, and snuffling thorow their noses.[78]

Such antics at least distracted attention from the sermon itself. Thus one ignorant, albeit zealous, Puritan allegedly dubbed Ovid a saint; another made Morgan Llewllyn an ancient Greek author; while a third in a desperate attempt to make Laud's name add up to 666 got the sums wrong.[79] Yet this was only to be expected from men who, if not mad, were con-artists interested simply in 'Reverence, Money, Meate, Drinke, new suits and apparell, [and] the solace of a Sister'. This last charge was by then a hackneyed feature of anti-Puritan rhetoric, but few Royalists were willing to ignore wonderful material on 'Shee that will lie, yet sweares shee hates a lyer, / Except it be that man that will ly by her'. Over the entire unsavoury crew loomed the spectre of Dutch religious radicalism; hence the stock Puritan, if not Dutch, had at least spent enough time there so that their goal was 'to see Great Britaine turn's to Amsterdam', where 'mad sects are sent, / Who have Religion all in pieces Rent'.[80]

Armed with such broad brushes, poets and polemicists on both sides fashioned their respective positions. Thus polarization, which had been such a marked feature of the 'underground' media, facilitated the abrupt formation of two increasingly antithetical camps in the early 1640s. While most eagerly devoured the latest tracts and used them to re-enforce their initial predilections to lean to one side or the other, a few contemporaries correctly identified the critical role of these works in the sharp division of the realm. In the summer of 1642, Isaac Massy launched an impassioned plea for reconciliation and unity. Yet this was impossible, he conceded, unless his contemporaries 'An intermission make of rigid writing' and 'of much indighting'.[81]

Amid hundreds of tracts all intent in intensifying the quarrel, Massy's plea stuck a note of much needed sanity. Unfortunately, while practically everyone acknowledged his proposal's wisdom, they differed sharply over which kind of 'rigid writing' to suppress. 'There is nothing more congruent to the nourishing of division in a State of Commonwealth,' one writer insisted,

> then diversity of Rumors mixt with Falsity and Scandall, nothing more preiudiciall to a Kingdome ... then abusive Pamphletts ... then to have the same spread over the world on [illigible] obnoxious Papers.

Yet the echoes of Massy's plea quickly faded as it became clear that what the author particularly wanted to check was Royalist tracts. Likewise, another author denounced the woeful influence of 'the temporizing Poets' who 'have broached such imprudent scurrilty ... that the whole City is embroyled with nothing but incredible lyes'. These political versifiers, he lamented, had exacerbated, if not created, all of the realm's problems in 1642:

> what a base humour is this in you, Poeticall Needy-braines, who for a sordid gaine or desire to have the Style of a witty Raylor, will thus impoyson you pen, and puzzle your sterile pates inventing such sencelesse stigmaticke ballad Balderdash.[82]

Yet here again, comparisons with Massy's work fail; this time the author simply wanted to close down the parliamentary polemicists. So well developed had both sides become that they handily managed to co-opt pleas for comprehension.

IV

After enduring years of 'the Libelling, the Slanders and the base Usage that hath been put upon me', Laud could only conclude in 1644 that 'I am fallen into a great Obloquoy.' In the disaster which had befallen him, the only certainty was that 'never man hath ... been made so notorious a subject for ridiculous pamphlets and ballads'.[83] The archbishop's dramatic farewell stretched the truth a little. Certainly Cecil and Buckingham would have objected to Laud's claim to the title of *the* most abused public figure. Their critics' failure to make it into print did nothing to mitigate the ferocity of the literary firestorms which raged around them in the 'underground' media. This point merits careful consideration, given recent arguments about the fundamentally consensual nature of early Stuart political culture. Parliament men, Conrad Russell has maintained, regarded division as an anathema; pending the arrival of Montesquieu, they were psychologically unable to imagine, much less employ, polarized language.[84] Likewise, Kevin Sharpe has argued against the notion of sharp polarities within early Stuart culture. Rather, contemporary criticism was easily contained within the complimentary conventions of the 'mundus politicus'.[85]

The brilliance of both arguments is undeniable. So too is the fact that both are based on a blinkered view of the evidence. As befits a 'high' political historian, Russell is at his most unconvincing once he steps out of the Palace of Westminster. His uneasiness can be seen in one of his rare forays outdoors to conduct a 'cursory exam' or the seditious words which he could find, with the help of the index, in the *Calendar of State Papers Domestic*; he uncovered only 'occasional hints'.[86] Had he examined the 'underground' poems, he would have found plenty of words that the regime found seditious. He would also have uncovered a world starkly different from that of Parliament, one which enshrined and institutionalized conflict, the more virulent the better.

Therefore there is no profound mystery about how contemporaries slipped so easily to violent confrontations in the early 1640s. Only a cursory examination of the pot-poets illustrates that conflict and seditious words were as English as kidney pie.

The same problem undercuts Sharpe's conclusions. Only in passing, and after 1640, does he employ manuscript verse; the implication seems to be that these were simply the development of the Scottish crisis. The danger of this assumption can be seen in his extended review of drama, poetry, diaries and newsletters. In the end, he found nothing seriously hostile which could not be reconciled to the regime. Yet had he broadened his examination, he might well have been less confident about his conclusion. By carefully focussing on what was available on booksellers' shelves, he cast a blind eye towards the less seemly material under the counter. Thus he missed the extended obituaries on Buckingham, the controversies over the 1629 session and its martyrs, the protracted mourning over Gustavus Adolphus and, above all, a veritable explosion of anti-Puritan verse. All of this is hard to imagine within the vaunted Caroline 'mundus politicus'. Aurelian Townshend damaged a budding career at court with an eulogy for the Swedish king which some at court found excessive.[87] Given his experience, it is impossible to see how the court's alleged tolerance could stretch to include, for example, the pot-poet who presided over the ritual sodomization of Buckingham's niece.

The historiographical significance of this neglected genre extends beyond these corrections. It suggests another, equally neglected, cause of the Civil War. Of late, explanations have tended to focus almost completely on the 'high' politics of Whitehall and Westminster. Without question, this new interest has produced a series of splendid works which have done much to sharpen our hitherto fuzzy understanding of the early Stuart elite. It has also generated nagging doubts that the recent interest in history from the top down might well have led us to lose sight of equally important changes taking place elsewhere in early Stuart England. The most important of these, I suggest, was the emergence of popular political awareness.

Compared to what went on a century later, politics in the Tudor age was a parlour game played by a comparatively small elite. Royal ministers generally found the House of Commons a pliant institution ready enough to defer to the government bench.[88] It is of course a commonplace that if subsequent generations of Parliament men had run true to form, the new Stuart monarchs would have found their new English possession decidedly less vexing. Yet behind this truism lies a profound question: what had changed to make the English less biddable? Religious controversies and growing social pressure plainly did much to disrupt the Tudor status quo. But there was another major agent of change which scholars would do well to remember – the prose, and particularly the poetry, of the 'underground' media. Thanks to the 'pot-poets' and the Pauls' walkers, the political crises of the early seventeenth century became crude adult education courses in contemporary politics, from which a rapidly growing percentage of the population graduated. From carefully observing politics, it was only a small step to participating in it. And for the toddlers of the expanding political nation, there was no more potent encouragement than the starkly binary political vision, which was available first in manuscript and then after 1640 in print.

The significance of the new political awareness emerges quite sharply when set against recent assessments of Charles I. Never particularly high, his ratings have of late plunged through the floor with some historians arguing that the Civil War is impossible to imagine without such an inept monarch. Over this point debate has recently been furious and doubtless will continue to rage for some time. Yet before abandoning the entire question as an insoluble enigma, it is worth considering whether the culprit was the declining quality of royal leadership or a rapidly changing political universe. If political culture underwent a fundamental transformation in the early seventeenth century, then it stands to reason that *any* monarch might well have had trouble in mid-century, even one of those formidable Tudors to whom Charles is so often compared unflatteringly.

The only means of testing this notion, it must be conceded, is to break the obsession with elite politics, which has gripped the field for the past two decades. This is not to argue for the wholesale abandonment of 'high' politics. Plainly, the recent work in this area has immeasurably improved our appreciation of the period, and more work in a similar mode needs to be done. Yet it is arguably now time to begin the task of setting our more sophisticated understanding of the centre against a broader context. There are, I submit, fewer broader and more promising avenues, down which political and social historians can amble, than that of political culture. To do otherwise is to remain baffled at a powerful archbishop's alarm over a few rude couplets.

Notes

A version of this essay was presented at the American Historical Association conference in January 1994; for their comments there, I am obliged to Richard Cust, Ann Hughes, Peter Lake and Rachel Weil. For their help with subsequent revisions, I would like to thank Alistair Bellany, Christopher Hill and Mark Summers.

[1] Laud to Strafford, 28 May and (August) 1637, *The Works of ... William Laud* (Oxford, 1860), vol. VII, pp. 349 and 371–2; and 28 August 1637, *The Earl of Strafforde's Letters and Dispatches* (London, 1740), vol. II, p. 99.

[2] Diary entries for 7 July and 23, 25 and 29 August, *Works* vol. III, pp. 228–9.

[3] Laud to Strafford, (August), 7 October and 16 November 1637, *Works*, vol. VII, pp. 371–2, 373 and 385; and Strafford to Laud, 28 August 1637, *Letters and Dispatches*, vol. II, p. 99.

[4] Thankfully this situation is changing. For more notable examples, see Richard Cust, 'New and politics in early seventeenth-century England', *Past and Present*, 112

(1986), pp. 60–90; Pauline Croft, 'The reputation of Robert Cecil: libels, political opinions and popular awareness in the early seventeenth century', *Transactions of the Royal Historical Society*, 6th series, 1 (1993), pp. 43–70; and Alastair Bellany, ' "Raylinge rymes and vaunting verse": libellous politics in early Stuart England, 1603–1628', in K. Sharpe and P. Lake (eds.), *Culture and Politics in Early Stuart England* (Stanford, 1994), pp. 285–310.

⁵ T. J., *The Christian Souldier* (London, 1642), Thomason Tracts (henceforth TT), E.114 (4), p. 3

⁶ W. W. Greg, *A Companion to Arber* (Oxford, 1967), p. 49. See also, Alvin Kernan, *Cankered Muse* (New Haven, 1959), pp. 81–2.

⁷ Thomas Bastard, 'Ad reginam Elizabethan', *Chrestoleros* (London, 1598), p. 148; and Everard Guiplin, *Skialetheia* (1598), ed. D. A. Carroll (Chapel Hill, 1974).

⁸ Whitgift's 1597 letter in Strype, *Whitgift* (London, 1822), vol. II. p. 387, quoted in G. R. Hibbard, *Thomas Nashe: a Critical Introduction* (Cambridge, MA, 1962), pp. 19–48.

⁹ Guilpin, *Skialetheia* (1598), p. 61; and Thomas Dekker, *The Guls Horne-booke* (1609), in A. Grosart (ed.), *The Non-Dramatic Works of Thomas Dekker*, (London, 1885), vol. II, p. 240.

¹⁰ Bastard, 'In Libellum', *Chrestoleros*, p. 70; and Joseph Hall, 'Of the Male-content', *Heaven upon Earth* and *Characters of Vertues and Vices*, ed. Rudolf Kirk (New Brunswick, 1948), p. 179.

¹¹ *The Whipper of the Satyre his Pennance* (London, 1601), sig. [A2]; W. I., *The Whipping of Satyre* (London, 1601), sig. [C6v] and E4; and [Star Chamber speeches] [1599], SP 12/273/35.

¹² John Marston, 'To him that hath perused mee', *The Scourge of Villanie* (London, 1599) [sig. 13].

¹³ W. I. *The Whipping of the Satyre*, sig. A2.

¹⁴ Bastard, Dedication, *Chrestoleros* [sig. A4].

¹⁵ C. H. Firth, 'Ballad history of the reign of Henry VII and Henry VIII'; and 'Ballad History of ... the late Tudors', *Transactions of Royal Historical Society*, 3rd series, vol. II, pp. 21–50; and vol. II, pp. 51–124. For an example of student verses, see Gabriel Harvey, *Marginalia*, ed. G. C. Moore Smith (Stratford, 1913).

¹⁶ Thomas Dekker, *Lanthorne and Candle-Light* (1609), *The Non-Dramatic Works*, vol. III, p. 178; and Sir Thomas Overbury, 'A Rymer', *The Miscellaneous Works*, ed. E. F. Rimbault (London, 1890), p. 151.

¹⁷ *A True Description of the Pot-Companion Poet* (London, 1642), TT E.143 (6), sig. A2; John Davies of Hereford, 'Against Dacus the pott-Poet', *The Scourge of Folly* (London 1611), p. 8; and I. W., *The Whipping of the Satyre*, sig. [C5v].

¹⁸ Sir John Harrington, 'A Comfort for poore Poets', *Letters and Epigrams of Sir John Harrington*, ed. N. E. McClure (Philadelphia, 1930), p. 164.

¹⁹ 'Sir Sackville Crowes Booke of Accomptes', B.L., Add. 12, 528, fo.15v.

²⁰ Preface, *Musarum Deliciae*, ed. E. Dubois (London, 1817), vol. I, pp. ix–x; and *Poems, Songs, etc., on George Duke of Buckingham*, ed. F. Fairholt (London, 1850), p. 1, note.

²¹ 'Upon the Lord Chancellor Bacons stinking breath', Nottingham University Library (henceforth NUL), Portland MSS, PwV 3, unfoliated.

²² For Harrington's original poem, see 'Of certain puritan wenches', *Letters and Epigrams*, p. 292; and for the altered version, see 'The conference of 6 puritanical

wenches', Folger Shakespeare Library, V.a. 345, p. 43. On Mr Prick, see also 'Upon Mr Prick', Houghton Library, Eng 686, fo. 34.

²³ 'Heaven Blesse King James', Bienecke Library, Osborn b197 [Alston Commonplace Book], pp. 186–8; and Fairholt, pp. 1–4.

²⁴ Edward Browne, *Sir James Cambels Clarks Disaster* (London, 1642), TT E.122 (22), pp. 7–8.

²⁵ *A True Description of the Pot-Companion Poet*, TT E.143 (6), sig. [A2v]–[A3]; and *A Good Wish for England* (London, 1641), TT 669f4 (40).

²⁶ Report on Holder et al *v.* Lee, 29 November 1634, Harvard Law School, LMS 1128, fo. 87. For examples of other poems set to music, see 'A proper new songe [on the signing of the Anglo-French marriage treaty, December 1624]'; and 'A Song [on social divisions in London taverns]', Bienecke Library, b197, pp. 53–5 and 43–4.

²⁷ J. H. Adamson and H. F. Holland, *The Shepherd of the Ocean* (Boston, 1969), pp. 437–442; and earl of Strafford, 'An Ellegy written by himselfe', *The true Copie of the three last Letters* (London, 1641), TT E.170 (6), sig. [A3–A3v]. For the suicide note in verse, see T. S., *The Arminian Haltered* (London, 1641), TT E.166 (9), pp. 5–6.

²⁸ 'Sir Francis Mitchell Appllogie for himselfe', B.L. Harleian 158, fos. 219–62; and *Diary of John Rous*, ed. M. A. Green (London, 1856), p. 77.

²⁹ John Davies of Hereford, 'To Mr Thomas Bastard and the Reader', *The Scourge of Folly* (London, 1611), p. 20; and Abraham Holland, 'A Continued Inquisition against Paper-persecuters', in Davies, *Scourge* (London, 1624), p. 81.

³⁰ Thomas Dekker, *The Dead Terme* (1608), in *The Non-Dramatic Works*, vol. III, p. 51.

³¹ *The Diary of John Rous* (London, 1856), p. 109.

³² *The Commons Petition of Long Afflicted England* (London, 1642), TT E.132 (31); variant edition (London, 1642), TT E.137 (15); and *The Humble Petition of the Wretched and most contemptible, the poore Commons of England* (London, 1642), TT E.108 (1).

³³ Anonymous note, University of London Library, MS 285, opening page.

³⁴ Garrard to Strafford, 9 October 1637, *Dispatches and Letters*, vol. II, p. 114.

³⁵ Mead to Stuteville, 23 January 1627, B.L. Harleian 390, fo. 181; and the poem itself, fo. 182. For examples of other verses, see fos. 186 and 249; and *The Letters of John Chamberlain* vol. II, pp. 427, 518, 523 and 532.

³⁶ Chantrell to Barrington, [1621], BL Egerton 2644, fo. 192. See also *The Barrington Letters*, ed. Arthur Searle (London, 1983), pp. 255.

³⁷ See for example, 'the case of the fidlers of Staines', Michaelmas 1627, Star Chamber Reports, B.L. Lansdowne 607, fo. 93v.

³⁸ Cited in Croft, 'The reputation of Robert Cecil', pp. 47, 49, 51 and 55.

³⁹ *Poems and Songs … of Buckingham*, pp. 10, 19, 21, 24, 32, 48 and 52.

⁴⁰ 'A libell of Ireland', Portland MSS, NUL, PwV 2, pp. 143–5.

⁴¹ *The diary of Simonds D'Ewes*, ed. E. Bourchier (Paris, 1974), pp. 122–3; and Thomas Dekker, *The Guls Horne-booke* (1609), in *The Non-Dramatic Works*, vol. II, pp. 243 and 253.

⁴² Examination, 27 April 1626, B.L. Add. MS 38,855, fo. 68–68v; and report on Gill and Grinkin, 7 November 1628, Harvard Law School, LMS 1128, fo. 16.

⁴³ Rogers to Scudamore, 23 July 1623, B.L. Add. MS 11,043, fo. 67; and 'the case of fidlers of Staines', Michaelmas 1627, BL Lansdowne 607, fo. 93v.

⁴⁴ See for example, Harrington, *Letters and Epigrams*; Sir John Stradling, *Beati*

Pacifici (London, 1623); *The English and Latin Poems of Sir Robert Ayton*, ed. C. B. Gullan (Edinburgh, 1963); and *The Poems of Richard Corbett*, ed. J. A. W. Bennett and H. R. Trevor-Roper, (Oxford, 1955).

⁴⁵ 'The wiper of the peoples teares', *The Poems of James VI of Scotland*, ed. James Craigie (Edinburgh, 1958), p. 183.

⁴⁶ 'By Prince Charles upon Mistress Diana Cecil', Houghton Library, English MS 703, p. 77.

⁴⁷ *The Works of Sir John Suckling*, ed. Thomas Clayton (Oxford, 1971); *The Poetical Works of Sir John Denham*, ed. T. H. Banks (New Haven, 1928); *The Poems of Thomas Carew*, ed. Rhodes Dunlap (Oxford, 1949); and *The Shorter Poems of Sir William Davenant*, ed. A. M. Gibbs (Oxford, 1972).

⁴⁸ William Lewis, 'A Defence to the Answer made for the Lord Bacon', Huntington Library, HM 198, pp. 134–6; 'Verses in defence of the late action on the Ile of Ree', Bodleian Library, Carte 77, fo. 328v; and 'In Answer of an Elegicall Letter', *Poems of Thomas Carew*, p. 77.

⁴⁹ 'Certaine Verses made when my Lord Cooke was made highe sheriffe of Buckingham', B.L. Add. MS 15,226, fo. 22v–24; 'Against the Opposing the Duke in Parliament in 1628', *The Poems of Richard Corbett*, pp. 82–3; and 'The copy of the Duke's Grace's most excellent rodomontade', in *Proceedings in Parliament, 1628* (New Haven, 1983), vol. V, pp. 243–5; and William Davenant, 'To him who Prophecy'd a Succesles end of the Parliament in the Year 1630', *The Shorter Poems and Songs*, ed. A. M. Gibbs (Oxford, 1972), pp. 123–4.

⁵⁰ *The Scots Scouts Discoveries* (London, 1642), TT E.153 (22), pp. 30 and 43–4. For similar examples, see also *Vox Borealis* (London, 1641), TT E.177 (5); and C. H. Firth, 'Ballads on the bishops' wars, 1638–1640', *Scottish Historical Review*, 3 (1906), pp. 257–73.

⁵¹ John Bond, *The Poets Recantation* (London, 1642), TT E.142 (13), pp. 1 and 5–6.

⁵² Laud to Johnson, 26 June 1640, *Works*, vol. VII, p. 603; *Canterbury's Will* (London, 1641), TT E.156 (5), p. 4; and *The History of the Troubles and Trial*, in *Works*, vol. III, pp. 445–6.

⁵³ *St. Hilliaries Teares Shed upon All Professions* (London, 1642), TT E.151 (16), pp. 3–4 and 6.

⁵⁴ *Mr Hampdens Speech occasioned upon the Londoners Petition* (London, 1642), TT 66986 (122); and *A Remonstrance of London Occurrences* (London, 1642), TT E.153 (5), sig. A2, [A2v] and [A4].

⁵⁵ *A disputation betwixt the Devil and the Pope* (London, 1642), TT E.132 (8), sig. [A3v]; and 'Upon the Valiant Collonell that beshitt himself', [1642], Huntington Library, El 8795.

⁵⁶ *An Elegie Upon the Death of ... Gustavus Adolphus* (n.p., (1641?), TT f669 (1); *Leycester's Ghost* (n.p., 1641), TT E.197 (3); and *The Dolefull Lamentations of Cheapside Crosse* (London, 1641), TT E.134 (9), p. 3.

⁵⁷ *A True Description of the Pot-Companion Poet* (London, 1642), sig. A2.

⁵⁸ Owen Dogerell, *A Brief Dialogue* (London, 1641), TT E.140 (5); *The Downfall of Temporizing Poets*, p. 1; and Martin Parker, *The Poet's Blind Mans Bough* (London, 1641), sig. [A3].

⁵⁹ *Taylors Physicke Has Purged the Divel* (London, 1641), TT E.163 (9), sig. [A2v]; and *A True Description*, sig. [A2v].

⁶⁰ Parker, *The Poets Blind Mans Bough*, sig. [A4v]; *Newes from Pauls* (London,

1642), TT E.126 (17), p. 5; and opening epigram, *Fortunes Tennis-ball* (London 1640).

⁶¹ John Taylor, *The Whole Life and Progresse of Henry Walker Ironmonger* (London, 1642), TT E.154 (29), sig. [Av]–A2; *A Cluster of Coxcombes* (London, 1642), TT E.154 (49), sig. [A4]; and *The Downfall of Temporizing Poets* (London, 1641), TT E.165 (5), p. 2.

⁶² *Sions Charity Towards Her Foes in Misery* (London, 1641), TT E.158 (13), p. 5. See also Wentworth's remarks on the mercuries in *A Description of the Passage of ... Strafford over the River of Styx* (London, 1641), TT E.156 (21), sig. [A4–A4v].

⁶³ *Sions Charity Towards Her Foes in Misery*, TT E.158 (13), pp. 3–4; and *Canterbury's Will* (London, 1641), TT E.156 (5), p. 3. On Laud, see also *Farewell Myter, or Canterburies Mediations* (London, 1641), TT E.134 (33); A. B., *A Canterbury Tale* (London, 1641), TT E.168 (5); *Canterburie Pilgrimage* (London, 1641), TT E.172 (28); and Richard Overton, *New Lambeth Faire* (London, 1642), TT E.128 (26).

⁶⁴ *A Second Message to Mr William Laud* (London, 1641), TT E.169 (9); and *A New Play called Canterburie his Change of Diet* (London, 1641), TT E.177 (8). On the attack, see Laud to Conway, 19 June 1640, *Works*, vol. VII, pp. 601–2; and Castle to Bridgewater, 12 May 1640, Huntington Library, EL 7833.

⁶⁵ Laud to the Vice-Chancellor of Oxford, [1640s], *Works*, vol. VI, p. 597; and [Archy Armstrong], *Archy's Dream* (London, 1641), TT E.173 (5).

⁶⁶ *The Bishops Last Good Night* (London, 1641), TT 669f4 (6); *The Wrens Nest Defild* (London, 1641), TT 165 (14); *A Rot Amongst the Bishops* (London, 1641), TT E.1102 (4); *The Bishops Downfall* (London 1641), TT E.181 (42); *The Prentices Prophecie of the Centainty of the Bishops destruction* (London, 1642), TT E.132 (4); *The Apprentices Advice to the XII Bishops* (London, 1642), TT E.131 (10); *A Shrove-Tuesday Banquet Sent to the Bishops* (London, 1641), TT E.135 (1); and *The Decoy Duck* (London, 1642), TT E.132 (35).

⁶⁷ *A Letter from Rhoan in France* (London, 1641), TT E.164 (6); and *The Petition and Articles ... against Dr Fuller* (London, 1641), TT E.175 (1).

⁶⁸ *The Organs Eccho* (London, 1641), TT 669f4 (32); *The Organs Funerall* (London, 1642), TT E.141 (6); *The Dolefull Lamentations of Cheap-side Crosse* (London, 1641), TT E.134 (9); *The Remarkable Funeral of Cheapside-Crosse* (London, 1641), TT E.132 (38); *A Dialogue betweene the Crosse in Cheap and Charing Crosse* (London, 1641), TT E.238 (9).

⁶⁹ *Times Alteration* (London, 1641), TT 669f4 (4).

⁷⁰ *Bishops, Iudges, Monopolists* (n.p., (1640?), TT E.171 (2); *The Frogges of Egypt* (London, 1641), TT E.166 (2); *Hogs Caracter [sic] of a Projector* (London, 1642), TT E.155 (8); *The Projectors Down-fall* (London, 1642), TT E.140 (22); and *A Pack of Patentees Opened* (London, 1641), TT E.163 (5).

⁷¹ *The Discontented Conference betwixt the Two Great Associates* (London, 1642), TT E.157 (3), sig. A2.

⁷² *A Deep Sigh Breathd Through the Lodgings at White-Hall* (London, 1642), TT E.119 (30), sig. [A2v]; and 'History of the Troubles', *Works* vol. III, p. 417; and *The Scots Scouts Discoveries*, p. 32.

⁷³ *The Scots Scouts Discoveries*, p. 30; *An Answer to as Foolish Pamphlet* (London, 1641), TT E.160 (15), p. 3; and *Mercuries Message Defended* (London, 1641), TT E.160 (13), p. 2.

⁷⁴ Thomas Herbert, *An Answer to ... Mercuries Message* (London, 1641), TT E.157 (7), p. 3; and *Tom Nash His Ghost* (London, 1642), TT E.110 (5), p. 6.

[75] Martin Parker, *The Poet's Blind Mans Bough* (London, 1641), TT E.172 (6), title-page and sig. [A4v]; and Thomas Herbert, *An Answer to ... Mercuries Message* (London, 1641), TT E.157 (7), pp. 4–5.

[76] *An Apology for Bishops* (London, 1641), TT E.167 (12), pp. 2–3; and H. P., *Square Caps Turned into Round-Heads* (London, 1642), TT E.149 (1), pp. 5–8.

[77] *The Country-Mans Care and the Citizens Feare* (London, 1641), TT E.179 (8), p. 6; and *The Resolution of the Roundheads* (London, 1642), TT E.132 (39), sig. [A3v]; and A. C. Generous, *A satyre against Seperatists* (London, 1642), TT E.126 (28), pp. 5–6.

[78] Owen Dogerell, *A Brief Dialogue*, sig [A4v]; and Richard Carter, *The Schismatick Stigmatized* (London, 1641), TT E.179 (14), p. 7.

[79] John Taylor, *A Swarme of Secretaries and Schismatiques* (London, 1641), TT E.158 (1), p. 20; [John Taylor], *A Full and Compleat Answer against ... A Tale in a Tub* (London, 1642), TT E.141 (9), p. 4; and Parker, *The Poets Blind Mans Bough*, sig. B2.

[80] H. P., *Square Caps*, p. 4; 'The Holy-Sisters Character', in *A Puritane Set Forth in His Lively Colours* (London, 1642), TT E.113 (11), p. 6; and John Taylor, *Mad Fashions, Od Fashions, All Out of Fashions* (London, 1642), TT E.138 (30), sig. [A3v].

[81] Isaac Massy, *Midsummers Prognostication of Pacification* (London, 1642), TT E.153 (11), p. 5.

[82] *A Presse Full of Pamphlets* (London, 1642), TT E.142 (9), sig. A2–[A2v]; and J. B., *The Poets Knavery Discovered, in all their lying Pamphlets* (London, [1642]), TT E.135 (11), sig. A2 and [A4].

[83] Speech at his trial, 1644, John Rushworth, *Historical Collections*, V, p. 776; and Laud to the Vice-Chancellor of Oxford [1643], *Works*, vol. VI, p. 597.

[84] Conrad Russell, *Politics and English Politics, 1621–1629* (Oxford, 1979), pp. 1–26; and 'The nature of a Parliament in early Stuart England', in H. Tomlinson (ed.), *Before the English Civil War* (London, 1983), pp. 123–50.

[85] Kevin Sharpe, *The Personal Rule of Charles I* (New Haven, 1992), p. 953 and *passim*; and *Criticism and Compliment* (Cambridge, 1986).

[86] Russell, *The Causes of the Civil War* (Oxford, 1990), pp. 8–9.

[87] Sharpe, *Personal Rule*, pp. 644–730; and 'Elegy on the death of the King of Sweden', *The Poems and Masques of Aurelian Townshend*, ed. Cedric Brown (Reading, 1983), pp. 48–9.

[88] G. R. Elton, *The Parliament of England, 1559–1581* (Cambridge, 1986); Elton, 'Parliament', *The Reign of Elizabeth I* (London, 1984), pp. 79–100; and M. A. R. Graves, 'Managing Elizabethan Parliaments', *The Parliaments of Elizabethan England* (Oxford, 1990), pp. 37–64.

13

'Wit in a Roundhead': the dilemma of Marchamont Nedham

Blair Worden

I

There have been few kind words for Marchamont Nedham, the principal journalist of Cromwellian England. While the panache and nimbleness of his prose have attracted admiration of a kind, his political opportunism, and his untiring reversals of political allegiance, have disconcerted past and present alike. Writing for the Long Parliament during the first Civil War and for the king in the second, then for the republic of 1649–53, then for the Cromwellian protectorate, then for the restored republic, and finally for the restored monarchy, he was uniform only in his willingness to sell or lend his pen to the prevailing power. Yet Nedham has larger claims on the attention of posterity than it has granted him: claims as large as those made by Peter Thomas, in a fine study,[1] for the Royalist newswriter Sir John Berkenhead, Nedham's rival in the first Civil War and his ally in the second. With Berkenhead, Nedham helped to shape the first age of journalism. The collapse of censorship in 1640, and the controversies of the civil wars, opened a market for newsbooks which the two men, better than any of their contemporaries, learned how to address. In doing so, they confronted the relationship of journalism to more traditional and less popular or ephemeral literary forms. Both men had high ambitions for their prose. Both were also poets and companions of poets. Yet it was in addressing a wide audience that they made their principal marks.

Berkenhead's career is a model of constancy. He was loyal to the Stuart cause in its darkest hours. Nedham's career is a model of inconstancy. He repeatedly found himself writing for politicians whom he had earlier betrayed, insulted or reviled. The readiness of those politicians to employ or re-employ him shows the importance, to Roundheads and Cavaliers alike, of the control of public opinion. So does the readiness with which successive parties and regimes were willing to sanction, from his pen, arguments more pragmatic and less elevated than those with which they justified their actions to themselves. Politicians needed him on their side. They dreaded the hostility of a writer who amply earned his motto: '*Nemo me impune lacessit.*'

Nedham may be important not only in spite of his mutability but because of it. He discovered, amidst the polarizations of the Puritan Revolution and the conflicting claims of oath and allegiance made by the groups which successively dominated it, that the very insincerities of journalism may protect a writer's independence of voice. A writer on temporary and provisional terms with the beliefs he professes may be a more intelligent observer of rapid changes of political fortune than the inflexible partisan. The ideals and hatreds of the Puritan Revolution produced some rigid postures and numb slogans. Nedham adopted the postures and slogans but thought beyond them. He is the first of a series of writers – Henry Stubbe and John Toland are his most obvious successors – who find a consistent identity in the adoption of external inconsistencies. Born in 1620, and so too young to share the scarring political emotions of the ensuing decade,[2] he found, as did others of his generation, that the party lines of the 1640s did not correspond to his own feelings. Again like others of his generation, he learned to survive in a conflict that was not of his making. His opportunism, like Stubbe's and Toland's, was intellectual as well as political. Stubbe penetrated the religious orthodoxy of Charles II's reign and moved towards deism. Toland penetrated both the religious and the political orthodoxies of the years after 1688 and moved towards deism and republicanism. Nedham moved beyond Roundhead and Cavalier orthodoxies alike. In doing so he made a pioneering and decisive contribution not only to the early history of journalism but to the history of political thought: particularly to the tradition of republican thought that Toland would revive.

Nedham's fame rests chiefly on the material he wrote as editor of three weekly newsbooks: *Mercurius Britanicus*, the leading parliamentary newsbook of the first Civil War: *Mercurius Pragmaticus*, the leading Royalist newsbook of the late 1640s; and *Mercurius Politicus*, the leading newsbook of the successive regimes of the 1650s. In each of those publications he had only limited room for manoeuvre. He had to toe a party line and please a publisher. Accepting those limits as facts of life, he tested and stretched them to the full. Nedham is the supreme literary brinkman of the Puritan Revolution. In every period of his career he found ways of saying things that must have troubled or angered his employers. Sometimes, by boldly declaring a controversial view, he overstepped the limits and incurred retribution or admonition, though he was rarely kept from favour for long. Sometimes, by ostensibly respectful references to his obligations to his employers, he contrived to indicate that his views might differ from theirs.[3] More often he achieved individuality of expression through a sideways glance or a choice of emphasis or a parenthetical or interlinear comment. His very brinkmanship gave his newsbooks much of their character and (we may suppose) of their appeal. His backers (we may suppose) took the point.

Nedham wrote under the pressures of time and space that journalism imposes. He learned to know what to leave out, a requirement that can tax the more committed writer. Even so, the editing and writing of newsbooks never satisfied his ambition. Though he seems to have hoped that his news-books would last and would immortalize the events they described,[4] he yearn-ed to write 'treatises' which would develop his arguments at more length and earn him a proper respect. Repeatedly he chafed at pressures of space, which imposed 'brevity' and restricted the 'instances' or 'examples' that could be adduced in support of his views. He would allude proudly to the 'collections' of notes that could give more authority to arguments he was constrained to submit in 'a few pages weekly'.[5] In 1645, concluding a series of editorial com-mentaries that had constituted the most significant contribution of *Britanicus* to political thought, he regretted that his 'pains' might prove of little value, since they had been committed to 'a poor inconsiderable pamphlet, the very name whereof is enough to raise a prejudice upon any other notions, how rea-sonable soever they be'; for 'serious truth' is 'not regarded in a pamphlet'.[6] Nedham did write 'treatises', which gave him more room, if to his mind never enough. Yet most of them, like his newsbooks, were works of propaganda. Though sometimes aimed at a narrower or more learned audience than his newsbooks, they relied for their effectiveness on a brisk style that eschewed complexities. Nedham's strength was as a synthesizer or simplifier rather than as an originator of ideas.[7] But he did see how to put ideas to original use.

He wrote more treatises than has been realized.[8] A number of them were anonymous. He helps us to identify them by his distinctive habits of style and content. He helps us too by his fondness for recycling his material, a feature of his prose that could take mischievous forms. In 1650 he informed his read-ers of his conversion from his Royalism of the previous three years to the regime that had sanctioned the regicide. 'I confess', he wrote airily, 'that for a time I was of an opinion contrary to what is here written, till some causes made me reflect with an impartial eye upon the affairs of this new govern-ment.'[9] The passage would reappear almost *verbatim* in a work with which he hailed the Restoration.[10] There are other moments too when, confronted by Nedham's inconsistency, we have to rub our eyes. Who was he, in 1676 (two years before his death), to attack the earl of Shaftesbury – who was almost exactly Nedham's contemporary – for his readiness to 'shift principles like shirts and quit an unlucky side in a fright at the noise of a new prevail-ing party'?[11] Arguments advanced by Nedham in the Roundhead cause were spurned by him in the Cavalier one. Roundhead leaders whom he hailed as heroes of the first Civil War became the butt of merciless satire by him in the second. The historical illustrations with which he liked to support his theses proved one thing in his Cavalier prose, another in his Roundhead prose, his arguments turning (as it were) on their footnotes to meet each change of alle-giance.

The breeziness with which Nedham liked to announce those changes con-

cealed the dangers under which he wrote. He took great risks. Sometimes he
did so to avoid greater ones. Sometimes he surrendered prudence to a love of
publicity.[12] Journalists on the opposing side marked him out as a candidate
for the death-sentence once their cause had prevailed. In the 1640s they proposed 'a rope for *Britanicus*': in 1660 they urged 'a rope for *Pol[iticus]*'.[13] His
Royalist writing in 1649, according to Anthony Wood, brought him 'into
danger of his life'.[14] His changes of side provoked bitter accusations of apostasy and venality. Yet his mutations never seem to have troubled his conscience. Did he have a conscience? Did he have principles? Or did he agree
with his friend and drinking-companion Henry Oxinden, who viewed the
contemporary world in terms of Machiavellian duplicity and regarded 'the art
of dissimulation' as essential to survival in it? Oxinden urged that a man
should be 'not startled nor troubled chameleon-like, as the necessity of occasion serves, to turn into all shapes. For the most constant men must be content to change their resolutions according to the alterations of time. Paul
himself became all things to all men.'[15]

We cannot know the terms on which Nedham lived with himself. But two
things we can say. First, his mutability was not the only impressive or interesting thing about him. He was, acknowledged Wood, 'a person endowed
with quick natural parts, was a good humanitarian, poet and boon droll; and
had he been constant to his Cavaliering principles, would have been beloved
by, and admired of, all'.[16] 'As a satiric poet', claims his biographer, 'Nedham
at his best is Dryden's equal.'[17] He kept cultivated company. There were the
Cavalier wits and poets who collaborated with him in the late 1640s. There
was Andrew Marvell, beside whom we often find him. And there was a still
greater figure, John Milton. Edward Phillips, Milton's nephew, called
Nedham a 'particular friend' of the poet. Anthony Wood, less amicably,
called him 'a great crony' of Milton.[18] So even if Nedham was a mercenary
hack, there must also have been something more attractive about him than
that.

The second thing we can say has a closer bearing on what follows.
Nedham's thought, amidst its flagrant inconsistencies, has its consistent patterns. While he can adopt almost any political voice, some voices come more
easily to him, and carry more conviction from him, than others. On Parliament's side he writes more happily as a critic of the king or of monarchy than
as a champion of Puritanism. On the Crown's side, both in the late 1640s and
after 1660, he writes more happily as a critic of Puritanism, and as a defender
of the cultural values to which Puritanism is opposed, than as a friend to the
king's prerogative or to the Church of England. Anti-Puritan republicanism,
the position which – amidst so much that contradicts it – we can watch growing in his writings of the 1640s and flowering in those of the 1650s, is an
underestimated force in the Puritan Revolution. It acquired its momentum in
spite of, perhaps even because of, the extent to which its adherents knew their
ideas to be eccentric to the main movements of the age. It was as the

spokesman for such men that Nedham produced, in the early 1650s, some of his most vital and incisive writing.

To that writing we shall come at the end of this essay. I have written elsewhere about Nedham's place in the republican movement of the 1650s.[19] I hope to write elsewhere about his relations with the leading poets of his age, Milton and Marvell (see n.272). Here I shall write about the Nedham of the years 1643–51: the Nedham who writes for the Roundhead cause in the first Civil War, deserts it afterwards, and then returns to it following the regicide.

II

Marchamont (or Marchmont) Nedham (or Needham: the surname should be pronounced, I think, so as virtually to rhyme with 'freedom'[20]) was born at Burford in Gloucestershire, into a family of some substance in the town. After studying at All Souls, Oxford, and obtaining a B.A. in 1637, he became an usher or assistant teacher at Merchant Taylor's School. The experience would leave him with a long-standing interest in teaching, and a long-standing grievance about its levels of pay.[21] In 1640 he found other employment, as a clerk at Gray's Inn. Then, in 1643, journalism gave him his chance.

From August 1643 to May 1646 there ran, with only occasional interruptions, the best-selling of the weekly parliamentary newsbooks, *Mercurius Britanicus*. In its prime it sold – it has been estimated – between 750 and 1,000 copies a week[22] – and was evidently seen or heard by a far larger number of readers. In editing it (reportedly for £3 a week) Nedham was responsible to, and worked alongside, the shadowy figure Captain Thomas Audley, who had apparently been in trouble in the late 1630s for publishing pamphlets against Charles I's policies in Scotland.[23] Audley seems to have collected the material for *Britanicus*, Nedham to have written it up.[24] *Britanicus* belonged to a syndicate of newsbooks which were owned by the printer Robert White and which, on most issues, took a broadly collective line.[25] Nedham's task was occasionally complicated by White's disputes with other printers or publishers, who produced rival or counterfeit versions of *Britanicus*. But Nedham's principal rival was not a parliamentary newsbook. It was a Royalist one. The celebrated feature of *Britanicus*, almost from its outset, was its weekly attack on Sir John Berkenhead's Royalist newsbook, *Mercurius Aulicus*. In the contest between *Aulicus* and *Britanicus* the battle for control of public opinion was joined.

So long as the king's cause held up on the battlefield, the advantages lay with *Aulicus*. Berkenhead commanded a supply of news and intelligence that Audley and Nedham could not rival.[26] Some of it, to Parliament's exasperation, was somehow gathered from within the Roundhead cause. *Aulicus* had a second advantage, in the primacy it was granted in Royalist propaganda: *Britanicus* had to compete with a spread of parliamentary newsbooks. Berkenhead was on close terms with the court, which liberally supplied him with information and opinion: Audley and Nedham scrambled for knowledge and encouragement.[27] *Britanicus* did, uniquely among the newsbooks of the first Civil War, establish an official relationship with the parliamentary army, whose lord general (first Essex, then Fairfax) was responsible for licensing it.[28] It also seems to have had contacts with prominent Roundhead politicians, particularly Lord Say and Sele and his sons,[29] and with lesser men at Westminster and in the armies and localities.[30] Yet, at least in the normal course of events, it acquired little privileged information. Its principal function was not to provide fresh intelligence but to challenge the news and views carried by *Aulicus*.[31]

Berkenhead returned the challenge. Behind the battle between him and Nedham there lay a comedy of pretence. Berkenhead represented *Britanicus'* spelling of its name as a symbol of Roundhead illiteracy, and declared that he would not refer to its rival again until the second 'n' had been inserted into the title. The embarrassed *Britanicus* proposed a strenuously arcane justification of the spelling and refused to back down. In consequence, though *Aulicus* found other ways of alluding to its rival, it rarely named it. On the occasions when the strength of *Britanicus'* claims obliged it to do so, Nedham's newsbook broke into cries of triumph.[32] For all Berkenhead's affection of disdain, he and his fellow Royalist journalists knew that *Britanicus* was the king's chief enemy in the propaganda war, and did what they could to discredit it.[33] *Britanicus* in turn strove to deflate *Aulicus'* accounts of the war: to convict Berkenhead, as Berkenhead sought to convict the parliamentary newswriters, of invention and exaggeration and distortion. Both authors struggled to sustain the morale and defend the integrity of their own side: both strove to depress the spirits and impugn the resolution of the other's. It is not least to that contest that we owe the images or caricatures of Cavalier and Roundhead. Cavaliers, whose 'long hair' *Britanicus* mocked,[34] were frivolous, sensual, irresponsible, snobbish. Roundheads were sullen, hypocritical, graceless, philistine. In the polarization of the nation the press played a full part. *Aulicus*, disowning the moderates on its own side, spoke for monarchical absolutism and for Laudianism. It portrayed the Parliament at Westminster as the tool of radicals bent on the destruction of monarchy and of all order and decency in religion. That representation widened the gap between the two sides and made a negotiated peace the more difficult. It also played into the hands of the parliamentary extremists.[35] Among those extremists, we shall see, was Nedham himself.

Nedham won his contest with Berkenhead because Parliament won the war. In 1645, especially after the battle of Naseby in June, *Aulicus* found intelligence ever harder to collect and high spirits ever harder to sustain. Yet its decline and disappearance, which marked Nedham's triumph, were a mixed blessing to him. His rivalry with Berkenhead had been the *raison d'être* of his newsbook, and he had relished the fight. Amidst its fury he had learned to respect his opponent. The two writers knew that the standards of their

journalism were higher than those of the (mainly) leaden gazettes that competed for their audiences but could not match their exuberance or wit or
repartee. From December 1645 to March 1646 the Royalists ran a pale successor to *Aulicus* entitled *Mercurius Academicus*. In comparing it
unfavourably with its predecessor, and voicing nostalgia for his combats with
Aulicus, Nedham was using an obvious tactic. Yet in doing so he offered
Berkenhead a genuine, if immodest, tribute: unlike our rivals 'we are both
Athenians'.[36]

Modesty was not Nedham's way. Repeatedly he boasted that he had
fulfilled the aim, which he proclaimed in his weekly heading and often
emphasized in his text, of providing 'for the better information of the people'.
'There is not now so much as a young apprentice that keeps shop', declared
Britanicus in September 1644, 'or a labourer that holds the plough, not one
from the city to the country,' whom the newsbook has not taught to see
through the 'lying' and 'juggling' of *Aulicus*. 'I have got the success I aimed
at, the uncheating, the undeluding, the undeceiving, the unmasquing, the
uncovering, the un-Oxfording, the unbishoping, and I hope the un-Common
Prayering of the kingdom too.'[37] In August 1645 Nedham claimed to have
'rendered prerogative, popery, prelacy, and the privy councils at Oxford, with
all their atheistical abettors, ridiculous unto the kingdom, thereby to make
way for a perfect reformation'.[38] Even his enemies allowed him to have had
'reasonable success among the empty vulgar'.[39] Aiming at a nation-wide audience, he offered frequent encouragement to zealous parliamentarians in the
regions. Yet he seems primarily to have envisaged a readership of Londoners,
among whom the success of *Aulicus*, against a Parliament unable to suppress
it, was especially galling to Roundheads. Nedham often paused to flatter the
inhabitants of 'that famous city', whose bravery and loyalty were, he
reminded them, the bases of Parliament's successes[40] – though later, under his
Royalist hat, he would subject the same citizens to persistent abuse.

Nedham drew attention to two features of his prose: jocularity and plainness. He presented himself as 'a merry fellow, who can laugh in my sleeve
now and then',[41] who liked to 'jest a little' or to 'bait my intelligence with
some sport'. He was 'pleasant', he explained, to a 'purpose', for since 'all the
serious treatises would not draw the people off from their liking for the king's
ways, I thought it the best to jeer them out of it'. He hoped, through the
appeal of his humour, 'to be read as well in the court as the city'.[42] He also
hoped, through the same means, to reach a popular audience. As he would
explain in 1650, in his prospectus for *Mercurius Politicus*, a newsbook can be
expected to 'undeceive the people' only if it is 'written in a jocular way, or
else it will never be cried up: for those truths which the multitude regard not
in a serious dress, being represented in pleasing popular airs, make music to
the common sense'.[43] *Politicus* wrote in the Lucianic tradition of *joco-serio*.
Its weekly heading invoked Horace's words in *Ars Poetica*: '*ita vertere seria
ludo*' (thus to turn seriousness to play).[44] In *Mercurius Pragmaticus*, which

had adopted the same principle, Nedham declared that 'in the midst of jest I am much in earnest'.[45]

Nedham and Berkenhead did battle in an age when, in Peter Thomas' words, 'satire was used for the first time on the grand scale as an instrument of political warfare'.[46] Nedham, who liked to acclaim the accomplishments of his own 'satire',[47] was greeted by Royalists with derision on its account. They had two objections. First, 'wit', the quality of nimble and lively intellect or invention, was held by Cavaliers to be the natural monopoly of the upper classes.[48] 'Were I able to say he hath a good wit', declared an anonymous attack on *Britanicus* which Berkenhead helped to write,[49] '(as to speak ingenuously I never knew a worse) yet to prostitute it to the recreation of a herd of readers ... is to defile and strumpet one of the greatest ornaments God and nature have bestowed upon us; and to make wit, which was born to rule, the fool and jester of the people.'[50] What *Britanicus* supplied, according to its enemies, was not 'true satire' but crude invective and foolery, full of 'flashes' and 'squibs' but 'thin of wit'. It was as subtle as the throwing of 'rotten eggs'. It recalled the 'clowning' and the 'frothy humour' of a less 'knowing' or sophisticated age. Nedham's 'style' was all 'rage' and no 'point'.[51] Those charges were not intended to be just. If they had justice in them, then comparable accusations might have been levelled at the more populist moments of *Aulicus*. But the second Royalist objection to Nedham's 'wit' pointed to a dilemma which afflicted Nedham and which Berkenhead was spared. As Thomas says, it was Berkenhead's 'first article of faith' that 'royalists have a sort of divine right' to wit.[52] 'Wit in a Roundhead', declared a Cavalier attack on *Britanicus*, was a 'monstrous' notion, a contradiction in terms.[53] Nedham's performance as 'a light fantastic, apish pretender of wit', though it might momentarily appeal to the vulgar or to youths in alehouses, could hope for no larger success, at least among the 'graver sort'.[54]

That was a palpable hit. Nedham wrote for the Puritan cause: a cause generally hostile to or ill at ease with wit and with merriment. It is true that there was Puritan humour (though less of it after 1640 than before), and that there were Puritans with aesthetic tastes. It is also true that on the other side there was some grave, even puritanical, Royalism. Yet the cultural division between the two sides could be profound. In Nedham's relationship to it we can sense the width of the divide. *Britanicus* endorsed the humourless stance of its party. It professed to be scandalized by the 'enormities at home', by the 'debauchery in apparel and behaviour', the 'patches' and 'paint' and 'rings' and 'curls' of female adornment, by 'so many stews in the suburbs', by the survival of 'the wondrous old heathen-customs ... with the meritorious maypoles, garlands, galliards, and jolly whitsun-ales', by 'dancing, drinking and rioting about a maypole' in the city.[55] It called for the stricter observation of days of public fasting and humiliation, and urged that such days be observed 'with more vigour of spirit'.[56] It enjoined proper respect for the sabbath and rebuked *Aulicus* for its 'sabbath blasphemy' in supplying intelligence on, and using the pagan name of, the first day of the week.[57] *Britanicus* adopted, too, the grim language of Puritan providentialism. Nedham reproached Round-heads for their 'carnal confidence' when they relied on God rather than man for military success.[58] He demanded inquests into the 'self-seeking'[59] and sin-fulness and idolatry of the nation and its capital. He called for the destruc-tion of 'the Babylonish stuff hid yet in our tents and temples', which angered the Lord and thus weakened the armies fighting in his cause. 'Know we not that God is most provoked by the rubbish in his own house, by the stains in the linen ephod, by the counterfeit jewel in the breastplate of Aaron?'[60] Yet, to win the nation over, Roundheads needed the support of readers indiffer-ent, if not opposed, to killjoy Puritanism. That is why Nedham's career flour-ished in the first Civil War and again in the 1650s. So he had to address two audiences. He wooed his readers, he explained, 'by being serious with the sadder judgements, and more pleasant with the sanguine'.[61] Skilfully as he pursued that double strategy, the moments of merriment in *Mercurius Bri-tanicus* were hard to reconcile with its professions of Puritan gravity.

So was his own personality. The few surviving letters to or from or about him testify to an epicurean and bibulous lifestyle and to some epic nights on the town.[62] Here again a clue to Nedham's thinking may lie in a remark of his companion-in-ale Henry Oxinden, who thought that a man should bring up his children 'in the profession of that religion you shall find established in the kingdom you and they live ... For the major part of men by far take up their religion upon trust, according to their education in the kingdom they are born in, without any scrutiny into the truth of it.'[63](Oxinden, a lifelong enemy of clerical pretension and Puritan hypocrisy, ran on an Anabaptist ticket in a parliamentary election in 1659, when he was said to be 'against tithing self-seeking ministers'. After the Restoration, to which he contributed verses of extravagant flattery in praise of Charles II,[64] he received Anglican ordination and became an absentee clergyman, eager for the collection of his tithes.)[65] Nedham's scepticism is no less transparent. But how could he square his outward Puritanism with his instinctive jocularity? A certain defensiveness is evident in his attempts to do so: in his assertion, for example, that *Britan-icus* used 'wit' to instruct those 'that would not read a serious rebuke'.[66] Some-times he would announce that the arrival of grave news had made humour unfitting, and resolve upon a more 'serious' tone.[67] Or he would reproach *Aulicus* for making 'jests', for trying to be 'witty', amidst the carnage wrought by the king's armies.[68] Nedham had to bridle or undermine his own wit too often for it to sustain an equal challenge to Berkenhead's. Sometimes the author or authors of the counterfeit issues of *Britanicus*, who were without Nedham's obligations, could be more extravagantly comic than he.

The second stylistic quality of *Britanicus* to which Nedham drew attention was plainness. That was the virtue, he claimed, that enabled him to strip away the pretences and self-deceptions of the Cavalier cause. He contrasted his own 'sincere and plain language', and the 'plain' preaching of godly ministers, with the evasive discourse of clergy in 'lawn and satin' and of 'court chaplains and pamphlets ... too soft and silken in their language'.[69] He spoke 'plain', 'bold', 'naked truth', and 'plain English', English 'as plain as a pikestaff', to a king whose flattering advisers had shielded him from those virtues.[70] Royalists covered truth by 'daubing' and 'painting' and 'masking', and wrought or subscribed to 'delusions'.[71] Nedham associated their deceptions and self-deceptions with the Cavalier taste for the escapist world of plays and masques, for Shakespeare and Jonson, for Beaumont and Fletcher, for Shirley and Davenant.[72] That view, which has its counterpart among modern historians and literary critics with Roundhead sympathies, barely concealed Nedham's own literary enthusiasms, with would emerge openly in his Royalist writing and which were close to those attacked in *Britanicus*.[73]

He found other means of identifying Royalism with the evasion of reality. Cavaliers and papists – and fainthearts on the Roundhead side – were 'blind', victims of 'blind superstition'. *Britanicus* resolved to 'open their eyes' and to dispel the 'clouds' or 'mists' of misunderstanding.[74] Or they were lost in 'sleep' or 'security', or had fallen victim to 'charms' or 'enchantment'.[75] They were, he insisted time and again, in thrall to the 'yoke' or 'dominion' of 'fancy' or 'fantasy'[76] – a charge which, under his Cavalier hat, he would level at the Roundheads. That rhetorical tactic, no less than his criticism of playwrights, was a pose, for, as his prospectus for *Mercurius Politicus* would acknowledge, his own purpose was to 'charm the fancy' of 'the multitude'.[77] He made the same point in writing *Mercurius Pragmaticus*, where he printed ballads 'only to tickle and charm the more vulgar fancies, who little regard truths in a serious garb.'[78]

III

Of the charges levelled by *Mercurius Aulicus* at the parliamentarians, the most damaging were those which exposed their divisions. 'The nerves and sinews of our cause', Nedham warned the Roundheads, lay in 'unity'.[79] Yet 'we are at difference, as if we meant to open a passage to let the enemy in amongst us'.[80] Nedham tried to paper over the differences. 'I thank God', he answered *Aulicus* in March 1644, 'our divisions are but calm agitations and peaceable disputes'.[81] As the war progressed, that defence became impossible to sustain. When the conflict between the war and peace parties reached its ugly climax in the quarrel between Cromwell and the earl of Manchester, Nedham urged that 'nothing should divide the love and affection between gallant men of one party'.[82] By 'bandying one against another ... see what a wide gap and door of reproach we open unto the enemy against ourselves'.[83] With divisions in politics went divisions in religion. Here too Nedham strove to play the conflicts down. When Berkenhead drew attention to the 'heats' that had arisen between Presbyterians and Independents, Nedham replied that they were preferable to the 'cold ... religion' of the prelates, whose souls ... are congealed and frozen. They stand all over with an ice, they have not so many sparks of grace to thaw them ... Oh the coldness of the Protestants at Oxford, oh the chillness upon their consciences; there is as much snow upon the spirits of their clergy as upon any mountain of Wales the last February ... Is it not better to be warming one another in holy controversies, and to walk on so fast in the way of reformation ... than to sit still as you do in Oxford in your old copes and surplices, freezing to the Common Prayer Book and popery?[84]

Yet those 'holy controversies', Nedham knew, gave Royalist propaganda a potent weapon. Cavalier writers, warned *Britanicus*, 'blow the coals, in matter of church-discipline, and endeavour to make the gap wider'.[85] Roundheads should suspend their differences until the common enemy had been defeated: 'let us first dispute it out with the papist, and then we shall have more time to argue it out amongst ourselves'.[86]

In pleading for irenicism on his own side, in religion and politics alike, Nedham followed the party line of Robert White's newsbooks.[87] Yet he had a line of his own, and with time he was increasingly willing to follow it. Later in his career he would breathe hatred, sometimes a bilious hatred, of the 'malign ulcer', the 'monstrous babe', the 'viperous brood' of Presbyterianism, of its clericalism and dogma and intolerance, of the Solemn League and Covenant, of 'the pharisees of our times', the 'pulpit-incendiaries', with their itch for 'kirk-domination' and for 'parochial tyranny'.[88] In those sentiments Nedham was at one with Berkenhead. Yet, in replying to *Aulicus'* charges, he was obliged to defend Parliament's Scottish allies and to praise the Presbyterian system which Parliament had resolved to introduce. The Covenant was thus 'a most heavenly engine', the Westminster Assembly 'a divine auxiliary'.[89] The Scots must be referred to affectionately, as 'our brethren'.[90] Yet Nedham's praise was selective. The merits of the Covenant, as he presented them, were that it committed Parliament first to the vigorous prosecution of the war[91] (a policy from which many Presbyterians drew back) and secondly to the extirpation of popery and prelacy[92] (a goal far from peculiar to Presbyterians).

Britanicus waged unrelenting war on 'prelacy' and on the Church of England, which the 'half-Reformation' of Edward VI had left riddled with popery.[93] The religion of the king was a 'statuous and windy religion',[94] with its organs and Prayer Book, its 'abundance of trumpery, as the cathedral dressings, paintings, and carvings'.[95] The Book of Common Prayer, 'against which we are Covenanted', was a 'devised worship of men'. It 'symbolises more with the Church of Rome than with the best reformed Churches'.[96] It robbed God of 'the purity of worship due unto him ... tickling men's ears, and puffing up their devotions with anthems, and responds blown out of organ pipes, as if there were no music left to the devout soul but what is let in at the ears'.[97] Why, asked *Britanicus*, was Parliament so slow to effect 'the removal of this ... superstitious, idolised stuff and prayers'?[98] Why did it permit the Covenant to remain 'but half-taken'? Why was the use of the Prayer Book in the suburbs and parishes winked at? How could Roundheads expect God's favour in battle 'so long as [the Royalists] and we have one service'? 'Must the people needs have a golden calf?'[99] When the Prayer Book was at last replaced by the Directory, Nedham rejoiced: 'Farewell then all superstitious First and Second Service, Te Deums, Litany, and the whole bundle of Collects, praying over the dead, enormities of Baptism, and Ashwednesday cursings', and 'the heathenish and obscene ceremony of the ring'.[100]

In religion as in politics, Nedham spoke for plainness against mystery, Considered as an enemy of popery and superstition and idolatry, Presbyterianism accorded with that principle and could be endorsed accordingly. Nedham's support for Presbyterianism ended when it took issue with Independency. The Independency he championed was moderate, respectable, Erastian. 'The Independents', he declared, 'are for set forms, and order.'[101] There is little sympathy in his writings for the sects or for the movement to divorce Church from State. (What there is of it, I hope to suggest elsewhere, can be explained by his friendship with Milton.) Scorning mechanic preaching, he stood for 'a godly pious ministry',[102] for the 'order' of the ministry and 'such as are ministers indeed'.[103] But he was with the Independents, and against the Presbyterians, in calling for liberty of conscience and in deprecating the smearing of godly men as Anabaptists or Brownists.[104] Even as he urged unity on Presbyterians and Independents he rebuked the former for intending to persecute the latter. He learned to speak the Independent language of progressive revelation, a process in which the believer reaches truth through the trial and error which liberty of conscience makes possible. 'Is there not', he asked, 'a passing from grace to grace, from glory to glory in gospel knowledge? Doth God reveal himself all at once? Have we attained perfection? Are we so acquainted with gospel mysteries, and gospel government, that we look after no further discoveries in the hidden things of God? ... we should all be Seekers in this kind.'[105]

Yet Nedham himself was no 'Seeker'. Adroit as his imitation of Independent rhetoric is, it cannot quite hide his own detachment from religious enthusiasm. Occasionally he lapses into phraseology more Gibbonian than Puritan – as when he refers to 'true celestial contemplations' or to the tactics adopted by Satan 'upon any irradiations of divine light'.[106] In his mind the argument for toleration is essentially political and secular. He conveys it in a characteristically secular simile: 'uniformity-mongers' are 'the only enemies of a state', for 'as a confinement of the wind torments nature with an earthquake, so to rob the soul of its freedom ... must cause a cholic (with inflammation) in the bowels of a kingdom'.[107]

In politics as in religion, Nedham discreetly supports the Independents. When praising Cromwell and Manchester, he contrives, by adjectival emphasis, to indicate his preference for 'the valiant Cromwell'.[108] He supports the Self-Denying Ordinance and demands its speedy and thorough implementation.[109] With characteristic impatience – one of his favourite terms is 'It is high time that' – he calls for the encouragement and speedy assistance of soldiers let down by apathy or foot-dragging in the supply lines or by dilatoriness among ill-affected commanders or at Westminster.[110] The recovery of territory from Royalist occupation is a process of liberation, which allows 'people' who have 'long groaned under oppressions' to 'taste the sweets of freedom' or to 'find what the liberty of the subject is, a thing they never heard of before'.[111] In the early 1650s he would use similar language in exhorting Cromwell and the Rump to liberate the peoples of the continent from political and social oppression.[112]

Though Nedham warned against divisions within the Roundhead cause, his more polemical utterances could only inflame them. Resolved to 'spare neither friend nor foe',[113] he confined his sympathies to the zealously 'well-affected' on Parliament's side. Time and again he condemned the 'neutrals' or 'neuters', the 'indifferents', the 'lukewarmed', 'the moderate sort of our friends'.[114] Among the ostensibly Roundhead clergy he attacked 'mere time-servers' who 'wheel about with their weather-cock divinity upon any occasion',[115] 'such as stand leering betwixt the pew and the pulpit ... betwixt king and parliament, betwixt prelate and presbyter ... These are such clergymen ... as will never burn; I warrant you, they are too moist for martyrdom.'[116] Everywhere *Britanicus* saw 'malignancy', that 'hydra', that 'fever against Reformation'.[117] Roundhead counsels were being penetrated by 'close false brethren of our own party'.[118] London was crowded with 'malignants' (those 'vultures'[119]), whose 'licentiousness in common discourse' was audible 'on every corner, to the great prejudice of our cause'. The result was 'the seducing of the ignorant, with the disheartening of the well-affected people. This is done under our noses, yet no special order taken for remedy.'[120] 'Malignants' lurked in the 'lodgings and chambers' of the Inns of Court[121] or in houses where parliamentary committees met.[122] As *Britanicus* 'often urged', a 'severe course' was 'needful' against them.[123] Men who 'maliciously utter any thing against the parliament' should be charged with 'high treason'.[124] The 'discontented soldier lurking at home' must be 'made an example'.[125] The county committees must be purged of 'malignants', whose estates are to be confiscated and awarded either to informers against them or to the commanders of the parliamentary armies.[126] The same committees should 'return the names of the delinquent ministers, for in all places that are bad, the people and ministers have agreed to wink at one another's faults'.[127] When in August 1645 Nedham provoked the indignation of the House of Lords and of fellow parliamentary journalists by the irreverence of his criticisms of the king, he declared that the attacks on his newsbook had illustrated the very danger against which he had been warning. It was true that he had erred, but 'my late slip proves very useful in the event. Now those secret enemies, which lurked here under the notion of neuters, or moderate friends, have made a large discovery of themselves. Now we can point them out, and I desire all well-affected persons to take notice of ... the lukewarm wretches' who 'conceive I have been too bold with the king'. 'Hatred against *Britanicus*', he concluded, was in itself 'a sign of malignancy'.[128]

There must be no sell-out to the king. Though Nedham – like Berkenhead[129] – was obliged to profess a longing for peace and blamed the intransigence of the other side for its delay, no more than Berkenhead did he favour concessions in peace negotiations. There was 'no likelihood of assurance but by the sword'.[130] Though the 'languishing multitude' would 'entertain peace at any rate',[131] MPs must be 'vigilant' and 'jealous' and 'wary ... upon all pretended overtures', for fear of being 'kept talking while the enemies are doing their designs'.[132] The Royalists 'never make overtures of peace but upon some by-ends'.[133] It was vital that Parliament hold to its 'just demands'.[134] Fortunately 'the people of England are not so tame as to be fooled out of their liberties'.[135]

Nedham contrasted those 'liberties' with the slavery endured by other peoples. In doing so he played on a tradition that went back at least as far as Fortescue. When *Aulicus* derided the county committee of Hertfordshire as a 'yeoman-committee', *Britanicus* answered that the Royalists, having

> a plot in hand to enslave the whole commons of the kingdom ... therefore cannot endure to hear that the yeomanry should be held of any esteem, or have anything to do in matters of the least public concernment. It was the old court-plot, ever to hoist up the prerogative of the king, and suppress the liberty of the subject; setting before [the king's] eyes the absolute power of France as a pattern of emulation, so that in time the ancient and free English title of yeoman should have been changed into that of peasant or slave; and so our whole estates and liberties been made a sacrifice to the avarice and flattery of courtiers.[136]

It was England's right 'to be governed by laws, and not by horses, as other nations: not according to the fancy or will of the prince or his favourite'.[137] The English government was properly 'a mixed government of monarchy, aristocracy and democracy', in which the monarch had 'a fiduciary interest of trust and depositoriness'. Supreme power had historically been 'divided' or 'shared' between king and Parliament, and 'though time and artifice had almost' raised the king above the other co-ordinate estates, 'yet when the balance is got right, you shall see the scales will scarce turn'.[138] It would be Parliament's responsibility to impose terms upon the king that would get that balance right.

Parliament itself was wary of professing any such right or aim. It told the nation that it fought for the king, not against him; that it aimed to restore him with honour; that it had no intention of revising the constitution. From time to time Nedham deferred to those suppositions. He vouched for the 'love and loyalty' felt by the parliamentary armies for their king,[139] and insisted that 'no change of government' was 'intended' by Parliament.[140] The target of his criticism, he affirmed, was the king's 'party', not his 'person'.[141] Those claims were disingenuous. If the people were to be instructed in their liberties,

Nedham saw, then not only kingship but the king himself must be stripped of awe and mystery. The plain prose of *Britanicus* would introduce plain politics. How far dared Nedham go? He did not hesitate to attack, sometimes in savage terms, Queen Henrietta Maria, whose 'matchless impudence', 'obstinacy', 'malice' and 'follies have made her the hate and jealousy of this nation, by perverting and incensing' the king.[142] Rupert and Maurice, those 'bloody princes', he also attacked without equivocation.[143] His treatment of Charles I had to be more subtle. Yet as early as December 1643 *Britanicus* was ready to intimate that Charles was a Machiavellian prince.[144] In September 1644 Nedham asked 'How long will Your Majesty triumph in the spoils of your subjects? Shall your robe be only of that purple which is coloured in the blood of your people?'[145] Next month he observed that the slaughter waged by Royalist commanders 'makes all good men wonder that His Majesty, who is or ought to be a common father to all, should still proceed so violently through blood and mischief ... even to the unpeopling of the kingdom'.[146]

In 1645 Nedham took a new line.[147] The king, whose duty is to protect his subjects,[148] has abandoned them and thus deserted his throne. Since his departure from London 'the royal robes begin to wax mouldy for want of use'.[149] Ought he not to abdicate and make way for Prince Charles, who would 'help to fill up that room in the monarchy which hath been too long empty'?[150] No longer was Nedham prepared to refer to the king as 'His Majesty', for – by separating his person from his office – 'he left his majesty behind him at Westminster'.[151] When Berkenhead called the king 'His Sacred Majesty', Nedham scathed his rival with sarcasm: 'if this be true, then [the king] is fitter for heaven than I thought him; for the truth is, when the false report of his being wounded [at Naseby] first came to town, I pitied him, in regard it might be mortal, and the man die with the guilt of so much blood about him, which made me pray heartily (as a loyal subject ought to do) that God would give him time and grace for repentance'.[152]

Naseby, the decisive battle of the war, brought a bonus to Parliament's propagandists in the capture of a cache of incriminating royal correspondence. The letters demonstrated what Nedham called the 'odious dissimulation'[153] with which the king had conspired, not least with Irish Catholics, to regain his throne. In the following months Nedham published a series of long excerpts from the king's letters and glossed them mercilessly. In August 1645, carried away by that opportunity, he wrote the most infamous of the issues of *Mercurius Britanicus*, which men would remember in coffee-house talk twenty years later.[154] The claim that the king had abandoned his subjects was now pushed to the limit in a moment of satirical inspiration that looks forward to Nedham's writings of the late 1640s. 'Where is King Charles', asked *Britanicus*; 'What's become of him?' The only solution to his apparent disappearance was 'to send Hue and Cry after him'. So *Britanicus* would reward 'any man' who 'can bring any tale or tiding of a wilful king, which hath gone astray these four years from his parliament, with a guilty conscience, bloody hands, a heart full of broken vows and protestations'.[155]

Nedham had gone too far. His printer and licenser were imprisoned by the House of Lords. 'I have overshot myself', he confessed in a public *Apologie* – 'though I hope', he added cheekily, 'not beyond recovery'.[156] The *Apologie* apologized for strikingly little, and the recovery was strikingly swift. Publication of *Britanicus* was resumed after only a week's delay. Thereafter Nedham was for a while more careful, but by December he was once more charging the king with having abandoned his duties and with the guilt of his subject's blood. In May 1646, when Charles had been defeated and Parliament had to decide what to do with him, Nedham demanded that 'a strict account be required for the blood of all the saints'.[157] He was raising the stakes. In what proved to be the final issue of *Britanicus*, he reminded 'the commons of the kingdom' that 'you have paid dear for your liberties'. 'Whosoever he was that endeavoured to rob you of them', he informed them, 'is *ipso facto* a tyrant, by common consent of all that ever wrote history or politics'. Indeed the history of Britain, as a reading of Buchanan would show, was full of the reigns of 'tyrants'.[158] With those assertions the acceptability of *Britanicus* to Parliament came to an end. Excesses which had been tolerated or forgiven in the cause of wartime propaganda and persuasion seemed intolerable or unforgivable once the war was over. In any case Robert White's syndicate, which the pressures of war had kept together, was falling apart.[159] Nedham was sent to the Fleet by the House of Lords, and released only on bond of good behaviour and on condition 'that he shall not write any more pamphlets without leave of this House first obtained'.[160] *Mercurius Britanicus* was dead.

IV

What had Nedham's assault on the majesty and mystery of kingship achieved? The men who carried out or supported the regicide in 1649 knew there was no divinity to hedge a king. Whether or how far they owed that knowledge to Nedham we cannot tell. Some of them retained the ideal, which enabled them to hold back from republicanism, of the just and virtuous king. They blamed Charles not for being a king but for failing to be one.[161] Nedham, in his protests against the king's absenteeism, had himself endorsed that idea. He contrasted Charles, to the king's disadvantage, with 'other princes'.[162] Yet in its final issues, when it claimed that the kings of both England and Scotland had most often been tyrants, *Britanicus* made a precocious advance in the political thought of the revolution. The argument that the history of monarchical rule shows the conventional distinction between (virtuous) kings and (wicked) tyrants to be untenable in practice would be a large strand in the republicanism with which Nedham strove to educate the nation in the 1650s. *Britanicus* looked ahead to that republicanism in other ways too. It anticipated, in its pleas for England's assertion of its maritime sovereignty[163] and for the reform of the Mint[164] the economic programme which in the early

1650s the republicans in Parliament, with Nedham as their spokesman, would combine (as we shall see) with their political programme.

More tellingly, *Britanicus* anticipated Nedham's later expressions of enthusiasm for the Dutch republic. During the first Civil War *Mercurius Aulicus* saw, in Parliament's use of the terms 'state' and 'states' in its proceedings and declarations, an opportunity to charge the Roundheads with intending to introduce a republic on the model of the 'States' of the United Provinces. Instead of denying that charge, Nedham championed the struggle of the Dutch republicans against the Stuarts' ally, the House of Orange, whose principles and ambitions he consistently identified with those of Charles I.[165] The 'free states' or the United Provinces, he declared in February 1644, 'know the miseries of tyranny and slavery'.[166] Next month, noting that *Aulicus* 'tells us of our parliament's striving to be like the States', Nedham replied that the term 'States' was properly applicable to the constitution of England.[167] *Britanicus* voiced, too, an enthusiasm for the social policies of the Dutch republic. In June 1644 it praised the 'State charity' towards the sick and wounded that 'makes the States of the Netherlands flourish'.[168] Next year Nedham recommended that tithes be abolished and provision for the payment of ministers established on the Dutch model.[169] He could not be openly republican in *Britanicus*. Yet within months of the closure of his newsbook he would show (as we shall see) that his republican thinking was well advanced.

If *Britanicus* was gingerly about republicanism, it was bolder on another front of political theory. In 1645, as *Aulicus* declined and as attacks on it came to serve an ever smaller purpose, Nedham looked for other ways to catch public attention. His commentaries on the royal correspondence captured at Naseby were one answer. Another was to introduce his readers to a novel view of the political landscape. Seventeenth-century England saw a growing understanding of the extent to which politics is governed not by ethics or rights but by the 'interests' of those who participate in it. Writers strove to identify those interests and to show how they operate or ought to operate. The principal historian of that development, J. A. W. Gunn, portrays Nedham as (with Charles Herle) one of the two 'pioneers' in the development of interest theory in the 1650s.[170] Nedham was an earlier and thus more remarkable pioneer than Gunn recognizes, for his study of 'interest' began not in the 1650s but in *Mercurius Britanicus* – even though, like other themes of that newsbook, it became more sophisticated in his later prose.[171] In his theory of interest, Nedham found another means of penetrating the exterior falsities of political behaviour and language.

His model was the Huguenot grandee, the duc de Rohan. Near the end of his life Nedham would praise 'that excellent prince' and his 'little but weighty book',[172] of which an English translation had been published in 1640 and again in 1641 as *A Treatise of the Interest of the Princes and States of Christendom*. It was Rohan's premise, quoted by Nedham, that states 'as they follow their proper interests ... thrive or fail in successes'.[173] The pursuit of 'interest', maintained Rohan, was the demand of 'reason': the neglect of it was a surrender to the 'passions'. For 'our proper interest' is 'guided by reason alone, which ought to be the rule of all our actions'.[174] Nedham in turn equated true interest – or what he called 'public' interest – with 'reason'. False or 'private' interest he equated, as he associated so many of his targets, with 'fantasies'.[175] Like Rohan in his treatise, Nedham in *Britanicus* put his philosophical premise to the use of his political party. Rohan aimed to demonstrate that it was the 'interest' of France and of its potential allies to stand up to the Habsburg threat. Nedham, in *Mercurius Britanicus*, addressed Royalists who held out against Parliament in the hope that relief might reach them from abroad. Examining 'week by week'[176] the conditions and priorities of the various continental states, he argued that it was in the 'interest' of none of them to come to Charles I's aid.

That 'there is no security for a state but in strict bent to its own interest'[177] would remain a cardinal principle of Nedham's writings. His innovation lay in the perception that the logic of 'interest' could be applied not only to international but to domestic politics. The political fragmentation of England in the 1640s enabled him to explain national developments in terms of the 'interests' that competed for control of them: Royalists, Presbyterians, Independents, Scots, Londoners, and so on. That approach, which *Britanicus* tried out in the Civil War,[178] would become the distinguishing feature of a number of Nedham's later pamphlets. There he would explain the interests of the various groups and urge them to act upon them. The path to political wisdom, he would argue, lay in men's understanding not only of their own interests but of those of their enemies or rivals or allies or neighbours.[179] The interests which he described, at home no less than abroad, conveniently proved to coincide with the aims of the parties in whose cause he variously wrote.

In Nedham's insistence on the sway of interest there is a sceptical and pessimistic streak. 'Interest', he maintained, 'is the true zenith of every state and person, according to which they may certainly be understood, though clothed never so much with the most specious disguise of religion, justice and necessity'.[180] 'It is a sure maxim', he declared, 'that the proceedings of states in relation to each other are not regulated by ordinary rules of courtesy and friendship; forasmuch as, in this corrupted state of mankind, they measure all their respects and observances only by power.'[181] In addressing the various interest groups in England, Nedham had in mind two kinds of reader, 'the conscientious man and the worldling'. It was the latter group that had the larger claim on his attention, 'the greater part of the world being led more by appetites of convenience and commodity than the dictates of conscience'.[182] Yet there was a more positive and hopeful vision too. If men would only be faithful to their interests, and suppress the passions that obscured them from themselves, then politics would lose its venom and violence. It would be possible, both in international and in national politics, to 'balance' the competition of interests that was an inescapable fact of political life.[183] There would

still be conflicts, but those conflicts, we are invited to infer, would be rational. Nedham is kinder to the groups against whom he writes when he finds
that their enmity to his own cause is to be explained in terms of interest rather
than of passion. He cannot 'blame' them, he tells us.[184] He even hints that
'conscience', and 'the consideration of right and wrong', oblige us to pursue
our interests and to shed the 'specious' or 'frivolous pretences' that we substitute for them.[185]

Nedham's claims about interest, like his claims about most things, are not
consistently sustained. Sometimes he yields them to a more conventional politics of virtue.[186] High-minded claims for 'the interest of religion' or 'the interest of freedom' leave us uncertain of his understanding of his terms.[187] Often,
in company with more conventional writers, he represents the Puritan Revolution as a struggle between a communal 'public interest' and selfish 'private'
ones. That language is particularly useful to him in his Roundhead and
republican modes, where he contrasts the 'private' or 'particular' interest of
monarchy with 'the people's interest' or 'the common good' or 'the common
interest of the people'.[188] Yet the contrast does not satisfy him, and we watch
him groping towards a more innovative approach. Like James Harrington,
whose *Oceana* his arguments so often anticipate, he sees the key to political
health not in the elimination of private interest but in the harmonizing of private with public interest. We can rely only on rulers whose 'own interest'
coincides with that of the 'public', on men who 'have made the public interest, and their own, all one'.[189]

Perhaps we tend to think of seventeenth-century knowledge of advanced
political theory as predominantly the preserve of members of the landed
classes, in whose papers and commonplace books the most vivid evidence of
it is often to be found. Yet the discussions of interest theory in *Mercurius Britanicus*, like the republican arguments of *Mercurius Politicus*, question any
such assumption. Nedham's republican editorials, which roam the histories
of ancient Greece and Rome, are especially suggestive in that respect. Grammar school boys, after all, read Livy and Plutarch. The debates on the franchise at Putney in 1647 were critically affected by an intervention of Colonel
Rich, who reminded his audience that the granting of political rights to the
plebeians of ancient Rome had given a social base to imperial tyranny.[190] In
1659, newsbooks other than Nedham's, evidently written with a wide readership in mind, assumed a basic knowledge of Roman history in their readers.[191] Nedham's writings, too, strengthen the impression given by much
recent writing on seventeenth-century England of a politically and intellectu-
ally alert electorate.

V

The period from the death of *Mercurius Britanicus* in May 1646 to the birth
of *Mercurius Pragmaticus* in September 1647 saw Nedham without full-time

employment, but far from inactive. He had already set up, and could now give more time to, a medical practice, which he would resume – if he had ever dropped it – after the Restoration. Then he would write a contentious treatise, his longest work, recommending the application of Baconian methods to medical practice and denouncing 'pedantic compliance', 'superstitious fooleries', and 'our dogmatical methodists'. Once more he presented himself as a spokesman for plainness and reality who had penetrated evasions and disguises and 'fantasies'.[192]

But it was as a writer, not as a doctor, that he remained in the public eye after the demise of *Britanicus*. In July 1646 his pamphlet *Independencie no Schisme* defended the congregational way, and liberty of conscience, from Presbyterian attack. Then, in November, there appeared an anonymous pamphlet, sympathetic to the Levellers, entitled *Vox Plebis, or the People's Outcry against Oppression, Injustice and Tyranny*, a large part of which is unmistakably by Nedham.[193] In the previous year he had supplied the preface to a pamphlet written in defence of, and apparently written by, John Lilburne, *An Answer to Nine Arguments*. Lilburne, like Nedham, was imprisoned by the House of Lords in the mid-1640s. His counsel was John Bradshaw, whom we know to have been, or at least to have become, an intimate friend of Nedham.[194] Nedham's relations with the Leveller movement, as with other movements, are contradictory. Both as a Royalist newswriter and as a servant of the Commonwealth he would ferociously criticize Lilburne and his allies. Under his Royalist hat, it is true, he also sought to embarrass the Roundheads by egging on the 'valiant' or 'gallant' or 'honest John Lilburne', or 'my friend John Lilburne', in his struggles for the liberty of the subject against Cromwell and Parliament;[195] but there he was following a common Royalist tactic.[196]

Even so, there were bonds of sympathy and agreement between Nedham and the Levellers. *Britanicus* had intermittently protested, in terms of which the Levellers would have approved, on behalf of the 'oppressed', of 'poor people',[197] of 'common townsmen'[198] or 'honest feltmaker[s]'[199] whom snobbish Royalists held in contempt, of victims of monopolies,[200] of 'the poor soldier' who endured 'extremity of weather' in the camp while others 'stretch [them]selves on beds of down'.[201] There was nothing socially revolutionary about Nedham's complaints. He expected 'men of quality' to guide the 'multitude',[202] and lamented the debasement of honour by the ennoblements and knighthoods bestowed by the king on his supporters.[203] He could be withering about the 'rabble'. 'The name of Levellers', he declared in his Royalist mode in 1647, was 'a most apt title for such a despicable and desperate knot to be known by, that endeavour to cast down and level the enclosures of nobility, gentry and propriety, to make us all even.'[204] Yet Lilburne and his friends, as Nedham must have known very well, had no such intentions.[205]

The section of *Vox Plebis* that is obviously by Nedham changes the character of the pamphlet. Until that point it has offered an embittered account of a dispute about the powers of the county committee of Lincolnshire. Nedham turns it into a disquisition on the history of republican Athens and Rome and of Renaissance Italy and on the lessons of Machiavelli and Guicciardini. He introduces his readers to a range of arguments and historical examples and tricks of style that would frequently recur in his writings of 1650–2, when his claims for republicanism received official encouragement and could be openly advanced. In 1646 he had no such opportunity. Yet the advice he slips into *Vox Plebis* on the conduct appropriate to a 'republic' or 'free state'[206] confirms what the discussions of tyranny and of the Dutch republic in *Britanicus* suggest: that his republican ideas were already maturing. Soon, however, those ideas would collide with very different ones. By the autumn of 1647 Nedham was writing in the cause not of Roundheads, Levellers or republicans, but of Royalists.

VI

The transformation of Nedham from Roundhead to Cavalier in 1647 was a subtle process. Its occasion was the attempt by the New Model Army during the summer of that year to outbid the Presbyterian majority in Parliament in the negotiations with the king. The army's *Heads of the Proposals* offered Charles terms more generous than Parliament's. As editor of *Britanicus* Nedham had been answerable to the army; he had formed contacts with the army that gave him a knowledge of its internal politics;[207] and in three pamphlets in the summer of 1647 he advanced an argument which the army leaders had every reason to promote.[208] The real enemy both of the king and of the army, he claimed, was the Presbyterian party, whose abuses of parliamentary privilege were an affront to the soldiery and to the liberty of the subject, and whose religion was incompatible both with episcopacy (the goal of the king) and with liberty of conscience (the goal of the army). The *Heads of the Proposals*, by contrast, would preserve episcopacy and guarantee toleration. It was thus the 'true' and 'only interest' of the defeated king to seek a 'wary compliance' with the Independents (the party of the army and its allies) and to 'close with' them.[209] The army, after all, was no more opposed to monarchy than to episcopacy. The goal of 'so potent, so religious, so resolute, so well-accomplished, well-disciplined and victorious an army' was 'the common freedom of the subject, with a restoration of the king in parliament with such honour and freedom as may gain a lasting repute to those acts that shall be provided for by the royal assent in that behalf'.[210]

The republican tendency which Nedham had disclosed in *Vox Plebis* was accordingly put into reverse. Classical and Renaissance history, and the writings of Machiavelli and Guicciardini, were now enlisted to show that 'monarchical government is of more ease and benefit to the subjects that live under it than the government or domination of a popular republic or free state'.[211] Perhaps Nedham calculated, in the summer of 1647, that the *Heads of the Pro-*

posals offered the likeliest outcome of the post-war settlement and the best, perhaps the only, means of his own advancement. With the waning of those negotiations he ceased to represent the army's position. In September 1647, reportedly after kneeling at the king's feet and obtaining his forgiveness for his Roundhead past, he began to write the weekly newsbook *Mercurius Pragmaticus*, the most successful of the six Royalist newsbooks founded about that time.[212] Its purpose, he declared, was 'to write his majesty back into his throne'.[213]

Pragmaticus would be Nedham's principal occupation until January 1649, though it left him time to write pamphlets. It also left him time to supplement his income, as he would at other times of his life, by writing newsletters for private patrons.[214] In producing *Pragmaticus* he led a precarious life. Berkenhead, writing *Mercurius Aulicus* in Oxford, had tantalized Roundheads by acquiring information about their inner counsels. *Pragmaticus*, which was apparently written (though perhaps not always written) in London, taunted Parliament with its weekly reports 'especially from Westminster' and from the army's 'headquarters'. In 1648 Nedham became, for the first time, a journalist to be reckoned with on account not only of his prose but of his news. He found a source, a sometimes very revealing if also an erratic one, that enabled him to report passages of parliamentary debates.[215] He mocked Parliament's vigorous efforts to trace his printer and suppress his newsbook. It would never, he claimed, track down his 'invisible intelligence' or catch his 'printing-press upon wheels'.[216]

From its outset, *Pragmaticus* attuned itself to the conventions of Cavalier propaganda. Free at last of the inhibitions of Puritan solemnity, Nedham could mock it at will. Like much other Royalist writing of the late 1640s, *Pragmaticus* describes a world gone mad, where the victorious Puritans parade grotesque slogans as holy truths, and where laughter provides the only remaining source of sense, perhaps even of sanity.[217] Is it a mere accident that the most colourful evidence of Nedham's drinking-bouts survives from the years 1648–9? There was now an unbuttoned, even a frenzied aspect to his satire. The 'presbytery and bag-pipes' of the Scots, and the hypocrisy of the 'saints', were his favourite targets. Burlesque and caricature, the chief weapons of the Royalist propaganda of the late 1640s, came easily to him. So did the writing of political ballads, those boons to the sales of newsbooks.[218] Each issue was introduced by a run of verses which derided the Scottish or English Presbyterians or the 'saints'.

Admittedly there is, as in much Royalist writing of that time, a tension. One side of the Cavalier culture of the late 1640s prides itself on its discrimination and exclusiveness, on its distance from the crudities of popular literature and opinion. The other side is desperate to capture that opinion for the royal cause. There is a similar tension elsewhere in Nedham's writings. On the one hand there is the Nedham who favours Latin tags and shows off his learning. On the other there is the champion of 'the common people of this kingdom', whom the truths he reveals 'most concern'. They deserve instant instruction in politics and history because they 'cannot attend to read chronicles'. They must be given translations of learned works 'so long locked up in a language unknown'.[219] Yet in general his journalism – and the journalism of his fellow Cavalier journalists of the late 1640s[220] – succeed in appealing both to a popular and to an elite readership.[221]

The first pages of *Pragmaticus* announced its commitment to 'wit' and scorned the Roundheads' incapacity for it.[222] *Pragmaticus*, Anthony Wood would recall, was 'very witty, satirical against the presbyterians, and full of loyalty'. It 'made [Nedham] known to, and admired by, the bravadoes and wits of those times'.[223] Nedham now adopted many of the postures, and some of the catchphrases, of *Mercurius Aulicus*, the former rival to *Britanicus*. His change of allegiance produced some startling transformations. The principle of liberty of conscience, which he had championed in *Britanicus*, was derided by *Pragmaticus*.[224] *Britanicus* had condemned the Cavaliers' wish for 'a more jovial kind of Christianity':[225] *Pragmaticus* appeared to share that taste. *Britanicus* had condemned the celebration of Christmas as 'the grand idol of papists and Cavaliers': *Pragmaticus* bemoaned Parliament's efforts to suppress it.[226] The principle of popular sovereignty, at which *Britanicus* had hinted and which would become a key theme of *Mercurius Politicus* in 1651–2, was likewise scorned by *Pragmaticus*.[227] The king's sovereignty, which *Britanicus* had held to be shared with or subordinate to the people's representatives, was now claimed to be independent of them.[228] The 'purple robe' of majesty, which *Britanicus* had associated with the blood shed in the king's name, was now held to be 'venerable and sacred', while the king's 'majesty', which *Britanicus* had accused him of discarding, was now 'the glory of a kingdom'.[229] The Dutch republic, which *Britanicus* had praised, was now presented, as Berkenhead had presented it, as the model of the seditious Roundheads.[230]

Yet if Nedham had parted company with the New Model, his Royalism was never as extreme as Berkenhead's – or as extreme as the Roundhead principles that had been expounded in *Britanicus*. Initially *Pragmaticus* hoped, as Nedham's pamphlets of the summer had done, for a negotiated settlement between king and army.[231] In the spring of 1648 he repeated his earlier argument that the 'interests' of king and army obliged them to come together. Even so, his attitude to the army leaders had hardened. Their readiness to negotiate in the previous summer, he now concluded, had been a front of Machiavellian hypocrisy.[232] Soon he was expressing sympathy for the 'moderate party' in Parliament which was repeatedly overruled by 'the faction' or 'the saints'.[233] Even so, he continued to see a deal between king and army as the best or likeliest outcome. In the weeks before the execution of the king he clung to the conviction that Cromwell would restore (in order to dominate) the king, without whom he could never secure an adequate power-base.[234]

Nedham was never comfortable with uncompromising Royalism. Was he ever comfortable with Royalism of any kind? Or did his heart – if he had a heart – lie in the emerging republicanism of the last issues of *Mercurius Britanicus* and of *Vox Plebis*? In 1656, when employed by the protectorate, he would publish a treatise, *The Excellencie of a Free State*, which was ostensibly an apologia for the regime but which supplied, between the lines, a clever and daring republican attack on it.[235] He is unlikely to have been attempting anything so two-faced or risky in 1647–9. If he was, then the outcome must have been counter-productive, for *Pragmaticus* strengthened the Cavalier cause and weakened the Roundhead one. Yet Nedham was no one's poodle. In the late 1640s, as so often in his career, he found ways of preserving his independence of voice even while mouthing the slogans of his political masters. We find him reminding his readers of the Dutch threat to England's maritime strength,[236] a point he would soon make, in a more dynamic form, as part of a republican programme; and we find him implying that a free State would mount a much more effective challenge to the Dutch, who had 'engrossed our trade' and exploited England's divisions, than a restored monarchy.[237]

In the late 1640s, too, he repeatedly analysed current political developments, as radicals on the Roundhead side were learning to do[238] (and as we have seen Nedham himself doing briefly in *Britanicus*), in terms of the classical classifications of government: of monarchy, aristocracy, democracy, oligarchy.[239] That language, admittedly, was not a Roundhead preserve. It had been first applied to the politics of the Puritan Revolution in the king's *Answer to the Nineteen Propositions* in 1642, which argued that the English government was a mixed government.[240] In 1676, writing on behalf of the Restoration regime, Nedham would dwell on the 'excellent delineation' of the English constitution to be found in that document.[241] In *Pragmaticus*, too, Nedham put the classical vocabulary to anti-republican use.[242] Even so, Royalists generally regarded the king's momentary adoption of that vocabulary in 1642 as a mistake, which had legitimized the questioning of the royal prerogative. The *Answer* prepared the ground for the conceptual breakthrough achieved by Nedham and others in the 1650s, when classical republicanism swept aside the sanctions of the ancient constitution. We cannot tell whether Nedham harboured republican intentions in 1647–9. What we can say is that his Royalism of those years advanced no political or constitutional theory to match those of his Roundhead and republican writings. Nedham's was the Royalism of an instinctive anti-Puritan, not of an instinctive monarchist.

In the weeks before the regicide, Nedham's freedom and safety were in mounting jeopardy.[243] He survived unscathed, but had to abandon *Pragmaticus*. From April until June 1649, to the exasperation of England's new rulers, he was able to resume its production. In that time he appears to have written much of his copy at Minster Lovell (close to his native Burford). There he was 'sheltered' in a 'high room' in the house of the Royalist divine and writer Peter Heylin, who had written the early numbers of *Mercurius Aulicus* before Berkenhead took over. But Nedham's partnership with Heylin would soon be shattered. In 1650, as Heylin's early biographer would recall, Nedham, 'like Balaam the son of Beor, hired with the wages of unrighteousness, corrupted with mercenary gifts and bribes, became the only apostate of the nation, and writ for the pretended Commonwealth ... for which the doctor could never after endure the mention of his name, who had so disobliged his country, and the royal party, by his shameful tergivisation'.[244]

VII

That 'tergivization' was conducted in desperate circumstances. In June 1649 there began what Nedham called his 'scene of calamity'. Having been (as he believed) betrayed, in circumstances which cannot be reconstructed, by his friend the treacherous attorney James Thompson, he was arrested and sent to Newgate.[245] In August he escaped, and wrote a pamphlet urging Parliament to do what, in the periods when he wrote for it, he consistently advised it not to do: to show leniency to its enemies.[246] Until November he was 'a pilgrim about the country'. Then, apparently, he saw in the Rump's Engagement of loyalty, which he quickly signed, a chance 'to preserve my peace upon rational terms'. He returned to London, where he wrote to his friend Henry Oxinden begging the loan of five pounds. The letter, which describes his predicament, is characteristic of Nedham's *joco-serio* vein:

> I dare not so much as peep abroad to converse with any, but am constrained to associate with rats, old books, and cobwebs, in the suburbs of hell, where I hope nobody will imagine to find me ... Nay, did you but see my clothes, you would suppose them plundered from half a dozen factions, or begged for God's sake in as many several nations; and this habit I rant in, partly out of necessity, partly on purpose to obscure myself; whereto my periwig likewise very much contributes, being red, and so looks like a cap-case dropped from some well-complexioned sinner that had been executed at Tyburn, begged by the College for an anatomy, and after converted at the 'pothecary's into mummy.

Then comes the seriousness: 'the truth in good earnest is, I am much distressed every way'.[247]

He had been brought to that pass, he explained, because he had 'been a little more religious than Mr. Thompson in point of friendship, and valued my integrity above my life or livelihood'.[248] Nedham was not normally free with professions of religion or integrity. Whatever the place of those virtues in his dealings with Thompson, they did not prevent him from writing, at the same time, to his friend John Bradshaw, the president of the Council of State, who secured his release.[249] It may be that William Lenthall, the Speaker of the House of Commons, who had an estate in Nedham's native Burford and who, says Wood, 'knew [Nedham] and his relations well', also helped him.[250] It may be too that Nedham had to hand over Royalist secrets to obtain his liberty.[251] At all events, within a few months he found himself not only free and safe but prosperously employed. In the summer of 1650 he became the leading propagandist of the Commonwealth. It was the turn of the Royalists to rub their eyes. *Mercurius Politicus*, which began its weekly issues in June 1650, was, wrote Anthony Wood, 'so extreme contrary to the former that the generality for a long time, especially the most generous royalists, could not believe that that intelligence could possibly be written by the same hand that wrote the *M. Pragmaticus*'.[252]

There was no doubting the success of the new newsbook. *Politicus*, Royalists acknowledged, was 'the Goliah of the Philistines ... whose pen was in comparison of others like a weaver's beam'. It 'had very great influence upon numbers of inconsiderable persons, such who have a strange presumption that all must needs be true that is in print'.[253] So different from *Pragmaticus* in its allegiance, *Politicus* none the less resumed, especially in its opening numbers, the satirical high spirits of the earlier newsbook (though the new publication contained no ballads). Presenting itself as the Commonwealth's 'fool',[254] *Politicus* was particularly close to its predecessor in its mockery of Scots and Presbyterians. The willingness of England's rulers to sanction writing of such exuberant irreverence in the summer of 1650, when the fortunes of the new rulers were at their nadir, indicates the urgency of their need to win over a hostile public. For it was at that time that the official Puritanism of the revolution was at its grimmest, and that fierce measures were taken against blasphemy and adultery and frivolity of dress.[255]

The unorthodoxy of Nedham's stance was facilitated by unorthodox backers. In the winter of 1650–1 *Politicus* became the spokesman for a group of MPs who were committed to a programme of political and economic radicalism. At their forefront were the republicans Henry Marten and Thomas Chaloner. They were supported from outside the Commons by Nedham's friend John Bradshaw.[256] In 1652, in dedicating his translation and edition of John Selden's *Mare Clausum* to Parliament, Nedham disclosed that he had been 'indebted' in his research '(as I am also for many other favours) to a Right Honourable Member of your own great assembly'.[257] We do not know who he meant, but the republican group perhaps supplies the likeliest candidates. As early as January 1646 Nedham had discreetly demonstrated his support for Henry Marten in one of those succinct asides that can suddenly illuminate his news reports. Marten, who had been expelled from the House and sent to the Tower for questioning the necessity of kingship, was readmitted to Parliament. 'I am glad of it', signalled *Britanicus*.[258] In 1648 Nedham's friend John Hall, who had revived *Britanicus* even as Nedham was writing *Pragmaticus*, used his columns to hail Marten as 'our English Brutus, that durst in the beginning of these times speak more than others could wish'.[259] *Pragmaticus*, it is true, vilified Marten and Chaloner, not least for their radical views. Yet the statements which Nedham there attributed to them, especially their anti-Scottish ones,[260] were close to statements made by Nedham himself under his Roundhead hat.

In the winter of 1650–1 the group headed by Marten and Chaloner made powerful headway in Parliament. To the discomfort of moderates, they persuaded the Rump to give official recognition to the 'courage and fidelity' of the men who had brought the king to justice and to recommend 'the memory thereof to posterity'. That decision by Parliament, declared *Politicus*, 'was well worthy their best resolutions'.[261] No less keenly than in *Britanicus* earlier, Nedham scorned 'moderate' and 'lukewarm' supporters of the Parliament.[262] He spoke for the 'honest party' or 'faithful party' in the Commons who resisted all inducements towards compromise.[263] He spoke too for the men characterized by David Underdown as the 'honest' radicals in the country at large, who had promoted the regicide and now demanded their reward:[264] for what Nedham called the Commonwealth's 'party of its own throughout the nation, men of valour and virtue'.[265]

The Marten-Chaloner group had not only a political but an economic programme. It secured the establishment of a Council of Trade and promoted measures for the encouragement of shipping, for the supply of convoys for merchant-ships, for the ending of the monopolies of big trading companies, for the reform of the Mint, for the abolition or the removal of abuses in the manufacture of gold and silver thread. Nedham, who maintained that "tis trade must make this nation rich and secure', went out of his way to advocate or advertise those measures.[266] The same group insisted on a tough negotiating stance towards foreign ambassadors, and steered the Commonwealth towards a recognition that its diplomatic interest lay in an alliance with the traditional enemy of English Protestantism, Spain. Here too Nedham signalled and supported the policies of the group.[267] Above all, his friends in Parliament sought, by building up England's sea-power, to give her the greatness of which they believed a republic to be uniquely capable. Chaloner longed for Cromwell to complete his land-war in Scotland and to look 'towards the sea, which [is] our main business now'.[268] Nedham echoed Chaloner's point: the Commonwealth was 'the greatest and most glorious republic that the sun ever saw, except the Roman. God hath made it so by land and will by sea; for without that the land is nothing'.[269]

Marten and Chaloner, and their close friend and parliamentary ally Henry Neville, were known as 'those wits'. Marten, recorded John Aubrey, had 'an incomparable wit for repartees'.[270] No less than Nedham, he and his friends disliked the solemnities and the theology of Puritanism. He, Chaloner and Neville were all renowned for their irreverence and suspected of atheism.[271] Those were the men in whose company, in the brief period of their political prominence in the early 1650s, Nedham was able to bring his republicanism and his anti-Puritanism together. 'Wit in a Roundhead' was legitimate at last.[272]

Notes

[1] P. W. Thomas, *Sir John Berkenhead 1617–1679* (Oxford, 1969).

[2] For the distinctive experience of the 1620s see H. R. Trevor-Roper, *Religion, the Reformation and Social Change* (London, 1967), pp. 246–7, 281–2.

[3] See, for example, *Mercurius Britanicus* (hereafter *Merc. Brit.*), 8 Dec. 1645, p. 960.

[4] *Ibid.*, 20 May 1644, p. 284; cf. *Mercurius Pragmaticus* (hereafter *Merc. Prag.*), 15 Aug. 1648, p. [1].

[5] *Merc. Brit.*, 25 Nov. 1644, p. 465; *Vox Plebis* (London, 1646), p. 61 (a passage written, as we shall see, by Nedham); [Nedham], *A Plea for the King and Kingdom* (London, 1648), pp. 10, 20, 25, 27; [Nedham?], *The Manifold Practices and Attempts of the Hamiltons* (London, 1648), p. 6; *Mercurius Politicus* (hereafter *Merc. Pol.*), 15 May 1651, p. 284, 12 Aug. 1652, p. 1789; [Nedham], *The Case Stated between England and the United Provinces* (London, 1652), p. 46; *New Idea of the Practice of Physic written by ... Franciscus de la Boe* (London, 1675), preface (by Nedham); M[archamont] N[edham], *A Discourse concerning Schools* (London, 1663), p. 14; M[archamont] N[edham], *Medela Medicinae* (London, 1665), pp. 18, 211; [Nedham], *The Excellencie of a Free State* (London, 1757 edn.), pp. 10, 24, 41, 55, 158. Cf. [Joh]n [Ha]ll, *A Letter written to a Gentleman in the Country touching the Dissolution of the Late Parliament* (London, 1653), p. 14. (For the pertinence of Hall's writings to Nedham's see below, n. 8.)

[6] *Merc. Brit.*, 1 Dec. 1645, p. 952; cf. John Hall, *The Grounds and Reasons of Monarchy* (Edinburgh, 1651), preface.

[7] That point is made by Philip Knachel in his edition of Nedham's *The Case of the Commonwealth of England Stated* (Folger Shakespeare Library, 1969), p. xlii, and by Joseph Frank, *Cromwell's Press Agent: A Critical Biography of Marchamont Nedham, 1620–1678* (Lanham, MD, 1980), p. 171. I am indebted to Frank's book, although I sometimes dissent from it.

[8] The internal evidence of Nedham's authorship in the works which I freshly attribute to him will normally be obvious enough to readers familiar with works already known to be his. He may sometimes have collaborated with other authors. A particularly close literary partner was John Hall of Durham. Much that was published in Nedham's name could have been written by Hall, and vice versa; much that was written anonymously could have been written by either or both of them.

[9] *Case of the Commonwealth*, p. 3.

[10] [Nedham], *The True Character of a Rigid Presbyter* (London, 1661), preface.

[11] Quoted by Knachel, *Case of the Commonwealth*, pp. xli–xlii, from Nedham's *A Pacquet of Advices and Animadversions* (London, 1676).

[12] Cf. N. P., *A Reply to that Malicious Letter, pretended to be sent from Brussels* (London, 1660).

[13] *Aulicus his Hue and Cry sent forth after Britanicus* (London, 1645), p. 4; *A Rope for Pol* (London, 1660). Cf. *Britanicus his Blessing* (London, 1646), p. 2; *Mercurius Britanicus his Welcome to Hell* (London, 1646); *The Downfall of Mercurius Brittanicus, Pragmaticus, Politicus* (London, 1660).

[14] Anthony Wood, *Athenae Oxonienses*, 4 vols. (Oxford, 1813–20), vol. III, p. 1181.

[15] British Library (hereafter B.L.), Additional MS. 28,001 (Oxinden papers), fos. 117, 118v.

[16] Wood, *Athenae Oxionienses*, vol. III, p. 1182.

[17] Frank, *Cromwell's Press Agent*, p. 171.

[18] Helen Darbishire (ed.), *The Early Lives of Milton* (London, 1965), pp. 44–5, 74.

[19] See my contribution to David Wootton (ed.), *Republicanism, Liberty, and Commercial Society* (Stanford, 1994), pp. 45–81, 111–12.

[20] *The Hue and Cry after those Rambling Protonotaries of the Times, Mercurius Elenticus, Britanicus, Melanchollichus, and Aulicus* (London, 1652), p. 4; *The Poor Committee-Man's Accompt, avouched by Britannicus* (n.p., [1647]).

[21] *Discourse concerning Schools*, p. 3.

[22] Joseph Frank, *The Beginnings of the English Newspaper 1620–1660* (Cambridge, MA, 1961), p. 57.

[23] C. M. Clyde, *The Struggle for the Freedom of the Press in England* (St Andrews, 1934), p. 45.

[24] Cf. *Mercurius Anti-Britanicus, or, The Second Part of the King's Cabinet Vindicated* ([Oxford], 1645), pp. 24–5. There is uncertainty on this subject, because contemporaries were uncertain. Anthony Cotton ('London newsbooks in the Civil War', D. Phil. thesis, University of Oxford, 1971, pp. 71–2) proposes a role for Audley in the writing of *Britanicus*, especially in the earlier numbers. His argument cannot be disproved, but those numbers do contain passages distinctively characteristic of Nedham.

[25] Cotton, 'London newsbooks', pp. 60ff.

[26] *Ibid.*, pp. 41, 43.

[27] Thomas, *Sir John Berkenhead*, p. 37.

[28] Cotton, 'English newsbooks', pp. 30–1, 74–5.

[29] *Merc. Brit.*, 5 Feb. 1644, pp. 163, 168, 18 Nov. 1644, pp. 459–60, 25 Nov. 1644, p. 465 (and see *ibid.*, 17 Oct. 1643, p. 60); *Mercurius Urbanus*, 9 Nov. 1643, p. 14; [William Prynne], *A Check to Brittanicus* (London, 1642), p. 3; [Nedham], *A Check to the Checker of Britanicus* (London, 1644). Berkenhead's frequent attacks on Say and his family would be enough to explain many, but by no means all, of *Britanicus'* kind words for them.

[30] Sir William Brereton is likely to have been one such contact (although he too was a regular target of *Aulicus*): *Merc. Brit.*, 30 Nov. 1643, pp. 106–7, 12 Feb. 1644, p. 176, 3 June 1644, p. 308, 9 Dec. 1644, p. 475, 17 Mar. 1645, p. 606, 9 Feb. 1646, p. 1031. For other probable and possible contacts in the army and regions see *Merc. Brit.*, 15 Apr. 1644, pp. 253–4 (Yorkshire), 20 May 1644, p. 284, 27 May 1644, p. 294, 8 July 1644, p. 329, 19 Aug. 1644, p. 374, 26 Aug. 1644, pp. 376–7 (all Kent), 29 Dec. 1645, p. 979 (Col. Birch), 12 Jan. 1646, p. 999, 2 Feb. 1646, pp. 1022–3 (Col. Sanderson's regiment).

[31] Cf. Cotton, 'London newsbooks', p. 41.

[32] For that saga see, for example, *Merc. Brit.*, 10 Oct. 1643, p. 55, 10 Mar. 1645, pp. 586, 588; *Mercurius Aulicus*, 25 Sep. 1643, p. 85, 1 Oct, 1643, pp. 101–3, 107, 29 June 1644, p. 1049, 10 Aug. 1644, pp. 1113–14, 11 May 1645, p. 1576.

[33] Thomas, *Sir John Berkenhead*, pp. 90, 117.

[34] *Merc. Brit.*, 2 Feb. 1646, p. 1022.

[35] Thomas, *Sir John Berkenhead*, pp. 42, 74–6.

[36] *Merc. Brit.*, 5 Jan. 1646, pp. 985–6.

[37] *Ibid.*, 30 Sep. 1644, p. 399; cf. *ibid.*, 28 Oct. 1644, p. 431, and *Check to the Checker of Britanicus*, sig. e2.

[38] *Merc. Brit.*, 18 Aug. 1645, p. 833; cf. *ibid.*, 5 Aug. 1644, p. 361.

[39] *The Spie*, 20 Feb. 1644, p. 32.

[40] *Merc. Brit.*, 13 May 1644, p. 278, 30 Sep. 1644, p. 402, 16 Mar. 1646, p. 1061, 18 May 1646, p. 1118; [Nedham], *Britanicus his Pill to Cure Malignancy* (London, 1644), p. 6; [Nedham], *Mercurius Britanicus his Apologie* (London, 1645), pp. 4–5. Cf. [Nedham], *The Lawyer of Lincolnes-Inne Reformed* (London, 1647), p. 9; [Nedham], *Reverend Alderman Atkins (The Shit-Breech)* (London, 1648), title-page; *New Idea of the Practice of Physic*, preface; [Nedham?], *Plaine English* (London, 1660), p. 7.

[41] *Merc. Brit.*, 3 Nov. 1645, p. 913.

[42] *Ibid.*, 5 Aug. 1644, p. 361.

[43] J. M. French (ed.), *The Life Records of John Milton*, 5 vols. (New Brunswick, NJ, 1949–58), vol. II, p. 311.

[44] See too John Fitzjames' invocation of those words in a letter to Nedham on 21 July 1658: B.L. microfilms, Northumberland MSS, 552. I am grateful to the duke of Northumberland for permission to read and cite that microfilm. See too [John Hall], *Lusus Serius: or, Serious Passe-Time* (London, 1654).

[45] *Merc. Prag.*, 4 Apr. 1648, pp. [1]–[2].

[46] Thomas, *Sir John Berkenhead*, p. ix.

[47] *Merc. Pol.*, 29 Aug. 1650, p. 192, 5 Sep. 1650, p. 203, 12 Sep. 1650, p. 209.

[48] Thomas, *Sir John Berkenhead*, p. 121.

[49] *Ibid.*, pp. 118–20.

[50] *Mercurius Anti-Britanicus, or, The Second Part of the King's Cabinet Vindicated*, p. 25. Cf. *Britanicus Vapulans* (n.p., [1643]), p. 3.

[51] *Mercurius Britanicus, or, Part of the King's Cabinet Vindicated* ([Oxford], 1645), p. 11; *Britanicus Vapulans*, pp. 2–4, 7.

[52] Thomas, *Sir John Berkenhead*, p. 120.

[53] *Britanicus Vapulans*, p. 3.

[54] *Ibid.*, p. 3.

[55] *Ibid.*, 12 May 1645, p. 745, 1 Sep. 1645, pp. 854–5, 12 Jan. 1646, p. 999; *Britanicus his Pill*, p. 7.

[56] *Merc. Brit.*, 22 Apr. 1644, p. 254, 13 May 1644, p. 278, 19 Aug. 1644, p. 374, 14 Oct. 1644, p. 422; cf. *ibid.*, 28 Dec. 1643, p. 137.

[57] *Ibid.*, 19 Sep. 1643, p. 26, 16 Nov. 1643, p. 89, 23 Nov. 1643, p. 97, 30 Nov. 1643, p. 105, 11 Jan. 1644, p. 153, 12 Mar. 1644, p. 199, 17 Feb. 1645, p. 551.

[58] *Merc. Brit.*, [1 July] 1644, p. 320; cf. *ibid.*, 27 May 1644, p. 230, 7 Oct. 1644, p. 414.

[59] *Ibid.*, 12 May 1645, p. 745.

[60] *Ibid.*, 30 Sep. 1644, p. 403; cf. *ibid.*, 22 Apr. 1644, p. 254, 2 Sep. 1644, p. 390.

[61] *Check to the Checker of Britanicus*, sig. e2.

[62] B.L., Add. MS. 28,002 (Oxinden papers), fos. 141, 328v; Dorothy Gardiner (ed.), *The Oxinden and Peyton Letters* (London, 1937), pp. 143, 161, 168, 199–200.

[63] B. L., Add. MS, 28,001, fos. 116v–117.

[64] Oxinden, *Charles Triumphant* (privately printed, 1660).

[65] Gardiner, *Oxinden and Peyton Letters*, pp. 227–9, 313–14.

[66] *Merc. Brit.*, 2 Sep. 1644, p. 387.

[67] *Ibid.*, 23 Mar. 1646, p. 1065.

[68] *Ibid.*, 10 Oct. 1643, p. 53; cf. *ibid.*, 20 Jan. 1645, p. 521.

[69] *Ibid.*, 30 Sep. 1644, p. 400, 14 Oct. 1644, p. 415.

[70] 5 Aug. 1644, pp. 361, 365, 30 Sep. 1644, p. 400, 28 Oct. 1644, p. 435, 3 Mar. 1645,

pp. 575–6, 17 Mar. 1645, p. 598, 16 June 1645, pp. 777–8, 28 July 1645, p. 817, 6 Apr. 1646, pp. 1081–2, 11 May 1646, p. 1110; *Mercurius Britanicus his Apologie*, p. 2.

[71] *Merc. Brit.*, 24 Oct. 1643, p. 65, 25 Mar. 1644, p. 222, 19 Aug. 1644, p. 368, 14 Oct. 1644, p. 415, 28 Oct. 1644, pp. 431, 438, 11 Nov. 1644, p. 454. Cf. [John Hall], *Mercurius Britannicus*, 13 June 1648, pp. 36, 38, 1 Aug. 1648, p. 90.

[72] *Merc. Brit.*, 11 Jan. 1644, p. 153, 2 Sep. 1644, p. 386, 22 Dec. 1645, p. 969. Cf. Hall, *Mercurius Britannicus*, 23 May 1648, p. 16, 30 May 1648, p. 19, 13 June 1648, p. 37, 27 June 1648, p. 54, 4 July 1648, pp. 61, 63, 11 July 1648, pp. 66, 68; J[ohn] H[all], *An Humble Motion to the Parliament of England concerning the Advancement of Learning* (London, 1649), p. 37; [John Hall], *A Serious Epistle to Mr. William Prynne* (London, 1649), p. 3; Thomas, *Sir John Berkenhead*, pp. 102–35.

[73] For Nedham's taste for Jonson see *Merc. Prag.*, 9 Nov. 1647, p. 63; [Nedham], *A Plea for the Kingdom* (London, 1648), p. 10; [Nedham], *Honesty's Best Policy* ([London, 1677]), pp. 7–8. Cf. the allusion to Shakespeare's *Richard II* in [Nedham], *A Cat May Look upon a King* (London, 1652), p. 26. (*A Cat* is usually attributed to Sir Antony Weldon. Perhaps it draws on material by Weldon, but it alludes to issues that arose only when Weldon was probably dead. The prose belongs to Nedham, to whom the work is attributed (as Steve Pincus has kindly pointed out to me) in *Manuscripts of the Harleian Collection*, 4 vols. (London, 1812–1818), vol. I, p. 609.)

[74] *Merc. Brit.*, 3 Oct. 1643, p. 47, [I July] 1644, p. 324, 8 July 1644, p. 328, 26 Aug. 1644, p. 377, 19 Jan. 1646, p. 1003; *Britanicus his Pill*, p. 7.

[75] *Merc. Brit.*, 15 Apr. 1644, p. 252, 29 Apr. 1644, p. 257, [1 July] 1644, p. 322, 8 July 1644, p. 329, 14 Oct. 1644, p. 415, 27 Jan, 1645, p. 528. Cf. *ibid.*, 20 May 1644, p. 304, 10 Feb. 1645, p. 541; Hall, *Grounds and Reasons of Monarchy*, pp. 5, 15. Here Nedham (and Hall) stood in a radical tradition: I hope to discuss elsewhere an earlier manifestation of it in the time and writing of Sir Philip Sidney.

[76] *Merc. Brit.*, 17 Feb. 1645, pp. 550, 554, 10 Mar. 1645, p. 584, 12 May 1645, pp. 745–6, 20 Oct. 1645, p. 900, 3 Nov. 1645, p. 920, 8 Dec. 1645, p. 958, 26 Jan. 1646, p. 1009. Cf. *Lawyer of Lincolnes-Inne Reformed*, p. 1; *Case of the Commonwealth*, pp. xli, 14; [Nedham], *A True State of the Case of the Commonwealth* (London, 1654), p. 50; *Excellencie of a Free State*, p. 21; Nedham, *Interest will not Lie* (London, 1659), pp. 9, 20: *New Idea of the Practice of Physic*, preface; *Medela Medicinae*, p. 242.

[77] French, *Life Records of John Milton*, vol. II, p. 311. Cf. Gardiner, *Oxinden and Peyton Letters*, p. 143.

[78] *Merc. Prag*, 4 Apr. 1648, p. [1].

[79] *Merc. Brit.*, 29 Dec. 1645, p. 984; cf. *ibid.*, 5 May 1645, p. 744.

[80] *Ibid.*, 6 May 1644, p. 270.

[81] 25 Mar. 1644, p. 217; cf. *ibid.*, 2 Sep. 1644, p. 389.

[82] *Ibid.*, 26 Aug. 1644, p. 378; cf. *ibid.*, 5 Jan. 1646, pp. 989–90.

[83] *Ibid.*, 9 Dec. 1644, p. 474.

[84] *Merc. Brit.*, 18 Mar. 1644, p. 209.

[85] *Ibid.*, 29 Dec. 1645, p. 979.

[86] *Ibid.*, [1 July] 1644, p. 323.

[87] Cotton, 'London newsbooks', p. 68.

[88] *Merc. Pol.*, 5 Sep. 1650, p. 193; *Case of the Commonwealth*, p. 4; *True Character of a Rigid Presbyter*, esp. pp. 1–2, 28; *Pacquet of Advices*, p. [63].

[89] *Merc. Brit.*, 30 Sep. 1644, pp. 401–2; cf. *ibid.*, 5 Aug. 1644, p. 361.

[90] *Ibid.*, 17 June 1644, p. 308.

[91] *Ibid.*, 3 Mar. 1645, p. 582.

[92] *Ibid.*, 5 Aug. 1644, p. 365, 3 Mar. 1645, pp. 578–9.

[93] *Ibid.*, 1 Sep. 1645, pp. 854–5.

[94] *Ibid.*, 28 Dec. 1643, p. 141.

[95] *Ibid.*, 7 Oct. 1644, p. 407.

[96] *Ibid.*, 9 Sep. 1644, p. 398.

[97] *Ibid.*, 13 Jan. 1645, p. 517.

[98] *Ibid.*, 8 July 1644, p. 334.

[99] *Ibid.*, 30 Sep. 1644, pp. 403–4, 28 Oct. 1644, p. 432; cf. *ibid.*, [1 July] 1644, p. 325.

[100] *Ibid.*, 12 Dec. 1644, p. 475–6.

[101] *Ibid.*, 18 Mar. 1644, p. 210.

[102] *Britanicus his Pill*, p. 7; *Merc. Brit.*, 25 Nov. 1644, p. 469, 12 May 1645, p. 745.

[103] *Merc. Pol.*, 7 Aug. 1651, p. 965.

[104] *Merc. Brit.*, [1 July] 1644, p. 323; cf. *ibid.*, 2 Sep. 1644, p. 387.

[105] Nedham, *Independencie no Schisme* (London, 1646), p. 10. Cf. *ibid.*, p. 11; *An Answer to Nine Arguments* (London, 1645), preface (by Nedham).

[106] *Merc. Brit.*, 13 Jan. 1645, p. 517; *Independencie no Schisme*, p. 2. Cf. John Hall, *The Grounds and Reasons of Monarchy* (Edinburgh, 1651), p. 12.

[107] Nedham, *The Case of the Kingdom Stated* (London, 1647), p. 8.

[108] *Merc. Brit.*, 7 Oct. 1644, p. 410, 21 Oct. 1644, pp. 428–9.

[109] *Ibid.*, 30 Dec. 1644, p. 502; cf. *Merc. Pol.*, 6 Nov. 1651, p. 1174.

[110] *Merc. Brit.*, 4 Jan. 1644, p. 149, 29 May 1644, p. 285, 9 Dec. 1644, pp. 474, 475–6, 7 Apr. 1645, p. 712, 16 June 1645, p. 784, 22 Dec. 1645, p. 971.

[111] *Ibid.*, 8 July 1644, p. 328, 6 Apr. 1646, p. 1088.

[112] See my contribution to Wootton, *Republicanism, Liberty, and Commercial Society*, pp. 72–3.

[113] *Merc. Brit.*, 30 Sep. 1644, p. 400.

[114] *Ibid.*, 26 Sep. 1643, p. 34, 25 Mar. 1644, p. 218, 22 Apr. 1644, p. 252, 14 Oct. 1644, pp. 415–16, 20 Jan. 1645, p. 526, 25 Aug. 1645, p. 848, 19 Jan. 1646, p. 1002.

[115] *Ibid.*, 28 Oct. 1644, p. 432.

[116] *Ibid.*, 2 Sep. 1644, p. 386.

[117] *Ibid.*, 29 Dec. 1645, p. 981, 12 Jan. 1646, p. 998.

[118] *Ibid.*, 29 Dec. 1645, p. 979.

[119] *Ibid.*, 8 July 1644, p. 331.

[120] *Ibid.*, 30 June 1645, p. 800. Cf. *ibid.*, 8 July 1644, p. 331, 27 Oct. 1645, p. 912, 12 Jan. 1646, p. 1000; Hall, *Humble Motion*, p. 3.

[121] *Merc. Brit.*, 24 June 1644, pp. 313–14.

[122] *Ibid.*, 19 Aug. 1644, p. 374.

[123] *Ibid.*, 30 June 1645, p. 800; cf. *ibid.*, 12 Jan. 1646, p. 1000.

[124] *Ibid.*, 29 Dec. 1645, p. 981.

[125] *Ibid.*, 30 Sep. 1644, p. 404.

[126] *Ibid.*, 28 Oct. 1644, p. 432, 11 Nov. 1644, p. 462, 7 July 1645, p. 808, 15 Dec. 1645, p. 968.

[127] *Ibid.*, 15 Apr. 1644, p. 254.

[128] *Ibid.*, 18 Aug. 1645, pp. 833, 840; cf. *ibid.*, 14 Oct. 1644, p. 415.

[129] Thomas, *Sir John Berkenhead*, p. 77.

[130] *Merc. Brit.*, 22 Dec. 1645, p. 971.

[131] *Ibid.*, 19 Jan. 1646, p. 1002.

132 *Ibid.*, 20 May 1644, p. 286, 12 Jan. 1646, p. 994.

133 *Ibid.*, 14 Oct. 1644, p. 415. Cf. *ibid.*, 29 July 1644, p. 351, 7 Oct. 1644, pp. 412–13, 9 Dec. 1644, p. 471, 23 Dec. 1644, p. 494, 6 Jan. 1645, p. 510.

134 *Ibid.*, 21 July 1645, p. 811; cf. *ibid.*, 18 Nov. 1644, p. 462.

135 *Ibid.*, 22 Dec. 1645, p. 971.

136 *Ibid.*, 28 Oct. 1644, p. 432.

137 *Britanicus his Pill*, p. 8. Cf. *Merc. Brit.*, 18 May 1646, p. 1118; *Cat May Look upon a King*, pp. 43, 66, 75; *Interest will not Lie*, p. 24.

138 *Merc. Brit.*, 6 Mar. 1644, p. 198, 12 Mar. 1644, p. 206. Cf. *ibid.*, 27 Apr. 1646, p. 1087; *Case of the Commonwealth*, pp. 24, 36; *Merc. Pol.*, 7 Nov. 1650, p. 358.

139 *Merc. Brit.*, 30 Sep. 1644, p. 400.

140 *Ibid.*, 18 May 1646, p. 1113.

141 *Ibid.*, 5 Aug. 1644, p. 365.

142 *Ibid.*, 10 Mar. 1645, pp. 586–7. Cf. *ibid.*, 16 Sep. 1643, p. 36, 17 June 1644, p. 304, 24 June 1644, p. 318, 9 Sep. 1644, p. 396, 19 Jan. 1646, p. 1004.

143 *Ibid.*, 26 Aug. 1644, p. 375.

144 *Ibid.*, 21 Dec. 1643, p. 136.

145 *Ibid.*, 30 Sep. 1644, p. 400; cf. *ibid.*, 19 Jan. 1646, p. 1004.

146 *Ibid.*, 21 Oct. 1644, p. 426.

147 Cf. Cotton, 'London newsbooks', p. 66; Frank, *Cromwell's Press Agent*, pp. 23–4.

148 *Merc. Brit.*, 4 Aug. 1645, p. 832, 22 Dec. 1645, p. 969.

149 *Ibid.*, 3 Mar. 1645, p. 576; cf. *ibid.*, 10 Feb. 1645, p. 541.

150 *Ibid.*, 3 Mar. 1645, pp. 575–6.

151 *Ibid.*, 16 June 1645, p. 778.

152 *Ibid.*, 30 June 1645, p. 794.

153 *Ibid.*, 4 Aug. 1645, p. 829.

154 Public Record Office, SP29/114, fo. 155. I owe my knowledge of that document to the kindness of Steve Pincus.

155 *Ibid.*, 4 Aug. 1645, p. 825.

156 *Mercurius Britanicus his Apologie*, p. 2.

157 *Merc. Brit.*, 11 May 1646, p. 1110.

158 *Ibid.*, 18 May 1646, p. 1111; cf. *ibid.*, 12 Jan. 1645, p. 997.

159 Cotton, 'London newsbooks', pp. 76, 101–3.

160 Frank, *Cromwell's Press Agent*, p. 29.

161 Cf. J. G. A. Pocock, 'A discourse of sovereignty', in Nicholas Phillipson and Quentin Skinner (eds.), *Political Discourse in Early Modern England* (Cambridge, 1993), p. 388.

162 *Merc. Brit.*, 12 Jan. 164 , p. 994.

163 *Ibid.*, 23 Nov. 1643, p. 99; cf. Hall, *Mercurius Britannicus*, 13 June 1648, pp. 34–5.

164 *Merc. Brit.*, 9 Sep. 1644, p. 396.

165 *Ibid.*, 9 Nov. 1643, p. 87, 12 Mar. 1644, p. 205, 25 Mar. 1644, pp. 216–17, 22 Apr. 1644, p. 249, 28 Oct. 1644, p. 433, 27 Jan. 1645, p. 528, 28 Apr. 1645, pp. 731–2, 2 June 1645, p. 771, 24 Nov. 1645, p. 944, 13 Apr. 1646, pp. 1000–3, 20 Apr. 1646, pp. 1080–7.

166 *Ibid.*, 5 Feb. 1644, p. 165.

167 *Ibid.*, 25 Mar. 1644, p. 216.

168 *Ibid.*, 24 June 1644, p. 312.

169 *Answer to Nine Arguments*, preface; cf. Hall, *Humble Motion*, pp. 23–4, 31.

[170] J. A. W. Gunn, *Politics and the Public Interest in the Seventeenth Century* (London, 1969), pp. 33–5, 43–4, 52.

[171] Gunn (*ibid.*, p. 48n.) does, however, suggest that Nedham probably wrote a pamphlet of 1648 which discusses 'interest', *Good English*. The pamphlet is plainly Nedham's, whose earlier writings it plunders. Nedham, as Gunn observes, commended it in *Merc. Prag.*, 2 May 1648, p. [8]. In 1648 Nedham may also have written *A Venice Looking-Glasse*; cf. *Merc. Prag.*, 29 Aug. 1648, p. [12].

[172] [Nedham], *Christianissimus Christiandus* (London, 1678), p. 67. Cf. *Merc. Pol.*, 6 Mar. 1651, pp. 623–4.

[173] *Case of the Kingdom Stated*, preface; cf. *ibid.*, p. 8.

[174] *A Treatise of the Interest of the Princes and States of Christendom ... by ... the Duke of Rohan* (Paris, 1640), pp. 338–9.

[175] *Excellencie of a Free State*, p. 29; cf. *Merc. Pol.*, 13 June 1650, p. 3.

[176] *Merc. Brit.*, 3 Nov. 1645, p. 920.

[177] John Selden, *Of the Dominion of the Seas*, trans. and ed. Marchamont Nedham (London, 1652), sig. d1.

[178] *Merc. Brit.* 12 Mar. 1644, p. 206, 15 Dec. 1645, p. 966, 18 May 1646, p. 1118.

[179] See especially *Interest will not Lie*, p. 3. Nedham's fullest discussions of domestic interests are in that pamphlet and in *Case of the Kingdom Stated*; *Good English*; *Case of the Commonwealth*.

[180] *Case Stated between England and the United Provinces*, p. 23.

[181] *Merc. Pol.*, 7 July 1653, p. 2560 (letter ostensibly from Amsterdam).

[182] *Case of the Commonwealth*, p. 4. Did Nedham here have in mind Shakespeare's *King John* II. ii. 574ff.?

[183] For Nedham's preoccupation with international 'balance': *Good English*, p. 5; *Merc. Pol.*, 5 Dec. 1650, p. 433; [Nedham] *The Pacquet-Boat Advice* (London, 1678), p. 20; *Christianissimus Christiandus*, pp. 67–8; with domestic 'balance': *Merc.Brit.*, 12 Mar. 1644, p. 206; *True State of the Case of the Commonwealth*, p. 10.

[184] *Merc. Prag.*, 21 Mar. 1648, p. [2]; *Merc. Pol.*, 24 July 1651, p. 945 (with which compare *Cat May Look upon a King*, pp. 30–1). Cf. *Merc. Brit.*, 25 Mar. 1644, pp. 216–17, 23 Dec. 1644, p. 488, 29 Dec. 1645, p. 982, 12 Jan. 1646, p. 994; Bodleian Library, Clarendon MS. 34, fos. 17, 88 (Nedham's newsletters, 25 Dec. 1648, 26 Jan. 1649); Hall, *Mercurius Britannicus*, 1 Aug. 1648, p. 90.

[185] *Merc. Pol.*, 15 July 1652, pp. 159–60; *Interest will not Lie*, p. 10.

[186] *Lawyer of Lincolnes-Inne*, p. 9; *Independencie no Schisme*, p. 8.

[187] *Merc. Brit.*, 24 Nov. 1645, p. 944; *Excellencie of a Free State*, pp. 1, 116.

[188] *True State of the Case of the Commonwealth*, p. 49 (cf. *ibid.*, p. 29); *Excellencie of a Free State*, pp. xxvi, 50, 58; *Interest will not Lie*, p. 28. Cf. *Merc. Prag.*, 26 Oct. 1647, p. 46.

[189] *Interest will not Lie*, p. 26; *Excellencie of a Free State*, p. 130.

[190] C. H. Firth (ed.), *The Clarke Papers*, 4 vols. (London 1891–1901), p. 315.

[191] *The Faithfull Scout*, 10 June 1659, pp. 49–50; *The Loyall Scout* vol. I (e.g.), 21 Oct. 1659, p. 199, 28 Oct. 1659, p. 201; *Merc. Prag.*, 6 Sep. 1659, pp. 2–3.

[192] *Medela Medicinae*, pp. 215, 218, 242, 311.

[193] The passage plainly by Nedham begins on p. 60. His hand may also be present on pp. 3–5, 58–60.

[194] I have discussed that friendship in a study of Nedham's relations with Milton, another close friend of Bradshaw: n.272.

[195] *Merc. Prag.*, 6 Oct. 1647, pp. 22, 24, 19 Oct. 1647, p. 35, 26 Oct. 1647, pp. 47–8, 2 Nov. 1647, p. 55, 4 Jan. 1648, pp. [7]–[8], 8 Aug. 1648, p. [8]. Cf. Austin Woolrych, *Soldiers and Statesmen* (London, 1987), p. 192.

[196] Cf. Thomas, *Sir John Berkenhead*, pp. 128, 155.

[197] *Merc. Brit.*, 9 Sep. 1644, p. 396, 21 Oct. 1644, p. 426, 9 Dec. 1644, p. 475. Cf. Hall, *Serious Epistle*, pp. 9–10; Nedham, *Medela Medicinae*, p. 216.

[198] *Merc. Brit.*, 4 Nov. 1644, p. 440.

[199] *Ibid.*, 26 Aug. 1644, p. 379.

[200] *Ibid.*, 26 May 1645, p. 767. Cf. *Merc. Pol.*, 12 June 1651, p. 860; *Good English*, p. 17; *Case Stated between England and the United Provinces*, p. 4; *Medela Medicinae*, title-page.

[201] *Merc. Brit.*, 15 Dec. 1644, p. 964; cf. *Merc. Pol.*, 3 July 1651, p. 887. Cf. *Plaine English* (London, 1643), p. 25. I think it possible, as I may try to explain elsewhere, that Nedham had a hand in that pamphlet.

[202] *Merc. Brit.*, [1 July] 1644, p. 320; cf. *Medela Medicinae*, pp. 216–17.

[203] *Merc. Brit.*, 29 July 1644, p. 353, 28 Oct. 1644, p. 435.

[204] *Merc. Prag.*, 16 Nov. 1647, p. 70.

[205] For another hint of an affinity between Nedham and Lilburne, compare *Merc. Prag.*, 12 Oct. 1647, p. 30 with *Plea for the King and Kingdom*, p. 27. See also *Match Me These Two: or the Conviction and Arraignment of Britannicus and Lilburne* (London, 1647).

[206] *Vox Plebis*, pp. 63, 65, 66 (cf. *ibid.*, p. 59).

[207] Nedham's evident knowledge of and remarks on the army politics of 1647 (*Merc. Prag.*, 21 Sep. 1647, p. 3, 12 Oct. 1647, p. 29; *Pacquet of Advices*, p. 51 (with which cf. *Vox Plebis*, p. 66); *Plea for the King and Kingdom*, p. 23; Woolrych, *Soldiers and Statesmen*, p. 277) raise some tantalizing possibilities. Was he involved in the penning of the declarations that emerged from them? See *Lawyer of Lincolnes-Inne*, p. 1. Did his association with the army secretary John Rushworth, who had licensed *Britanicus* for the army (Cotton, 'London newsbooks', pp. 30–1), give him privileged knowledge? See *Merc. Pol.*, 29 Aug. 1650, p. 186; B.L., Add. MS. 28,003 (Oxinden papers), fo. 43.

[208] *Case of the Kingdom*; *Lawyer of Lincolnes-Inne*; and [Nedham], *A Parallel of Governments* (London, 1647). Cf. [Joh]n [Ha]ll, *A True Account of the Character of the Times*, (London, 1647).

[209] *Case of the Kingdom Stated*, pp. 1, 6.

[210] *Lawyer of Lincolnes-Inne*, pp. 1, 3–4.

[211] *Parallel of Governments*, p. 2 and *passim*.

[212] Thomas, *Sir John Berkenhead*, pp. 62–3, 150.

[213] *Merc. Prag.*, 11 Jan, 1648, p. [8], 12 Sep. 1648, p. [1].

[214] For Nedham as newswriter: Bodleian Library, Clarendon MS. 34, fos. 7–8, 12–13, 17–19, 72–4, 86–8; Northumberland MS. 552, Fitzjames' letters Apr. 1658–Jan. 1659; Longleat, Whitelocke MS. XIII, fos. 49–50, 52–3; Gardiner, *Oxinden and Peyton Letters*, pp. 149–50; *The Character of Mercurius Politicus* (London, 1650), p. 5.

[215] Cf. David Underdown, *Pride's Purge* (Oxford, 1971), pp. 114–15, 138, 214.

[216] *Merc. Prag.*, 21 Dec. 1647, p. [2]. Cf. *ibid.*, 22 Feb. 1648, p. [8], 14 Mar. 1648, pp. [1]–[2], 21 Nov. 1648, pp. [7]–[8].

[217] Cf. Thomas, *Sir John Berkenhead*, p. 167.

[218] Hyder E. Rollins, *Cavalier and Puritan* (New York, 1923), pp. 32ff.

[219] *Cat May Look upon a King*, pp. 32–3; Selden, *Of the Dominion of the Seas*, sig.

A2v. The similarities between those two passages are among the numerous indications that Nedham wrote *Cat*.

220 Thomas, *Sir John Berkenhead*, p. 179.

221 For Nedham's elite readership see, for example, *Historical Manuscripts Commission Reports, De Lisle and Dudley*, vol. VI, p. 601; my contribution to Wootton, *Republicanism, Liberty, and Commercial Society*, p. 434; cf. Underdown, *Pride's Purge*, p. 175.

222 *Merc. Prag.*, 21 Sep. 1647, p. [2].

223 Wood, *Althenae Oxonienses*, vol. III, p. 1181.

224 *Merc. Prag.*, 6 Oct. 1647, p. 18, 21 Mar. 1648, p. [6], 6 June 1648, p. [2], 8 Aug. 1648, pp. [4], [8], 5 Sep. 1648, p. [3].

225 *Merc. Brit.*, 28 Dec. 1643, p. 137.

226 *Merc. Brit.*, 26 Jan. 1646, p. 1110; *Merc. Prag.*, 28 Dec. 1647, p. [1].

227 *Merc. Prag.*, 2 Nov. 1647, p. 54, 12 Dec. 1648, pp. [1]–[2].

228 *Ibid.*, 12 Dec. 1648, p. [2]; cf. *Plea for the King and Kingdom*, p. 22.

229 *Ibid.*, 15 Aug. 1648, pp. [8]–[9], 26 Sep. 1648, p. [6], 12 Dec. 1648, p. [1].

230 *Ibid.*, 11 Jan. 1648, p. [2], 15 Feb. 1648, p. [8].

231 *Ibid.*, 21 Sep. 1647, p. 3; cf. *ibid.*, 28 Sep. 1647, p. 16 (but that issue may be a counterfeit).

232 *Good English*, p. 11.

233 *Merc. Prag.*, 5 Sep. 1648, p. [10], 12 Sep. 1648, pp. [2]–[3]; cf. *ibid.*, 28 Nov. 1648, p. [3].

234 *Merc. Prag.*, 26 Dec. 1648, pp. [2], [8]; Bodleian Library, Clarendon MS. 34, fos. 12–13, 17, 72.

235 See my contribution to Wootton, *Republicanism, Liberty, and Commercial Society*, pp. 77–9.

236 *Merc. Prag.*, 15 Feb. 1648, p. [8]; *Good English*, pp. 5–6; cf. Hall, *Mercurius Britannicus*, p. 34.

237 Bodleian Library, Clarendon MS. 34, fo. 88v.

238 *The Moderate Intelligencer*, 14 Sep. 1648, p. 1529; C. H. Firth (ed.), *Memoirs of Edmund Ludlow*, 2 vols. (London, 1894), vol. I, pp. 184–5.

239 *Merc. Prag.*, 12 Oct. 1647, p. [28], 12 Dec. 1648, p. [2], 26 Dec. 1648, pp. [2], [8], 9 Jan. 1649, p. [2]; *Good English*, pp. 9, 12; Clarendon MS. 34, fos. 13, 17, 72v.

240 Corinne Comstock Weston, *English Constitutional Theory and the House of Lords* (London, 1965), pp. 9–23.

241 *Pacquet of Advices*, pp. 63–6.

242 Cf. D. P., *Severall Politique and Militarie Observations* (London, 1648), esp. pp. 3, 27.

243 Bodleian Library, Clarendon MS. 34, fo. 73; Gardiner, *Oxinden and Peyton Letters*, pp. 146–8.

244 *The Historical and Miscellaneous Works of ... Peter Heylin* (London, 1681), p. xix; cf. Wood, *Athenae Oxonienses*, vol. III. p. 1181.

245 Gardiner, *Oxinden and Peyton Letters*, pp. xxiv, 160–1; cf. B.L., Add. MS. 28,003, fo. 205.

246 *Certain Considerations Tendered ... to an Honourable Member of the Council of State* (London, 1649).

247 Gardiner, *Oxinden and Peyton Letters*, pp. 160–1. Cf. (for the periwig) *The Character of Mercurius Politicus*, p. 2.

[248] Gardiner, *Oxinden and Peyton Letters*, pp. 160–1.

[249] *Ibid.*, p. 161.

[250] Wood, *Athenae Oxonienses*, vol. III, p. 1181; cf. Clarendon MS. 34, fo. 17.

[251] *Character of Mercurius Politicus*, p. 5.

[252] Wood, *Athenae Oxonienses*, vol. III. pp. 1181–2.

[253] *Ibid.*, p. 1182; cf. *Rope for Pol*, preface.

[254] *Merc. Pol.*, 13 June 1650, p. 1.

[255] Keith Thomas, 'The Puritans and adultery', in Donald Pennington and Keith Thomas (eds.), *Puritans and Revolutionaries. Essays … presented to Christopher Hill* (Oxford, 1978), pp. 257–82; Blair Worden, *The Rump Parliament 1648–1653* (Cambridge, 1974), pp. 233–4; Worden, 'Cromwellian Oxford 1652–1660', in *History of [Oxford] University*, vol. IV, ed. Nicholas Tyacke (forthcoming).

[256] Worden, *Rump Parliament*, pp. 251–61.

[257] Selden, *Of the Dominion of the Seas*, sig. A2v.

[258] *Merc. Brit.*, 12 Jan. 1646, p. 1000.

[259] Hall, *Mercurius Britannicus*, 13 June 1648, p. 35.

[260] *Merc. Prag.*, 28 Sep. 1647, p. 4, 18 Jan. 1648, pp. [7]–[8].

[261] *Merc. Pol.*, 19 Dec. 1650, p. 464.

[262] *Ibid.*, 13 Feb. 1651, p. 575, 13 Mar. 1651, p. 647, 24 July 1651, p. 923, 21 Aug. 1651, p. 997, 6 Nov. 1651, p. 1174–5.

[263] *Interest will not Lie*, p. 28.

[264] David Underdown, '"Honest" radicals in the counties', in Pennington and Thomas, *Puritans and Revolutionaries*, pp. 186–205.

[265] *Case of the Commonwealth*, p. 114.

[266] *Merc. Pol.*, 7 Nov. 1650, pp. 359–60, 5 Dec. 1650, pp. 436–7, 26 Dec. 1650, pp. 479–80, 6 Mar. 1651, p. 627, 13 Mar. 1651, pp. 647, 650, 20 Mar. 1651, pp. 664–5, 24 July 1651, p. 945, 19 Feb. 1652, p. 1424, 2 Sept. 1652, p. 1835, 2 Dec. 1652, p. 2056, 23 June 1653, p. [2532], 17 Nov. 1653, p. 2870; Selden, *Of the Dominion of the Seas*, ep. ded.; *Cat May Look upon a King*, pp. 30–1, 100–1.

[267] J. Nickolls (ed.), *Original Letters and Papers of State addressed to Oliver Cromwell* (London, 1743), pp. 39–40, 42–3; *Case of the Commonwealth*, pp. 54–5; *Merc. Pol.*, 23 June 1650, pp. 37–8, 4 July 1650, p. 64, 18 July 1650, p. 95, 15 Aug. 1650, p. 173, 5 Dec. 1650, p. 433, 27 Feb. 1651, p. [620], 6 Mar. 1651, pp. 623–4.

[268] Worden, *Rump Parliament*, p. 254.

[269] Selden, *Of the Dominion of the Seas*, p. 483.

[270] Worden, *Rump Parliament*, pp. 36, 261.

[271] *Ibid.*, p. 260; Worden, 'Classical republicanism and the Puritan Revolution', in Hugh Lloyd-Jones et al. (eds.), *History and Imagination. Essays in Honour of H. R. Trevor-Roper* (London, 1981), p. 195. See, too, the commitment of Neville's close friend and republican ally James Harrington to 'wit and gallantry': J. G. A. Pocock (ed.), *The Political Works of James Harrington* (Cambridge, 1977), pp. 353–4. Neville, as the author of the anonymous *The Parliament of Ladies*, was (loosely) linked with Nedham in *Match Me These Two*.

[272] On Nedham and the 1650s I have now written 'Milton and Marchamont Nedham', in David Armitage, Armand Himy and Quentin Skinner (eds), *Milton and Republicanism* (Cambridge, 1995).

14

Turning frogs into princes: Aesop's *Fables* and the political culture of early modern England

Mark Kishlansky

For nothyng is better than lyberte/ For lyberte shold not be wel sold for alle the gold and syluer of all the world.

(Epimythia, 'Of the Frogs and of Jupiter', 1484)[1]

No Government can th'unsetled vulgar please,
Whom change delight's think quiet a disease.

(Moral, 'Of the Frogs desiring a King', 1651)[2]

So that Government, or No Government; A King of God's Making, or of the Peoples, or none at all; the Multitude are never to be satisfied.

(Moral, 'The Frogs Chuse a King', 1692)[3]

I

Sometimes a fable is just a fable. This was once a truism and is now a paradox. It has been the post-modern project to reduce all cultural productions and human relations to Political acts. It is hard to unthink the thought. For the past decade historians and literary critics of early modern England have been exposing the Political agenda 'inherent' in forms of elite and popular culture from Shakespeare to charivaris. Culture either reinforces the power structure or subverts it. In both cases it is Political. In a world in which publishing is a state monopoly and in which all printers are licensed and all publications censored, writing is a Political act. It can speak directly to political subjects if its voice is that of orthodoxy, or obliquely to them if its voice is that of dissent. Sophisticated readers know that Hobbes' translation of Thucidides is a veiled critique of the Petition of Right and that the revival of Tacitus and Seneca is a covert expression of republicanism. Jonson's masques empower the Stuart monarchy while pastoral poetry is a flight from the corruption of the court.

The Political lens of modern scholars has magnified aspects of human activity that had once seemed obscure, even if on occasion it has made it difficult to see the acorn through the moss. Moreover, the reduction of forms of cultural production to Political acts has itself empowered the objects of study. The light entertainments of poets and playwrights, the orderly ceremonies of the elites and the disorderly festivals of the people are now seen as part of the political power struggle which dominated early modern England. Revel and riot are raised to the level of rebellion. In this context it seems conceptually unsophisticated to argue that there was a time in the early modern period when the stories told to children were not part of a process of indoctrination and did not exist in an arena of political contestation.[4] It seems perversely naive to argue that sometimes a fable is just a fable.

But the creation of the Political as a transcendant 'large P' construct, makes it difficult to study the political as a functional 'small p' mode of behaviour. Indeed, it makes it impossible to study politicization as a process that took place in the early modern period at all. Yet, it can be argued that over the course of the sixteenth and seventeenth centuries contemporaries first become aware of the political dimensions of their lives. This is not to suggest that before then English people lived in an apolitical or pre-political world, that they did not understand power relations, or the nature and forms of government. But it is to suggest that they did not view their world through a political prism at the beginning of this period and that they did so by the end. Not surprisingly, it was the events of the middle of the seventeenth century which, if they did not initiate the process, certainly accelerated it. Before the English Revolution political power was in the hands of a small segment of the social elite and co-ordinated thinking and writing about politics was the occupation of a tiny group of intellectuals. After the English Revolution political power was widely dispersed and the subject of near constant speculation.

Though it would be difficult to establish tests to prove such assertions even without the modern predilection that all acts are Political acts, there are ways to illustrate them. One is through comparison of the publication of standard texts throughout the early modern era. The production of English editions of Aesop's *Fables* provides such an opportunity, for it allows us to observe how 'translators' treated the same material over a 200-year period.[5] The first English edition was published by William Caxton in 1484 and makes a natural starting point. It was also the dominant edition throughout the sixteenth century. The publication of Sir Roger L'Estrange's *Fables of Aesop And other Eminent Mythologists with Morals and Reflexions* in 1692 makes an artificial end point. It became the most influential of the seventheenth-century editions, the Tory Aesop to stand against Croxall's eighteenth-century Whig one. Between Caxton and L'Estrange there is an embarrassment of riches, a host of English editions in all sizes and all formats. Some were published as grammar textbooks, others as light poetic entertainment, and a few as vehicles for elaborate illustrations. None, however, were produced as political tracts.

They were created by schoolmasters, by language reformers, by poets, by etchers and by 'classicists'. Their trajectory, of course, follows the path of literacy in general and of the publishing industry in particular, with the number of editions and the number of different editions constantly growing.[6] But from the 1550s not a decade passed without the publication of another English edition of Aesop. It was one of the most popular books in early modern England.

For these reasons Aesop's *Fables* is an excellent object for the study of English political culture and the ways in which it changed. Early editions appear to have little direct political application, subsequent editions to be self-consciously political and late seventeenth-century ones to be overtly ideological. In the sixteenth century most editions were directed at the school market, for the teaching of English and Latin. They were mainly close translations, though from a variety of sources. Early editors justified their work as being more accurate or as containing a larger number of fables than their competitors. While some seventeenth-century editors continued in this vein, others made verse translations, added a biography of Aesop, or adorned their work with illustrations. Having the same basic text available in editions published across a 200-year period allows for direct comparisons and a reasonable estimation of what a particular editor set about to change in his or her edition.[7]

But the use of this type of literature to study political culture is not without its problems. The two that have most vexed historians and literary critics are authorial intent and reader response. It is argued on the one hand that the creative demands of literary genres, the workings of the subconscious, and the limitations of language all militate against the ability of the author to have an intention, to know it, or to communicate it. It is argued on the other hand that the ways in which readers respond to literary productions encompass so wide a spectrum as to ensure that all texts ultimately subvert themselves. Incomprehension meets the uncomprehending. While these conundrums have had a liberating effect on literary criticism, they have been less helpful to historians who have, on the whole, tended to be more literal minded. Thus it can be argued that the fable by its very nature is well designed to plumb authorial intent, being composed of an opaque story that is then explicitly moralized.

If it can be argued that the didactic element of the fable can reasonably be taken as the author's 'intent', there is no equally good proxy for the reader's response. When L'Estrange justified the publication of yet another edition of Aesop in the 1690s he observed that when Aesop was read in the schools it was for pronunciation and grammar rather than for lessons and morals: 'The boys break their teeth upon the shells, without ever coming near the kernel. They learn the fables by lessons and the moral is the least part of our care in a child's institution'.[8] L'Estrange set out to crack this nut by adding 'Reflexions' upon the fables he translated which were many times the length of the moral itself. But it remains true that the meaning which the author wished to convey was not necessarily the meaning that the reader received. This is obviously the case with stories that are repeated from generation to generation and which move across geographical and cultural divides. The story of a black slave who wins his freedom through his intelligence will resonate differently in ancient Rome, early modern England or modern America.[9] But it is also the case when the same story is told in the same culture across time. A fable about democracy and monarchy will be read differently before, during and after the English Revolution even if told in the same words. All we will be able to conclude is that across the seventeenth century the Aesopian fable came to be politicized in a particular way and a variety of translators used its morals to inculcate a particular set of political values. This politicization followed the same path by which the literary production of the fables changed. New audiences were sought, new editors felt less bound to translate and more empowered to create.

In order to view these changes concisely, this essay will follow the telling of a single fable through all of the sixteenth and seventeenth-century English editions of Aesop. The fable chosen is variously entitled 'The Frogs and Jupiter' or 'The Frogs Desiring a King'. It is one of the early fables in nearly all editions of Aesop, the first fable of the second book in Caxton, the seventeenth fable in the standard schoolbooks. It appears in every edition of Aesop published in the period and it appears largely in the same form, though as we shall see the selection of words and phrases and the construction of the moral left much room for interpretation. The fable of the Frogs and Jupiter is especially appropriate in trying to follow the political uses to which Aesop was put, for it is potentially one of the most explicitly political of the fables, focusing on forms of government and the relationship between rulers and ruled. Tracing changes in the telling of this story and in the way it came to be moralized across the period should provide a good proxy for overall changes in the editions themselves.[10]

II

The translation history of the English versions of Aesop is complex and esoteric. Its finer points need not detain us. The Greek and Latin sources from which medieval editions were compiled have been exhaustively studied and there are only a few significant facts which affect the English tradition.[11] The first is that all English versions derive ultimately from Phaedrus, a Romanized Greek who lived in the first century CE and who wrote Latin verses on the basis of a Greek manuscript.[12] The second is that both the Greek manuscript and Phaedrus' verses were lost by the early middle ages. The text known as 'Aesop's fables' in the middle ages was a prose version made by the pseudonymous Romulus some time between 350 and 600 CE. In rendering verse into prose, Romulus gave the fables a Latin patina – thus Jupiter rather than Zeus – and this was overlaid with a Christian finish in various subse-

quent renditions of Romulus' compilation.[13] By the fifteenth century the manuscript texts of Aesop that circulated in Europe were well removed from their
source and offered the early printers wide latitude in their translations into
the vernacular. The most important of these, for our story, was a translation
into German of the Romulus collection published by Heinrich Steinhöwel in
1476 and translated into French by Julien Macho in 1480.[14] The first English
translation was made by William Caxton in 1484, directly from Macho's
French translation of Steinhöwel.[15] Caxton's Aesop was the most important
English edition for nearly 200 years. It was reprinted at least nine times in the
sixteenth century and five times in the seventeenth, the last in 1676.[16]

The second source for English translations was probably the Latin edition
published by Wynkyn de Worde in the early 1530s and commonly reprinted
thereafter.[17] This version was a conflation of a variety of continental editions
including those of Lorenzo Valla and Erasmus. It was the basis of William
Bullokar's 1585 edition, *Æsopz fabl'z in tru ortography with grammar-nótz.*[18]
Bullokar was a grammarian who invented a system for English pronunciation
and published a small number of works using marked vowels and phonetic
spelling. His purpose in publishing Aesop was to aid the teaching of Latin by
providing a literal English translation of this common schoolbook. Bullokar
had to overcome many obstacles: he kept running out of his specially cast
type; his printers introduced scores of errors; and where the public was not
indifferent to his 'tru ortography' it was hostile. All of this delayed his edition of Aesop and when it was finally ready he sadly admitted that he had
lost the Latin originals from which he had made his translation.

Bullokar's *Æsopz fabl'z* is of interest not only because it is not based on
Caxton, but because it brought into the English tradition the structure that is
thought to be characteristic of the Aesopian fable: a story followed by a
moral.[19] The prose tradition that culminated in Caxton's edition was one in
which promythia and/or epimythia were used. These were brief epitome
which preceded or followed the fable, though their use was unsystematic.
Many fables, like 'Of the Frogs and of Jupiter', contained both, while many
others contained neither. It has been speculated that the promythia were originally designed as an indexing device that would allow the reader easily to
scan the fables by theme, while the epimythia gave the meaning or application of the story.[20] But not all of the 'Romulus' fables contained epimythia,
even though 'Romulus' added many epimythium in converting Phaedrus'
verse into prose. The morals that Bullokar translated from Wynkyn de
Worde's 1535 Latin edition are comparatively brief. Earlier Latin editions
published in England contained long commentaries on the fables, but Bullokar's rarely ran past several lines and many are pithy apothegms.[21] They
became the basis for subsequent English editions, and established the structure of the Aesopian fable: a story followed by a moral.[22]

The final source for the English editions of Aesop was a Latin edition of
what were thought to be the original verses of Phaedrus. This was translated

into English prose by Simon Sturtevant in 1602 in a volume which also contained a translation of the same Latin text used by Bullokar.[23] Like Bullokar, Sturtevant's purpose was the teaching of Latin to schoolchildren and his book was directed at the schoolmasters who might use it. Sturtevant published the Latin test of each fable sentence by sentence. He then reordered the Latin words into English grammatical structure and translated them. Thus 'Gens ranarum cum esset libera,' was reorderd to 'Cum gens renarum esset libera' and translated as 'When the nation of the frogs was free from subjection'.[24] Sturtevant did not reprint the Latin morals in the first part of his work and Phaedrus' original verse did not contain them.[25]

The publication of the fables in Latin verse encouraged their composition in English verse, the first edition being published by R. A. in 1634.[26] R. A. followed the order of the fables as set out by Bullokar and Sturtevant, but produced his edition as light entertainment rather than as a grammar textbook. His fables and morals were in cleverly conceived rhymed couplets. These were followed five years later by a more elaborate poetic edition by William Barret. Barret's *Fables of Aesop* began with a self-deprecating prologue, contained celebratory verses from his friends, and restored the tradition, followed by Caxton, of including woodcuts – 'Emblematically Illustrated with Pictures'. Barret's verse was in pentameter couplets and it became the standard verse version of the fables for over a century, achieving its twentieth edition by 1750.[27]

The verse editions of R.A and William Barret (and that of Leonard Willan published in 1650) changed the direction of English publications of Aesop. They were produced as entertainment rather than as language instruction and they were intended for adults rather than children.[28] R. A. took his epigraph from Horace, and when Barret's verses were paired with a prose translation and printed in Cambridge in 1651 the new editor took as his epigraph 'Go and Learn of the Ant'. He excused the nature of the Aesopian fables with the biting observation, 'thou mayest well allow owls, daws, buzzards, woodcocks, apes and asses to talk together in old times, when as we now find the same creatures ordinarily in every pulpit'.[29] This shift in focus and audience culminated in the publication of the first of the many editions of John Ogilby's *The Fables of Æsop Paraphras'd in Verse* (1651).[30] Ogilby was an astonishing virtuoso: he was successively a Scots dancer who caught the fancy of James I; a theatrical impresario who became Master of Revels in Ireland; a client of Buckingham, Strafford and both kings Charles. He made himself into one of the great classical translators of the time, though he had no formal education and did not begin the study of Latin until past the age of forty. He was even more famous for his lavish atlases of America, Africa and Asia which he began publishing after he was seventy. 'Cosmographer Royal and Geographick Printer', he oversaw a survey of the roadways of England (for which he hired both John Aubrey and Gregory King); invented the statute mile; and published in *Britannia* (1675) the standard English road maps for the next century.

Ogilby's *Æsop* was distinguished in a number of ways. In the first place it was a quarto, the first edition since the beginning of the sixteenth century to be published in a volume larger than an octavo. This gave way, after the Restoration, to folio editions, in 1665 and 1668.[31] Secondly, it was lavishly illustrated, 'adorned with sculpture' as its title-page proclaimed. The quarto edition contained eighty-one etchings, one full page for all but one of the fables, most by the skilled etcher Francis Cleyn, who did the portrait of Ogilby (rather than of Aesop) with which the book opened. The folio edition contained new and more sophisticated etchings by Wenceslaus Hollar.[32] The third significant aspect of Ogilby's *Æsop* is that it was purely a literary production. 'Having tasted the sweetness of a little fame ... [I] endeavored to sore [*sic*] a little higher ... Æsop the Prince of Mythologists became my Quarry, on his Plain Song I Descanted, on his short and pithy Sayings, Paraphras'd raising my voice to such a height, that I took my degree among the Minor Poets.'[33] Ogilby dedicated the book to literary patrons – the first edition to Heneage Finch, earl of Winchelsea and Henry Seymour, Lord Beauchamp, the second edition to the earl of Ossory – and he probably used them as financial backers.[34] It is a dead certainty that both editions were expensive to produce – Ogilby printed on quality paper and paid premium prices for his etchings – and expensive to own. Unbound copies of the folio retailed at £3 each and even subsequent down-market bound octavos cost 16*s*.[35] This gives rise to a final point. While earlier editions of Aesop were produced largely for students or as light entertainment, Ogilby's production was for educated gentlemen and urban professionals, though it might be unwarranted speculation that his loose 'paraphrases' reflected their tastes and their politics.[36]

At precisely the same time that Ogilby was publishing his lavish folio, Francis Barlow, 'the father of English sporting artists', was producing his. Barlow contributed etchings to Ogilby's folio, though it is unclear what relationship – other than a competitive one – the two projects had to each other. Barlow's *Æsop's Fables, with his Life: in English, French and Latin* (1666), was a vehicle for his own drawings. In the first edition, which was readied for press in 1665 but not actually published until 1666, the French and Latin was by Robert Codrington, the English verse by Thomas Philipott. Most of the first edition perished in the Fire of London, though the copperplates and some folded sheets survived. The 1687 edition contained thirty-one new etchings to illustrate *The Life of Aesop*, to which were added English verse by Aphra Behn.[37] But Barlow appears to have intermixed new and old sheets in some copies of the 1687 edition, as both contained his own etchings.

Barlow's *Æsop's Fables* was clearly a vehicle for his etchings and not for the text. In his introduction he addressed himself 'to young Gentlemen and ladies' and offered his polyglot texts to satisfy their supposed interests in reading languages. But most of his preface was taken up in explaining his illustrations; none of the three language versions of the texts of the fables are translations of each other; and the nature of the texts are determined by space considerations. Thus the French versions of the fables are the longest for they fill the entire folio page facing the illustration. The Latin texts occupy less than a quarter of a folio underneath each etching, while the English text was cut on to the plate itself. This may have been done so the the pages containing both English and Latin could be sold as separates as had some of Barlow's earlier cartoons. This strategy created unforeseen problems once the fire destroyed most of the sheets and it was necessary to substitute Behn's verses for Philipott's. The verses of the first edition had to be burred out (not entirely successfully) and Behn had to write to these space limitations. Her decision to create an entire set of fables in two couplets followed by a single couplet for the moral is not the least remarkable of her achievements.[38]

The final significant edition of Aesop's fables published in the seventeenth century was that of Sir Roger L'Estrange.[39] A staunch Royalist all his life, L'Estrange was captured during the first Civil War, court-martialled and sentenced to death. Reprieved on the condition that he emigrate, he joined the Royalist court in exile, but returned to England in the mid-1650s where he was a shadowy figure in the Royalist underground. In the chaotic year before the Restoration he published several pamphlets in support of the resumption of monarchy. Part pugilist, part journalist, L'Estrange was rewarded in 1663 with the office of surveyor of printing and became a licenser of the press. In this capacity he was fanatical against religious extremists and took advantage of the post to enhance his own publishing career. He founded the *Observator*, one of the first political newspapers in England. At the apex of the Restoration crisis, L'Estrange held out against the hysteria of the Popish Plot, impugning the testimony of Titus Oates and his confederates. For these opinions he was forced to flee abroad, but he relentlessly pursued his exposé until he was vindicated. Again in favour under James II, L'Estrange resumed his career as a translator of classics, which during his life included works of Erasmus, Tully and Seneca. But the Revolution of 1688 brought the final turn to his political wheel. He was persecuted, intermittently imprisoned and forced to abandon political pamphleteering for literary pursuits. In 1690 he was approached by a combine of booksellers to prepare a translation of Aesop.

L'Estrange set out to create the most compendious Aesop ever, expanding his definition to include fables from all sources. The two parts (1692, 1699) contained over 500 fables of which L'Estrange identified 383 as Aesopic.[40] They were both high quality folios which belied Sir Roger's stated purpose of introducing them into the English classroom in place of those 'wooden' versions most commonly used. Though his preface was directed at schoolmasters, and his stated concern was teaching the fables through their morals rather than their stories, the publication was aimed at the well-heeled who were more likely to read then in the drawing room than the nursery. His real innovation, the kiss of L'Estrange, was the introduction of 'Reflextions' at the end of each story and moral. These 'Reflextions' were undisguised social and political commentary that contained more than a tint of Jacobitism. His entire production, as he makes clear in the preface, was didactically political.[41] L'Estrange's *Aesop* was so popular that it achieved three editions in seven years and then was followed by a second volume of non-Aesopic fables in the same format.

III

Through its many retellings, the fable that Caxton called 'Of the Frogs and of Jupiter' preserved its essential elements. A community of frogs asks Jupiter to give them a king. He is bemused by the request and throws a log into their pond.[42] Though at first in dread of their king, the frogs discover it to be inanimate, jump upon it, and ask Jupiter for another monarch. This time he sends them a stork.[43] The stork arrives in the pond and devours whatever frogs he can catch. For a third time the frogs appeal to Jupiter, but now he refuses them, saying that the stork shall be their king.[44] Caxton's version, in seventeenth-century language, runs thus:

> Divers frogs were in ditches and ponds at their own liberty, they all together with one consent made request unto Jupiter, that he would give them a King, and Jupiter thereof began to marvel and for their King he cast them down a great piece of wood, which with the fall thereof made a great sound in the water, whereof they had great dread and fear: and after as they approached to their King for to make to him obeisance, and perceived that it was but a piece of wood, they turned again to Jupiter, praying him earnestly that he would give to them another King. Then Jupiter gave to them the heron to be their King. Then the heron entered into the water and ate them one after another. And when the Frogs saw that their King did so devour them they began to weep to Jupiter and to say unto him right high and mighty Jupiter, we pray to thee to deliver us from the throat of this tyrant, which eats us one after another. And then says Jupiter to them, the King which you have demanded shall be your master.[45]

The same fable is told more economically by Aphra Behn:

> The Frogs implore a king, and Jupiter
> To please the Rable does king Log preffer,
> But too unactive he – again they implore,
> Jove sends the Stork who does the fooles devour.[46]

The fable admits of a number of ambiguities and it is these that form the basis of its interpretative history. The first concerns its title. Caxton called it 'Of the Frogs and of Jupiter', which gave no hint of its subject matter or its moral.[47] Several translators inverted the order to 'Jupiter and the Frogs' and it is commonly found under 'J' in those editions with indexes.[48] But many other editions entitle the fable 'Of Frogs and their King', and Ogilby begins the tradition of calling it 'Of the Frogs desiring a King', which is picked up in *Æsop Explained* and by Philip Ayres.[49] L'Estrange is more accusatory, naming it 'The Frogs Chuse a King'.[50] The title given to the fable is not simply a matter of convenience. As interpretations shift across the seventeenth century from the deficiencies inherent in the petition to those inherent in the petitioners, so words like 'desire' and 'chuse' become more ascriptive. The second ambiguity derives from the form of government that first existed in the frog pond. Caxton describes the frogs as being 'at theyre lyberte', Sturtevant as 'free from subjection', and R. A. makes them 'a free and populous nation'.[51] But Sturtevant's translation from Phaedrus had the frogs 'wandering free or without controlment' and after the Civil Wars translators rendered 'liberty' in this sense.[52] Ogilby describes the state of the Frogs as factious and unruly – 'In several Interests we divided are.' In his account King Frogmoreton had been killed by a kite doing a war with the mice and the frogs were left leaderless.[53] The anonymous translator of *Æsop Improved* has the frogs 'Thinking a Commonwealth but a mean thing'.[54] Philip Ayres in 1689 was even less flattering of free frogs, 'Whether under an Anarchy or Democracy ... the Frogs in a great lake grown wanton'; while Sir Roger L'Estrange denied the efficacy of liberty altogether: 'In the days of Old, when the Frogs were all at liberty in the Lakes, and grown quite weary of living without Government'.[55]

The explanations as to why the frogs wanted a king run a similar gamut. Caxton is silent on the question, saying only that the request came 'all together with one consent'. Most others attributed it to pride. 'Frogs swell'd like Toads with pride croakt for a King', opened the version provided in *Æsop Improved*. 'The Frogs a King set o're them, did desire;/For to a high degree they did aspire,' began *Æsop Explained*.[56] All translations agree that Jupiter was bemused by the request, either smiling or laughing, which probably accounts for the decision to send a log. However, later translators suggest that Jupiter was reluctant to accede to it: 'they made him do it whether he will or no'.[57] This stridency, the 'croaking of the Frogs', beginning in the 1630s is significantly described as 'petitioning', whereas Caxton had used the words 'request' and 'prayer' in his account.[58]

With the appearance of King Log, the story takes its first turn toward the behaviour of subjects. The log is thrown into the pond, making a great 'sound' and its frightens the frogs: 'That vast weight shakes the water with a huge crash. The frogs being terrified are silent.'[59] This fear or 'dread' is universally seen as appropriate behaviour of subjects toward their monarch and described as 'obeisance', 'adoration', 'reverence', or 'homage': 'A Logg hee tumbles downe whose weightier blow/So aw'd the Froggs, themselves they prostrate throw.'[60] But as king log remained 'sluggish' – in Brinsley's deft understatement – the bolder among the frogs approach their monarch and discover his inadequacies. In Caxton's rendition they simply 'perceive that it was but a piece of wood', but in all subsequent accounts the frogs commit *lèse-majesté*, jumping upon their king or playing 'Leap-Frog'.[61] The language used is powerful, 'The sluggish king is made a scorne and a contempt', 'their mild King deride', 'And make in sport their suff'ring King their scoff', 'threw aside all manner of respect, leaped upon it, and made their King their sport and scorn'.[62] Sturtevant describes the scene as doubly transgressive, 'one stilly or without noise putteth up *her* head out of the pond and having made trial of the king *she* calleth all her fellows'.[63] This is the only suggestion in any of the fables that it was a female frog who subverted the reign of King Log. But subverted the reign was as the frogs renewed their appeal to Jupiter for a king 'who would be strong and stirring'.[64] This time Jupiter casts fire from heaven in the form of the stork. While there is never any direct connection made between the frogs' misconduct toward their first king and the character of the next, nor do any of the compilers defend the justice of a king who literally feeds off his subjects. King stork's behaviour is variously described as 'tyranny', 'cruelty', or 'rigour'.[65] Ogilby describes it with the unmistakable catchphrase of the Revolution: 'This cruel Prince that made his will a law'.[66]

The denouement of the story provides its first moral. In Caxton's version the frogs 'weep' and 'pray' for deliverance. In the rendititions from Phaedrus, like Sturtevant and Brinsley, they 'secretly complain' or 'by stealth ... they prefer a supplication'.[67] There is even the etiological suggestion that the croaking of frogs derives from these night battles in their efforts to avoid being heard by the stork (low murmuring) during their unrelenting appeal to Jupiter (hoarseness). And unrelenting it is for, 'They talk to one that hears them not.'[68] Jupiter refuses to grant their final petition. In the Caxton version he simply says, 'the king you have demanded shall be your master', but in most other versions Jupiter's response is more pointed: 'The Crane must governe still; since (not content)/They murmur'd at a peacefull Government', concludes William Barret. 'They that petitioned against a gracious king, should now endure one that had no mercy in him', was Hoole's translation. Ogilby's interpretation – published in 1651 before it could apply to Cromwellian government but reprinted across the 1660s – was the most striking:

Then th'angry God in thunder answr'd these;
To change your government great Jove did please,
And you I gave a peacefull Soveraign:
Since he dislik'd you, by the Stygian lake
   A vow I make,
   The Stork shall reign,
And you evermore repent in vain.[69]

IV

Though interpretation could enter into the telling of the fable, subtly in the choice of keywords or overtly in the looser verse editions, there was little need for coyness. With the exception of the Caxton editions, the English versions of Aesop all contained morals and it was within the morals that point of view could be most directly expressed. Since the story of the Frogs and Jupiter was inherently about forms of government, it is not surprising that it should carry some political freight right from the start. But political freight could come in differently shaped containers. There could be the perfect circles of idealized peace and harmony for which writers and readers might yearn but not expect to experience. There could be boxes in which speculation about forms of government was an intellectual rather than a practical exercise. There could also be polyhedrons in which the lessons were so opaque that every reader could fly off along their own angle. And there could be the straight line of direct application to immediate political circumstances.

The morals of the Frogs and Jupiter story appear to move through such a continuum. In its early tellings it is hard to discern an overt political application or to believe that it is addressed to English political conditions. But as the seventeenth century progressed, more 'translators' became authors and more of a direct political message is both intended and conveyed. By the end of the century, the fable and its moral are didactically political and directly relevant both to historical memories of the English Revolution and to the current political situations of the 1680s and 1690s. The fable has become politicized. It is told to convey a precise political lesson, one that readers might have drawn from it anyway, but one which its authors now consider so important that it cannot be left to interpretation.

Although neither the texts on which Caxton relied nor the original verses of Phaedrus contained explicit morals, the fable Of the Frogs and of Jupiter nevertheless was given an application in both of the sources. In Caxton's edition it was the first fable of the second book and was preceded by a general introduction: 'All manner of fables are found to show men what they should ensue and follow, and also what they ought to leave and flee; for fable is as much to say in poetry as words in theology.' But this general introduction quickly gave way to a specific context for Of the Frogs and of Jupiter.

> And therefore I write fables, to show the good conditions of good men; for the law is given for trespassers and misdoers: and because the good and just be not subject to the law, as we find and read of the Athenians, which living after the law of nature, and also at their liberty, would needs have a king for to punish all evil: but because they were not accustomed to be informed when any of them was corrected and punished they were greatly troubled when their King executed any justice: because that before that time they had never been under any man's subjection, it was grievous to them to be in servitude, wherefore they were sorrowful that ever they had demanded any King. Against the which Aesop rehearses this fable following.[70]

This introduction is an example of the Christian overlay that many of the Latin fables had acquired during the middle ages. The law is for 'trespassers and misdoers', not for the 'good and just'. This suggests that the state of nature in which the Athenians were living was less than ideal and that the king they had acquired was more than necessary. The epimythia to the fable, however, seems less opaque. 'Wherefore when men have that which is convenient, they ought to be joyful and glad, and he that hath liberty ought to keep it well, for nothing is better than liberty, for liberty should not be sold for all the gold and silver in the world.' This lesson can be allied to two conditions in the fable, most obviously to the state of nature before the appearance of evil, when the frogs lived 'at their own liberty', but also under the benevolent rule of their wooden king when the frogs had 'that which is convenient'.

In Caxton's version the fable does not seem directly to raise the issues about forms of government that are so obviously embedded in it when read from a modern perspective. There are no animadversions on the caprice of Jupiter or the shortcomings of the two kings. Nor are the frogs harshly judged. After the Heron begins to eat them, thy 'began [tenderly] to weep'. We are led to sympathize with their plight and with their frailties. Despite its ringing phrases, the fable is less an encomium upon liberty than a caution to leave high matters well enough alone.

That it could be read another way can hardly be disputed. Its first edition was published at the end of the Wars of the Roses and might well have suggested that kings could bring tyranny. Tudor historians of the reign of Richard III would have found resonance in the image of king heron eating his subjects. But it is hard to believe that the fable was taught to successive generations of Henrician and Elizabethan schoolchildren in an anti-monarchial vein. What thoughts it provoked when republished in 1628, 1647 or 1658 is another matter. Following the debates over the Petition of Right, 'liberty' assumed a contextualized political meaning which it had not held before, and following the Civil War and then the Revolution it became a keystone of political discourse. John Milton certainly read the fable as being explicitly anti-monarchical: 'the true moral shews rather the folly of those being free seek a King', but this was in a debate with those who read it the other way and at a time when England did not have a king. Indeed, if this fable had been used for generations as a means of inculcating a love of democratic liberty, it is surprising both that there are few reprintings of Caxton in the 1650s and that there were no new editions that emphasized this interpretation.

The verses of Phaedrus that were newly discovered in the seventeenth century also set the fable of the Frogs and Jupiter within the context of ancient Athenian politics, though more concretely than did Caxton.

When Athens flourished with equal laws, malepart liberty mingled or marred the city and licentiousness let loose the ancient bridle of government. From hence parts or parties of diverse factions being in a conspiracy, Prince Pisistratus taketh and holdeth the tower and when the Athenians lamented that sorrowful or heavy subjection, bondage or service, not for that he was cruel or tyrannous but because it was a grievous burthen to them who were altogether unaccustomed with government and when they began to complain, Aesop told such a tale.[71]

This version ended with the exhortation: 'Oh ye also o citizens, saith he, sustain this evil patiently lest that there come upon you a greater mischief.' Though Phaedrus' verse fable emphasized the obligation of citizens to endure their government and attributed the origins of monarchy to the degeneration of life in the state of nature, it was also the only rendition to condemn the great frog massacre. In this version it was a water serpent with sharp teeth who made a meal of his subjects, but he is explicitly labelled 'evil and a tyrant'.[72] More strongly than in Caxton, this epimythium suggests that the mistake of the frogs was the overthrow of their first king, rather than desiring a monarchy in the first place. The last two lines of the story run: 'since you would not bear your good gentle king endure ye now your evil or tyrant'.

The moral translated from the standard Latin edition placed more responsibility on the frogs, but did not yet suggest that they possessed some moral or psychological failing that justified their fate. Both Bullokar, Brinsley and the editions based on *Aesopi Phrygris et vita et fabellae*, contained the moral 'It is wont to fall out to the common people, even as to the frogs. Who if they have a king somewhat more mild, they charge him to be sluggish and cowardly ... and contrarily if at any time they get a stout king they condemn his cruelty and praise the clemency of the former: whether for that we always mislike our present estate; or because it is a true word, that new things are better than old.'[73] Here the frogs are analogized to the common people, a theme which became central once the fable came to be placed into a direct political context. But the lesson still remains general – the lilies are always greener on the other side of the pond – and the frogs' failing is nothing other than a general human weakness, the belief that 'new things are better than old'.

By the 1630s this same theme had acquired much sharper edges. R. A., the first of the Aesopian versifiers, concluded his story 'For with mild King who will not live content,/Are justly plagued with Tyrants government.' He then provided a stinging moral:

> Like Frogs the vulgar people bee,
> Contented neither bond, nor free;
> Who governed by a gentle hand,
> Account their softness, weakness, and
> For stirring Magistrates they call,
> Then such account tyrannicall.
> Unconstant as the Moon or wave,
> Love change, and loath the thing they have.[74]

The transformation of the 'common people' to the 'vulgar people' marks a dramatic step forward in turning the fable into a commentary upon democracy and monarchy. While R. A. has not gone very far down this path, he has added psychological depth to the 'vulgar' frogs. They are 'unconstant as the moon'. They do not simply yield to the temptations of new things, rather they 'Love change and loath the thing they have'. The association of the common people with inconsistency was a familiar trope of ancient history, while the phrase 'unconstant as the moon' was commonly descriptive of women. Both associations served to deligitimize the frogs and to divert attention from the activities of their kings. Indeed, in William Barret's popular verse edition of 1639, it is kings rather than people who are to be pitied:

> How good so ere the King, we daily see
> Subjects repine; and if he peaceful be,
> They count him dull: if much severe, they cry
> And mummer hourly against his tyranny.[75]

Thus while it is hard to draw a specific political message from the morals of either of these fables, by the 1630s the language in which it is told is more highly charged than it has been before and the frogs have acquired implicitly negative political characteristics.

It is only to be expected that the Civil Wars and Revolution would intensify the political reading of all publications. The breakdown of censorship in the 1640s and the ravenous appetite of the public for information led to a flood of publications of all kinds. With the execution of Charles I and the establishment of the commonwealth, it might also be expected that the fable would revert to the language of liberty that had been so prominent in Caxton's edition or to reflections on the conduct of kings stork and log that float so obviously on the surface of the story. But there was only one Caxton edition published between the execution of the king and the Restoration, and most of the editions of the 1650s were reprints of Barret's verse and the conventional prose editions of Bullokar and Brinsley.[76]

Indeed, the two new editions of this period are exclusively monarchist in nature. 'God cannot please the giddy multitude', concluded Leonard Willan in his blandly titled 'The Frogs and their King'.[77] John Ogilby was even more explicit. His paraphrased Aesop allowed for his own dilations upon the meaning of this story, and there was no mistaking his staunch Royalism. Throughout his telling of the tale he introduced kingship as the only means of a settled state. His frogs were divided into 'severall interests' and 'Small hope is left well ground peace t'obtain'. While democratic government was theoretically possible, it was, in Ogilby's view, Utopian. 'That Supreme power may on the people be/Setle'd, tis true; but who that day shal see?', he wrote in 1651. Monarchy was the natural state: 'Men, beasts, and birds; nay Bees their King obey'. But the frogs were fickle. They did not want just any king, they wanted 'an active Prince, a Monarch stout', and when king log was not to their liking, 'streight they proclaim a fast' and decide to petition for another king. This was the stork, the 'cruell Prince that made his will a law'. Jove would hear no more petitions and the stork would reign for ever. Ogilby left no doubt as to the contemporary meaning of the tale:

> No government can th' unsetled vulgar please,
> Whom change delight's think quiet a disease,
> Now anarchie and Armies they maintain,
> And wearied, are for King and Lords again.

Ogilby's versions powerfully evoked the language and rhetoric of the Revolution. Catchphrases like 'made his will a law', and parodies of the Long Parliament's proclivity to fasts and prayers to heaven were unmistakable echoes. So was his analysis of the factions and self-interest that led to the change of government, for by 1651 even many who had supported the parliamentary cause believed that it had degenerated into the rule of a single faction backed by the army.[78] But however persuasive this reading of the fable might have been in the 1650s, it was prescient when reprinted in its many post-Restoration editions. By then the concluding lines, 'Now anarchie and Armies they maintain/And wearied are for Kings and Lords again', became the official assessment of the Revolution which was widely blamed for allowing the 'unsetl'd vulgar' a role in political affairs.

This contemporary tilt became the fashion in succeeding editions, though Ogilby dominated the 1660s and 1670s. Barlow's first edition, with the English verse of Thomas Philipott seemed more a comment on the reign of Charles II than of his father: 'If Kings are milde they're dull, if active we still blast them with the guilt of tyrannie.'[79] The anonymous *Æsop Explained* (1682) which presented side by side Latin and English versions designed for classroom use, nevertheless declared that it was 'accommodated to the Lives and Manners of Men in this present Age.' The author of *Æsop Improved* (1673) urged 'Æsop's Fables is a book not only to be read, and contemplated, but, to be followed and practis'd; and many serve to guide and govern our civil, domestical, and political affairs.' It too found a moral for those disillusioned with Charles II:

> Too mild is a good fault in them that rule,
> (If any fault be good,) and they who pule
> And whine at rulers too great clemency,
> Deserve to feel the smart of tyranny.
> A beam doth nothing like a Crane annoy:
> If it can't save, neither will it destroy.[80]

By the time of Barlow's second edition in 1687 the use of Aesop for political commentary was well established. Aphra Behn's verses deliberately recalled contemporary events. She celebrated Charles II's miraculous escape after the battle of Worcester in the moral of 'The Lion and the Mouse': 'Do not despise the service of a slave/ An oak did once a glorious monarch save.' The moral of the Ringdove and the Fowler provided an unmistakable reference to Monmouth's rebellion: 'The young usurper who designed t'invade /Another's right, himself the victim made.'[81] As had Ogilby, Behn inculcated the lessons that were to be learned from civil war: 'So petty feuds by the Rout persu'd/Have often mighty common wealths subdu'd.' The 'rout' or the commonality was her special target. 'Ungratefull People thus on Princes fall,/ And given some liberties rebell for all.'[82] Behn also adorned Barlow's new etchings of the life of Aesop with her conservative political philosophy. 'Th' unthinking rabble thus wise states-men blame/ Where ere they act beyond their duller aime.'[83] To the final sculpture, that which depicted the shame the Delphians felt at having killed Aesop, Behn provided a paean to Charles I:

Thus did not our ungratfull Brittish brood
To expiate for guiltless Royall blood,
Had we thy sacred name great Charles importall made,
Wee'd shund those Plagues the wiser Delphian stayd.[84]

Though it is not known how long before publication Barlow and Behn actually did their work – as with the first edition, the English poetry was etched on to the plates rather than typeset – their Aesop looks back to the reign of Charles II rather than ahead to that of his brother. The moral Behn attaches to Jupiter and the Frogs is simply, 'If Kings be mild they'r dull, if active they/ We blast them with the guilt of Tyrants way.'[85] This was little different to the moral which appeared in the first edition twenty years earlier, though in 1687 it could easily have been read as a contrast between the last years of Charles II and the first of James II. Indeed, beginning in 1687 the fable dovetailed neatly with the debate over passive obedience. The context in which Phaedrus had told the story was of the Athenian dissatisfaction with Pisistratus, and his lesson was 'sustain this evil patiently lest that there come upon you a greater mischief'. In *Mythologia Ethica* (1689), Philip Ayres again set the fable in this Athenian context. Athenian democracy degenerated into factiousness which allowed Pisistratus to set up a tyranny against which the people then complained. His moral to the fable was: 'A multitude was an unruly thing, without all manner of Prudence and Foresight.'[86]

This emphasis upon the unruly multitude whose fickleness made them unsuitable political participants was the central message of L'Estrange. His edition contained both morals and what he called 'Reflextions'. His moral to 'The Frogs Chuse a King' was: 'The Mobile are Uneasy without a Ruler: They are as Restless with one: and the oftn'er they shift, the Worse they Are; so that Government, or No Government; a King of God's Making, or of the Peoples, or none at all; the Multitude are never to be satisfied.' This was amplified, if amplification was needed, in the Reflexion. Here L'Estrange launched a diatribe against 'the unsteadiness of the Common People'. They don't know what they have, they don't like it and they don't like what comes next: 'They are never satisifed with their present condition.' 'Redress of Grievances is the question', he proclaims sarcastically, 'and the devil of it is that the Petitioners are never to be pleased.'[87] The common people have no business meddling in government, L'Estrange asserts and his conclusion is an open defence of passive obedience:

> They Beg and Wrangle, and Appeal, and their Answer is at last, that if they shift again, they shall be still Worse; By this, the Frogs are given to Understand the very truth of the Matter, as we find it in the World, both in the Nature, and Reason of the Thing, and in Policy and Religion; which is, That Kings are from God, and that is a Sin, a Folly, and a Madness, to struggle with his Appointments.[88]

Ironically, this was a moral that would soon suit the Whigs better than the Tories!

V

L'Estrange's *Aesop* was quickly seen for what it was – thinly disguised political propaganda. It was followed by a succession of parodies, some of which lampooned L'Estrange as a modern-day Aesop. These transparent satires depended entirely upon familiarity with the politics of the moment and much of the wit has receded with the events.[89] When Samuel Croxall set out in the eighteenth century to combat the influence of L'Estrange he did so by presenting his own highly politicized versions. L'Estrange was an agent of popery and arbitrary government who made arguments 'to justify slavery'. They were not fit for the 'children of Britain ... for they are born with free Blood in their veins: and suck in Liberty with their very Milk'. Aesop's *Fables* had become a political battleground for the loyalties of babes while their minds were still 'blank paper'.[90]

It is not surprising that the English Revolution should transform the political culture of the generation that endured it. For twenty years the nation was inundated by a flood of political writing while political experimentation cut new channels into all aspects of daily life. The intensity of the Civil Wars, the quite literal revolutions of government – monarchy to monarchy in little more than a decade – naturally left their mark. The English Revolution politicized culture and this could be seen in the poetry of Lovelace, Denham and Marvell as well as the theory of Hobbes, Harrington and Milton. The Restoration might end constitutional experimentation, repudiate land settlements and restore orthodoxy in Church and State, but it could not unthink a political perspective.

Indeed, it could only reinforce the viewpoint. The conscious undoing of the past took the form of a deadening repetition of stock lessons. The rule of the king was divinely ordained, the participation of the people inherently destabilizing. Challenging constituted authority led to misery and chaos, obedience led to peace and prosperity. Religious orthodoxy was true piety, religious nonconformity impious stubbornness. The constant attention to political forms in sermons and tracts, in newsbooks and broadsides enlarged the tendency to see the world in political terms. The change from one generation to the next is neatly symbolized by the literary apprenticeships of Milton and Dryden. The first cut his teeth on love poetry and court masque, the second on political panegyric and satire. In such circumstances the politicization of stock works like Aesop's *Fables* was all but inevitable. Even if subconsciously, translators and editors, schoolmasters and poets had learned that sometimes a fable is not just a fable.

Notes

[1] R. T. Lenaghan (ed.), *Caxton's Aesop* (Cambridge, MA, 1967), p. 91. This is a collation of the surviving copies of the 1484 translation.

[2] John Ogilby, *The Fables of Æsop Paraphras'd in Verse* (1651) [A689], p. 31. All place of publication is London unless otherwise noted. Because so many of the editions cited below have nearly identical titles, STC and Wing numbers will be used for identification.

[3] Sir Roger L'Estrange, *Fables of Æsop and other Eminent Mythologists with Morals and Reflexions* (1692) [A706], p. 20.

[4] This constitutes my principal (and principle) objection to Annabel Patterson's admirable *Fables of Power* (Durham, NC, 1991).

[5] Although all of the editions of Aesop's *Fables* discussed in this essay are technically translations, some of them are loose ones.

[6] STC lists eighteen editions, mostly Caxtons, between 1484 and 1640. There were, by my count, twenty-nine editions between 1641 and 1700.

[7] There is at least one translation done by a woman – the elegant quatrains of Aphra Behn. Francis Barlow, *Aesop's Fables, with his Life: in English, French, and Latin* (1687) [A703].

[8] L'Estrange (1692) [A706], Preface B3.

[9] For the story in Roman context see Keith Hopkins, 'Novel evidence for Roman slavery', *Past and Present*, 138 (1993), pp. 3–27. For its reception in England see Patterson, *Fables of Power*.

[10] I have sampled several other fables in these editions and find 'The Frogs and Jupiter' to be representative for the purposes of my analysis.

[11] Ben E. Perry, *Aesopica* (Urbana, 1952).

[12] There are two 'ancient' sources for Aesop: the Latin verse of Phaedrus and the Greek verse of Babrius. As English editions of Aesop grew in the seventeenth century they added on fables that derived from Babrius. Ben E. Perry, *Babrius and Phaedrus* (Cambridge, MA, 1965).

[13] Thus the epimythia of the fable, 'Of the Beasts and of the Birds', reads, 'For as the Evangel sayth/None may serve both god and the devil.' Lenaghan, *Caxton's Aesop*, p. 107.

[14] Steinhöwel's version contained both Latin and German prose texts and Latin verse for the first three books of fables. For a full discussion of Steinhöwel's sources see Joseph Jacobs, *The fables of Aesop, as first printed by William Caxton in 1484*, 2 vols. (London, 1889), vol. I.

[15] The best guide to the origins of Caxton's edition is Lenaghan, *Caxton's Aesop*,

pp. 4–18.

16 The pre-1640 printing history can be followed in STC, vol. 1, p. 9. There were three editions based on Caxton published after 1640, in 1647 [A687] (which Wing mis-dates to 1674); one in 1658 [A692]; and the last in 1676 [A702B]. These various editions were not identical, but they were all directly derived from Caxton's text and they did not involve the rewriting of his fables.

17 *Aesopi Phrygis et vita et fabellae* (1535) [STC 171]. This is based on the Latin edition printed in Holland and ascribed to William of Gouda. David Hale, 'Aesop in Renaissance England', *The Library*, 5th series, 27 (1972), p. 119. It is possible that de Worde's edition was a reprint of the 1531 edition printed by Peter Treveris [STC 170.7]. De Worde reprinted a number of Treveris' publications, stating on other occasions that they were defective. H. S. Bennett, *English Books and Readers 1475–1557* (Cambridge, 1970), p. 224.

18 William Bullokar, *Æsopz fabl'z in tru ortography with grammar-notz* (1585) [STC 187].

19 The first edition of fables that used this structure was Thomas Blague, *A Schole of Wise Conceytes*, which had editions in 1569 and 1572 (STC 3114 and 3115). These included fables from a variety of sources including Aesop and appear to be wholly Blague's creation. They were not a source for the English editions of Aesop.

20 Ben Perry, 'The origin of the epimythium', *Transactions of the American Philological Association*, 71 (1940), pp. 408–12.

21 In contrast see the long commentaries in *Esopus cum commento optimo et morali* (1502) [STC 168] printed by Richard Pynson or those in *Fabule Esopi cum commento* (1503) [STC 169], another edition printed by de Worde.

22 Bullokar, or more likely his source text, became the basis for Brinsley, Hoole and the first part of Sturtevant, all of which are nearly identical texts.

23 Simon Sturtevant, *The Etymologist of Aesop's Fables Containing the Construing of his Latin fables into English : also ... of Phædrus fables* (1602?) [STC 23410]. It seems unlikely that Bullokar's 'tru ortography' was the direct source for Sturtevant. De Worde's Latin text had at least three, and perhaps as many as five, editions between 1535 and 1602. David Hale asserts that Sturtevant translated from a Latin edition printed in Holland David Hale, 'Aesop in Renaissance England', p. 120.

24 Sturtevant (1602?) [STC 23410], p. 28.

25 Sturtevant's edition is reprinted without acknowledgement, *Æsop's Fables*, By I. L. (1646) [A686].

26 R. A., *The Fabulist Metapmorphosed, and Mythologized, or the Fables of Esop Translated out of Latine into English verse, and moralized* (1634) [STC 188.5].

27 [STC 189]. Though both Wing and the British Museum catalogue trace these oft-reprinted verses to R. D., *Æsop's Fables with their Morals* (1650) [A688], they are in fact the verses of Barret (slightly modified) to which have been juxtaposed a stock prose version of the same fables. This had reached its fourteenth edition by 1698 [A708]. For Barret's sources see, David Hale, 'William Barret's "The fables of Aesop"', *The Papers of the Bibliographical Society of America*, 64 (1970), pp. 285–6.

28 L. Willan, *The Phrygian Fabulist* (1650) [A732].

29 R. A. (1634) [188.5] 'Omne tulit punctum qui miscuit utile dulci'. R. D., *Æsop's Fables with their Morals* (1651) [A690] Sig A3. This version was reprinted three times during the 1650s.

30 Ogilby (1651) [A689]. There are, by my count, six editions of Ogilby's *Æsop Para-*

phras'd published between 1651 and 1675 [A689, 693, 697, 700, 701, and 702]. Its publishing history is complicated by the author's companion volume *Æsopics*, first published in 1668 and ultimately bound together with his *Æsop Paraphras'd*. *Æsopics*, in large part, are satirical fables of Ogilby's own devising. Miner lists only five by not counting the 1673 edition [A 700]. Earl Miner (ed.), *John Ogilby, The Fables of Æsop Paraphras'd in Verse* (Los Angeles, 1965), p. iii.

31 This is substantially a reprint of the 1651 edition with the addition of one fable and copious marginal notations.

32 A thorough (and critical) analysis of these etchings is in E. Hodnett, *Francis Barlow, First Master of English Book Illustration* (Ilkley, Yorks., 1978), pp. 143–53.

33 Quoted in Marian Eames, 'John Ogilby and his Æsop', *New York Public Library Bulletin*, 65 (1961), p. 76.

34 Beauchamp's father, the Marquess of Hertford had backed Ogilby's production of Virgil and it is likely that Winchelsea and Beauchamp backed the Aesop.

35 Eames, 'John Ogilby and his Æsop', p. 86.

36 Pepys owned copies of both the 1651 and the 1665 editions, though he won the latter in the lottery that Ogilby organized to reduce his stock and raise money for his Atlases.

37 There are only two 'editions' of Barlow, those of 1666 [A696] and 1687 [1703]. The so-called 1703 edition 'printed by R. Newcomb' is simply a new collation of the 1687 version. It is wrongly attributed '1666?' in Wing [A 695].

38 The circumstances surrounding Behn's involvement in the project remain obscure. See Germaine Greer (ed.), *The Uncollected Verse of Aphra Behn* (Cambridge, 1989), pp. 191–2.

39 Three other editions appeared between Barlow and L'Estrange. Two were anonymous, *Æsop Improved* (1673) [A 742], and *Æsop Explained* (1682) [A727], and Philip Ayres, *Mythologia ethica* (1689) [A731].

40 L'Estrange (1692) [A706], Preface B2. George Kitchen identifies 201 of them as Aesopic in *Sir Roger L'Estrange* (1913), p. 298.

41 See the discussion in Patterson, *Fables of Power*, pp. 139–43.

42 Variously a 'great piece of wood' (Lenaghan, *Caxton's Aesop* p. 90); a 'beam' (Sturtevant (1602?) [STC 23410], p. 29, *Æsop Explained* (1682) [A727], Ayres (1689) [A731], p. 59) and a 'block' (Brinsley (1617) [STC 187.5], Ogilby (1651) [A689]).

43 Variously a 'Heron' (Lenaghan, *Caxton's Aesop*, p. 90); 'Crane', (Barret (1639) [STC 189], Willan (1650) [A732], *Æsop Improved* (1673) [A742], p. 11, *Æsop Explained* (1682) [A727]); 'Sea-serpent' (Sturtevant (1602?) [STC 23410], p. 105. L'Estrange (1692) [A706], p. 20).

44 'The kynge which ye haue demaunded shalle by your mayster', Lenaghan, *Caxton's Aesop*, p. 91.

45 *The Fables of Esop in English* (1628) [STC 183], pp. 67–8.

46 Francis Barlow, *Aesop's Fables with his Life: in English, French and Latin* (1687) [A703], p. 73.

47 Lenaghan, *Caxton's Aesop*, p. 90.

48 Barret (1639) [STC 189]; Francis Barlow (1666) [A695].

49 Brinsley (1617) [STC 187.5], p. 14, R. A. (1634) [STC 188.5], Willan (1650) [A732], p. 18, Hoole (1657) [A691], C2, Ogilby (1665) [A693], p. 31, *Æsop Explained* (1682) [A727], p. 25, Ayres (1689) [A731], p. 58.

50 L'Estrange (1692) [A706], p. 19.

⁵¹ Lenaghan, *Caxton's Aesop*, p. 90; Sturtevant (1602?) [STC 23410], p. 28; R. A. *The Fabulist Metamorphosed and Mythologized* (1634) (STC 188.5), p. 15.

⁵² Sturtevant (1602?) [STC 23410], p. 103, Sturtevant's work derives from two separate sources and thus he translates some fables twice. Since he attempts a 'literal' construal, the stories have different details. In his translation from 'Aesop' he has a beam and a stork as the two kings; in his translation from Phaedrus, they are a great block and a serpent.

⁵³ John Ogilby, *The Fables of Æsop Paraphras'd in Verse* (1665) [A693], pp. 31, 17. This explains the first line of the fable 'Since good Frogmoreton Jove thou didst translate'.

⁵⁴ *Æsop Improved* (1673) [A742], p. 10.

⁵⁵ Ayres (1689) [A731], p. 5; L'Estrange (1692) [A706], p. 19.

⁵⁶ *Æsop Improved* (1673) [A742], p. 10; *Æsop Explained* (1682) [A727], p. 25. Ogilby called it a 'vain Sute', while L'Estrange opined that Jupiter 'knew the vanity of their hearts'. Ogilby (1665) [A693], p. 31; L'Estrange (1692) [A706], p. 20.

⁵⁷ Hoole (1657) [A691], C2; 'tired with their cries', Barret (1639) [STC 189], Fab 18; 'tired with their importunity', Ayres (1689) [A731], pp. 58–9.

⁵⁸ For example R. A. (1634) [STC 188.5], p. 15 and Willan (1650) [A732], p. 18.

⁵⁹ Brinsley (1617) [STC 187.5], p. 14.

⁶⁰ Lenaghan, *Caxton's Aesop*, p. 90; Brinsley (1617) [STC 187.5], p. 14; Ogilby (1665) [A693], p. 31; Barlow (1666) [A 696], p. 73.

⁶¹ Lenaghan, *Caxton's Aesop*, p. 90; Ogilby (1665) [A693], p. 31.

⁶² Brinsley (1617) [STC 187.5], pp. 14–15; Barret (1639) [STC 189], Willan (1650) [A732], p. 18, Ayres (1689) [A731], p. 59.

⁶³ Sturtevant (1602) [STC 23410], p. 30. The only other author to identify a single frog as the instigator of the usurpation identifies a male. L'Estrange (1692) [A706], p. 20.

⁶⁴ Sturtevant (1602) [STC 23410], p. 30. 'Stout', Brinsley (1617) [STC 187.5], p. 15; 'Valorous', Hoole (1657) [A691], p. C2; 'awefull power', Willan (1650) [A732], p. 18; 'awful scepter', Barlow (1666) [A696], p. 73.

⁶⁵ Barret (1639) [STC 189], Fable 18; Willan (1650) [A732], p., 18; Hoole (1657) [A691], p. C2; Barlow (1666) [A 696], p. 73.

⁶⁶ Ogilby (1651) [A792], p. 30.

⁶⁷ Lenaghan, *Caxton's Aesop*; Sturtevant (1602) [STC 23410], p. 30, Brinsley, (1617) [STC 187.5], p. 15.

⁶⁸ Hoole (1657) [A691], p. C2.

⁶⁹ Ogilby (1651) [A792], p. 30.

⁷⁰ Caxton (1628) [STC 183], p. 67.

⁷¹ Sturtevant (1602) [STC 23410], pp. 102–3. The clumsiness of Sturtevant's prose is the result of it being a literal translation.

⁷² Sturtevant (1602) [STC 23410], pp. 102–3. The fable moves back and forth between condemning the frogs and judging the actions of their kings. It also uniquely suggests a vengeful Jupiter.

⁷³ Brinsley (1617) [STC 187.5], pp. 14–15.

⁷⁴ R. A. (1634) [STC 188.5].

⁷⁵ Barret (1639) [STC 189], Fable 18.

⁷⁶ There are three editions of the same compilation ascribed to R. D: (1650) [A688]; (1651) [A690]; (1655) [A690A].

⁷⁷ Willan (1650) [A732], p. 18. The only interesting aspect of Willan's verses is his attribution of motive to the frogs. They want glory in the form of a warrior king: 'Jove they importune, once again, to send/A King, whose valor might from Foes defend'.

⁷⁸ Other fables like 'The Parliament of Birds' were transparent accounts of the events of the 1640s. See Miner, *John Ogilby, The Fables of Aesop*, pp. 95–100.

⁷⁹ Barlow (1666) [A 696], p. 73.

⁸⁰ *Æsop Improved* (1673) [A742], A3, p. 11.

⁸¹ Barlow (1687) [A703], M, R2. Other references to the Duke of Monmouth can be found in fables XXIV and XXXV.

⁸² Barlow (1687) [A703], p. Ccc; Iii.

⁸³ Barlow (1687) [A703], at plate 4.

⁸⁴ Barlow (1687) [A703], at plate 31.

⁸⁵ Barlow (1687) [A703], p. Aa.

⁸⁶ Ayres (1689) [A731], p. 60.

⁸⁷ L'Estrange (1692) [A706], p. 20.

⁸⁸ L'Estrange (1692) [A706], p. 21.

⁸⁹ For example, *Æsop at Amsterdam* (1698) [A734]; *Æsop at Bath* (1698) [A735]; *Æsop at Epsom* (1698) [A736]; *Æsop At Richmond* (1698) [A738]; *Æsop at Tunbridge* (1698) [A739].

⁹⁰ Samuel Croxall, *Fables of Aesop and Others* (1722), p. B5.

Index